D0552546

teach yourself

dutch and english dictionary

**dutch–english/
english–dutch**
gerdi quist &
dennis strik

For over 60 years, more than
50 million people have learnt over
750 subjects the **teach yourself**
way, with impressive results.

be where you want to be
with **teach yourself**

The publisher has used its best endeavours to ensure that the URLs for external websites referred to in this book are correct and active at the time of going to press. However, the publisher and the author have no responsibility for the websites and can make no guarantee that a site will remain live or that the content will remain relevant, decent or appropriate.

For UK order enquiries: please contact Bookpoint Ltd, 130 Milton Park, Abingdon, Oxon, OX14 4SB. Telephone: +44 (0) 1235 827720. Fax: +44 (0) 1235 400454. Lines are open 09.00–18.00, Monday to Saturday, with a 24-hour message answering service. Details about our titles and how to order are available at www.teachyourself.co.uk

For USA order enquiries: please contact McGraw-Hill Customer Services, PO Box 545, Blacklick, OH 43004-0545, USA. Telephone: 1-800-722-4726. Fax: 1-614-755-5645.

For Canada order enquiries: please contact McGraw-Hill Ryerson Ltd, 300 Water St, Whitby, Ontario, L1N 9B6, Canada. Telephone: 905 430 5000. Fax: 905 430 5020.

Long renowned as the authoritative source for self-guided learning – with more than 50 million copies sold worldwide – the **teach yourself** series includes over 500 titles in the fields of languages, crafts, hobbies, business, computing and education.

British Library Cataloguing in Publication Data: a catalogue record for this title is available from the British Library.

Library of Congress Catalog Card Number: on file.

First published in UK 2003 by Hodder Education, 338 Euston Road, London, NW1 3BH.

First published in US 2003 by The McGraw-Hill Companies, Inc.

This edition published 2003.

The **teach yourself** name is a registered trade mark of Hodder Headline.

Copyright © 2003 Gerdi Quist & Dennis Strik

Typeset by Transet Limited, Coventry, England.
Printed in Great Britain for Hodder Education, a division of Hodder Headline, 338 Euston Road, London NW1 3BH, by Cox & Wyman Ltd, Reading, Berkshire.

Hodder Headline's policy is to use papers that are natural, renewable and recyclable products and made from wood grown in sustainable forests. The logging and manufacturing processes are expected to conform to the environmental regulations of the country of origin.

Impression number   10 9 8 7 6 5
Year   2010 2009 2008 2007

3

contents

introduction

This dictionary contains the most frequently used Dutch words, which are given translated from Dutch into English, and also from English into Dutch. It is intended for learners of Dutch from beginner's level to intermediate and advanced. The selection of words has been based on the original edition by Peter and Margaretha King but has been extensively adapted and revised to make it more up to date and reflect contemporary usage of the Dutch language. In order to ensure that this dictionary matches the needs of learners of Dutch today, words from a wide variety of different contexts – including the media and I.T. – have been included, and terminology of a highly specialized technical nature, such as nautical and scientific terminology, has been omitted.

Dictionaries are a very important and useful tool for understanding a foreign language and improving your language skills. However, it is important that you do not simply take a given translation from a dictionary and use it without further thought. Never assume, for instance, that a particular translation is always applicable. Most words have various different meanings depending on the context in which they are used, i.e. the meaning of a word can change from one situation to another. English *hard*, for instance, can refer to the hardness of a material (**hard** in Dutch), or it can mean *difficult* (**moeilijk** in Dutch). Similarly, the Dutch word **hard** has more than one meaning as well. It can mean *hard* (referring to the hardness of a material), but it can also mean *fast*. Another Dutch example is **bank**, which can mean *bank* (where you put your savings) or *sofa*.

Some entries display more than one translation or meaning, but others are given with only one translation. Wherever the latter is the case, there may still be other meanings, but these are not frequently used. In allowing as many entries as possible, we have often included only the dominant meaning of a word.

More subtle differences also exist between different translations, where different words carry different stylistic values. English *man*, for instance, can be translated as **man**, but also as **kerel** (besides various other possible translations). However, **kerel** is much more informal than **man** and generally is not used in formal situations. Such information has been included wherever possible.

How to use this dictionary

General

Each entry is given in **bold**, followed by a comma and the translation.

auto (de), car

Multiple meanings are separated by a semi-colon.

daverend, thunderous; resounding

Translations which are close in meaning are separated by a comma.

com'mercie (de), commerce, trade

When different forms of a word exist, this is indicated by brackets, in this example: **vriendin** or **vriendinnetje**.

girlfriend, vriendin(netje)

Where deemed helpful, entries which belong to different grammatical categories are listed separately, otherwise they are separated by a colon.

kussen, to kiss
kussen (het) pillow, cushion
lijden, to suffer: suffering

Articles

Dutch nouns are accompanied by either the article **het** or **de**. This is indicated in brackets straight after the entry. Articles are only given in the Dutch–English section.

bankoverval (de), bank robbery

Occasionally a noun takes either **de** or **het**, in which case both articles are listed.

de'bacle (het, de), disaster, failure

When a noun has a different meaning depending on which article it takes, they are listed as separate entries.

bal (de), ball (*e.g. football*)
bal (het), ball (*dance*)

Stress

The stress in most words in Dutch is on the first syllable. When another syllable is stressed, this is indicated by an apostrophe in front of the stressed syllable.

fi'nesses, details

Context

When translated meanings could cause confusion, an explanation is given in brackets after the translation.

hé, hey, hello, oh (really)? (greeting/pleasant surprise)

If a word has a particular stylistic value, for example, if it is informal or vulgar, this is indicated in brackets before the translation.

boob, flater, blunder; borst, (*inf*) tiet

Expressions

Frequently used expressions are entered after the translation. The keyword is then substituted by –.

haarfijn, minutely:
iets – uitleggen,
to explain something in great detail

When keywords are used mainly as part of an expression, no separate translation is given of the keyword.

aanklampen: iemand –,
to accost someone

Forms

Entries are listed in their basic form:

verbs (including separable verbs) are given in the infinitive (no past tenses are given – you need to refer to a grammar book to find the past tense forms of irregular verbs);

klagen, to complain

nouns are given in the
singular form;

fa'cet (het), aspect,
facet

adjectives are listed without the
added -e.

e'xotisch, exotic

Abbreviations

For most abbreviations, the full
Dutch form is given after a colon.

a.s.: aanstaande,
coming: **9 juli a.s.,**
9 July next

Dutch–English dictionary

A

aaien, to stroke
aak (de), (Rhine) barge
aal (de), eel
aalbes (de), red, black or white currant
aalmoes (de), alms
aambeeld (het), anvil
aambeien, piles
aan, at; on; to
aan, on, at, by, of:
  – het hoofd staan, to head, to manage (an institution or company)
  ik woon – zee, I live by/near the sea;
  zij heeft een leuke rok –, she's wearing a nice skirt
  ik heb daar niets –, that's of no use to me
aanbeeld (het), anvil
aanbellen, to ring the bell
aanbesteden, to put out to contract
aanbevelen, to recommend
aanbeveling (de), recommendation
aan'bidden, to worship, to adore
aanbieden, to offer
aanbieding (de), offer
aanbinden, to tie on
aanblik (de), sight, spectacle
aanbod (het), offer
aanbouw (de): in –, under construction
aanbranden, to burn (in cooking)
aanbreken, to come; break into (money or supplies); break, dawn
  een nieuw tijdperk is aangebroken, a new age has begun/dawned

aandacht (de), attention
aan'dachtig, attentive
aandeel (het), share, portion
aandeelhouder (de), shareholder
aandenken (het), memory; memento
aandienen, to announce
aandikken, to thicken; to lay it on
aandoen, to put on; to move; to affect; to call at a place
  hoe kun je me dat – ? how can you do such a thing to me?
aandoening (de), infection (of the throat, etc.)
aan'doenlijk, moving
aandrang (de), insistence; urgency; impulse
aandringen op, to press for; to insist on
  op – van, at the insistence of
aanduiden, to indicate
aan'een, together; consecutively
aanfluiting (de), mockery
aangaan, to begin; to enter into; to concern:
  dat gaat jou niks aan, that's none of your business!
aan'gaande, concerning
aangapen, to gape at
aangeboren, innate
aangedaan, moved, affected
aange'legenheid (de), affair, concern
aangenaam, agreeable, pleasant
aangenomen, adopted; assumed
aangeschoten, tipsy
aangetrouwd, connected by marriage
aangeven, to give; to hand; to indicate; to register (luggage); to notify; to inform the police

aangezien, seeing that, since

aangifte (de), notification, declaration

aan'grenzend, adjacent

aangrijpen, to grasp; to seize, to assail

aan'grijpend, moving, touching

aangroeien, to increase, to grow

aanhalen, to tighten; to quote; to fondle, to paw

aan'halig, physically demonstrative

aanhalingsteken (het), inverted comma

aanhang (de), following; supporter

aanhangen, to follow, support

aanhanger (de), follower, supporter

aan'hangig, pending, *sub judice*

aanhangsel (het), appendix

aanhangwagen (de), trailer

aan'hankelijk, affectionate

aanhebben, to have on, to wear

aanhef (de), opening words

aanheffen, to start, to strike up

aanhoren, to listen to, to hear out

aanhouden, to keep on; to persist; to arrest

aan'houdend, constant; persistent

aanhouding (de), arrest, detention

aanjagen: schrik –, to give a fright

aankijken, to look at

aanklacht (de), charge, accusation

aanklagen, to charge, to accuse

aanklager (de), plaintiff, prosecutor

aanklampen, to accost

aankleden, to dress

aankloppen, to knock at the door; to appeal

aanknopen, to tie on; to enter into

  een gesprek –, to start a conversation

aanknopingspunt (het), point of contact

aankomen, to arrive

  daar komt het juist op aan, that is just the point

aankomst (de), arrival

aankondigen, to announce

aankondiging (de), announcement

aankoop (de), purchase

aankopen, to purchase

aankoppelen, to couple

aankunnen, to be a match for, to cope (with)

aankweken, to cultivate, to grow; to foster

  een gewoonte –, to foster/cultivate a habit

aanleg (de), layout; (natural) aptitude

  in – , under construction

aanleggen, to lay out; to build; to moor; to manage

aanlegplaats (de), berth (at a wharf)

aanlegsteiger (de), landing stage

aanleiding (de), occasion

  naar – van, with reference to

aanlengen, to dilute

aanleren, to learn, to acquire

aanleunen, to lean against

aan'lokkelijk, tempting, attractive

aanloop (de), preliminary run; preamble

  veel – , many callers

aanlopen tegen, to collide with; to come across

aanmaken, to manufacture; to light (a fire)

aanmanen, to urge, to exhort, to press

aanmatigen
zich – , to presume

aan'matigend, arrogant, presumptuous

aanmelden, to announce
zich – , to present oneself

aan'merkelijk, considerable

aanmerken op, to find fault with

aanmerking (de), critical remark
in – nemen, to take into consideration

aanmoedigen, to encourage

aanmoediging (de), encouragement

aan'nemelijk, acceptable, plausible

aannemen, to accept; to assume; to adopt; to contract for

aannemer (de), contractor

aanpakken, to take hold of; to tackle

aanpappen, to chum up

aanpassen, to try on
zich – bij, to adapt oneself to

aanpassingsvermogen (het), adaptability

aanplakbiljet (het), poster

aanplanten, to plant

aanpraten, to talk (a person) into

aanprijzen, to recommend strongly

aanraden, to advise

aanraken, to touch

aanraking (de), contact

aanranden, to assault

aanrander (de), assailant

aanrecht (het), draining board

aanreiken, to hand

aanrekenen, to account
iemand iets – , to hold something against a person

aanrichten, to cause, to do

aanrijden, to run into
komen – , to drive up

aanrijding (de), collision, crash

aanroeren, to touch (on); to mix

aanschaffen, to procure, to purchase

aan'schouwen, to behold

aanschrijven, to notify officially
hij staat goed aangeschreven, he is well thought of

aanslaan, to strike (a note); to assess (for tax); to catch on (a trend)

aanslag (de), attack; (tax) assessment; fur, scale

aanslibben, to silt (up)

aansluiten, to connect, to link up
zich – bij, to join

aansluiting (de), connection

aansmeren, to foist on

aansnijden, to start cutting; to broach

aanspannen, to tighten up
een proces –, institute legal proceedings

aanspoelen, to drift ashore

aansporen, to urge on

aanspraak (de), claim; contacts
– maken op geld, claim money
hij heeft weinig –, he has few contacts, not many people talk to him

aan'sprakelijk, answerable

aanspreken, to address

aanstaan, to please
aanstaande, next; prospective
   mijn aan'staande, my *fiancé(e)*
aanstalten maken, to get ready
aan'stekelijk, infectious
aansteken, to light; to infect
aansteker (de), (cigarette)
   lighter
aanstellen, to appoint
   zich – , to put on airs
aanstelle'rij (de), affectation,
   showing off
aanstelling (de), appointment
aansterken, to recuperate
aanstichten, to instigate
aanstippen, to touch (on)
aanstoot (de), offence
aan'stotelijk, offensive
aansturen op, to head for, to
   aim at
aantal (het), number
aantasten, to attack; to impair
aantekening (de), note
aantonen, to demonstrate
aan'toonbaar, demonstrable
aantreffen, to meet, to find
aan'trekkelijk, attractive
aantrekken, to attract; to put on
   **trek je daar maar niets van
   aan!** forget it!
aan'vaarden, to begin; to
   assume; to accept
aanval(len) (de), (to) attack
aanvaller (de), assailant
aanvang (de), beginning, start
aanvangen, to begin, to start
aan'vankelijk, initial
aanvaren, to collide
aan'vechtbaar, debatable
aanvechting (de), sudden
   impulse
aanvoelen, to feel; to sense
aanvoer (de), supply

aanvoerder (de), leader
aanvoeren, to supply; to
   command
aanvraag (de), application
aanvragen, to apply for
aanvullen, to supplement
aanwakkeren, to rouse; to fan
aanwenden, to apply
aanwennen: zich – , to acquire
   (a habit)
aanwerven, to recruit
aan'wezig, present
aanwijzen, to point out
aangewezen, obvious
**aan'wijzend voornaamwoord
   (het),** demonstrative pronoun
aanwijzing (de), indication
aanwinst (de), acquisition, asset
aanwippen, to drop in
aanwrijven, to rub against; to
   impute, to blame
   iemand iets –, to pin
   something on someone
aanzetten, to put on: to hone;
   to tighten up; to egg on
aanzien, to look at: **(het),**
   distinction, reputation
aanzien voor, to (mis)take for
aan'zienlijk, notable;
   considerable
aanzoek (het), request, proposal
aanzwellen, to swell
aap (de), monkey
   de – uit de mouw, the cat out
   of the bag
aardappel (de), potato
aardbei (de), strawberry
aardbeving (de), earthquake
aarde (de), earth; soil
aarden, to thrive
   – naar, to take after
aardewerk (het), earthenware
aardgas (het), natural gas

aardig, nice, pleasant
  – wat, a fair amount
aardigheid (de), joke, fun
aardrijkskunde (de), geography
aardrijks'kundig, geographical
aards, earthly
aardschok (de), earth tremor
aard(ver)schuiving (de),
  landslide
aarts-, arch-
aarzelen, to hesitate
aarzeling (de), hesitation
aas (het), ace; bait; carrion
ab'ces (het), abscess
ab'dij (de), abbey
ABN: Algemeen Beschaafd
  Nederlands (het), Standard
  Dutch
abnor'maal, abnormal
abomi'nabel, abominable
abon'nee (de), subscriber
abonne'ment (het), subscription;
  season ticket
abon'neren: zich – op, to
  subscribe to
abri'koos (de), apricot
ab'sent, absent(-minded)
ab'sentie (de), absence
absoluut, absolute, absolutely
absor'beren, to absorb
ab'stract, abstract(ed)
abstra'heren, to abstract
absurdi'teit (de), absurdity
abt (de), abbot
a'buis (het), (in) error
abu'sievelijk, erroneously
aca'demie (de), university;
  academy
aca'demisch, academic
accent (het), accent; stress
  het – leggen op to stress
accentu'eren, to accent(uate)
accep'teren, to accept

ac'cijns (de), excise duty
ac'countant (de), chartered
  accountant, auditor
accu (de), accumulator, battery
accu'raat, accurate
ach! ah! oh! alas!
acht, eight
  acht slaan op, to heed
  in acht nemen, to observe
achtbaan (de), rollercoaster
achteloos, negligent
achten, to consider; to esteem
achtens'waardig, estimable
achter, behind
  van achter(en), from behind
achter'aan, last, in the rear
achter'af, on second thoughts
  zich – houden, to keep in the
  background
achterbak (de), boot
achter'baks, underhand
achterblijven, to stay, to lag
  behind
achterblijver (de), straggler
achterdocht (de), suspicion
achter'dochtig, suspicious
achter'een, at a stretch
achtereen'volgend, consecutive
achtereen'volgens, successively
achtergrond (de), background
achter'halen, to overtake; to
  recover
achterhoede (de), rearguard
achterhouden, to keep back
achter'in, at, in the back
achterkleinkind (het), great-
  grandchild
achterklep (de), lid of the boot,
  hatchback, tailgate
achterlaten, to leave behind
achterlijk, backward
achter'nalopen, to run after
achternaam (de), surname

achterneef (-nicht) (de), great-nephew (-niece), second cousin

achter'om, round the back

achter'op, behind

achter'over, back(wards)

achterstaan, to be inferior to; to be behind

achter'stallig, in arrear

achterstand (de), arrears
  een – hebben, to trail behind

achterstellen bij, to discriminate against

achter'uit (de), reverse gear

achter'uit, back(wards)

achter'uitgaan, to move backwards; to fall (off); to deteriorate

achter'uitgang (de), decline; deterioration

achtervoegsel (het), suffix

achter'volgen, to pursue

achter'volging (de), pursuit

achter'wege laten, to omit

achthoek (de), octagon

achtste, eighth, quaver

ac'quit, discharge

acro'baat (de), acrobat

acroba'tiek (de), acrobatics

a'cryl (het), acrylic

ac'teren, to act

ac'teur (de), actor

actie (de), action, campaign

ac'tief, active

activi'teit (de), activity

ac'trice (de), actress

actuali'teit (de), topic(ality)

actu'eel, topical

adder (de), viper

adel (de), nobility

adelaar (de), eagle

adem(loos), breath(less)

buiten –, out of breath
  op – komen, to recover one's breath

ademen, ademhalen, to breathe

ader (de), vein

aderverkalking (de), hardening of the arteries

administra'teur (de), manager

admini'stratie (de), book-keeping; management

administra'tief, administrative

admini'stratiekosten (de), administrative costs, service charges

a'dres (het), address; petition
  je bent aan het goede – , you've come to the right place

a'dresboek (het), directory

arbeidsduurverkorting (de), reduction of working hours

adver'tentie (de), advertisement

adver'teren, to advertise

ad'vies (het), advice

advi'seren, to advise

advi'seur (de), adviser

advo'caat (de), lawyer

af, off; down; finished
  – en aan, to and fro
  – en toe, now and then

afbakenen, to buoy; to stake out; to define

afbeelden, to depict

afbeelding (de), picture

afbellen, to ring off

afbetalen, to pay off

afbetaling (de), hire purchase, credit

afboeken, to write off

afbraak (de), demolition, rubble

afbreken, to demolish; to break off

afbrengen, to put off, to get off

het er goed –, to make a good job of it

afbreuk doen aan, to injure; to detract from

afbrokkelen, to crumble (away)

afdak (het), lean-to

afdalen, to descend

afdammen, to dam

afdanken, to discard; to dismiss, to disband

afdankertje (het), hand-me-down

afdeling (de), division, section, detachment, department

afdingen, to haggle

afdoen, to take off; to settle
  die theorie heeft afgedaan, that theory is quite exploded

afdoend, conclusive

afdrogen, to dry (up)

afdruipen, to drip off; to slink off

afdruk (de), copy, print; imprint

afdrukken, to print (off)

afdwalen, to stray; to digress

afdwingen, to extort; to compel

af'faire (de), affair

af'fiche (het), poster

afgaan, to go down; to go off; to flop
  van school –, to leave school
  het gaat hem goed af, it comes easily to him
  op iemand –, to go up to a person
  afgaande op de feiten, judging by the facts

afgang (de), flop, embarrassing moment

afgelegen, remote

afgemeten, measured; formal

afgescheiden van, apart from

afgevaardigde (de), deputy

afgeven, to hand over; to hand in; to emit
  de verf geeft af, the paint comes off

afgezaagd, hackneyed

afgezant (de), envoy

afgezien van, apart from

afgietsel (het), (plaster) cast

afgifte (de), delivery; issue

afgod (de), idol

af'grijselijk, horrible

afgrond (de), abyss

afgunst (de), jealousy

afhalen, to take down; to collect; to strip; to string (beans)

afhandelen, to settle (business)

af'handig: iemand iets – maken, to con someone out of something

afhangen, to hang down; to depend

af'hankelijk van, dependent on

afhebben, to have finished

afhelpen, to rid of, to relieve of; to help off; to help down

afhouden, to keep off; to deduct

afkammen, to disparage

afkeer (de), aversion

af'kerig van, averse to

afketsen, to glance off; to reject; to come to naught

afkeuren, to disapprove of; to reject as unfit, to condemn

afkeurens'waardig, reprehensible

afkijken, to crib; to look down

afkloppen, to beat off; to 'touch wood'

afkomen, to come down
  er –, to get off
  ergens van –, to get rid of a thing

afkomst (de), origin, birth

af'komstig van, originating from

afkondigen, to proclaim

afkondiging (de), proclamation

afkooksel (het), decoction

afkoopsom (de), ransom

afkopen, to buy off

afkorten, to abbreviate

afkrijgen, to get off; to get finished

afkunnen, to be able to manage

afleggen, to cover (a distance); to take (an oath)

   het – tegen iemand, be no match for someone

afleiden, to distract; to deduce; to derive

afleiding (de), distraction; derivation

afleren, to unlearn; to break off a habit

afleveren, to deliver

aflevering (de), delivery; number, instalment, episode

afloop (de), end, outcome; expiry

aflopen, to run down; to slope; to end; to expire

   ik heb alle winkels afgelopen, I have been to every shop in town

af'losbaar, redeemable

aflossen, to redeem; to relieve

afluisteren, to eavesdrop

afmaken, to finish; to kill; to break off

af'mattend, exhausting

afmeten, to measure (off)

afmeting (de), dimension

afnemen, to take off; to take down; to clear away; to decrease

afnemer (de), customer

afpakken, to snatch out of one's hand

afpersen, to extort

afpoeieren, to send packing

afraden, to dissuade

afraffelen, to rush through (a task or a speech)

afranselen, to thrash

afrastering (de), (wire) fence

afreageren, to work off (one's emotions)

afrekenen, to settle accounts

afrekening (de), settlement

afremmen, to slow down, to break; to curb

afroepen, to call

afronden, to round off

afruimen, to clear away

afschaffen, to abolish

afschaffing (de), abolition

afscheid (het), parting

   – nemen, to take one's leave

afscheuren, to tear off

afschepen, to fob off

afschilderen, to depict

afschrift (het), copy

   afschrijven, to copy; to write off; to cancel

afschrikken, to frighten away

afschrikkingsmiddel (het), deterrent

afschuw (de), loathing

af'schuwelijk, loathsome, hideous

afslaan, to beat off; to decline

   rechts – , to turn to the right

afslachten, to butcher

afslag (de), exit (on motorway); Dutch auction; erosion

afsloven: (zich) – , to wear (oneself) out

afsluitboom (de), gate, barrier

afsluitdijk (de), dam; causeway
afsluiten, to lock; to close; to turn off; to cut off; to balance; to conclude
afsnauwen, to snap at
afsnijden, to cut off
afspelen, to play (a CD on a CD player)
  zich –, to occur, to happen
afspiegelen, to reflect
afspoelen, to rinse (off)
afspraak (de), appointment, date, arrangement
afspreken, to agree, to arrange
afstaan, to cede
afstammen, to descend
afstamming (de), descent
afstand (de), distance
afstappen, to step down
afsteken bij, to contrast with
afstemmen, to tune (a radio); to attune, to gear towards
afstempelen, to stamp
afsterven, to die off
afstoffen, to dust
afstompen, to blunt
afstormen op, to rush at
afstoten, to push off; to repel
af'stotelijk, repellent
afstraffen, to punish; to reprimand
afstraffing (de), punishment, dressing-down
afstudeerrichting (de), main subject (of study)
afstuderen, to graduate, to complete one's studies
afsturen op, to head for; to unleash
aftakelen, to dismantle; to age badly
af'tands, worn out
aftappen, to tap; to draw off

aftekenen, to outline
  zich – tegen, to stand out against
aftocht (de), retreat
aftrap (de), kick-off
aftrappen, to kick off; to kick down
aftreden, to resign
af'trekbaar, (tax) deductible
aftrekken: zich –, to masturbate (men)
aftroeven, to trump
aftroggelen, to wheedle out of
aftuigen, to give a hiding
afvaardigen, to delegate
afvaart (de), departure, sailing
afval (het), refuse; waste
afvalbak (de), dustbin, rubbish bin
afvallen, to fall down, to fall away; to lose weight
af'vallig, disloyal
afvalprodukt (het), by-product, waste product
afvaren, to (set) sail
afvegen, to wipe (off)
afvloeien, to flow down; to be discharged
afvoer (de), removal; discharge; waste (pipe)
afvoeren, to carry away
afvragen: zich – , to wonder
afwachten, to await, to wait and see (about)
afwachting (de), expectation
afwas (de), washing-up, dishes
afwasbak (de), washing-up bowl
afwassen, to wash up or off
afwateren, to drain
afweergeschut (het), anti-aircraft guns
afwegen, to weigh up

afwenden, to avert
  zich –, to turn away
afwennen, to break a habit
afweren, to ward off
afwerken, to finish off
af'wezig, absent
af'wezigheid (de), absence
afwijken, to deviate
afwijking (de), deviation
afwijzen, to turn down or away,
  to reject
afwikkelen, to unroll; to wind
  up
afwisselen, to alternate, to vary
  elkaar –, to take turns
af'wisselend, alternating; varied
afzakken, to come down
afzeggen, to cancel
afzetgebied (het), market
afzetten, to take off; to depose;
  to amputate; to trim; to
  cordon off; to cheat
  een ge'voel van zich –, to
  shake off a feeling
afzette'rij (de), swindle
af'zichtelijk, hideous
afzien van, to give up
  afgezien van, apart from
  binnen af'zienbare tijd, within
  the not too distant future
af'zijdig, aloof
afzonderen, to isolate, to
  segregate
afzondering (de), seclusion
af'zonderlijk, separate
afzweren, to abjure
a'genda (de), agenda; diary
a'gent (de), agent; policeman
a'gentschap (het), agency,
  branch (bank)
a'geren, to agitate
air (het), air, demeanour
akelig, nasty, unpleasant; unwell

akker (de), (arable) field
ak'koord (het), agreement;
  chord: agreed!
akoes'tiek (de), acoustics
akte (de), deed; contract
  – van geboorte, birth
  certificate
aktentas (de), briefcase
al, all: already; even though
  – te, too
a'larmcentrale (de), emergency
  centre, emergency number
alarmeren, alert; to startle, to
  frighten
alcoholhoudend, alcoholic
alcoholvrij, non-alcoholic
aldoor, all the time
al'dus, thus
alge'meen, general, common
  over het –, in general
alhoe'wel, although
a'linea (de), paragraph
Allah, Allah
alle'bei, both
alle'daags, commonplace, of
  daily occurrence
al'leen, alone; only
al'leenspraak (de), soliloquy
al'leenstaand, single
alle'gaartje (het), hotchpotch
alle'maal, all; altogether
  – tegelijk, all together
alle'machtig, terrific, fantastic;
  wel –, I'll be damned
allen, all
al'lengs, gradually
aller'liefst, most charming
aller'eerst, first of all
aller'lei, aller'hande, all sorts of
aller'minst, (the) very least; not
  in the least
alles, everything
  van –, all sorts of things

van – en nog wat, anything and everything

al'licht, quite likely: I should think so!

　we kunnen het – proberen, no harm in trying!

allochtoon (de), (im)migrant, alien; foreign(er)

al'lure (de), air, style

　iemand met –, someone with a certain presence

al'machtig, almighty

almanak (de), almanac

al'om, everywhere

alomtegen'woordig, ubiquitous

als, as; like; if; when

alsje'blieft, please; here you are

als'mede, as well as

als'nog, as yet

als'of, as if

alstu'blieft, (see alsje'blieft)

alt (de), alto

altaar (het), altar

al'thans, at least

altijd, always

al'vast, meanwhile

al'vorens, before

al'wetend, omniscient

a'mandel (de), almond

a'mandelen (de), tonsils

amanu'ensis (de), laboratory assistant

ambacht (het), trade

ambas'sade (de), embassy

ambassa'deur (de), ambassador

ambi'ëren, to aspire to

am'bitie (de), ambition

ambiti'eus, ambitious

ambt (het), function; office

ambtelijk, official

ambtenaar (de), official, civil servant

ambtena'rij (de), red tape

ambu'lance (de), ambulance

amfi'bie (de), amphibian

ampel, ample

amper, scarcely

ampu'teren, to amputate

amu'seren, to amuse

ana'loog, analagous

ana'lyse (de), analysis

analy'seren, to analyse

ana'lytisch, analytical

ananas (de), pineapple

ander, different; other

　om de andere dag, every other day

　onder andere (o.a.), inter alia

anderhalf, one and a half

anders, different; else

　net als – , just as usual

anders'om, the other way round

anders'talige, non-native speaker

anderzijds, on the other hand

an'dijvie (de), endive

ane'moon (de), anemone

angel (de), sting; fishhook

an'gina (de), tonsillitis

angst (de), fear, terror

angstig, afraid, fearful

angst'vallig, scrupulous, timid

angst'wekkend, alarming

angstzweet (het), cold sweat

a'nijszaad (het), aniseed

ani'matiefilm (de), animation film

animo (het, de), zest

anker (het), anchor

ankeren, to anchor

an'nex (de), annexe; enclosed, attached

an'nexeren, to annex, incorporate

anno, in the year

　– 1876, in the year 1876

annu'leren, to cancel
annu'lering (de), cancellation
ano'niem, anonymous
ansicht(kaart) (de), picture postcard
an'sjovis (de), anchovy
an'tenne (de), aerial
anti'climax (de), anticlimax
an'tiek (de), antique(s)
antipa'thiek, antipathetic
antiquari'aat (het), secondhand bookshop, antique shop
antiqui'teiten, antiques
antivries (de), antifreeze
antropolo'gie (de), anthropology
antwoord (het), answer
antwoordapparaat (het), answering machine, ansaphone
antwoorden, to answer
AOW (abbrev) **(de),** state pension
a'part, apart, separate
  iets zeer –, something very special
a'pathisch, apathetic
apegapen: op – liggen, to be at one's last gasp
apenstaartje (het), @ sign
a'postel (de), apostle
apo'theek (de), (dispensing) chemist('s)
apo'theker (de), pharmacist
appa'raat (het), apparatus
appartement (het), flat, apartment
ap'pel (het), appeal, rollcall
appel (de), apple
appelgebak (het), apple pie
appel'leren, to appeal
appelsap (de), apple juice
appelstroop (de), apple spread

ap'plaus (het), applause
applaudiss'eren, to applaud
april, April
apro'pos (het): van zijn – raken, to be unnerved
aqua'rel (de), watercolour
arbeid (de), labour
arbeiden, to labour
arbeider (de), labourer
arbeidsduurverkorting (de), reduction of working hours
arbeidsinten'sief, labour-intensive
arbeidsonge'schikt, unable to work
  – verklaard worden, be declared as unable to work
arbeidstijdverkorting (de), reduction of working hours
arbeidsvoorwaarde (de), condition of employment
ar'chief (het), archives; record office
archi'tect (de), architect
architec'tuur (de), architecture
are (de), 100 square metres
arend (de), eagle
argeloos, unsuspecting
arg'listig, crafty
argwaan (de), suspicion
arg'wanend, suspicious
arm, poor
arm (de), arm; branch (of a river)
armband (de), bracelet, armlet
armleuning (de), elbow rest
armoe (de), poverty
ar'moedig, needy; shabby
arm'zalig, pitiful
armslag (de), elbow room
ar'rest (het), arrest, detention
arres'tant (de), prisoner
arres'teren, to arrest

arrondise'mentsrechtbank (de), district court, county court
ar'senicum (het), arsenic
ar'tiest (de), variety artist
artille'rie (de), artillery
arti'sjok (de), artichoke
arts (de), doctor
a.s.: aanstaande, coming: **9 juli a.s.,** 9 July coming
as (de), ash(es): axle; axis
asbakje (het), ashtray
as'best (het), asbestos
a'siel (het), asylum; refuge
asjemenou, well, I never!
as'perge (de), asparagus
astro'loog (de), astrologer
astro'noom (de), astronomer
ate'lier (het), studio, workshop
at'leet (de), athlete
atle'tiek (de), athletics
at'tent, attentive; considerate
at'tentie (de), attention; act of courtesy
at'test (het), certificate, testimonial
at'tractie (de), attraction
at'tractiepark (het), theme park, amusement park
ATV (abbrev), reduction of working hours
au pair (de), au pair
auber'gine (de), aubergine, eggplant
auditie (de), audition, screentest
au'gurk (de), gherkin
augustus, August
aula (de), auditorium
au'teur (de), author
au'teursrecht (het), copyright
auto (de), car
autobiogra'fie (de), autobiography
autochtoon (de), autochthonous, indigenous; aboriginal

autodi'dact (de), self-taught (person)
autogordel (de), seatbelt
autokaart (de), roadmap, road atlas
auto'maat (de), automaton; slot machine
auto'noom, autonomous
autori'seren, to authorize
autori'tair, high-handed; authoritarian
autoweg (de), motorway
averechts, wrong
avond (de), evening
avondeten (het), supper
avon'tuur (het), adventure
avon'tuurlijk, adventurous
azen op, to prey on
a'zijn (de), vinegar

B

baai (de), bay
baal (de), bale, bag
baaldag (de), (inf) day off, sickie
baan (de), way, track; orbit; (tennis) court; job
baanbreker (de), pioneer
baard (de), beard
  hij heeft de – in de keel, his voice is breaking
baarmoeder (de), womb
baas (de), master; boss
baat (de), benefit
  – hebben/vinden bij, to benefit from
  ten bate van, for the benefit of
baatzucht (de), selfishness
babbelen, to chatter; to gossip
babysit (de), babysitter
bad (het), bath

baden, to bath, to bathe
 zich in weelde – , to wallow in luxury
badkleding (de), bathing costume, swimwear
badkuip (de), bathtub
ba'gage (de), baggage, luggage
baga'tel (het, de), trifle
bagger (de), mud
baggeren, to dredge; to squelch
bak (de), tray; bin; pan
bakbeest (het), huge thing
bakermat (de), birthplace
bakkebaarden, side whiskers
bakken, to bake; to roast; to fry
 versgebakken broodjes, freshly baked rolls
bakker (de), baker
bakke'rij (de), bakery
baksteen (de), brick
 zakken als een – to fail (an exam) utterly
bal (de), ball (e.g. football)
bal (het), ball (dance)
ba'lans (de), balance(sheet), scales
bal'dadig, wanton, destructive
balen, to be fed up
balie (de), railing, counter
balk (de), beam, rafter
 over de – gooien, to squander
bal'kon (het), balcony
bal'let (het), ballet, dance
balling(schap) (de), exile
bal'lon (de), balloon
ba'lorig, refractory; ill-tempered
balpen (de), ballpoint pen
balsemen, to embalm
ban (de), excommunication; spell
 in de – zijn van iets, to be/fall under the spell of something
ba'naal, banal

ba'naan (de), banana
band (de), band, tape; ligament; waveband; tyre; bond
 aan banden leggen, to put under restraint
 uit de – springen, to let one's hair down
bandje (het), band; cassette, tape
ban'diet (de), bandit
bandrecorder (de), tape recorder
banen: de weg – voor, to pave the way for
 zich een weg –, to force one's way (through)
bang, afraid
bangmake'rij (de), intimidation
bank (de), bench, settee; bank
bankbiljet (het), banknote
ban'ket (het), banquet; fancy cakes
ban'ketbakker (de), pastry cook
ban'kier (de), banker
bankkluis (de), safe-deposit box
bankoverval (de), bank robbery
bankpas (de), bankcard; debit card
bank'roet (het), bankrupt(cy)
bankstel (het), sitting-room suite
bannen, to banish
bar (de), bar
 – slecht, very bad
 hij maakt het al te – , he is going too far
ba'rak (de), hut, barracks
bar'baars, barbaric
baren, to give birth to
ba'ret (de), cap, beret
barm'hartig, charitable, merciful
 de –e Samaritaan, the Good Samaritan
barrevoets, barefoot
bars, gruff, stern

barst (de), crack
barsten, to burst, to crack; to
  explode
bas (de), bass
ba'seren, to base
basis (de), basis, base; footing
basisonderwijs (het), primary
  education
basisschool (de),
  primary/elementary school
bast (de), bark
basterdsuiker (de), moist
  (brown) sugar
baten, to avail
batig saldo (het), credit balance
batikken, to do batik
batte'rij (de), battery
bavi'aan (de), baboon
ba'za(a)r (de), bazaar; sale of work
bazelen, to talk nonsense
bazig, bossy
ba'zuin (de), trumpet, trombone
be'ambte (de), official;
  employee
be'amen, to assent
be'angstigen, to alarm
be'antwoorden, to answer; to
  return; to correspond
be'bloed, bloody
be'boeten, to fine
be'bossen, to afforest
be'bouwen, to cultivate; to
  build on (or up)
be'cijferen, to calculate
bed (het), bed
be'daard, calm, composed
be'dacht op, alive to, mindful of
be'dachtzaam, circumspect
be'danken, to thank; to decline;
  to resign
be'dankje (het), word of thanks
be'daren, to calm down
beddengoed (het), bedding

bede (de), prayer, request
be'deesd, timid; coy
be'dekken, to cover
bedelaar (de), beggar
bedelen, to beg
be'delen, to endow; to
  distribute relief
be'delven, to bury
be'denkelijk, grave; precarious;
  questionable
be'denken, to recollect; to
  consider; to think up
  zich – , to change one's mind
be'derf (het), corruption; decay
be'derven, to spoil; to go bad
bedevaart (de), pilgrimage
be'diende (de), servant
be'dienen, to serve; to
  (ad)minister (to)
be'diening (de), service
be'dieningspaneel (het), control
  panel
be'ding (het): onder geen – , not
  in any circumstances
be'dingen, to stipulate
be'disselen, to see to
be'doelen, to mean
be'doeling (de), intention
be'dompt, close; stuffy
be'donderen, to bamboozle
  ben je bedonderd? are you
  crazy?
be'dotten, to fool, take in
be'drading (de), (electric) wiring
be'drag (het), amount
be'dragen, to amount to
be'dreigen, to threaten
be'dremmeld, shy, confused
be'dreven, proficient
be'driegen, to deceive
bedriege'rij (de), deception
be'drieg(e)lijk, deceptive,
  deceitful

be'drijf (het), industry, business, undertaking; act

be'drijfscultuur (de), corporate culture

be'drijfseconomie (de), business economics

be'drijfskapitaal (het), working capital

be'drijfsleider (de), manager

be'drijfsvoering (de), management

be'drijvigheid (de), bustle, activity

be'drinken: zich – , to get drunk

be'droefd, sad
– weinig, precious little

be'droevend, sad, depressing; miserable

be'drog (het), deceit, trickery

be'drukt, depressed; printed

be'ducht, apprehensive

be'duidend, significant, considerable

be'dwang (het), restraint
zich in – houden, to restrain oneself

be'dwelmen, to stun; to drug; to intoxicate

be'dwingen, to suppress, to curb

be'ëdigen, to swear in

beek (de), brook

beeld (het), image; picture; statue; beauty
zich een – vormen van, to visualize

beeldbuis (de), television screen
voor de – zitten, sit in front of the box

beeldhouwen, to sculpt

beeldhouwer (de), sculptor

beeldmerk (het), logo

beeldspraak (de), metaphor

been (het), leg; bone

beenbreuk (de), fracture

beer (de), bear; boar; buttress

beerput (de), cesspit

beest (het), animal, beast

beestachtig, beastly

beestenboel (de), filthy mess, pigsty

beet (de), bite, sting

beet hebben, to have got hold of

beetje (het), (little) bit

beetnemen, to take in

beetpakken, to take hold of

be'faamd, famous, notorious

be'gaafd, gifted

be'gaan, to tread; to commit (a murder or blunder)

be'gaan zijn met, to feel sorry for

be'gaanbaar, passable

be'gane grond (de), ground level

be'geerte (de), desire

bege'leiden, to accompany

bege'leiding (de), supervision, support; accompaniment, accompanying

bege'nadigen, to pardon, to bless

be'geren, to desire, to covet

be'gerig, desirous, covetous

be'geven, to give way; to bestow
zich – , to go, to proceed

be'gin (het), beginning

be'ginneling (de), beginner

be'ginnen, to start, to begin
wat moet ik nu – ? whatever shall I do now?
er is niets met hem te – , there is no doing anything with him

be'ginpunt (het), starting point

be'ginsel (het), principle
be'ginstadium (het), initial stage
be'graafplaats (de), cemetery
be'grafenis (de), funeral
be'graven, to bury
be'grenzen, to bound, to limit
be'grijpelijk, understandable
be'grijpen, to understand;
 include
be'grip (het), concept(ion);
 notion; comprehension
 vlug van –, quick on the
 uptake
be'groeid, overgrown
be'groeten, to greet
be'groten, to estimate
be'groting (de), estimate, budget
be'gunstigen, to favour
be'ha (de), bra
be'haaglijk, pleasant,
 comfortable
be'haard, hairy
be'halen, to gain, to win
be'halve, except, apart from
be'handelen, to treat, to deal
 with
be'handeling (de), treatment
be'hang(sel) (het), wallpaper
be'hangen, to paper, to drape
be'hartigen, to have at heart, to
 look after
be'heer (het), management
be'heerder (de), manager,
 administrator
be'heersen, to rule; to control;
 to command (a language); to
 dominate
be'helpen: zich –, to make do,
 to rough it
be'hendig, dexterous
be'hept met, afflicted with
be'heren, to manage, to
 administer

be'hoedzaam, cautious
be'hoefte (de), need
be'hoefte (hebben) aan, (to have
 a) need for
be'hoeve: ten – van, for the
 sake of, in aid of
be'hoorlijk, proper; decent
be'horen, to belong; to be
 fitting
 naar –, properly
be'houd (het), preservation
be'houden, to retain; to
 preserve
be'houdend, conservative
be'hulp: met – van, with the aid
 of
be'hulpzaam, helpful
beide(n), both; two
 geen van –, neither (of them)
be'ijveren: zich –, to do one's
 utmost
be'ïnvloeden, to influence
beitel (de), chisel
beits (de), (wood) stain
beitsen, to stain (wood)
be'jaard, aged
be'jaarde (de), old-age
 pensioner
be'jaarden(te)huis (het), old
 people's home, home for the
 elderly
be'jammeren, to lament
be'jegenen, to treat
bek (de), mouth, beak
be'kaaid: er – afkomen, to come
 off badly
bekaf, dog tired
be'kakt, snooty, affected
be'kend, (well-)known;
 acquainted
 ik ben hier niet –, I'm a
 stranger here: I don't know
 the area

be'kende (de), acquaintance

be'kendheid (de), acquaintance; reputation, notoriety

 van algemene – , generally known

be'kendmaken, to announce; to make public; to familiarize (with)

be'kendmaking (de), announcement

be'kennen, to admit, to confess; to follow suit

be'kentenis (de), admission, confession

beker (de), cup, mug

be'keren, to convert

be'keuring (de), charge, fine

be'kijken, to look at; to look into

be'kijk(s) hebben, to attract attention

bekken (het), basin; pelvis

be'klaagde (de), accused

be'kladden, to besmirch

be'klagen, to pity

 zich – , to complain

be'kleden, to cover; to upholster

 een ambt – , to hold an office

be'kleding (de), covering, upholstery; lagging

be'klemd, oppressed; stressed

be'klemdheid (de), oppression; constriction

be'klimmen, to climb

be'klinken, to rivet; to settle

be'kneld, locked, jammed

be'knopt, concise

be'kocht, cheated

be'koelen, to cool down

be'kogelen, to pelt

be'kokstoven, to wangle

be'komen, to recover; to agree with

be'kommeren: zich – om, to bother about

be'konkelen, to scheme

be'kopen (met de dood), to pay (with one's life)

be'korten, to curtail

be'kostigen, to pay for

be'krachtigen, to confirm, to ratify

be'krassen, to cover with scratches

bekriti'seren, to criticize, to find fault with

be'krompen, narrow-minded; restricted

be'kronen, to crown, to award a prize

be'kruipen, to take by surprise

 het gevoel bekroop me, the feeling came over me

bekvechten, to wrangle noisily

be'kwaam, capable

be'kwaamheid (de), ability

bel (de), bell; bubble

be'labberd, rotten

be'lachelijk, ridiculous

be'landen, to land (up)

be'lang (het), interest; importance

be'langeloos, disinterested

be'langrijk, important

belang'stellend, interested

be'langstelling (de), interest

belangwekkend, interesting

be'lastbaar, taxable, dutiable

be'lasten, to burden; to tax; to charge; to debit

 zich – met, to take upon oneself

be'lasteren, to slander; to libel

be'lasting (de), tax(ation); load

be'lastingaangifte (de), tax return

be'lastingaanslag (de), tax assessment

be'lastingdienst (de), Inland Revenue, Internal Revenue Service (Am)

be'lastingheffing (de), taxation

be'lastingontduiking (de), tax evasion

be'lazeren, to bamboozle
  ben je belazerd? are you mad?

be'ledigen, to insult

be'lediging (de), insult

be'leefd(heid) (de), polite(ness)

beleefdheids'halve, out of politeness

be'leg (het), siege

be'legen, mature (cheese)

be'leggen, to cover; to call (a meeting); to invest

be'leid (het), administration; prudence

be'lemmeren, to hamper

be'lendend, adjacent

be'letsel (het), obstacle, hindrance

be'letten, to prevent

be'leven, to experience, to live through
  avonturen – , to have/experience adventures

be'lezen, well-read

be'lichamen, to embody

be'lichten, to throw light on; to expose

be'lijden, to confess; to profess

be'lijdenis (de), confession, creed; confirmation

belknop (de), bell-pull; bell-push

bellen, to ring (the bell)

belletje (het), call, buzz, ring

be'loeren, to spy upon

be'lofte (de), promise

be'lonen, to reward

be'loop: op zijn – laten, to let (something) take its course

be'loven, to promise

be'luisteren, to listen to

be'lust op, eager for

be'machtigen, to secure

be'mannen, to man

be'manning (de), crew; garrison

be'merken, to perceive

be'mesten, to manure

be'middelaar (de), intermediary

be'middeld, well-to-do

be'middelen, to mediate

be'middeling (de), mediation

be'mind, much loved

be'moedigen, to encourage

be'moeial (de), busybody

be'moeien: zich – met, to concern oneself with, to meddle with

be'moeienis (de), concern

be'moeilijken, to hinder

be'moeiziek, meddlesome

be'nadelen, to harm

be'naderen, to estimate; to get near

be'nadering: bij – , approximately

be'nard, critical; perilous

be'nauwd, close, stuffy; constricted; afraid
  ik heb het – , I can't breathe

be'nauwdheid, closeness; constriction; fear

bende (de), gang; mess

be'neden, below, downstairs; under, beneath

be'nedenhuis (het), bottom flat

be'nedenverdieping (de), ground floor

be'nemen, to take away
  de moed – , to discourage

be'nepen, cramped; narrow-minded; timid

be'nevelen, to befog, to fuddle

bengelen, to dangle

be'nieuwen: het zal me – , I wonder

be'nieuwd, curious to know

be'nijden, to envy

benijdens'waard(ig), enviable

be'nodigd, required

be'noemen, to appoint; to nominate

be'nul (het), notion

  ik heb geen flauw –, I haven't got a clue

be'nutten, to make use of

ben'zine (de), petrol

ben'zinepomp (de), petrol station; fuel pump

be'oefenen, to study, to practise

be'ogen, to have in view

be'oordelen, to judge, to review

be'oordeling (de), assessment, evaluation, judgement

bepaald, positive; definite; appointed

  in een – geval, in a given case

  niet – beleefd, not exactly polite

be'pakken, to pack

be'palen, to determine, to define

  zich – tot, to confine oneself to

be'paling (de), definition; regulation; stipulation

be'perken, to limit, to confine

be'planten, to plant

be'pleiten, to plead

be'praten, to talk over

  zich laten – , to be persuaded

be'proefd, well-tried

be'proeven, to try, to put to the test; to afflict

be'raad (het), deliberation, consideration

be'raadslagen, to deliberate

be'raden: zich – (op), to consider

be'ramen, to devise

berde: te – brengen, to broach

be'rechten, to adjudicate

be'redderen, to arrange

be'reden, mounted

berede'neren, to reason out

be'reid, ready, prepared

be'reiden, to prepare

bereid'vaardig, bereid'willig, ready to help

be'reik (het), reach; range

be'reiken, to reach, to achieve

be'reikbaar, attainable

be'rekenen, to calculate; to charge

  niet berekend voor het werk, not equal to the work

be'rekening (de), calculation

berg (de), mountain

bergachtig, mountainous

berg'afwaarts, downhill

bergen, to store; to salvage; to accommodate

bergingswerk (het), salvage operations

bergkam (de), bergrug (de), mountain ridge

bergkloof (de), ravine, gorge

bergruimte (de), storage space

bergwand (de), mountain face

be'richt (het), news, report; notice

be'richten, to inform

be'rispen, to rebuke, to reprimand

berk (de), birch

berm (de), shoulder (roadside)

be'roemd, famous

be'roemdheid (de), fame, celebrity

be'roemen: zich – op, to pride oneself on

be'roep (het), profession; appeal
in hoger – gaan, to appeal

beroepen: zich – op, to appeal to, to plead, to refer to

be'roeps-, professional

beroeps'halve, in one's professional capacity

be'roerd, rotten

be'roeren, to stir, to disturb

be'roerte (de), stroke, fit

be'rokkenen, to cause
iemand schade – , to cause damage to someone

be'rooid, penniless

be'rouw (het), repentance

be'rouwen: het zal je – , you will be sorry (for it)

be'rouwvol, repentant

be'roven, to rob, to deprive

be'rucht, notorious

be'rusten in, to be resigned to

be'rusten op, to rest on; to be due to
dit moet op een misverstand –, this must be due to a misunderstanding

bes (de), berry, (red) currant

be'schaafd, well-bred; civilized

be'schaamd, ashamed

be'schadigen, to damage

beschamen, to shame; to dash (hope); to betray (confidence)

beschamend, humiliating

be'schaving (de), culture, civilization

be'scheiden, modest, retiring

be'schermeling (de), protégé(e)

be'schermen, to protect

be'schermengel (de), guardian angel

be'scherming (de), protection, patronage

be'schikbaar, available

be'schikken over, to have at one's disposal

be'schikking: ter – , available

be'schilderde ramen, stained glass windows

be'schimmelen, to go mouldy

be'schouwen, to regard, to contemplate
wel beschouwd, all things considered

be'schrijven, to describe; to cover with writing

be'schrijving (de), description

be'schroomd, timid

be'schuldigde (de), accused, defendant

be'schuldigen, to accuse

be'schuldiging (de), accusation

be'schutten, to shelter

be'sef (het), realization; notion

be'seffen, to realise, to be aware of

be'slaan, to take up (space); to mount (with silver, etc.); to shoe; to get blurred; to tarnish

beslag (het), batter; fitting
zijn – krijgen, to settle, to be put into effect
– leggen op, to take up; to secure; to claim

be'slissen, to decide

be'slist, decided, for certain

be'sloten, private; close

be'sluipen, to steal up on

be'sluit (het), conclusion; decision

be'sluiteloos, irresolute

be'sluiten, to conclude, to decide

be'smettelijk, contagious, infectious

be'smetten, to infect, to contaminate

be'sneeuwd, snow-covered

be'snijden, to circumcise

be'snoeien, to lop, to prune; to cut down

be'sparen, to save

be'spatten, to bespatter

be'spelen, to play

be'speuren, to perceive

be'spieden, to spy on

be'spiegelend, contemplative

be'spiegeling (de), contemplation

be'spoedigen, to speed up

be'spottelijk, ridiculous

be'spotten, to ridicule

be'spraakt, never at a loss for words

be'spreken, to book, to reserve; to discuss, to review

be'sprenkelen, to sprinkle

be'springen, to pounce upon

be'sproeien, to spray

best, best; very good; dear; very well

  het is mij – , it is all right by me

  ten beste geven, to contribute

be'staan (het), existence, livelihood

bestaan, to exist

  – uit, to consist of

  – van, to subsist on

be'staanbaar, possible

be'staansmiddel (het), means of support

be'staansminimum (het), subsistence level

be'staansrecht (het), right to exist

be'stand (het), truce

be'stand tegen, be immune to

be'standdeel (het), ingredient, component

be'steden, to spend; to devote

be'stedingspatroon (het), pattern of spending

be'steedbaar, disposable

be'stelen, to rob

be'stellen, to order; to deliver

be'stelwagen (de), (delivery) van

be'stemmen, to destine; to intend

be'stempelen, to stamp; to designate

be'stendig, constant; lasting; steady

be'sterven: hij bestierf het van schrik, he nearly died of fright **dat woord ligt in zijn mond bestorven,** he is always using that word

be'stijgen, to mount, to ascend

be'stormen, to storm

be'straffen, to punish

be'straten, to pave

be'strijden, to combat; to defray

be'strijdingsmiddel (het), pesticide; weed killer

be'strijken, to cover

be'strooien, to strew, to sprinkle

bestu'deren, to study

be'stuiven, to (cover with) dust; to pollinate

be'sturen, to govern; to drive; to steer

be'stuur (het), government, administration; committee

bèta, science subjects

be'taalpasje (het), cheque card, debit card

be'talen, to pay (for)

  ik zal het hem betaald zettten, I'll get even with him

be'tamelijk, seemly
be'tasten, to feel
be'tegelen, to tile
be'tekenen, to mean
  het heeft niets te – , it is of no
  consequence
be'tekenis (de), meaning;
  significance
beter, better
beterschap (de), recovery
be'teugelen, to curb
be'teuterd, taken aback
be'tichten, to accuse
be'timmeren, to panel with wood
be'titelen, to style
be'togen, to argue
be'toging (de), demonstration,
  march
be'ton (het), concrete
be'tonmolen (de), concrete
  mixer
be'tonnen, concrete
be'toog (het), argument;
  exposition
be'toveren, to bewitch, to
  fascinate
be'traand, tear-stained
be'trachten, to do, to show
be'trappen, to catch
  iemand op heterdaad –, to
  catch someone red-handed
be'treden, to tread; to set foot on
be'treffen, to concern
  wat mij betreft, as far as I am
  concerned
be'trekkelijk, relative
be'trekken, to move into; to
  involve; to cloud over
be'trekking (de), post, job
  met – tot, with reference to
be'treuren, to regret
betreurens'waardig, regrettable
be'trokken, overcast

be'trokken bij, concerned
  (with, in)
be'trouwbaar, reliable
be'tuigen, to express; to protest;
  to profess
betweter (de), knowall
be'twijfelen, to doubt
be'twistbaar, contestable
be'twisten, to dispute, to
  contest
beu, fed up
beuk (de), beech
beuken, to beat, to pound
beul (de), executioner; brute
beunhaas (de), bungler
beunhazen, to dabble, to
  moonlight
beurs, overripe; bruised
beurs (de), purse; scholarship;
  exchange
beurt (de), turn
  een goede – maken, make a
  good impression, earn
  brownie points;
  jij bent aan de – , it's your turn
be'vallen, to please; to be
  confined
be'valllig, graceful
be'vatten, to contain; to
  comprehend
be'veiligen, to safeguard
be'vel (het), order, command
be'velen, to command
be'velhebber (de), commander
beven, to tremble
bever (de), beaver
beverig, shaky
be'vestigen, to fasten; to
  consolidate; to confirm; to
  induct
be'vinden, to find
  zich – , to be (situated)
be'vlekken, to stain

be'vlieging (de), sudden impulse, whim

be'vochtigen, to moisten

be'voegd, competent, qualified

be'volking (de), population

be'volkingsdichtheid (de), population density

be'volkingsgroep (de), section of the population

be'voordelen, to benefit

be'vooroordeeld, prejudiced

be'voorrechten, to privilege

be'vorderen, to promote

be'vorderlijk voor, conducive to

be'vredigen, to satisfy; to appease

be'vreesd voor, afraid of

be'vriend, on friendly terms

be'vriezen, to freeze, to get frost-bitten

be'vrijden, to liberate, to release

be'vrijdingsdag (de), liberation day

be'vruchten, to fertilize

be'vuilen, to soil

be'waken, to guard

be'wapenen, to arm

be'waren, to keep, to preserve

be'waring (de), keeping, custody

in – geven, to deposit

be'weegbaar, movable

be'weeglijk, mobile, fidgety

be'weegreden (de), motive

be'wegen, to move; to induce

be'weging (de), movement, motion

uit eigen – , of one's own accord

be'weren, to assert, to contend

be'werkelijk, laborious

be'werken, to till; to work on or up; to adapt; to bring about

bewerk'stelligen, to bring about

be'wijs (het), proof; certificate; evidence

be'wijsgrond (de), argument

be'wijzen, to prove; to show

be'wind (het), government, rule

be'wolken, to cloud over

be'wolking (de), cloud(s)

be'wonderen, to admire

be'wonen, to inhabit

be'woner (de), resident, occupant, inhabitant

be'woonbaar, liveable, habitable

be'wust, conscious; concerned

zich – zijn van, to be aware of

de bewuste brief, the letter in question

be'wusteloos, unconscious

be'wustzijn (het), consciousness

buiten – , unconscious

be'zaaien, to strew; to dot; to litter

het is bezaaid met bloemen, it is strewn/dotted with flowers

be'zadigd, sober-minded

be'zegelen, to seal

bezem (de), broom

be'zeren, to hurt

be'zet, occupied, engaged; set

be'zeten, possessed

be'zetten, to occupy; to set

be'zetting (de), occupation; cast (of a play)

be'zichtigen, to view

be'zielen, to inspire

wat bezielt je? what has come over you?

be'zien, to look at

dat staat nog te – , that remains to be seen

bezig, occupied, busy

druk – , hard at work

bezigheid (de), occupation

bezighouden, to keep occupied

be'zinken, to settle (down); to sink in

be'zinksel (het), sediment

be'zinnen: zich –, to reflect; to change one's mind

bezinning (de): tot – komen, to come to one's senses

be'zit (het), possession(s), estate

be'zittelijk voornaamwoord (het), possessive pronoun

be'zitten, to possess

be'zittingen (de), property, possessions

be'zoedelen, to defile

be'zoek (het), visit
  we krijgen –, we are expecting visitors

be'zoeken, to visit; to afflict

be'zondigen: zich – aan, to be guilty of

be'zopen, tipsy; crazy

be'zorgd, anxious; provided for

be'zorgen, to procure; to give; to deliver

be'zuinigen, to economize

be'zuren, to suffer for

be'zwaar (het), objection; drawback

be'zwaard, weighted; burdened, oppressed

be'zwaarlijk, scarcely
  bezwaarlijk vinden, to object to

be'zwaarschrift (het), petition

be'zwarende omstandigheden, aggravating circumstances

be'zweet, sweating

be'zweren, to adjure; to exorcise

be'zwijken, to succumb, to collapse

be'zwijmen, to faint

bibberen, to shiver

bibliothe'caris (de), librarian

biblio'theek (de), library

bidden, to pray, to say grace

biecht (de), confession

biechten, to confess; to go to confession

bieden, to offer; to bid

biefstuk (de), rump steak

bier (het), ale, beer

biet (de), beet
  rode –, beetroot

bietsuiker (de), beet sugar

biezen, (made of) rushes

big (de), piglet

bij, near, at, with, by; present; in addition; bee
  hij is goed –, he is all there
  er staat me iets van –, I seem to remember something about it

bij-, secondary, in addition

bijbedoeling (de), ulterior motive

bijbel (de), bible

bijblijven, to keep pace with; to stick in the memory

bijbrengen, to impart; to bring round

bijde'hand, smart

bijdraaien, to heave to; to come round

bijdrage (de), contribution

bijdragen, to contribute; to tend

bij'een, together

bij'eenkomen, to come together

bij'eenkomst (de), meeting, gathering

bij'eengenomen: alles –, all things considered

bijenkorf (de), beehive

bijgaand, enclosed

bijgedachte (de), implication; association

bijgeloof (het), superstition
bijge'lovig, superstitious
bijhouden, to keep up to date; to keep up with
bijkeuken (de), utility room
bijknippen, to trim
bijkomen, to come to, to revive
  er komt nog bij, what is more
bijkomend, bij'komstig, attendant; incidental
bijl (de), hatchet, axe
  het bijltje erbij neerleggen, to chuck it (in)
bijlage (de), enclosure; appendix
bijleggen, to make up (a quarrel); to add (money) to
bijna, almost
  – niet, hardly
bijnaam (de), nickname
bijpassen, to pay the difference
bijpassend, matching
bijschenken, to fill up
bijscholen, to get/give further training
bijschrijven, to include
bijslag (de), bonus, extra allowance; extra charge;
  kinderbijslag, child benefit
bijsluiter (de), information/instruction leaflet
bijsmaak (de), trace, tang
bijspijkeren, to brush up (skills), to catch up
bijspringen, to help
bijstaan, to assist
bijstand (de), assistance; social security, welfare
bijstandsmoeder (de), (single) mother on social security
bijstandsuitkering (de), social security payment
bijstelling (de), readjustment
bijster: het spoor – zijn, to have lost one's way
  niet – , not particularly
bijten, to bite
  van zich af – , to bite back
bijtend, caustic; cutting; corrosive
bij'tijds, in good time
bijtrekken, to pull up; to improve
bijvak (het), subsidiary subject
bijval (de), approbation; applause
bijvallen, to back up
bijverdienen, to earn a little on the side
bijvoegen, to add
bij'voeglijk naamwoord (het), adjective
bijvoegsel (het), supplement
bij'voorbeeld, for instance
bijwerken, to touch up; to bring up to date; to give extra coaching
bijwonen, to attend
bijwoord (het), adverb
bijzaak (de), matter of secondary importance
bijzettafeltje (het), occasional table
bij'ziend, short-sighted
bijzijn (het), presence
bijzin (de), subordinate clause
bij'zonder, special, particular; private
  niets bijzonders, nothing out of the ordinary
bij'zonderheden (de), particulars
bil (de), buttock
bil'jart (het), billiard table, billiards
bil'jet (het), (bank)note; ticket
billijk, fair
binden, to bind, to tie (up); to thicken

binnen, within, inside, in
   het schoot me te – , it
   (suddenly) struck me
binnenband (de), inner tube
binnen'door gaan, to take a
   short cut
binnengaan, to go in
binnenkomen, to come in
binnen'kort, shortly
binnenlands, internal, home ...
   **Ministerie van Binnenlandse
   Zaken,** Home Office
binnens'huis, indoors
binnens'monds, under one's
   breath, indistinctly
binnenste'buiten, inside out
binnenvaart, inland navigation
bio'loog (de), biologist
bios'coop (de), cinema
bisschop (de), bishop
bitter, bitter
   bitter weinig, next to nothing
bitterkoekje (het), macaroon
bivak (het), bivouac
blaadje (het), petal; leaflet;
   tray
   ik sta bij hem in een goed –,
   I am in his good books
blaar (de), blister
blaas (de), bladder; bubble
blaasinstrument (het), wind
   instrument
blad (het) (pl bladen), leaf; sheet
   of paper; newspaper; tray: **(pl
   bladeren),** leaf of a tree
   **hij neemt geen – voor de
   mond,** he does not mince his
   words
bladgroente (de), greens
bladzij(de) (de), page
blaffen, to bark
bla'mage (de), disgrace, blunder
blanco, blank

blank, white; pure; naked;
   flooded
blaten, to bleat
blauw, blue
blauwe'regen (de), wisteria
blazen, to blow; to spit (cat)
   hoog van de toren –, to brag
bleek, pale
bleken, to bleach
bles'sure (de), wound, injury (in
   sport)
blij(de), glad
blijdschap (de), gladness
blijk: – geven van, to show signs
   of
blijkbaar, apparently
blijken, to appear, to transpire
   't moet nog –, it remains to be
   seen
blijspel (het), comedy
blijven, to stay, to remain
blijvend, lasting, permanent
blik (de), glance, look
blik (het), tin, can; dustpan
blikgroente (de), tinned
   vegetables
blikken: zonder – of blozen,
   without turning a hair
blikopener (de), tin opener
blikschade (de), bodywork
   damage (to a car)
bliksem (de), lightning
blikvanger (de), eyecatcher
blind, blind
   zich – staren op, to be
   obsessed by
blinddoeken, to blindfold
blinde'darmontsteking (de),
   appendicitis
blindelings, blindly
blindheid (de), blindness
bloed (het), blood
bloedarmoede (de), anaemia

bloedbad (het), carnage, bloodbath
bloeden, to bleed
bloederig, bloody
bloedneus (de), nose bleed
bloedsomloop (de), circulation (of the blood)
bloei (de), bloom, blossom(ing); prosperity
bloeien, to bloom; to flourish
bloeitijd (de), blossom time; heyday
bloem (de), flower; flour
  de bloemetjes buiten zetten, to paint the town red
bloembol (de), bulb
bloe'mist (de), florist
bloemkool (de), cauliflower
bloemlezing (de), anthology
bloemrijk, florid
bloemstuk (het), bouquet
bloesem (de), blossom
blok (het), block; log
blokfluit (de), recorder
blokje (het), cube; square
blok'kade (de), blockade
blokken, to swot, to grind
blok'keren, to block; to blockade
blond, fair
bloot, bare, naked; sheer
blootgeven: zich –, to lay oneself open (to attack)
blootje: in je –, in the nude
blootleggen, to reveal
blootshoofds, bareheaded
blootstaan aan, to be exposed to
blootstellen, to expose
blos (de), blush; bloom
blozen, to blush
blubber (de), mud
bluffen, to brag

blunder (de), blunder
blussen, to extinguish; to quell
blut, broke
bobbel (de), bump; bubble
bobbelig, lumpy
bobslee (de), bob (sleigh)
bochel (de), hump; hunchback
bocht (de), bend
bochtig, winding
bod (het), bid
bodem (de), bottom; soil; territory
bodemloos, bottomless
boed'dhisme (het), Buddhism
boedel (de), household goods; personal estate
boeg (de), bow (s)
  veel werk voor de –, a lot of work on hand
boei (de), buoy
boeien (de), fetters: to fetter; to hold the attention
boeiend, fascinating
boek (het), book
  te – staan als, to have the reputation of
  je gaat buiten je boekje, you are overstepping the mark
boekdeel (het), volume
boekenlegger (de), bookmark
boeken, to book
boekenkast (de), bookcase
boekenwijsheid (de), book learning
boekhandel (de), bookshop
boekhouden, to keep accounts
boeking (de), booking, reservation; caution (in football)
boel: een –, a lot
  een armoedig boeltje, a shoddy outfit
boemeltrein (de), slow train

boenen, to scrub
boenwas (de), wax polish
boer (de), farmer; knave (at cards); boor; belch
boerde'rij (de), farm
boeren, to belch
boeren'jongens, brandy and raisins
boeren'kool (de), kale
boerenverstand (het), common sense
boe'rin (de), farmer's wife
boers, boorish
boete (de), penalty, fine; penance
boeten voor, to atone for
boet'seren, to model
boezem (de), bosom
bof (de), stroke of luck; mumps
boffen, to be lucky
bok (de), buck; billy goat
bokkensprong (de), caper, prank
boksen, to box
bol (de), globe, sphere; crown (of hat); bulb; head: convex, bulging
bolhoed (de), bowler hat
bollen, to bulge
bollenteelt (de), bulb-growing (industry)
bollentijd (de), bulb season
bolletje (het), little ball; roll
bolletjesslikker (de), someone who smuggles drugs by swallowing them
bolster (de), shell, husk
bolwerk (het), bulwark
bolwerken: hij kon het niet –, he could not manage it
bom (de), bomb
bomaanslag (de), bomb attack
bombar'deren, to shell; to bomb(ard)

bom'melding (de), bomb alert
bon (de), voucher; coupon
bond (de), alliance, union
bondgenoot (de), ally
bondig, terse
bondscoach (de), national (football) coach
bondselftal (het), national (football) team
bonne'fooi: op de – ergens heen gaan, go somewhere on the off chance
bons (de), bump, thud
de – geven, to sack, to throw over
bont (het), fur
bont, many-coloured; gaudy; piebald; varied; motley
je maakt het te –, you are going too far
bonzen, to throb; to pound; to bump
boodschap (de), message, errand
boodschappen doen, to go shopping
boog (de), arch, arc; bow
boogschieten, (to do) archery
Boogschutter (de), Sagittarius
boom (de), tree; barrier; pole
boomgaard (de), orchard
boomstam (de), tree trunk
boon (de), bean
boor (de), drill, gimlet
boord (het, de), collar; (ship)board
aan –, on board
boordevol, brim-full
booreiland (het), oilrig
boormachine (de), (electric) drill
boos, angry; evil
boos'aardig, malicious
boosheid (de), anger

boot (de), boat
bootreis (de), voyage, cruise
bord (het), plate; board
bor'deel (het), brothel
bor'des (het), (flight of) steps
bordkrijt (het), chalk
bor'duren, to embroider
boren, to drill, to bore
borg (de), surety, security, bail
borgsom (de), deposit; security (money)
borgstelling (de), security; bail
borgtocht (de), security, bail
borrel (de), dram, shot (of an alcoholic drink); a social occasion
borrelen, to (have a) drink; to bubble
borst (de), breast, chest
  tegen de – stuiten, to go against the grain
borstbeeld (het), bust
borstel (de), brush; bristle
borstelen, to brush
borstelig, bristly
borstkanker (de), breast cancer
borstkas (de), chest
borstplaat (de), fondant
borstvoeding (de), breastfeeding
borstzak (de), breast pocket
bos (de), bunch, bundle, tuft
bos (het), bundle, bunch; forest
bosachtig, wooded
bosbes (de), bilberry, blueberry
bosbouw (de), forestry
boswachter (de), (forest)keeper
bot (het), bone
  bot blunt
  – vangen, to meet with a curt refusal
botvieren, to give rein to
boter (de), butter
boterbloem (de), buttercup

boterham (de), slice of bread; sandwich
botsen, to collide, to bump
botsing (de), collision
botweg, flatly
boud, bold
bou'gie (de), sparking plug
bouil'lon (de), beef tea, stock
bout (de), bolt; wooden pin; leg cut of meat
bouw (de), build, construction; cultivation; structure
bouwen, to build
bouw'kundig, architectural
bouwkunst (de), architecture
bouwterrein (het), building site
bouwval (de), ruin
bouw'vallig, tumble-down, dilapidated
boven, above, over
  te – gaan, to exceed
  te – komen, to get over
bovenaan, at the top
boven'dien, moreover
bovenmodaal, above average
boven'menselijk, superhuman
bovenna'tuurlijk, supernatural
bovenop, on (the) top of
bovenste, topmost
boventoon (de), overtone
  de – voeren, to (pre)dominate
bovenverdieping (de), top floor
bowl (de), punch
box (de), playpen
braaf, good, decent, upright
braak, fallow
braaksel (het), vomit
braam (de), blackberry
Brabançonne (de), 'Brabançonne' (national anthem of Belgium)
braden, to roast
braille (de), Braille

brak, brackish
braken, to vomit
brallen, to brag
bran'card (de), stretcher
branche (de), sector (of industry or business), branch, department
brand (de), fire
  in – vliegen, to catch fire
brandbaar, inflammable
brandblusser (de), fire extinguisher
branden, to burn
brandgevaar (het), fire hazard, fire risk
brandkast (de), safe
brandmerken, to brand
brandnetel (de), stinging nettle
brandpunt (het), focus
brandschoon, spotless
brandstapel (de), stake; funeral pile
brandstof (de), fuel
brandweer (de), fire brigade
bra'voure (de), bravado
breed, broad, wide
breed'sprakig, long-winded
breedte (de), breadth, width; latitude
breed'voerig, detailed
breekbaar, breakable, fragile
breekijzer (het), crowbar
breien, to knit
brein (het), brain
breiwerk (het), knitting
breken, to break
brengen, to bring, to take
  er toe –, to induce
bres (de), breach
bre'tels (de), braces
breuk (de), fracture, fraction, rupture
bre'vet (het), (flying) certificate

brief (de), letter
briefkaart (de), postcard
briefwisseling (de), correspondence
bries (de), breeze
briesen, to snort
brievenbus (de), letterbox
brij (de), pulp; porridge
bril (de), glasses
brilmontuur (het), glasses frame
Brits, British
broche (de), brooch
bro'chure (de), brochure; prospectus
broeden, to brood
broeder (de), brother
broeien, to brood; to brew; to heat
broeierig, sultry
broeikas (de), greenhouse
broeikaseffect (het), greenhouse effect
broeinest (het), hotbed
broek (de), (pair of) trousers, knickers
broekje (het), panties, knickers
broekspijp (de), trouser leg
broer (de), brother
brok (het), fragment; lump
bro'kaat, bro'caat (het), brocade
brokkelen, to crumble
brommen, to growl, to grumble
bromvlieg (de), bluebottle
bron (de), spring, source
brons (het), bronze
bronzen, bronze
brood (het), bread, loaf
  zijn – verdienen, to earn one's living
broodbeleg (het), sandwich filling
broodje (het), (bread)roll
broodjeszaak (de), sandwich bar

broos, brittle, fragile, frail
brouwen, to brew
brouwe'rij (de), brewery
  leven in de – brengen, to liven
  things up
brug (de), bridge
  over de – komen, to pay up
brui (de): er de – aan geven, to
  chuck it
bruid (de), bride
brui(de)gom (de), bridegroom
bruidsjapon (de), wedding dress
bruidsmeisje (het), bridesmaid
bruidspaar (het), bride and
  bridegroom
bruidsschat (de), dowry
bruikbaar, usable
bruikleen: in –, on loan
bruiloft (de), wedding (feast)
bruin, brown
bruisen, to effervesce; to seethe
brullen, to roar
bru'taal, impudent
bru'taalweg, calmly
brutali'teit (de), insolence
bruto, gross (weight)
brutosalaris (het), gross salary
bruusk, brusque
bruut, brutish
bruut (de), brute
btw (de), VAT
buffel (de), buffalo
buf'fet (het), sideboard; buffet
bui (de), shower (of rain); fit
buigbaar, flexible
buigen, to bend, to bow; to
  submit
buiging (de), bow, bend;
  inflexion
buigtang (de), (pair of) pliers
buigzaam, pliable; yielding
buiig, showery
buik (de), belly

buikje (het), tummy
buikpijn (de), stomach ache
buikspreker (de), ventriloquist
buil (de), bump (on someone's
  head)
  **daar kun je je geen – aan
  vallen,** you can't go far wrong
  with that
buis (de), tube, pipe; jacket
buiten, outside; beyond;
  without; in the country
  het ging – mij om, it occurred
  without my knowledge
  van – kennen, to know by
  heart
buitenband (de), tyre
buitenbeentje (het), odd one
  out, outsider
buitenge'meen, buitenge'woon,
  uncommon, extraordinary
buite'nissig, odd
buitenkansje (het), stroke of
  luck
buitenkant (de), outside
buitenland: in het –, abroad
buitenlander (de), foreigner
buitenlands, foreign
buitenlucht (de), open air
buitens'huis, out of doors
buiten'spel (de), off-side
buiten'sporig, excessive
buitenstaander (de), outsider
buitenste, outermost
buitenwijk (de), suburb
bukken, to duck, to stoop
  gebukt gaan onder, to be
  weighed down by
bul (de), bull; diploma
bulderen, to roar
bulken, to bellow
  – van het geld, to roll in
  money
bult (de), hump, lump

bundel (de), bundle; collection (of poems etc.)
bungelen, to dangle
burcht (de), castle, citadel
bu'reau (het), office; desk
bureaucra'tie (de), bureaucracy
bureaulamp (de), desk lamp
burger (de), citizen, civilian
burger-, civil(ian), civic
burgerlijk, bourgeois, civil
burgelijke stand (de), registry of births, marriages and deaths
burgeroorlog (de), civil war
bus (de), tin, canister; bus
buschauffeur (de), bus driver
busdienst (de), bus service
buurman (de), buurvrouw (de), neighbour
buurt (de), neighbourhood
buurtbewoner (de), local resident
buurthuis (het), community centre
buurtvereniging (de), residents' association
b.v.: bijvoorbeeld, e.g.

C

ca'cao (de), cocoa
ca'deau (het), present
ca'deaubon (de), gift voucher
calcu'leren, to calculate, to compute
ca'mee (de), cameo
camou'fleren, to camouflage
cam'pagne (de), campaign
camper (de), camper
camping (de), campsite
capaci'teit (de), capacity; ability
capitu'leren, to capitulate
capri'ool (de), caper, prank; antics

carbu'rator (de), carburettor
carri'ère (de), career
cas'setteband (de), cassette, tape
cas'settedeck (de), tape deck
cassis (de), cassis, sparkling blackcurrant drink
casta'gnetten (de), castanets
cas'treren, to castrate
catalogi'seren, to catalogue
ca'talogus (de), catalogue
catechi'satie (de), confirmation class, religious instruction
cate'gorie (de), category
cate'gorisch, categorical
cd (de), CD
ceder (de), cedar
cein'tuur (de), belt, sash
cel (de), cell
celi'baat (het), celibacy
celiba'tair, celibate
cel'list (de), violoncellist
cello (de), cello
Celsius, Centigrade
censu'reren, to censor
cen'suur (de), censorship
cent (de), cent
  eurocent, eurocent (1/100 of one euro)
cen'traal, central
cen'trale (de), power station
centrum (het), centre
ceremoni'eel, ceremonial
cere'moniemeester (de), master of ceremonies
certifi'ceren, to certify
cha'grijn (het), chagrin
cha'grijnig, cantankerous
champi'gnon (de), mushroom
chan'tage (de), blackmail
cha'otisch, chaotic
char'mant, charming
char'meren, to charm
chef (de), head, manager, chief

chemi'caliën, chemicals
chemicus (de), (analytical) chemist
che'mie (de), chemistry
chemisch, chemical
cheru'bijn (de), cherub
chip (de), chip
chipknip (de), smart card
chips (de), crisps, chips (Am)
chi'rurg (de), surgeon
chirur'gie (de), surgery
chi'rurgisch, surgical
chloor, chlorine
choco'laatje (het), chocolate (drop)
choco'la(de) (de), chocolate
choco'la(de)melk (de), cocoa
christelijk, Christian
christen (de), Christian
Christus, Christ
chromo'soom (het), chromosome
chronisch, chronic
chronolo'gie (de), chronology
chry'sant (de), chrysanthemum
cider (de), cider
cijfer (het), figure, digit, mark
ci'linder (de), cylinder
ci'lindrisch, cylindrical
cim'baal (de), cymbal
ci'pier (de), warder
ci'pres (de), cypress
circa, approximately
circu'latie (de), circulation
circu'leren, to circulate
cirkel (de), circle
cirkelen, to circle
cirkel'vormig, circular
ci'taat (het), quotation
ci'teren, to quote
ci'troen (de), lemon
ci'troenpers (de), lemon squeezer
ci'viel, civil; moderate

claim (de), claim
claimen, to (file a) claim
clande'stien, clandestine; illicit; bootleg
clau'sule (de), clause; proviso
cle'ment, lenient
cle'mentie (de), clemency
clo'set (het), water-closet, toilet
club (de), club
coa'litie (de), coalition
co'con (de), cocoon
codi'cil (het), codicil
cogni'tief, cognitive
cohe'rent, coherent
co'hesie (de), cohesion
coke (de), coke; snow (cocaine)
col (de), rollneck, polo neck; mountain (pass)
col'bert (het), jacket
collec'tant (de), person collecting money
col'lecte (de), collection
collec'teren, to collect money
col'lega (de), colleague
col'lege (het), board; college; university lecture
– geven, to lecture
collegi'aal, friendly, harmonious
col'loquiem (het), symposium
co'lonne (de), column (of soldiers)
comeback (de), comeback
comfor'tabel, comfortable
comi'té (het), committee
comman'dant (de), commandant, commander, ship's captain
comman'deren, to command, to order about
com'mando (het), command
commen'taar (het), commentary
com'mercie (de), commerce, trade

commerci'eel, commercial
commissari'aat (het), directorate
commis'saris (de), chief inspector of police
com'missie (de), committee, commission
com'mune (de), commune
communi'catie (de), communication
communica'tief, communicative
communi'ceren, to communicate
communi'qué (het), statement, bulletin
  een – uitgeven, to put out a statement
com'pact, compact, dense
compact disc (de), compact disk
compa'gnon (de), (business) partner
comparti'ment (het), compartment
compen'satie (de), compensation
compen'seren, to compensate
compe'tent, competent, capable
compi'latie (de), compilation
compi'leren, to compile
com'pleet, complete
comple'teren, to complete
compli'catie (de), complication
compli'ment (het), compliment
complimen'teren met, to compliment on,
complimen'teus, complimentary
com'plot (het), conspiracy
compo'neren, to compose (music)
compo'nist (de), composer
compromit'teren, to compromise
com'puter (de), computer
com'puteren, to work/play on the computer
concen'tratievermogen (het), power of concentration
concen'treren, to concentrate
con'cept (het), draft (document)
con'cert (het), concert, recital; concerto
con'certgebouw (het), concert hall
con'certzaal (de), concert hall; auditorium
con'cessie (de), concession
con'ciërge (de), caretaker, hall porter
con'creet, concrete(ly)
concur'rent (de), competitor
concur'rentie (de), competition
concur'reren, to compete
concur'rerend, competitive
conden'sator (de), condenser
conden'seren, to condense
con'ditie (de), condition
  in conditie, fit
condo'leren, to offer one's condolences
conduc'teur (de), guard, tram, or bus conductor
con'fectie (de), ready-made (clothes)
con'fessie (de), confession
confessio'neel, confessional, denominational
confidenti'eel, confidential
con'flict (het), conflict
con'form, in accordance with
confor'meren: zich –, to conform (to), to comply (with)
confron'tatie (de), confrontation
confron'teren, to confront
con'gres (het), conference, congress
conjunc'tuur (de), market conditions

con'fuus, confused, abashed
conse'quent, consistent
conse'quentie (de), consequence, consistency
conser'vator (de), curator
con'serven (de), preserves
con'sorten (de), confederates
consta'teren, to establish
constru'eren, to construct
consulaat (het), consulate
consu'lent (de), expert adviser
con'sult (het), consultation
consul'tatie (de), consultation
consul'tatiebureau (het), clinic, health centre
consu'ment (de), consumer
consu'mentenbond (de), consumers' organization
con'sumptie (de), consumption, food and/or drink(s)
con'tact (het), contact, connection, touch
con'tactadvertentie (de), personal ad
con'tactdoos (de), socket; appliance inlet
con'tant, (in) cash, ready money
context (de), context
continu'eren, to continue
continuï'teit (de), continuity, continuation
contra, contra, against, versus
contra'ceptie (de), contraception
con'tract (het), contract, agreement
contrac'teren, to contract
contramine: in de –, in a contrary mood
con'trole (de), check, supervision
contro'leren, to check, to inspect
contro'leur (de), inspector

cor'rect, correct; right
cor'rectie (de), correction, adjustment; marking
cor'rectiewerk (het), marking, correcting
correspon'deren, to correspond
correspon'dentie (de), correspondence
corri'geren, to correct
cou'lant, obliging, accommodating
cou'lissen (de), wings (theatre)
cou'pé (de), compartment
cou'veuse (de), incubator
cre'peren, to perish; to suffer:
  – van de pijn, to be racked with pain
cricketen, to play cricket
crisis (de), crisis
cri'terium (het), criterion
crois'sant (de), croissant
cru, crude
culi'nair, culinary
culmi'neren, to culminate
cultfiguur (de/het), cult figure
cultu'reel, cultural
cul'tuur (de), culture
cum laude: – geslaagd zijn, to pass with a distinction/ credit/a first
cura'tele (de), guardianship; legal restriction
  onder – staan, be under legal restriction, in receivership
cur'ator (de), curator
curiosi'teit (de), curio
cur'riculum (het), curriculum; **curriculum vitae (CV, cv),** CV, résumé (Am)
cur'sief, italicized
cur'sist (de), learner, student
cursus (de), school year, course of studies

cursusboek (het), textbook, course book

cynicus (de), cynic

cynisch, cynical

D

daad (de), deed, act(ion)

daad'werkelijk, actual

daags, daily

daar, there; as, because

daar'achter, behind it

daar'aan, on (to) that
  wat heb je –?, what good is that?

daarbe'neden, down there, below

daarbij, near it; moreover

daar'binnen, in there, inside

daar'door, through it, as a result

daaren'tegen, on the other hand

daar'ginds, over there

daar'heen, there

daargelaten, (quite) apart from

daar'net, just now

daarom, therefore

daarom'trent, thereabouts

daar op, on that; on top of that

daarop'volgend, subsequent, next

daarover, over it, about it

daar'tegen, against that, next to that

daarvan'daan, from there

daar'voor, in front of it, before that; that's why

dadel (de), date

dadelijk, immediate

dader (de), perpetrator

dag (de), day(light)

dag! hello!, goodbye

om de drie dagen, every third day

dagblad (het), daily paper

dagboek (het), diary

dagdeel (het), part of the day; shift

dagelijks, daily

dagen, to summon; to dawn

dageraad (de), dawn

dagkaart (de), day ticket

dagkoers (de), current rate (of exchange)

dagloner (de), day labourer

dagopvang (de), day nursery

dagretour (het), day return

dagschotel (de), today's special

dagtekenen, to date

dagtocht (de), day trip

dagvaarden, to summon

dagvaarding (de), summons

dagverblijf (het), day nursery, crèche; outside pen (for animals)

dak (het), roof

dakgoot (de), gutter

dakkapel (de), dormer (window)

dakloos, homeless

dakkamer (de), attic room

dakloze (de), homeless person

dakpan (de), tile

dakraam (het), skylight

dal (het), valley

dalen, to go or come down

daling (de), descent; drop

daluren (de), off-peak hours

dam (de), dam, causeway; king (in draughts)

dambord (het), draught board

dame (de), lady

damesmode (de), ladies' fashion

damhert (het), fallow deer

dammen, to play draughts

damp (de), vapour
dampkring (de), atmosphere
dan, then; still; than
 – ook, so (consequence)
 (hoe, wat, wie) – ook,
 (how-, what-, who-) ever
danig, exceeding; greatly
dank, thanks
 dank zij, thanks to
dankbaar, grateful, gratifying
dankbaarheid (de), gratitude
danken, to thank, to say grace
dans (de), dance
dansen, to dance
dapper, brave
darm (de), intestine
dartel, frisky
dartelen, to frolic, to gambol
das (de), (neck)tie, scarf; badger
dat, that; which
data (de), data; dates
databank (de), data bank
da'teren, to date
datgene, that (one)
datum (de), date
dauw (de), dew
daveren, to thunder, to resound
daverend, thunderous;
 resounding
de, the
de'bacle (het, de), disaster,
 failure
de'bat (het), debate
debat'teren, to debate
debet (het), debit; overdrawn
de'biel (de), (term of abuse)
 moron, cretin
debi'teren, to debit
debi'teur (de), debtor
de'buut (het), début
december, December
decentrali'seren, to decentralize
decla'meren, to recite

decla'ratie (de), expenses claim
de'cor (het), décor, scenery,
 setting
decora'tief, decorative
de'creet (het), decree
decre'teren, to decree
deeg (het), dough; mixture
deel (het), part, share; volume
deel'achtig, participating in
deelbaar, divisible
deelgenoot (de), participant;
 partner
deelgenootschap (het),
 partnership
deelnemen (aan), to participate
 (in)
deelnemer (de), participant
deelneming (de), participation;
 sympathy
deels, partly
deelteken (het), division sign
deeltijdbaan (de), part-time job
deeltje (het), particle
deelwoord (het), participle
dee'moedig, meek
Deen(se) (de), Dane, Danish
 woman
deernis (de), compassion
deernis'wekkend, pitiable
de'fect (het), faulty, out of
 order; defect, fault
de'fensie (de), (national)
 defence
defi'lé (het), parade, procession
defi'leren, to march past
defini'ëren, to define
defini'tief, definite, definitive
de'flatie (de), deflation
deftig, dignified; distinguished
degelijk, sound; substantial
 hij weet het wel –, he knows
 (it) perfectly well
degen (de), sword

de'gene die, the one who

degra'deren, to degrade, to downgrade

deinen, to heave; to bob

deining (de), swell; commotion

dek (het), cover; bedclothes; deck

deken (de), blanket; dean

dekhengst (de), stallion

dekken, to cover; to lay (the table); to serve (a mare)
　zich –, to take cover

dekking (de), cover
　– zoeken, to take cover

deksel (het), lid, cover

dekzeil (het), tarpaulin

delen, to divide, to share, to split

deling (de), division

delin'quent (de), delinquent, offender

delfstof (de), mineral

delica'tesse (de), delicacy

delven, to dig

de'ment, demented

demo'craat (de), democrat

democra'tie (de), democracy

demon'stratie (de), demonstration, display; march

demonstra'tief, demonstrative

demon'streren, to demonstrate; to protest (against)

demon'teren, to dismantle

dempen, to fill in (with earth); to subdue

den, denneboom (de), pine(-tree)

Den Haag, the Hague

denderend, smashing

Denemarken, Denmark

denkbaar, conceivable

denkbeeld (het), idea

denk'beeldig, imaginary; fictitious; hypothetical

denkelijk, probably

denken (aan), to think (of)
　doen – aan, to remind of

denkvermogen (het), intellectual capacity

dennenappel (de), fir cone

dennenhout (het), pinewood

depo'neren, to deposit, to file, to register

de'pot (het), depot; branch establishment

depri'meren, to depress

derde, third
　– wereld (de), Third World
　–'wereldwinkel (de), Third World shop
　ten –, thirdly

derdemachtswortel (de), cube root

derde'rangs, third rate

deren, to harm

dergelijk, such (like)
　iets dergelijks, something of the sort

der'halve, hence

dermate, to such a degree

dertien(de), thirteen(th)

dertig, thirty

derven, to lack

des, of the
　des te (meer), all the (more)

desalniette'min, nevertheless

desas'treus, disastrous

desbe'treffend, relating to this

desge'lijks, likewise

desge'wenst, if desired

desillusie (de), disillusionment

des'kundig(e) (de), expert

des'noods, if need be; at a pinch

deson'danks, nevertheless

des'poot (de), despot

des'sin (het), design

des'tijds, at the time

de'tail (het, de), detail; retail

de'tailhandel (de), retail trade

de'tentie (de), detention, custody

determi'neren, to determine; to identify

deti'neren, to detain

deto'neren, to detonate; to be out of tune, to be out of keeping

deugd (de), virtue

deugdelijk, reliable

deugdzaam, virtuous

deugen: niet –, to be no good

deugniet (de), rascal, good-for-nothing

deuk (de), dent

  ik lag in een –, (inf) I was laughing my head off

deuken, to dent

deuntje (het), tune

deur (de), door

  met de – in huis vallen, to come straight to the point

deurwaarder (de), bailiff

de'vies (het), motto, device

de'viezen (de), (foreign) currency

deze, this, these

  – of gene, (some)one or other

de'zelfde, the same

dhr.: de heer, Mr

diag'nose (de), diagnosis

diago'naal, diagonally

di'aken (de), church worker; deacon

dia'loog (de), dialogue

dia'mant (de), diamond

dia'manten, (made of) diamond

dia'mantslijper (de), diamond cutter

diameter (de), diameter

diar'ree (de), diarrhoea

dicht, closed; dense

dicht'bij, near (to), close by

dichtbevolkt, densely populated

dichten, to write poetry; to stop a leak

dichter('es) (de), poet(ess)

dichterlijk, poetic(al)

dichtkunst (de), (art of) poetry

dichtstbij'zijnd, nearest

dichtvriezen, to freeze over (of a canal, lake)

dic'taat (het), dictation; lecture-notes; notebook

dictatori'aal, dictatorial

dicta'tuur (de), dictatorship

dic'tee (het), dictation

die, that, those; who, which; he, she, it, they

di'eet (het), diet

dief (de), thief

diefstal (de), theft

die'gene, he, she

dienaar (de), servant

diender (de), cop(per)

dienen, to serve

  waar dient dit voor? what is the use of this?

  daar ben ik niet van gediend, I take exception to that

dienovereen'komstig, accordingly

dienst (de), service, duty

dienstbode (de), (house)maid

dienstensector (de), services sector

dienstplicht (de), compulsory (military) service

dienstregeling (de), timetable

dienstverlening (de), services; caring profession

dienstweigeraar (de), conscientious objector

dientenge'volge, in consequence
diep, deep; profound
diepgaand, searching
diepgang (de), depth; profundity
diepte (de), depth
diepvries (de), freezer
  spinazie uit de –, frozen spinach
diep'zinnig, profound; abstruse
dier (het), animal
dierbaar, dearly loved
dierenbescherming (de), prevention of cruelty to animals
dierenmishandeling (de), cruelty to animals
dierenriem (de), zodiac
dierenwinkel (de), pet shop
dierlijk, animal; bestial
die'vegge (de), female thief
digi'taal, digital
dij (de), thigh
dijbeen (het), thighbone
dijk (de), dike, embankment; dam
  aan de – zetten, to sack someone
dik, thick; fat; dense
dikkerd (de), fatty
dikte (de), thickness
dikwijs, often
dimmen, to dim, to dip
di'neren, to dine
ding (het), thing
dingen, to bargain
  – naar, to compete for, to sue for
dinsdag, Tuesday
diplo'maat (de), diplomat(ist)
diplo'matenkoffertje (het), attaché case
diploma'tie (de), diplomacy

direc'teur (de), director, manager, head(master)
di'rectie (de), management
diri'gent (de), conductor
diri'geren, to conduct
discu'teren, to discuss, to argue
dis'puut (het), dispute; debating society
disser'tatie (de), thesis for a doctorate
distel (de), thistle
distilla'teur (de), distiller
distilleerde'rij (de), distillery
distri'butie (de), distribution, (food) allocation; radio-diffusion
dit, this, these
ditmaal, this time
di'versen (de), miscellaneous, sundries
diversi'teit (de), diversity, variety
divi'dend (het), dividend
di'visie (de), division; league (in sport)
dobbelaar (de), gambler, dice player
dobbelen, to play dice
dobbelstenen (de), dice
dobber (de), float
  een harde – hebben, to be hard put to it
dobberen, to bob up and down
do'cent (de), teacher
do'ceren, to teach
doch, but; however
dochter (de), daughter
docto'raal (e'xamen) (het), examination for master's degree
docto'randus, person who has passed the *doctoraalexamen*
docu'ment (het), document, paper

documen'taire (de), documentary

dode (de), dead (wo)man, deceased

dodelijk, mortal, deadly

doden, to kill

dodenherdenking (de), commemoration of the (war) dead

doedelzak (de), bagpipes

doel (het), target, goal; aim

doe-het-zelfzaak (de), DIY shop

doelbe'wust, purposeful

doeleinde (het), purpose

doelen op, to allude to

doelloos, aimless, pointless

doel'matig, appropriate; efficient

doel'treffend, effective

doemdenken (het), doom-mongering

doemen, to doom

doen, to do, to make; to ask; to put

  ik kan er niets aan –, I can't help it

  ik heb met je te –, I am sorry for you

  het doet er niet(s) toe, it makes no difference

  – in, to deal in

  – en laten, behaviour, doings

doetje (het), softy

doezelen, to drowse

dof, dull, dim

dok (het), dock

dokken, to dock; to fork out

  je zult moeten –, you'll have to fork out

dokter (de), doctor

doktersbehandeling (de), medical treatment

doktersrecept (het), medical prescription

dol, mad, frantic

dolblij, overjoyed

dolen, to wander

dol'fijn (de), dolphin

dolgraag, only too gladly

dolheid (de), frenzy

dolk (de), dagger

dolleman (de), madman

dollen, to romp

dom, stupid; **(de)** cathedral, dome

do'mein (het), domain

domheid (de), stupidity

dominee (de), minister, clergyman

domi'neren, to dominate; to play dominoes

domkop (de), blockhead

dommelen, to doze

dompelaar (de), diver (bird); plunger

dompelen, to plunge

dona'teur (de), donor, supporter

donder (de), thunder

  iemand op zijn – geven, to give a person a good hiding

  het kan me geen – schelen, I don't give a damn

donderbui (de), thunderstorm

donderdag, Thursday

donderen, to thunder

donderjagen, to be a nuisance, to mess about

donderslag (de), thunderclap

do'neren, to donate

donker, dark

donor (de), donor

donorcodocil (het), donor card

dons (het), down

donzig, downy

dood (de), death

dood, dead

doodbloeden, bleed to death

doodeen'voudig, perfectly simple

doodgaan, to die

doodgraver (de), gravedigger

doodop, dead beat

doods, deathly, mortally

doodsbang, scared to death

doodskist (de), coffin

doodslag (de), homicide

doodsnood: in –, in the throes of death

doodstraf (de), capital punishment

doodsstrijd (de), death struggle, throes of death

doodzwijgen, to hush up, to keep quiet

doof, deaf

doof'stom, deaf mute

dooi (de), thaw

dooien, to thaw

dooier (de), yolk

doolhof (het), labyrinth

doop (de), baptism

doopsge'zind, Baptist

doopvont (het), font

door, through; by
 – de week, on weekdays

doorbladeren, to glance through

doorbrengen, to spend

door'dacht, carefully considered, well thought-out

door'dat, owing to

doordraaien, to keep going; to remain unsold

doordrammen, to nag, to go on about something

doordrijven, to get one's own way

doordringen, to penetrate

door'eenmengen, to mix together

dooreten, to go on eating, to eat up

doorgaan, to go on
 – voor, to pass for
 er van doorgaan, to bolt

doorgaande trein (de), through train

doorgaans, usually

doorgang (de), passage, way through

doorgeven, to pass (on)

doorgewinterd, seasoned, experienced

door'gronden, to fathom

doorhalen, to strike out (words); to pull through

door'heen, through

door'kneed in, well-versed in

doorkomen, to get through

door'kruisen, to traverse

doorleren, to stay at school, to continue with one's education

doorlichten, to screen; to X-ray; to investigate

door'lopen, to complete, to pass through

doorlopen, to walk to run on; to get a move on; to run (of colours); to walk through

door'lopend, continuous, continual

doormaken, to go through

door'midden, in half

doorn (de), thorn

doornat, wet through

door'schijnend, translucent

doorslaand bewijs, convincing proof

doorslag (de), dip, turn; carbon copy
 de – geven, to turn the scale

doorslaggevend, decisive

doorsnede (de), cross-section; diameter

doorsnee, average

doorsneemens (de), the average person

door'staan, to stand, to endure

door'tastend, vigorous, thorough-going, go-ahead

door'trapt, cunning; villainous

door'trokken, soaked; imbued

doorvertellen, to pass on (a secret or information)

door'voed, well-fed

door'waadbare plaats, ford

doorzakken, to make a night of it

doorzetten, to persevere

door'zichtig, transparent

doos (de), box, case

  uit de oude –, antiquated

dop (de), shell, husk, pod; top

dopen, to baptize, to dip

doperw (de), (green) pea

doppen, to shell

dor, dry, arid

dorp (het), village

dorpeling (de), villager

dorsen, to thresh

dorst (de), thirst

dosis (de), dose

dos'sier (het), file, document, records

dot (de), tuft; pet

dou'ane (de), Customs

dove (de), deaf person

doven, to extinguish, to dim

do'zijn (het), dozen

draad (de), thread, wire

draadloos, wireless

draagbaar, stretcher; portable

draagkracht (de), carrying capacity, range

draaglijk, tolerable

draagmoeder (de), surrogate mother

draagstoel (de), sedan chair

draagvlak (het), basis, support

  het maatschappelijk –, the public support

draai (de), turn, twist

  een – om de oren, a box on the ears

  zijn – vinden, to find one's niche

draaibaar, revolving

draaibank (de), lathe

draaiboek (het), scenario, script

draaideur (de), revolving door

draaien, to turn, to revolve; to prevaricate

draaierig, dizzy

draaikolk (de), whirlpool

draaimolen (de), roundabout

draaiorgel (het), barrel organ

draaitafel (de), turntable

draak (de), dragon

  de – steken met, to make fun of

drab (de), dregs

dracht (de), dress, wear

draderig, stringy

draf (de), trot

dragen, to bear; to wear; to carry

dralen, to tarry

drang (de), pressure; urge

drank (de), drink

  aan de – zijn, to be addicted to drink

dra'peren, to drape

drassig, marshy

drastisch, drastic

draven, to trot

dreef (de), avenue, lane; mead(ow)

  op –, in/on form

dreggen, to drag

dreige'ment (het), threat

dreigen, to threaten

dreinen, to whine

drempel (de), threshold
drenkeling (de), drowning person
drentelen, to saunter
drenzen, to whine
dres'seren, to train (animals)
dres'soir (het), sideboard
dreumes (de), toddler
dreun (de), drone; blow
dreunen, to drone, to rumble
drie, three
drie'delig, tripartite; three-piece
driedimensio'naal, three-dimensional
drie'dubbel, triple
driehoek (de), triangle
driekwart, three-quarter(s)
drieling (de), triplet(s)
drieluik (het), triptych
driepoot (de), tripod
drietjes: met z'n –, the three of us/them
drievoud, treble; triplicate
driewieler (de), tricycle
drift (de), passion; drift
driftig, hot-tempered; in a temper
driftkop (de), hothead
drijfhout (het), driftwood
drijfkracht (de), drive
drijfnat, sopping wet
drijfveer (de), mainspring; incentive; motive
drijfzand (het), quicksand(s)
drijven, to float, to drift; to drive; to run (a business)
dringen, to crowd, to jostle; to press
de tijd dringt, time presses
dringend, urgent
drinken, to drink
droef, sad
droefenis (de), sorrow

droef'geestig, mournful
droefheid (de), sadness
droevig, sad
droge (het), dry land
drogen, to dry
drogiste'rij (de), chemist's (shop)
dromen, to dream
dromerig, dreamy
dronk (de), drink, draught, toast
dronkaard (de), drunkard
dronken, drunk(en)
droog, dry
droogleggen, to drain, to reclaim
droogrek (het), clotheshorse
droogte (de), dryness; drought
droogtrommel (de), tumble dryer
droom (de), dream
droomprins (de), Prince Charming
droomwereld (de), dreamworld
drop (de), liquorice; drop
drug (de), drug, narcotic
drugsbeleid (het), drug policy
drugshandel (de), dealing (in drugs)
drugsverslaafde (de), drug addict
druif (de), grape
druilerig: het is – weer, there is rain in the air
druipen, to drip
druipsteen (het, de), stalactite, stalagmite
druisen, to roar, to churn
druk, busy; fussy; gaudy; pressure; print
maak je niet –, be calm
een – bezochte vergadering, well-attended meeting
drukfout (de), misprint
drukken, to (de)press; to oppress; to print; to shake (hands)

drukkend, oppressive
drukker'ij (de), printer('s works)
drukletters (de), type
drukte (de), bustle; pressure of business; fuss
drukwerk (het), printed matter
druppel (de), drop, drip
druppelen, to drip
dubbel, double
dubbeldekker (de), double-decker
dubbelganger (de), double
dubbeltje (het), ten-cent piece
dubbel'zinnig, ambiguous
dubbel'zinnigheid (de), ambiguity
dubi'eus, doubtful
dubio: in –, in doubt
duchten, to dread
duchtig, thorough, strong
duf, musty
duidelijk, clear, obvious
duidelijkheidshalve, for clarity's sake
duiden op, to point to
duif (de), dove, pigeon
duikboot (de), submarine
duikelen, to tumble
duiken, to dive; to plunge
duim (de), thumb
duin (het), dune
duister (de), dark: darkness
duisternis (de), darkness
Duitser (de), German
Duitsland, Germany
duivel (de), devilish
duivels, devilish
duiventil (de), dovecote(e)
duizelen, to get dizzy or giddy
duizelig, dizzy, giddy
duizeling (de), (fit of) dizziness, giddiness
duizeling'wekkend, dizzy

duizend, a thousand
duizendpoot (de), centipede
dulden, to bear, to endure
dumpen, dump
dun, thin
dunk (de), opinion
dunken, be of the opinion
  me dunkt, indeed!
  het dunkt mij…, I am of the opinion…
dunnen, to thin
duo (het), duo, pair
duobaan (de), job share
du'peren, to hit; to let down
dupli'caat (het), duplicate
duplo: in –, to duplicate
duren, to last
durven, to dare
dus, so
dus'danig, (in) such (a way)
dusver: tot –, thus far
dutje (het): een – doen, to have a nap
dutten, to doze
duur, expensive; duration
  op de(n) –, in time
duurzaam, durable
duw (de), push, shove
duwen, to push, to shove
dwaalspoor (het), wrong track
dwaas (de), fool: foolish
dwaasheid (de), foolishness
dwalen, to wander; to err
dwaling (de), error
dwang (de), compulsion
dwangarbeid (de), hard labour
dwangarbeider (de), convict
dwangbuis (de), straightjacket
dwarrelen, to whirl
dwars, transverse; cross-grained
  het zit me –, it worries me, it annoys me

dwarsbomen, to thwart
dwars door, straight through
dwarsdoorsne(d)e (de), cross-section
dwarsfluit (de), flute
dwarsliggen, to be obstructive
dwarsligger (de), sleeper; troublemaker
dwarsschip (het), transept
dwarsstraat (de), side street: **neem maar een –,** just an example
dweepziek, fanatic
dweil (de), floorcloth; slut
dwepen met, to think the world of; to rave about
dweper (de), zealot; fan(atic)
dwerg (de), dwarf, midget
dwingeland (de), tyrant; bully
dwingen, to force
d.w.z.: dat wil zeggen, i.e.
dyna'miek (de), dynamics, vitality
dy'namisch, dynamic
dy'namo (de), dynamo
dys'lectisch, dyslexic
dys'lexie (de), dyslexia

E

e.a.: en andere(n), et al.
eb (de), ebb (tide)
ebbenhout (het), ebony
echo (de), echo; ultrasound
echt, real, genuine, thorough
echtelijk, matrimonial
echter, however
echtgenoot (de), husband
echtgenote (de), wife
echtheid (de), genuineness
echtpaar (het), married couple
echtscheiding (de), divorce
e'clips (de), eclipse

ecolo'gie (de), ecology
econo'mie (de), economy; economics
eco'nomisch, economic; economical(ly)
eco'noom (de), economist
ec'zeem (het), eczema
e.d.: en dergelijke, and the like
edel, noble
Edel'achtbare, Your Honour
edelgesteente (het), precious stone(s)
edel'moedig, generous
edelsteen (de), gem
e'ditie (de), edition
educa'tief, educational
eed (de), oath
eekhoorn (de), squirrel
eelt (het), hard skin
een, a(n); one
– en al, all; nothing but
eend (de), duck
eender, the same
een'drachtig, united
eenge'zinswoning (de), (small) family home
eenheid (de), unit(y)
eenheidsprijs (de), unit price; uniform price
eenhoorn (de), unicorn
een'jarig, yearling
een'kennig, shy
eenletter'grepig, monosyllabic
eenmaal, once
het is nu – zo, but there it is
eenper'soonskamer (de), single room
een'richtingsverkeer (het), one-way traffic
eens, once, one day; just
het – zijn, to agree
eensge'zind, as one, unanimous

eensge'zindheid (de), harmony, unanimity

eensklaps, suddenly

eensluidend, similar, true

een'stemmig, in unison; with one accord

een'stemmig, unanimous

eentje, one
 in je –, on your own

een'tonig, monotonous

een'voudig, simple

eenvoud (de), simplicity

eenzaam, lonely, solitary

eenzaamheid (de), solitude

een'zelvig, self-contained

een'zijdigheid (de), one-sidedness, bias

eer (de), honour
 – aandoen, to do credit to

eerbetoon (het), eerbewijs (het), mark of honour, homage

eerbied (de), respect

eer'biedig, respectful

eer'biedigen, to respect

eerder, before, sooner; rather

eer'gisteren (de), the day before yesterday

eerlijk, honest, fair

eerst, first, former
 de eerste de beste, the first (man, opportunity) that comes along
 ten eerste, in the first place
 voor het –, for the first time

Eerste Kamer (de), Upper Chamber/House (of the Dutch parliament)

eersteklas, first-rate, first-class

eervol, honourable

eerzaam, respectable

eerzucht (de), ambition

eer'zuchtig, ambitious

eetbaar, edible

eetgelegenheid (de), eating place

eetkamer (de), dining room

eetlepel (de), tablespoon

eetlust (de), appetite

eetservies (het), dinner service

eetstokje (het), chopstick

eetwaren (de), provisions

eetzaal, dining hall

eeuw (de), century, age

eeuwfeest (het), centenary

eeuwig, eternal, everlasting

eeuwigheid (de), eternity

ef'fecten, stocks (and shares)

effec'tief, effective

effen, level, smooth

effenen, to level, to smooth (down)

effici'ënt, efficient

e'gaal, smooth, uniform

egel (de), hedgehog

ego (het), ego

ego'centrisch, egocentric, self-centred

EHBO (de), first aid

ei (het), egg

eicel (de), ovum

eierdooier (de), eggyolk

eierdopje (het), eggcup

eierstok (de), ovary

eigen, (of one's) own; private

eigenaar (de), owner

eigen'aardig, peculiar, strange

eigen'aardigheid (de), peculiarity

eigenbaat (het), egoism

eigenbelang (het), self-interest

eigendom (het), property

eigendomsbewijs (het), title-deeds

eigendunk (de), self-conceit

eigenge'maakt, home-made

eigenge'reid, opinionated

eigenlijk, actual, proper, real

eigennaam (de), proper name
eigenschap (de), quality, property
eigenwaarde (de), self-respect
eigen'wijs, self-opinionated, pig-headed, cocky
eigen'zinnig, self-willed
eik (de), oak
eikel (de), acorn; glans (penis); oaf
eiland (het), island
eind (het), end(ing); length, distance
  ten einde raad, at one's wits' end
einddiploma (het), school-leaving certificate
eindelijk, at last
eindeloos, endless, superb
eindexamen (het), school-leaving exam; final exam
eindigen, to finish (off)
eindje (het), piece, bit; short distance
eindproduct (het), finished article
eindpunt (het), eindstation (het), terminus
eindsignaal (het), final whistle (in sport)
eis (de), demand, claim
  aan de eisen voldoen, to satisfy the requirements
eisen, to demand, to claim
eiser (de), plaintiff, prosecutor
eiwit (het), white of egg; protein
EK: Euro'pees Kampi'oenschap (het), European Championship
ekster (de), magpie
e'lan (het), élan
eland (de), elk
elas'tiek (het), elastic
elas'tiekje (het), rubber band

elders, elsewhere
electo'raat (het), electorate
elektri'ciën (de), electrician
electrici'teit (de), electricity
e'lectrisch, electric
elektro'cutie (de), electrocution
elek'tronisch, electronic
ele'ment (het), element, component
elemen'tair, elementary, basic
elf, eleven; elf
  op zijn elf-en-dertigst, at a snail's pace
elfde, eleventh
elf'stedentocht (de), skating marathon in Friesland
elftal (het), eleven, team
elimi'neren, to eliminate, to remove
eli'tair, elitist
e'lite (de), elite
elk, each, any
el'kaar, el'kander, each other, one another
  alles bij – genomen, all things considered
  ik kan ze niet uit – houden, I can't tell one from the other
  alles is voor –, everything has been arranged
elleboog (de), elbow
el'lende (de), misery
el'lendeling (de), rotter
el'lendig, wretched, miserable; rotten
e-mail (de), e-mail
e-mailen, to send an e-mail
e'mail (het), enamel
e'maillen, enamelled
emanci'patie (de), emancipation, liberation
embleem (het), emblem
emi'greren, to emigrate

emmer (de), pail
e'motie (de), emotion
emotio'neel, emotional
em'pirisch, empirical
emplo'yé (de), employee
en, and
  – ... –, both ... and
encyclope'die (de),
  (en)cyclopaedia
end (het), distance
enenmale: ten –, absolutely
ener'gie (de), energy
ener'giek, energetic
ener'giebedrijf (het), power
  company
ener'giebesparing (de), energy-
  saving
enerlei, of the same kind
enerzijds, on the one hand
en'fin, in short
  maar –, but there (it is)
eng, narrow; horrible, creepy
engel (de), angel
Engeland, England
Engels, English
enig, only, unique; marvellous;
  some, any, a few
  zij is de enige, she is the only
  one
enigs'zins, somewhat, in a way
enkel (de), ankle
enkel, single, only
enkeling (de), individual
enkelvoud (het), singular
e'norm, enormous
en'quête (de), poll, survey
en'quêteformulier (het),
  questionnaire
ensce'neren, to stage(manage)
enten, to graft
enthousi'ast, enthusiastic
en'tree (de), entrance; entrée;
  admission

en'treegeld (het), admission
  charge
enz(ovoort), etc(etera), and so
  on
epide'mie (de), epidemic
epi'loog (de), epilogue
epos (het), epic
equivalent (het), equivalent
er, there: of it, of them
  – zijn –, die ..., there are those
  who ...
  wat is –? what's the matter?
er'aan, on (it)
  ik kom eraan, I'm on my way
er'achter, behind (it)
er'barmelijk, pitiable
er'bij, there, included at; at it
erboven'op, on top of it
ere-, honorary, of honour
e'rectie (de), erection
eredienst (de), divine worship
eren, to honour
erf (het), (farm)yard
erfelijk, hereditary
erfelijkheid (de), heredity
erfenis (de), heritage, legacy
erfgenaam (de), heir
erfgename (de), heiress
erfgoed (het), inheritance
erfstuk (het), heirloom
erg, bad; very (much)
  zonder –, unintentionally
  ik had er geen – in, I was not
  aware of it
ergens, somewhere, anywhere
ergeren, to annoy; to scandalize
  zich –, to be vexed, to take
  offence
  het is om je dood te –, it's
  infuriating
ergerlijk, annoying, offensive
ergernis (de), annoyance,
  offence

er'kend, recognized; acknowledged

er'kennen, to recognize; to acknowledge, to admit

er'kentelijk, grateful

erker (de), bay window

ernst (de), seriousness

ernstig, serious

ertegen'aan, on to it;
we gaan –, we're going for it/ to tackle it

ertussen'in, in between; in the middle

ertussen'uit, out of it
een dagje –, a day out

er'uitzien, to look; to look like;
ze ziet er niet goed uit!, she looks awful!

er'varen, experienced

er'varen, to experience

er'varing (de), experience

erven, to inherit

erwt (de), pea

es (de), ash tree

esca'leren, to escalate

esdoorn (de), maple tree

es'kader (het), eska'dron (het), squadron

es'sentie (de), essence

essenti'eel, essential

esta'fette (de), relay race

e'tage (de), floor, storey

e'tagewoning (de), flat

eta'lage (de), shop window

e'tappe (de), stage, lap

eten (het), food; meal

eten, to eat, to have a meal

etenstijd (de), dinnertime

etentje (het), dinner, (special) meal

e'thiek (de), ethics

ethisch, ethical

eti'ket (het), label

etmaal (het), (space of) 24 hours

ets (de), etching

etsen, to etch

ettelijke, several

etter (de), pus; a pain in the neck, a nasty piece of work

etteren, to fester

é'tui (het), pencil case

EU: Euro'pese Unie (de), European Union

euro (de), euro

eurocent (de), eurocent

Eu'ropa (het), Europe

europarlement (het), European Parliament

Europe'aan (de), European

euthana'sie (de), euthanasia

euvel (het), evil

evacuatie (de), evacuation

evacu'eren, to evacuate

evalu'atie (de), evaluation, assessment

evalu'eren, to evaluate, to assess

evan'gelisch, evangelical

even, even, equally; just (as)
het is mij om het –, it's all the same to me
– … als, as … as

evenaar (de), equator

evenals, just as

eve'naren, to equal

evenbeeld (het), image; likeness

even'eens, likewise

evene'ment (het), event

evengoed, (just) as well

evenmin … als, no more … than

even'redig, proportional

eventjes, just (for) a moment

eventu'eel, possible; by any chance

evenveel, as much, as many

even'wel, however

evenwicht (het), balance

evenwichtig, (well-)balanced, level-headed

evenwichtstoestand (de), equilibrium

even'wijdig, parallel

even'zeer, as much

even'zo, likewise

everzwijn (het), wild boar

e'xamen (het), examination

  een – afnemen, to examine

excentrek, eccentric

excu'seren, to excuse

ex'cuus (het), excuse, apology

exem'plaar (het), specimen; copy

expe'ditie (de), expedition

exploi'tatie (de), operation; exploitation

expo'sitie (de), exhibition

e'xotisch, exotic

experimen'teel, experimental

ex'pres, express

ex'tase (de), ecstasy

exteri'eur (het), exterior

ex'tern, non-resident; external

extra, extra; special

extraatje (het), bonus

ezel (de), ass, donkey; easel

ezelsbrug (de), mnemonic

ezelsoor (het), dog ear, donkey's ear

F

f., fl. (= florijn), guilder(s)

faam (de), fame, repute

fabel (de), fable, fabrication

fabelachtig, fabulous

fabri'ceren, to manufacture

fa'briek (de), factory

fabri'kaat (het), manufacture

fabri'kant (de), manufacturer

fa'cet (het), aspect, facet

facili'teit (de), facility, amenity

fac'tuur (de), invoice

facul'teit (de), faculty

fa'got (de), bassoon

fail'liet, bankrupt

faillisse'ment (het), bankruptcy

fakkel (de), torch

falen, to fail

fal'set (het), falsetto

fa'meus, famous, wonderful

familiair, familiar, informal

fa'milie (de), family, relation(s)

fa'miliekwaal (de), hereditary disease

fa'naticus (de), fanatic

fanatiek, fanatical

fana'tisme (het), fanaticism

fanta'seren, to indulge in fantasies

fanta'sie (de), fantasy, fancy, imagination

fan'tastisch, fantastic, fabulous

fas'cisme (het), fascism

fasci'neren, to fascinate, captivate

fase (de), phase

fa'taal, fatal

fat'soen (het), decency, good manners

  houd je –, behave yourself

fat'soenlijk, decent, respectable

fau'teuil (de), armchair

faxen, to fax

fa'zant (de), pheasant

febru'ari, February

fee (de), fairy

feeë'riek, fairy-like

feeks (de), shrew

feest (het), feast, festival, fête

feestelijk, festive

feestje (het), party

feestmaal (het), banquet

feestvarken (het), person giving a party

feestvieren, to celebrate, to go on a spree

feilbaar, fallible

feilloos, faultless

feit (het), fact

feitelijk, actual

fel, fierce

felici'tatie (de), congratulation

felici'teren met, to congratulate on

femi'nistisch, feminist

fenome'naal, phenomenal

ferm, firm; brave

fes'tijn (het), feast

fê'teren, to fête

feuille'ton (de), serial story

fi'asco (het), disaster, failure, flop

fiche (het), counter; token (in a game)

fic'tief, fictitious

fier, proud, undaunted

fiets (de), bicycle

fietsen, to cycle

figu'rant (de), extra (films); super (numerary)

figu'reren, to figure

fi'guur (het, de), figure; character

   een gek – slaan, to cut a ridiculous figure

fi'guurlijk, figurative, metaphorical

fijn, fine; subtle

fijnge'voelig, sensitive

fijnproever (de), connoisseur

fijntjes, nicely, subtly

fik (de), (inf) fire

fikken, (inf) to burn

fiks, robust, vigorous; brave

fiksen, to fix (something); manage

file (de), line, row; traffic jam

fi'leren, to fillet

fi'let (het, de), fillet, filet (of meat)

   – américain, steak tartare

filhar'monisch, philharmonic

fili'aal (het), branch (establishment)

filmkeuring (de), film censorship, board of film censors

filmopname (de), film shot; to make a film of

filter (de, het), filter; percolator

filteren, to filter

fi'naal, final; quite

financi'eel, financial

fi'nanciën (de), finance(s)

finan'cieren, to finance

fi'neer (het), veneer

fi'neren, to veneer; to refine

fi'nesses (de), details

finishen, to finish

fin'geren, to feign; to invent

firma (de), firm

fiscus (de), treasurer, treasury

fit, fit, fresh

fix'eren, to fix; to look intently at

fladderen, to flutter; to flit

flakkeren, to flicker

fla'neren, to saunter, to parade, to stroll

flan'keren, to flank

flappen: eruit –, to blurt out

flapuit (de), blabber

flarden (de), tatters

   aan –, in rags; to shreds

flater (de), blunder

   een – slaan, to make a blunder

flat'teren, to flatter, to be becoming

flat'teus, flattering

flauw, insipid, feeble, faint

flauwe'kul (de), nonsense, rubbish

flauwte (de), fainting fit

flauwtjes, faintly

flensje (het), thin pancake

fles (de), bottle

flesopener (de), bottle opener

flesvoeding (de), bottle feeding; baby milk/formula

flets, lacklustre, pale

fleurig, colourful

flikkeren, to flicker

flink, tough, capable; considerable

flits (de), flash

flitsend, stylish, snappy

flodderig, shapeless, flimsy

flonkeren, to sparkle, to twinkle

floppen, to flop

floppydisk (de), floppy disk

flo'reren, to flourish

floris'sant, flourishing

fluisteren, to whisper

fluit (de), flute

fluiten, to whistle

fluitje (het), whistle

fluitketel (de), whistling kettle

flu'weel (het), velvet

fnuiken, to break, to ruin

fnuikend, fatal

foefje (het), trick, dodge

foei'lelijk, as ugly as sin

foelie (de), mace

foeteren, to rage, to grumble

föhn (de), hair dryer, blow dryer

fokken, to breed

folder (de), leaflet, brochure

folie (de), (tin) foil

folteren, to torture

fonds (het), fund

fonkelen, to sparkle

fon'tein (de), fountain

fon'teintje (het), small handbasin

fooi (de), tip

foppen, to hoax

fopspeen (de), baby's dummy

for'ceren, to force; to strain

fo'rel (de), trout

fo'rens (de), season ticket holder, commuter

for'maat (het), size; stature

formali'teit (de), formality

formateur (de), person charged with forming a new government

for'meel, formal

formi'dabel, formidable

for'mule (de), formula

formu'lier (het), form

for'nuis (het), cooker

fors, robust, strong, vigorous

fort (het), forte; fort(ification)

for'tuin (het), fortune

for'tuinlijk, fortunate

fos'siel (het), fossil

fotogra'feren, to photograph, to take a photograph (of)

fouil'leren, to search (a person)

fourni'turen (de), haberdashery

fout (de), mistake, fault, error

fou'tief, wrong, erroneous

fraai, nice; handsome

fractie (de), fraction; group

fractieleider (de), leader of a parliamentary party

fragmen'tarisch, fragmentary

fram'boos (de), raspberry

franje (de), fringe

fran'keren, to stamp

Frankrijk, France

frap'pant, striking

frase (de), phrase
fratsen (de), pranks
fraude (de), fraud
fraudu'leus, fraudulent
fre'gat (het), frigate
fre'quent, frequent
friemelen, to fumble
fries (het, de), frieze
Fries, Frisian
friet (de), chips, fries
fris (het, de), soft drink
fris, fresh, refreshing; airy; chilly, cool
  het is frisjes vanavond, it's chilly this evening
frisdrank (de), soft drink
fri'turen, to deep-fry
fruitautomaat (de), slot machine
fri'vool, frivolous
frommelen, to crumple
fronsen, to frown
fruiten, to fry, to sauté
frus'tratie (de), frustration
functie (de), to function
functio'naris (de), functionary
functio'neren, to function
fun'dering (de), foundation
fu'nest, fatal
fun'geren, to function
fu'seren, to merge (with)
fusie (de), merger, fusion
fut (de), spirit, go
futloos, lifeless

G

gaaf, sound, whole; great
gaai (de), jay
gaaies (het), riffraff
gaan, to go
  hoe gaat het? how are you (getting on)?

  het gaat om ... it is a question of ...; it is about
gaande, afoot, going
gaandeweg, gradually
gaar, cooked, done
gaarkeuken (de), communal kitchen
gaarne, gladly
gaas (het), gauze; wire netting
gaatje (het), small hole
  ik heb nog een – op donderdag, I can just fit (that) in on Thursday
gabber (de), mate, pal
gade, spouse
gadeslaan, to watch
gading (de), liking
  iets van je – vinden, to find something you like
gal (de), bile, gall
gal'lant, courteous
gale'rie (de), (art) gallery
gale'rij (de), gallery, walkway
galg (de), gallows
galmen, to resound, to reverberate
ga'lop (de), gallop
gammel, ramshackle
gang (de), passage; gait; way
  aan de –, going, working
  op –, in form; (in) working (order)
  ga je –, go ahead; help yourself
gangbaar, current, available
gans (de), goose
gapen, to yawn; to gape
gappen, to pinch
ga'rage (de), garage
garan'deren, to guarantee
ga'rantie (de), guarantee, warranty
garde (de), guard(s); whisk

garde'robe (de), wardrobe; cloakroom

ga'reel (het), horse collar, harness

  in het – lopen, to toe the line

garen (het), thread

garen, to gather

gar'naal (de), shrimp

gasfabriek (de), gasworks

gasleiding (de), gas pipe(s), gas main(s)

gasmeter (de), gas meter

gaspedaal (het, de), accelerator

gaspit (de), gasring, gas jet

gasstel (het), gas ring(s)

gast (de), guest

gastarbeider (de), immigrant worker

gastheer (de), host

gastvrij, hospitable

gast'vrijheid (de), hospitality

gastvrouw (de), hostess

gat (het), hole

  in de gaten krijgen, to spot

  in de gaten houden, to keep an eye on

gauw, quick

gave (de), gift

ga'zon (het), lawn

ge'aardheid (de), disposition

ge'acht: Geachte Heer/Mevrouw, Dear Sir/Madam

geaffec'teerd, affected

gealli'eerd, allied

geani'meerd, animated, lively

ge'armd, arm in arm

ge'baar (het), gesture

ge'baard, bearded

ge'bak (het), fancy cake(s)

ge'barentaal (de), sign language

ge'bed (het), prayer

ge'bergte (het), mountain range

ge'beten zijn op, to have a grudge against

ge'beuren, to happen

ge'beurtenis (de), event

ge'bied (het), territory; field, realm

ge'bieden, to order

ge'bit (het), set of teeth

ge'bladerte (het), foliage

ge'bod (het), command(ment)

ge'boorte (de), birth

ge'boortecijfer (het), birth rate

ge'boortekaartje (het), birth announcement card

ge'boorteland (het), native country

ge'boren, born

ge'bouw (het), building

ge'brek (het), lack; failing; infirmity

ge'brekkig, defective, faulty; deformed

ge'broeders (de), brothers

gebrouil'leerd, not on speaking terms

ge'bruik (het), use; custom

ge'bruikelijk, customary

ge'bruiken, to use; to partake of

gebruikers'vriendelijk, user-friendly

ge'bruiksaanwijzing (de), directions for use

gechar'meerd: ik ben niet zo – van, I am not that keen on/I am not really taken with

gecompli'ceerd, complicated

ge'daagde (de), defendant

ge'daante (de), form, shape

ge'daanteverwisseling (de), metamorphosis

gedachte (de), thought

ge'dachteloos, thoughtless

ge'dachtengang (de), train of thought

ge'dagvaarde (de), person
  summoned
ge'deelte (het), part
ge'deeltelijk, partly
gedele'geerde (de), delegate
ge'dempt, subdued, muffled,
  hushed
ge'denkdag (de), anniversary
ge'denken, to commemorate
ge'denkteken (het), monument
gedenk'waardig, memorable
gedepu'teerde (de), deputy
ge'dicht (het), poem
ge'dienstig, obliging
ge'dijen, to thrive
ge'ding (het), lawsuit; issue
gediplo'meerd, qualified
gedistil'leerd, distilled
gedistin'geerd, distinguished-
  looking
ge'doe (het), fuss; business
ge'dogen, to permit
ge'donder (het), thunder;
  trouble; messing around
ge'drag (het), behaviour
ge'dragen: zich –, to behave
ge'dragslijn (de), policy
ge'drang (het), crowd, crush
ge'drocht (het), monstrosity
ge'drongen, thick-set; impelled
ge'druis (het), rumbling, roaring
ge'ducht, formidable
ge'duld (het), patience
ge'duldig, patient
ge'durende, during
ge'durfd, daring; risky
ge'dwee, submissive
geel, yellow
geelzucht (de), jaundice
geen, not a, not any, no
geënga'geerd zijn, to be
  committed
geenszins, by no means

geest (de), spirit; mind; wit
geest'dodend, soul-destroying
geestdrift (de), enthusiasm
geestelijk, spiritual, mental
geestelijke (de), priest
geestig, witty
geestigheid (de), wit, witticism
geestkracht (de), fortitude
geestverruimend, mind-
  expanding; hallucinogenic
geestverwant (de), kindred
  spirit
geeuw(en), (to) yawn
gefortu'neerd, wealthy
ge'gadigde (de), prospective
  buyer; applicant
ge'gevens (de), data
ge'goed, well-off
ge'grond, well-founded
ge'haaid, canny
ge'hakt (het), minced meat
  (beef)
ge'halte (het), content; quality
ge'hard, seasoned; injured;
  tempered
ge'harrewar (het), bickering
ge'havend, battered
ge'heel (het), whole, all, quite
  in het – niet, not at all
ge'heelonthouder (de),
  teetotaller
ge'heim (het), secret
ge'heimschrift (het), (secret) code
geheim'zinnig, mysterious
ge'hemelte (het), palate
ge'heugen (het), memory
ge'hoor (het), hearing, ear;
  audience, congregation
ge'hoorapparaat (het), hearing aid
ge'hoorzaal (de), auditorium
ge'hoorzaam, obedient
ge'hoorzaamheid (de),
  obedience

ge'hoorzamen, to obey

ge'horig, far from sound- proof, noisy

ge'hucht (het), hamlet

ge'huichel (het), hypocrisy

ge'huisvest, housed

gehu'meurd: goed –, good- tempered

ge'ijkt, standard, traditional, common

geil, horny, randy; rank

gein (de), fun

geinig, funny

geintje (het), joke

geïrri'teerd, irritated; irritable

geiser (de), geyser

geit (de), goat

ge'jaagd, agitated

gek, mad, foolish; idiot

  voor de – houden, to make a fool of

gekheid (de), foolishness, joke

gekkekoeienziekte (de), BSE, mad cow disease

ge'kleurd, coloured

  je staat er – op, you look silly

ge'klungel (het), bungling

gekostu'meerd, in fancy dress

ge'knipt voor, cut out for

gekscheren, to joke

ge'kunsteld, artificial

ge'laat (het), countenance; face

ge'laatskleur (de), complexion

ge'laatstrek (de), feature

ge'lang: naar – van, according to

ge'lasten, to order

ge'laten, resigned

geld (het), money

gelden, to apply, to count

  zich doen –, to assert oneself

  de algemeen geldende mening, the generally accepted view

geldig, valid

geldstuk (het), coin

geldwolf (de), money grubber

geldzuivering (de), currency reform

ge'leden, ago

ge'leerd, learned

ge'leerde (de), scholar, scientist

ge'legen, situated; convenient

  er is veel aan –, much depends on it

ge'legenheid (de), occasion, opportunity; place

ge'leide (de), escort

ge'leidelijk, gradually

ge'leiden, to conduct

ge'letterd, lettered

ge'lid (het), rank, file, order

ge'liefd, beloved, popular

ge'liefkoosd, favourite

ge'lieven, to please

ge'lijk, equal, alike; level

  je hebt –, you are right

  iemand – geven, to agree with a person

ge'lijkenis (de), resemblance; parable

gelijkge'zind, like-minded

ge'lijkheid (de), equality

gelijk'matig, equable; even

gelijk'tijdig, simultaneous

gelijk'vloers, on the ground floor; on the same floor

ge'lofte (de), vow

ge'loof (het), belief, faith

geloof'waardig, credible

ge'loven, to believe, to think

ge'lovig, faithful

gelovige (de), believer

ge'luid (het), sound

ge'luidloos, noiseless

ge'luidshinder (de), noise pollution

ge'luidsinstallatie (de), sound equipment

ge'luk (het), luck, good fortune; happiness

ge'lukkig, happy; fortunate, lucky

ge'luksvogel (de), lucky one

ge'lukwens (de), congratulation

ge'lukwensen, to congratulate

ge'maakt, affected, feigned; ready-made

ge'maal (het), pumping engine

ge'mak (het), ease; comfort; convenience

ge'makkelijk, easy, comfortable; convenient

ge'makshalve, for the sake of convenience

gemak'zuchtig, lazy

ge'matigd, temperate; moderate

gember (de), ginger

ge'meen, (in) common; foul, nasty

ge'meend, sincere

ge'meenplaats (de), platitude

ge'meenschap (de), community; (sexual) intercourse

gemeen'schappelijk, common, joint

ge'meenschapsgevoel (het), public spirit

ge'meente (de), municipality; congregation; parish

ge'meentebelasting (de), (local) rates

ge'meentelijk, municipal

ge'meenteraad (de), council

ge'meenteraadsverkiezing (de), council elections

ge'meentereiniging (de), environmental health department of the council

gemelijk, peevish

ge'middeld, average

ge'mis (het), lack, want, loss

ge'moed (het), heart, mind, feeling(s)

ge'moedelijk, kindly, informal

ge'moedsrust (de), peace of mind

ge'moeid, involved

gems (de), chamois

ge'mutst: goed –, in a good mood

ge'naamd, named

ge'nade (de), grace; mercy; pardon

ge'nadeloos, merciless

ge'nadeslag (de), finishing stroke

gen (het), gene

gene, that; the other

  deze en –, several people

ge'neesheer (de), physician

genees'krachtig, curative

ge'neeskunde (de), medicine

ge'neesmiddel (het), remedy; medicine

ge'negen, willing; inclined, disposed

ge'negenheid (de), affection

ge'neigd, inclined, prone

gene'raal (de), general

generale repetitie (de), dress rehearsal

generen, to embarrass

  zich –, to feel embarrassed

ge'netisch, genetic

ge'nezen, to cure, to heal; to recover

ge'nezing (de), cure; recovery

geni'aal, brilliant

ge'nie (het), military; engineers; (man of) genius

ge'niepig, underhand

ge'nieten (van), to enjoy

ge'nodigden (de), invited guests
ge'noeg, enough
ge'noegdoening (de), satisfaction, reparation
ge'noegen (het), pleasure
ge'noeglijk, pleasant
ge'noegzaam, sufficient
ge'nootschap (het), society, association
ge'not (het), joy, delight
genuan'ceerd, subtle
geo'graaf (de), geographer
geo'loog (de), geologist
ge'oorloofd, permitted
ge'ordend, regulated, orderly
georgani'seerd, organized
georiën'teerd (op), with leanings towards, minded
ge'paard gaan met, to be accompanied by
ge'past, fitting, seemly
– geld, the exact amount
ge'peins (het), pondering
ge'peperd, peppered, pungent
gepi'keerd, offended, piqued, nettled
ge'prikkeld, irritated, irritable
gepromo'veerd, promoted; holding a doctor's degree
ge'raamte (het), skeleton
ge'raden, advisable
geraffi'neerd, refined; unmitigated; artful
ge'raakt, offended, moved
ge'raken, to become, to get
ge'raspt, grated
ge'recht (het), dish (food)
ge'rechtelijk, judicial, legal
ge'rechtigd, entitled
ge'rechtigheid (de), justice
ge'rechtshof (het), court of justice
ge'reed, ready

ge'reedschap (het), tools
gerefor'meerd, Dutch Reformed, Calvinist(ic)
ge'regeld, regular
ge'remd, inhibited
gerenom'meerd, renowned
ge'rief(e)lijk, comfortable
ge'ring, small, slight
ge'roezemoes (het), buzz, bustle
gerouti'neerd, experienced
ge'rucht (het), rumour; noise
ge'ruchtmakend, sensational
ge'ruim, ample
ge'ruisloos, noiseless
ge'ruit, checked
ge'rust, easy
  neem (het) maar –, you're welcome (to it)
ge'ruststellen, to reassure
ge'schater (het), peals of laughter
ge'schenk (het), present
ge'schieden, to happen, to come about
ge'schiedenis (de), history; story; affair
geschied'kundig, historical
ge'schiedschrijver (de), historian
ge'schift, nuts, crazy
ge'schikt, suitable; decent
ge'schil (het), dispute
ge'schoold, trained, skilled
ge'schrift (het), writing
ge'schut (het), artillery
gesel (de), whip
geselen, to whip, to lash
gesterili'seerd, sterilized
ge'situeerd: goed –, well-off
ge'slaagd, successful
ge'slacht (het), stock; generation; sex; gender
ge'slachtsdelen (de), genitals

ge'slachtsziekte (de), venereal
  disease
ge'slepen, cunning; sharpened
  – glas, cut glass
ge'sloten, close(d);
  uncommunicative
ge'sluierd, veiled
gesp (de), buckle, clasp
ge'spannen, tense, strained
gespen, to buckle
ge'spierd, muscular
ge'spikkeld, speckled, dotted
ge'sprek (het), conversation
ge'spuis (het), rabble
ge'stadig, steady
ge'stalte (de), figure; stature
ge'stel (het), constitution
ge'steldheid (de), condition;
  nature, character
ge'stemd, tuned; disposed
ge'sticht (het), institution
ge'streept, striped
ge'strest, stressed
ge'stroomlijnd, streamlined
getai'lleerd, tailored, close-
  fitting
ge'tal (het), number
ge'tand, toothed, cogged
ge'tij (het), tide
ge'tikt, crazy
ge'tint, tinted
ge'tob (het), worry(ing)
ge'tralied, barred, latticed
ge'troosten: zich veel moeite –,
  to take great pains
ge'trouw, faithful
ge'trouwd, married
ge'tuige (de), witness
ge'tuigen, to testify
ge'tuigenis (de), testimony,
  evidence
ge'tuigschrift (het), certificate;
  testimonial

geul (de), channel; gully
geur (de), scent
  **iets in geuren en kleuren
  vertellen**, to go into elaborate
  details about something
geuren, to smell
geurig, fragrant
ge'vaar (het), danger
ge'vaarlijk, dangerous
ge'vaarte (het), huge object
ge'val (het), case
  in geen –, on no account
ge'vangene (de), prisoner
ge'vangenis (de), prison
ge'vangenschap (de),
  imprisonment
gevari'eerd, varied
ge'vat, quick-witted
ge'vecht (het), fight
gevel (de), façade
geven, to give
  het geeft niets, it does not
  matter; it is no use
gever (de), donor
ge'vestigd, settled,
  established
ge'vleugeld, winged
**ge'vlij: bij iemand in het –
  komen**, to worm oneself into a
  person's favour
ge'voel (het), feeling, sense
ge'voelig, sensitive; tender
ge'voelloos, numb; unfeeling
ge'voelsmens (het), emotional
  person
ge'vogelte (het), birds, poultry
ge'volg (het), consequence;
  retinue
  – geven aan, to comply with
ge'volgtrekking (de), conclusion
ge'waad (het), garment
ge'waagd, bold, *risqué*
  aan elkaar –, well-matched

ge'waarworden, to become aware of

ge'waarwording (de), sensation

gewapender'hand, by force of arms

ge'was (het), vegetation, crops

ge'weer (het), gun, rifle

ge'wei (het), antlers

ge'weld (het), violence, force
– **aandoen,** to violate

geweld'dadig, violent

ge'weldig, terrific

ge'welf (het), vault

ge'welfd, vaulted, domed

ge'wennen, to accustom

ge'west (het), region

ge'westelijk, regional

ge'weten (het), conscience

ge'wetenloos, unprincipled

ge'wetensbezwaar (het), conscientious objection

ge'wezen, late, ex-

ge'wicht (het), weight; importance

ge'wichtig, weighty; important
– **doen,** to be pompous

ge'wiekst, smart

ge'wild, in demand

ge'willig, willing

ge'wond, wounded, injured

ge'woon, usual, ordinary, accustomed

ge'woonlijk, usually

ge'woonte (de), custom, habit

ge'woonweg, simply

ge'wricht (het), joint

ge'wrongen, laboured; twisted

ge'zag (het), authority, command

ge'zaghebbend, authoritative

ge'zagvoerder (de), captain, pilot

ge'zamenlijk, joint; complete

ge'zang (het), singing; hymn

ge'zant (de), ambassador, minister

ge'zapig, slow, lethargic

ge'zegde (het), (old) saying; predicate

ge'zel (de), mate, companion

ge'zellig, cosy; pleasant; sociable

ge'zelschap (het), company, party

ge'zet, corpulent; set

ge'zicht (het), sight; face

ge'zichtsbedrog (het), optical illusion

ge'zichtsvermogen (het), (eye)sight

ge'zichtspunt (het), point of view

ge'zichtsveld (het), field of vision

ge'zien, seen; highly thought of; in view of

ge'zin (het), family

ge'zind, disposed, minded

ge'zocht, sought (after), far-fetched

ge'zond, healthy, sound

gezondheid (de), health

ge'zwel (het), tumour, swelling

ge'zwollen, swollen; bombastic

gids (de), guide

giechelen, to giggle

gier (de), vulture

gierig, miserly

gierigheid (de), avarice

gietbui (de), downpour

gieten, to pour; to cast

gieter (de), watering can

gietijzer (het), cast iron

gif(t) (het), poison

gift (de), donation, contribution

giftig, poisonous; venomous

gi'gantisch, gigantic, huge
gij, thou, ye, you
gijzelaar (de), hostage
gijzelen, to take as a hostage
gil (de), scream, shriek
gilde (de), guild
gillen, to yell
ginder, ginds, over there
ginnegappen, to giggle
gips (het), gypsum, plaster (of Paris)
gipsafgietsel (het), plaster cast
gi'reren, to pay by giro
giro (de), giro; giro account; bank/giro transfer
girobe'taalkaart (de), giro cheque
gissen, to guess
gissing (de), guess
gist (de), yeast
gisten, to ferment
gisteren, yesterday
gister'avond, last night
gisting (de), ferment(ation)
gi'taar (de), guitar
gitzwart, jet-black
glaasje (het), small glass
glad, smooth, slippery; glib, cunning
gladheid (de), slipperiness
glans (de), gloss, sheen, lustre
glansrijk, brilliant
glanzen, to shine, to gleam
glanzig, glossy
glas (het), glass
glashelder, crystal clear
glazen, (made of) glass
glazenwasser (de), window-cleaner
glazenwisser (de), squeegee
glazig, glassy, waxy
gla'zuren, to glaze, to ice
gletscher, gletsjer (de), glacier

gleuf (de), groove, slit, slot
gleufhoed (de), trilby
glibberen, to slither
glijbaan (de), slide
glijden, to slide; to glide
glimlach (de), smile
glimlachen, to smile
glimmen, to shine, to gleam
glimp (de), glimpse
glimworm (de), glow-worm
glinsteren, to glitter, to glisten
glippen, to slip
glo'baal, rough, broad
gloed (de), glow; blaze; ardour
gloednieuw, brand-new
gloeidraad (de), filament
gloeien, to glow
  gloeiend heet, burning hot
gloeilamp (de), electric light bulb
glooien, to slope
glooiing (de), slope
glorie (de), glory
glorierijk, glori'eus, glorious
gluiper(d) (de), sneak
gluiperig, sneak
glunderen, to beam (with joy)
gluren, to peer
gniffelen, gnuiven, to laugh in one's sleeve
goddelijk, divine
goddeloos, godless
godgeklaagd, crying (to heaven)
godgeleerdheid (de), theology
go'din (de), goddess
godsdienst (de), religion
godsdienstwaanzin (de), religious mania
godslasteraar (de), blasphemer
gods'lasterlijk, blasphemous
goed, good; well
goe'daardig, good-natured; benign

goederen (de), goods
goed'geefs, generous
goedge'lovig, credulous
goedge'zind, well-disposed
goed'hartig, kind-hearted
goedheid (de), kindness
goedig, sweet-natured
goedje (het), stuff
goedkeuren, to approve of
goedkeuring (de), approval,
 assent
goed'koop, cheap
goed'lachs, easily amused
goed'moedig, good-natured
goedpraten, to explain away
goedschiks of kwaadschiks,
 willing or unwilling
goedvinden, to approve
goeierd (de), kind soul
gokken, to gamble, to chance
gokker (de), gambler
golf (de), wave; bay; gulf
golfbreker (de), breakwater
golflengte (de), wave-length
golfslag (de), dashing of the
 waves
golven, to wave, to undulate
gom (de), gum; rubber
gondel (de), gondola
gonzen, to buzz
goochelaar (de), conjurer,
 juggler
goochela'rij (de), conjuring,
 juggling
goochelen, to conjure, to juggle
goochem, smart
gooi (de), throw
gooien, to fling, to throw
goor, dingy; rank
goot (de), gutter; drain
gootsteen (de), (kitchen) sink
gordel (de), belt; girdle
gordelroos (de), shingles

gor'dijn (het), curtain
gorgelen, to gargle
gort (de), pearl barley
gortig: het te – maken, to go too
 far
 dat is me toch te –, that's more
 than I can take
gotisch, gothic
goud (het), gold
gouden, gold(en)
goudmijn (de), goldmine
graad (de), degree, rank, grade
gradenboog (de), protractor
graaf (de), count, earl
graafschap (het), county
graafwerk (het), excavation(s)
graag, eager; gladly
 (ja) –, yes please
 ik zou – willen weten, I would
 (dearly) like to know
graaien, to rummage; to grab
graan (het), grain, corn
graanschuur (de), granary
graansoorten (de), cereals
graat (de), fishbone
grabbel: te – gooien, to throw
 away
grabbelen, to scramble; to win
 in lucky dip
grabbelton (de), lucky dip
gracht (de), (town) canal; moat
graf (het), grave, sepulchre
gra'fiek (de), graph
grafkelder (de), (family) vault
grafschrift (het), epitaph
grafstem (de), sepulchral voice
grafzerk (de), tombstone
gram (het), gram
gram'matica (de), grammar
gra'naat (de), shell, grenade
gra'naatappel (de), pomegranate
gra'naatscherf (de), (piece of)
 shrapnel

gra'niet (het), granite
grap (de), joke
  voor de –, for fun
**grapjas (de), grappenmaker
  (de),** wag
grappig, funny
gras (het), grass
grasduinen, to browse
grashalm (de), grasspriet (de),
  blade of grass
graszode (de), turf, sod
gratie (de), grace; free pardon;
  favour
  uit de – zijn, being out of
  favour
grati'eus, graceful
gratifi'catie (de), bonus
grauw, grey, drab
grauwen, to snarl, to growl
graven, to dig
gra'veren, to engrave
gra'vin (de), countess
gra'vure (de), engraving
grazen, to graze
  iemand te – nemen, to take
  someone for a ride
greep (de), grip; grasp; hilt
grendel (de), bolt
grendelen, to bolt
grenen (de), deal; pinewood
grens (de), bound(ary), frontier,
  limit
grensgeval (het), borderline case
grensrechter (de), linesman
grenzen aan, to border on
grenzeloos, boundless
greppel (de), field drain; narrow
  ditch
gretig, eager
Griekenland, Greece
Griek(s)(se) (de), Greek
  (woman)
grienen, to sniffle

griep (de), flu
griezel, monstrosity
griezelen, to shudder
griezelig, gruesome
grif, readily
grif'fier (de), clerk of the court
grijns (de), grin, sneer
grijnzen, to sneer, to grin
grijpen, to seize
grijs, grey
grijsaard (de), old man
gril (de), caprice
grillig, capricious
gri'mas (de), grimace
grime (de), (stage) make-up
grimmig, grim
grinniken, to chuckle, to snigger
grint (het), gravel
grissen, to snatch
groef (de), groove; furrow
groeien, to grow
groeistuipen (de), growing pains
groen, green
groente(n) (de), vegetables
groenteboer (de), greengrocer
groep (de), group
groe'peren, to group, to cluster
  (around)
groepsgewijze, in groups
groet (de), salute, greeting
  de groeten doen, to give one's
  kind regards
groeten, to greet, to nod good-day
groezelig, grubby
grof, coarse; rude; gross
  – geld verdienen, to earn big
  money
grommen, to growl, to grumble
grond (de), ground, earth, soil
  in de – van de zaak, basically
  te gronde gaan, to go to pieces
grondbeginsel (het), basic
  principle

grondbelasting (de), land tax
grondbezitter (de), landowner
grondgebied (het), territory
grondig, thorough
grondslag (de), foundation
grondstof (de), raw material
grondverf (de), undercoat
grondwet (de), constitution
grond'wettelijk, constitutional
groot, large, big, great, tall
 in het –, on a large scale
grootbrengen, to bring up
groothandel (de), wholesale
 trade
grootheid (de), magnitude
grootheidswaanzin (de),
 megalomania
groothouden: zich –, to put a
 brave face on it
grootmoeder (de), grandmother
groot'moedig, magnanimous
grootouders (de), grandparents
groots, grand(iose)
grootscheeps, large-scale
grootsheid (de), grandeur
grootspraak (de), boasting
grootte (de), size
grootvader (de), grandfather
gros (het), gross; majority
gros'sier (de), wholesaler
grot (de), grotto, cave
grotendeels, for the greater part
gruis (het), grit, slack
gruizele'menten (de),
 smithereens
grut: klein –, little ones
gruwel (de), atrocity, horror
gruweldaad (de), atrocity
gruwelijk, horrible
gruwen, to shudder; to abhor
guitig, mischievous
gul, open-handed
gulden (de), guilder

gulheid (de), generosity
gulp (de), fly
gulzig, greedy
gum (de), rubber, eraser
gunnen, to grant
 het is je gegund, you're
 welcome to it
gunst (de), favour
gunstig, favourable
gutsen, to gush
guur, bleak, raw
gym (de), gymnastics;
 gym'nasium (het), grammar
 school
gymnas'tiek (de), gymnastics
gymnas'tiekzaal (de),
 gymnasium
gympen, gym shoes, trainers

H

haag (de), hedge
(Den) Haag, The Hague
haai (de), shark
haak (de), hook
 niet in de –, not all that it
 should be
 tussen haakjes, in brackets;
 by the way
haaknaald (de), haakpen (de),
 crochet hook
haal (de), (pen) stroke; pull
haalbaar, attainable,
 feasible
haan (de), cock
 daar kraait geen – naar,
 nobody will be any the wiser
haar (het), hair
 het scheelde maar een –, it
 was touch and go
haar, her
haard (de), stove; centre; hotbed
 open – (de), fireplace

haardos (de), head of hair

haarfijn, minutely
  iets – uitleggen, to explain something in great detail

haarklove'rij (de), hair-splitting

haarspeld (de), hairclip

haarspeldbocht (de), hairpin bend

haarspoeling (de), hair colouring

haaruitval (de), hair loss

haas (de), hare

haast, almost; haste

haasten: zich –, to hurry

haastig, hasty

haat (de), hatred

haat'dragend, vindictive

hachelijk, precarious

hachje (het): bang voor zijn –, afraid to risk one's life

hage'dis (de), lizard

hagel (de), hail; shot

hagelen, to hail

hagelwit, white as snow

hak (de), (shoe)heel
  van de – op de tak springen, to jump from one subject to another
  iemand een – zetten, to play a person a dirty trick

hakblok (het), chopping block

haken, to crochet; to hook

hakenkruis (het), swastika

hakkelen, to stammer

hakken, to chop, to hack

hakmes (het), cleaver

hal (de), hall

halen, to fetch, to get; to catch
  hij haalt het nooit, he will never manage it
  dat haalt er niet bij, there's no comparison

half, half, semi-
  – zes, half past five

half'gaar, underdone; half-witted

halfgod (de), demigod

halfrond (het), hemisphere

half'slachtig, half-hearted

half'stok, at half mast

halm (de), stalk, blade

hals (de), neck

halsband (de), (dog)collar

halssnoer (het), necklace

hals'starrig, stubborn

halte (de), stop(ping place)

hal'veren, to halve

halverwege, half-way

hamer (de), hammer, mallet

hameren, to hammer

hamsteren, to hoard

hand (de), hand
  handen thuis! hands off!
  de handen uit de mouw steken, to get down to it
  er is niets aan de –, there is nothing wrong
  met de handen in het haar, at one's wits' end
  op handen dragen, to worship
  van de – doen, to dispose of
  voor de – liggen, to be obvious

handbagage (de), hand luggage

handboeien (de), handcuffs

handdoek (de), towel

handdruk (de), handshake

handel (de), trade
  in de –, in business; on the market

handelaar (de), dealer

handelbaar, handy; pliant

handelen, to act; to trade

handeling (de), act(ion)

handelsakkoord (het), trade agreement

handelsbetrekkingen (de), trade relations

handelsrecht (het), commercial law

handelswaren (de), merchandise

handelswijze (de), method(s) (of dealing), behaviour

handgemeen worden, to come to blows

handgreep (de), grip, handle

handhaven, to maintain

handig, handy, deft

handlanger (de), accomplice

handleiding (de), manual

handrem (de), hand break

handschoen (de), glove

handschrift (het), manuscript; handwriting

hand'tastelijk, aggressive, violent

– zijn, to touch up

handtastelijkheden (de), blows, fighting; pawing

handtekening (de), signature; autograph

handvat (het), handle

handvest (het), charter

handwerk (het), (handi)craft; needlework

handwerken, to do needlework

hangen, to hang

hangend(e), drooping; pending

hanger (de), (coat)hanger; pendant

hangerig, listless

hangmat (de), hammock

hangslot (het), padlock

han'teerbaar, manageable

han'teren, to handle, to operate

hap (de), mouthful, bite

haperen, to falter

er hapert iets, there is a hitch somewhere

happen, to take a mouthful

happig, keen, eager

hard, hard

– nodig, very necessary

ik heb er een – hoofd in, I have my doubts (about the result)

harden, to harden, to temper

ik kon het niet langer –, I couldn't stand it any longer

hard'horig, hard of hearing

hardlopen, to run

hard'nekkig, stubborn

hardop, aloud

hard'vochtig, callous

harig, hairy

haring (de), herring; tent peg

hark (de), rake; gawk

harken, to rake

harlekijn (de), harlequin

har'monica (de), accordion, mouth organ

harmo'nie (de), harmony

harmoni'ëren, to harmonize

har'monisch, harmonious; harmonic

harnas (het), armour

iemand in het – jagen, to put a person's back up

harrewarren, to squabble

hars (het, de), resin, rosin

hart (het), heart

heb het – niet! don't you dare!

hart- en vaatziekten (de), cardiovascular diseases

hartaanval (de), heart attack

hartelijk, cordial, hearty

harteloos, heartless

hartelust: naar –, to one's heart's content

hart'grondig, whole-hearted

hartig, savoury; forthright

hartinfarct (het), heart attack

hart'roerend, touching

hartstikke, (inf) very, terribly, completely

  ik heb het – druk, I'm incredibly busy

hartstocht (de), passion

harts'tochtelijk, pasionate

hartverlamming (de), heart failure

hartver'scheurend, heartbreaking

hatelijk, spiteful

hatelijkheid (de), spite(ful remark)

haten, to hate

haveloos, ragged; shabby

haven (de), harbour

havenarbeider (de), dock worker

havenstad (de), port

haver (de), oats

  van – tot gort kennen, to know inside out

haverklap: om de –, at the slightest provocation; every other minute

havermout (de), porridge (oats)

havik (de), hawk

haviksneus (de), aquiline nose

hazelnoot (de), hazelnut

hazenlip (de), harelip

hbo: hoger be'roepsonderwijs (het), higher vocational education

hé, hey, hello, oh (really)? (greeting/pleasant surprise)

hè, oh, what? (unpleasant surprise)

  leuk hè?, great, isn't it?

hebben, to have

  hoe laat heb je het? what time do you make it?

  wat heb ik eraan? what's the good of it to me?

het – over, to talk about

hebberig, greedy

hebzucht (de), greed

heb'zuchtig, grasping

hecht, firm, solid

hechten, to attach; to stitch (up)

  ge'hecht aan, fond of, attached to

hechtenis (de), custody

hechting (de), stitch

hechtpleister (de), adhesive plaster

heden, today

  – ten dage, nowadays

hedendaags, present-day

heel, whole, entire; quite, very

heelhuids, unscathed

heen, gone; on the way out

  daar kun je niet –, you can't go there

  – en weer, to and fro

  waar wil je –? where do you want to go? what are you driving at?

heengaan, to go away

heenweg: op de –, on the way there

heer (de), gentleman; master; lord

heerlijk, delicious; delightful

heerschap'pij (de), dominion, rule

heersen, to rule; to prevail

heerser (de), ruler

heers'zuchtig, ambitious

hees, hoarse

heester (de), shrub

heet, hot

heetge'bakerd, quick-tempered

hefboom (de), lever

heffen, to raise

heffing (de), levy

heft (het), handle, haft
heftig, violent; vehement
heg (de), hedge
heibel, din, racket
heide (de), moor, heath(er)
heiden (de), heathen, pagan
heidendom (het), paganism,
  pagan world
heidens, heathen(ish), pagan
heien (het), pile-driving
heiig, hazy
heilbot (de), halibut
heilig, holy, sacred
heiligdom (het), sanctuary,
  sanctum
heilige (de), saint
heiligen, to hallow; to keep holy
heiligschennis (de), sacrilege
heiligverklaring (de),
  canonization
heilloos, evil; disastrous, fatal
heilzaam, salutary
heimelijk, secret, furtive
heimwee (het), homesickness,
  nostalgia
heinde en ver, near and far
heining (de), fence
heipaal (de), (concrete) pile
hek (het), railings; gate
hekel (de), hackle
  ik heb er een – aan, I dislike it
  intensely
  over de – halen, to criticize
  sharply
hekelen, to heckle, to satirize
hekkensluiter (de), last comer
heks (de), witch; hag
heksenketel (de), cacophony
heksentoer (de), insuperable
  task
hel (de), hell
he'laas, alas
held (de), hero

helder, clear, lucid; bright; clean
helder'ziend, clairvoyant
held'haftig, heroic
hel'din (de), heroine
helemaal, completely
  hele'maal niet, not at all
helen, to receive stolen goods;
  to heal
helft (de), half
hellen, to slope, to slant
helling (de), slope, incline,
  slipway
helm (de), helmet; beach-grass
helpen, to help, to be effective
hels, infernal, hellish
  – zijn, to be wild (with rage)
hem, him
hemd (het), vest, shirt
hemel (de), heaven, sky; canopy
hemellichaam (het), celestial
  body
hemels, heavenly
  hemelsbreed verschil, all the
  difference in the world
hemelsvaartdag (de), Ascension
  Day
hen, them
hengel (de), fishing rod
hengelaar (de), angler
hengelen, to angle, to fish
hengsel (het), handle; hinge
hengst (de), stallion
hennep (de), hemp
her: van eeuwen –, from times
  immemorial
  van oudsher, of old
her-, re-, again
her'ademen, to breathe again
heral'diek (de), heraldry
herberg (de), inn
herbergen, to accommodate; to
  harbour
herber'gier (de), inn keeper

her'denken, to commemorate; to recall

her'denking (de), commemoration

herder (de), shepherd; herdsman

herdershond (de), sheepdog

her'drukken, to reprint

her'enigen, to reunite

herfst (de), autumn

her'haald(elijk), repeated(ly)

her'halen, to repeat; to revise

her'haling (de), repetition; revision

herinneren, remember; remind
– **aan,** to remind of
zich –, to remember

her'innering (de), recollection, memory

herintreden, return to work (a woman after a childcare break)

her'kauwen, to chew the cud; to ruminate

her'kenbaar, recognizable

her'kennen, to recognize

her'kiezen, to re-elect

herkomst (de), origin

her'leiden, to convert, to reduce

her'leven, to revive; to live again

her'nemen, to resume; to take again

her'nieuwen, to renew

hero'ïne (de), heroin

herontdekken, to rediscover

her'overen, to recapture

herrie (de), row, hullabaloo

her'roepen, to revoke

hersenen (de), brain(s)

hersenpan (de), cranium

hersenschim (de), chimera

hersenschudding (de), concussion

her'stel (het), recovery, convalescence

her'stellen, to mend; to restore; to recover

her'stellingsoord (het), convalescent home

hert (het), deer, stag

hertenkamp (de), deer park

hertog (de), duke

hertogdom (het), duchy

herto'gin (de), duchess

her'trouwen, to remarry

her'vatten, to resume

her'vormd, reformed; protestant

her'vorming (de), reform(ation)

her'winnen, to regain

her'zien, to revise; to review

het, it: the

heten, to be called

hetero'geen, heterogeneous

heteroseksu'eel, heterosexual

het'geen, (that) which

het'zelfde, the same

het'zij ... of (or dan wel), either or whether ... or

heugen: dat zal je –, you won't forget that in a hurry

heuglijk, joyful

heulen met, to be in league with

heup (de), hip

heus, real; courteous

heuvel (de), hill

hevig, violent

hi'aat (het), hiatus

hiel (de), heel

hier, here

hierheen, this way

hier'naast, next to this; next door

hier'namaals (het), (life) hereafter

hieruit, out (of) here; from this

hij, he

hijgen, to pant
hijsen, to hoist
hijskraan (de), crane
hik (de), hiccups
hikken, to have hiccups
hilari'teit (de), hilarity, mirth
hinderen, to hinder; to annoy
hinderlaag (de), ambush
hinderlijk, annoying;
  inconvenient
hindernis (de), hinderpaal (de),
  obstacle
hinken, to limp; to hop
hinniken, to neigh
his'torisch, historic(al)
hitte (de), heat
hobbel (de), bump
hobbelen, to jolt
hobbelig, bumpy
hobbelpaard (het), rocking
  horse
hobo (de), oboe
hoe, how
  – eerder – beter, the sooner the
  better
  – dan ook, however
hoed (de), hat
hoe'danigheid (de), quality
hoeden, to guard
hoef (de), hoof
hoefijzer (het), horseshoe
hoegenaamd niets, nothing
  whatever
hoek (de), angle; corner, nook
hoekig, angular
hoenderhok (het), hen coop
hoepel (de), hoop
hoer (de), whore
hoes (de), loose cover; dustsheet
hoest (de), cough
hoesten, to cough
hoeveel, how much, how many
hoe'veelheid (de), quantity

hoeveelste: de – is het
  vandaag? what is the date
  today?
hoeven, to need
hoe'ver, how far
  in hoeverre, to what extent
hof (het), court
  het – maken, to court
hoffelijk, courteous
hofhouding (de), royal
  household
hoge'school (de), institution of
  higher education
hok (het), kennel, pen, sty, hutch
hokken, to shack up with
hol (het), den, cave
hol, hollow, concave
Hollands, Dutch
hollen, to run
holte (de), cavity
hommel (de), bumble bee, drone
homoseksu'eel, homosexual
homp (de), lump, chunk
hond (de), dog, hound
  rode –, German measles
hondeweer (het), foul weather
honderd, a hundred
  honderduit praten, to talk
  nineteen to the dozen
honds'dolheid (de), rabies
honen, to scoff at
Honga'rije, Hungary
honger (de), hunger
hongerig, hungry
hongerloon (het), starvation
  wage
hongersnood (de), famine
honing (de), honey
honingraat (de) honeycomb
honk (het), base, home
hono'rair, honorary
hono'rarium (het), fee
hono'reren, to honour; to pay

hoofd (het), head; principal, chief

hoofdartikel (het), leading article

hoofdbreken (het), brain racking

hoofddoek (de), scarf; veil

hoofdgetal (het), cardinal number

hoofdkussen (het), pillow

hoofdkwartier (het), headquarters

hoofdletter (de), capital letter

hoofdpijn (de), headache

hoofdstad (de), capital, principal town

hoofdstraat (de), main street

hoofdstuk (het), chapter

hoofdzaak (de), main thing

hoofd'zakelijk, mainly

hoofs, courtly

hoog, high, tall
drie –, on the third floor

hoogachten, to esteem

hoogachtend, yours faithfully, yours sincerely

hoog'dravend, bombastic

hoog'hartig, haughty

Hoogheid (de), Highness

hooghouden, to uphold

hoog'leraar (de), professor

hoogmoed (de), pride

hoog'moedig, proud

hoogmoedswaanzin (de), megalomania

hoog'nodig, very necessary

hoogoven (de), blast furnace

hoogst, highest; extremely
ten hoogste, at most

hoogseizoen (het), high season

hoogspanning (de), high voltage

hoogstaand, of high moral character

hoogstens, at most

hoogstnodig, absolutely necessary

hoogte (de), height, altitude
op de –, well-informed
uit de –, supercilious

hoogtepunt (het), acme, zenith

hoogtezon (de), sun-lamp; ultra-violet light

hoogtij vieren, to be rampant

hoogtijdag (de), heyday; high day

hoogvlakte (de), plateau

hoogvlieger (de): hij is geen –, he's no genius

hoog'waardigheidsbekleder (de), (high) dignitary

hoog'water (het), high tide

hooi (het), hay
teveel – op zijn vork nemen, to bite off more than one can chew
te – en te gras, haphazardly

hooiberg (de), haystack

hooien, to make hay

hooivork (de), pitchfork

hoon (de), scorn

hoop (de), hope; heap, stack

hoopvol, hopeful

hoorbaar, audible

hoorn (de), horn, bugle; telephone receiver

hoornvlies (het), cornea

hoorspel (het), radio play

hopeloos, hopeless

hopen, to hope

hor (de), gauze screen

horde (de), horde, mass; hurdle:
hordeloop (de), hurdle race

horen, to hear; to belong (to); to be right (and proper), ought

horizon'taal, horizontal

hor'loge (het), watch

horrelvoet (de), clubfoot

hort: met horten en stoten, jerkily

horzel (de), horsefly

hospes (de), hospita (de), landlord, landlady

hossen, to sing and dance arm in arm

hotsen, to jolt

houdbaar: – tot, best before

houden, to hold; to keep
 – van, to like, to love
 – voor, to take for
 zich goed –, to control oneself

houding (de), position, pose; attitude, manner
 zich geen – weten te geven, feel awkward

hout (het), wood

houten, wooden

houterig, wooden, stiff

houtje (het), bit of wood
 iets op eigen – doen, do something on your own (initiative)

houtskool (de), charcoal

houtsne(de)e (de), woodcut

houtsnijwerk (het), wood carving

houvast (het), hold

hou'weel (het), pickaxe

hozen, to bale/bail; to pour (with rain)

huichelaar (de), hypocrite

huichela'rij (de), hypocrisy

huichelen, to be hypocritical; to feign

huid (de), skin, hide

huidig, present-day

huifkar (de), covered wagon

huilebalk (de), cry baby

huilen, to cry, to howl

huis (het), house, home

huisarts (de), family doctor

huisbaas (de), landlord

huisdier (het), pet

huiselijk, domestic(ated); homely

huisgenoot (de), member of the household

huis'houdelijk, domestic, household

huishouden (het), household; housekeeping

huishouden, to keep house
 vreselijk –, to play havoc

huishoudkunde (de), domestic science

huishoudster (de), housekeeper

huiskamer (de), living room

huisraad (het), household goods

huis-tuin-en-keuken, suburban, common

huisvesten, to house

huiswerk (het), homework

huiveren, to shudder

huiverig voor, wary of

huivering (de), shudder

huivering'wekkend, horrible

hulde (de), homage

huldigen, to pay tribute to

hulp (de), help

hulpbehoevend, in need of help, infirm, invalid

hulpeloos, helpless

hulpmiddel (het), remedy; aid; means

hulptroepen (de), auxiliaries

hulp'vaardig(heid) (de), helpful(ness)

hulpverlening (de), assistance; caring profession

hulpwerkwoord (het), auxiliary verb

huls (de), pod; case; cover

hulst (de), holly

humeur (het), mood; temper

hu'meurig, moody

hummel (de), tiny tot

humor (de), humour

hun, their; (to) them
hunkeren naar, to hanker after
huppelen, to hop
huren, to hire, to rent
hurken, to squat
hut (de), cabin, hut
hutkoffer (de), trunk
hutspot (de), traditional Dutch stew; hotpot
huur (de), rent
huurder (de), tenant
huurling (de), hireling, mercenary
huurmoordenaar (de), assassin
huurovereenkomst (de), rental agreement
huursubsidie (de), rent subsidy
huwbaar, marriageable
huwelijk (het), marriage
huwelijksaanzoek (het), proposal (of marriage)
huwelijksreis (de), honeymoon
huwelijksvoltrekking (de), marriage ceremony
huwen, to marry
hygi'ëne (de), hygiene
hypermodern, ultramodern
hypo'theek (de), mortgage
hy'sterie (de), hysteria
hys'terisch, hysterical

I

ide'aal (het), ideal
ideali'seren, to idealize
idea'lisme (het), idealism
i'dee (het, de), idea
ide'ëel, imaginary; idealistic
idem, ditto
iden'tiek, identical
identifi'ceren, to identify
identi'teit (de), identity
identi'teitsbewijs (het), ID card

idi'oom (het), idiom
idi'oot (de), idiot
idi'oot, idiotic
ido'laat van, infatuated with
ieder, every, each, any
ieder'een, everyone, anyone
iemand, someone, anyone
iep (de), elm
Ier (de), Irishman
Iers, Irish
Ierland, Ireland
iets, something, anything
ietsje, ietwat, somewhat
ijdel, vain
ijdelheid (de), vanity
ijdeltuit (de), vain person
ijken, to calibrate, to verify
ijl: in aller –, hastily
ijl, thin; rarefied
ijlen, to be delirious; to hasten
ijs (het), ice
ijsbaan (de), skating rink
ijsbeer (de), polar bear
ijsberen, to pace up and down
ijsberg (de), iceberg
ijsblokje (het), ice cube
ijselijk, horrible
ijskast (de), refrigerator
ijskoud, icy, (cold), iced
IJsland, Iceland
ijsschots (de), ice floe
ijstijd (de), ice age
ijver (de), diligence
ijverig, diligent, keen
ijzel (de), ice on the roads
ijzen, to shudder
ijzer (het), iron
ijzerdraad (het), wire
ijzerhoudend, ferrous
ijzig, icy; frightful
ijzing'wekkend, ghastly
ik, I
  het –, the ego

ille'gaal, illegal
il'lusie (de), illusion
illus'treren, to illustrate
i'mago (het), image
imam (de), imam
imker (de), beekeeper
immer, ever
immers, surely; after all
immi'grant (de), immigrant
immi'gratie (de), immigration
immo'reel, immoral
im'muun, immune
impo'neren, to impress
impo'sant, impressive
imperia'lisme (het), imperialism
im'perium (het), empire
impli'ceren, to imply
impor'teren, to import
improviseren, to improvise
impul'sief, impulsive, impetuous
in, in, at, to, into, on, inside
in'achtneming (de), observance
inademen, to breathe in
inbeelden: zich –, to imagine
inbeelding (de), imagination; conceit
inbegrepen, including
inbegrip: met – van, inclusive of
inbe'slagneming (de), seizure (of goods)
inbinden, to bind
je moet je wat –, you must climb down
inboedel (de), household effects
inboeten, to forfeit
hij heeft er het leven bij ingeboet, the attempt cost him his life
inboezemen, to inspire
inbraak (de), burglary
inbreken, to burgle, to break in
inbreker (de), burglar

inbrengen, to bring in; to put forward
hij heeft niets in te –, he has no say in the matter
inbreuk (de), infringement
inburgeren, to naturalize; to settle down
inburgeringscursus (de), integration course
incas'seren, to cash; to collect
in'cluis, included
inclu'sief, including, inclusive (of)
incom'pleet, incomplete
inconse'quent, inconsistent
indampen, to evaporate
indelen, to class(ify), to allocate
indeling (de), classification, grouping
indenken: zich –, to imagine, to visualize, to conceive
inder'daad, indeed
inder'tijd, at one time, at the time
indeuken, to dent
India, India
Indië , Dutch East Indies
in'dien, if
indienen, to introduce, to submit
indijken, to surround with dikes
indivi'du (het, de), indiviual
individu'eel, individual
indommelen, to doze off
Indo'nesië, Indonesia
indringen: zich –, to intrude
in'dringend, penetrating
indroevig, very sad
indrogen, to dry up
indruisen tegen, to run counter to
indruk (de), impression
indruk'wekkend, impressive

industriali'seren, to industrialize

indus'trie (de), industry

indu'striebond (de), industrial union

industri'eel, industrial

indu'strieterrein (het), industrial zone

indutten, to doze off

in'een, together

in'eengedoken, hunched up

in'eenkrimpen, to cower, to double up

in'eens, at once

in'eenstorten, to collapse, to come crashing down

in'eenzakken, in el'kaar zakken, to collapse, to cave in

inenten, to inoculate, to vaccinate

infante'rie (de), infantry

inferi'eur, inferior

influisteren, to whisper in a person's ear

informateur (de), politician charged with investigating a proposed cabinet formation

infor'matie (de), information

infor'meren (naar), to inquire (about)

in'fuus (het), drip; infusion

ingaan, to enter; to take effect
  niet – op, to ignore

ingang (de), entrance
  met – van, as from

ingebeeld, imaginary; conceited

ingeboren, innate

ingehouden, restrained

ingeni'eur (de), (qualified) engineer

ingeni'eus, ingenious

ingenomen met, pleased with

ingespannen, strenuous; intent

ingetogen, modest, subdued

inge'val, in case

ingeven, to prompt; to administer; to inspire

ingeving (de), inspiration

inge'volge, in accordance with

ingewanden (de), intestines

ingewijde (de), old hand; insider

inge'wikkeld, complicated

ingeworteld, deep-seated

ingezetene (de), inhabitant

ingezonden stuk (het), letter to the editor

ingooien, to throw in(to); to smash

ingreep (de), intervention

ingrijpen, to intervene

in'grijpend, far-reaching

inhalen, to catch up, to overtake; to take in

inha'leren, to inhale

in'halig, grasping

inham (de), creek

in'hechtenisneming (de), arrest

in'heems, indigenous

inhoud (de), content(s); capacity

inhouden, to contain; to restrain; to dock

inhoudsmaat (de), cubic measure

inhoudsopgave (de), table of contents

inhuldigen, to inaugurate

inkeer: tot – komen, to repent

inkleden, to put into words

inkomen (het), income

inkomen, to come in
  dar kan ik –, I can understand that
  daar komt niets van in, that's out of the question

inkomsten (de), income, revenue

inkopen, to buy, to purchase

inkorten, to shorten , to curtail

inkrimpen, to shrink, to cut down
inkt (de), ink
inktvis (de), squid
inkwartieren, to billet
inlassen, to fit in, to insert
inlaten, to let in
  zich – met, to have dealings
  with
inleiden, to introduce
inleiding (de), introduction
inleven: zich – in, to imagine
  oneself as
inleveren, to hand in
inlichten, to inform
inlichting (de), information
inlijsten, to frame
inlijven, to incorporate
inlossen, to redeem
inluiden, to ring in
inmaak (de), preserving;
  preserves
inmaken, to preserve
inmenging (de), interference
in'middels, meanwhile
innemen, to take (in, up); to
  capture; to please
innen, to collect
innerlijk, inner; intrinsic
innig, heartfelt, intimate
inpakken, to pack (up), to wrap
  up
inpalmen, to grab; to inveigle
inpikken, to grab; to tackle
inpolderen, to reclaim (land)
inpompen, to pump in; to cram
inprenten, to instil, to imprint
inrichten, to arrange, to rig up,
  to furnish
inrichting (de), institute;
  institution; arrangement,
  furnishing
inrijden, to ride, or drive into; to
  break or run in

inrit (de), entrance
inroepen, to call in, to invoke
inruilen, to trade in, to exchange
inruimen, to clear, to vacate; to
  put back
inschakelen, to switch on; to
  put into gear
inschenken, to pour out
inschepen: zich –, to embark
inschieten: erbij –, to go by the
  board
in'schikkelijk, accommodating
inschikken, to move in closer
inschrijven, to register; to
  tender; to subscribe
insge'lijks, likewise
in'signe (het), badge
inslaan, to smash (in); to stock
  up on; to turn into (a street)
inslapen, to fall asleep
insluiten, to enclose, to
  surround; to include, to
  comprise
inspannen, to exert, to strain
in'spannend, strenuous
inspanning (de), exertion
inspec'teur (de), inspector
inspi'rerend, inspiring
inspraak (de), involvement,
  having a say
inspreken: iemand moed –, to
  put heart into a person
inspringen, to stand in (for a
  colleague)
inspringende regel (de),
  indented line
inspuiten, to inject
instaan voor, to vouch for
instal'leren, to install; to induct
in'standhouden, to maintain
in'stantie (de), authority
  in laatste instantie, in the
  last resort

instellen, to institute; to focus
　er op ingesteld zijn, to be
　used to it
instelling (de), institution
instemmen, to agree
instemming (de), approval
instinc'tief, instinct'matig,
　instinctive
instoppen, to tuck in
instorten, to collapse
instru'eren, to instruct
instuderen, to practise; to study
inteelt (de), inbreeding
in'tegendeel, on the contrary
inte'grerend, integral
intekenen op, to subscribe to
in'tentie (de), intention
interen, to live on one's capital
interes'sant, interesting
interes'seren: zich – voor, to be
　interested in
in'tern, internal
inter'naat (het), boarding school
inter'neren, to intern
internetten, to work/surf on the
　internet
interpre'tatie (de), interpretation
inter'punctie (de), punctuation
interrum'peren, to interrupt
interviewen, to interview
in'tiem, intimate
intimi'teit (de), intimacy
intocht (de), (ceremonial) entry
intoetsen, to key in
intomen, to curb; to rein in
intrappen, to kick open; to
　tread down
intreden, to enter (upon), to set in
intrek: zijn – nemen in, to take
　up residence at
intrekken, to draw in; to move
　in; to withdraw; to retract

in'trige (de), intrigue
intuïtie (de), intuition
intuï'tief, intuitive, instinctive
in'tussen, meanwhile
inval (de), invasion; raid;
　brainwave
inva'lide (de), disabled person
invalidi'teit (de), disablement
invallen, to fall in; to deputize;
　to enter, to raid
inven'taris (de), inventory
inventari'satie (de), stock taking
inves'teren, to invest
investering (de), investment
invetten, to grease
invliegen: er –, to fall for a trick
invloed (de), influence
invloedrijk, influential
invoegen, to insert
invoer (de), import(s)
invorderen, to collect (debts)
in'vrijheidstelling (de), release
in'wendig, internal, inward
inwerken op, to act on
inwijden, to consecrate; to
　initiate
inwilligen, to comply with
inwinnen, to obtain
inwisselen, to (ex)change, to
　cash
inwrijven, to rub in(to)
inzage: ter –, for inspection, on
　approval
in'zake, with reference to
inzakken, to collapse
inzamelen, to collect
inzegenen, to consecrate
inzender (de), contributor;
　exhibitor
inzending (de), contribution;
　exhibit(s)
inzepen, to soap
inzet (de), stake(s)

in'zetbaar, usable, available (e.g. for work)

inzetten, to put in; to start; to stake

inzicht (het), insight, understanding

inzien, to glance through; to realize

    iets ernstig –, to take a grave view of something

    bij nader –, on second thoughts

    mijns inziens, in my opinion

inzinken, to subside; to decline

inzinking (de), subsidence; relapse

inzitten: erover –, to be worried about something

    de inzittende, the occupant

iro'nie (de), irony

i'ronisch, ironical

irre'ëel, unreal

irrele'vant, irrelevant

irri'tant, irritating, annoying

irri'teren, to irritate

ischias (de), sciatica

isla'mitisch, Islamic

iso'latie (de), insulation

isole'ment (het), isolation

iso'leren, to isolate, to insulate

i'voor (het), ivory

I'vriet, (modern) Hebrew

J

ja, yes

jaagpad (het), towpath

jaap (de), gash

jaar (het), year

jaarbeurs (de), industries fair

jaargang (de), a year's issue (of a periodical), volume

jaargenoot (de), classmate

jaargetij (het), season

jaarkaart (de), annual season ticket

jaarlijks, annual

jaartal (het), date

jaartelling (de), era

jaarwisseling (de), turn of the year

jacht (de), hunt(ing); shoot(ing), pursuit

jacht (het), yacht

jachten, to hurry

jachthaven (de), marina

jachthond (de), hound

jachtschotel (de), hotpot

jagen, to hunt; to shoot; to race

jager (de), hunter, sportsman

jakhals (de), jackal

jakkeren, to hustle

ja'loers, jealous

ja'loersheid (de), jealousy

jaloe'zie (de), jealousy; Venetian blind

jammer (de, het), distress

    – genoeg, unfortunately

    wat –! what a pity!

jammeren, to lament

jammerlijk, miserable

Jan en alle'man, every Tom, Dick and Harry

Jan met de pet, the (ordinary) man in the street

janboel (de), muddle

janken, to whine; to badger

ja'pon (de), dress

jarenlang, for years

jarig, one year old

    ik ben –, it is my birthday

jarige (de), birthday boy or girl

jarre'telle (de), suspender, garter

jas (de), coat

jasje (het), jacket

jas'mijn (de), jasmine

jassen, to peel (spuds)
ja'wel, certainly
jawoord (het), consent
je, you; your
jegens, towards
je'never (de), Dutch gin
je'neverbes (de), juniper berry or tree
jengelen, to whimper
jeugd (de), youth
jeugdherberg (de), youth hostel
jeugdig, youthful, young
jeuk (de), itch
jeuken, to itch; to scratch
je'zelf, yourself
jihad (de), jihad
jij, you
j.l.: jongst'leden, last
  15 maart j.l., 15th of March last
jochie (het), kid, lad(die)
jodendom (het), Jews; Judaism
jodium (het, de), iodine
joelen, to cheer; to howl
jokken, to fib
jokkebrok (de), fibber
jol (de), yawl, dinghy
jolig, jolly
jonassen, to swing a child by its arms and legs
jong, young
jonge'lui (de), young people
jongen (de), boy
jongen, to give birth (animals)
jongensachtig, boyish
jong'leur (de), juggler
jongs: van – af aan, right from childhood
jongst'leden, last
jood (de), Jew
joods, Jewish
Joost: – mag het weten, (I have) no idea, search me

jota (de), iota
jou, you
jour'naal (het), logbook; journal; newsreel
journalis'tiek (de), journalism
jouw, your
jouwen, to hoot
jubelen, to shout for joy
jubi'laris (de), man celebrating some personal anniversary
jubi'leren, to celebrate some anniversary in one's life
jubi'leum (het), jubilee, anniversary
juf (de), female teacher, Miss
juffrouw, Miss, Madam
juichen, to shout for joy
juist, correctly; exactly; right; just
  daarom –, for that very reason
juk (het), yoke
jukbeen (het), cheekbone
juli, July
jullie, you (people)
juni, June
ju'ridisch, juridical, legal
ju'rist (de), lawyer
jurk (de), dress
jury (de), jury
jus (de), gravy
jus'titie (de), judicature; justice, law
ju'weel (het), jewel; gem
juwe'lier (de), jeweller

K

kaak (de), jaw
  aan de – stellen, to expose
kaakje (het), biscuit
kaal, bald; bare; threadbare
kaalslag (de), deforestation
kaap (de), cape

kaars (de), candle
kaarsrecht, bolt upright
kaarsvet (het), candle grease
kaart (de), card; map, chart; hand (at cards)
kaarten, to play cards
kaartenbak (de), index box
kaartje (het), card; ticket
kaartsysteem (het), card index
kaas (de), cheese
  ik heb er geen – van gegeten, I don't know the first thing about it
kaasschaaf (de), cheese slicer
ka'baal (het), racket, din
kabbelen, to lap, to ripple
kabel (de), cable
kabelbaan (de), cable lift
kabel'jauw (de), cod
kabi'net (het), cabinet
ka'bouter (de), goblin, gnome
kachel (de), stove
ka'daster (het), land registry
kade (de), quay
kader (het), cadre, framework, scope
ka'detje (het), soft roll
kaf (het), chaff
kaft (de), (book) cover, book jacket
kaftan (de), kaftan
kajak (de), kayak
ka'juit (de), saloon, cabin (of a ship)
kakelbont, gaudy, motley
kakelen, to cackle, to chatter
kake'toe (de), cockatoo
kakkerlak (de), cockroach
kale'bas (de), gourd
ka'lender (de), calendar
kalf (het), calf
kalfsvlees (het), veal
ka'liber (het), calibre

kalk (de), lime; mortar
kalkaanslag (de), limescale
kal'koen (de), turkey
kalm, calm
kal'meren, to calm
kalmerend, calming
  – middel (het), sedative
kalmpjes, calmly
kalmte (de), calm(ness), composure
ka'lotje (het), skullcap
kalven, to calve
kalverliefde (de), puppy love
kam (de), comb; crest; bridge (of a violin)
  over één – scheren, to treat alike
ka'meel (de), camel
kamer (de), room, chamber
kame'raad (de), comrade
kameraad'schappelijk, friendly
kamergenoot (de), roommate
kamerjas (de), dressing gown
kamerlid (het), member of parliament
kamerscherm (het), screen
ka'mille (de), camomile
kammen, to comb
kamp (het), camp; contest
kam'peerterrein (het), campsite
kam'peerwagen (de), camper; campervan
kampen, to fight; to contend
kam'peren, to camp
kamper'foelie (de), honeysuckle
kampi'oen (de), champion
kampi'oenschap (het), championship
kan (de), jug, can
ka'naal (het), canal; channel
Ka'naaltunnel (de), Channel Tunnel
ka'narie (de), canary

kandelaar (de), candlestick

kandi'daat (de), candidate

kan'dijsuiker (de), sugar candy

ka'neel (de), cinnamon

kanjer (de), whopper

kanker (de), cancer

kankeren, to grumble

kankerver'wekkend, carcinogenic

kanni'baal (de), cannibal

kano (de), canoe

ka'non (het), gun

kans (de), chance

kans'arm, deprived

kansel (de), pulpit

kansspel (het), game of chance

kant (de), side, edge; lace

  dat raakt – nog wal, that is quite irrelevant

  iets over zijn – laten gaan, to put up with something

  zich van – maken, to do oneself in

  op 't kantje af, only just

kant-en-klaar, ready-to-use

kan'teel (het), battlement

kantelen, to topple over; to tilt

kanten, (made of) lace

  zich – tegen, to oppose

kan'tine (de), canteen

kantklossen (het), lace making

kantlijn (de), margin

kan'tongerecht (het), district court

kan'toor (het), office

kan'toorbaan (de), office job

kan'toorbenodigdheden (de), (*pl*) stationery

kap (de), cap; hood; bonnet; lampshade

ka'pel (de), chapel; band

kape'laan (de), curate

kapen, to hijack

kaper (de), hijacker; privateer

  kapers op de kust, rivals

kapi'taal (het), capital

kapitaal'krachtig, financially strong

kapitali'seren, to capitalize

kapita'lisme (het), capitalism

kapi'tein (de), captain

kaplaars (de), top boot, wellington

ka'pot, broken

kappen, to cut or chop down; to dress hair

kapper (de), hairdresser

kapsalon (de), hairdresser's, barbershop

kapseizen, to capsize

kapsel (het), hairstyle/cut

kapstok (de), hallstand, coathooks

kar (de), cart

ka'raat (het), carat

kara'bijn (de), carbine

ka'raf (de), carafe, decanter

ka'rakter (het), character

karakteri'seren, to characterize

karakteris'tiek, characteristic

kara'vaan (de), caravan

karbo'nade (de), chop

kardi'naal (de), cardinal

karig, parsimonious; sparing, scanty

karnemelk (de), buttermilk

karnen, to churn

karper (de), carp

kar'tel (het), cartel, trust

kar'ton (het), cardboard; carton

kar'wei (het), job (of work)

kar'wijzaad (het), caraway seed

kas (de), socket; greenhouse; cash (desk)

  goed bij kas, in funds

kassa (de), pay desk, box office; till

kas'sier (de), cashier

kast (de), cupboard; case

kas'tanje (de), chestnut

kaste (de), caste

kas'teel (het), castle

kaste'lein (de), publican

kas'tijden, chastise

kastje (het), locker

  van het – naar de muur, from pillar to post

kastpapier (het), lining paper

kat (de), cat

  de – uit de boom kijken, to play a waiting game

kater (de), tomcat; hangover

ka'theder (de), lectern

kathe'draal (de), cathedral

katho'liek, (Roman) Catholic

katje (het), kitten; catkin

ka'toen (de), cotton

ka'trol (de), pulley

kattenbak (de), litter tray (of a cat)

kattenkwaad (het), mischief

kattenpis: dat is geen –, no kidding!

kattig, catty

katzwijm (de), feigned swoon

kauwen, to chew

kauwgom (het, de), chewing gum

ka'zerne (de), barracks

keel (de), throat

  het hangt me de – uit, I'm sick and tired of it

keelpijn (de), a sore throat

keer (de), turn; time(s)

  een doodenkele –, once in a blue moon

  te – gaan, to storm

keerkringen (de), tropics

keerpunt (het), turning point

keerzijde (de), reverse side

keet (de), shed, hut

keet trappen, (inf) to kick up a racket

keffen, to yap

kegel (de), cone; skittle

kegelen, to play skittles

kei (de), boulder, cobblestone, set; 'wizard'

keihard, rock-hard

keilen, to fling

keizer (de), emperor

keize'rin (de), empress

keizerlijk, imperial

keizerrijk (het), empire

keizersnede (de), caesarian

kelder (de), cellar, vault

kelderen, to go to the bottom; to slump

kelk (de), chalice; calyx

kelner (de), waiter

kemphaan (de), fighting cock

kenau (de), amazon

kenbaar, distinguishable

  – maken, to make known

kenmerk (het), characteristic

kenmerken, to characterize

kennelijk, apparent, clear

kennen, to know

  te – geven, to intimate

  men heeft mij er niet in gekend, I was not consulted

kenner (de), connoisseur

kennis (de), knowledge; acquaintance

  – geven van, to announce

  buiten –, unconscious

kennisgeving (de), notification

kenschetsen, to characterize

kenteken (het), registration/ licence number (of a car)

kentekenplaat (de), number/ licence plate

kerel (de), fellow
keren, to turn, to stem
kerf (de), notch
kerfstok (de): hij heeft veel op zijn –, he has a lot to answer for
kerk (de), church
kerkbank (de), pew
kerkdienst (de), (divine) service
kerkelijk, ecclesiastical; church (going)
kerker (de), dungeon
kerkhof (het), churchyard
kermen, to moan
kermis (de), fair
kern (de), kernel, core; crux, gist
kernachtig, pithy
kerncentrale (de), nuclear power station
kerngezond, fit as a fiddle
kernwapen (het), nuclear weapon
kerrie (de), curry
kers (de), cherry
kerst (de), Christmas
  eerste kerstdag, Christmas Day; **tweede kerstdag,** Boxing Day
kers'vers, quite fresh
kerven, to carve, to notch, to cut
ketel (de), kettle, boiler
ketelsteen (de), scale, fur
keten (de), chain(s)
ketenen, to chain
ketjap (de), soysauce
ketsen, to misfire
ketter (de), heretic
ketteren, to swear, to rage
ketting (de), chain; necklace
keu (de), (billiard) cue
keuken (de), kitchen; cuisine
keukenfornuis (het), kitchen range
keukengerei (het), kitchen utensils

keuren, to examine; to inspect; to sample
keurig, trim, very nice
keuring (de), medical examination; inspection
keurslijf (het), bodice; straitjacket
keus (de), choice
keutel (de), dropping
keuvelen, to chat(ter)
keuze (de), choice
kever (de), beetle
kibbelen, to squabble
kicken, to get a kick (out of)
kidnappen, to kidnap
kiepen, to topple (over)
kieken, to take a snapshot of
kielzog (het), wake
kiem (de), germ; seed
kiemen, to germinate
kier (de), chink
  op een –, ajar
kies (de), molar
kiesbaar, eligible
kiesdistrict (het), constituency
kies'keurig, fastidious
kiespijn (de), toothache
kiesrecht (het), franchise
kietelen, to tickle
kieuw (de), gill
kievit (de), lapwing
kiezelsteen (de), pebble
kiezen, to choose, to elect
kiezer (de), voter; (pl) electorate
kijf: buiten –, beyond dispute
kijk (de), outlook, insight
kijk- en luistergeld (het), TV and radio licence fee
kijken, to (have a) look
kijker (de), telescope, binoculars; viewer
kijkgat (het), peephole

kijven, to quarrel

kik: hij gaf geen –, he did not utter a sound

kikken: je hebt maar te –, you've only to say the word

kikker (de), frog; cleat

kikvors (de), frog

kil, chilly

kilo(gram) (het, de), kilogram

kin (de), chin

kind (het), child

kinderachtig, childish

kinder'bijslag (de), child benefit

kinder'dagverblijf (het), crèche, day nursery

kinderlijk, childlike

kinderloos, childless

kinderopvang (de), crèche, day nursery; childcare

kindersterfte (de), infant mortality

kinderwagen (de), pram

kinds, infantine

kindsbeen: van – af, ever since childhood

kink (de), kink
een – in de kabel, a hitch

kinkhoest (de), whooping cough

kip (de), chicken, hen

kippengaas (het), chicken wire

kippenhok (het), hen house

kippenvel (het), goose bumps

kippig, short-sighted

kirren, to coo

kist (de), (packing), case, chest; coffin

kittig, spirited

klaaglied (het), lamentation, dirge

klaar, clear; ready, finished
– wakker, wide awake

klaar'blijkelijk, evident

klaarkomen, to (be) finished, to complete; to come (sex)

klaarlichte dag (de), broad daylight

klaarspelen : het –, to manage it

klacht (de), complaint

klad (het), rough draft
iemand bij de kladden pakken, to grab hold of a person

kladden, to daub, to scrawl

kladpapier (het), scribbling paper

klagen, to complain

klakkeloos, groundless, off-hand, rash

klam, clammy

klampen, to clamp

klan'dizie (de), custom(ers)

klank (de), sound

klankbord (het), sounding board

klankloos, toneless

klant (de), customer, client

klantenservice (de), customer service

klap (de), blow, smack, crack

klappen: in de handen –, to clap

klappertanden, to shiver

klaproos (de), poppy

klapstoel (de), tip-up seat, folding chair

klapwieken, to flap the wings

klari'net (de), clarinet

klas, klasse (de), class(room), form (grade)

klassenstrijd (de), class war

klas'siek, classic(al)

klateren, to splatter, to cascade

klauteren, to clamber

klauw (de), claw, talon

klave'cimbel (de, het), harpsichord

klaver (de), clover

kla'vier (het), keyboard

kleden, to dress; to clothe

klederdracht (de), local costume

kle'dij (de), kleding (de), clothes, attire

kledingstuk (het), garment

kleed (het), carpet; cloth; gown

kleedje (het), rug, (table)cloth

kleedkamer (de), dressing room, changing room

kleermaker (de), tailor

klei, sticky, soggy

klef (de), clay

kleimasker (het), mudpack

klein, little, small
– geld, small change

kleindochter (de), granddaughter

klei'neren, to belittle

klein'burgerlijk, narrow-minded, petty bourgeois

klein'geestig, narrow- minded

kleinigheid (de), trifle

kleinkind (het), grandchild

kleinkrijgen, to break (a person)

kleintje (het), baby, little one

klein'zerig, easily hurt, soft

klein'zielig, petty(-minded)

kleinzoon (de), grandson

klem (de), trap; clip; emphasis

klemmen, to pinch, to clench
een klemmend betoog (het), a convincing argument

klemtoon (de), stress

klep (de), valve; flap; peak

klepel (de), clapper

kleppen, to clang, to clatter

klepperen, to rattle, to bang to and fro

kleren (de), clothes

klerenkast (de), wardrobe

klerk (de), clerk

kletsen, to chatter; to talk rubbish

kletskous (de), gossip, chatter-box

kletteren, to clatter, to patter

kleur (de), colour; suit (cards)
– bekennen, to follow suit; to show one's colours

kleur'echt, colour-fast (dyed)

kleuren, to colour; to blush

kleurenpracht (de), blaze of colour

kleurloos, colourless

kleurstof (de), colouring matter

kleuter (de), toddler

kleven, to cleave, to stick

kleverig, sticky

kliederen, to make a mess

kliek (de), clique

kliekje (het), leftovers (of food)

klier (de), gland
wat een –, he is a real pain in the neck

klieven, to cleave

klif (het), cliff

klikspaan (de), telltale

kli'maat (het), climate

klimato'logisch, climatic

klimmen, to climb

klimop (de), ivy

klingelen, to tinkle

kli'niek (de), clinic

klink (de), latch

klinkbout (de), rivet

klinken, to sound, to ring (out); to clink glasses, to rivet

klinker (de), vowel; riveter

klinkklaar, utter, pure

klinknagel (de), rivet

klip (de), rock, reef

klis (de), klit (de), burr, burdock; tangle

klodderen, to clot; to daub

kloek, brave; stout; substantial

klok (de), clock; bell
alles wat de – slaat, all one hears about

klokhuis (het), core
klokkenspel (het), carillon, chimes
klokslag (de), stroke (of the clock)
klomp (de), clog; lump; nugget
klompvoet (de), clubfoot
klont(er) (de), lump, clod, clot
klonteren, to clot
klonterig, lumpy
kloof (de), cleft, crevice; rift
klooster (het), monastery, convent
klop (de), knock, throb
klopjacht (de), round-up
kloppen, to knock, to tap, to beat; to tally
 dat klopt als een bus, that tallies all along the line
klos (de), bobbin, reel; coil
klotsen, to slosh, to splash
kloven, to cleave, to split
klucht (de), farce
kluif (de), knuckle of pork; (meaty) bone
 een hele –, quite a job
kluis (de), safe, safe-deposit box
kluisteren, to fetter
kluit (de), clod, lump
 flink uit de kluiten gewassen, strapping
kluiven, to gnaw a bone
kluizenaar (de), hermit
klungel (de), bungler
klungelen, to bungle
klus (de), job, chore
 een hele –, a tough job
kluts (de): de – kwijtraken, to lose one's head
klutsen, to whisk
knaagdier (het), rodent
knabbelen, to nibble

knagen, to gnaw
knakken, to snap, to break
knakworst (de), Frankfurt sausage
knal (de), bang
knallen, to bang, to ring out
knalpot (de), silencer
knap, handsome, pretty; clever; neat
knappen, to snap; to crackle
knarsen, to grate; to crunch
knarsetanden, to gnash one's teeth
knauwen, to gnaw, to munch; to damage or hurt seriously
knecht (de), (man)servant
knechten, to enslave
kneden, to knead; to mould
kneedbaar, malleable
kneep (de), pinch; dodge
knel: in de – zitten, to be in a fix
knellen, to pinch
knetteren, to crackle
kneuzen, to bruise
kneuzing (de), bruise
knevelen, to gag, to pinion
knibbelen, to haggle
knie (de), knee
 onder de knie krijgen, to master
kniebuiging (de), curtsey
knielen, to kneel
knieschijf (de), kneecap
kniezen, to mope
knijpen, to pinch
 ik knijp 'm, I've got the wind up
knijper (de), clothespeg
knik (de), crack; buckle; twist
knikkebollen, to nod (with sleep)
knikken, to nod
knikker (de), marble

knip (de), snap; trap; catch; clasp; purse

knipogen, to wink; to blink

knippen, to cut (off/out), to clip
geknipt voor, cut out for

knipperen, to flicker

knipsel (het), cutting

knobbel (de), bump

knobbelig, gnarled

knoei: in de – zitten, to be in difficulties

knoeiboel (de), mess; swindle

knoeien, to make a mess; to bungle

knoeie'rij (de), corruption; bungling

knoeiwerk (het), shoddy work

knoest (de), knot (in wood)

knoflook (het, de), garlic

knok(kel) (de), knuckle

knokken, to scrap

knokploeg (de), gang of thugs, henchmen

knol (de), tuber; turnip

knolraap (de), swede

knoop (de), knot; button; node

knooppunt (het), junction

knoopsgat (het), buttonhole

knop (de), button

knopje (het), (push)button, switch

knopen, to tie, to knot

knorren, to grunt; to grumble

knorrig, peevish

knot (de), knot

knotwilg (de), pollard willow

knuffelen, to cuddle

knuist (de), fist

knul (de), fellow

knuppel (de), cudgel

knus(jes), snug

knutselen, to make things (for a hobby)

koe (de), cow
oude koeien uit de sloot halen, to rake up the past

koek (de), gingerbread

koeke'loeren, (*inf*) to stare inquisitively

koekenpan (de), frying pan

koekje (het), sweet biscuit

koekoek (de), cuckoo

koel, cool

koel'bloedig, cool-headed

koelen, to cool (down)
zijn woede –, to vent one's anger

koelkast (de), fridge

koelte (de), cool(ness)

koepel (de), dome

koe'rier (de), courier

koers (de), course; price (of stocks); rate of exchange

koesteren, to cherish
zich –, to bask

koetjes en kalfjes (de), trifling matters

koets (de), coach

koffer (de), suitcase

kofferbak (de), boot, trunk

koffie (de), coffee

koffiemelk (de), coffee cream, evaporated milk

kogel (de), bullet; ball

kogellager (het), ball bearing

kok (de), cook

koken, to cook; to boil

koker (de), (long) case

kokette'rie (de), flirtation

kokhalzen, to retch

kokosmat (de), coconut mat(ting)

kokosnoot (de), coconut

kolen (de), coal(s)
op hete –, on tenterhooks

kolendamp (de), carbon monoxide

kolenhok (het), coalshed
kolf (de), (rifle) butt; retort
kolk (de), whirlpool
ko'lom (de), column
koloni'aal, colonial
kolonia'lisme (het), colonialism
ko'lonie (de), colony
kolos'saal, colossal
kom (de), basin, bowl; the
  populous part, centre
kom'af (de), descent, birth
komedi'ant (de), (play-) actor,
  comedian
ko'medie (de), comedy play;
  theatre; comedy
ko'meet (de), comet
komen, to come
  hoe komt dat? how did that
  happen?
komisch, comic(al)
kom'kommer (de), cucumber
komma, comma, (decimal)
  point
kommer (de), sorrow, distress
kom'pas (het), compass
kom'plot (het), plot
komst (de), coming
ko'nijn (het), rabbit
koning (de), king
koning'in (de), queen
Koning'innedag (de), Queen's
  birthday
koningsgezind, royalist
koninklijk, royal, regal
koninkrijk (het), kingdom
konkelen, to scheme
kon'vooi (het), convoy
kooi (de), cage, pen; bunk
kook (de), boil
  water aan de – brengen, bring
  water to the boil
kookboek (het), cookery book
kool (de), cabbage; coal(s); carbon

koolhydraat (het), carbohydrate
koolmees (de), great tit
koolzaad (het), rape seed
koolzuur (het), carbonic acid
koop (de), purchase
  te –, for sale
  te – lopen met, to show off
  op de – toe, into the bargain
koopakte (de), title deed
koopcontract (het), contract of
  sale, title deed
koophandel (de), commerce
koopje (het), bargain
koopkracht (de), purchasing
  power
koopman (de), merchant
koopvaar'dij (de), merchant
  service
koopwaar (de), merchandise
koor (het), choir, chorus;
  chancel
koorbank (de), choir stall
koord (het), cord
koorddansen (het), tightrope
  walking
koorts (de), fever
  – hebben, to have a
  temperature
koorts(acht)ig, feverish
kop (de), head; large cup; bowl
  (of a pipe)
  de – indrukken, to nip in the
  bud
  op de – tikken, to pick up, to
  find (a bargain)
  op de – af, precisely
kopen, to buy
koper (de), purchaser
koper (het), copper, brass
kopergroen (het), verdigris
ko'pie (de), copy
kopi'ëren, to copy
ko'pij (de), copy, manuscript

kopje (het), (tea)cup
  kopje duikelen, to turn somersaults
koplamp (de), headlight
koploper (de), leader, frontrunner
koppel (de), leash
koppel (het), couple
koppelaar (de), matchmaker
koppelen, to couple, to join
koppeling (de), coupling; clutch
koppelteken (het), hyphen
koppig, obstinate
kopstuk (het), head/big man
kopzorg (de), worry
ko'raal (het), choral(e); coral
kor'daat, resolute
koren (het), corn
korenschuur (de), granary
korf (de), basket; hive
korfbal (het), korfball
korrel (de), grain; pellet
korrelig, granular
korst (de), crust, rind; scab
korstdeeg (het), short pastry
kort, short, brief
  – en bondig, terse
  – maar krachtig, short and snappy
kort'ademig, short of breath
kort'af, curt
kortheids'halve, for the sake of brevity
korting (de), discount, deduction
kor'tom, in short
kortsluiting (de), short circuit
kort'stondig, short-lived
kortweg, without wasting words
kortwieken, to clip the wings of
kort'zichtig, short-sighted
korzelig, grumpy
kost (de), food; living; board

– en inwoning (de), board and lodging
kostbaar, expensive; precious
kostbaarheden (de), valuables
kostelijk, superb; priceless
kosteloos, (cost-)free
kosten (de), expense(s), cost, charges: to cost
koster (de), verger
kostganger (de), boarder
kostgeld (het), board
kostschool (de), boarding school
kostwinner (de), breadwinner
kotsen, to puke
kou (de), cold
  – vatten, to catch cold
koud, cold
koukleum (de), chilly person
kous (de), stocking
kouwelijk, sensitive to cold
ko'zijn (het), windowsill, windowframe
kraag (de), collar, ruff
kraai(en), (to) crow
kraakbeen (het), cartilage
kraakstem (de), grating voice
kraal (de), bead
kraam (de), booth, stall
kraambed (het), childbed, confinement
kraan (de), tap; crane
kraanwagen (de), breakdown truck
krab (de), crab
krabbel (de), scratch, scrawl
krabbelen, to scratch, to scrawl
krabben, to scratch
kracht (de), force, strength, power
  volle – vooruit, full speed ahead
  op krachten komen, to regain strength

kracht'dadig, vigorous
krachteloos, powerless
krachtens, by virtue of
krachtig, powerful
krachtsinspanning (de), exertion
kra'kelen, to quarrel
kraken, to crack; to creak; to crunch
kramp (de), cramp; spasm
kramp'achtig, desperate; taut
kranig, smart; brave; brilliant
krank'zinnig, insane
krans (de), wreath
krant (de), newspaper
krap, tight; short of money
kras, scratch; strong (for one's age)
krassen, to scratch; to screech
krat (de), crate
krater (de), crater
kreeft (de), lobster
kreek (de), creek
kreet (de), cry, scream
kregel, peevish
kreng (het), carrion; rotter, bitch
krenken, to offend
krent (de), currant; skinflint
krenterig, niggardly
kreukel (de), crease
kreukelen, to crease
kreunen, to groan
kreupel, lame
kreupelhout (het), thicket
krib(be) (de), manger, crib
kribbig, testy
kriebelen, to itch, to tickle; to write a niggling hand
kriebelig, itchy
kriek (de), black cherry
krieken: bij het – van de dag, at the crack of dawn
krielkip (de), bantam hen
krijgen, to get

te pakken –, to get hold of
krijger (de), warrior
krijgertje (het), hand-me-down
krijgsgevangene (de), prisoner of war
krijgs'haftig, warlike
krijgslist (de), stratagem
krijgsmacht (de), armed forces
krijgsraad (de), council of war; court martial
krijgstocht (de), campaign
krijgstucht (de), military discipline
krijgs'zuchtig, bellicose
krijsen, to screech
krijt (het), chalk
krijtrots (de), chalk cliff
krimp: geen – geven, to not falter
krimpen, to shrink; to back
krimpvrij, unshrinkable
kring (de), circle
kringloop (de), cycle
kri'oelen, to swarm
kris'tal (het), crystal
kri'tiek (de), criticism; review
kritisch, critical
kriti'seren, to criticize
kroeg (de), pub
kroegbaas (de), landlord; innkeeper
kroep (de), croup
kroepoek (de), prawn crackers
kroes (de), mug, crucible
kroeshaar (het), frizzy/curly hair
krokusvakantie (de), spring half-term/semester break
krols, on heat
krom, crooked, bent, curved
je – lachen, to double up with laughter
kromliggen, to pinch and scrape

kromtrekken, to warp
kronen, to crown
kro'niek (de), chronicle
kroning (de), coronation, crowning
kronkel (de), twist, kink
kronkelen, to twist, to wind
kronkelig, winding
kronkeling (de), convolution
kroon (de), crown; corolla, chandelier
  dat spant de –, that beats everything
kroongetuige (de), crown witness
kroonlijst (de), cornice
kroos (het), duckweed
kroost (het), progeny
kropsla (de), lettuce
krot (het), hovel
kruid (het), herb
kruiden, to season
kruide'nier (de), grocer
kruidenthee (de), herbal tea
kruide'rijen (de), spices
kruidnagel (de), clove
kruien, to wheel (in a barrow); to break up, to drift (of ice)
kruier (de), (luggage) porter
kruik (de), stone bottle; hot water bottle
kruimelig, crumbly
kruin (de), crown, top
kruipen, to creep; to crawl; to cringe
kruiperig, cringing
kruis (het), cross; sharp (in music); croup, crupper, crutch; seat
  – of munt, head or tails
kruisbeeld (het), crucifix
kruisbes (de), gooseberry
kruiselings, crosswise
kruisen, to cross; to cruise

kruisigen, to crucify
kruispunt (het), point of intersection, crossroads
kruisraket (de), cruise missile
kruistocht (de), kruisvaart (de), crusade
kruit (het), (gun)powder
kruiwagen (de), (wheel)barrow; influential friend
kruk (de), crutch; doorhandle; crank; stool
krul (de), curl; scroll
krullebol (de), curly-head
kubiek, cubic
kubus (de), cube
kuch (de), dry cough
kuchen, to give a slight cough
kudde (de), herd, flock
kuieren, to stroll
kuif (de), quif, crest
kuiken (het), chicken
kuil (de), pit; (pot)hole
kuiltje (het), dimple
kuip (de), tub
kuis, chaste
kuisheid (de), chastity
kuit (de), calf (of the leg); spawn; roe
kuitschieten, to spawn
kul (de): flauwe –, nonsense, rubbish
kundig, able; knowledgeable
  ter zake –, expert
kundigheden (de), accomplishments
kunnen, to be able to, may
  dat kan (wel), that is (quite) possible, maybe
kunst (de), art; trick
  daar is geen – aan, there's nothing to it
kunst-, artificial; art
kunstenaar (de), artist

kunstgeschiedenis (de), history of art

kunstgreep (de), trick, manoeuvre

kunstig, ingenious

kunstijsbaan (de), skating rink

kunstkenner (de), connoisseur

kunst'matig, artificial

kunstmest (de), fertilizer

kunst'nijverheid (de), applied art

kunstrijden (het), figure skating

kunstschaatsen, figure skating

kunststof (de), man-made/synthetic material

kunststuk (het), work of art

kunst'vaardig, skilful

kunst'zinnig, artistic

kurk (de), cork

kurkentrekker (de), corkscrew

kus (de), kiss

kussen (het), pillow, cushion

kussen, to kiss

kussensloop (het), pillow case

kust (de), coast, shore
  te – en te keur, in plenty

kustvaart (de), coastwise trade

kut (de), (vulg) cunt

kuur (de), whim; cure

kwaad, bad; angry
  – geweten, guilty conscience
  het te – krijgen, to break down

kwaad (het), evil; harm

kwaad'aardig, malicious

kwaad'denkend, suspicious

kwaadschiks, with an ill grace

kwaadspreke'rij (de), scandal-mongering

kwaad'willig, malevolent

kwaal (de), complaint, ailment

kwabbig, flabby

kwa'draat (het), square

kwa'jongen (de), (young) rascal

kwa'jongensachtig, mischievous

kwak (de), thud; blob

kwaken, to quack; to croak

kwakkelen, to have poor health

kwakkelwinter (de), mild winter

kwakzalver (de), quack

kwal (de), jellyfish; jerk

kwalifi'ceren, to describe

kwalijk, evil
  – nemen, to blame
  neem me niet –, I am sorry

kwanti'teit (de), quantity

kwark (de), cottage cheese, soft curd cheese

kwart (het), quarter

kwar'taal (het), quarter, term

kwartel (de), quail

kwartje (het), 25 cents of a guilder

kwar'tier (het), quarter of an hour; quarter(s)

kwarts (het), quartz

kwast (de), brush, tassel; knot (in wood); coxcomb; smart alec

kwebbelen, to chatter

kweek (de), cultivation, growth, culture

kweken, to grow; to foster

kweker (de), nurseryman

kweke'rij (de), nursery

kwekken, to yap; to chatter

kwelen, to warble

kwellen, to torment

kwelling (de), torment

kwestie (de), question

kwetsbaar, vulnerable

kwetsen, to wound, to injure

kwet'suur (de), wound

kwetteren, to twitter

kwiek, spry

kwijlen, to dribble

kwijnen, to languish

kwijt, rid (of)
  – zijn, to have lost

kwijtraken, to lose
kwijten: zich – van, to discharge
kwijtschelden, to remit, to
  forgive
kwik (het), mercury
kwispel(staart)en, to wag the
  tail
kwistig, lavish
kwi'tantie (de), receipt

L

la(de) (de), drawer, till
laadvermogen (het), loading
  capacity
laag (de), layer, stratum
  hij gaf me de volle –, he let me
  have it
  lager onderwijs, primary
  education
laag, low(-pitched)
laag-bij-de-'gronds, crude
laag'hartig, base
laagseizoen (het), low season,
  off-season
laagte (de), low level, dip
laag'water (het), low tide
laaien, to blaze
laan (de), avenue
laantje (het), path, lane
laars (de), boot
laat, late
laat'dunkend, arrogant
laatst, last, latest; recently
laatstge'noemde (de), latter
la'biel, unstable
labora'torium (het), laboratory
lach (de), laugh
lachen, to laugh
lachlust: de – opwekken, to
  raise a laugh
lachspiegel (de), distorting
  mirror

lach'wekkend, laughable
la'cune (de), gap
ladder (de), ladder
laden, to load, to charge
ladenkast (de), chest of drawers
lading (de), load, cargo; charge
laf, cowardly
lafaard (de), lafbek (de), coward
laf'hartig, cowardly
lafheid (de), cowardice
lager (de), bearing(s)
Lagerhuis (het), Lower House,
  House of Commons
la'gune (de), lagoon
lak (het, de), sealing wax;
  lacquer
  ik heb er – aan, a fat lot
  I care
laken (het), cloth, sheet
  de lakens uitdelen, to rule the
  roost
  **hij kreeg van hetzelfde – een
  pak,** he was treated in just the
  same way
lakken, to lacquer; to seal
laks(heid) (de), lax(ity)
lam (de), lamb
lam, paralysed; nasty
lam'lendig, wretched, indolent
lammeling (de), wretch
lammetje (het), little lamb
lamp (de), lamp, bulb, valve
  tegen de – lopen, to get into
  trouble
lampi'on (de), Chinese lantern
lamstraal (de), wretch
lamsvlees (het), lamb (meat)
lan'ceren, to launch
land (het), land, country, field
  ik heb er het – aan, I hate it
  aan – gaan, to go ashore
landaanwinning (de), land
  reclamation

landarbeider (de), agricultural labourer

landbouw(kunde) (de), agriculture

landbouw'kundige (de), agriculturalist

landelijk, rural; nation-wide

landen, to land

landengte (de), isthmus

landerig, in the dumps

landgenoot (de), compatriot

landgoed (het), estate

landingsbaan (de), runway

landkaart (de), map

landmacht (de), army, land forces

landmijn (de), landmine

landschap (het), landscape

landverraad (het), high treason

lang, long, tall
  – van stof, long-winded
  – niet, not nearly

lang'dradig, long-winded

lang'durig, lengthy

langge'rekt, protracted

langs, along, past
  – elkaar heen praten, to talk at cross purposes

langskomen, to come past; to drop by

lang'uit, at full length

lang'werpig, oblong, elongated

langzaam, slow

langzamerhand, gradually

lank'moedig, long-suffering

lans (de), lance

lan'taarn (de), lan'taren (de), lantern; skylight; lamp

lan'taarnpaal (de), lamppost

lanterfanten, to loaf

lap (de), piece (of cloth), rag; patch; steak

lapmiddel (het), makeshift

lappen, to patch; to wipe; to manage

lappendeken (de), patchwork quilt

larie (de), stuff and nonsense

larve (de), larva

lassen, to weld

last (de), load, burden; instruction(s); trouble

lasteren, to slander

lasterlijk, slanderous

lastig, difficult, tiresome
  lastig vallen, to trouble

lastpost (de), nuisance

lat (de), lath, slat

laten, to let; to leave (off)
  ik kan het niet –, I can't help it
  iets – doen, to have something done

later, afterwards, later

La'tijn (het), Latin

latwerk (het), trellis

lau'rier (de), laurel

lauw, tepid

lauweren (de), laurels

la'vendel (de), lavender

la'waai (het), din

la'wine (de), avalanche

la'xeermiddel (het), laxative

la'xeren, to purge

lbo: lager beroepsonderwijs, (abbrev) lower vocational education

lebberen, to lap, to sip

lector (de), university lecturer

lec'tuur (de), reading (matter)

ledematen (de), limbs

ledig, empty

ledi'kant (het), bed(stead)

leed (het), sorrow

leedvermaak (het), pleasure at other people's misfortune

leedwezen (het), regret

leefbaar, liveable, endurable
leefgemeenschap (de), commune; community
leeftijd (de), age
  op –, elderly
leeftijdsgenoot (de), peer
leeftijdsgrens (de), age limit
leefwijze (de), manner of living
leeg, empty
leeggieten, to empty/pour (out)
leegte (de), emptiness, void
leek (de), layman
leem (het), loam
leemte (de), gap, hiatus
leep, cunning
leer (de), doctrine
  in de – bij, apprenticed to
leer (het), leather
leerboek (het), textbook
leergang (de), course of study
leer'gierig, studious
leerjongen (de), apprentice
leerkracht (de), teacher
leerling (de), pupil
leerlooien, to tan (leather)
leermeester (de), teacher
leerplan (het), curriculum
leerplicht (de), compulsory education
leerrijk, instructive
leerstoel (de), chair
leerstof (de), subject matter
leertje (het), washer (in a tap)
leerzaam, instructive
leesbaar, readable, legible
leesblind, dyslexic
leesteken (het), punctuation mark
leeszaal (de), reading room; public library
leeuw('in) (de), lion(ess)
leeuwerik (de), (sky)lark
lef (het, de), guts, nerve

le'gaal, legal
le'gaat (het), legacy
legbatterij (de), battery (cage)
legen'darisch, legendary
le'gende (de), legend
leger (het), army
  Leger des Heils, Salvation Army
leggen, to lay, to put
legio (de), countless
legi'oen (het), legion, army
legiti'matiebewijs (het), identification paper
legiti'meren: zich –, prove one's identity
legpuzzel (de), jigsaw
lei (de), slate
leiden, to lead
leider (de), leader
leiding (de), guidance, direction, lead; pipe(line)
leidingwater (het), tap water
leidraad (de), guideline
leien: alles ging van een – dakje, everything went smoothly
lek (het), leak(y)
  een lekke band, a puncture
lekken, to leak
lekker, nice
  ik ben niet –, I am not very well
  iemand – maken, to rouse a person's expectations
lekkerbek (de), gourmet
lekker'nij (de), delicacy
lel (de), lobe; clout
lelie (de), lily
lelijk, ugly; badly
  dat treft –, that's awkward
lende (de), small of the back, loin
lendenen (de), loins
lenen, to lend; to borrow

lengte (de), length, height; longitude

lenig, supple, lithe

lening (de), loan

lente (de), spring

lepel (de), spoon, ladle

lepra (de), leprosy

leraar (de), (male) teacher

lera'res (de), (female) teacher

leren, to teach; to learn

  de tijd zal het –, time will tell

leren, (made of) leather

les (de), lesson

les'bienne (de), lesbian

lesbisch, lesbian

lesgeld (het), tuition fee

lesgeven, to teach

lesrooster (het), timetable

lessen, to quench, to slake

letsel (het), injury

letten op, to pay attention to; to look after

  let wel!, mark you!

letter (de), letter, type

letteren, literature

lettergreep (de), syllable

letterkunde (de), literature

letterlijk, literal

letterteken (het), character

leugen (de), lie

leugenaar (de), liar

leugenachtig, mendacious

leuk, nice, cute, amusing

leukweg, coolly

leunen, to lean

leuning (de), (hand)rail; parapet; back, arm(rest)

leunstoel (de), armchair

leuren met, to hawk

leus (de), **leuze (de)**, slogan, device

leut (de), fun

leuteren, to talk drivel; to loiter

leven (het), life; noise

leven, to live, to be alive

levend, (a)live, living

levendig, lively

levenloos, lifeless

levensbehoefte (de), necessity of life

levensbeschouwing (de), philosophy of life

levensbeschrijving (de), biography

levensge'vaarlijk, perilous

levensgroot, life-size(d)

levenslang, lifelong

levensloop (de), course of life; curriculum vitae

levenslust (de), *joie de vivre*

levensmiddelen (de), provisions

levensonderhoud (het), subsistence

levensstandaard (de), standard of living

levensstijl (de), lifestyle

levens'vatbaar, viable

levensverzekering (de), life insurance

lever (de), liver

leveran'cier (de), purveyor, retailer

leve'rantie (de), delivery, supply

leveren, to supply, to deliver

levertraan (de), codliver oil

leverworst (de), liver sausage

lezen, to read; to gather

lezer('es) (de), reader

lezenaar (de), lectern

lezing (de), lecture; version

li'bel (de), dragonfly

libe'raal, liberal

lichaam (het), body

lichaamsbeweging (de), exercise

lichaamsbouw (de), physique

li'chamelijk, bodily, physical

licht (het), light
licht, light, mild, slight; easily
lichtbundel (de), beam of light
lichtelijk, slightly
lichten, to weigh, to lift
lichte(r)laaie: in –, ablaze
lichtge'raakt, touchy
lichtgevend, luminous
lichting (de), draft, class, levy; collection (of mail)
lichtpunt (het), point of light; lighting point; ray of hope
lichtsignaal (het), light signal
licht'vaardig, rash, lightly
licht'zinnig, frivolous, flighty
lid (het), limb, finger joint; member; sub-section; term
  uit het –, dislocated
lidmaatschap (het), membership
lidwoord (het), article
lied(eren) (het), song(s)
lieden, people
liedje (het), ditty, song
  het is het oude –, it's the same old story
lief, dear, sweet, nice
  meer dan me – is, more than I care for
  voor – nemen, to put up with
lief'dadig, charitable
lief'dadigheid (de), charity
liefde (de), love
liefdeloos, loveless
liefderijk, loving
liefdeslied (het), love song
lief(e)lijk, charming, sweet
liefhebben, to love
liefhebber (de), lover, enthusiast
liefhebbe'rij (de), hobby
liefkozen, to fondle
liefst, dearest; preferably
lief'tallig, sweet, winsome
liegen, to tell lies

lies (de), groin
lieve'heersbeestje (het), ladybird
lieveling (de), darling
liever, rather, sooner
lieverd, darling
liften, to hitch-hike
liggen, to lie
  waar ligt het aan? what is the cause of it?
ligging (de), situation
ligplaats (de), berth
lijden, to suffer
  ik mag hem wel –, I rather like him
  lijdend voorwerp (het), direct object
lijdzaam, submissive
lijf (het), body; bodice
  het heeft weinig om het –, it is of little importance
lijfsbehoud (het), self-preservation
lijfspreuk (de), motto
lijfwacht (de), bodyguard
lijk (het), corpse
lijken (op), to resemble; to seem
lijkschouwer (de), coroner
lijkschouwing (de), post-mortem
lijm (de), glue
lijmen, to glue
lijn (de), line; route
lijndienst (de), scheduled service (of transport)
lijnen, to diet
lijnolie (de), linseed oil
lijnrecht, straight; diametrically
lijnvlucht (de), scheduled flight
lijnzaad (het), linseed
lijst (de), list; frame
lijster (de), thrush
lijsterbes (de), mountain ash
lijvig, corpulent, bulky

lijzig, drawling
lik (de), lick; swipe
likdoorn (de), corn
li'keur (de), liqueur
likkebaarden, to lick one's lips
likken, to lick
lila, lilac(-coloured)
li'miet (de), limit
limo'nade (de), (fruit) cordial
linde (de), lime tree
lini'aal (de), ruler
linie (de), line
  over de hele –, all round
linker-, left
links, (to the) left; left-handed;
  gauche
  – laten liggen, to cold-shoulder
linksaf, linksom, to the left
linnen (het), linen
lint (het), ribbon
lintje (het), ribbon
  een – krijgen, to be
  decorated
lintworm (de), tapeworm
linzen (de), lentils
lip (de), lip
lippenstift (de), lipstick
liqui'deren, to wind up (a
  business)
lispelen, to lisp
list (de), ruse
listig, cunning
lite'rair, literary
lite'rator (de), man of letters
litera'tuur (de), literature
litera'tuurlijst (de), reading list;
  bibliography
litteken (het), scar
lobbes (de), big good-natured
  person or animal
lobbyen, to lobby
locomo'tief (de), (railway)
  engine

lodderig, drowsy
loden, lead(en)
loeder (het, de), swine, bitch
loeien, to low; to roar
loempia (de), spring roll
loensen, to squint
loep (de), magnifying glass
  iets onder de – nemen, to
  scrutinize something
loer: op de – liggen, to lie in
  wait
  iemand een – draaien, to play
  a dirty trick on a person
loeren, to peer; to spy
lof (de), praise
log, unwieldy; log
loge (de), lodge; (theatre) box
lo'gé(e) (de), guest
lo'geerkamer (de), spare room
loge'ment (het), inn
lo'geren, to stay
logica (de), logic
lo'gies (het), accommodation
  – met ontbijt, bed and
  breakfast
logisch, logical
logischer'wijs, logically
logo (het), logo
logope'die (de), speech therapy
lok (de), lock (of hair)
lo'kaal (het), room
lokaas (het), bait
lo'ket (het), counter, booking
  office
lokken, to (al)lure
lokmiddel (het), lure, bait
lokvogel (de), decoy
lol (de), lark, fun
lollig, funny
lommer (het), shade; foliage
lomp, boorish, clumsy
lompen (de), rags
lomperd (de), lout

lonen, to (re)pay
long (de), lung
longontsteking (de), pneumonia
lonk(en), (to) ogle
lont (de), fuse
 – ruiken, to smell a rat
loochenen, to deny
lood (het), lead
 – om oud ijzer, six of one and
 half a dozen of the other
 uit het – geslagen, bewildered
loodgieter (de), plumber
lood'recht, perpendicular,
 vertical
loods (de), shed; pilot
loodsen, to pilot
loodvrij, unleaded
loodwit (het), white lead
loofboom (de), deciduous tree
loom, languid
loon (het), wages
loonbelasting (de), income tax
loondienst (de), salaried
 employment
loop (de), gait; course; (gun)
 barrel
loopbaan (de), career
loopgraaf (de), trench
loopjongen (de), errand boy
loopneus (de), runny nose
loopplank (de), gangway
loops, on heat
loor: te – gaan, to be lost
loos, cunning; false
lootje (het), lottery ticket,
 raffle ticket
 – s trekken, draw names
 (out of a hat)
lopen, to walk, to go, to run
lopend , running; current
loper (de), walker; carpet strip;
 bishop (in chess); master key
los, loose, detachable

 er op –, recklessly
los'bandig, dissolute
losbarsten, to burst out
losbinden, to untie
los'bladig, loose-leaf
losgeld (het), ransom
losjes, loosely
loskopen, to ransom
loskoppelen, to disconnect
loslaten, to let go
los'lippig, indiscreet
loslopen, to run free
 het zal wel –, it won't be all
 that bad
lossen, to discharge, to unload
loszinnig, frivolous
lot (het), fate; lottery ticket
loten, to draw lots
lote'rij (de), lottery
lotgenoot (de), partner in
 adversity
lotgevallen (de), adventures
louche, shady
loupe (de), magnifying glass
louter, pure, sheer
louteren, to purify
loven, to praise
 – en bieden, to haggle
lo'yaal, loyal
lozen, to get rid of; to drain
lucht (de), air; sky; smell
 – geven aan, to vent
luchtaanval (de), air raid
luchtafweer (het), anti-aircraft
 defence
luchtalarm (het), air raid alarm
luchtballon (de), (hot-air) balloon
luchtbed (het), inflatable bed
luchtdruk (de), atmospheric
 pressure
luchten, to air, to vent(ilate)
 ik kan hem niet –, I can't abide
 him

luchter (de), candelabrum, chandelier
lucht'hartig, light-hearted
luchthaven (de), airport
luchtig, airy
luchtje (het), odour
luchtkoker (de), ventilating shaft
lucht'ledig, vacuum
luchtmacht (de), airforce
luchtpijp (de), windpipe
luchtvaart (de), aviation
luchtverfrisser (de), air freshener
luchtvervuiling (de), air pollution
lucht'vochtigheid (de), humidity
lucifer (de), match
lucra'tief, profitable
lu'guber, lugubrious
luiaard (de), sloth
lui, (*pl*) people
lui, lazy
luid, loud
luiden, to ring
  de brief luidt als volgt, the letter reads as follows
luidkeels, at the top of one's voice
luid'ruchtig, noisy
luidspreker (de), loudspeaker
luier (de), nappie
luieren, to laze
luifel, canopy
luiheid (de), laziness
luik (het), hatch; trapdoor; shutter
luilak (de), lazybones
luilakken, to (be) idle
luis (de), louse
luister (de), splendour
luisteraar (de), listener
luisteren, to listen
luisterrijk, splendid, glorious
luister'vaardigheid (de), listening skill

luistervink (de), eavesdropper
luitenant (de), lieutenant
luiwammes (de), lazybones
lukken, to succeed
  het lukt me nooit, I shall never manage it
lukraak, haphazard
lul (de), (inf) prick; (term of abuse) dickhead
lullen, (inf) to talk (drivel)
lumi'neus, luminous
  een – idee, a brainwave
lummel (de), lout
lummelen, to loiter
lurven: bij de – pakken, to take by the scruff of the neck
lus (de), loop; noose
lust (de), inclination, liking
  een – voor het oog, a sight for sore eyes
lusteloos, listless
lusten, to like, to fancy
lustig, lusty
lustobject (het), sex object
luttel, little
luwte (de), sheltered (from the wind)
luxaflex (de), Venetian blinds
luxe (de), luxury
luxu'eus, luxurious
lyrisch, lyrical

M

maag (de), stomach
maagd (de), virgin, maid(en)
maagdelijk(heid) (de), virgin(ity)
maagpijn (de), stomach ache
maagzuur (het), gastric acid; heartburn
maagzweer (de), gastric ulcer
maaien, to mow
maal (het), meal

tienmaal, ten times

maalstroom (de), whirlpool

maaltijd (de), meal

maan (de), moon

  loop naar de –, go to hell

maand (de), month

maandag, Monday

maandblad (het), monthly periodical, magazine

maandelijks, monthly

maandenlang, for months on end

maandverband (het), sanitary towel

maanjaar (het), lunar year

maansverduistering (de), eclipse of the moon

maar, but; only; just

maarschalk (de), marshal

maart, March

maas (de), mesh; loophole

maat (de), measure, size; time, bar; mate, partner

maatje (het), decilitre; pal

maatregel (de), measure

maat'schappelijk, social

maatschap'pij (de), society; company

maatstaf (de), criterion

maatwerk (het), clothing made to measure; bespoke work

machi'naal, mechanical

ma'chine (de), engine, machine

ma'chinegeweer (het), machine gun

machine'rieën (de), machinery

machi'nist (de), ship's engineer; engine driver

macht (de), power, might

  – der ge'woonte, force of habit

  niet bij machte, unable

machteloos, powerless

machtig, mighty, terrific; rich (food)

  een taal – zijn, to have command of a language

machtigen, to authorize

machtiging (de), authorization

machtspositie (de), position of authority

made'liefje (het), daisy

maffen (*inf*), to snooze

maga'zijn (het), store(s), storehouse; magazine

mager, thin, lean, meagre

ma'gie (de), magic

magisch, magic(al)

magi'straal, imposing

mag'naat (de), magnate

mag'neet (de), magnet

mag'netisch, magnetic

magneti'seren, to magnetize; to mesmerize

magne'tron (de), microwave

magni'fiek, magnificent

maïs (de), maize

maïskolf (de), cob of corn

maï'zena (de), cornflour

majesteit (de), majesty

majestu'eus, majestic

ma'joor (de), major

mak, tame, gentle

makelaar (de), broker, estate agent

maken, to make; to mend

  dat heeft er niets mee te –, that has nothing to do with it

  hoe maakt u het? how do you do?

makkelijk, easy

makker (de), comrade, mate

ma'kreel (de), mackerel

mal (de), mould, template; stencil: foolish

malen, to grind

maling: – hebben aan, to not give a damn/hoot

in de – nemen, to make a fool of

mal'loot (de), silly creature, fool

mals, tender; lush; gentle (rain)

man (de), man; husband

aan de – brengen, to sell

op de – af, point blank

man'chet(knopen) (de), cuff (links)

mand (de), basket

door de – vallen, to fail as

man'daat (het), mandate

manda'rijn (de), mandarin; tangerine

ma'nege (de), riding school

maneschijn (de), moonlight

man'haftig, manly

ma'nie (de), mania

manier (de), manner, way

mani'fest (het), manifesto, manifest

manifes'tatie (de), manifestation, demonstration

manipu'leren, to manipulate

mank, lame, crippled

man'keren, to be lacking or absent; to fail

wat mankeert je? what's come over you?

man'moedig, manful

man(ne)lijk, male, masculine, manly

mannetje (het), little man; male (animal)

manoeu'vreren, to manoeuvre

mans: niet veel –, not very strong

manschappen (de), men

mantel (de), coat, cloak

mantelpak (het), (woman's) suit

manusje van alles (het), odd job man

manziek, man-made

map (de), folder, file

ma'quette (de), model

mar'cheren, to march

marechaus'see (de), military constabulary

marge (de), margin

ma'rine (de), navy

mari'neren, to marinate, to marinade

mari'nier (de), marine

mar'kant, striking

mar'keren, to mark

mar'kies (de), marquis; sunblind

markt(plein) (het), market(place)

marktkraam (de), stall

marmer (het), marble

mar'mot (de), marmot; guinea pig

mars (de), march

hij heeft heel wat in zijn –, he has a lot to offer

marse'pein (het), marzipan

martelaar, martela'res (de), martyr

martelen, to torture, to torment

marteling (de), torture

masker (het), mask

mas'keren, to camouflage

massa (de), mass, crowd

mas'saal, massive

mas'seren, to massage

mas'sief, solid

mast (de), mast

mat, weary; matt; dim

mat (de), mat; checkmate

mateloos, boundless

materi'aal (het), material(s)

ma'terie (de), matter

materi'eel (het), material

matglas (het), frosted glass
matig, moderate
matigen, to moderate
matje (het), (table)mat; mullet
(hairstyle)
  op het – roepen, to be called
  to account
ma'tras (de), mattress
ma'troos (de), sailor
mattenklopper (de), carpet beater
mazelen, measles
mecani'cien (de), mechanic
me'chanica (de), mechanics
mecha'niek (het, de),
  mechanism
me'chanisch, mechanical
me'daille (de), medal
medail'lon (het), medallion;
  locket
mede, with, also: fellow-
mede'deelzaam, communicative
mededelen, to inform
mededeling (de),
  communication; information
mededingen, to compete
mede'klinker (de), consonant
me(d)eleven, to sympathize
me(d)elij(den) (het), pity
mede'plichtig, accessory
me(d)evoelen met, to feel for
me(d)ewerken, to cooperate
medewerker (de), co-worker
medewerking (de), active
  support, co-operation
medeweten (het), knowledge
medezeggenschap (de), say (in
  the matter)
medi'cijn (het), medicine
medisch, medical
mee, with
meebrengen: met zich –, to
  bring with one; to entail
meedoen, to take part

mee'dogenloos, merciless
meegaan, to go, to come
  (along)
mee'gaand, accommodating
meekomen, to come (along); to
  keep pace
meel (het), meal, flour
meemaken, to experience
meenemen, to take (along)
meepraten, to join in the
  conversation; to go along
  with, to parrot
meer (het), lake
meer, more
meerdere (de), superior; several
meerderheid (de), majority
meerder'jarig, of age
meerekenen, to include
meerijden, to drive with, to be
  given a lift
meermalen, more than once
meermin (de), mermaid
meervoud (het), plural
mees (de), titmouse
meeslepen, to drag along; to
  carry away
meest(al), most(ly)
meester (de), master
meeste'res (de), mistress
meesterstuk (het), masterpiece
meeuw (de), seagull
meevallen, to be better than one
  expected
  dat valt niet mee, that is not
  easy
meevaller (de), bit of luck
mei, May
meid (de), young woman, girl
meineed (de), perjury
meisje (het), girl, girlfriend
meisjesachtig, girlish
meisjesnaam (de), maiden
  name; girl's name

me'juffrouw (de), Madam, Miss

mekk(er)en, to bleat

me'lange (de), blend

melden, to report; to announce

meldens'waard(ig), worth mentioning

melding maken van, to mention

melig, corny

melk (de), milk

melkboer (de), milkman

melken, to milk

melkweg (de), Milky Way

me'loen (de), melon

men, one, people, they, you

me'neer (de), Sir; (gentle)man

menen, to think, to mean

't wordt menens, it's getting serious

mengelmoes (de), jumble

mengen, to mix, to mingle, to blend

zich – in, to meddle with

mengsel (het), mixture, blend

menig, many a

menigeen, many a person

menigmaal, many a time

menigte (de), crowd

menig'vuldig, manifold

mening (de), opinion

mennen, to drive (a carriage)

mens, man; human being

het is een goed –, she is a good soul

mensdom (het), mankind

menselijk, human

menselijkheid (de), humanity

mensenkenner (de), judge of character

mensheid (de), mankind

mep (de), smack, whack

meppen, to smack

meren, to moor

merendeel (het), greater part

merendeels, mostly

merk (het), mark, brand, brandname

merkbaar, noticeable

merrie (de), mare

mes (het), knife

Mes'sias (de), Messiah

mest (de), dung, manure

mesten, to fatten; to manure

mesthoop, mestvaalt (de), dunghill

met, with, of; plus, and; by, through, in; at

tot en –, up to and including

– wie spreek ik? who am I speaking to? (on the phone)

ik kom – de trein, I'm coming by train

hij komt – zijn vriendin, he's coming with (bringing) his girlfriend

me'taal (het), metal

meta'foor (de), metaphor

me'teen, straight away; presently

meten, to measure

meter (de), metre; meter

metgezel('lin) (de), companion

me'thodisch, methodical

metselaar (de), bricklayer

metselen, to build (using mortar)

metselwerk (het), masonry

metten: korte – maken met, to make short work of

meubel (het), piece of furniture

meubelmaker (de), cabinet maker

meubi'lair (het), furniture

meubi'leren, to furnish

me'vrouw (de), Mrs; Madam; lady

middag (de), midday; afternoon

middageten (het), middagmaal (het), midday meal

middel (het), waist; remedy, means

middelbaar, average, medium

middelbaar onderwijs (het), secondary education

middeleeuwen (de), Middle Ages

middeleeuws, medieval

Middellandse Zee (de), Mediterranean

middellijn (de), diameter

middel'matig, mediocre, average

middelpunt (het), centre, pivot

middelste, middlemost, centre

midden (het), middle, midst

midden'in, in the middle (of)

middenstand (de), self-employed; middle classes

midder'nacht (de), midnight

mier (de), ant

mierenhoop (de), anthill

miezerig, drizzly; puny

mijden, to shun

mijl (de), mile; kilometre

mijlpaal (de), milestone

mijmeren, to muse

mijn, my

mijn (de), mine: pit

mijnenveger (de), mine sweeper

mijnenveld (het), minefield

mijn'heer (de), Sir; Mr; (gentle)man

mijnwerker (de), miner

mijter (de), mitre

mikken (op), to aim (at)

mikpunt (het), aim, target, butt

mild, liberal; mild

mili'tair (de), soldier; military

mil'joen (het), million

mille (het), (one) thousand (euros)

millimeter (de), millimetre

millimeteren, to crop (hair) close

min, minus; little, few

minachten, to regard with disdain

minachting (de), contempt

minder, less(er), fewer

minderen, inferiors; to decrease

minderheid (de), minority

minder'jarig, under age

minder'waardig, inferior

minder'waardigheidscomplex (het), inferiority complex

mini'maal, minimum

mi'nister (de), minister, secretary (of state)

president (de), prime minister

mini'sterie (het), ministry, office

minnaar (de), (male) lover

minna'res (de), (female) lover

minnen, to love

minnetjes, poorly

minst, least

minstens, at least

minuti'eus, meticulous

mi'nuut (de), minute

minzaam, affable

mis, wrong

mis (de), Mass

misbruik (het), abuse

misbruik maken van, to abuse

mis'bruiken, to abuse, to misuse

misdaad (de), crime

mis'dadig, criminal

misdadiger (de), criminal

mis'dragen: zich –, to misbehave

misdrijf (het), offence

mis'gunnen, to begrudge

mis'handelen, to maltreat

miskraam (de), miscarriage

mis'leiden, to mislead

mislopen, to go wrong

mis'lukken, to fail
mis'lukking (de), failure
mis'maakt, deformed
mis'plaatst, misplaced, out of place
mis'prijzen, to disapprove of
mis'schien, perhaps
misselijk, sick; disgusting
missen, to miss; to lack
missie (de), mission
missio'naris (de), (RC) missionary
misstand (de), abuse
misstap (de), false step, slip
mist (de), fog
misten, to be foggy
misvatting (de), misunderstanding
misverstaan, misunderstand
misverstand (het), misunderstanding
mis'vormd, misshapen
mitrail'leur (de), machine gun
mits, provided (that)
modder (de), mud
mode (de), fashion
mo'del (het), model; pattern
modeshow (de), fashion parade
modi'eus, fashionable
moe, tired
moed (de), courage
moedeloos, dejected
moeder (de), mother; matron
moederlijk, motherly
moederschap (het), motherhood
moedertaal (de), mother tongue
moedervlek (de), birthmark, mole
moederziel alleen, quite alone
moedig, courageous
moed'willig, wilful
moeien: de politie in een zaak –, to call in the police

er is een week mee ge'moeid, it will take a week
moeilijk, difficult, with difficulty
moeilijkheid (de), difficulty
moeite (de), trouble; difficulty
de – waard, worthwhile
moeizaam, laborious
moer (de), nut
moe'ras (het), marsh
moe'rassig, marshy
moes (de, het), mash, pulp
moesson (de), monsoon
moestuin (de), kitchen garden
moeten, must, to have to
wat moet dat? what's going on (there)?
je moest je schamen, you ought to be ashamed of yourself
moffelen, to smuggle away
mogelijk, possible
mogelijker'wijs, possibly
mogelijkheid (de), possibility
mogen, to be allowed, may; to like
mogendheid (de), power
mokka (de), mocha
mokken, to sulk
mol (de), mole; flat, minor (key)
molen (de), mill
molenaar (de), miller
molenwiek (de), sail of a windmill
mollen, to do (a person) in, to destroy
mollig, chubby
molshoop (de), molehill
momen'teel, momentary; at present
mo'mentopname (de), snapshot
mompelen, to mutter
mond (de), mouth; muzzle
met de – vol tanden, tongue-tied

iemand naar de – praten, to play up to a person

mon'dain, fashionable

mondeling, oral

mond-en-'klauwzeer (het), foot and mouth disease

mondig, of age

mondje (het), mouthful, taste

zij is niet op haar – gevallen, she gives as good as she gets, she has a ready tongue

mondjes'maat (de), bare minimum

monnik (de), monk

monnikenwerk (het), drudgery, donkey work

mono'toon, monotonous

monster (het), monster; (free) sample

monsterachtig, monstrous

monstru'eus, monstrous

mon'tage (de), assembly, mounting

monter, lively

mon'teren, to assemble, to set (up)

mon'teur (de), fitter, mechanic

mon'tuur (het), (spectacle) frame

mooi, beautiful, fine

moord (de), murder

moordaanslag (de), murderous attempt

moord'dadig, murderous

moordenaar (de), murderer

moordpartij (de), massacre

moors, moorish

moot (de), fillet (of fish)

mop (de), joke

een schuine –, a dirty joke

mopperen, to grumble

mo'raal (de), moral(s)

morali'seren, to moralize

mo'reel (het), moral; morale

mores (de), manners, customs

morgen (de), morning; tomorrow

's morgens, in the morning, every morning

morgen'ochtend, tomorrow morning

mormel (het), freak

verwend –, spoiled brat

mor'fine (de), morphine

morrelen, to fumble

morren, to grumble

mors'dood, stone-dead

morsen, to spill, to make a mess

mos (het), moss

mos'kee (de), mosque

Moskou, Moscow

mossel (de), mussel

mosterd (de), mustard

(als) – na de maaltijd, a bit late in the day

mot (de), moth; bust-up

motie (de), motion, vote

mo'tief (het), motive; motif

moti'veren, to justify, to defend

motor (de), motor, engine

motorpech (de), engine trouble

motregen (de), drizzle

mous'seren, to effervesce

mouw (de), sleeve

ergens een – aanpassen, to manage somehow

iemand iets op de – spelden, to fool a person

moza'ïek (het), mosaic

muf, musty

mug (de), gnat

muggenzifte'rij (de), hair splitting

muilkorf (de), muzzle

muis (de), mouse; ball of the thumb

muisjes (de), aniseed comfits
muiten, to mutiny
muite'rij (de), mutiny
muizenval (de), mouse trap
mul, loose, sandy
multiplex (het), plywood
mummie (de), mummy
mu'nitie (de), ammunition, munitions
munt (de), coin(age); currency; mint
  kruis of –, heads or tails
munteenheid (de), monetary unit
munten, to mint
  dat was op mij gemunt, that (remark) was aimed at me
muntstuk (het), coin
murmelen, to babble
murw, soft, tender
  iemand – maken, break someone's spirit
mus (de), sparrow
musi'ceren, to make music
musicus (de), musician
mus'kiet (de), mosquito
muts (de), hat
muur (de), wall
muurschildering (de), mural
muurvast, firm as a rock
mu'ziek (de), music
mu'ziekkorps (het), band
mu'ziektent (de), bandstand
muzi'kaal, musical
muzi'kant (de), street musician; bandsman
mys'terie (het), mystery
mysteri'eus, mysterious
mythe (de), myth

N

na, after; close
  op één –, all but one

  de op één – duurste, the second most expensive one
  iedereen komt, op mijn moeder –, everyone is coming, except for my mother
naad (de), seam
  het naadje van de kous willen weten, to want to know every detail
naaien, to sew; to screw (vulg)
naaister (de), needlewoman
naakt, naked, nude
naald (de), needle
naaldbos (het), pinewood
naam (de), name
naambord (het), nameplate
naamgenoot (de), namesake
naamloze vennootschap (de), limited company
naamval(suitgang) (de), case (ending)
naäpen, to ape
naar, to, for
  we gaan – Rome, we're going to Rome
  ik ben op zoek –, I'm looking for
naar'mate, (according) as
naarstig, diligent
naast, next to; nearest
nabestellen, to put in a further order
na'bij, near, close
na'bijgelegen, neighbouring
nablijven, to stay behind
nabootsen, to imitate
na'burig, neighbouring
nacht (de), night
  bij – en ontij, at all hours of the day and night
nachtbraken, to make a night of it
nachtegaal (de), nightingale

nachtelijk, nocturnal
nachtgoed (het), nightwear
nachtmerrie (de), nightmare
nachtploeg (de), night shift
nachtpon (de), nightdress
nachtverblijf (het), lodging for the night
nadat, after
nadeel (het), disadvantage, detriment
na'delig, disadvantageous, detrimental
nadenken, to reflect
nader, nearer; further
　bij – inzien, on second thoughts
nader'bij, nearer
　van –, more closely
naderen, to approach
nader'hand, afterwards
na'dien, since (then)
nadoen, to imitate
nadruk (de), emphasis; reprint
na'drukkelijk, emphatic
nagaan, to examine, to trace
nagedachtenis (de), memory
nagel (de), nail
nagellak (de), nail varnish
nagelriem (de), cuticle
nagemaakt, imitation, spurious
nagenoeg, almost
nagerecht (het), dessert
nageslacht (het), posterity
nageven: dat moet ik hem –, I'll say that for him
nahouden: er op –, to maintain
na'ïef, naïve
najaar (het), autumn
nakijken, to gaze after; to check
na'komeling (de), descendant
nakomen, to carry out
nalaten, to leave (behind); to omit

ik kon niet – u te vertellen, I could not help telling you
na'latig, negligent, remiss
naleven, to observe; to comply with
nalezen, to read over or again
nalopen, to run after; to be slow
namaak (de), imitation
namaken, to imitate, to forge
namelijk, namely, i.e.; because
namens, on behalf of
namiddag (de), afternoon
naoorlogs, post-war
napluizen, to examine in detail
napraten, to parrot; to stay behind talking
napret (de), fun after the event
nar (de), jester
nar'cis (de), daffodil
nar'cose (de), narcosis
narekenen, to check
narigheid (de), unpleasantness
na'saal, nasal
naschrift (het), postscript
naslaan, to look up
nasleep (de), aftermath
nasmaak (de), aftertaste
nastaren, to (turn round and) stare
nastreven, to strive after
nat, wet
natafelen, to linger at the dinner table
natellen, to check, to count (again)
natie (de), nation
nationali'seren, to nationalize
nattigheid (de), moisture
　– voelen, to smell a rat
na'tura: in –, in kind
natu'rel, natural
na'tuur (de), nature; scenery
　van nature by nature

na'tuurgetrouw, true to nature
na'tuurkunde (de), physics
natuur'kundige (de), physicist
na'tuurlijk, natural; of course
na'tuurverschijnsel (het), natural phenomenon
nauw, narrow, tight, close
  hij neemt het niet te –, he is not very particular
nauwelijks, scarcely
nauwge'zet, conscientious
nauw'keurig, accurate
nauw'sluitend, close-fitting
navel (de), navel
navelstreng (de), umbilical cord
navertellen, to repeat
navraag (de), enquiries
naweeën (de), aftereffects
nawerken, to make its effect felt
nazien, to check
nazomer (de), late summer
neder, down
nederig, humble
nederlaag (de), defeat
Nederlander (de), Dutchman
Nederlands, Dutch
Nederlandse (de), Dutch woman
nederpop (de), Dutch pop music
nederzetting (de), settlement
neef (de), cousin, nephew
nee, no
neer, down
neer'buigend, condescending
neerhalen, to haul down; to run down
neerkomen, to come down
  het komt hierop neer, it boils down to this
neerleggen, to put down; to resign
neerslaan, to strike down; to precipitate

  de ogen –, to cast down one's eyes
negen, nine
negende, ninth
negentien(de), nineteen(th)
negentig, ninety
neger (de), negro
negeren, to bully
ne'geren, to ignore
nege'rin (de), negress
neigen, to incline
neiging (de), inclination, tendency
nek (de), (nape of the) neck
  met de – aankijken, to cold-shoulder
nekken, to break, to ruin
nemen, to take
  we zullen het er eens van –, let's enjoy ourselves
nergens, nowhere
  ik weet – van, I know nothing about it
ner'veus, nervous
nest (het), nest; minx
nestelen, to nest
  zich –, to ensconce oneself; to nestle
net (het), net(work); system
  achter het – vissen, to miss the boat
net, tidy, neat; respectable, decent; just, exactly
  we waren – op tijd, we were just in time
netel (de), nettle
netjes, tidily, neat, nice, decent
netto, nett
netvlies (het), retina
neuriën, to hum
neu'rose (de), neurosis
neus (de), nose, nozzle
  het is maar een wassen –,

there is nothing to it
met de – in de boter vallen, to come at the right moment
neusgat (het), nostril
neushoorn (de), rhinoceros
neusvleugel (de), nostril
neu'traal, neutral
neuzen in, to pry into
nevel (de), mist, haze
nicht (de), niece, cousin; fairy, queen, poofter, faggot
niemand, nobody
nier (de), kidney
niet, not
nieten, to staple
nietig, null and void; diminutive; trivial
nietje (het), staple
nietmachine (de), stapler
niets, nothing
nietsbe'duidend, nietsbe'tekenend, insignificant
nietsnut (de), good-for-nothing
niets'zeggend, meaningless
niette'min, nevertheless
niet'waar, is(n't) it?, do(n't) you?, does(n't) she? etc.
　jij spreekt Japans, –? you speak Japanese, don't you?
nieuw, new
nieuw'bakken, new-fangled
nieuweling (de), novice
nieuws (het), news
nieuwsblad (het), newspaper
nieuws'gierig, inquisitive
nieuwtje (het), piece of news
niezen, to sneeze
nihil, nil
nijdig, angry
nijlpaard (het), hippopotamus
nijptang (de), (pair of) pliers
niks, nothing
nimf (de), nymph

nimmer, never
nippertje: op het –, in the nick of time
nis (de), niche, alcove
ni'veau (het), level
nivel'leren, to level
n.l. (namelijk), i.e.; you see
nobel, noble-minded
noch … noch, neither … nor
nochtans, nevertheless
nodig, necessary
　– hebben, to need
noemen, to name, to call; to mention
noemens'waard(ig), worth mentioning
nog, still, yet
　vandaag –, this very day
　– vele jaren! many happy returns!
nogal, rather, fairly
nogmaals, once again
nok (de), ridge of the roof
no'made (de), nomad
non (de), nun
nonsens (de), nonsense
nood (de), need, emergency; distress
noodge'dwongen, from necessity
noodgeval (het), emergency
nood'lijdend, destitute
noodlot (het), fate
nood'lottig, fatal
noodrem (de), safety brake
noodtoestand (de), state of emergency; untenable situation
noodweer (het), deluge
noodgebouw (het), temporary building
noodzaak (de), necessity
nood'zakelijk, necessary

nooit, never
Noor (de), Norwegian
noord, north
noordelijk, northern, northerly
noorden (het), North
noorderlicht (het), northern
  lights
noorderzon: met de –
  vertrekken, to cut and run
noordpool (de), north pole
noordwaarts, northward(s)
Noors (het), Norwegian
Noorwegen, Norway
noot, not
noot (de), not: nut
  hele, halve –, kwartnoot etc,
  breve, minim, crotchet etc
  hij heeft veel noten op zijn
  zang, he is hard to please,
  pretentious
nootmus'kaat (de), nutmeg
nor (de) (vulg), clink
nor'maal, normal
nor'maliter, normally
nota (de), note; bill, account
no'taris (de), notary
notendop (de), nutshell
notenkraker (de), nut cracker
no'teren, to note (down)
notie (de), notion
no'titie (de), note; notice
no'tulen (de), minutes
nou, now: you bet!
no'velle (de), short story
nu, now (that)
  van – af aan, from now on
nuchter, sober, level-headed
  op de nuchtere maag, on an
  empty stomach
nukkig, wayward
nul (de), nought, nil, zero;
  nonentity
nulpunt (het), zero

nummer (het), number; issue
  iemand op zijn – zetten, to put
  a person in his place
nummeren, to number
nurks, grumpy
nut (het), use, benefit
nutteloos, useless
nuttig, useful
nuttigen, to partake of
N.V., ltd (company)

O

o.a.: onder andere, *inter alia*;
  including
o'ase (de), oasis
o-benen (de), bandy legs
ober (de), waiter
ob'ject (het), object(ive)
obli'gatie (de), bond
ob'sceen, obscene
obser'vator (de), observer
oce'aan (de), ocean
och, ah!, oh
ochtend (de), morning
  's ochtends, in the morning(s)
oc'taaf (de), octave
oc'trooi (het), patent; charter
oefenen, to train, to practise
oefening (de), exercise, practice
oer-, primal
Oeral (de), Urals
oermens (de), prehistoric man
oerwoud (het), virgin forest,
  jungle
oester (de), oyster
oever (de), bank, shore
of, or; whether, if
  – ... –, either .... or;
  whether ... or
offer (het), sacrifice, victim
offeren, to sacrifice; to offer up
of'ferte (de), offer; tender

offici'eel, official
offi'cier (de), officer
  – van justitie, public
  prosecutor
offici'eus, semi-official
of'schoon, although
ogen, to eye; to be attractive
ogenblik (het), moment
ogen'blikkelijk, immediate
ogen'schijnlijk, seemingly
ogenschouw: in – nemen, to
  look over
oksel (de), armpit
olie (de), oil
oliën, to oil
olifant (de), elephant
o'lijf (de), olive
om, round, about; at
  – de andere dag, every other day
  – te, in order to
  de tijd is –, time is up
oma (de), grandma
om'armen, to embrace
ombrengen, to kill
omdat, because
omdoen, to put on, to wrap
  round
omdraaien, to turn (round), to
  twist
omduwen, to knock over
omgaan, to go round; to
  associate; to manage/deal
  het hoekje –, to peg out
omgaande: per –, by return (of
  post)
omgang (de), social intercourse,
  dealings; procession; gallery
omgangstaal (de), everyday
  speech
omgangsvormen, manners
omgekeerd, upside-down;
  reverse(d)
om'geven, to surround

om'geving (de), surroundings
omgooien, to knock over
omhakken, to cut down
om'heen, round (about)
om'heinen, to fence in
om'heining (de), fence,
  enclosure
om'helzen, to embrace
om'hoog, up(wards)
om'hulsel (het), cover,
  wrapping, casing
omkantelen, to topple over
omkeren, to turn (round)
omkijken, to look round
omkleden, to change clothes
omkomen, to perish
omkopen, to bribe
om'laag, down (below)
om'lijnen, to outline
om'lijsten, to frame
omloop (de), circulation, course;
  gallery
omlopen, to walk round
ommekeer (de), change; turn
omploegen, to plough up
ompraten, to talk round
omrekenen, to convert,
  to work out
om'ringen, to surround
omroep (de), broadcasting
  service
omroepen, to broadcast
omroeper (de), announcer
omroeren, to stir
omruilen, to exchange
omschakelen, to switch over
om'schrijven, to define; to
  circumscribe
om'schrijving (de), definition;
  paraphrase
om'singelen, to encircle
omslaan, to turn (over); to
  knock over

omslag (de), cuff; cover
om'sluiten, to enclose
omsmelten, to melt down
omspitten, to dig (over)
omspoelen, to rinse
omspringen met, to handle, to manage
omstander (de), bystander
om'standigheid (de), circumstance, condition
om'streden, contested
omstreken (de), environs
omstreeks, about
omtoveren, to transform as if by magic
omtrek (de), outline, contour; neighbourhood; circumference
omvallen, to fall over
omvang (de), extent, girth
om'vangrijk, extensive
om'ver, down; over
om'verwerpen, to overthrow
omwaaien, to (be) blow(n) down
omweg (de), detour, roundabout way
omwenteling (de), revolution, rotation
omwerken, to remodel, to rewrite
omwisselen, to (ex)change
om'zeilen, to get round
omzet (de), turnover
omzetbelasting (de), sales tax
omzetten, to transpose; to convert; to sell
om'zichtig, circumspect
omzien, to look after
on'aangenaam, unpleasant
onaan'nemelijk, unacceptable, implausible
onaan'tastbaar, unassailable

onaan'zienlijk, insignificant
on'aardig: niet –, not at all bad
on'afgebroken, continuous
onaf'hankelijk, independent, irrespective
onaf'scheidelijk, inseparable
onbe'dorven, unspoilt
onbe'duidend, trivial
onbe'gonnen werk (het), hopeless task
onbe'heerd, unattended
onbe'holpen, awkward
onbe'kend, unfamiliar
onbe'kwaam, incapable
onbe'lemmerd, unrestricted
onbe'nullig, inane
onbe'paald, indefinite
onbe'perkt, unrestricted
– vert'rouwen, implicit faith
onbe'rekenbaar, incalculable
onbe'schaafd, ill-mannered; uncivilized
onbe'schaamd, shameless; brazen
onbe'schoft, impertinent
onbe'schrijfelijk, indescribable
onbe'slecht, onbe'slist, undecided
onbe'streden, uncontested
onbe'suisd, reckless
onbe'taalbaar, priceless
onbe'tekenend, insignificant
onbe'twist, undisputed
onbe'twistbaar, indisputable
onbe'vangen, unbiased
onbe'voegd, not qualified; unauthorized
onbe'vredigend, unsatisfactory
onbe'waakt, unguarded
onbe'weeglijk, motionless, immovable
onbe'werkt, untreated
onbe'wogen, unmoved

onbe'woonbaar, uninhabitable
onbe'woond, uninhabited
onbe'wust, unconscious
onbe'zorgd, carefree
on'breekbaar, unbreakable
on'bruikbaar, useless
on'dankbaar, ungrateful, thankless
ondanks, despite
on'denkbaar, unthinkable
onder, under(neath); among; during
onder'aan, at the foot of
onder'in, at the bottom (of)
onder'aards, subterranean
onderafdeling (de), subdivision
onderbewust, subconscious
onder'breken, to interrupt
onderbrengen, to accommodate, to place
onderbroek (de), (under)pants
onderdak (het), shelter, accommodation
onder'danig, submissive
onderdeel (het), part
onderdoen: niet – voor, to be in no way inferior to
onderdompelen, to immerse
onder'door, under, through
onder'drukken, to oppress, to suppress
onderduiken, to dive; to go into hiding
onder'gaan, to go down; to perish
onder'gaan, to undergo
ondergang (de), downfall, ruin
ondergeschikt, subordinate; secondary
onderge'tekende (de), (the) undersigned
ondergoed (het), underwear

onder'graven, to undermine
ondergrond (de), subsoil; foundation
onder'handelaar (de), negotiator
onder'handelen, to negotiate
onder'handelingen (de), negotiations
onderhoud (het), maintenance; interview
onder'houden, to maintain, to support
onder'houdend, entertaining
onder'huids, subcutaneous, hyperdermic
onderjurk (de), slip
onderkant (de), underside
onderkin (de), double chin
onderkomen (het), shelter
onderkoning (de), viceroy
onderling, mutual
onderlopen, to get flooded
onder'mijnen, to undermine
onder'nemen, to undertake
onder'nemend, enterprising
onder'nemer (de), employer; contractor
onder'neming (de), enterprise; company
onder'onsje (het), friendly get-together
onderpand (het), pledge, security
onder'schatten, to underestimate
onderscheid (het), difference, distinction
onder'scheiden, to distinguish
onder'scheiding (de), distinction, honour
onder'scheidingsvermogen (het), discrimination
onder'scheppen, to intercept
onderschrift (het), caption

onderspit: het – delven, to get the worst of it

onderstaand, (mentioned) below

onderste, bottom(most)

onderste'boven, upside down; upset

onder'steunen, to support

onder'steuning (de), support, relief

onder'strepen, to underline

onder'tekenen, to sign

ondertrouw (de), registration of intended marriage

onder'tussen, meanwhile

onderverhuren, to sub-let

onder'vinden, to experience

onder'voed, under-nourished

onder'vragen, to interrogate

onder'weg, on the way

onderwerp (het), subject

onder'werpen, to subject; to subdue; to submit

onder'wijl, meanwhile

onderwijs (het), education

onder'wijzen, to teach

onder'wijzer (de), schoolteacher

onder'worpen, submissive

onder'zeeboot (de), submarine

onderzoek (het), enquiry, investigation, examination, research

onder'zoeken, to investigate, to examine

onder'zoekingstocht (de), exploratory expedition

on'deugend, naughty

on'diep, shallow

ondoor'dacht, thoughtless

ondoor'dringbaar, impenetrable

ondoor'grondelijk, inscrutable

ondoor'schijnend, opaque

ondoor'zichtig, not transparent

on'draaglijk, unbearable

ondubbel'zinnig, unequivocal

on'duidelijk, indistinct

onecht, spurious; illegitimate

on'eens: het – zijn, to disagree

oneer'biedig, disrespectful

on'effen, uneven

on'eindig, infinite

on'enigheid (de), discord

oner'varen, inexperienced

oneven, odd

oneven'redig, disproportionate

onfat'soenlijk, improper

on'feilbaar, infallible

ongeacht, irrespective of

onge'bonden, unbound; dissolute

onge'daan maken, to undo

onge'deerd, unhurt

ongedierte (het), vermin

ongeduld (het), impatience

onge'duldig, impatient

onge'durig, restless

onge'dwongen, unconstrained

ongeëvenaard, unequalled

onge'frankeerd, unstamped, carriage forward

onge'hinderd, unimpeded

onge'hoord, unheard of

onge'huwd, unmarried

on'geldig, invalid

onge'legen, inopportune

onge'lijk, uneven, unequal

ongelijk (het) (hebben), (to be) wrong

ongelikte beer (de), rough customer

ongelimiteerd, unlimited

onge'lofelijk, incredible

ongeloof'waardig, improbable

ongeluk (het), accident, misfortune

onge'lukkig, unhappy, unfortunate, unlucky

ongemak (het), inconvenience, discomfort

onge'makkelijk, uncomfortable; hard to please; awkward

ongemeubi'leerd, unfurnished

onge'moeid laten, to leave in peace

onge'naakbaar, unapproachable

ongenade (de), disgrace, disfavour

onge'nadig, merciless

onge'neeslijk, incurable

onge'nietbaar, unpalatable; unbearable

ongenoegen (het), displeasure

onge'past, improper

onge'regeld, irregular

onge'regeldheden (de), disturbances

onge'rust, anxious, uneasy

onge'schikt, unfit, unsuitable

onge'schonden, undamaged; unimpaired

onge'schoold, untrained

onge'steld: zij is –, she's having her period

onge'stoord, undisturbed

onge'straft, unpunished; with impunity

onge'trouwd, single, unmarried

onge'twijfeld, undoubtedly

ongeval (het), accident

onge'veer, approximately

onge'voelig, unfeeling

onge'wapend, unarmed

onge'wenst, undesirable

onge'wijzigd, unaltered

onge'wild, unintentional

onge'woon, unusual

onge'zellig, unsociable; cheerless

onge'zouten, unsalted; plain

on'gunstig, unfavourable

on'guur, sinister, unsavoury

on'handelbaar, intractable

on'handig, clumsy; awkward

onheil (het), calamity

onheil'spellend, ominous

onher'bergzaam, inhospitable

onher'roepelijk, irrevocable

onher'stelbaar, irreparable

on'houdbaar, untenable

on'juist, inaccurate

onkosten (de), expenses

onkostendeclaratie (de), expenses claim

onkostenvergoeding (de), payment/reimbursement of expenses; mileage allowance

onkruid (het), weed(s)

onlangs, recently

on'leesbaar, illegible

onlusten (de), disturbances

onmacht (de), impotence, powerlessness

onmens (de), brute

on'menselijk, inhuman

on'merkbaar, imperceptible

on'metelijk, vast

on'middellijk, immediate

on'misbaar, indispensable

onmis'kenbaar, unmistakable

on'mogelijk, impossible, not possible

onna'volgbaar, inimitable

on'nodig, unnecessary

on'noembaar, on'noemelijk, immeasurable

on'nozel, silly; innocent

onom'stotlelijk, incontestable

onom'wonden, frank

ononderbroken, uninterrupted

onont'beerlijk, indispensable

onont'koombaar, inescapable

on'ooglijk, unsightly

onop'houdelijk, incessant

onop'lettend, inattentive

onover'gankelijk, intransitive

onover'troffen, unsurpassed

onover'winnelijk, invincible

onpar'tijdig, impartial

on'passelijk, sick

onper'soonlijk, impersonal

onrecht (het), injustice

  ten onrechte, wrongly

onrecht'matig, unlawful

on'redelijk, unreasonable

onroerende goederen (de), immovable property

onrust (de), unrest

onrust'barend, alarming

on'rustig, restless

onruststoker (de), onrustzaaier (de), troublemaker

ons (het), 100 grams

ons, us

onsamen'hangend, incoherent

on'schadelijk, harmless

on'schatbaar, priceless; invaluable

on'schendbaar, inviolable

onschuld (de), innocence

on'schuldig, innocent

on'smakelijk, unsavoury

on'sterfelijk, immortal

onsympa'thiek, uncongenial, unpleasant

ont'aard(en), (to) degenerate

on'tastbaar, intangible

ont'beren, to lack

ont'bieden, to summon

ont'bijt (het), breakfast

ont'bijten, to have breakfast

ont'binden, to undo; to decompose, to disintegrate, to dissolve; to disband

ont'binding (de), decomposition, disintegration, dissolution

ont'bloot, bare; devoid

ont'bloten, to bare, to uncover, to strip

ont'brandbaar, inflammable

ont'branden, to catch fire; to flare up

ont'breken, to be missing

  het ontbrak me aan moed, I lacked the courage

ont'cijferen, to decipher

ont'daan, cut up, shaken

ont'dekken, to discover

ont'dekking (de), discovery

ont'dekkingsreiziger (de), explorer

ont'dooien, to thaw (out)

ont'duiken, to elude, to evade

ont'eigenen, to expropriate

on'telbaar, innumerable

on'tembaar, indomitable

ont'eren, to dishonour

ont'erend, degrading

ont'erven, to disinherit

onte'vreden, discontented, dissatisfied

ont'fermen: zich – over, to take pity on; to take care of

ont'futselen, to filch

ont'gaan, to elude

ont'ginnen, to reclaim (land); to cultivate

ont'glippen, to slip (out); to escape

ont'groeien, to outgrow; to become estranged to

ont'groenen, to initiate

ont'haal (het), reception

ont'halen, to regale

ont'haren, to depilate

ont'heffen, to relieve; to exempt

ont'heiligen, to desecrate

ont'hoofden, to behead

ont'houden, to remember; to withhold

  zich – van, to abstain from

ont'hullen, to unveil; to reveal
ont'hutst, disconcerted
ont'kennen, to deny
ont'kenning (de), denial, negation
ont'ketenen, to unchain; to unleash
ont'kiemen, to germinate
ont'kleden, to undress
ont'knoping (de), denouement
ont'komen, to escape
ont'kurken, to uncork
ont'lasten, to unburden, to relieve, to discharge
ont'leden, to analyse; to dissect
ont'lenen, to borrow, to derive
ont'lokken, to elicit
ont'lopen, to evade
ont'luiken, to open, to blossom (out)
ont'mantelen, to dismantle
ont'maskeren, to unmask, to expose
ont'moedigen, to discourage
ont'moeten, to meet
ont'moeting (de), encounter, meeting
ont'nemen, to deprive of
ont'nuchteren, to disillusion
ontoe'gankelijk, inaccessible
ontoe'geeflijk, unaccommodating
ontoe'laatbaar, inadmissible
ontoe'reikend, inadequate
ontoe'rekenbaar, not responsible for one's actions
on'toombaar, uncontrollable
on'toonbaar, not fit to be seen
ont'plofbare stof, explosive
ont'ploffen, to explode
ont'plooien, to develop; to display; to unfold
ont'poppen: zich – als, to turn out to be

ont'raden, to advise against
ont'rafelen, to unravel
ont'roeren, to move, to touch
ont'roering (de), emotion
on'troostbaar, inconsolable
ontrouw (de), disloyal(ty)
ont'roven, to rob of
ont'ruimen, to vacate, to evacuate
ont'rukken, to snatch away from
ont'schepen, to disembark
ont'schieten, to escape (one's memory)
ont'sieren, to disfigure, to mar
ont'slaan, to discharge
ont'slag (het), discharge
 – nemen, to resign
ont'sluieren, to unveil
ont'sluiten, to open up
ont'smetten, to disinfect
ont'smettingsmiddel (het), disinfectant
ont'snappen, to escape
ont'spannen, to relax
ont'spanning (de), relaxation, recreation
ont'sporen, to (be) derailed
ont'springen, to have its source
 de dans –, to have a narrow escape
ont'spruiten, to sprout; to arise from
ont'staan, to originate, to come into being; **(het),** origin
 doen –, to bring about
ont'steken, to kindle, to ignite; to inflame
ont'steking (de), inflammation; ignition
ont'steld, alarmed
ont'stemd, upset, put out
ont'trekken, to withdraw
 zich – aan, to shirk

ontuig (het), riffraff

ont'vangstbewijs (het), receipt

ont'vangen, to receive

ont'vanger (de), recipient

ont'vangst (de), reception, receipt

ont'vankelijk, susceptible

ont'vlambaar, inflammable; excitable

ont'vlammen, to inflame

ont'vluchten, to escape from

ont'voeren, to abduct

ont'vouwen, to unfold

ont'vreemden, to steal

ont'waken, to wake up

ont'wapenen, to disarm

ont'warren, to disentangle

ont'wennen, to lose the habit of

ont'werp (het), project; design

ont'werpen, to design, to plan

ont'wijken, to evade, to avoid

ont'wijkend, evasive

ont'wikkeld, educated, developed

ont'wikkelen, to develop, to generate

ont'wikkeling (de), development, education

ont'wortelen, to uproot

ont'wrichten, to dislocate

ont'zag (het), awe

ont'zaglijk, tremendous

ontzag'wekkend, awe-inspiring

ont'zeggen, to deny, to refuse

ont'zenuwen, to unnerve; to disprove

ont'zet, appalled

ont'zetten, to relieve; to deprive; to put out

ont'zettend, terrible, appalling: awfully

ont'zien, to spare, to save

on'uitgesproken, unspoken

onuit'puttelijk, inexhaustible

onuit'spreekbaar, unpronounceable

onuit'staanbaar, intolerable

onuit'voerbaar, impracticable

onuit'wisbaar, indelible

onvast, unstable, unsteady

onver'anderd, unaltered

onver'anderlijk, invariable

onver'antwoord, irresponsible

onverant'woordelijk, irresponsible, inexcusable

onver'beterlijk, incorrigible

onver'biddelijk, inexorable

onver'bloemd, plain

onver'brekelijk, indissoluble

onver'deeld, undivided, unqualified

onverdiend, undeserved

onver'dienstelijk, undeserving

onver'draagzaam, intolerant

onver'droten, indefatigable

onver'enigbaar, incompatible

onver'gankelijk, imperishable

onver'geeflijk, unpardonable

onver'getelijk, unforgettable

onver'hinderd, unimpeded

onver'klaarbaar, inexplicable

onver'kort, unabridged

onver'krijgbaar, unobtainable

onver'mijdelijk, unavoidable

onver'minderd, undiminished

onver'moed, unsuspected

onver'moeibaar, indefatigable

onver'moeid, untiring

onvermogen (het), inability; powerlessness

onver'murwbaar, inexorable, unyielding

onverrichter zake, with nothing accomplished

onver'schillig, indifferent, unconcerned

onver'schrokken, intrepid
onver'slijtbaar, indestructible, very hard-wearing
onver'staanbaar, unintelligible
onver'standig, unwise
onver'stoorbaar, imperturbable
onver'togen, unseemly
onver'wacht, unexpected
onver'wijld, immediate
onver'woestbaar, inextinguishable
onver'zettelijk, stubborn
onver'zoenlijk, irreconcilable
onver'zorgd, unattended; careless, untidy
onvol'daan, unsatisfied; unpaid
onvol'doende (de), unsatisfactory mark, fail
onvol'doende, insufficient, unsatisfactory
onvol'prezen, beyond praise
onvol'tooid, unfinished; imperfect (tense)
on'voorbereid, unprepared
onvoor'delig, unprofitable, uneconomical
onvoor'waardelijk, unconditional
on'vriendelijk, unkind
on'vrij, not free, without any privacy
on'vruchtbaar, infertile, fruitless
onwaarde: van –, null and void
on'waardig, unworthy, undignified
onwaar'schijnlijk, improbable
onweer (het), thunder storm
onweer'staanbaar, irresistible
on'wel, unwell
on'wennig, ill at ease
onweren, to thunder
on'wetend, ignorant

on'wettig, unlawful, illegal, illegitimate
on'wezenlijk, unreal
on'wijs, fabulously, terrifically, unbelievably
  – gaaf, unbelievably fab/cool/fantastic
onwil (de), unwillingness
onwille'keurig, involuntary
on'willig, unwilling, obstinate
on'wrikbaar, unshakable
onze, our(s)
on'zedelijk, immoral
on'zeker, uncertain
onze-lieve-'heersbeestje (het), ladybird
on'zichtbaar, invisible
on'zijdig, neutral, neuter
onzin (de), nonsense
on'zinnig, absurd
on'zuiver, impure, inaccurate, out of tune
oog (het), eye
oogarts (de), ophthalmologist
ooggetuige (de), eye witness
oogharen, eyelashes
oogholte (de), oogkas (de), eye socket
oogkleppen, blinkers
ooglid (het), eyelid
oogluikend toelaten, to turn a blind eye (to something)
oogopslag (de), glance, look
oogpunt (het), point of view
oogst (de), harvest, crop
oogvlies (het), cornea
oogwenk (de), twinkling of an eye
ooievaar (de), stork
ooit, ever
ook, also, too; either
  wat (dan) –, whatever
  waar (dan) –, wherever

oom (de), uncle
oor (het), ear; handle
oorbel (de), earring
oord (het), place, region, resort
oordeel (het), opinion, judgement
oordelen, to judge
oorkonde (de), charter, (ancient) document
oorlel (de), earlobe
oorlog (de), war(fare)
oorpijn (de), earache
oorsprong (de), origin, source
oor'spronkelijk, original
oorver'dovend, deafening
oorzaak (de), cause
oost, east, Orient
oostelijk, easterly, east (of)
oosten (het), east
Oostenrijk, Austria
oosters, eastern, oriental
oostwaarts, eastward(s)
Oost'zee (de), Baltic
op, on; at; in; up
  het bier is –, the beer is finished
  ik heb veel met hem –, I like him a lot
opa (de), grandad
opbellen, to ring up
opbergen, to put away
opbeuren, to lift up; to cheer up
opbiechten, to own up
opblazen, to inflate
opbloei (de), revival
opbouwen, to build up
opbreken, to break up
opbrengen, to yield
opbrengst (de), yield, proceeds
opdagen, to turn up
op'dat, in order that
opdienen, to dish up, to serve
opdissen, to dish up

opdoeken, to close down, to clear out
opdoemen, to loom (up)
opdonderen: donder op! get the hell out of here!
opdracht (de), instruction(s), commission; dedication
opdragen, to instruct, to order; to dedicate
opdrijven, to force up; to drive
opdringen, to thrust on (a person)
op'dringerig, obtrusive
opduiken, to bob up, to crop up
op'een, together, on top of one another
op'eens, all at once
opeen'volgend, successive
opeisen, to claim, to demand
open, open
open'baar, public
open'baren, to reveal
open'baring (de), revelation
opendoen, to open; to answer the door
openen, opengaan, to open
open'hartig, frank
open('hartig)heid (de), frankness
opening (de), opening
openlijk, public, open
openmaken, to open, to undo
openrijten, to rip open
openslaan, to open
  openslaande deur (de), folding door(s), French window
  – raam (het), casement window
openstaande rekening (de), unsettled account
openstellen, to (throw) open (to the public)
openvouwen, to open out
ope'ratie (de), operation

ope'ratiekamer (de), operating theatre

ope'reren, to operate (on)

ope'rette (de), operetta

opeten, to eat (up), to finish (up)

opfrissen, to refresh

opgaaf, opgave (de), statement, return; task, problem, (examination) paper

opgaan, to rise, to go up; to be absorbed; to come off
  dat gaat niet altijd op, that does not always hold good

opgeblazen, puffed-up, bumptious

opgelucht, relieved

opgeruimd, cheerful

opgesloten, locked up; implied

opgetogen, enraptured

opgeven, to give (up); to cough up; to state
  hoog – van, to speak highly of

opgevreten, eaten away, consumed

opgewassen tegen, a match for

opgewekt, cheerful

opgewonden, excited

opgezet, swollen; stuffed
  groot(s) opgezet, ambitious

opgooien, to toss (up)

opgraven, to dig up

ophaalbrug (de), drawbridge

ophalen, to draw up; to pick up; to shrug; to sniff (up)

ophef (de), fuss

opheffen, to lift up; to abolish, to close (down)

ophelderen, to elucidate; to clear

ophemelen, to extol

ophitsen, to incite, to set on

ophopen, to pile up; to accumulate

ophouden, to hold up; to uphold; to cease; to delay

o'pinie (de), opinion

opkikkeren, to perk up

op'klapbaar, folding

opklapbed (het), tip-up bed

opklaren, to clear up

opknappen, to smarten up; to cope with; to get well

opkomen, to come up, to (a)rise; to come on; to stick up (for)
  het kwam bij me op, it occurred to me

opkomst (de), rise; attendance

opkrassen, to clear out

opkroppen, to bottle up

oplaag (de), oplage (de), number of copies printed

oplaaien, to flare up

oplaten, to fly

oplawaai (de), wallop

opleggen, to impose; to lay on; to store

opleiden, to train

opleiding (de), training, education

opletten, to pay attention

op'lettend, attentive

opleven, to revive

opleveren, to produce, to present

oplichten, to lift (up); to swindle

oplichter (de), swindler

oplopen, to run up; to rise; to mount; to incur

op'losbaar, soluble

oplossen, to (dis)solve

oplossing (de), solution

opluchting (de), relief

opluisteren, to add lustre to

opmaak (de), layout

opmaken, to make (up); to gather
op'merkelijk, remarkable
opmerken, to observe
opmerking (de), remark
op'merkzaam maken op, to call attention to
opname (de), recording, photograph; admission
opnemen, to take/lift (up); to take in; to record; to answer (telephone)
op'nieuw, anew
opnoemen, to enumerate; to call (out)
opofferen, to sacrifice
oponthoud (het), delay
oppas (de), babysitter, childminder
oppassen, to take care (of); to beware
oppasser (de), caretaker, attendant
opper'best, excellent
opperbevel (het), supreme command
opperbevelhebber (de), commander-in-chief
opperen, to propose
opperhoofd (het), chief(tain)
oppervlak (het), (outer) surface
opper'vlakkig, superficial
oppervlakte (de), surface, area
oppikken, to pick up
opprikken, to pin up
oprakelen, to poke (up); to rake up
oprapen, to pick up
op'recht, sincere
oprichten, to erect; to establish
oprichter (de), founder
oprijlaan (de), drive
oprit (de), drive
oproep (de), summons, call

oproepen, to call (up)
op'roerig, rebellious
oproerkraaier (de), agitator
opruien, to incite to rebellion
opruimen, to clear (away)
opruiming (de), clearance sale
oprukken, to press onward
opscharrelen, to dig up
opschepen met, to saddle with
opscheppen, to serve; to brag
opschepper (de), braggart
opschieten, to get (a move) on
met elkaar –, to get on (well) together
opschorten, to suspend
opschrift (het), inscription, caption
opschrijven, to note down
opschrikken, to start, to be startled
opschrokken, to gobble up
opschudding (de), commotion
opschuiven, to push up, to move up
opslaan, to raise; to turn up; to lay in; to rise (in price)
opslag (de), rise; storage
opslorpen, opslurpen, to drink noisily; to absorb
opsluiten, to lock (up)
opsommen, to enumerate, to recount
opspelen, to kick up a row
opsporen, to track (down)
opspraak (de), disrepute
opstaan, to rise
opstand (de), rising; elevation
in – komen, to rebel
opstandeling (de), rebel
op'standig, rebellious
opstap (de), step
opstapelen: zich –, to accumulate

opstappen, to go away; to go up

opsteken, to put up; to light; to get up

– **van,** to profit by

opstel (het), essay

opstellen, to draft; to place

opstijgen, to rise; to climb up, to mount

opstoken, to stir up (animosity)

opstootje (het), disturbance

opstrijken, to run an iron over; to rake in

opstropen, to roll up

optekenen, to note down

optellen, to add up

optocht (de), procession

optreden (het), action; performance, show

optreden, to appear; to act

optrekken, to pull up; to raise

– **tegen,** to march against

– **met,** to go about with

optrommelen, to round up

optuigen, to decorate

opvallen, to be conspicuous, to strike

op'vallend, conspicuous

opvangen, to catch; to overhear

opvatten, to take (up), to interpret, to conceive

opvatting (de), conception, opinion

opvoeden, to educate

opvoeding (de), upbringing

lichamelijke –, physical training

opvoeren, to raise; to perform

opvoering (de), performance

opvolgen, to succeed; to carry out

opvolger (de), successor

op'vouwbaar, collapsible

opvreten, to devour

opvrolijken, to cheer up

opwaarts, upward(s)

opwachten, to wait for

opwegen tegen, to offset

opwekken, to arouse, to stimulate, to generate

op'wekkend, encouraging

opwerken: zich –, to work one's way up

opwinden, to wind (up), to excite

opwinding (de), excitement

opzeggen, to recite; to terminate, to cancel

zijn baan –, to give notice

opzet (de), plan, intent(ion)

op'zettelijk, met opzet, deliberate

opzetten, to set up; to put on; to turn (against); to swell

opzichter (de), superintendent

op'zichtig, flashy

opzien tegen, to look up to; to dread

opzien'barend, sensational

opzoeken, to look up

o'ranje (het), orange

orchi'dee (de), orchid

orde (de), order

aan de –, up for discussion

ordelijk, orderly

ordenen, to (put in) order

order (de), order, command

ordi'nair (de), vulgar

ordner (de), file

or'gaan (het), organ

organi'seren, to organize

orgel (het), organ

orgeldraaier (de), organ grinder

oriën'teren zich –, to find one's bearings

origi'neel, original

or'kaan (de), hurricane

or'kest (het), orchestra

os (de), ox, bullock

oud, old, ancient

  bij het oude laten, to leave (things) as they were

oud'bakken, stale

oude van dagen (de), aged

oudejaars'avond (de), New Year's Eve

ouder (de), older, elder; parent

ouderdom (de), (old) age

ouderlijk, parental

ouder'wets, old-fashioned

oudheid (de), antiquity

oudje (het), old (wo)man

oudoom (de), great-uncle

oudsher: van –, (from) of old

oudst, oldest, elder; senior

oudtante (de), great-aunt

ouwel (de), wafer

ouwelijk, elderly

o'vaal, oval

oven (de), oven, furnace, kiln

over, over, across; via; past; about; left (over)

  – en weer, mutually

  tijd te –, time to spare

  ik heb veel voor hem –, I would do anything for him

  – een paar dagen, in a few days' time

over'al, everywhere

overbekend, widely known

overbelasten, to overburden; to overload

overbelicht, over-exposed

overblijfsel (het), remains, relic

overblijven, to be left; to stay (at school for lunch)

over'bodig, superfluous

over'boord, overboard

overbrengen, to convey

over'bruggen, to bridge

overbuur (de), neighbour across the road

overdaad (de), excess

over'dadig, excessive

over'dag, during the day

over'dekt, covered

over'denken, to consider

overdoen, to do again; to pass on

over'donderen, to overwhelm

overdracht (de), transfer

over'drachtelijk, metaphorical

overdragen, to transfer, to convey

over'dreven, exaggerated

over'drijven, to exaggerate

over'duidelijk, obvious

over'dwars, across, athwart

over'eenkomen, to agree

over'eenkomst (de), agreement, similarity

overeen'komstig, corresponding (to)

over'eenstemmen, to agree

over'eind, upright, on end

overgaan, to cross over; to pass (on); to go up (to a higher form)

overgang (de), transition, change; crossing; menopause

overgangsmaatregel (de), temporary measure

over'gankelijk, transitive

overgave (de), surrender

overgelukkig, over-joyed

overgeven, to hand over, to surrender; to vomit

overge'voelig, hypersensitive

overgieten, to transfer, to decant

overgooier (de), tunic

overgordijn (het), (running) curtain

over'goten met, bathed in

overgrootmoeder (de), great-grandmother

overgrootvader (de), great-grandfather

overhalen, to pull over; to persuade

overhand (de), upper hand

over'handigen, to hand (over)

over'heen, across, over
  er gaan jaren –, it takes years

overheerlijk, exquisite

over'heersen, to (pre)dominate

overheid (de), authorities

overhellen, to incline, to lean over

overhemd (het), shirt

overhevelen, to siphon

over'hoop, in a mess

over'horen, to test

overhouden, to have left

overig, remaining

overigens, for the rest; anyway

overkant (de), opposite side

over'kapping (de), roof(ing)

over'koepelend, coordinating

over'komen, to happen to

overkomen, to come over (to visit); to come across

overladen, to transfer

over'langs, lengthwise

overlast (de), inconvenience, nuisance

overlaten, to leave

over'leden, deceased

over'leg (het), deliberation, consultation

over'leggen, to deliberate

over'leven, to survive

over'levende (de), survivor

overleveren, to hand down; to deliver up

over'levering (de), tradition

overlezen, to read through, to read again

over'lijden, to die

overloop (de), landing

overlopen, to run over; to go over

overloper (de), deserter, traitor

overmaat, excess
  tot – van ramp, to crown it all

overmacht (de), superior force; force majeure

overmaken, to do again; to transfer

over'mannen, to overpower; to overcome

over'meesteren, to overpower

over'moedig, overconfident

over'morgen, the day after tomorrow

over'nachten, to stay the night

overnemen, to take over; to adopt

overplaatsen, to transfer

overplanten, to transplant

over'reden, to persuade

over'rijden, to run over

over'rompelen, to take by surprise

overschenken, to decant

overschot (het), remainder, surplus

over'schreeuwen, to shout down

over'schrijden, to exceed; to step across

overschrijven, to copy (out); to transfer

overslaan, to skip; to estimate; to crack

over'spannen, overwrought, suffering from severe stress

overspel (het), adultery

overstaan: ten – van, in the presence of

overstappen, to change
oversteekplaats (de), (pedestrian) crossing
oversteken, to cross
over'stelpen, to overwhelm
over'stemmen, to drown, to shout down
over'stromen, to flood, to inundate
over'stuur, upset
overtocht (de), crossing, passage
over'tollig, superfluous
over'treden, to transgress; to infringe
over'treffen, to surpass
  overtreffende trap (de), superlative
overtrek (de), (loose) cover
over'tuigen, to convince
over'tuiging (de), conviction
overuren (de), overtime
overval (de), surprise attack
over'vallen, to surprise
over'vleugelen, to surpass; to outflank
overvloed (de), abundance
over'vloedig, abundant
over'vragen, to overcharge
overwaaien, to blow over
overweg (de), level crossing
over'weg kunnen, to get on well
over'wegen, to consider
over'wegend, preponderant
over'weging (de), consideration
over'weldigen, to overpower
over'weldigend, overwhelming
overwerken, to work overtime
over'werken, to overwork
overwicht (het), preponderance, authority
over'winnaar (de), victor
over'winnen, to conquer
over'winning (de), victory

overzicht (het), summary
over'zichtelijk, well organized; clearly set out
over'zien, to survey
overzijde (de), opposite side
OV-'jaarkaart (de), annual season ticket/travel card
oxi'deren, to oxidize
ozon (de), ozone

P

paadje (het), (foot)path
paal (de), pole, pile, post
  als een – boven water, as clear as daylight
paar (het), pair, couple; few
paard (het), horse
paardenbloem (de), dandelion
paardenkracht (de), horsepower
paars, violet, purple
paarsgewijs, in pairs
paartijd (de), mating season
paasdag (de): de eerste –, Easter Day
  de tweede –, Easter Monday
paasvakantie (de), Easter holidays
pachter (de), tenant farmer
pad (de), toad
pad (het), path
paddestoel (de), toadstool, mushroom
padvinder (de), boy scout
padvindster (de), girl guide
paf staan, to be dumbfounded
pafferig, puffy
pagina (de), page
pais en vree (de), peace and quiet
pak (het), pack(age); suit
  – slaag, thrashing
pakhuis (het), warehouse

pakje (het), parcel, packet
pakken, to pack; to seize; to hug
  iemand te – krijgen, to get hold of a person
  ik heb het erg te –, I've got it badly
pakkend, fascinating; catchy
pakkerd (de), hug and kiss
pakpapier (het), brown paper
pal (de), catch: directly; due
  – oost, due east
pa'leis (het), palace
Pales'tijn (de), Palestinian
Pales'tijns, Palestinian, Palestine
Pales'tina, Palestine
paling (de), eel
palm (de), palm
Palm'pasen, Palm Sunday
pam'flet (het), pamphlet lampoon
pan (de), pan; tile; shindy
  in de – hakken, to make mincemeat of
pand (het), forfeit; premises; (coat)tail
pandjeshuis (het), pawn shop
pa'neel (het), panel
pa'neermeel (het), breadcrumbs
pa'niek (de), panic
panne (de), breakdown
pannenkoek (de), pancake
panta'lon (de), trousers
panter (de), panther
pan'toffel (de), slipper
pan'toffelheld (de), henpecked husband
pantser (het), armour
pantserdier (het), armadillo
pantseren, to armour; to brace
pap (de), milk pudding, porridge
pa'paver (de), poppy

pape'gaai (de), parrot
pa'pier (het), paper
  pa'pieren, papers; stocks and shares; credentials
papje (het), paste
pappie (de), daddy
paprika (de), (sweet) pepper
pa'raaf (de), initials
pa'raat, ready
para'chute (de), parachute
pa'rade (de), review, parade
para'dijs (het), paradise
para'feren, to initial
para'graaf (de), paragraph, section
paral'lel, parallel
parano'ïde, paranoid
paranor'maal, paranormal
para'plu (de), umbrella
para'siet (de), parasite
par'cours (het), course
par'does, slap(bang)
par'don (het), pardon; mercy
parel (de), pearl
parel'moer (het), mother of pearl
paren, to mate
  zich – aan, to be coupled with
par'fum (het), scent
parfu'meren, to scent
park (het), park
par'keerautomaat (de), (car park/parking lot) ticket machine
par'keerboete (de), parking fine
par'keerbon (de), parking ticket
par'keergarage (de), (underground) car park, parking garage
par'keergeld (het), parking money
par'keerplaats (de), parking place/space, parking lot, car park

par'keerterrein (het), car park

par'keerverbod (het), parking ban, no parking (on signs)

par'keren, to park

par'ket (het), public prosecutor's office; parquet
 in een lastig –, in a predicament

par'kiet (de), parakeet

parle'ment (het), parliament

parlemen'tair, parliamentary

parlemen'tariër (de), member of parliament, representative

pa'rochie (de), parish

paro'die (de), parody

parodi'ëren, to parody

par'terre (de), pit; ground floor

particu'lier, private

par'tij (de), part(y); game; consignment
 – kiezen, to take sides

par'tijdig, biased

pas (de), step; pass, passport

pas, only (just)
 te – en te onpas, at random
 te –, van –, (be)fitting

Pasen, Easter

pasfoto (de), passport photo

pasge'boren, new-born

pasge'trouwd, newly wed

paskamer (de), fitting room

pasklaar, ready for fitting

paspoort (het), passport

paspoortcontrole (de), passport control

pas'sage (de), passage; arcade

passa'gier (de), passenger

passen, to fit; to try on; to match; to be fitting; to pass
 ik pas ervoor, I won't do it
 – op, to take care (of)

passend, fitting, appropriate

passer (de), pair of compasses

pas'seren, to pass (over); to happen

passie (de), passion

pas'sief, passive

passievrucht (de), passion fruit

pasta (de), paste, pasta

pas'tei (de), patty; paste

pas'toor (de), parish priest

pasto'rie (de), parsonage

pa'tat (de), chips, fries
 – met, chips with mayonnaise

pa'tatje (het), (portion of) chips/fries

pa'tent (het), licence; patent

patisse'rie (de), pastries; pastry shop

pa'trijs (de), partridge

pa'trijspoort (de), porthole

pa'troon (de), cartridge

pa'troon (het), pattern, design

pa'trouille (de), patrol

pats (de), smack; bang!

patser (de), show-off

patserig, macho

pauk (de), kettledrum

paus (de), pope

pauselijk, papal

pauw (de), peacock

pauze (de), interval, pause

pavil'joen (het), pavilion; marquee

pech (de), bad luck

pechvogel (de), unlucky person

pe'daal (het), pedal

pe'daalemmer (de), pedal bin

pe'dant, pedant(ic)

peddelen, to pedal; to paddle

pedi'cure (de), chiropodist

peen (de), carrot

peer (de), pear; light bulb
 met de gebakken peren zitten, to be left holding the baby

pees (de), tendon; gristle

peet (de), godparent

peetoom (de), godfather

peil (het), gauge, level
  er is op hem geen – te trekken, he is quite unpredictable

peilen, to gauge, to sound

peinzen, to muse

peinzend, thoughtful

pelgrim (de), pilgrim

pelgrimstocht (de), pilgrimage

pellen, to peel, to shell

pelo'ton (het), platoon; pack, bunch

pels (de), pelt; fur coat

pen (de), pen, nib, quill; peg, pin

penalty (de), penalty (kick, shot)

pe'narie: in de –, in a fix

pendelen, to commute

pe'nibel, grim

peni'tentie (de), penitence; ordeal

pennen, to pen

penning (de), medal; official badge

penningmeester (de), treasurer

pens (de), paunch; tripe

pen'seel (het), (artist's) brush

pen'sioen (het), pension
  met – gaan, to retire (on a pension)

pen'sion (het), guesthouse; board

peper (de), pepper

peperduur, very expensive

peperkoek (de), gingerbread

peper'munt (de), peppermint

pepernoot (de), ginger nut

per'ceel (het), plot; premises

percen'tage (het), percentage

per'centsgewijze, proportional

perfectio'neren, to perfect

peri'ode (de), period

perio'diek, periodical

perk (het), flower bed; limit

perka'ment (het), parchment

permit'teren, to permit

per omgaand, by return (of post)

per'plex, perplexed

per'ron (het), platform

per se, at all cost

pers (de), press; Persian (rug)

persbureau (het), press agency

persen, to press, to squeeze

persfotograaf (de), press photographer, newspaper photographer

perso'neel (het), staff, personnel

perso'neelschef (de), personnel manager, staff manager

perso'neelszaken (de), personnel/staff matters; personnel department

per'sonenauto (de), private car, passenger car

per'soon (de), person

per'soonlijk, personally, private, individual

per'soonlijkheid (de), personality

per'soonsbewijs (het), identity card

perspec'tief (het), perspective

perti'nent, emphatic, positive

per'vers, perverse

perzik (de), peach

Perzisch, Persian

pest (de), plague, pest(ilence)

pesten, to bait, to tease the life out of

pestkop (de), bully

pet (de), cap
  dat gaat boven mijn –, it beats me

petekind (het), godchild

peter'selie (de), parsley
pe'troleum (de), paraffin
peukje (het), cigar(ette) butt
peultjes (de), mange tout peas
peulvruchten (de), legumes
peuter (de), tiny tot
peuteren, to fiddle, to tinker
peuterwerk(je) (het), finicky job
pi'anokruk (de), music stool
pi'as (de), clown
piccolo (de), piccolo; pageboy
picknick (de), picnic
picknicken, to picnic
picknickmand (de), picnic
  hamper
piek (de), peak, spike
piekeren, to puzzle, to brood
piekfijn, smart, posh
pienter, bright, smart
piepen, to squeak, to cheep
piepjong, very young
pier (de), pier, jetty;
  (earth)worm
  ik ben altijd de kwaaie –, I get
  the blame for everything
pierenbad (het), paddling pool
piet'luttig, petty
pietsje (het), wee bit
pijl (de), arrow
pijler (de), pillar
pijn (de), pain, ache
  – doen, to hurt
pijnigen, to torture, to rack
pijnlijk, painful
pijn'stillend, sedative, soothing
pijnstiller (de), painkiller
pijn (de), pipe; tube; funnel;
  trouser leg
pik (de), (vulg) penis, dick
  een stijve –, a hard-on
pi'kant, piquant, spicy
pik'donker (het), pitch
  blackness, pitch darkness

pikhouweel (het), pickaxe
pikken, to peck; to pinch, steal;
  to put up with
pil (de), pill; chunky book
pi'laar (de), pillar
pi'loot (de), pilot
pimpelaar (de), tippler
pin (de), peg, pin
pin'cet (het), tweezers
pinda(kaas) (de), peanut (butter)
pindasaus (de), peanut sauce
pingelen, to haggle
pinguïn (de), penguin
pink (de), little finger
  bij de pinken, all there
Pinksteren, Whitsun(tide)
pinnen, to pay by bankcard;
  withdraw money from a
  cashpoint
pinpas (de), cash card,
  bankcard
pi'oenroos (de), peony
pi'on (de), pawn
pio'nieren, to pioneer
pi'pet (de), pipette
pips, off colour
pi'raat (de), pirate
pis'tool (het), pistol
pit (de), kernel, stone, pip;
  burner; pith
pittig, pithy, spicy; tough
pizza (de), pizza
pk (paardenkracht) (de),
  horsepower
plaag (de), nuisance, plague
plaat (de), plate; slab;
  (gramophone) record; picture
plaats (de), place; room; yard;
  seat
  in – van, instead of
  ter plaatse on the spot
plaatsbewijs (het), ticket
plaatselijk, local

plaatsen, to place
plaatsvervanger (de), deputy
pla'fond (het), ceiling
plagen, to tease, to worry
plage'rij (de), teasing
plagi'aat (het), plagiarism
plak (de), slice; slab
  onder de – zitten, to be under a person's thumb
plakband (het), adhesive tape
plakboek (het), scrapbook
plakken, to stick
pla'muren, to fill cracks
plan (het), plan, project
  van – zijn, to intend
pla'neet (de), planet
plank (de), plank, board; shelf
plankenkoorts (de), stage fright
plant (de), plant
plant'aardig, vegetable
plan'tage (de), plantation
planten, to plant
plantengroei (de), vegetation
plantkunde (de), botany
plant'soen (het), gardens, flower bed
plas (de), pool, puddle; lake
plassen, to go to the loo/toilet, to (have a) pee
plat, flat; vulgar
pla'taan (de), plane tree
platenspeler (de), record player
platenzaak (de), record shop
platina (het), platinum
platte'grond (de), (ground)plan
platte'land (het), country(side)
platte'lands, country, rural
plattrappen, to trample down
plat'vloers, coarse, crude
platzak, penniless, empty-handed
pla'veien, to pave
pla'vuis (de), flagstone

plebs (het), hoi polloi
plecht('stat)ig, solemn
plechtigheid (de), ceremony, solemnity
pleeg-, foster-
plegen, to commit
  overleg –, to consult together
plei'dooi (het), plea, (address for the) defence
plein (het), square, open space
pleister (de), plaster, bandaid
pleiten, to plead
  dat pleit voor hem, that's a point in his favour
plek (de), spot
pletten, to roll out, to crush
pletter: te – slaan, to smash to smithereens
plexiglas (het), plexiglass
ple'zier (het), pleasure
ple'zierig, pleasant
plicht (de), duty
plicht(s)getrouw, plicht'matig, dutiful
plint (de), plinth; skirting board
ploeg (de), plough: gang, shift, team
ploegen, to plough
ploegendienst (de), shift work
ploegleider (de), team manager
ploeteren, to splash; to plod; to drudge
plof(fen) (de), (to) thud, (to) plop
plomp, plump, squat
plons (de), splash
plonzen, to (s)plash
plooi (de), fold, pleat, crease
  uit de – komen, to unbend
plooibaar, pliable
plooien, to fold, to pleat
plotseling, sudden
pluche (de), plush

pluim (de), plume, feather; tuft
pluimpje (het), compliment
pluimvee (het), poultry
pluis: niet –, fishy
pluisje (het), piece of fluff
plukken, to pick, to pluck
plunderen, to plunder
plunjezak (de), kitbag
plus'minus, approximately
pluspunt (het), plus, asset
pochen, to boast
podium (het), stage, platform
poedel (de), poodle
poedel'naakt, stark naked
poeder (de, het), powder
poedersuiker (de), icing sugar
poe'ha (de), fuss, la-di-da
poeieren, to powder
poel (de), pool, puddle
poe'lier (de), poulterer
poen (de), dough, dosh
poep (de), crap, shit
poepen, to (have a) crap
poes (de), (pussy)cat
  niet voor de –, no chicken feed
poeslief, honey-lipped, smooth
poespas (de), fuss about
  nothing
poetsen, to polish, to brush
poë'zie (de), poetry
poffen, to puff; to pop; to roast
poffertjes (de), small pancakes
pogen, to endeavour
poging (de), attempt
pokken (de), smallpox
pokkewerk (het),
  nasty/unpleasant work
polderpop (de), Dutch pop
  music
Polen, Poland
po'lijsten, to polish
polikliniek (de), out-patients' clinic
polis (de), insurance policy

po'liticus (de), politician
po'litie (de), police
po'litieagent (de), policeman
po'litiebureau (het), police station
poli'tiek (de), politics
poli'tiek, political
pollepel (de), wooden spoon
pols (de), pulse, wrist
polsen, to sound someone out
  about
polsslag (de), pulse, pulsation
polsstokspringen (het), pole
  vaulting
pomp (de), pump
pompen, to pump
pom'peus, pompous
pom'poen (de), pumpkin
pompstation (het), petrol/
  service station
pond (het), (British) pound,
  500 grammes
pont (de), ferry boat
pony (de), pony; fringe
pooier (de), pimp
pook (de), poker
pool (de), pole
poolcirkel (de), polar circle
Pools, Polish
poolshoogte nemen, to see how
  the land lies
poolster (de), pole star
poolzee (de), (ant)arctic sea
poort (de), gate(way)
poos(je) (het, de), (little) while
poot (de), paw, leg
pootjebaden, to paddle
pop (de), doll; puppet; dummy
  **nu heb je de poppen aan het
  dansen!** now we're in for it!
popelen, to quiver, to itch
poppenhuis (het), doll's house
poppenkast (de), puppet show,
  Punch and Judy show

popperig, diminutive
popu'lair, popular
populari'teit (de), popularity
popu'lier (de), poplar
popzanger(es) (de), pop/rock singer
por (de), prod
po'reus, porous
porie (de), pore
porno(gra'fie) (de), porno(graphy)
porren, to poke, to prod
porse'lein (het), china(ware)
por'taal (het), porch; hall
porte'feuille (de), portfolio; wallet
portemon'nee (de), wallet, purse
portie (de), share, helping
por'tiek (de, het), porch, doorway
por'tier (de), (hall) porter; (car) door
por'tierraampje (het), car window
porto (de), postage
por'tret (het), portrait
po'seren, to pose, to sit
po'sitie (de), position, situation
posi'tief, positive
po'sitiekleding (de), maternity clothes
posi'tieven (de), wits
post (de), post; mail; item; picket
  op –, on duty
postbode (de), postman
postbus (de), post office box
postcode (de), postal code, ZIP code (Am)
posten, to post; to picket
poste'rijen (de), postal service
postkantoor (het), post office
postorderbedrijf (het), mail-order company

pos'tuum, posthumous
pos'tuur (het), figure; posture
postwissel (de), money order
postzegel (de), postage stamp
pot (de), pot, jar; (chamber) pot; saucepan, pot; kitty, pool; (inf) lesbian, dyke/dike
pot'dicht, shut tight
poten, to plant, to dibble
poten'tieel, potential
potig, hefty
potlood (het), pencil; black lead
potten, to pot; to hoard
pottenbakker (de), potter
pottenkijker (de), nosy parker, snooper
potvis (de), sperm whale
pover, poor, meagre
praal (de), pomp, splendour
praat(je) (het, de), talk, chat, gossip
  veel praats hebben, to talk big
praatgraag, praatziek, garrulous
praatpaal (de), emergency telephone
pracht (de), splendour
prachtig, splendid, magnificent
practicum (het), practical (work)
prak (de), hash
prakken, to mash (up)
prak'tijk (de), practice
praktisch, practical
prakti'seren, to practise
pralen, to shine; to flaunt
prat gaan op, to pride oneself on
praten, to talk
pre'cair, precarious
pre'cies, precise, exact
predi'kant (de), minister, vicar
prediken, to preach
preek (de), sermon
preekstoel (de), pulpit

prefe'reren, to prefer
prei (de), leek
preken, to preach
premie (de), premium
pre'mier (de), prime minister
prent (de), print, picture
prenten, to imprint
presen'teren, to offer; to present
pre'sentielijst (de), attendance list
pressen, to press
presse-pa'pier (de), paper weight
pressie uitoefenen, to bring pressure to bear
pres'tatie (de), achievement
pres'teren, to achieve
pret (de), fun
pre'tentie (de), pretension
  zonder pretenties, unassuming
preten'tieus, pretentious
pretje (het), bit of fun
prettig, pleasant, nice
  – vinden, to like
preuts, prudish, squeamish
preva'leren, to prevail
prevelen, to mutter
priester (de), priest
prijken, to (be) display(ed)
prijs (de), price; prize
  op prijs stellen, to appreciate
prijsbe'wust, cost-conscious
prijsdaling (de), fall in price
prijsgeven, to abandon, to give up
prijskaartje (het), price tag
prijsklasse (de), price range, price bracket
prijslijst (de), price list
prijsopgave (de), estimate, quotation, tender

prijsuitreiking (de), distribution of prizes, prize-giving ceremony
prijsverhoging (de), rise, price increase
prijsverlaging (de), price cut/reduction
prijsvraag (de), competition
prijzen, to praise; to price, to mark
prijzig, expensive
prik (de), prick, stab; pop, fizz
prikbord (het), noticeboard, bulletin board
prikkel (de), sting, goad; spur
prikkelbaar, irritable
prikkeldraad (het), barbed wire
prikkelen, to prickle; to irritate, to provoke; to stimulate
prikken, to prick; to tingle
pril, tender, vernal
prima, first-rate
pri'mair, primary
pri'meur (de), scoop
primi'tief, primitive, crude
prin'cipe (het), principle
principi'eel, fundamental, of or on principle
prins (de), prince
  van de – geen kwaad weten, to be as innocent as an unborn babe
prinselijk, princely
prin'ses (de), princess
printen, to print
printer (de), printer
priori'teit (de), priority
privati'seren, to privatize
privé, private
pro'beren, to try (out)
pro'bleem (het), problem
pro'bleemloos, trouble-free, uncomplicated, smooth

procé'dé (het), process
proce'deren, to take it to court
pro'cent (het), percent
pro'ces (het), lawsuit; process
  iemand een – aandoen, to bring
  an action against a person
pro'ces-ver'baal (het), official
  report
procu'reur (de), attorney
pro deo, voluntarily, for love
produ'cent (de), producer
produ'ceren, to produce
pro'duct (het), product(ion)
pro'ductie (de), production
pro'ductiekosten (de), cost(s) of
  production
productivi'teit (de), productivity
proef (de), test; proof
proefkonijn (het), laboratory
  rabbit; guinea pig
proefschrift (het), thesis
proeftijd (de), apprenticeship;
  probation
proefwerk (het), test (paper)
proesten, to splutter
proeven, to taste
pro'feet (de), prophet(ess)
pro'fessor (de), professor
pro'fiel (het), profile; cross-
  section
pro'fijt (het), profit, advantage
profi'teren van, to profit by, to
  take advantage of
prog'nose (de), prognosis;
  forecast
pro'gramma (het), programme
program'meertaal (de),
  computer language
program'meren, to program
  (computers); to programme,
  to schedule
progres'sief, progressive
projec'teren, to project, to plan

pro'jectie (de), projection
prole'tariër (de), proletarian
prolon'geren, to continue
pro'loog (de), prologue
pro'motie (de), promotion,
  graduation (ceremony)
promo'veren, to obtain a
  doctor's degree
pronk: te – staan, to be on show
pronken, to show off
pronkstuk (het), show piece
prooi (de), prey
proost! cheers!
prop (de), plug, wad
  **met een voorstel op de
  proppen komen,** to come out
  with a suggestion
propa'geren, to propagate
proper, clean and tidy
propvol, chock-full
prostitu'ée (de), prostitute
prosti'tutie (de), prostitution
prote'ïne (de), protein
protes'teren, to protest
pro'these (de), artifical teeth (or
  limb etc.)
protserig, ostentatious
provi'and (de), provisions
provinci'aal, provincial
pro'vincie (de), province
pro'visie (de), provision;
  commission
provi'sorisch, provisional
provo'ceren, to provoke
proza (het), prose
pruik (de), wig
pruilen, to pout
pruim (de), plum
prul (het), trash
prullenmand (de), wastepaper
  basket
prut (de), mud, mire,
  grounds

prutsen, to mess about, to botch

pruttelen, to simmer; to grumble

pseudo'niem (het), pseudonym

psychi'ater (de), psychiatrist

psychi'atrisch, psychiatric

psychisch, psychological, mental

psycho'loog (de), psychologist

puber (de), adolescent

pube'raal, adolescent

puber'teit (de), adolescence

publi'ceren, to publish

pu'bliek (het), public, audience

pu'bliekstrekker (de), crowd puller, box-office hit

puffen, to puff

puin (het), rubble

puinhoop (de), ruins; mess

puist (de), spot, pimple

puistje (het) pukkel, pimple

pulken, to pick

pu'naise (de), drawing pin, thumbtack

punctu'eel, punctual

punt (de) (het), point, tip; full stop

  dubbel(e) –, colon

  – komma, semi-colon

  als puntje bij paaltje komt, when push comes to shove

  geen –, no problem

puntig, pointed, jagged

pu'pil (de), pupil

put (de), pit, well

  in de – zitten, to be depressed

putten, to draw, to derive

puur, sheer, neat

puzzelen, to do puzzles; solve crosswords, jigsaw puzzles

Q

qua, as regards, as far as ... goes

quaran'taine, quarantine

quitte, quits

quiz (de), quiz

quizleider (de), quiz master

quota (de), quota, share

R

raad (de), advice; council, board

raadgevend, advisory

raadhuis (het), council offices

raadplegen, to consult

raadsel (het), riddle, puzzle; enigma

raadselachtig, mystifying

raadslid (het), councillor

raadsman (de), adviser

raadsverkiezingen (de), municipal election

raadzaam, advisable

raaf (de), raven

raak, well-aimed, to the point

  maar raak, at random

raam (het), window; frame

raamkozijn (het), window frame, window sill

raar, strange, funny, odd

ra'barber (de), rhubarb

rab'bijn (de), rabbi

race (de), race

  nog in de –, still in the running

raceauto (de), racecar

racebaan (de), (race)track

racefiets (de), racing bicycle

racen, to race

ra'cisme (het), racism

ra'cist (de), racist

rad (het), wheel

radbraken, to wreck, to mangle

radeloos, at a loss, distraught

raden, to guess; to advise
radi'caal, radical, fundamental
ra'dijs (de), radish
radioac'tief, radioactive
rafelen, to fray
raffinade'rij (de), refinery
rage (de), craze
ragfijn (de), gossamer(y)
rakelings langs gaan, to skim
  past
raken, to hit, to touch; to
  concern; to get
ra'ket (de), rocket, missile
rakker (de), rascal
ram (de), ram
Ram, Aries, the Ram
ramadan (de), Ramadan
ramen (op), to estimate
rammelaar (de), rattle
rammelen, to rattle, to clank
  door elkaar –, to give a
  thorough shaking to
rammen, to ram
ramp (de), disaster
ramp'zalig, disastrous, wretched
ran'cune (de), rancour
rand (de), edge, (b)rim
randgemeente (de), suburb
randgroep'jongere (de), young
  dropout
randstad (de): de – Holland,
  urban area in western Holland
rang (de), rank, grade
rangschikken, to arrange
rangtelwoord (het), ordinal
  number
ranja (de), orange squash,
  orangeade
rank (de), slender, sleek-lined:
  (de) tendril
ranselen, to thrash
rans(ig), rancid
rant'soen (het), ration

rap, nimble
rapen, to gather
rap'port (het), report
rap'portcijfer (het), report mark
rappor'teren, to report
rari'teit (de), curio(sity)
ras (het), race, breed, variety
ras, quick, soon
rasartiest (de), born artist
rasecht, true-born
rasp (de), grater, rasp
raspen, to grate, to rasp
rassendiscriminatie (de), racial
  discrimination
rasta (de), Rasta(farian)
rat (de), rat
ratel (de), rattle; tongue
ratelen, to rattle, to roll
rationali'seren, to rationalize
ratio'neel, rational
ratje'toe (de), hotchpotch
rauw, raw; raucous
  dat valt me – op het lijf, that's
  an unexpected blow
rauwkost (de), uncooked
  vegetables or fruit
ra'vage (de), ravage(s), havoc;
  debris
ra'vijn (het), ravine
ra'votten, to romp
ra'yon (het), district, territory
razen, to roar, to rage
razend, furious, wild, frantic
razer'nij (de), frenzy
re'actie (de), reaction
rea'geerbuis (de), test tube
rea'geerbuisbaby (de), test tube
  baby
rea'geren, to react, to respond
reali'seerbaar, realizable,
  feasible
reali'seren, to realize
rea'lisme (het), realism

reali'teit

reali'teit (de), reality

reani'matie (de), resuscitation, reanimation

reani'meren, to resuscitate, revive

re'bel (de), rebel

rebel'leren, to rebel

recen'sent (de), reviewer

re'censie (de), review

re'cept (het), recipe; prescription

re'ceptie (de), reception

re'cherche (de), criminal investigation department

recher'cheur (de), detective

recht (het), straight; right; law

rechtbank (de), (law) court(s)

rechter (de), judge

rechter-, right

rechterhand (de), right hand (side)

rechtelijk, judicial

rechthoek (de), rectangle

recht'hoekig, rectangular, right-angled

recht'op, upright, erect

rechts, (on) the right; right-handed; right

rechts'af, to the right

rechtsom'keert! about turn!

rechtspositie (de), legal status

rechtspraak (de), administration of justice

rechtspreken, to administer justice

rechtstreeks, direct

rechtzaak (de), lawsuit

rechtzaal (de), court room

recht'uit, straight (on)

recht'vaardig, just

recht'vaardigen, to justify

reci'teren, to recite

re'clame (de), advertisement

– maken voor, to advertise

re'clameaanbieding (de), special offer

re'clameblaadje (het), advertising leaflet, pamphlet

re'clameboodschap (de), commercial

re'clamefolder (de), advertising brochure, pamphlet

re'clamespot (de), commercial

reclas'sering (de), (prisoner) rehabilitation

reconstru'eren, to reconstruct

recre'atie (de), recreation, leisure

recrea'tief, recreational

recru'teren, to recruit

rector (de), principal, master

– mag'nificus, vice- chancellor

re'çu (het), receipt, ticket

re'cyclen, to recycle

redac'teur (de), editor

re'dactie (de), editorial staff

reddeloos, irretrievable

redden, to save, to rescue

ik kan me wel –, I can manage (all right)

reddingsboot (de), lifeboat

reddingspoging (de), rescue attempt

rede (de), reason; speech

in de – vallen, to interrupt

redelijk, reasonable; rational

reden (de), reason

rede'natie (de), rede'nering (de), reasoning

rede'neren, to reason; to hold forth

reder(ij) (de), ship owner(s)

redetwisten, to dispute

redevoering (de), speech, oration

redi'geren, to edit

redu'ceren, to reduce, to decrease

re'ductie (de), reduction

ree(bok) (de), roe(buck)

reeds, already

re'ëel, real(istic)

reeks (de), series, row, string

reep (de), strip, bar; rope

reet (de), (vulg) crack, arse/ass, backside

refe'rentie (de), reference

refe'reren, to refer

refor'matie (de), reformation

re'frein (het), refrain

regel (de), rule; line

regelen, to arrange; to regulate
  zich – naar, to conform to

regeling (de), arrangement

regelmaat (de), regularity

regel'matig, regular

regelrecht, straight

regen (de), rain
  van de – in de drop, from the frying pan into the fire

regenachtig, rainy

regenbui (de), shower (of rain)

regenen, to rain

regenkleding (de), rainproof clothing

regenjas (de), raincoat

regenpijp (de), drainpipe

re'gent (de), regent, governor

regenval (de), rain fall

re'geren, to govern, to rule

re'gering (de), government, reign

re'geringsbeleid (het), government policy

re'geringspartij (de), party in office/power, government party

re'gie (de), production

regis'seur (de), producer

re'gister (het), register; index; organ stop

regis'treren, to register

regle'ment (het), regulation(s)

reglemen'tair, regulatory; regulation

regu'leren, to regulate

reiger (de), heron

reiken, to reach, to stretch

reikhalzend, longingly

rein, clean; chaste
  je reinste, utter
  in het reine brengen, to straighten out

reinigen, to clean(se)

reinigingsmiddel (het), detergent

reis (de), journey, voyage

reisbureau (het), travel agency

reischeque (de), traveller's cheque

reisgids (de), travel brochure; guidebook, (travel) guide (both book and person)

reiskosten (de), travelling expenses

reisorganisatie (de), travel organization, tour operator

reisverzekering (de), travel insurance

reizen, to travel

reiziger (de), traveller, passenger

rek (de), elasticity

rek (het), rack, shelves

rekbaar, elastic

rekenen, to reckon, to count; to charge
  reken maar! you bet!

rekenfout (de), (mathematical) error

rekening (de), bill, account
  – houden met, to take into consideration

rekening-cou'rant (de), current account

rekenmachine (de), calculator

rekensom (de), sum; problem, question

rekken, to stretch; to protract

rekstok (de), horizontal bar

rel (de), riot

re'latie (de), (business) relation, connection

rela'tief, relative

re'ligie (de), religion

reling (de), (ship's) rail(s)

relletje (het), disturbance

relschopper (de), rioter, hooligan

rem (de), brake

remmen, to brake; to restrain; to retard

remspoor (het), skid mark

remweg (de), braking distance

renbaan (de), race course; speedway

ren'dabel, profitable, paying

rende'ment (het), return, yield, output; efficiency, output, performance

ren'deren, to pay (its way)

rendier (het), reindeer

rennen, to run

renpaard (het), racehorse

rentabili'teit (de), productivity, cost effectiveness, profitability

rente (de), interest

renteloos, free of interest

rente'nieren, to live on private means

rentevoet (de), interest rate

reorgani'satie (de), reorganization

reorgani'seren, to reorganize

rep en roer (de), uproar

repa'ratie (de), repair(s)

repa'reren, to repair, to mend

repatri'ëren, to return home, to repatriate

repe'teren, to repeat; to rehearse; to coach (for an examination)

repe'titie (de), (revision) test; rehearsal

repor'tage, commentary

reppen: – van, to make any mention of

zich –, to hurry (up)

representa'tief, representative, typical (of); presentable

rep'tiel (het), reptile

repub'liek (de), republic

republi'kein (de), republican

repu'tatie (de), reputation

reser'vaat (het), reserve

re'serve (de), reserve(s)

reser'veren, to reserve, put aside; book, reserve

een tafel –, to book a table

reser'vering (de), booking, reservation

re'servesleutel (de), spare key

re'servewiel (het), spare wheel

resi'dentie (de), royal residence; residency

reso'luut, resolute

respec'tievelijk, respectively

rest (de), rest, remainder

res'tant (het), remnant

restau'ratie, restoration, renovation; refreshment room, dining car

restau'reren, to restore

resten, to remain

res'teren, to be left, to remain

res'terend, remaining

resul'taat (het), result

resu'meren, to summarize

re'torisch, rhetorical

re'tour (het), return

re'tourtje (het), return, round trip
reuk (de), smell, scent, odour
reukwater (het), scent
reuma, rheumatism
reü'nie (de), reunion
reus (de), giant
reus'achtig, gigantic; great
reuze, enormous, wizard
reuzenrad (het), Ferris wheel
re'vanche (de), revenge
re'visie (de), revision
revolutio'nair, revolutionary
re'vue (de), review; revue
riant, ample, spacious
rib (de), rib
ribbel(ig) (de), rib(bed)
ribbenkast (de), rib cage
richel (de), ledge, ridge
richten, to direct, to aim; to
  address
  zich – naar, to conform to
richting (de), direction, trend
  iets in die –, something of the
  sort
richtingaanwijzer (de),
  (direction) indicator
richtinggevoel (het), sense of
  direction
richtlijn (de), guiding principal
ridder (de), knight
ridderlijk, chivalrous
ridderorde (de), order of
  knighthood
rieken, to smell
riem (de), strap, belt; oar; ream
riet (het), reed; cane
rieten dak (het), thatched roof
rietje (het), (drinking) straw
rietsuiker (de), cane sugar
rif (het), reef
rij (de), row
rijbaan (de), riding track;
  carriageway

rijbewijs (het), driving licence
rijbroek (de), riding breeches
rijden, to ride, to drive, to run
rijdier (het), mount
rijexamen (het), driving test
rijk (het), state, kingdom,
  empire; government, state
rijk, rich, wealthy, sumptuous
rijkdom (de), riches, wealth
rijkelijk, richly, amply
rijke'lui (de), rich people
rijksambtenaar (de), civil
  servant
rijksuniversiteit (de), state
  university
rijks'waterstaat (de),
  Department/Ministry of
  Waterways and Public Works
rijksweg (de), trunk road
rijkswege: van –, on
  government authority
rijles (de), driving lesson, riding
  lesson
rijm (het), rhyme
rijmen, to rhyme; to tally, to
  reconcile
rijmpje (het), rhyme, short verse
Rijn (de), Rhine
rijpen, to ripen, to mature
  het heeft gerijpt, there has
  been a hoar frost
rijschool (de), riding school
rijst (de), rice
rijstebrij (de), rijstepap (de),
  rice pudding
rijstrook (de), (traffic) lane
rijsttafel (de), meal of savoury
  dishes with rice
rijtjeshuis (het), terrace(d) house
rijtuig (het), carriage
rijweg (de), carriage way
rijwiel (het), (bi)cycle
rijwielhandel (de), bicycle shop

rijwielstalling (de), bicycle parking area

rijzen, to (a)rise

rijzig, tall

riksja (de), rickshaw

rillen, to shiver, to shudder

rilling (de), shiver, shudder, tremble

rimboe (de), jungle

rimpel (de), wrinkle; ripple

rimpelen, to wrinkle, crinkle

ring (de), ring

rinkelen, to jingle, to tinkle

rio'lering (de), sewerage

ri'ool (het), sewer, drain

risico (het), risk

ris'kant, risky

ris'keren, to risk

rit (de), (tram, bus) ride, drive, rally

ritme (het), rhythm

ritmisch, rhythmic(al)

rits (de), zipper, zip; string, batch, battery

ritselen, to rustle

ritssluiting (de), zip fastener

ritu'eel (het), ritual

rivali'teit (de), rivalry

ri'vier (de), river

rob (de), seal

ro'bijn (de), ruby

ro'buust, robust

rochelen, to rattle, to ruckle

roddel (de), gossip

roddelblad (het), gossip magazine

roddelen, to gossip

roddelpers (de), gutter press, gossip papers

rode'hond (de), German measles

Rode 'Kruis (het), Red Cross

roe(de) (de), rod, birch; rood

roeiboot (de), rowing boat

roeien, to row

roeispaan (de), oar

roekeloos, reckless

roem (de), glory; renown

roemen, to praise; to boast

Roe'menië, Rumania

roemrijk, roemvol, glorious

roep (de), call, cry; fame

roepen, to call (out)

roeping (de), calling, vocation

roer (het), rudder, helm

roerbakken, to stir fry

roerei (het), scrambled egg

roeren, to stir; to move

roerend, moving, pathetic

  roerende goederen, movables

roerig, restless, lively

roerloos, motionless: rudderless

roes (de), intoxication, fever of excitement

roest (de), rust, blight

  oud –, scrap iron

roesten, to rust

roestig, rusty

roestvrij, rustproof, stainless

roet (het), soot

  – in het eten gooien, to throw a spanner in the works

roezemoezig, rowdy

roffel (de), (drum) roll

rogge (de), rye

roggebrood (het), rye bread, pumpernickel

rok (de), skirt; tails

roken, to smoke

roker (de), smoker

rokerig, smoky

rokkostuum (het), dress suit

rol (de), roll; part, role

rolgordijn (het), blind

rol'lade (de), rolled meat

rollen, to roll

rollenspel (het), role playing

rolletje (het), roll, packet; castor
rolluik (het), roller shutter
rolschaats (de), roller skate/
  blade
rolschaatsen, to roller skate/
  blade
rolstoel (de), wheelchair
roltrap (de), escalator
rolverdeling (de), cast; division
  of roles
roman (de), novel
roman'tiek (de), romanticism
romantisch, romantic
Ro'mein(s), Roman
rommel (de), mess, rubbish,
  junk
rommelen, to rummage; to
  rumble
rommelig, untidy
rommelmarkt (de), flea market,
  jumble sale
rompslomp (de), fuss and bother
rond, round; surrounding
rondhangen, to hang around
ronde (de), round(s), lap, heat
rondje (het), round (of drinks or
  cards)
rondkomen, to make ends meet
rondneuzen, to nose about,
  prowl
rondom, all round
rondreis (de), tour
rondrit (de), (coach) tour
rondtasten, to grope about
rondte: in de –, in a circle,
  round about
ronduit, outright
rondvaart (de), boat trip
rondvertellen, to spread
rondvraag (de), question time
rondwaren, to haunt
ronken, to snore; to roar
röntgenfoto (de), X-ray

rood, red
roodborstje (het), robin
roodgloeiend, red-hot
roodharig, red-haired, red-
  headed
Rood'kapje, Little Red Riding
  Hood
roof (de), plunder, robbery, prey
roofdier (het), beast of prey
roofoverval (de), hold-up
rooftocht (de), foray
rooien, to dig (up); to manage
rook (de), smoke
rookgordijn (het), smoke screen
rookverbod (het), ban on smoking
rookvlees (het), smoked beef
rookwolk (de), cloud of smoke
room (de), cream
roomboter (de), butter
roomijs (het), ice cream
Rooms(-Katholiek), Roman
  (Catholic)
roomsoes (de), cream puff
roos (de), rose; dandruff; bull's
  eye
roos'kleurig, rosy
rooster (het), grating, grate,
  grill, ventilator; rota, timetable
roost(er)en, to roast, to grill, to
  toast
ros (het), steed
rosbief (het), roast beef
rose, pink
rot, rotten
  zich – lachen, to laugh oneself
  stupid
ro'teren, to rotate
rotjong (het), brat, little pest
rots (de), rock, cliff
rotsachtig, rocky
rotsblok (het), boulder
rotstreek (de), dirty trick, mean
  trick

rotsvast, firm as a rock
rotten, to rot, to decay
rotzak (de), (inf) bastard, jerk
rotzooi (de), ruddy mess (up)
rou'leren, to circulate
rouw (de), mourning
rouwdienst (de), memorial service
rouwen, to be in mourning
rouwig, sorry
roven, to pillage, to steal, to kidnap
rover (de), robber
ro'yaal, generous, sporting, lavish, ample
rozenbottel (de), rosehip
rozenkrans (de), rosary; garland of roses
ro'zijn (de), raisin
rubber (de, het), rubber
ru'briek (de), heading, rubric, column
rug (de), back, ridge
  achter de –, over and done with
ruggegraat (de), backbone
ruggelings, backward(s), back to back
rugleuning (de), back of the chair
rugnummer (het), (player's) number
rugpijn (de), backache
rugzak (de), rucksack
ruig, shaggy, hairy; rough
ruiken, to smell, to scent
ruil (de), exchange
ruilen, to (ex)change, to swap
ruim, ample, spacious, wide
ruimen, to clear (away)
  het veld –, to give way to
ruimschoots, amply
ruimte (de), room, space

ruimtegebrek (het), lack of space
ruimtevaarder (de), astronaut
ruimtevaartuig (het), spacecraft
ru'ïne (de), ruin(s), wreck
ruï'neren, to ruin
ruisen, to rustle, to rush, to swish
ruit (de), (glass) pane(l); check; diamond
ruiten, diamonds; checked, chequered:
ruitenheer, king of diamonds
ruitenwisser (de), windscreen wiper
ruiter (de), horseman, trooper
ruiterpad (het), bridle path
ruk (de), jerk, tug; gust (of wind); time, spell
  in één – door, in one stretch
rukken, to jerk/tug (at); tear, wrench
rukwind (de), squall, gust (of wind)
rul, loose, running
ru'moer (het), clamour
ru'moerig, noisy
rund (het), ox
rundergehakt (het), minced beef, mince
rundvee (het), (horned) cattle
rundvlees (het), beef
rups (de), caterpillar
Rus(sisch), Russian
rust (de), rest, quiet, peace; half time
  op de plaats –! stand easy!
rusteloos, restless, untiring
rusten, to rest
  wel te –! night night!
rustgevend, comforting, restful, calming
rustig, quiet, tranquil

ruw, rough, coarse, raw
ruwweg, roughly
ruzie (de), quarrel, row
ruziën, to quarrel

S

saai, dull, drab
saam'horigheid (de), solidarity
saam'horigheidsgevoel (het), team spirit
sabbat (de), sabbath
sabbelen, to suck
sabo'teren, to sabotage
sa'disme (het), sadism
saf'fier (de), sapphire
saf'fraan (de), saffron
sage (de), saga, legend
sa'lade (de), salad
sa'laris (het), salary
sa'larisverhoging (de), (salary) increase, (pay) rise
saldo (het), balance
per –, after all
sa'lon (de), drawing room; saloon
salu'eren, to salute
sa'luut (het), salute; cheerio!
salvo (het), salvo, volley; round
samen, together
samendoen, to put together; to go shares
samengesteld, compound(ed), complex, composite
samenhangen, to be connected
samenkomen, to come together
samenleven, to live together
samenleving (de), society
samenlevingscontract (het), cohabitation agreement
samenloop van omstandigheden (de), coincidence

samenscholing (de), gathering
samensmelten, to fuse, to amalgamate
samenspel (het), ensemble, team work
samenstellen, to compose
samenstelling (de), composition, compound
samenvallen, to coincide
samenvatten, to summarize
samenvloeien, to unite; to merge, to blend
samenvoegen, to join
samenzweerder (de), conspirator
samenzwering (de), conspiracy
sanctie (de), sanction
san'daal (de), sandal
sa'neren, to put in order; to reorganize, redevelop
sani'tair (het), sanitary fittings
sani'tair, sanitary
sap (het), sap, juice
sappig, juicy, luscious
sar'castisch, sarcastic
sarren, to bait, to provoke
sa'tanisch, fiendish
sa'té (de), satay
sa'téstokje (het), skewer
sa'tijn (het), satin
sau'cijzenbroodje (het), sausage roll
Saudi-A'rabië, Saudi Arabia
sauna (de), sauna
saus (de), sauce
saxo'foon (de), saxophone
Scandi'navië, Scandinavia
Scandi'navisch, Scandinavian
schaaf (de), plane, slicer
schaafwond (de), graze, abrasion
schaakbord (het), chessboard

schaakmat (de), checkmate; stale mate

schaakspel (het), game of chess; chess set

schaakstuk (het), chess piece

schaal (de), scale; shell; dish

schaaldier (het), crustacean

schaalverdeling (de), graduation

schaamdelen (de), private parts

schaamhaar (het), pubic hair

schaamrood, blush of shame

schaamte(loos), shame(less)

schaap (het), sheep; ninny
  zwart –, black sheep, scapegoat

schaar (de), (pair of) scissors, shears

schaars, scarce, sparse

schaats (de), skate

schaatsen, to skate

schaatser (de), skater

schacht (de), shaft

schade (de), damage, harm, detriment
  de – inhalen, to make up arrears

schadeclaim (de), insurance claim (for damage)

schadelijk, harmful, noxious

schadeloos stellen, to indemnify

schaden, to harm, to do damage to

schadevergoeding (de), compensation

schaduw (de), shadow, shade

schaduwzijde (de), shaded side; drawback

schaften, to knock off for lunch

schakel (de), link

schakelaar (de), switch

schaken, to play chess: to abduct

scha'kering (de), shade

schamel, meagre, wretched

schamen: zich –, to be ashamed

schan'daal (het), scandal, shame

schan'dalig, disgrace, shameful

schande (de), disgrace, shame

schandelijk, disgraceful

schappelijk, fair, decent

schar'minkel (het), scrag(gy person)

schar'nier (de, het), hinge

scharrelen, to rummage; to get along somehow

schat (de), treasure, wealth; darling

schatbewaarder (de), treasurer

schateren, to scream (with laughter)

schatkist (de), treasury

schatrijk, fabulously rich

schattebout (de), poppet, sweetheart

schatten, to value; to estimate

schattig, sweet

schatting (de), estimate, valuation; tribute

schaven, to plane, to graze; to polish

schedel (de), skull

scheef, crooked, lop-sided, raked

scheve voorstelling, misrepresentation

scheve verhouding, wry relationship

scheel, cross-eyed

scheelkijken, scheelzien, to squint

scheenbeen (het), shin bone

scheepsjournaal (het), log(book)

scheepvaart (de), shipping

scheerapparaat (het), (safety) razor

scheermes (het), razor

scheermesje (het), razor blade

scheerzeep (de), shaving soap

scheidbaar, separable

scheiden, to separate, to part; to divorce

scheiding (de), separation; parting; divorce

– van tafel en bed, legal separation

scheidslijn (de), dividing line

scheidsrechter (de), umpire, referee; arbitrator

scheikunde (de), chemistry

schei'kundig, chemical

schel, shrill, glaring

schelden (op), to swear (at)

scheldnaam (de), (rude) name

scheldpartij (de), slanging match

scheldwoord (het), term of abuse

schelen, to matter; to make a difference

het kan me niet –, I don't mind

we – maar twee jaar, there are only two years between us

schelp (de), shell, scallop

schelpdier (het), shellfish

schema (het), sketch diagram, rough draft

sche'matisch, schematic

schemer(ing) (de), twilight, dusk

schemeren, to dawn, to grow dusk; to be dimly visible

schemerlamp (de), floor lamp

schenden, to violate; to damage, to disfigure; to desecrate

schenken, to pour (out); to present with, to grant

schenking (de), gift

schep (de), shovel, scoop

een – geld, heaps of money

schepje (het), spoonful

er een – (boven) opdoen, to go one better

scheppen, to scoop, to shovel, to ladle; to create

schepper (de), creator

schepping (de), creation

schepsel (het), creature

scheren, to shave, to shear, to skim

scherf (de), fragment, splinter

scherling en inslag (de), warp and weft; everyday occurrence

scherm (het), screen, curtain

achter de schermen, behind the scenes

schermen, to fence

scherp, sharp, keen; trenchant

scherpe hoek, acute angle; sharp corner

scherpschutter (de), marksman

scherp'ziend, keen-sighted; penetrating

scherp'zinnig, acute, astute

schets (de), sketch

schetsen, to sketch

schetteren, to blare; to rant

scheur (de), tear, crack

scheuren, to tear; to crack

scheutig, open-handed

schichtig, shy, skittish

schiereiland (het), peninsula

schietbaan (de), rifle range

schieten, to shoot, to fire

een plan laten –, to drop a plan

te binnen –, to come back to mind

schietschijf (de), target

schiften, to curdle

schijf (de), disk; slice; target, dial

schijn (de), light; appearance, semblance

schijnaanval (de), sham attack

schijnbaar, seemingly

schijnbeweging (de), apparent movement

schijnen, to shine; to seem

schijn'heilig, hypocritical

schijnsel (het), light, glimmer

schijnwerper (de), spotlight, searchlight, floodlight

schijt (de), shit

schijten, (inf) to shit, crap

schijter(d) (de), scaredy-cat

schijterig, chicken-hearted

schik: in zijn – zijn, to be pleased (with life)

schikken, to arrange, to settle, to be convenient (to)

  zich – in, to resign onself to

schikking (de) arrangement, agreement

schil (de), peel, skin

schild (het), shield

  iets in het – voeren, to be up to something

schilder (de), painter; decorator

schilderachtig, picturesque

schilderen, to paint; to depict

schilde'rij (het), painting, picture

schilderkunst (de), painting, art

schildpad (de), tortoise(shell), turtle

schildwacht (de), sentry

schilferen, to peel, to flake off

schillen, to peel

schim (de), shadow, ghost

schimmel (de), mould, mildew

schimmelen, to go mouldy

schip (het), ship; nave

  schoon – maken, to clear out (or up)

schipbreuk lijden, to be ship-wrecked

schipper (de), skipper

schipperen, to give and take

schitteren, to glitter, to be brilliant; to be conspicuous

schitterend, brilliant, splendid

schlager (de), popular song

schmink (de), stage make-up

schminken, to make someone up

  zich –, to make oneself up

schoen (de), shoe

  de stoute schoenen aantrekken, to pluck up courage

  iemand iets in de schoenen schuiven, to lay something at a person's door

schoener (de), schooner

schoenmaker (de), shoe repairer

schoensmeer (de), shoe polish

schoenenzaak (de), shoe shop

schoft (de), bastard

schok (de), shock, jolt

schokbreker (de), shock absorber

schokken, to shake, to jerk, to jolt

schol (de), plaice

scholengemeenschap (de), comprehensive school

scho'lier (de), pupil

schommel (de), swing

schommelen, to swing, to rock, to roll; to fluctuate

schooier (de), beggar, tramp

school (de), school; shoal

schoolblijven, to be kept in (after school)

schoolbord (het), blackboard

schoolgeld (het), school fees

schooljuffrouw (de), schoolmistress

schoolmeester (de), schoolmaster; pedant

schoolplein (het), playground
schoolreisje (het), school outing
schools, school(ish); scholastic
schoolslag (de), breast stroke
schoolverzuim (het), absence(s)
schoon, clean; beautiful, fine
schoonfamilie (de), in-laws
schoonheid (de), beauty
schoonheidsmiddel (het), beauty preparation
schoonhouden, to keep clean
schoonmaak (de), (spring) cleaning; clear-out
schoonmaken, to clean
schoonouders, schoonvader en schoonmoeder (de), father- and mother-in-law
schoonrijden, figure skating
schoonzoon (de), son-in-law
schoonzuster (de), sister-in-law
schoorsteen (de), chimney (pot); funnel
schoorsteenmantel (de), mantel piece
schoorsteenveger (de), chimneysweep
schoot (de), lap; womb
schop (de), spade; shovel; kick
schoppen, to kick (up)
schoppen'heer (de), etc.; king etc. of spades
schor, hoarse
schor (de), mud flat
schorem (het), riffraff, scum
schorpi'oen (de), scorpion
schors (de), bark (tree)
schorsen, to suspend; to adjourn
schort (de, het), apron, pinafore
schort: wat – eraan? what is the matter?
schot (het), shot; partition, bulkhead

Schot (de), Scot(sman)
schotel (de), dish; saucer
schots (de), (ice)floe
schouder (de), shoulder
schouderblad (het), shoulder blade
schouw (de), fireplace; scow
schouwburg (de), theatre
schouwspel (het), spectacle
schraal, meagre, lean, bleak
schram (de), scratch
schransen, to gorge
schrapen, to scrape; to clear
schrappen, to scrap(e), to cross out
schreeuw (de), yell, cry
schreeuwen, to shout, yell, scream, screech
schreeuwlelijk (de), bawler
schriel, frail; meagre; mingy
schrift (het), (hand)writing; exercise book
schriftelijk, written, in writing
schrijden, to stride
schrijfster (de), (female) writer
schrijver (de), (male) writer
schrijftaal (de), formal language
schrijven, to write
schrik (de), fright, terror
schrikaanjagend, terrifying
schrik'barend, appalling
schrikbeeld (het), nightmarish vision
schrikbewind (het), reign of terror
schrikkeljaar (het), leap year
schrikken, to have a (nasty) fright, to be taken aback
wakker –, to wake with a start
schrik'wekkend, terrifying
schril, shrill, glaring
schrobben, to scrub

schroef (de), screw, propeller
  op losse schroeven staan, to
  be uncertain
schroeien, to scorch, to singe
schroevendraaier (de), screw
  driver
schroeven, to screw
schrokken, to gorge
schroom, diffidence
schroot (het), scrap metal
schub (de), scale
schuchter, bashful
schudden, to shake; to shuffle
schuieren, to brush
schuif (de), bolt
schuifdak (het), sun roof
schuifdeur, sliding door
schuifelen, to shuffle, to slither
schuifladder (de), extending
  ladder
schuifraam (het), sash window
schuilen, to (take) shelter, to
  lurk
schuilhouden, to lie low
schuilkelder (de), air raid shelter
schuilkerk (de), clandestine
  church
schuilplaats (de), hiding place
schuim (het), foam, froth,
  lather; scum; meringue
schuimbekken, to foam at the
  mouth
schuimen, to foam, to froth, to
  lather; to skim
schuin, slanting, oblique;
  smutty
schuit (de), boat, barge
schuiven, to push
  laat hem maar –, he can fend
  for himself
schuld (de), debt; fault, blame,
  guilt

schuldbekentenis (de), IOU;
  confession of guilt
schuldeiser (de), creditor
schuldenaar (de), debtor
schuldgevoel (het), feeling of
  guilt, guilty conscience
schuldig, guilty
  – zijn, to be guilty; to owe
schuldige (de), culprit, guilty
  party
schunnig, shabby; filthy
  (language)
schuren, to scour, to sandpaper;
  to graze
schurft (de), scabies
schurk (de), scoundrel, villain
schutkleur (de), camouflage
schutsluis (de), lock
schutter (de), marksman
schutting (de), fence
schuur (de), barn; shed
schuurmachine (de), sander,
  sanding machine
schuurmiddel (het), abrasive
schuurpapier (het), sandpaper
schuw, timid, shy
schuwen, to shun, to fight shy
  of
scriptie (de), thesis
secon'dair, secondary
se'conde(wijzer) (de), second(s)
  (hand)
secreta'resse (de), (female)
  secretary
secretari'aat (het), secretariate
secre'taris (de), secretary
sectie (de), section; incision,
  autopsy
secu'lair, secular
se'cuur, safe; accurate; certain
sedert, since, for
sein (het), signal

seinen, to signal, to wire

sei'zoen (het), season

sei'zoenkaart (de), season ticket

sei'zoenopruiming (de), (clearance) sale(s)

seks (de), sex

sekse (de), sex, gender

sek'sisme (het), sexism, male chauvinism

sek'sist (de), sexist, male chauvinist

sek'sistisch, sexist; like a sexist

seksuali'teit, sexuality

seksu'eel, sexual

sekte (de), sect

selderij (de), celery

se'naat (de), senate

se'niel, senile

sen'satie (de), sensation

sensatio'neel, sensational, spectacular

sensu'eel, sensual

sentimen'teel, sentimental

septisch, septic

serie (de), series, serial

seriemoordenaar (de), serial killer

seri'eus, serious

serieux: au – nemen, to take seriously

seroposi'tief, HIV-positive

ser'pent (het), serpent; shrew

serre (de), conservatory, sun parlour

ser'veren, to serve

ser'vet (het), napkin

servicebeurt (de), service

ser'vies (het), dinner service, tea set

sfeer (de), (atmo)sphere

sferisch, spherical

shag (de), (rolling) tobacco

sho'arma (de), doner kebab

schoenveter (de), shoelace

sidderen (voor), to quake (at the thought of)

sieraad (het), ornament, (piece of) jewellery

sieren, to adorn, to enhance

dat siert hem, that is to his credit

sierlijk, elegant

sierplant (de), ornamental plant

si'gaar (de), cigar

si'garenwinkel (de), tobacconist's (shop)

siga'ret (de), cigarette

si'gnaal, signal

signale'ment (het), (police) description

signa'leren, to see, to signal

sijpelen, to seep

sik (de), goatee

sikkel (de), sickle, crescent

simpel, simple, silly

simu'leren, to simulate

sinaasappel (de), orange

sinaasappelsap (de), orange juice

sinds('dien), (ever) since (then)

singel (de), (street on either side of a) town canal

sint (de), saint

Sinter'klaas (de), Santa Claus

sinterklaas'avond (de), St Nicholas' Eve (Dec. 5)

sip kijken, to look glum

Sire, your Majesty

si'rene (de), siren

si'roop (de), syrup

sissen, to hiss, to sizzle

sisser: met een – aflopen, to fizzle out, to blow over

sjaal (de), shawl

sjacheren, to run a shady business; to haggle

sjansen, to flirt, make eyes at someone

sjekkie (het), (hand-rolled) cigarette, roll-up

sjerp (de), sash

sjoelbak (de), shovelboard

sjofel, shabby

sjokken, to trudge

sjorren, to lash (up); to haul

sjouwen, to lug; to drudge

skeeleren, to rollerblade

ske'let (het), skeleton

skelterbaan (de), go-kart (race)track

skelteren, to go-kart

skiën, to ski

skileraar (de), ski instructor

sla (de), salad; lettuce

slaaf (de), slave

slaafs, slavish, servile

slaags raken, to come to blows

slaan, to hit, to strike, to beat, to smack

  dat slaat op mij, that applies to me

slaap (de), sleep; temple

  – hebben, to feel sleepy

slaapdronken, not fully awake

slaapje (het), nap; bedmate

slaapkop (de), sleepyhead

slaapliedje (het), lullaby

slaapver'wekkend, sleep-inducing, soporific; tedious

slaapwandelaar (de), sleepwalker

slaapwandelen, to walk in one's sleep

slaap'wekkend, soporific

slaapzaal (de), dormitory

slaatje (het), salad

slab (de), bib

slachten, to slaughter

slachting (de), slaughter

slachtoffer (het), victim

slag (de), blow, stroke, beat, crash; battle; knack; turn; kind

  een – om de arm houden, not to commit oneself

slagader (de), artery

slagbal (het), rounders

slagboom (de), boom, barrier

slagen, to succeed, to pass

slager('ij) (de), butcher('s) shop

slaghout (het), bat

slagregen (de), downpour

slagroom (de), (whipped) cream

slagtand (de), fang, tusk

slagwerk (het), striking mechanism; percussion (section)

slagzin (de), slogan

slak (de), snail, slug: slag

slaken, to utter, to heave

slakkengang (de), snail's pace

slakkenhuis (het), snailshell; cochlea

slang (de), snake, serpent; hose(pipe)

slangenbezweerder (de), snake charmer

slank, slim, slender

slaolie (de), salad oil

slap, slack, soft, flabby, weak; spineless

slape'loosheid (de), insomnia

slapen, to (be a)sleep

slaperig, sleepy

slapjanus (de), wimp, weed

slapjes, slack, weak

slappeling (de), weakling, wimp

slavenarbeid (de), slavery

slavendrijver (de), slave driver

slaver'nij (de), slavery, servitude

Slavisch, Slav(onic)

slecht, bad, poor

slechten, to level (out); to demolish; to settle

slechts, only

sle(d)e (de), sled(ge)

  een – van een wagen, a large luxury car

sleep (de), train, trail, tow

sleepboot (de), tug

sleepnet (het), dragnet

sleeptouw (het), towrope

slenteren, to saunter

slepen, to drag; to tow

slet (de), slut

sleuf (de), groove; slot

sleur (de), rut, humdrum routine

sleuren, to drag (on)

sleutel (de), key; clef

sleutelbeen (het), collar bone

sleutelbos (de), bunch of keys

sleutelen, to work (on), repair; to fiddle/tinker (with)

sleutelgat (het), keyhole

sleutelhanger (de), keyring

slier(t) (de), stream(er); winding trail

slijk (het), mire, slime

slijm (het), slime, phlegm, mucus

slijmvlies (het), mucous membrane

slijpen, to sharpen, to grind; to cut and polish

slij'tage (de), wear (and tear)

slijten, to wear out, to wear off; to spend, to retail

slijter (de), wine merchant, liquor dealer

slijte'rij (de), off-licence

slikken, to swallow

slim, clever, crafty; bad

slinger (de), festoon; pendulum; sling; (crank) handle

slingeren, to swing; to lurch; to wind; to lie about; to fling

slingerplant (de), creeper

slinken, to shrink (to nothing), to subside

slinks, sly, underhand

slipgevaar! beware of skidding!

slip'over (de), pullover

slippen, to slip, to skid

slippertje: een – maken, to have a bit on the side

slissen, to lisp

sloddervos (de), slob

sloep (de), (ship's) boat, (naval) barge

sloerie (de), slut

slof (de), slipper; briquette; carton

  het op zijn sloffen doen, to take things easy

sloffen, to shuffle

slok (de), gulp, draught

slokdarm (de), gullet

slokje (het), sip, drop

slokken, to guzzle

slons (de), slattern, frump

sloom, languid

sloop (de), demolition; scrapyard (cars)

sloop (het), pillowcase

sloot (de), ditch

slopen, to demolish, to break up

sloppenwijk (de), slums, slum area

slordig, untidy, slipshod

slot (het), lock; castle; conclusion

  ten slotte, finally

  per – van rekening, when all is said and done

slotscène (de), final scene

slotsom (de), conclusion; upshot

sluier (de), veil
sluimeren, to slumber
sluipen, to steal, to creep
sluis (de), lock; floodgate
sluisdeur, lockgate
sluiten, to shut (up), to close (down), to lock (up); to conclude; to fit
sluiting (de), closing (down); fastening
slungel (de), beanpole; oaf
slurf (de), trunk, proboscis
slurpen, to sip noisily, to gulp
sluw, sly, wily
smaad (de), libel
smaak (de), taste, flavour; relish; palate
in de – vallen, to be popular, to be to a person's liking
smaakvol, in good taste
smachten, to pine (away)
smak (de), thud
smakelijk, toothsome
– eten! enjoy your meal!
smakeloos, tasteless; in bad taste
smaken (naar), to taste (of)
smakken, to fall with a thud; to fling; to smack (one's lips)
smal, narrow
smaragd (de), emerald
smart (de), grief, anguish
smartelijk, grievous
smartlap (de), tear jerker
smeden, to forge; to plan
smede'rij (de), smithy, forge
smeedijzer (het), wrought iron
smeer (de), grease
smeerkaas (de), cheese spread
smeermiddel (het), lubricant
smeerolie (de), lubricating oil
smeerpoets (de), dirty tyke
smeerworst (de), pâté

smeken, to implore, to beseech
smelten, to (s)melt, to fuse
smeltkroes (de), crucible
smeren, to spread; to grease, to lubricate
'm –, to beat it
smerig, filthy, shabby
smeris (de), cop(per)
smetteloos, spotless, blameless
smeuïg, smooth, creamy; vivid
smeulen, to smoulder
smid (de), blacksmith
smidse (de), forge
smiezen: ik heb het in de –, I've got it taped
smijten (met), to chuck; to throw (about)
smoesje (het), excuse
smoezelig, soiled
smoezen, to whisper together
smoking (de), dinner jacket
smokkelaar (de), smuggler
smokkelen, to smuggle; to cheat
smokkelwaar (de), contraband
smoor: de – hebben, to be utterly fed up
smoor'heet, sweltering
smoorver'liefd, madly in love, smitten
smoren, to strangle, to stifle
smullen, to tuck in
snaar (de), string, chord
snakken naar, to yearn for, to gasp for
snappen, to get, to understand
ik snap 'm, I get it
hij snapt het niet, he doesn't get it
ik snap er niets van, I don't get it at all
snateren, to quack, to cackle
snauwen, to snarl
snavel (de), beak, bill

sne(d)e (de), cut; slice

sneeuw (de), snow

sneeuwbal (de), snowball

sneeuwen, to snow

sneeuwklokje (het), snowdrop

sneeuwpop (het), snowman

snel, quick, fast

snelheid (de), speed

snellen, to hurry

sneltrein (de), express train, intercity (train)

snelweg (de), motorway, freeway

snerpend, biting, piercing

snert (de), pea soup; trash(y)

sneu, rotten (luck)

sneuvelen, to be killed (in action)

snijboon (de), French bean, string bean

rare –, strange fellow

snijden, to cut (in), to carve; to intersect

snijtand (de), incisor

snik (de), sob, gasp

niet goed –, not all there

snik'heet, sweltering

snikken, to sob

snipperdag (de), day off

snoeien, to prune, to lop, to clip

snoek (de), pike

snoep (de), sweets

snoepen, to eat sweets, to tuck in

snoepgoed (het), confectionery, sweets/candy

snoer (het), flex; string; line

snoeren: iemand de mond –, to shut a person up

snoet (de), snout; face

snoezig, sweet, dinky

snor (de), moustache

snorren, to roar, to drone, to hum

snotaap (de), brat

snotjongen (de), brat

snotneus (de), runny nose; little kid; brat

snowboarden, to go snowboarding

snuffelen, to sniff; to ferret (about)

snugger, bright, brainy

snuiste'rij (de), trinket

snuit (de), snout, trunk; (little) face

snuiten, to blow (one's nose); to snuff

snuiter (de), chap, fellow

snuiven, to (give a) sniff, to snort

snurken, to snore

soci'aal, social(ly); socially minded

socia'lisme (het), socialism

socië'teit (de), club(-house)

soep (de), soup

soepel, supple

soezen, to doze

software (de), software

sojasaus (de), soysauce

sok (de), sock

sol'daat (de), soldier

sol'deerbout (de), soldering iron

sol'deren, to solder

soli'dair, loyal, sympathetic; to show solidarity

solidari'teit (de), solidarity

so'lide, sound, substantial

so'list (de), soloist

sollici'tant (de), applicant

sollici'tatiebrief (de), letter of application

sollici'tatiegesprek (het), (job) interview

sollici'tatieprocedure (de), selection procedure

sollici'teren, to apply (for a job)
solocarrière (de), solo career
som (de), sum
somber, gloomy, sombre
sommige(n), some
soms, sometimes; perhaps
so'nate (de), sonata
soort (de), brand, species
soort (het), sort, type, kind
soortge'lijk, similar
soos (de), club
sop (het), broth; (soap) suds
  het ruime –, the sea
soppen, to sop, to steep
so'praan (de), soprano, treble
sor'teren, to (as)sort, to grade
sor'tering (de), assortment
soulmuziek (de), soul music
sou'peren, to sup
souter'rain (het), basement
souvereini'teit (de), sovereignty
spaak (de), spoke, rung
  – lopen, to come to grief
Spaans, Spanish
spaarbank (de), savings bank
spaargeld (het), savings
spaarlamp (de), low-energy light
  bulb
spaarpot (de), money box
spaarvarken (het), piggy bank
spaarzaam, sparing, thrifty
spade (de), spade
spalk (de), splint
spalken, to put in splints
span (het), span; team, yoke
spandoek (de, het), banner
Spanje, Spain
spannen, to stretch, to strain
  het zal er om –, it will be
  touch and go
spannend, tense, thrilling
spanning (de), tension; span

spanwijdte (de), span
spar (de), spruce (tree)
sparen, to save (up); to spare
spartelen, to sport, to splash, to
  kick
spatader (de), varicose vein
spatbord (het), mudguard
spatie (de), space (word
  processing)
spatiebalk (de), space bar
spatten, to splash, to spatter
spece'rij (de), spice
specht (de), woodpecker
speci'aal, special
speciali'satie (de), specialization
speciali'seren: zich – (in), to
  specialize (in)
specia'lisme (het), specialism
specia'list (de), specialist;
  (hospital) consultant
specie (de), mortar
specifi'ceren, to specify
speci'fiek, specific
specu'laas (de), a kind of ginger
  biscuit
specu'leren, to speculate
speeksel (het), saliva
speelautomaat (de), slot
  machine
speelbal (de), cue ball; plaything
speelgoed (het), toy(s)
speelgoedafdeling (de), toy
  department
speelplaats (de), playground
speels, playful
speeltuin, playground
speen (de), teat, dummy
speer (de), spear, javelin
spek (het), bacon, fat pork;
  blubber
spekken: zijn beurs –, to line
  one's purse
spek'takel (het), spectacle

spel (het), game; pack, hand (of cards), play(ing), acting
  op het – staan, to be at stake
spelbreker (de), spoilsport
speld (de), pin
spelen, to play, to act; to chime
speler (de), player, musician, actor
spelfout (de), spelling mistake
speling (de), (free) play; scope
spellen, to spell
spelletje (het), game
spelregel (de), rule (of the game): spelling rule
spen'deren, to spend
sperma (het), sperm
spermabank (de), sperm bank
spermadonor (de), sperm donor
sperzieboon (de), French bean
spett(er)en, to spatter
speuren, to search
speurhond (de), tracker dog
spiegel (de), mirror
spiegelbeeld (het), reflection; phantom
spiegelei (het), fried egg
spiegelen: zich – aan, to learn from
spiegel'glad, as smooth as glass; icy (roads)
spiegeling (de), reflection
spieken, to crib
spier (de), muscle
spierbal (de), muscle
spierkracht (de), muscular strength, muscle (power)
spier'naakt, stark naked
spierpijn (de), aching/sore muscles, muscular pain
spier'wit, white as a sheet
spies (de), spear, pen
spijbelen, to play truant
spijker (de), nail

spijkers met koppen slaan, to get down to business
spijkers op laag water zoeken, to make a song and dance about nothing; to quibble
spijkerbroek (de), (pair of) jeans
spijkerjasje (het), denim jacket
spijkerstof (de), denim
spijl (de), bar, spike
spijskaart (de), menu
spijsvertering (de), digestion
spijt (de), regret
  daar krijg je – van, you'll regret that
  het – me, I'm sorry
spijtig: het is –, it is a pity
spiksplinter'nieuw, brand new, gleaming new, spanking new
spil (de), pivot, axis; capstan
spilziek (de), spendthrift
spin (de), spider
spi'nazie (de), spinach
spinnen, to spin; to purr
spinnenweb (het), cobweb; spider's web
spinnewiel (het), spinning wheel
spinrag (het), cobweb
spi'on (de), spy
spio'neren, to spy
spi'raal (de), spiral; woven bedspring
spiritus (de), methylated spirits
spit (het), spit; lumbago
spits, point(ed), sharp: peak
  spitse toren (de), steeple, pinnacle
  op de – drijven, to bring to a head
spitsuur (het), rush hour, peak hour
spits'vondig, smart, sophisticated
spitten, to dig

spleet (de), slit, split
splijten, to split, to cleave
splinter (de), splinter
splinter'nieuw, brand new
split (de), slit, placket
splitsen, to split (up), to fork
splitsing (de), split(ting up), fork, fission
spoed (de), haste
spoedcursus (de), crash course, intensive course
spoedgeval (het), emergency case
spoedig, soon, speedy
spoelen, to rinse, to wash
spoken, to haunt; to be astir
spons (de), sponge
spon'taan, spontaneous
spook (het), ghost; freak, bogey
spookhuis (het), haunted house
spoor (het), platform (at railway station)
spoorbaan (de), railway
spoorboekje (het), (railway) timetable
spoorboom (de), level-crossing barrier
spoorlijn (de), railway (line)
spoorloos, without a trace
spoorverbinding (de), railway communication; connection
spoorweg (de), railway
spoorwegovergang (de), level crossing
spo'radisch, sporadic
sport (de), sport
sportbroekje (het), shorts
sportclub (de), sports club
sporten, to do/play sports
sporter (de), sportsman
spor'tief, sports, sporty; sports-loving; sportsmanlike, be sporting

sporttas (de), sports bag
spot, mockery
spotgoedkoop, dirt-cheap
spotprent (de), caricature, cartoon
spotten (met), to mock; to defy
spraak (de), speech
spraakgebrek (het), speech defect
spraakgebruik (het), usage
spraakzaam, talkative
sprake (de), talk, question
ter –, up for discussion
sprakeloos, speechless
sprankelen, to sparkle
spreekbeurt (de), talk, lecturing engagement
spreekbuis (de), mouthpiece
spreekkamer (de), consulting room
spreektaal (de), conversation(al) language
spreekuur (het), office hours, surgery (hours)
spreek'vaardigheid (de), fluency, speaking ability
spreekwoord (het), proverb
spreek'woordelijk, proverbial
spreeuw (de), starling
sprei (de), bedspread
spreken, to speak (to), to mention
het spreekt vanzelf, it stands to reason
sprekend, striking, telling
spreker (de), speaker
sprenkelen, to sprinkle
spreuk (de), motto, maxim
spriet (de), blade (of grass); antenna
springen, to jump; to snap, to burst, to become insolvent
ik zit erom te –, I just can't wait for it

spring'levend, very much alive

springplank (de), springboard

springstof (de), explosive

springtij (het), spring tide

springtouw (het), skipping rope

sprinkhaan (de), locust, grasshopper

sprint (de), sprint

sprinten, to sprint

sproeien, to sprinkle, to spray

sproet (de), freckle

sprokkelen, to gather (wood)

sprong (de), jump, leap, bound

sprookje (het), fairytale

sprookjesachtig, make-believe, dream-like

spruit (de), sprout; offspring

spruiten, to sprout; to spring

spruitjes (de), Brussel sprouts

spugen, to spit

spuien, to sluice; to vent(ilate)

spuigaten: dat loopt de – uit, that's going too far

spuit (de), syringe; needle; shot

spuiten, to gush, to spray, to squirt, to inject

spul (het), stuff; trouble

　spullen (de), bits and pieces; togs

sputteren, to sputter

spuug (het), spit

squashbaan (de), squash court

squashen, to play squash

staaf (de), bar, rod

staal (het), steel; sample, piece

staal(draad)kabel (de), steel-wire rope

staan, to stand, to be; to suit

　laat –, leave alone; let alone

　erop –, to insist on it

　hoe staat hij ervoor? how is he doing?

　zich staande houden, to keep

on one's feet; to hold one's own

　op staande voet, then and there

staanplaats (de), standing room; terrace (football)

staar (de), cataract

staart (de), tail; pigtail

staat (de), state; rank; list

　in – zijn, to be able

staatsgreep (de), *coup d'état*

staatshoofd (het), head of state

staatsman (de), statesman

staatsrecht (het), constitutional law

staatsschuld (de), national debt

staatssecretaris (de), state secretary

sta'biel, stable

stad (de), town, city

stad'huis (het), town hall, city hall

stadion (het), stadium

stadium (het), stage, phase

stadslichten, sidelights

stadsmens (de), city dweller, townsman

stadsschouwburg (de), municipal theatre

staf (de), staff; mace, crosier

stage (de), work placement; teaching practice

stageplaats (de), trainee post

stagi'air(e) (de), student on work placement, student teacher

stag'neren, to stagnate

sta-in-de-weg (de), obstacle

staken, to stop, to strike

staking (de), stoppage, suspension, strike

stakker(d) (de), poor devil, poor thing

stal (de), stable, cowshed, stall

stallen, to stable, to put away

stalling (de), garage; shelter

stam (de), stem, trunk; tribe, race

stamboom (de), family tree

stamcafé (het), favourite pub/bar; local; hangout

stamelen, to stammer

stamgast (de), regular (customer)

stammen, to hail, to date

stampen, to pound, to mash; to stamp, to drum; to pitch

stamper (de), pestle, (potato) masher; pistil

stamppot (de), mashed potatoes and cabbage, hotchpotch

stampvoeten, to stamp (one's foot)

stamp'vol, packed

stamvader (de), ancestor

stand (de), position, attitude; score; class, order, state
  tot – komen, to come into being

standaard, standard; stand

standbeeld, statue

standhouden (het), to hold (one's own)

standje (het), position, posture; rebuke
  iemand een – geven, to tell someone off

standplaats (de), stand, pitch, (taxi) rank; post, living

standpunt (het), point of view

stand'vastig, steadfast

stang (de), bar, rod, stave; crossbar
  op – jagen, to bait, to needle

stank (de), stench

stap (de), step, pace; move
  op –, on (our) way

stapel (de), pile, heap
  hard van – lopen, to go too fast

stapelen, to stack, to heap

stapel('gek), mad, crazy

stappen, to step, to get

stapvoets, at a walking pace

star, fixed, rigid

staren, to stare, to gaze

startbaan (de), runway

starten, to start

Statenbijbel (de), Authorized Version (of the Dutch Bible)

Staten-Gene'raal (de), States General, the Upper and Lower Chambers

sta'tief (het), tripod, stand

statiegeld (het), refundable deposit (on glass bottles)

statig, stately, majestic

sta'tion (het), station

stati'onshal (de), station concourse

statis'tiek (de), statistics

sta'tuut (het), statute, regulation

stedelijk, urban, municipal

stedeling (de), townsman/woman

steeds, ever, still; town(ish)

steeg (de), alley, lane

steek (de), stitch, sting, stab, dig
  in de – laten, to leave in the lurch; to abandon

steekproef (de), sample taken at random

steekvlam (de), (burst of) flame

steel (de), stem, stalk; handle

steelpan (de), saucepan

steen (de), stone

steenbok (de), ibex; Capricorn

steengroeve (de), quarry

steenhouwer (de), stonemason

steenkool (de), coal

steenpuist (de), boil

steentijd (de), stone age

steentje (het), stone, pebble
  een – bijdragen, to do one's (little) bit

steevast, regularly

steiger (de), landing stage; scaffolding

steigeren, to rear

steil, steep, sheer

stek (de), cutting

stekel (de), prickle, spine

stekelig, prickly

stekelvarken (het), porcupine

steken, to sting, to stab, to smart; to stick
  van wal –, to push off, start

stekker (de), plug (top)

stel (het), set; couple

stelen, to steal

stellen, to put; to adjust; to suppose; to manage

stellig, definite

stelling (de), proposition, thesis; position; scaffolding

stelpen, to staunch

stelsel (het), system

stelsel'matig, systematic

stelten (de), stilts
  op – zetten, to raise hell

stem (de), voice, part; vote

stembanden, vocal chords

stembiljet (het), voting paper

stembureau (het), polling station

stembus (de), ballot box

stemge'rechtigd, entitled to vote

stem'hebbend, voiced; entitled to vote

stemloos, voiceless

stemmen, to vote; to tune (up)

stemmig, demure, sober

stemming (de), mood, atmosphere: vote

stempel (de, het), (post)mark; stigma

stempelen, to stamp, to (post-hall-) mark

stemrecht (het), right to vote

stemvork (de), tuning fork

stengel (de), stalk, stem

stenigen, to stone (to death)

steno(gra'fie) (de), shorthand

step (de), scooter

ster (de), star

stereo (de), stereo; hi-fi system, music centre

stero'tiep, stereotype(d)

stereotoren (de), hi-fi system, music centre

stereo'type (de), stereotype

sterfbed (het), deathbed

sterfelijk, mortal

sterfgeval (het), death

sterftecijfer (het), mortality rate

ste'riel, sterile

sterk, strong; extraordinary; greatly
  – verhaal, tall story

sterken, to strengthen; to comfort

sterkte, strength; all the best!

sterrenkijker (de), telescope

sterrenbeeld (het), constellation

sterrenwacht (de), observatory

sterretje (het), star, asterisk

sterveling (de), mortal

sterven (aan), to die (from)

steun (de), support

steunen, to support, to lean; to groan

steunpilaar (de), pillar, mainstay

steuntrekken, to be on the dole

stevig, firm, substantial, sturdy

stichten, to found, to establish; to edify

stichting (de), foundation, institution; edification

stief(moeder) (de), step(mother)

stiekem, on the quiet

stier (de), bull, Taurus

stierlijk: zich – vervelen, to be bored stiff

stift (de), stylo, pin, pencil (lead)

stifttand (de), crowned tooth

stijf, stiff, starchy

stijfjes, stiff, formal

stijfkop (de), pig-headed person

stijgen, to rise; to (dis)mount

stijl (de), style

stijldansen (het), ballroom dancing

stik'donker (het), pitch dark(ness)

stikken, to stifle, to suffocate; to stitch

stikstof (de), nitrogen

stil, silent, quiet; still

stilhouden, to stop; to keep quiet

stilleggen, to stop

stillen, to quiet(en), to alleviate

stilletjes, quietly, stealthily

stilliggen, to lie still, to lie idle

stilstaan, to stand still; to pull up
– **bij**, to give (some) thought to

stilstaand, stationary, stagnant

stilstand (de), standstill

stilte (de), silence
in –, quietly, privately

stilzwijgen (het), silence

stil'zwijgend, tacit

stimu'lans (de), stimulant, stimulus

stimu'leren, to stimulate

stinkdier (het), skunk

stinken, to stink

stip(pel) (de), dot, speck

stippellijn (de), dotted line

stipt, punctual, prompt; strict

stiptheidsactie (de), work-to-rule, go-slow, slow-down (strike)

stoeien, to romp

stoel (de), chair

stoelendans (de), musical chairs

stoelgang (de), (bowel) movement

stoep (de), front doorstep(s); pavement, kerb

stoer, sturdy, tough

stoet (de), procession

stof (de), material, (subject) matter

stof (het), dust
– **afnemen**, to dust
lang van –, long-winded

stofdoek (de), duster

stoffelijk, material, mortal

stoffen, to dust

stoffer (de), brush

stof'feren, to upholster

stoffig, dusty

stofje (het), speck of dust; bit of material

stofwisseling, metabolism

stofzuiger (de), vacuum cleaner

stoï'cijns, stoical

stok (de), stick; perch, roost; truncheon

stok'doof, stone deaf

stoken, to burn, to keep a fire going, to distil; to stir up

stokje (het), stick, baton
er een – voor steken, to put a stop to something

stok'oud, ancient

stokpaard (het), hobby (horse)

stok'stijf, rigid

stollen, to congeal

stom, dumb, mute, speechless; stupid

stomen, to steam, to smoke; to dry clean; to cram
stome'rij (de), dry cleaners
stommelen, to clump (about)
stommeling (de), idiot, fool
stommerik (de), idiot, fool
stommi'teit (de), stupidity, blunder
stomp (de), blunt, obtuse: stump: punch, dig
stompen, to punch, to jab
stomp'zinnig, obtuse
stomverbaasd, stupefied
stomvervelend, deadly dull
stoom (de), steam
stoomboot (de), steamboat
stoomcursus (de), crash course, intensive course
stoot (de), punch, thrust, stab, blow, gust; (vulg) sexually attractive woman
stoornis (de), disturbance
stop (de), plug, stopper; fuse
stopcontact (het), (wall) socket
stoppel (de), stubble
stoppen, to stop (up); to put; to fill; to darn; to constipate
stoptrein (de), slow train
stopverf (de), putty
stopwoord (het), stopgap
stopzetten, to stop, to shut down
storen, to disturb, to interrupt
zich – aan, to bother about
storing (de), interference, failure, dislocation
storm (de), gale, storm
stormen, to storm, to blow a gale
stormlamp (de), hurricane lamp
stormloop (de), rush, stampede
stormvloed (de), gale-swept high water

stortbui (de), heavy shower
storten, to plunge, to dump, to shed; to pay in
stortregenen, to pour with rain
stortvloed (de), torrent
stoten, to bump, to knock, to butt
zich – aan, to take offence at
stotteren, to stammer
stout, naughty
stoven, to stew
straal (de), ray; radius; jet
straalaandrijving (de), jet propulsion
straalvliegtuig (het), jet plane
straat (de), street, road; straits
straat'arm, penniless
straatlantaarn (de), street lamp
straatweg (de), high road
straf (de), punishment, penalty
strafbaar, punishable
straffen, to punish
strafrecht (het), criminal law
strafschop (de), penalty kick
strafwet (de), criminal law
strak, tight, hard
strak(je)s, in a moment, soon
stralen, to shine, to beam
stralend, radiant
stram, stiff, rigid
strand (het), beach
stranden, to (be) strand(ed)
strandjutter (de), beachcomber
stra'teeg (de), strategist
stratenmaker (de), road worker, paviour
streber (de), careerist, (social) climber
streek (de), district, region; trick; stroke
van –, upset
streekroman (de), regional novel

streep (de), stripe, stroke, line
 er een – onder zetten, to call it
 a day
streepje (het), dash, hyphen
streepjescode (de), barcode
strekken, to stretch
strekking (de), purport
strelen, to stroke; to tickle
streng, severe, strict, strand,
 skein
stress (de), stress, strain
stressen, to be under strain, to
 be stressed
streven naar, to strive for
strijd (de), fight, struggle,
 conflict
strijden met, to fight (against),
 to go against
strijdig, contrary
strijdkrachten (de), military
 forces
strijd'lustig, bellicose,
 pugnacious
strijkbout (de), iron
strijken, to iron; to haul down;
 to stroke, to brush
strijkgoed (het), ironing
strijkijzer (het), iron
strijkinstrument (het), stringed
 instrument
strijkkwartet (het), string quartet
strijkplank (de), ironing board
strik (de), bow(tie); snare
strikken, to tie; to (en)snare
strikt, strict
strikvraag (de), trick question
stripboek (het), comic (book)
stripfiguur (de), comic (strip)
 character
stripheld (de), comic (strip) hero
strippenkaart (de), bus and tram
 card/ticket
stripverhaal (het), comic (strip)

stro (het), straw
stroef, stiff, harsh
stromen, to flow
stroming (de), current; trend
strompelen, to hobble
strooien, to strew, to sprinkle:
 straw
strook (de), strip; frill;
 counterfoil
stroom (de), stream, flood,
 current
stroom'af(waarts), downstream
stroomgebied (het), river basin
stroom'op(waarts), upstream
stroomversnelling (de), rapid(s)
stroop (de), syrup, treacle
strooplikken, to curry favour
strooptocht (de), marauding
 expedition
strop (de), noose; tough luck
stropdas (de), stock, tie
stropen, to skin, to strip; to
 poach, to pillage
stroper (de), poacher
strot (de), throat
strottenhoofd (het), larynx
struc'tuur (de), structure
struik (de), bush, shrub
struikelblok (het), stumbling block
struikelen, to stumble, to trip
 (up)
struisveer (de), ostrich feather
struisvogel (de), ostrich
stu'deerkamer (de), study
stu'dentenflat (de), (block of)
 student flats; hall of residence,
 student apartments
stu'dentenhaver (de), almonds
 and raisins
studenti'koos, undergraduate,
 varsity
stu'deren, to study, to read; to
 practise; to be at university

studie (de), study, studies

studiebeurs (de), grant

studieboek (het), textbook

studiefinanciering (de), student grant(s)

studiepunt (de), credit

studierichting (de), subject, course, discipline, branch of studies

stuff (de), dope, stuff; pot; grass, weed

stug, dour, gruff; tough

stuiptrekking (de), convulsion

stuitbeen (het), tailbone, coccyx

stuiten, to check; to bounce
  – op, to encounter
  tegen de borst –, to go against the grain

stuitend, offensive

stuiven, to blow dust about; to dash

stuiver (de), 5-cent coin (of guilder)

stuk (het), piece; play; document; broken, to pieces
  een – of vier, three or four
  aan één – door, without a break
  op geen stukken na, not by a long chalk
  klein van –, small
  iemand van zijn – brengen, to upset a person

stuka'door (de), plasterer

stukhakken, to chop up

stukslaan, to smash (to pieces)

stumper(d) (de), wretch

stuntelig, clumsy

stunten, to stunt

stuntprijs (de), very low price

sturen, to send; to steer

stutten, to prop (up)

stuur (het), handlebar(s), (steering) wheel, helm

stuurboord, starboard

stuurknuppel (de), control column

stuurman (de), mate; cox(swain)

stuwdam (de), (flood-control) dam, barrage

stuwen, to drive; to stow; to dam up

stuwkracht (de), driving force

subjec'tief, subjective, personal

su'bliem, sublime

sub'sidie (de), subsidy, aid, grant, allowance

subsidi'ëren, to subsidize, grant (an amount)

sub'stantie (de), substance

substitu'eren, to substitute

sub'tiel, subtle

sub'tropisch, subtropical

suc'ces (het), success

succes'sievelijk, successively

suc'cesvol, successful

suf, dopey, groggy

suffen, to day dream

suffer(d) (de), dope, fathead

sugge'reren, to suggest, to prompt

suiker (de), sugar

suikergoed (het), candy

suikerklontje (het), lump of sugar, sugar cube

suikeroom, (de), rich uncle

suikerpot (de), sugar bowl

suikerriet (het), sugar cane

suikerziekte (de), diabetes

suizen, to whisper, to murmur

sukkel (de), idiot, dope, twerp

sukkelaar (de), weakling; booby

sukkelen, to be in poor health; to plod

sul (de), nincompoop

summum (het), height

supermarkt (de), supermarket
super'sonisch, supersonic
supple'ment (het), supplement
sup'poost (de), attendant
sup'porter (de), supporter
surfen, to be surfing/ surfboarding; to surf (also on the internet)
surfer (de), surfer, windsurfer
surfplank (de), surfboard, sailboard
Suri'name, Surinam
Suri'namer (de), Surinamese
surro'gaat (het), substitute
surveil'leren, to supervise, to invigilate
sussen, to soothe; to salve
s.v.p. (s'il vous plaît), please
sweater (de), sweatshirt
sweatshirt (het), sweatshirt
symbo'liek (de), symbolism
sym'bool (het), symbol
symfo'nie (de), symphony
sympa'thiek, congenial, engaging
symp'toom (het), symptom
syno'niem, synonymous
syn'thetisch, synthetic
sys'teem (het), system
sys'teembeheerder (de), system manager

T

taak (de), task
taal (de), language
taal'kundige (de), linguist
taart (de), tart, *gâteau*
ta'bak (de), tobacco
  ergens – van hebben, to be fed up with something
ta'bel (de), table, index
ta'blet (de), tablet

tachtig, eighty
tachtiger (de), octogenarian; writer of the movement of 1880
tac'tiek (de), tactic(s)
tactloos, tactless
tafel (de), table
tafelblad, tabletop, tableleaf
tafeldekken, to lay the table
tafelen: lang –, to linger over a meal
tafelkleed (het), table cover
tafellaken (het), tablecloth
tafeltennissen, to play table tennis
tafeltennisser (de), table-tennis player
tafe'reel (het), scene
taille (de), waist(line)
tak (de), branch
takel (de), tackle, rigging
takelen, to rig (out); to hoist
takelwagen (de), breakdown lorry
tal (het), number
  een viertal, twaaftal, twintigtal etc., (about) four, a dozen, a score etc.
talenknobbel (de), gift for languages, linguistic talent
talenpracticum (het), language lab

talkpoeder (het), talcum powder
talloos, countless
talrijk, numerous
tam, tame(d), domestic(ated)
tamboe'rijn (de), tambourine
tamelijk, fair(ly), rather
tam'pon (de), tampon
tand (de), tooth, prong
  iemand aan de – voelen, to put a person through his paces

tandarts (de), dentist
tandem (de), tandem
tandenborstel (de), toothbrush
tandenstoker (de), toothpick
tandpasta (de), toothpaste
tandplak (de), (dental) plaque
tandsteen (de), tartar
tandvlees (het), gum(s)
tang (de), (pair of) tongs,
  forceps; witch
  **dat slaat als een – op een
  varken,** that is neither here
  nor there
tanken, to (re)fuel
tankschip (het), tanker
tante (de), aunt
tantième (het), bonus
tapdansen, to tap dance
tapdanser (de), tap dancer
ta'pijt (het), carpet
tapkast (de), bar
tappen, to tap; to crack
taps, tapering
ta'rief (het), tariff, terms, fare
tarten, to defy, to flout
tarwe (de), wheat
tas (de), (hand)bag, briefcase
tast: op de –, by feeling
tastbaar, tangible
tasten, to feel, to grope
tatoe'age (de), tattoo
tatoe'ëren, to tattoo
  zich laten –, to have oneself
  tattoed
t.a.v. (ten aanzien van), with
  regard to
t.a.v. (ter attentie van), (for the)
  attention (of)
tau'gé (de), beansprouts
taxa'teur (de), valuer
tax'eren, to value, to assess
t.b.v. (ten behoeve van), on
  behalf of

te, at, in; too; to
T-biljet (het), tax reclaim
  form
tech'niek (de), technique;
  technics
technisch, technical
te(d)er, tender, delicate
teef (de), bitch, vixen
teelbal (de), testicle
teelt (de), cultivation, culture,
  breeding
teen (de), toe
teer (de, het), tar (*see* **teder**)
tegel (de), tile
tege'lijk(ertijd), at the same time
tege'moet-, to … to meet
tege'moetkomend,
  accommodating
tegen, against; towards; at
  ik kan er niet –, I cannot
  stand it
tegen-, counter-
tegen'aan, against, into
tegendeel (het), contrary
tegengaan, to counter(act)
tegengesteld, opposite
tegengif (het), antidote
tegenhanger (de), counterpart
tegenhouden, to check, to hold
tegenkandidaat, opposing
  candidate
tegenkomen, to come across
tegenligger (de), oncoming
  vehicle or vessel
tegenlopen: het liep me tegen, I
  had bad luck
tegen'over, opposite (to), (as)
  against, towards
tegen'overgesteld, contrary
tegenpartij (de), opponent
tegenpool (de), antipole
tegenprestatie: als –, in return
tegenslag (de), setback

tegenspartelen, to struggle; to protest

tegenspeler (de), opponent; opposite number

tegenspoed (de), adversity

tegenspreken, to contradict

tegenstaan, to be repugnant to

tegenstand (de), resistance

tegenstander (de), adversary

tegenstelling (de), contrast

tegenstemmen, to vote against

tegenstribbelen, to struggle; to protest

tegen'strijdig, conflicting

tegenvallen, to be disappointing **het viel tegen,** it was worse than (or not what) I'd expected

tegenvaller (de), blow

tegenwerken, to oppose

tegenwind (de), headwind; opposition

tegen'woordig, present(-day), nowadays

tegen'woordigheid (de), presence

tegenzin (de), aversion **met –,** reluctantly

tegenzitten: alles zit me tegen, I'm up against it

te'goed (het), credit: owing

te'goedbon (de), credit note

te'huis (het), home

teil (de), (zinc, enamel) bowl or bath

te'keergaan, to rant (and rave)

teken (het), sign, token **in het – staan van,** to be overshadowed by

tekenaar (de), artist; draughtsman

tekenen, to draw; to sign

tekenfilm (de), cartoon

tekening (de), drawing, plan; marking(s)

te'kort (het), shortage, deficit, deficiency **te'kort doen,** to stint; to wrong

tekst (de), text, script, words

tekstverklaring (de), close reading

tekstverwerker (de), word processor

tel (de), count; second **in – zijn,** to be highly thought of

telebankieren (het), computerized banking

telecommunicatie (de), telecommunication

tele'foon (de), telephone

tele'foonaansluiting (de), (telephone) connection

tele'fooncel (de), telephone box/booth

tele'fooncentrale (de), telephone exchange

tele'foongids (de), telephone directory

tele'foonrekening (de), telephone bill

tele'foontje (het), (telephone) call

teleshoppen (het), teleshopping

te'leurstellen, to disappoint

te'leurstelling (de), disappointment

telg (de), offspring

telkenmale, telkens (weer), again and again, every time

tellen, to count, to total

telwoord (het), numeral

temmen, to tame

tempel (de), temple

tempera'mentvol, temperamental

tempera'tuur (de), temperature

temperen, to temper, to moderate

tempo (het), tempo, pace

ten'dens (de), tendency

teneinde, so that, in order to

tenger, slight, delicate

tenge'volge van, as a result of

te'nietdoen, to nullify, to vitiate

ten'minste, at least

tennis (het), tennis

tennisbaan (de), tennis court

tennishal (de), indoor tennis court(s)

tennissen, to play tennis

tennisser (de), tennis player

tent (de), tent, booth, joint

ten'tamen (het), preliminary examination

ten'toonstelling (de), exhibition, show

te'nue (het): (groot) –, (full) dress

ten'zij, unless

tepel (de), nipple, teat

ter'dege, thoroughly

te'recht, rightly

te'rechtbrengen, to make a job of

te'rechtkomen, to turn out all right; to turn up; to end up

te'rechtstaan, to stand trial

teren op, to live on

tergen, to provoke

tering (de), consumption, TB

ter'loops, incidental

term (de), term, expression

ter'mijn (de), term; instalment
op korte –, at short notice; short term

ter'nauwernood, scarcely

ter'neergeslagen, disheartened

terpen'tijn (de), turpentine

terpen'tine (de), white spirit

ter'ras (het), terrace

ter'rein (het), terrain, ground, field

ter'reur (de), terror

terrori'seren, to terrorize

terro'risme (het), terrorism

terro'rist (de), terrorist

terro'ristisch, terrorist(ic)

ter'stond, at once

te'rug, back

te'rugblik (de), retrospect(ion)

te'rugdenken aan, to recall (to mind)

te'rugfluiten, to call back

te'ruggeven, to give back, to return

te'rugkeer (de), return

te'rugkeren, to return, to turn back

te'rugkomen, to come back, to return

te'ruglopen, to walk back; to decline

te'rugnemen, to take back, to withdraw

te'rugreis (de), return journey, way back

te'rugroepen, to call back, to recall

te'rugslaan, to hit back, to repulse; to backfire

te'rugtraprem (de), back-pedal brake

te'rugtrekken, to draw back, to retract; to retreat
zich –, to retire

te'rugverdienen, to recover the costs on

ter'wijl, while; whereas

testa'ment (het), will, testament

testen, to test

teugel (de), rein

teugje (het), sip

teuten, to dawdle
te'veel, surplus
tevens, as well
tever'geefs, to no purpose
te'vreden, content(ed), satisfied
tex'tiel (de, het), textile
te'zamen, together
thans, at present
thea'traal, theatrical
thee (de), tea
theedoek (de), tea towel
theelepel (de), teaspoon
theelepeltje (het), teaspoon, teaspoonful
theeleut (de), inveterate tea drinker
theelichtje (het), (heated) tea pot stand
Theems (de), Thames
theemuts (de), teacosy
theeservies (het), tea set
theezeefje (het), tea strainer
thema (het), theme; exercise
theo'loog (de), theologian, theological student
theo'retisch, theoretical
theo'rie (de), theory
thera'pie (de), therapy, therapeutics
thermosfles (de), thermos (flask)
thermo'pane (de, het), double glazing
thuis, (at) home
thuisbankieren (het), home banking
thuisbezorgen, to deliver (to the house/door)
thuisbrengen, to take home; to place
thuisfront (het), home front
thuishoren, to belong
tien, ten

tiend(e), tenth
tien'delig, ten-piece, in ten parts; decimal
tien'tallig, decimal
tientje (het), ten-guilder note
tier(e)lan'tijntje (het), frill, furbelow
tieren, to thrive; to rage
tij (het), tide
tijd (de), time; tense
tijdelijk, temporary; temporal
tijdens, during
tijdgenoot (de), contemporary
tijdig, timely, in good time
tijdlang: een –, for some time
tijdopname (de), time exposure; timing
tijdperk (het), period
tijd'rovend, protractive
tijdsbestek (het), space of time
tijdschrift (het), periodical, magazine
tijdstip (het), epoch, moment
tijdsverloop (het), lapse of time
tijdvak (het), period
tijdverdrijf (het), pastime
tijdverspilling (de), waste of time
tijger (de), tiger
tijm (de), thyme
tik (de), tap, rap
tikje (het), gentle tap; touch, shade
tikken, to tap; to tick; to type
tillen, to raise, to lift
timmeren, to carpenter, to hammer
timmerman (de), carpenter
tingelen, to tinkle
tint (de), tint, shade
tintelen, to sparkle, to twinkle; to tingle
tip (de), tip, corner
tippelen, (prostitution) to be on the streets, to solicit

ti'ran (de), tyrant
tiranni'seren, to bully
titel (de), title, heading
titelrol (de), title role
tja, well
tjilpen, to chirp
tjok'vol, chock-full
tl-buis (de), strip light, neon light
tl-verlichting (de), neon light(ing)
tobben, to brood; to slave; to have a tough time
toch, still, for all that; surely, after all
  zeg het –! do tell me!
  waarom –? whatever for?
tocht (de), draught; trip, drive
tochten, to be draughty
tochtig, draughty
toe, to
  – maar!, – nou! go on!
  er slecht aan – zijn, to be in a bad way
  het is tot daar aan –, it is bad enough
toebrengen, to inflict on; to administer
toedekken, to cover up; to mulch
toedienen, to administer, to serve up
toeëigenen: zich –, to appropriate
toegaan: het gaat er raar toe, there are strange goings-on there
toegang (de), admission, entry
toegangsbewijs (het), ticket of admission
toe'gankelijk, accessible, open
toe'geeflijk, lenient
toegeven, to admit; to give way (to)

toegewijd, devoted
toegift (de), encore
toehoorders (de), audience, observers
toejuichen, to applaud; to welcome
toekennen, to confer on, to attach to
toekijken, to look on
toekomen, to come to(wards); to make ends meet; to be due to
toe'komend, future; due
toekomst (de), future
toelage (de), allowance
toelaten, to admit, to permit
toelatingsexamen (het), entrance examination
toelichten, to elucidate
toeloop (de), concourse, rush
toelopen, to run (up) to; to taper
toen, then; when
toenaam: met naam en –, in detail
toenadering (de), advance, approach
toename (de), increase
toenemen, to increase
toenmaals, at that time
toen'malig, then, of the day
toe'passelijk, applicable, appropriate
toepassen, to apply
toepassing: van –, applicable
toer (de), tour; feat; rev(olution); row (of knitting)
  een hele –, quite a job
toereiken, to hand (to)
toe'reikend, sufficient
toe'rekenbaar, responsible
toeren: gaan –, to go for a drive
toe'risme (het), tourism

toe'rist (de), tourist
toer'nooi (het), tournament
toe'schietelijk, responsive, obliging
toeschouwer (de), spectator, onlooker
toeschrijven, to attribute
toeslaan, to hit home, strike
toeslag (de), excess (fare); bonus
toespeling (de), allusion
toespraak (de), address
toespreken, to speak to, to address
toestaan, to allow, to grant
toestand (de), state of affairs, situation, position, condition
toestel (het), apparatus, machine
toestemmen (in), to consent (to)
toestemming (de), permission
toestoppen, to slip into (a person's) hand; to tuck in
toestromen, to pour (in)
toetakelen, to doll up; to knock about
toetasten, to help oneself
toeten: hij weet van – noch blazen, he doesn't know a thing (about it)
toeter (de), horn
toeteren, to hoot, to honk
toetje (het), pudding, second course
toetreden tot, to join
toets (de), key; test
toetsen, to test
toetsenbord (het), keyboard
toeval (het), accident; epileptic fit
toe'vallig, (by) chance
wat –! what a coincidence!
toevalstreffer (de), chance hit, stroke of luck

toevertrouwen, to (en)trust with
dat is hem wel toevertrouwd, you can leave that to him
toevlucht (de), recourse
toevoegen, to add
toevoer (de), supply
toewensen, to wish
toewijding (de), devotion
toewijzen, to allocate
toezeggen, to promise
toezicht (het), supervision
toezien, to look on; to take care (of)
tof, great, ok
toi'letreiniger (de), toilet cleaner
toi'letrol (de), toilet paper
toi'lettafel (de), dressing table
toi'lettas (de), toilet bag
toi'letverfrisser (de), toilet freshener
tokkelen, to pluck, to strum
tol, toll; top
tole'reren, to tolerate
tolk (de), interpreter; spokesman
tollen, to play with a top, to spin round
tolweg (de), toll road
to'maat (de), tomato
to'matenketchup (de), tomato ketchup
to'matenpuree (de), tomato purée
to'matensap (de), tomato juice
to'matensoep (de), tomato soup
tomeloos, unbridled
tom'poes (de), cream slice
ton (de), barrel; buoy; ton; 100,000 euros
ton'deuse (de), hair clippers
to'neel (het), stage; scene, theatre
to'neelgezelschap (het), theatre company
to'neelschool (de), school of dramatic art

to'neelschrijver (de), playwright

to'neelspeler (de), actor

to'neelstuk (het), play

tonen, to show

tong (de), tongue; sole

tongval (de), accent

tongzoen (de), French kiss

tooien, to adorn

toom (de), bridle

  in – houden, to keep in check

toon (de), tone; pitch

toonaan'gevend, leading

toonbaar, presentable

toonbank (de), counter

toonbeeld (het), model

toonladder (de), scale

toonsoort (de), key

toontje lager zingen, to come down (a) peg or two

toorts (de), torch

toost (de), toast

top, top, tip, peak

topatleet (de), top-class athlete

topconditie (de), top condition/form

topkwaliteit (de), top quality, (the) highest quality

topo'grafisch, topographical, ordnance

topprestatie (de), record/top performance

toppunt (het), summit, height; limit

tor (de), beetle

toren (de), tower

toren'hoog, towering

torenspits (de), spire

tornen, to unpick; to meddle

torpe'deren, to torpedo; to scotch

tor'pedojager (de), destroyer

torsen, to labour under (the weight of)

tossen, to toss

tot, till, (up) to; as

  – aan, as far as

  – op, to within; up till

to'taal, total, utter

totdat, until

tou'cheren, to touch (up)

tour'nee (de), tour

touw (het), rope, string

  op – zetten, to plan, start something

  ik kon er geen – aan vastknopen, I couldn't make head or tail of it

touwtje (het), piece of string

touwtjespringen, to skip

touwtrekken (het), tug-of-war

tovenaar (de), magician

toverachtig, magic, enchanting

toverdrank (de), magic potion

toveren, to work charms, to conjure (up)

traag, slow, sluggish

traan (de), tear; oil

trachten, to attempt, to try

tra'ditie (de), tradition

tra'gedie (de), tragedy

tra'giek (de), tragedy

tragisch, tragic

trainen, to train, to coach

trainer (de), trainer, coach

training (de), training, practice; workout

trainingspak (het), tracksuit, jogging suit

tra'ject (het), stretch, stage, line

trak'tatie (de), treat

trak'teren (op), to treat (to)

tralies (de), bars, grating

tram(halte) (de), tram (stop)

transfor'mator (de), transformer

tran'sistorradio (de), transistor radio

tran'sito(haven) (de), transit (port)

transpi'reren, to perspire

transplan'tatie (de), transplant(ation)

transplan'teren, to transplant

transpor'teren, to transport; to bring forward

transseksu'eel (de), transsexual

trant (de), style, manner

trap (de), kick; stairs; degree
  een hele –, quite a way (by bike)

trapgevel (de), step gable

trapje (het), step, stair

trapleuning (de), banisters

traploper (de), stair carpet

trappelen, to stamp
  ik sta te –, I'm raring to go

trappen, to kick; to tread; to pedal

trappenhuis (het), stairwell

trappers (de), pedals; brogues

trapsge'wijs, step by step

traves'tiet (de), transvestite

trechter (de), funnel, hopper

trede (de), step, stair

treden, to tread; to go, to come

treffen, to hit, to strike; to meet
  het (goed) –, to be lucky

treffend, striking, touching

treffer (de), good shot, hit

trein (de), train

treinongeval (het), train/railway accident

treinramp (de), train/railway disaster

treinreis (de), train journey

treinreiziger (de), rail(way) passenger

treintaxi (de), train taxi

treinverkeer (het), train/rail traffic

treiteren, to torment

trek (de), pull, draught; stroke; feature, trait; inclination, appetite; migration
  in –, in demand

trekken, to pull, to draw, to drag; to migrate, to trek

trekker (de), trigger; hiker

trekking (de), (lottery) draw

trekpleister (de), attraction

trektocht (de), hiking tour

treuren, to grieve

treurig, sad

treurspel (het), tragedy

treurwilg (de), weeping willow

treuzelen, to dawdle

triatlon (de), triathlon

tri'bune (de), platform, gallery, stand

trillen, to vibrate, to quiver

tri'omf (de), triumph

triom'fantelijk, triumphant

triom'feren, to triumph

triplex (de, het), three-ply

trippelen, to trip

troebel, turbid, cloudy

troef (de), trump(s)

troep (de), mess; crowd, troop, company

troepenmacht (de), military forces

troetelkind (het), spoiled child

troeven, to trump

trom (de), drum

trommel (de), tin, (bread)bin; drum

trommeldroger (de), tumble dryer

trommelen, to drum; to strum

trommelvlies (het), eardrum

trom'pet (de), trumpet

tronie (de), mug

troon (de), throne

troonrede (de), queen's/king's speech
troost (de), consolation
troosteloos, cheerless, dreary
troosten, to comfort
tropen (de), tropics
tros (de), cluster, bunch
trots (de), proud: pride
trot'seren, to brave, to face
trot'toir (het), pavement
trouw (de), faithfulness, loyalty
trouw-, marriage-, wedding-
trouwakte (de), marriage certificate
trouwen (met), to marry, to be married (to)
  zo zijn we niet getrouwd, that's not on
trouwens, for that matter
truc (de), trick, stunt
trui (de), jersey, sweater
T-shirt (het), T-shirt
Tsjech (de), Czech
Tsjechië, Czech Republic
tsjirpen, to chirp
tuimelen, to tumble, to topple over
tuin (de), garden
tuinboon (de), broad bean
tuinbouw (de), horticulture
tuinder (de), market gardener
tuinhuisje (het), summerhouse
tui'nieren, to garden
tuinkabouter (de), garden gnome
tuinman (de), gardener
tuinstoel (de), garden chair
tuit (de), spout
tuk op, keen on
tukje (het), snooze
tulband (de), turban; ring(cake)
tulp (de), tulip
tunnel (de), tunnel, subway

ture'luurs, dotty
turen, to peer, to pore over
turf (de), peat
Turk (de), Turk
Tur'kije, Turkey
Turks, Turkish
turnen, to do gymnastics
turner (de), (male) gymnast
turnster (de), (female) gymnast
tussen, between, among
  iemand er – nemen, to pull a person's leg
tussen'beide komen, to intervene
tussen'door, through
tussenhandel (de), middleman's trade
tussen'in: er –, in between
tussenkomst (de), intervention
tussenmuur (de), partition wall
tussenpersoon (de), middleman; go-between
tussenpoos (de), interval
tussenstand (de), score (so far), score at halftime
tussentijd (de), interim
tussentijdse verkiezing (de), by-election
tussenuur (het), free period
tussenvoegen, to insert
tussenwoning (de), terrace(d) house
tutoy'eren, to drop the formalities
tv-serie (de), TV series
twaalf, twelve
twaalf'uurtje (het), midday meal
twee, two
tweebaansweg (de), two-lane road; dual carriageway, divided highway
tweede, second
tweede'hands, second-hand

Tweede-'Kamerlid (het), member of the Lower House

tweede'rangs, second-rate

tweedracht (de), discord

tweegevecht (het), dual

tweeklank (de), diphthong

twee'ledig, twofold, dual

tweeling (de), (pair of) twin(s)

Tweelingen (de), Gemini

tweemaal, twice

twee-onder-een-'kapwoning (de), semi-detached house, (one side of a) duplex

tweepersoons, double

twee'slachtig, amphibious; ambiguous

tweesprong (de), fork; crossroads

twee'stemmig, two-part

tweestrijd (de), inner conflict

twee'talig, bilingual

tweeverdieners (de), couple with two incomes, double income family/couple

tweevoud (het), double, duplicate; binary, double

twee'zijdig, bilateral

tweezitsbank (de), two-seater sofa, settee for two people

twijfel(achtig) (de), doubt(ful)

twijfelen (aan), to doubt

twijg (de), twig

twintig, twenty

twist(en) (de), (to) quarrel

twistgesprek (het), dispute

twistpunt (het), vexed question

twistziek, quarrelsome

typefout (de), typing error, typo

ty'peren, to typify

ty'perend voor, typical of

tyfus, typhus (de), typhoid

typisch, typical; quaint

U

u, you

überhaupt, at all; anyway

ufo (de), UFO

ui (de), onion

uier (de), udder

uil (de), owl

uilskuiken (het), numbskull

uit, out (of), from; finished
  ergens op – zijn, be out for (bent on) something

uitbeelden, to depict, to render

uitbesteden, to put out to contract; to board out

uitblijven, to stay away; to fail to materialize

uitblinken, to excel

uitbouw (de), extension

uitbouwen, to build out, to add onto (a house); to develop, to expand

uitbraak (de), escape (from prison)

uitbraken, to vomit; to belch out

uitbrander (de), dressing-down

uitbreiden, to extend

uitbuiten, to exploit

uit'bundig, exuberant

uitdagen, to challenge

uitdelen, to distribute

uitdenken, to think up

uitdiepen, to deepen

uitdijen, to expand

uitdokteren, to work out, to figure out

uitdoen, to take off; to put out

uitdraaien, to turn out
  zich er –, to wriggle out of it
  op (ruzie) –, to end in (a quarrel)

uitdrage'rij (de), junk shop

uit'drukkelijk, express

uitdrukken, to express; to stub out

uitdrukking (de), expression

uitduiden, to point out

uit'eengaan, to separate

uit'eenlopend, divergent

uit'eenzetten, to state, to explain

uiteinde (het), extremity, tip, (far) end; end, close, end of the year

uit'eindelijk, ultimate

uiten, to utter, to express

uiten'treuren, on and on (and on)

uiter'aard, naturally

uiterlijk (het), outward appearance

uiterlijk, outward(ly), external, from the outside; at the latest, no later than

uitermate, exceedingly

uiterst, ut(ter)most, extreme

uiterste (het), extreme

uiterwaarden (de), water meadows

uitfoeteren, to blow up, to call names

uitgaan, to go out

uitgang (de), exit; ending

uitgangspunt (het), point of departure

uitgave (de), expense; publication, edition

uitgebreid, extensive

uitgehongerd, famished

uitgekookt, sly, shrewd

uitgelaten, elated

uitgemergeld, emaciated, exhausted

uitgeslapen, wide awake, (fully) rested

uitgestreken: met een – gezicht, without batting an eyelid

uitgeven, to spend; to issue; to publish

zich – voor, to pose as

uitgever (de), publisher

uitgezonderd, except (for)

uitgieren: het – van het lachen, to scream with laughter

uitgifte (de), issue

uitglijden, to slip

uitgommen, to rub out

uitgroeien, to (out)grow

uithalen, to turn out; to unpick; to be up to (tricks)

de kosten er –, to cover the costs

uithangbord (het), sign(board)

uithangen, to hang out; to act

uit'heems, foreign; outlandish

uithoek (de), out-of-the-way place

uithollen, to hollow out

uithoren, to wheedle information from

uithouden: het –, to stand (it)

uithoudingsvermogen (het), stamina, staying power, endurance

uithuw(elijk)en, to marry off

uiting (de), expression

uitje (het), jaunt; small onion

uitjouwen, to jeer (at)

uitkeren, to pay

uitkering (de), pay(ment), benefit

uitkienen, to figure (out)

uitkiezen, to select

uitkijk (de), view; lookout

uitkijken, to look out, to look forward; to be careful

uitkleden, to undress, to strip

uitknijpen, to squeeze out; to do a bunk; to peg out

uitkomen, to come out, to work out
  ervoor –, to state openly
uitkomst (de), result; remedy
uitkramen, to spout, to parade
uitlaat (de), exhaust (pipe), muffler; funnel
uitlaatgas (het), exhaust fumes/gases
uitlaatklep (de), outlet valve, exhaust valve, escape valve; outlet
uitlaatpijp (de), exhaust pipe (of a car)
uitlachen, to laugh at, to have a good laugh
uitlaten, to let out; leave off (wearing)
  zich –, to express an opinion
uitleentermijn (de), lending period
uitleg (de), explanation
uitleggen, to lay out; to explain; to let out
uitlenen, to lend (out), loan
uitleven: zich –, to live one's (own) life (to the full)
  uitgeleefd, decrepit
uitleveren, to deliver up
uitlezen, to finish (reading)
uitloggen, to log off/out
uitlokken, to invite
uitlopen, to run out; to sprout
  – op, to lead to
uitloper (de), runner; spur
uitmaken, to break off (a relationship), finish, terminate; to matter, to be of importance; determine, establish; call, brand
uitmesten, to clear out
uitmonden in, to discharge into; to end in

uitmoorden, to massacre
uit'munten, to excel
uitmuntend, excellent
uitnodigen, to invite
uitnodiging (de), invitation
uitoefenen, to exercise; to carry on, to hold
uitpakken, to unpack
uitpluizen, to go through with a fine toothcomb
uitpraten, to finish talking; to talk over; to hear someone out
  zich ergens –, to talk one's way out of something
uitpuilen, to bulge
uitputten, to exhaust
uitreiken, to distribute, to issue
uitrekenen, to calculate
uitroeien, to root out, to exterminate
uitroep (de), exclamation
uitroepen, to call (out), to exclaim; to proclaim
uitroepteken (het), exclamation mark
uitrusten, to rest; to equip
uitrusting (de), outfit, equipment
uitschakelen, to switch off, disconnect; eliminate
uitscheiden (met), to stop
uitschelden, to call names
uitschot (het), scum, dregs
uitslag (de), result; rash
uitslapen, to sleep long enough, to lie in; to sleep off
uitsloven: zich –, to slave away
uitsluiten, to exclude
  uitgesloten! out of the question!
uit'sluitend, exclusively
uitsmijter (de), bouncer; fried egg on bread and ham
uitsparen, to save

uitspatting (de), extravagance, excess

uitspelen, to finish (a game); to play (off)

uitspoken, to be up to (mischief)

uitspraak (de), pronunciation; verdict

uitspreiden, to spread (out)

uitspreken, to pronounce, to express; to finish speaking

uitstaan, to stick out, protrude; bear, endure, stand

ik kan hem niet –, I can't stand him

uitstallen, to display

uitstapje (het), outing

uitstappen, to alight, to get out

uitstek: bij –, pre-eminently

uitsteken, to put out, to stick out

uitstekend, protruding

uit'stekend, excellent

uitstel (het), postponement

uitstellen, to postpone

uitsterven, to die (out), to become extinct

uitstippelen, to work out (in detail)

uitstorten, to pour out

uitstralen, to radiate

uitstrekken, to stretch (out)

uitstrijkje (het), (cervical) smear, swab

uitstulping (de), bulge

uittocht (de), exodus

uittreden, to resign

uittrekken, to pull out; to take off; to march out

uittreksel (het), extract; summary

uitvaardigen, to issue

uitvaart (de), funeral/burial (service)

uitval (de), explosion; outburst; hair loss

uitvallen, to fall out; to turn out; to flare up; to make a sortie

uitvaren, to sail (out)

uitverkocht, sold out

uitverkoop (de), (clearance) sale

uitverkoren, chosen

uitvinden, to invent

uitvinding (de), invention

uitvissen, to fish out; to ferret out

uitvlucht (de), pretext

uitvoer (de), export(s)

ten – brengen, to put into effect

uit'voerbaar, practicable

uitvoeren, to export; to carry out, to perform

uit'voerig, detailed, fully

uitwaaien, to blow out, to be blown out; to get a breath of fresh air

uitwedstrijd (de), away match

uitweg (de), way out, escape, outlet

uitweiden, to digress

uit'wendig, external

uitwerken, to work out, to elaborate; to mature, to wear off

uitwerking (de), effect; elaboration

uitwerpselen (de), excrements

uitwijken, to move to one side; to flee the country

uitwijzen, to show; to decide; to expel

uitwisselen, to exchange

uitwisseling (de), exchange, to swap

uitwissen, to wipe out, to erase

uitzendbureau (het), temp(ing) agency, (temporary) employment agency

uitzenden, to send out; to broadcast

uitzendkracht (de), temp, temporary worker

uitzet (de), outfit; trousseau

uitzetten, to expand; to turn out; to set (out); to lower (boats)

uitzicht (het), view, prospect

uitzieken, to get over an illness

uitzien, to look out; to look forward to

uitzingen: het –, to hold out

uitzitten: zijn straf –, to serve one's sentence

uitzoeken, to pick out; to sort/figure out

uitzondering (de), exception

uitzuigen, to suck out; to bleed dry; to exploit

uk (de), nipper

una'niem, unanimous

unicum (het), unique specimen

unie (de), union

u'niek, unique

univer'seel, universal; sole

universi'tair, university

universi'teit (de), university

un'zippen, to unzip, decompress, unpack

urenlang, for hours

uur (het), hour; o'clock

uurloon (het), hourly wage, hourly pay

uurtarief (het), hourly rate

uurtje (het), hour
  de kleine uurtjes, the small hours

uurwerk (het), timepiece

uw, your

uwerzijds, for your part

V

vaag, vague

vaak, often

vaal, faded, sallow

vaandel (de), banner, flag

vaardig, skilful; ready

vaargeul (de), fairway, channel

vaart (de), speed; waterway
  (grote) –, (ocean-going) trade

vaartuig (het), vessel

vaarwater (het), fairway
  iemand in het – zitten, to thwart a person

vaar'wel (het), farewell

vaas (de), vase

vaat (de), washing-up, dishes

vaatdoek (de), dishcloth

vaatwasmachine (de), dishwasher

vaatwasser (de), dishwasher

vaca'ture (de), vacancy

vacci'neren, to vaccinate

vacht (de), pelt, coat

vader (de), father

vagina (de), vagina

vaderlander (de), patriot

vaderlands'lievend, patriotic

vaderlands, native, national

vaderschap (het), paternity, fatherhood

vadsig, fat, lazy

vagevuur (het), purgatory

vak (het), compartment, panel; subject, trade

va'kantie (de), holiday(s), vacation
  op/met – gaan, to go on holiday
  prettige –!, have a nice holiday!

va'kantiebestemming (de), holiday destination

va'kantiegeld (het), holiday pay

va'kantiewerk (het), holiday/summer job

vakbeweging (de), trade union

vakblad (het), trade journal

vakbond (de), (trade) union

vakbondsleider (de), (trade) union leader

vakgebied (het), field (of study)

vakje (het), pigeonhole

vakman (de), expert

vakterm (de), technical term

val (de), (down)fall; trap

valbrug (de), drawbridge

Valentijnsdag, St Valentine's Day

valhelm (de), (crash) helmet

valk(e'nier) (de), falcon(er)

valkuil (de), pitfall

val'lei (de), valley

vallen, to fall

  er valt niets aan te doen, nothing can be done about it

valluik (het), trapdoor

valreep: op de –, at the last moment

vals, false; vicious

  – spelen, to cheat; to play out of tune

valsheid in geschrifte (de), forgery

valstrik (de), trap

va'luta (de), currency

van, of; from

  – de week, this week

van'af, (as) from

van'avond, this evening

van'daag, today

van'daal (de), vandal

van'daan, from

van'daar, hence

  – dat, that is why

vanda'lisme (het), vandalism

van'door: er – (gaan), to be off

vangen, to catch

vangnet (het), safety net

vangrail (de), crash barrier

vangst (de), haul, catch

va'nille (de), vanilla

va'nilleijs (het), vanilla ice cream

va'nillevla (de), vanilla custard

van-, this (afternoon, morning)

van'nacht, last night, tonight

van'ouds (her), of old

van'waar, whence

van'wege, on account of

vanzelf'sprekend, self-evident, quite obvious

varen, to sail, to fare

  laten –, to give up, to drop

varen (de), fern

varia, miscellaneous (items)

vari'ëren, to vary

varië'teit (de), variety, diversity

varken (het), pig

varkensvlees (het), pork

vast, fixed, permanent, firm, regular, stock; solid; certainly

  maar –, in the meantime

vastbe'raden, resolute

vastbinden, to tie up (tight)

vaste'land (het), continent, mainland

vasten, to fast

vastenavond (de), Shrove Tuesday

vastentijd (de), Lent

vastgrijpen, to catch hold of

vasthouden, to hold (on to), to clutch; to detain

vast'houdend, tenacious; conservative

vastklampen: zich – aan, to cling to

vastleggen, to fix, to tie up; to record

vastlopen, to run aground; to jam; to bog down

vastmaken, to fasten
vastpakken, to seize, grab hold
vastraken, to run aground; to get jammed
vastroesten, to rust (solid); to get stuck (in one's ways)
vaststaan, to stand firm; to be definite
vaststellen, to fix, to establish
vastzetten, to fix (in position); to corner
vastzitten, to be stuck
 er aan –, to be entailed, to have to go through with something
vat (het), cask, vat, vessel; hold
vatbaar, susceptible
Vati'caan (het), Vatican
Vati'caanstad (de), Vatican City
vatten, to catch; to understand; to get
v.Chr (voor Christus), BC
vechten, to fight
vecht'lustig, pugnacious
vechtpartij (de), fight
vee (het), cattle
veearts (de), veterinary surgeon (cattle)
veeg (de), streak, smudge
veel, much, a good deal, many
veelal, often
veelbe'lovend, promising
veelbe'tekenend, significant, suggestive
veelbe'wogen, eventful
veel'eisend, exacting, demanding
veelom'vattend, comprehensive
veel'soortig, manifold
veelvoud (het), multiple
veelvraat (de), glutton
veel'vuldig, frequent; manifold
veel'zeggend, significant

veel'zijdig, many-sided, versatile
veen (het), peat(moor)
veer (de), feather; spring; **(het)**, ferry(boat)
veerkracht (de), resilience, elasticity
veer'krachtig, resilient
veertien, fourteen
veertig, forty
veertig'plusser (de), over-40
veestapel (de), livestock
veeteelt (de), stock breeding
vegen, to sweep, to brush, to wipe
vege'tariër (de), vegetarian
vege'tatie (de), vegetation
veilen, to auction
veilig(heid) (de), safe(ty)
veiligheidsagent (de), security officer
veiligheidsdienst (de), security forces
veiligheidsgordel (de), safety belt, seat belt
veiligheidshalve, for safety's sake
veiligheidsraad (de), security council
veiling (de), auction
veinzen, to feign, to sham
vel (het), skin, hide; sheet
 om uit je – te springen, enough to make you wild
veld (het), field
 het – ruimen, to make way
 uit het – geslagen, taken aback
veldfles (de), water bottle, flask
veldslag (de), battle
velen, many (people)
veler'lei, all kinds of
ve'nijn (het), venom
ve'nijnig, venomous
ven'noot (de), partner

ven'nootschap (de), partnership, company

venster (het), window

vensterbank (de), window sill

vent (de), chap

ven'tiel (het), valve

venti'latie (de), ventilation

venti'lator (de), fan, ventilator

venti'leren, to ventilate

ver, far, distant

ver'aangenamen, to make pleasant

ver'achtelijk, contemptible, contemptuous

ver'achten, to despise

ver'ademing (de), relief

veraf, far (away)

ver'afgoden, to idolize

ver'afschuwen, to detest

ver'anderen, to change, to alter

ver'andering (de), change, transformation

ver'anderlijk, changeable, variable, inconstant

verant'woordelijk, responsible

verant'woordelijkheid(sgevoel) (het), sense of responsibility

ver'antwoorden, to answer for; to justify

ver'antwoording (de), account; justification

ver'armen, to impoverish; to become poor

ver'band (het), connection; context; bandage, dressing; bond

ver'bannen, to exile

ver'bazen: zich –, to be astonished, to be amazed

ver'beelden, to represent
  zich –, to imagine, to fancy

ver'beelding (de), imagination, (self-)conceit

ver'bergen, to hide

ver'beteren, to improve; to correct

ver'bieden, to forbid, to prohibit

ver'bijsteren, to bewilder

verbijten: zich –, to clench one's teeth

ver'binden, to join, to connect
  zich – tot, to commit oneself to

ver'binding (de), connection, communication

ver'bindingsstreepje (het), hyphen

ver'bitterd, embittered

ver'bleken, to grow pale; to fade

ver'blijden, to cheer (up)

ver'blijf (het), stay; residence

ver'blijfskosten (de), hotel, living expenses

ver'blijven, to stay, to remain

ver'blinden, to blind, to dazzle

ver'bloemen, to disguise

ver'bluffend, staggering

ver'bod (het), prohibition, ban

ver'bolgen, incensed

ver'bond (het), alliance; covenant

ver'bouwen, to carry out alterations (to a building); to grow

verbouwe'reerd, flabbergasted

ver'branden, to burn (down); to be burnt (down, out, up), to tan

ver'breden, to widen

ver'breiden, to spread

ver'breken, to break (off), to cut (off)

ver'brijzelen, to shatter

ver'brokkelen, to crumble

ver'bruien: het bij iemand –, to get into a person's bad books

ver'bruik (het), consumption
ver'bruiken, to consume,
  to use up
ver'buigen, to bend, to buckle;
  to decline
ver'dacht, suspect(ed);
  suspicious
ver'dampen, to evaporate
ver'dedigen, to defend
ver'dediger (de), defender,
  council for the defence
ver'dediging (de), defence
ver'deeld, divided
ver'dekt, under cover
ver'delen, to divide (up)
ver'denken, to suspect
verder, further(more)
ver'dienen, to earn; to deserve
ver'diepen: zich – in, to become
  engrossed in
verdieping (de), floor, storey
ver'doemenis (de), damnation
ver'doen, to waste
ver'domd, damn(ed)
ver'dommen, to flatly refuse
ver'dorie! damn!
ver'dorren, to wither, to parch
ver'dorven, depraved
ver'doven, to deaden, to
  benumb, to stun, to give an
  anaesthetic; to deafen
ver'dovingsmiddel (het),
  anaesthetic, narcotic
ver'draagzaam, tolerant
ver'draaien, to distort, to twist
ver'drag (het), treaty
ver'dragen, to bear
ver'driet (het), grief; regrets
ver'drietig, pained, sad, sullen
ver'drijven, to drive off; to
  dispel; to while away
ver'dringen, to oust
  zich – om, to crowd round

ver'drinken, to be drowned; to
  drown; to squander on drink;
  to inundate
ver'drogen, to dry up
ver'drukking: in de – komen,
  to suffer
ver'dubbelen, to (re)double
ver'duidelijken, to elucidate,
  make clear
ver'duisteren, to eclipse, to
  black out; to embezzle
ver'dunnen, to thin, to dilute
ver'duren, to put up with
ver'dwaasd, vacant
ver'dwijnen, to disappear
vereen'voudigen, to simplify
vereen'zelvigen, to identify
ver'eeuwigen, to immortalize
ver'effenen, to settle
ver'eisen, to require
ver'eiste (de, het),
  requirement
veren, to (be) spring(y)
verend, springy, elastic
Verenigd 'Koninkrijk (het),
  United Kingdom
**Verenigde 'Staten (van Amerika)
  (de),** United States of America
ver'eniging (de), association,
  union
ver'eren, to honour
ver'ergeren, to deteriorate, to
  aggravate
verf (de), paint; dye
ver'fijnen, to refine
ver'filmen, to film
ver'flauwen, to flag, to fade
ver'foeien, to detest
ver'fomfaaien, to dishevel
ver'fraaien, to beautify
ver'frissen, to refresh; freshen up
verfroller (de), paint roller
ver'frommelen, to crumple up

ver'gaan, to perish, to decay, to go down

  hoe zal het ons –? what is in store for us?

ver'gaderen, to assemble

ver'gadering (de), meeting

ver'gallen, to embitter, to spoil

ver'gankelijk, transitory

vergapen: zich – aan, to gape at (in admiration)

ver'garen, to collect

ver'gassen, to vaporize; to gas

ver'geeflijk, pardonable

ver'geefs, (in) vain

ver'geetachtig, forgetful

ver'gelden, to repay, to pay for

ver'geldingsmaatregel (de), retaliatory measure

ver'gelen, to turn yellow

verge'lijken, to compare

verge'lijkend, comparative, competitive

verge'lijking (de), comparison, simile; equation

verge'makkelijken, to make easier

vergen, to make demands on, to require

verge'noegd, contented

ver'geten, to forget

ver'geven, to forgive

ver'gevensgezind, forgiving

vergevorderd, (far) advanced

verge'zellen, to accompany

verge'zocht, far-fetched

ver'giet (het), colander

ver'gieten, to shed

ver'gif(t) (het), poison

ver'giffenis (de), forgiveness

ver'giftig, poisonous

ver'giftigen, to poison

ver'gissen: zich –, to be mistaken, to make a mistake

ver'gissing (de), mistake, slip

ver'goeden, to compensate (for), to reimburse

ver'gooien, to throw away

  zich –, to throw oneself away; to play the wrong card

ver'grijp (het), offence, breach

ver'grijpen: zich – aan, to lay hold on

ver'grijzen, to age/get old (usually of a population)

ver'grijzing (de), ageing (usually of a population)

ver'grootglas (het), magnifying-glass

ver'groten, to enlarge, to increase, to magnify

ver'gruizen, to crush

ver'guizen, to vilify

ver'guld, gilt; delighted

ver'gulden, to gild

ver'gunnen, to permit

ver'gunning (de), permission, licence

ver'haal (het), story; redress

  op zijn – komen, to take it easy (for a bit)

ver'halen, to relate; to vent

  het – op, to take it out of

ver'handelen, to deal in; to discuss

ver'harden, to harden

ver'haren, to moult

ver'heerlijken, to glorify, to elate

ver'heffen, to lift (up), to raise, to exhalt

ver'helderen, to clarify

ver'helpen, to remedy

ver'hemelte (het), palate

ver'heugen, to delight

  zich –, to rejoice

  zich – op, to look forward to

ver'hinderen, to prevent, to hinder

ver'hitten, to heat

ver'hogen, to raise, to heighten

ver'hoging (de), increase; platform; temperature

ver'hongeren, to starve (to death)

ver'hoor (het), interrogation, hearing

ver'horen, to hear, to grant; to interrogate

ver'houding (de), relation(ship), proportion

ver'huisbedrijf (het), removal firm/company

ver'huisbericht (het), change of address card

ver'huizen, to move (house)

ver'huizing (de), move

ver'hullen, to conceal

ver'huren, to let

ver'huur (de), hire, hiring out

ver'huurder (de), landlord

verifi'ëren, to verify

ver'ijdelen, to frustrate

vering (de), springiness, springs; suspension (of cars)

ver'jaard, out of date

ver'jaardag (de), birthday

ver'jaardagscadeau (het), birthday present

ver'jaardagsfeest (het), birthday party

ver'jaardagskaart (de), birthday card

ver'jaardagskalender (de), birthday calendar

ver'jagen, to drive away

ver'kalken, to harden, to calcerate

ver'keer (het), traffic; intercourse

ver'keerd, wrong, misunderstood, etc.

ver'keersagent (de), traffic policeman

ver'keersbord (het), road sign, traffic sign

ver'keersdrempel (de), speed ramp

ver'keersheuvel (de), traffic island

ver'keerslicht (het), traffic lights

ver'keersongeval (het), traffic accident, road accident

ver'keersovertreding (de), traffic offence

ver'keersregel (de), traffic rule

ver'keerstoren (de), control tower

verkeers'veiligheid (de), road safety, traffic safety

ver'keersweg (de), thoroughfare

ver'kennen, to reconnoitre

ver'kenner (de), scout

ver'keren, to be, to move

ver'kering (de), courtship
– hebben, to go steady

ver'kiezen, to prefer; to elect, to chose

ver'kiezing (de), election; preference

ver'kiezingsprogramma (het), (electoral) platform

ver'kijken: zich – op, to make a mistake (with)
je kans is verkeken, you've missed your chance

ver'klappen, to let on (about)

ver'klaren, to explain; to declare, to certify

ver'klaring (de), explanation; declaration; certificate

ver'kleden: (zich) –, to change; dress up

ver'kleinen, to reduce, to cut down; to belittle

ver'kleinwoord (het), diminutive

ver'kleumen, to get numb with cold

ver'kleuren, to fade

ver'klikken, to give away, to spill the beans

ver'klikker (de), telltale

ver'kneukelen, ver'kneuteren:
  zich –, to gloat

ver'knippen, to cut up; to spoil by cutting wrongly

ver'knocht, devoted

ver'knoeien, to bungle; to waste

ver'kondigen, to proclaim

verkoop (de), sale(s)

verkoopdatum (de), date of sale
  uiterste –, sell-by date

ver'koopster (de), shop assistant (female)

ver'kopen, to sell

ver'korten, to shorten; to reduce

ver'kouden: – worden, to catch cold
  je bent –, you've got a cold

ver'koudheid (de), cold

ver'krachten, to violate, to rape

ver'kreuk(el)en, to crumple (up)

ver'krijgbaar, obtainable

ver'krijgen, to obtain

ver'kroppen, to swallow

ver'kropt, pent-up

ver'kruimelen, to crumble (away)

ver'kwisten, to waste, to dissipate

ver'lammen, to paralyse

ver'lamming (de), paralysis

ver'langen, to desire, to long; to require

ver'langlijst (de), list of gifts wanted

ver'laten, to leave, to desert: lonely, deserted
  zich – op, to rely on

ver'leden, last: **(het),** past

ver'legen, shy, embarrassed

ver'legenheid (de), shyness, embarrassment

ver'leggen, to shift, move

ver'leidelijk, tempting

ver'leiden, to tempt, to seduce

ver'lenen, to grant, to give

ver'lengen, to lengthen, to extend

ver'leppen, to wilt; to jade

ver'leren, to lose the art

ver'licht, lit (up); enlightened; relieved

ver'lichten, to light (up), to illuminate; to lighten; to alleviate

ver'liefd, in love, amorous

ver'liefdheid (de), being in love

ver'lies (het), loss

verlies'gevend, loss-making

ver'liezen, to lose

ver'lof (het), leave, permission; licence

ver'lokken, to entice

ver'loochenen, to deny, to belie

verloofde (de), *fiancé(e)*

ver'loop (het), course, (re)lapse

ver'lopen, to elapse; to go down(hill); to go (off): expired; down and out

ver'loren gaan, to get lost; to be wasted

verlos'kundige (de), midwife

ver'loten, to raffle

ver'loven, to get engaged

ver'loving (de), engagement

ver'lovingsring (de), engagement ring

ver'lummelen, to laze away

ver'maak (het), pleasure, amusement

ver'mageren, to reduce or lose weight

ver'mageringskuur (de), slimming course

ver'makelijk, amusing

ver'maken, to amuse; to alter; to bequeath

ver'meend, supposed

ver'meerderen, to increase

ver'melden, to mention, to record

ver'mengen, to mix, to mingle

vermenig'vuldigen, to multiply

ver'mijden, to avoid, to evade

vermil'joen (het), vermilion

ver'minderen, to reduce, to diminish

ver'minken, to maim, to mutilate

ver'mist, missing

ver'moedelijk, presumably, probably

ver'moeden, to presume; to suspect: **(het),** conjecture, suspicion

ver'moeid(heid) (de), tired(ness), fatigue(d)

ver'moeiend, tiring

ver'mogen (het), fortune; ability, capacity

ver'mogend, wealthy

ver'mogensbelasting (de), property tax

ver'mommen, to disguise

ver'moorden, to murder

ver'morzelen, to crush

ver'murwen, to mollify

ver'nauwen, to take in, to narrow

ver'nederen, to humble, to humiliate

ver'nemen, to learn, to hear

ver'nielen, to destroy, to wreck

ver'nielziek, verniel'zuchtig, destructive

ver'nietigen, to destroy; to annul, to reverse

ver'nieuwen, to renew

ver'noemen naar, to name after

ver'nuft (het), ingenuity, wit

veronder'stellen, to suppose, to assume

ver'ongelijkt, hurt, injured

ver'ongelukken, to be wrecked, to crash, to be killed

veront'reinigen, to pollute

veront'rusten, to alarm

veront'schuldigen, to excuse **zich –,** to apologize, to excuse oneself

veront'waardigd, indignant

veront'waardiging (de), indignation

ver'oordelen, to condemn, to convict

ver'oorloofd, allowed, permissible

ver'oorloven: zich –, to permit oneself, to take the liberty of; to afford

ver'oorzaken, to cause

ver'ordening (de), regulations, by-law

ver'ouderd, obsolete, aged

ver'overen, to conquer, to capture

ver'pakken, to pack, to wrap in paper

ver'pakking (de), packing, wrapping paper

ver'pakkingsmateriaal (het), packing material

ver'patsen, to flog

ver'pesten, to contaminate; to wreck

ver'plaatsen, to move, to transfer

  zich –, to imagine oneself

verpleeg'kundige (de), nurse

ver'pleegster (de), nurse (female)

ver'plegen, to nurse

ver'pleger (de), (male) nurse

ver'pletteren, to shatter

ver'plicht, obliged, indebted; compulsory

ver'plichten, to oblige; to compel

ver'plichting (de), obligation, commitment

ver'pozen: zich –, to relax

ver'praten: tijd –, to spend time talking

  zich verpraten, to let on

ver'prutsen, to muck up

ver'raad (het), treason

ver'raden, to betray

ver'rader (de), traitor

ver'raderlijk, treacherous, insidious

ver'rassen, to surprise

ver'rassing (de), surprise

ver'regend, washed out (by the rain)

ver'reikend, far-reaching

ver'rek, gosh, get away, get out of here

ver'rekenen, to settle

  zich –, to miscalculate

verrekijker (de), binoculars

ver'rekken, to sprain, to strain; to go to hell

verre'weg, by far

ver'richten, to carry out, to do

ver'rijken, to enrich

ver'rijzen, to (a)rise, to spring up

ver'roeren, to stir

ver'roest, rusty

ver'rotten, to rot

ver'ruimen, to broaden

ver'rukkelijk, delicious; gorgeous

ver'rukt, delighted

vers, fresh, new-(laid): **(het),** verse, poetry, poem

ver'schaffen, to provide

ver'scheiden, various, several

ver'scheidenheid (de), diversity

ver'schepen, to (tran)ship

ver'scherpen, to intensify

ver'scheuren, to tear (to pieces), to rend

ver'schieten, to use up; to turn pale, to fade

ver'schijnen, to appear

ver'schijning (de), appearance; figure

verschijnsel (het), phenomenon; symptom

verschil (het), difference

ver'schillen, to differ

ver'schillend, different

ver'schonen, to put on clean sheets or clothes; to excuse; to spare

ver'schrikkelijk, terrible

ver'schroeien, to scorch

ver'schrompelen, to shrivel (up)

ver'schuilen, to hide, to shelter

ver'schuiven, to shift

ver'schuildigd, indebted, due

versie (de), version

ver'sieren, to decorate; to pick up (someone), to get off (with someone)

ver'siering (de), decoration

ver'siersel (het), ornament

ver'sjouwen, to shift

ver'slaafd, addicted

ver'slaan, to beat, to defeat; to cover

ver'slag (het), report

ver'slagen, defeated; put out

ver'slaggever (de), reporter, commentator

ver'slapen: zich –, to oversleep

ver'slappen, to weaken, to flag

ver'slepen, to tow away, to shift

ver'slijten, to wear out; to while away

waar verslijt je me voor? what do you take me for?

ver'slikken: zich –, to choke

ver'slinden, to devour

ver'slingeren: zich – aan, to throw oneself away

ver'sloffen, ver'slonzen, to neglect

ver'smachten, to pine away

ver'smelten, to melt, to blend

ver'snapering (de), titbit, refreshment

ver'snellen, to accelerate

ver'snelling (de), acceleration; gear

ver'snellingsbak (de), gearbox

ver'snipperen, to cut up; to fritter away

ver'snoepen, to spend on sweets

ver'spelen, to throw away

ver'sperren, to block (up)

ver'spillen, to waste

ver'spilling (de), waste, wasting

ver'splinteren, to (break into) splinter(s)

ver'spreiden: (zich) –, to spread, to scatter

ver'spreken: zich –, to make a slip (of the tongue)

verspringen (het), long jump

ver'staan, to understand, to hear

ver'staanbaar, audible, intelligible

ver'stand (het), sense(s), mind; knowledge

met dien verstande, on the understanding

daar staat mijn – bij stil, it is beyond me

ver'standelijk, intellectual, rational

ver'standhouding (de), understanding, terms

ver'standig, sensible

ver'standskies (de), wisdom tooth

ver'stard, rigid

ver'steend, petrified; fossilized

ver'stekeling (de), stowaway

ver'stelbaar, adjustable

ver'steld, stunned

– staan, to be dumbfounded

ver'stellen, to adjust; to mend

ver'sterken, to fortify, to reinforce, to intensify; to amplify

ver'sterker (de), amplifier

ver'stevigen, to consolidate

ver'stijven, to stiffen; to grow numb

ver'stikken, to stifle

ver'stoord, disturbed; vexed

ver'stoppen, to block (up); to hide

ver'stoppertje spelen, play hide-and-seek

ver'storen, to disturb, to upset

ver'strekken, to issue

verstrekkend, far-reaching, sweeping

ver'strijken, to expire, to elapse

ver'strooid, scattered; absent-minded

verstrooien: zich –, to disperse; to find amusement

ver'stuiken, to sprain
ver'stuiven, to (be) blow(n) about
ver'suft, stupefied
ver'takken: zich –, to branch
ver'taalbureau (het), translation agency
ver'taalster (de), (female) translator
ver'talen, to translate
ver'taler (de), (male) translator
ver'taling (de), translation
verte (de), distance
ver'tederend, tender
ver'teerbaar, digestible
vertegen'woordigen, to represent
ver'tellen, to tell, to say
ver'telling (de), ver'telsel (het), story
ver'teren, to consume, to spend; to digest; to perish
ver'tikken, to jib, to refuse flatly
ver'tillen, to lift
  zich –, to strain oneself (lifting something)
ver'timmeren, to make alterations to
ver'tolken, to interpret
ver'tonen, to show, to produce
ver'toon (het), show, presentation
ver'tragen, to slow down; to delay
ver'traging (de), delay
ver'trappen, to trample under foot
ver'trek (het), room; departure
ver'trekhal (de), departure hall
ver'trekken, to leave; to distort
ver'trektijd (de), time of departure
ver'troebelen, to confuse

ver'troetelen, to pamper
ver'trouwd, trusty, safe; conversant
ver'trouwelijk, confidential; intimate
ver'trouwen, to (en)trust; to rely; **(het),** trust, confidence
ver'twijfeld, desperate
ver'twijfeling (de), desperation
veruit, by far
ver'vaardigen, to manufacture
ver'vagen, to fade
ver'val (het), decline; disrepair; fall
ver'vallen, to lapse, to be cancelled, to expire, to fall (due); to go to ruin
ver'valsen, to fake
ver'vangen, to replace
ver'velen: (zich) –, to (be) bore(d)
  tot vervelens toe, *ad nauseam*
ver'velend, boring; annoying
ver'veling (de), boredom
ver'vellen, to peel
verven, to paint; to dye
ver'versen, to refresh; to renew
ver'vliegen, to evaporate, to vanish
ver'vloeken, to curse
ver'voer (het), transport
ver'voeren, to transport
ver'voermiddel (het), (means) of transport
ver'volg (het), sequel, continuation; future
ver'volgen, to continue; to pursue; to persecute, to prosecute
ver'volgens, after that
ver'vreemden, to alienate, to grow estranged
ver'vroegen, to put forward

ver'vuilen, to get filthy
ver'vullen, to fill, to fulfil
ver'waaid, dishevelled
ver'waand, conceited
ver'waarlozen, to neglect
ver'wachten, to expect
ver'wachting (de), expectation
ver'want, related
ver'wanten (de), relatives
ver'wantschap (de), relationship, affinity
ver'warmen, to heat
ver'warren, to confuse, to (en)tangle
ver'warring (de), confusion, disorder
ver'wedden, to bet
ver'weerd, weather-beaten
ver'wekken, to arouse; to beget, to father
ver'welken, to wither, to wilt
ver'welkomen, to welcome
ver'wennen, to spoil
ver'wensen, to curse
ver'weren, to weather; to defend
ver'werken, to cope with; to work up
ver'werpen, to reject
ver'werven, to acquire
ver'wezenlijken, to realize
  zich –, to materialize
ver'wijderen, to remove, to turn out
  zich –, to withdraw
ver'wijfd, effeminate
ver'wijlen, to linger
ver'wijt(en) (het), (to) reproach
ver'wijzen, to refer
ver'wikkelen, to implicate, to complicate
ver'wikkeling (de), complication, plot

ver'wilderen, to run wild, to degenerate
ver'wisselen, to (ex)change
ver'wittigen, to notify
ver'woed, furious
ver'woesten, to devastate
ver'wonden, to injure, to wound
ver'wonderen: zich –, to be surprised
ver'wonen, to pay in rent
ver'zachten, to alleviate; to soften
ver'zadigen, to saturate; to satisfy
ver'zaken, to forsake
ver'zakken, to sag, to subside
ver'zamel-cd (de), compilation CD
ver'zamelen, to collect, to muster (up)
ver'zameling (de), collection
ver'zamelplaats (de), meeting place, assembly point
ver'zanden, to silt up; to get bogged down
ver'zegelen, to seal (up)
ver'zekeren, to assure, to insure; to secure
ver'zekering (de), assurance, insurance
ver'zekeringsmaatschappij (de), insurance company
ver'zekeringspremie (de), insurance premium
ver'zenden, to send (off)
ver'zet (het), resistance
ver'zetje (het), divergence
ver'zetten, to move; to get through; to get over
  zich –, to oppose, to resist
ver'zien: het – hebben op, to be out to get
verziend, long-sighted

ver'zilveren, to silver (plate); to convert into cash
ver'zinnen, to think (up)
ver'zitten, to move to another chair; to shift one's position
ver'zoek (het), request
ver'zoeken, to request; to tempt
ver'zoekschrift (het), petition
ver'zoenen, to reconcile
ver'zorgen, to take care of
ver'zot op, mad on
ver'zuchten, to sigh
ver'zuim (het), omission; non-attendance
   zonder –, without fail
ver'zuimen, to fail (in); to miss
ver'zuipen, to drown
ver'zuren, to (turn) sour
ver'zwakken, to weaken
ver'zwijgen voor, to keep from
ver'zwikken, to sprain
vest (het), waistcoat; cardigan
vestigen, to establish; to fix
   zich –, to settle
vesting (de), fortress
vet, fat; greasy; rich: **(het),** fat
   vet gedrukt, in heavy type
vetarm, low-fat
vete (de) feud
veter (de), (shoe)lace
vete'raan (de), veteran
vetgehalte (het), fat content
vetmesten, to fatten (up)
vetplant (de), succulent plant
vettigheid (de), richness, greasiness
vet'vrij, greaseproof
vetzak (de), fatty
vetzucht (de), obesity
veulen (het), foal
vezel (de), fibre
vgl. (vergelijk), cf.
V-hals (de), V-neck

via'duct (het), (railway) bridge, viaduct
vi'breren, to vibrate
video (de), video (tape, recorder)
videocamera (de), video camera
videocassette (de), video cassette
video-opname (de), video recording
videorecorder (de), video (recorder), VCR, video cassette recorder
video'theek (de), video shop
vief, lively
vier, four
   onder – ogen, in private
vierbaansweg (de), four-lane motorway, dual carriageway, divided highway
vierdelig, four-part, four-piece
vieren, to celebrate: to ease off
vierkant (het), square
vierkantswortel (de), square root
viervoud (het), quadruple
viervoudig, fourfold, quadruple
vies, dirty, filthy; wry
   ik ben er – van, it turns my stomach
viezerik (de), pig, slob
vijand (de), enemy
vij'andelijk, enemy('s)
vij'andig, hostile
vijf, five
vijftien, fifteen
vijftig, fifty
vijftiger (de), someone in his/her fifties
vijg (de), fig
vijl(en) (de), (to) file
vijver (de), pond
vijzel (de), mortar

villa (de), villa
villawijk (de), (exclusive) residential area
villen, to skin, to fleece
vin (de), fin
vinden, to find; to think; to get on
vindingrijk, inventive
vinger (de), finger
  door de vingers zien, to overlook
vingerafdruk (de), fingerprint
vingerhoed (de), thimble
vink (de), finch
vinnig, cutting, sharp
vio'list (de), violinist
vi'ool (de), violin; violet, pansy
virtu'oos (de), virtuoso
vis (de), fish
visboer (de), fishmonger
visgraat (de), fishbone
vishandelaar (de), fishmonger, fish dealer
visie (de), vision
visi'oen (het), vision
vismarkt (de), fish market
Vissen, Pisces
vissen, to fish, to angle; drag, dredge
vi'site (de), visit(or)(s)
visser (de), fisherman
vissersboot (de), fishing boat
visse'rij (de), fishing (industry)
visvangst (de), fishing
vi'taal, vital
vi'trage (de, het), (curtain) net
vi'trine (de), showcase
vitten op, to find fault with
vla (de), custard
vlaag (de), gust; fit
Vlaams, Flemish
Vlaamse (de), Flemish woman
Vlaanderen, Flanders

vlag (de), flag
vlaggen, to put out the flag(s)
vlak, flat, smooth; right, close; **(het),** (sur)face
vlakte (de), plain, stretch
vlam (de), flame
vlammen, to blaze, to be ardent
Vlaming (de), Flemish man
vlecht (de), plait
vlechten, to plait, to weave
vleermuis (de), bat
vlees (het), meat, flesh
vleesmes (het), carving knife
vleeswaren, meat products, meats
vleet: geld bij de –, pots of money
vleien, to flatter, to coax
vlek (de), blot, spot, stain
vlekkeloos, spotless
vleugel (de), wing; grand piano
vleugje (het), breath, touch
vlezig, fleshy, plump
vlieg (de), fly
vliegdekschip (het), aircraft carrier
vliegen, to fly
  in brand –, to burst into flames
vliegenmepper (de), (fly) swat
vliegensvlug, as quick as lightning
vlieger (de), kite; airman
vlieghaven (de), airport
vliegramp (de), plane crash
vliegticket (het, de), airline ticket
vliegtuig (het), aircraft, plane
vliegveld (het), airport
vliegwiel (het), flywheel
vliering (de), loft
vlies (het), fleece; film, membrane
vlijmscherp, sharp as a razor
vlijtig, industrious

vlinder (de), butterfly
vlo (de), flea
vloed (de), flood (tide), flow
vloedgolf (de), tidal wave
vloeibaar, liquid
vloeien, to flow; to blot
vloeiend, flowing; fluent
vloeistof (de), liquid
vloeitje (het), cigarette paper
vloek (de), curse, oath
vloeken, to swear, to curse; to
   clash
vloer (de), floor(ing)
vloerbedekking (de), floor
   covering, carpet
vloeren, to floor
vloerkleed (het), carpet
vlonder (de), plank (thrown
   across a ditch); wooden
   platform
vloot (de), fleet
vlot, fluent, smooth, slick,
   sprightly; afloat: **(het),** raft
vlotten, to float; to proceed
   smoothly
vlucht (de), flight
vluchteling (de), fugitive, refugee
vluchten, to fly, to flee
vluchtheuvel (de), traffic island;
   mound
vluchtig, cursory, fleeting,
   volatile
vlug, quick
VN (Verenigde Naties) (de), UN
VN-'vredesmacht (de), UN
   peacekeeping force
vocabu'laire (de, het),
   vocabulary
vocht (het), fluid, moisture
vochtig, damp, moist
voeden, to feed, to nourish
voeding (de), feeding, nutrition;
   food; power supply

voedingsbodem (de), breeding
   ground
voedsel (het), food
voedselhulp (de), food aid
voedselpakket (het), food parcel
voedselvergiftiging (de), food
   poisoning
voedzaam, nourishing
voeg (de), joint
voegen, to join, to add; to point
   zich –, to join; to comply
voegwoord (het), conjunction
voelbaar, perceptible
voelen, to feel
voer (het), fodder; load
voeren, to take, to carry (on), to
   wield, to conduct, to feed: to
   line
voering (de), lining
voertaal (de), official language
voertuig (het), vehicle
voet (de), foot; footing
   – bij stuk houden, to stick to
   one's guns
voetbal (het), football
voetbalclub (de), football club
voetbalcompetitie (de), football
   competition
voetbalelftal (het), football team
voetbalfan (de), football fan
voetbalknie (de), cartilage trouble
voetballen, to play football
voetballer (de), football player
voetbalschoen (de), football
   boot
voetbalvandaal (de), football
   hooligan
voetbalveld (het), football pitch
voetbalwedstrijd (de), football
   match
voet(en)bank (de), footstool
voet(en)einde (het), foot (of the
   bed)

voetganger (de), pedestrian

voetgangersbrug (de), footbridge, pedestrian crossing, zebra crossing

voetnoot (de), footnote; note in margin, critical remark/comment

voetspoor (het), footmark; track

voetstuk (het), pedestal

voetzoeker (de), (jumping) cracker

vogel (de), bird

vogelnest (het), bird's nest

vogelverschrikker (de), scarecrow

vogelvlucht (de), bird's-eye view

vogel'vrij, outlawed

vol, full

volautomatisch, fully automatic

volbloed (de), thorough(bred)

vol'brengen, to accomplish

vol'daan, satisfied; paid

vol'doen, to satisfy, to give satisfaction, to pay
 – **aan**, to fulfil

vol'doend, satisfactory; sufficient

vol'doende (de), pass (mark)

vol'doening (de), satisfaction; settlement

volgauto (de), car in procession

volgeboekt, booked up

volgeling (de), follower

volgen, to follow

volgend, following, next

volgens, according to

volgieten, to fill

volgnummer (het), serial number

volgorde (de), order, sequence

volgzaam, docile

vol'harden, to persevere

volhouden, to keep up, to maintain, to insist

voli'ère (de), aviary

volk (het), nation, people

volkenkunde (de), ethnology

vol'komen, complete

vol'korenbrood (het), wholemeal bread

volksaard (de), national character

volksbuurt (de), working-class quarter

volksdans (de), folk dance

volksdansen (de), folk dancing

volksdracht (de), national costume

volksge'zondheid (de), public health, national health

volkslied (het), national anthem; folksong

volksmond: in de – heten, to be popularly called

volkstelling (de), census

volkstuin (de), allotment

volksverhuizing (de), mass migration

vol'ledig, complete, full

vollopen, to fill up

vol'maakt, perfect

volmacht (de), power of attorney, proxy

vol'mondig, whole-hearted

volop, plenty (of)

volproppen, to stuff, to clutter up

vol'slagen, utter, total

vol'staan: laat ik – met te zeggen, suffice it to say

vol'strekt, absolute, at all

vol'tallig, complete, plenary

vol'tooien, to complete

voltreffer (de), direct hit

vol'trekken, to execute

vol'uit, in full

vol'waardig, sound (in body and mind), able

vol'wassen(e) (de), grown-up, full-grown, adult

vondst (de), find

vonk(en) (de), (to) spark

vonnis (het), sentence, verdict

voogd('es) (de), guardian

voog'dij (de), guardianship

voor, for; before; in front of: furrow

– ... uit, ahead of

voor'aan, in front, at this end

voor'aanstaand, prominent

vooraanzicht (het), front view

voor'af, beforehand

voor'afgaand, foregoing, preliminary

voor'al, especially, by all means, on any account

voorals'nog, as yet

vooravond (de), early evening; eve

voorbaat: bij –, in anticipation

voor'barig, premature

voorbedachte: met – rade, with malice aforethought

voorbeeld (het), example, model

voor'beeldig, exemplary

voorbehoedmiddel (het), contraceptive

voorbereiden, to prepare

voorbereiding (de), preparation

voor'bij, past

voor'bijgaan, to pass (by)

voor'bijganger (de), passer-by

voor'bijstreven, to outstrip, to overshoot

voordat, before

voordeel (het), advantage, profit

voor'delig, economical, advantageous

voordeur (de), front door

voor'dien, until then

voordoen, to give a demonstration; to put on

zich –, to arise; to (re)present oneself

voordracht (de), recitation, lecture; delivery, rendering; nomination

voordragen, to recite; to propose

voorgaan, to lead (the way); to come first

voorgaand, preceding

voorganger (de), predecessor; minister

voorgerecht (het), entrée

voorgeslacht (het), ancestors

voorgevel (de), façade

voorgevoel (het), presentiment

voor'goed, for good

voorgrond (de), foreground, fore(front)

voor'handen, available

voorhebben, to intend; to have the advantage

voor'heen, formerly

voorhoofd (het), forehead

voorhoofdsholteontsteking (de), sinusitis

voorhuid (de), foreskin

voor'in, in (the) front

voor'ingenomen, prejudiced

voorjaar (het), spring

voorkamer (de), front room

voorkauwen, to repeat over and over again

voorkennis (de), (fore)knowledge

voorkeur (de), preference

voorkomen, to occur; to seem; to drive up; to get ahead; to appear: **(het),** appearance; incidence

voor'komen, to prevent, to anticipate

voor'komend, charming, considerate

voorlaatst, penultimate, last but one

voorleggen, to submit to

voorletter (de), initial

voorlezen, to read (out) to

voorlichten, to light the way; to enlighten

voorlichting (de), information

voorliefde (de), preference

voorlopen, to go in front; to gain, to be fast

voor'lopig, interim, provisional, for the time being

voor'malig, one-time

voornaam (de), Christian name

voor'naam, distinguished, prominent

het voornaamste is, the main point is

voornaamwoord (het), pronoun

voor'namelijk, principally

voornemen: zich –, to resolve, to propose

voornemen (het), intention

vooroordeel (het), prejudice

voor'oorlogs, pre-war

voor'op, in front

voor'opgezet, preconceived

voor'opstellen, to take for granted; to put first and foremost

voorouders (de), ancestors

voor'over, forward

voorpagina (de), front page

voorproefje (het), foretaste

voorraad (de), stock, store

voor'radig, in stock

voorrang (de), precedence; right of way

voorrangsweg (de), major road

voorrecht (het), privilege

voorruit (de), windscreen

voorschieten, to advance

voorschijn: te – brengen, to produce

te – halen, to take out

te – komen, to appear

te – roepen, to evoke

voorschot (het), advance

voorschrift (het), regulation, order

voorschrijven, to prescribe, to lay down

voor'spellen, to predict; to presage

voor'spiegelen, to hold out prospects of

voorspoed (de), prosperity

voor'spoedig, prosperous, successful

voorsprong (de), start, lead

voorstad (de), suburb

voorstander (de), advocate

voorste, foremost, front

voorstel (het), proposal, suggestion

voorstellen, to (re)present, to introduce; to propose

zich –, to introduce oneself; to imagine; to intend

voorstelling (de), performance; representation

zich een – maken van, to visualize

voortaan, in future, from now on

voortbestaan (het), future life; survival

voortbrengen, to produce, to beget

voort'durend, continual, continuous

voortgang (de), progress

voortkomen uit, to emanate from

voortmaken, to make haste

voortplanten, to propagate
voor'treffelijk, excellent
voortrekken, to favour
voortrekker (de), pioneer
voorts, further(more)
voortslepen, to drag along
voortspruiten uit, to arise from
voortuin (de), front garden
voor'uitbetalen, to pay in
  advance
voort'varend, go-ahead
voort'varendheid (de),
  enterprise, drive
voorverkoop (de), advance
  booking
voortvloeien uit, to result from
voort'vluchtig, at large, fugitive
voortwoekeren, to spread
voortzetten, to continue
voor'uit, forward, ahead;
  before(hand); come on!
voor'uitbetalen, to pay in
  advance
voor'uitgaan, to go on ahead; to
  make progress
voor'uitgang (de), progress,
  improvement
voor'uitkomen, to get on
voor'uitlopen op, to anticipate
vooruit'strevend, progressive
voor'uitzicht (het), prospect
voorvader (de), ancestor
voorval (het), incident
voorvoegsel (het), prefix
voorwaarde (de), condition
voorwaarts, forward(s)
voorwendsel (het), pretext,
  pretence
voorwerp (het), object
voorwoord (het), foreword
voorzeggen, to prompt
voorzetsel (het), preposition
voor'zichtig, careful, cautious

voor'zien, to foresee; to provide
  (for)
voorzitter (de), chairman
voorzorg(smaatregel) (de),
  precaution(ary measure)
vorderen, to (make) progress; to
  requisition, to demand
voren: naar –, to the front
  te –, before(hand)
  van –, (from) in front
  van – af aan, from the
  beginning
vorig, last, previous
vork (de), fork
vorm (de), form, shape, mould
vormen, to form, to constitute
vorming (de), formation;
  education
vorm(e)loos, shapeless
vorst (de), frost; prince,
  monarch
vorstelijk, royal, regal
vorstendom (het), principality
vorstin (de), queen
vos (de), fox
vouw (de), fold, crease
vouwen, to fold
vouwfiets (de), folding bike,
  collapsible bike
vraag (de), question, request,
  demand
vraaggesprek (het), interview
vraagstuk (het), problem
vraagteken (het), question mark
vracht (de), freight, load, cargo
vrachtauto (de), lorry
vrachtgoed (het), goods, cargo
vrachtverkeer (het), cargo trade,
  goods transport(ation), lorry
  traffic
vrachtwagen (de), lorry
vragen, to ask; to charge; to
  require

vrede (de), peace
vredesmacht (de), peacekeeping force
vredesnaam: in –, for goodness' sake
vredestichter (de), peacemaker
vredig, peaceful
vreedzaam, peaceable
vreemd, strange; foreign, alien
vreemde: in den –, abroad
vreemdeling (de), stranger; foreigner
vreemdelingenverkeer (het), tourist traffic
vreemd'soortig, unusual
vrees (de), fear
vreetzak (de), greedy-guts
vrek(kig) (de), miser(ly)
vreselijk, frightful
vreten, to devour, to eat, to stuff
vreugde (de), joy
vreugdevol, joyful
vrezen, to fear
vriend (de), (boy)friend
vriendelijk, kind, friendly
vriendendienst (de), kind turn
vriendjespolitiek (de), favouritism, nepotism
vrien'din (de), (girl)friend
vriendschap (de), friendship
vriend'schappelijk, friendly, amicably
vriespunt (het), freezing point
vriezen, to freeze
vrij, free: rather, quite
vrij'af, time off
vrij'blijvend, subject to alteration in price; without obligation
vrijdag, Friday
vrijen, to make love, to go to bed with someone; to neck, to pet

vrije'tijdsbesteding (de), leisure activities, recreation
vrije'tijdskleding (de), casual clothes
vrijgeven, to decontrol; to give (time) off
vrij'gevig, liberal
vrijgevochten, undisciplined
vrijge'zel (de), bachelor
vrijge'zellenavond (de), stag-night, hen-party; singles night
vrijheid (de), liberty, freedom
vrijheidsbeeld (het), Statue of Liberty
vrijkomen, to get off; to fall vacant; to be decontrolled; to be liberated
vrijlaten, to release, to emancipate; to leave free
vrijmarkt (de), unregulated street market
vrij'metselaar (de), freemason
vrij'moedig, frank, outspoken
vrijpleiten, to exonerate
vrij'postig, forward, impertinent
vrijspreken, to acquit
vrijstaand, detached
   een – huis, a detached house
vrijstellen, to exempt, to excuse
vrij'uit, freely
vrijwel, practically
vrij'willig, voluntary
vrij'williger (de), volunteer
vrij'zinnig, liberal
vroedvrouw (de), midwife
vroeg, early
   – of laat, sooner or later
vroeger, earlier, former, previous
   ik woonde daar –, I used to live there
vroeg'tijdig, early
vrolijk, cheerful
vroom, pious

vrouw (de), woman; wife

vrouwelijk, female, feminine

vrouwenarts (de), gynaecologist

vrouwenbeweging (de), feminist movement, women's (rights) movement

vrouwtje (het), woman; mistress; female

vrucht (de), fruit; foetus

vruchtbaar, fertile; fruitful, prolific

vruchteloos, fruitless, in vain

vruchtvlees (het), pulp

vuil, dirty: **(het),** dirt, muck

vuilak (de), dirty/filthy person, pig

vuilbek (de), foul-mouthed fellow

vuil(ig)heid (de), filth; obscenity

vuilmaken, to (make) dirty; to waste

vuilnis (het), refuse, rubbish, garbage

vuilnisbak (de), dustbin

vuilnisbelt (de), rubbish dump

vuilnisman (de), dustman

vuilverbranding (de), (waste, garbage) incinerator

vuist (de), fist
  voor de – (weg), *ad lib*

vul'gair, vulgar

vul'kaan (de), volcano

vul'kaanuitbarsting (de), volcanic eruption

vullen, to fill, to stuff

vulpen (de), fountain pen

vuns, vunzig, musty, fusty; dirty; obscene

vuren, to fire

vurig, fiery; fervent, ardent

VUT (vervroegde uittreding) (de), early retirement

vuur (het), fire
  – geven, to fire; to give (a person) a light

vuurpeloton (het), firing squad

vuurpijl (de), rocket
  de klap op de –, the crowning sensation

vuurproef (de), ordeal by fire; crucial test

vuur'rood, flaming red

vuurtje (het), (small) fire; light
  een – geven, give a light
  het nieuws ging als een lopend – door de school, the news spread through the school like wildfire

vuurtoren (de), lighthouse

vuurvast, fire-proof

vuurwapen (het), firearm

vuurwerk (het), firework(s) (display)

VVV (Vereniging voor Vreemdelingenverkeer) (de), tourist information

VVV-kantoor (het), tourist information office

vwo (voorbereidend wetenschappelijk onderwijs) (het), pre-university education

W

waag (de), weighhouse

waaghals (de), daredevil

waagstuk (het), risky enterprise

waaien, to blow, to fan

waaier (de), fan

waakhond (de), watchdog

waaks, waakzaam, watchful

waakzaamheid (de), vigilance

Waals, Walloon

waanzin (de), madness

waan'zinnig, mad, crazy

waar, where; true; **(de),** ware(s), commodity, stuff
  niet –? isn't that so?

waar-(aan etc.), (to etc.) what, which, whom

waarborg (de), guarantee, security

waarborgen, to guarantee

waarborgsom (de), deposit, bail

waard (de), landlord; worth

waarde (de), value

waardebon (de), (gift) voucher/coupon

waardeloos, worthless

waar'deren, to appreciate, to value

waardevol, valuable

waarheen, waar … heen, where (… to)

waarheid (de), truth

waarmaken, to verify

waarmerk (het), hallmark

waar'neembaar, perceptible

waarnemen, to observe; to deputize; to discharge

waar'om, why

waar'schijnlijk, probable

waarschuwen, to warn

waarschuwing (de), warning; demand note, reminder

waarzegster (de), fortune teller

waas (de), film, haze; air

wacht (de), watch(man), guardduty
  in de – slepen, to scrounge, to rake in

wachten (op), to wait (for)

wachter (de), watchman

wachtgeld (het), reduced salary, retainer

wachtkamer (de), waiting room

wachtlijst (de), waiting list

wachtwoord (het), password

wad (het), mudflat

waden, to wade

wafel (de), waffle, wafer

wagen (de), car, cart; to risk, to venture

wagenziek, trainsick, carsick

waggelen, to totter, to waddle

wa'gon (de), (railway) carriage, van, truck(load)

wak (het), hole (in the ice)

waken, to (keep) watch; to wake

wakker, awake
  – schrikken, to wake with a start

wal (de), quay(side); bank
  aan –, ashore
  van – steken, to push off; to fire away
  van twee wallen eten, to have it both ways

walg(e)lijk, disgusting

walgen, to be nauseated

walkman (de), walkman

Wal'lonië, the Walloon provinces (Belgium)

walm(en) (de), (to) smoke

walnoot (de), walnut

wals (de), waltz; *(motor) roller*

walvis (de), whale

wanbetaling (de), non-payment

wand (de), wall

wandelaar (de), walker, stroller

wandelen, to walk, to wander
  gaan –, to go for a walk

wandeling (de), walk, stroll

wandelkaart (de), large-scale map

wandelpad (het), footpath

wandelstok (de), walking stick

wandmeubel (het), wall unit

wandschildering (de), mural

wandtapijt (het), hanging carpet,

tapestry
wang (de), cheek
wangedrag (het), misconduct
wanhoop (de), despair
wanhopen, to despair
wan'hopig, desperate,
despairing, hopeless
wankel, unsteady, rickety
wankelbaar, unstable
wankelen, to stagger, to sway
from side to side; to waver
wanneer, when(ever)
wanorde (de), disorder
wan'staltig, deformed
want, for, because: **(de),** mitten
wantoestand (de), chaotic
situation
wantrouwen (het), (to) distrust
wan'trouwend, wan'trouwig,
suspicious
WAO (Wet op de
Arbeidsongeschiktheids-
verzekering) (de), disability
insurance act
WAO'er (de), recipient of
disablement insurance benefit
wapen (het), weapon, arm; coat
of arms
wapenen, to arm, to reinforce
wapenspreuk (de), heraldic
device
wapenstilstand (de), armistice,
truce
wapenwedloop (de), arms race
wapperen, to flutter
war: in de –, in a muddle, upset
warboel (de), muddle, clutter
ware (de), right person (or
thing) (for the job); true one
wa'rempel, truly, actually
warenhuis (het), department
store
warm, warm, hot

warmen, to warm
warmpjes, warmly
warmte (de), warmth, heat,
temperature
warrelen, to whirl
wars van, averse to
Warschau, Warsaw
was (de), wax: wash(ing)
  goed in de slappe – zitten, to
  have plenty of dough
wasautomaat (de), washing
machine
wasbaar, washable
wasbak (de), wash basin
wasgoed (het), washing,
laundry
washandje (het), flannel, face
cloth
wasknijper (de), clothes peg
wasmachine (de), washing
machine
wasmiddel (het), detergent
waspoeder (het), washing
powder, soap powder
wassen, to wash; to shuffle; to
swell, to wax
wassenbeeld (het), waxwork
(model)
wasse'rij (de), laundry
wastafel (de), wash basin, wash
stand
wat, what, which; how;
some(thing), any(thing);
somewhat
  – voor, what (sort of)
  – (dan) ook, – maar, whatever
  – blij, only too pleased
water (het), water
waterbouwkunde (de),
hydraulic engineering
waterdamp (de), vapour
water'dicht, waterproof,
watertight

waterfiets (de), pedal boat, pedalo

waterhoen (de), moorhen

waterig, watery

waterijsje (het), ice lolly, popsicle

waterkant (de), water's edge, waterfront

waterkering (de), weir

waterlanders (de), tears

waterlinie (de), flooding defence line

watermeloen (de), watermelon

waterpas (de), spirit level

waterpokken (de), chicken pox

waterschade (de), water damage

waterschap (het), district controlled by polder board

watersnood (de), floods

waterspiegel (de), water level

waterstand (de), water (level)

waterstof (de), hydrogen

watertanden: doen –, to make the mouth water

waterverf (de), watercolour

watervliegtuig (het), seaplane

watje (het), wad of cotton wool; wally

watten (de), cotton wool, wadding

wattenstaafje (het), cotton bud

wat'teren, to pad, to quilt

wauwelen, to blather

WA-verzekering (de), third-party insurance

wa'xinelichtje (het), tealight

wazig, hazy, filmy

wc (de), WC, toilet, lavatory

wc-bril (de), toilet seat

web (het), web

website (de), website

wedden, to bet

weddenschap (de), wager

weer, again, re-

weer (het), weather
  in de – zijn, to be on the move; to be busy

weder'kerend, reflexive

weder'kerig, mutual

weder'om, (once) again

weder'opbouw (de), rebuilding, reconstruction

wederzijds, mutual

wedijveren, to compete

wedloop (de), (running) race

wedstrijd (de), match, competition

weduwe (de), widow

weduwnaar (de), widower

wee, sickly, faint: **(de), woe,** labour pain

weefsel (het), tissue, fabric, texture

weegschaal (de), (pair of) scales, weighing machine

week, soft

week (de), week

weekblad (het), weekly (paper)

weekdier (het), mollusc

weeklagen, to (be)wail

weelde (de), luxury, profusion

weelderig, luxurious, luxuriant

weemoed (de), melancholy

Weens, Viennese

weerbaar, defensible; able-bodied

weer'barstig, unruly

weerbericht (het), weather forecast

weer'galmen, to reverberate

weergeven, to render, to reflect

weerhaak (de), barb(ed hook)

weerhaan (de), weathercock

weer'houden, to restrain, to suppress

weer'kaatsen, to reflect, to (re)echo

weerklank (de), echo
weer'klinken, to resound
weer'leggen, to refute
weerlicht (het), lightning
weerloos, defenceless
weermacht (de), (fighting) services
weersgesteldheid (de), weather conditions
weerskanten, both sides
weer'spiegelen, to reflect
weer'staan, to resist
weerstand (de), resistance
weersverwachting (de), weather-forecast
weerzien (het), meeting, reunion
weerzin (de), aversion
weerzin'wekkend, repugnant
wees (de), orphan
weeshuis (het), orphanage
weetal (de), knowall
weg (de), way, road: away, gone
  veel van iemand – hebben, to be very like a person
wegbergen, to put away
wegbrengen, to take away; to see off
wegdek (het), road surface
wegen, to weigh
wegennet (het), road system
wegens, on account of
wegenwacht (de), AA patrol, RAC patrol, AAA road service
weggaan, to leave, to go away
weggooien, to throw away/out, discard
weggooiverpakking (de), disposable packaging/package
wegkomen, to get away
weglaten, to omit, to leave out
wegleggen, to put aside
  weggelegd zijn voor, to be in store for; to be meant for

wegmaken, to get rid of, to lose; to put under an anaesthetic
wegnemen, to take away, to allay
  dat neemt niet weg dat, that does not alter the fact that
wegomlegging (de), diversion, detour
wegpraten, to explain away
wegraken, to get lost
wegrestaurant (het), transport café, wayside restaurant
wegtrekken, to pull away; to march away
wegvallen tegen, to cancel (out)
wegwerken, to get rid of
wegwerpartikel (het), disposable article
wegwezen, to clear off/out, push off, buzz off
  wegwezen jij!, buzz off, you!
wegwijs maken, to show the ropes
wegwijzer (de), signpost
wei (de), meadow; whey
weide, meadow, pasture
weids, grandiose
weifelen, to waver
weigeren, to refuse
weiland (het), pasture
weinig, little, few
wekelijks, weekly
weken, to soak, to soften
wekken, to wake, to arouse
wekker (de), alarm clock
wekkerradio (de), radio alarm (clock), clock radio
wel, well; very much; certainly, probably, quite
  ik geloof van –, I think so
  ik zie het –! I do see it!
wel'dadig, beneficial, pleasant

weldoener (de), benefactor
weldoordacht, well thought-out
weldra, soon
wel'eer, of old
welge'steld, well-to-do
welgezind, kindly disposed
welig, lush
weliswaar, it is true
wel'ja, yes
welk(e), which, what
welkom (het), welcome
welkomstgroet (de), (word of) welcome
wellen, to weld
welletjes, enough
wellicht, perhaps
wel'luidend, melodious
wel'nee, no
wel'nu, well (now)
weloverwogen, (well-) considered
welp (de), cub
wel'sprekend, eloquent
welte'rusten, goodnight, sleep tight
welvaartsmaatschappij (de), affluent society
welvaart (de), prosperity
welvaartsstaat (de), welfare state
wel'willend, obliging, sympathetic
welzijn (het), welfare, health
wemelen van, to swarm with
wenden: (zich) -, to turn; to apply
wending (de), turn
Wenen, Vienna
wenen, to weep
wenkbrauw (de), eyebrow
wenken, to beckon
wennen, to get used to
wens (de), wish
wenselijk, desirable

wensen, to wish, to desire
wentelen, to roll (over)
wenteling (de), revolution
wenteltrap (de), winding staircase
wereld (de), world
  uit de - helpen, to dispose of
wereldberoemd, world-famous
wereldbevolking (de), world population
werelddeel (het), continent
wereldkampioen (de), world champion
wereldkampioenschap (het), world championship(s)
Wereldna'tuurfonds (het), World Wildlife Fund
wereldoorlog (de), world war
  de Tweede Wereldoorlog, the Second World War
wereldrecord (het), world record
wereldrecordhouder (de), world record holder
wereldreiziger (de), globetrotter
werelds, worldly (minded)
wereldstad (de), metropolis
wereldtaal (de), universal language
wereldtentoonstelling (de), world fair
weren, to avert, to present, to keep out
werf (de), shipyard, dockyard; wharf
werk (het), work, job
  er - van maken, to do something about it
werkdruk (de), pressure of work
werkelijk, real
werkelijkheid (de), reality
werkeloos, unemployed, idle
werke'loosheid (de), unemployment

werken, to work, to be active
  naar binnen –, to get down
  (one's throat)
werkervaring (de), work
  experience
werkgever (de), employer
werking (de), action, operation
werkkamer (de), workroom,
  study
werkkracht (de), worker,
  employee
werkloos, unemployed, idle
werkloze (de), unemployed
  person
werkman (de), workman,
  working man
werknemer (de), employee
werkplaats (de), workshop
werkster (de), cleaner
werktuig (het), tool
werktuigkunde (de), mechanics
werk'tuiglijk, mechanical
werkwoord (het), verb
werkzaam, active,
  employed (in)
werkzaamheden (de), activities,
  duties, tasks
werk'zoekende (de), job seeker,
  person looking for work
werpen, to throw
wervelkolom (de), spinal
  column
wervelwind (de), whirlwind,
  tornado
werven, to rope in, to enlist
wesp (de), wasp
wespennest (het), wasps' nest
westelijk, westerly, western
westen (het), west
  buiten –, unconscious
westerling (de), westerner
westers, western
wet (de), law, act

de – voorschrijven, to lay
  down the law
wetboek (het), code
weten, to know; to manage
  er iets op –, to know the
  answer/solution
weten (het), knowledge
wetenschap (de), science;
  learning, knowledge
wetenschappelijk, scientific
wetgevend, legislative
wethouder (de), councillor
wetsontwerp (het), bill
wettelijk, wettig, legal, lawful
weven, to weave
wezen (het), being, essence
wezenloos, vacant
wichelroede (de), divining rod
wicht (het), creature (usu. young
  woman)
wie, who(m), anyone who
  – (dan) ook, whoever
wiebelen, to wobble
wieden, to weed
wieg (de), cradle
  in de – gelegd voor, cut out for
wiegen, to rock
wiek (de), wing, sail
wiel (het), wheel
wielklem (de), wheel clamp
wielrennen (het), cycle racing
wielrenner (de), (racing) cyclist,
  bicyclist, cycler
wielrijder (de), cyclist
wier (het), seaweed
wierook (de), incense
wij, we
wijd, wide, spacious
wijd en zijd, far and wide
wijdbeens, with legs apart
wijdte (de), width
wijdvertakt, widespread
wijf (het), bitch, woman, wife

wijfje (het), female (animal)

wijk (de), district

wijken, to yield; to pass (off)

wijkverpleegster, wijkzuster, (de), district nurse

wijlen, (the) late

wijn (de), wine

wijnfles (de), wine bottle

wijngaard (de), vineyard

wijnhandelaar (de), wine merchant

wijnkaart (de), wine list

wijnkenner (de), connoisseur of wine

wijs, wise: **(de)**, manner, way; tune; mood

van de –, at sea, in a muddle

– maken, to convince; to dupe

wijsbegeerte (de), philosophy

wijselijk, wisely

wijsheid (de), wisdom

wijsje (het), tune, air

wijsneus (de), knowall

wijsvinger (de), forefinger

wijten, to impute

het is aan het weer te –, it is due to the weather

wijze (de), manner, way

wijzen, to point (out), show

wijzer, pointer, hand

wijzerplaat (de), (clock) face

wijzigen, to modify

wikkelen, to wrap (up)

wikken en wegen, to weigh (up)

wil (de), will, wish

tegen – en dank, against one's will

ter wille van, for the sake of

wild (het), game; wild

in het wild(e weg), wildly, at random

wilde (de), savage

wildernis (de), wilderness

wildvreemd, utterly strange

wilg (de), willow

Wil'helmus (het), Wilhelmus (the Dutch national anthem)

willekeur: naar – handelen, to do as one pleases

wille'keurig, arbitrary

willen, to want, to like, to be willing

dat wil zeggen, that is to say

willens, on purpose

willig, willing

wilsbeschikking (de), will

wilskracht (de), will power

wimper (de), eyelash

winden, to wind

winderig, windy

windhond (de), greyhound

windhoos (de), whirlwind

windmolenpark (het), wind park/farm

windstil(te) (de), calm

windstoot (de), gust of wind

windstreek (de), point of the compass

windvaan, windwijzer (de), weather vane

winkel (de), shop

winkelbediende (de), shop assistant

winkelcentrum (het), shopping centre, mall

winkeldief (de), shoplifter

winkelen, to shop, to go shopping

winke'lier (de), shopkeeper, retailer

winnaar (de), winner

winnen, to win, to gain

winst (de), profit, gain

winst'gevend, profitable

winstmarge (de), profit margin

winter (de), winter
winters, wintry
winterslaap (de), hibernation
winterspelen (de), winter Olympics
wintersport (de), winter sports
wip (de), seesaw
wipneus (de), snub nose
wippen, to rock (to and fro), to nip; to unseat
wirwar (de), tangle
wiskunde (de), mathematics
wispel'turig, fickle
wissel (de), points; bill of exchange
wisselbeker (de), challenge cup
wisselen, to (ex)change; to shed milk teeth
wisselgeld (het), small change
wisselkoers (de), exchange rate
wisselstroom (de), alternating current
wissel'vallig, changeable; precarious
wisselwerking (de), interaction
wissen, to wipe
wissewasje (het), slightest little thing, trifle
wit, white
witlof (de, het), chicory
wittebroodsweken (de), honeymoon
witten, to whitewash
WK (wereldkampioenschap) (de, het), world championship(s)
wodka (de), vodka
woede (de), rage
woedeaanval (de), tantrum, fit (of anger)
woedend, furious
woekeren, to be rife
woelen, to toss and turn
woelig, turbulent, restless

woensdag, Wednesday
woest, wild, waste, desolate
woesteling (de), ruffian
woeste'nij (de), wilderness
woes'tijn (de), desert
wol (de), wool
wolf (de), wolf
wolk (de), cloud
wolkenkrabber (de), skyscraper
wolkje (het), little cloud; puff, drop
wollen, woolen
wollig, woolly
wond (de), wound
wonder (het), wonder, miracle
wonder'baarlijk, miraculous, stupendous
wonderkind (het), infant prodigy
wonderlijk, strange, surprising
wondermiddel (het), panacea
wonen, to live
woning (de), house, flat
woningbouwvereniging (de), housing association/corporation
woningnood (de), housing shortage
woon'achtig, resident
woongroep (de), commune
woonhuis (het), private house
woonkamer (de), living room
woonkeuken (de), open kitchen, kitchen–dining room
woonplaats (de), (place of) residence
woonschip (het), woonschuit (de), houseboat
woonwagen (de), caravan, trailer
woonwagenbewoner (de), caravan dweller, trailer park resident

woonwagenkamp (het), caravan camp, trailer camp

woon-'werkverkeer (het), commuter traffic

woonwijk (de), residential district

woord (het), word
  het hoogste – hebben, to monopolize the conversation
  het – voeren, to speak, to be spokesman
  onder woorden brengen, to put into words
  iemand te – staan, to speak to a person

woordenboek (het), dictionary

woordenschat (de), vocabulary

woordspeling (de), play on words, pun

woordvoerder (de), spokesman

woordvolgorde (de), word order

worden, to be(come)

worm (de), worm, grub

worp (de), throw; litter

worst (de), sausage

worstelen, to struggle, to wrestle

wortel (de), root; carrot

wortelen, to be rooted

woud (het), forest

wraak (de), revenge

wraak'gierig, wraak'zuchtig, vindictive

wrak, rickety, dilapidated: **(het)**, wreck

wrakhout (het), wreckage

wrang, sour, tart; bitter

wrat (de), wart

wreed, cruel

wreef (de), instep

wreken, to revenge, to avenge

wrevel (de), resentment

wrevelig, resentful

wriemelen, to crawl, to tickle

wrijfwas (de), furniture polish

wrijven, to rub; to polish

wrijving (de), friction

wrikken, to jerk

wringen, to wring, to wrench
  zich –, to wriggle

wroeging (de), remorse

wroeten, to root, to rummage

wrok (de), rancour

wuiven, to wave

wurgen, to strangle

wurmen, to wriggle

WVC (Welzijn, Volksgezondheid en Cultuur), (the Ministry of) Welfare, Health and Cultural Affairs

WW (Werkloosheidswet) (de), unemployment insurance act
  in de – lopen/zitten, to be on the dole/unemployment benefit

WW-uitkering (de), unemployment benefit

Y

yoga (de), yoga

yoghurt (de), yogurt

Z

zaad (het), seed; semen, sperm

zaag (de), saw

zaagmeel (het), zaagsel (het), sawdust

zaaien, to sow

zaak (de), thing, object; matter, business, affair; deal; shop, business; case; issue; lawsuit
  bemoei je met je eigen zaken, mind your own business

op kosten van de –, on the house

een auto van de –, a company car

zaakgelastigde (de), agent

zaal (de), hall, ward, auditorium

zaalvoetbal (het), indoor football

zacht, soft, mild, gentle

zacht'aardig, gentle

zachtjes, gently, quietly

zachtjes aan, gradually

zacht'moedig, gentle

zacht'zinnig, good-natured

zadel (het), saddle

zadelen, to saddle

zagen, to saw; to harp (on a subject)

zak (de), pocket; sack, bag

zakdoek (de), handkerchief

zakelijk, business-like, to the point

zakenbrief (de), business letter

zakenleven (het), business (life), commerce

zakenman (de), businessman

zakenreis (de), business trip

zakenvrouw (de), businesswoman

zakformaat (het), pocket size

zakken, to sink, to fall; to fail (an exam)

zakkenroller (de), pickpocket

zaklantaarn (de), torch

zaklopen (het), sack race

zalf (de), ointment

zalig, blessed; heavenly

zalm (de), salmon

zand (het), sand

zandbak (de), sandbox, sandpit

zanderig, sandy

zandloper (de), hourglass

zandplaat (de), sandbank

zandweg (de), sandy lane

zang (de), song, canto

zanger('es) (de), singer

zangerig, melodious, sing-song

zangles (de), singing lesson

zangstem (de), singing voice; voice part

zaniken, to nag, to moan

zat, drunken; fed up; plenty

zaterdag, Saturday

zatlap (de), drunk

ze, they, them; she

zede (de), custom

zeden, morals; manners

zedelijk, moral

zedeloos, immoral

zedig, modest, demure

zee (de), sea

zeebanket (het), seafood

zeef (de), sieve, strainer

zeegat (het), entrance to channel

zeegezicht (het), seascape

zeehond (de), seal

zeem (de), wash leather

zeemacht (de), naval forces

zeeman (de), seaman

zeemeermin (de), mermaid

zeemeeuw (de), seagull

zeemleer (het), chamois leather

zeep (de), soap

zeepaard(je) (het), seahorse

zeepbel (de), soap bubble

zeepsop (het), soapsuds

zeer, very (much): sore

– doen, to hurt

zeerob (de), seal

zeerste: ten –, highly, greatly

zeespiegel (de), sea level

zeester (de), starfish

Zeeuw(se) (de), inhabitant of Zeeland

zeevaart (de), shipping

zeevarend, seafaring
zee'waardig, seaworthy
zeewering (de), seawall
zeewier (het), seaweed
zeeziek, seasick
zege (de), victory, triumph
zegel (de), seal; stamp
zegelen, to seal
zegelring (de), signet ring
zegen(ing) (de), blessing
zegenen, to bless
zegevieren, to triumph
zeggen, to say, to tell
  liever gezegd, rather
  er valt niets op te –, there is
  nothing to be said against it
  dat zegt niets, that doesn't
  mean a thing
zeil (het), sail; tarpaulin;
  lino(leum)
zeildoek (het), canvas, oilcloth
zeilen, to sail
zeilplank (de), sailboard
zeis (de), scythe
zeker, certain, (for) sure
zekerheid (de), certainty;
  security
  voor alle –, to be on the safe
  side
zekerheidshalve, for safety('s
  sake)
zekering (de), fuse
zelden, seldom, rarely
zeldzaam, rare, scarce;
  exceptionally
zelf, (one)self
  ik (etc.) zelve, I (etc.) myself
  de eenvoud zelve, simplicity itself
zelfbediening (de), self-service
zelfbedieningsrestaurant (het),
  self-service restaurant
zelfbeheersing (de), self-control

zelfbehoud (het), self-preservation
zelfbe'wust, self-assured
zelfge'noegzaam, self-sufficient
zelfmoord (de), suicide
zelfs, even
zelfstandig, independent
  – naamwoord (het), noun
zelfvertrouwen (het), self-
  confidence
zelfvol'daan, self-satisfied
zelfver'zekerd, self-confident
zendeling (de), missionary
zenden, to send
zender (de), sender; transmitter
zending (de), mission;
  consignment
zendmast (de), (radio, TV)
  mast, radio tower, TV tower
zendstation (het), broadcasting
  station
zenuw (de), nerve; tendon
zenuwachtig, nervous, nervy;
  flustered
zenuwgestel (het), nervous
  system
zenuwpees (de), bundle of
  nerves
zenuw'slopend, nerve-racking
zes(de), six(th)
zeshoek (de), hexagon
zestien(de), sixteen(th)
zestig, sixty
zestig'plusser (de), over-60,
  senior citizen
zet (de), move, coup; push
zetel (de), seat
zetmeel (de), starch
zetten, to set, to put; to make;
  to stake
zeug (de), sow
zeulen, to lug
zeuren, to whine, to nag

zeurkous (de), zeurpiet (de), grouser

zeven, seven: to sieve, to strain

zeventien(de), seventeen(th)

zeventig, seventy

zgn. (zoge'naamd), so-called

zich, one (him, her, it, your)self, themselves

zicht (het), sight; visibility
 op –, on approval; at sight

zichtbaar, visible

zich'zelf, one (him, her, it)self, themselves
 uit –, of his own accord

zieden, to seethe

ziek, ill, sick; diseased

zieke (de), patient

ziekelijk, sickly, in bad health

ziekenauto (de), ambulance

ziekenbezoek (het), visit to a patient

ziekenfonds (het), national health insurance

ziekenhuis (het), hospital

ziekenhuisopname (de), hospitalization

ziekte (de), illness, disease

ziektekosten (de), medical expenses

ziektewet (de), health law
 in de – zitten/lopen, be on sickness benefit/sick pay

ziel (de), soul; heart, lifeblood

zielig, pitiful, pathetic

zien, to see, to look
 er uit –, to look (like)
 laten –, to show

zienderogen, visibly

ziens: tot –, goodbye

ziezo, there we are

ziften, to sift

zi'geuner('in) (de), Gypsy

zij, she; they

zijbeuk (de), aisle (in church)

zij(de), side; silk
 op zij, ter zijde, aside
 ter zijde staan, to help

zijdelings, sidelong, indirect, oblique

zijden, silk(en)

zijderups (de), silkworm

zijkant (de), side

zijn, to be: his, its, one's
 dat mag er –, that takes a lot of beating

zijrivier (de), tributary

zijspiegel (de), wing mirror

zijspoor (het), siding

zijtak (de), side branch, branch

zijwaarts, sideways, sideward

zijwind (de), sidewind, crosswind

zilver(en) (het), silver

zin (de), sense; mind, way; sentence
 er – in hebben, to feel like it
 naar mijn –, to my liking

zindelijk, clean; toilet-trained

zingen, to sing

zink (het), zinc

zinken, to sink: **(de),** zinc

zinloos, senseless

zinnelijk, sensual, sensory

zinspelen op, to hint at

zinsverband (het), context

zintuig (het), sense

zin'tuiglijk, sensory

zinvol, significant, advisable, a good idea

zit: een hele –, a long time sitting down

zitbad (het), hipbath

zitbank (de), settee

zitje (het), seat (of bicycle); seating area

zitkamer (de), sitting room

zitplaats (de), seat
zitten, to sit; to be; to fit
  gaan –, to sit down
  iemand laten –, to walk out on a person
  er zit niets anders op, there's no alternative
  ik zit met de gebakken peren, I'm left holding the baby
zittend, sitting, sedentary
zitting (de), session; seat
zitvlak (het), bottom
zo, so, like that; in a minute; just now: if
  de zaak zit –, it's like this
  – gaat het niet, that won't do
  – iets, such a thing
zoals, (such) as, like
zo'danig, such, in such a way
zodat, so that
zo'doende, in that way
zo'dra, as soon as
zoek, missing
  op – naar, in search of
zoeken, to look (for), to seek
zoeklicht (het), searchlight
zoekmaken, to mislay
zoekraken, to get lost
zoektocht (de), search (for)
zoemen, to buzz, to drone
zoen (de), kiss
zoet, sweet
zoetekauw: een – zijn, to have a sweet tooth
zoethout (het), liquorice (root)
zoetig, slightly sweet
zoetigheid (de), sweet things
zoetjes aan, gradually
zoet'sappig, mealy-mouthed; saccharine
zoetwater (het), fresh water
zoëven, just now
zogen, to suckle

zoge'naamd, so-called; ostensibly
zolang, as long as; meanwhile
zolder (de), loft, attic
zolderkamer (de), garret, attic room
zomaar, just like that; for no reason in particular
zomen, to hem
zomer (de), summer
zomers, summery
zomerspelen (de), summer games, summer Olympics
zomersproeten (de), freckles
zomertijd (de), summer; summer time
zomervakantie (de), summer holiday
zo'n, such (a), a sort of
zon (de), sun
zondag, Sunday
zonde (de), sin; shame; waste
zondebok (de), scapegoat
zonder, without
zondigen, to sin, to offend
zondvloed (de), Flood
zon-en-feestdagen (de), Sundays and bank holidays
zonlicht (het), sunlight
zonnebank (de), sunbed, solarium
zonnebril (de), sunglasses
zonne-energie (de), solar energy
zonnehemel (de), sunbed
zonneklaar, clear as daylight
zonnen, to bask (in the sun)
zonnescherm (het), sunshade, sunblind
zonneschijn (de), sunshine
zonnesteek (de), sunstroke
zonnestelsel (het), solar system
zonnestraal (de), sunbeam; ray of sunshine

zonnewijzer (de), sundial
zonnig, sunny
zons'ondergang (de), sunset
zons'opgang (de), sunrise
zonsverduistering (de), eclipse of the sun
zonwering (de), awning, sunblind
zoogdier (het), mammal
zooi (de), mess, heap, load
zool (de), sole
zoom (de), seam, hem; edge; outskirts
zoon (de), son
zootje (het), mess; lot
zorg (de), care, concern, worry
  het zal mij een – zijn! fat lot I care!
  – baren, to cause anxiety
zorgeloos, carefree
zorgen voor, to look after; to provide (for)
  zorg dat je op tijd bent, mind you're not late
zorg'vuldig, careful
zorg'wekkend, worrying, alarming
zorgzaam, careful, conscientious
zot (de), fool
zout (het), salt
zoutje (het), nibbles; salt(y) biscuit
zoutloos, salt-free
zoutvaatje (het), saltcellar
zoutzak (de), sack of potatoes
zoutzuur (het), hydrochloric acid
zoveel, so much, so many
zover, so far, thus far
  in zover(re), to the extent, in so far as
  voor –, as far as

zo'waar, believe it or not
zo'wel, as well
z.o.z. (zie ommezijde), p.t.o., please turn over
zo'zeer, so much
z.s.m. (zo spoedig mogelijk), a.s.a.p., as soon as possible
zucht (de), sigh
zuchten, to sigh
zuid, south
Zuid-'Afrika, South Africa
Zuid-Afri'kaan (de), South African
Zuid-A'merika, South America
Zuid-Ameri'kaans, South American
zuidelijk, southern, south(erly), southward(s)
zuiden (het), south
Zuidoost-'Azië, South-East Asia
zuid'wester (de), sou(th)wester
zuigeling (de), infant (in arms)
zuigen, to suck
zuiger (de), piston
zuigfles (de), feeding bottle
zuil (de), pillar, column
zuinig, economical
zuipen, to booze, to swill
zuiplap (de), boozer
zuivel (de), dairy produce
zuivelproduct (het), dairy product
zuiver, pure, sheer; clear
zuiveren, to purify, to clean(se), to refine; to clear
zuivering (de), purge
zulk, such
zullen, shall, will
  dat zal wel, I quite believe it
  wat zou dat? so what!
zus en zo, so-and-so, this and that
zus (de), sister

zuster (de), sister; nurse

zuur, sour; **(het)**, acid; pickles

zuurkool (de), sauerkraut

zuurpruim (de), grouch

zuurstof (de), oxygen

zuurtje (het), acid drop

zwaai (de), swing, sweep

zwaailicht (het), flashing light

zwaaien, to wave, to wield, to swing

zwaan (de), swan

zwaar, heavy; hard; severe; full-bodied, podgy

zwaard (het), sword

zwaardvechter (de), gladiator

zwaargewapend, heavily armed

zwaar'lijvig, corpulent

zwaartekracht (de), gravitation

zwaartepunt (het), centre of gravity; crux

zwabber (de), swab, mop
 aan de zwabber, on the razzle

zwabberen, to swab, to mop

zwachtel (de), bandage

zwachtelen, to swathe

zwager (de), brother-in-law

zwak, weak, delicate, feeble

zwakkeling (de), weakling

zwakte (de), weakness

zwak'zinnig, mentally disabled

zwalken, to drift about

zwaluw (de), swallow

zwaluwstaart (de), swallowtail; dovetail

zwam (de), fungus

zwanger, pregnant

zwangerschap (de), pregnancy

zwart, black
 zwart maken, to blacken (someone's name)

zwartkijker (de), pessimist; TV licence dodger

zwartrijden (het), evade paying road/highway tax; dodge paying the fare (bus/train)

zwartrijder (de), road tax dodger; faredodger (bus/train)

zwartwerk (het), moonlighting

zwartwerken, to moonlight, to work on the side

zwavel (de), sulphur

zwavelzuur (het), sulphuric acid

Zweden, Sweden

Zweeds, Swedish

zweefvliegen, to glide

zweefvliegtuig (het), glider

zweem (de), trace

zweep (de), whip, hunting crop

zweepslag (de), lash (with the whip)

zweer (de), ulcer

zweetdruppel (de), drop/bead of sweat

zweethanden (de), sweaty hands

zweetvoeten (de), sweaty feet

zwelgen, to guzzle; to revel

zwellen, to swell

zwembad (het), swimming pool

zwembroek (de), swimming trunks

zwemmen, to swim

zwemvest (het), lifejacket

zwemvlies (de), web, flipper

zwendel (de), swindle, racket

zwengel (de), pumphandle, crank

zwenken, to swing round, to swerve

zweren, to swear; to fester

zwerftocht (de), ramble, trek

zwerm (de), swarm

zwermen, to swarm

zwerven, to roam, to wander

zwerver (de), wanderer; vagabond, tramp

zweten, to sweat
zwetsen, to blather; to brag
zweven, to float, to glide, to
   hover
zwichten voor, to yield to
zwijgen, to be silent, to keep
   quiet
   tot – brengen, to silence
zwijgend, silent, tacit
zwijgzaam, taciturn

zwijm (de), swoon
zwijmelen, to swoon
zwijn (het), hog, swine
zwikken, to sprain
Zwitserland, Switzerland
Zwitser(s), Swiss
zwoegen, to toil
zwoel, sultry

English–Dutch dictionary

A

a(n), een

abandon, opgeven, ver'laten;
   overgave

abashed, ver'legen

abate, ver'minderen, afnemen

abbey, ab'dij

abbot, abt

abbreviate, afkorten, ver'korten

abbreviation, afkorting

abdicate, afstand doen van

abdomen, buik

abduct, ont'voeren

aberration, afwijking

abhor, ver'afschuwen

abhorrent, weerzin'wekkend

abide, toeven; uitstaan
   to abide by, zich houden aan

ability, ver'mogen,
   be'kwaamheid

abject, ver'slagen

abjure, afzweren

ablaze, in lichterlaaie

able, in staat; be'kwaam
   to be – to, kunnen

abnegation, ver'loochening

abnormal, abnor'maal

aboard, aan boord

abolish, afschaffen

abolition, afschaffing

abominable, af'schuwelijk

abomination, afschuw, gruwel

abortion, a'bortus

abound, in overvloed zijn

abounding in, rijk aan

about, om(streeks), onge'veer;
   over; in de buurt
   – to go, op het punt te gaan

above, boven
   the –, het bovenstaande

abrasion, schaafwond

abrasive, schuurmiddel;
   afschurend

abreast, naast el'kaar; ter (or op
   de) hoogte (van)

abridge, ver'korten

abroad, in (or naar) het
   buitenland

abrupt, ab'rupt, kort'af

abscess, ab'ces

absence, af'wezigheid

absent, af'wezig

absentee, af'wezige

absenteeism, absente'ïsme

absent-minded(ness),
   ver'strooid(heid)

absolute, vol'slagen, vol'strekt;
   defini'tief; abso'luut

absolution, abso'lutie

absolve, ver'geven, vrijspreken

absorb, (in zich) opnemen

absorbed, ver'diept

absorbent, absor'berend

absorbing, boeiend

abstain, zich ont'houden

abstinence, ont'houding

abstract, ab'stract; uittreksel

absurd, onge'rijmd;
   be'lachelijk, gek

abundance, overvloed

abundant, meer dan
   vol'doende

abundantly, in overvloed,
   rijkelijk

abuse, misbruik,
   scheldwoorden; mis'bruiken;
   uitschelden

abusive, be'ledigend

abut on, grenzen aan

abysmal, bodemloos,
   grenzeloos

abyss, afgrond

academic(al), aca'demisch

academy, aca'demie

accede to, be'stijgen,
   aan'vaarden; toestemmen in

accelerate, ver'snellen, gas
geven; in snelheid toenemen
acceleration, ver'snelling
accelerator, gaspedaal
accent, ac'cent, klemtoon
accent(uate), accentu'eren
accept, aannemen
acceptable, be'vredigend;
welkom
acceptance, gunstige ont'vangst
access, toegang
accessible, (gemakkelijk)
be'reikbaar; ge'naakbaar
accession, (troons)bestijging;
toetreding, aanwinst
accessories, toebehoren
accessory, mede'plichtige
accident, ongeluk; toeval
accidental, toe'vallig; per
ongeluk
acclaim, toejuiching; toejuichen
acclimatize, acclimati'seren
accolade, ridderslag; acco'lade
accommodate, onderdak
ver'lenen, (her)bergen;
aanpassen
accommodating, in'schikkelijk
accommodation,
accommo'datie
accompaniment, bege'leiding
accompany, verge'zellen,
ge'paard gaan met; bege'leiden
accomplice, mede'plichtige
accomplish, vol'brengen
accomplished, ta'lentvol;
vol'dongen (fact)
accomplishment, gave,
pres'tatie
accord, over'eenstemming;
ver'lenen; over'eenstemmen
of my own –, uit eigen
be'weging
according to, volgens

accordingly,
dienovereen'komstig
accost, aanklampen
account, ver'slag; rekening;
rekenschap; be'lang
to – for, ver'klaren
to take into –, in aanmerking
nemen
on – of, van'wege
on no –, in geen ge'val
accountancy, boekhouding
accountant, (hoofd)boekhouder
accredit, toeschrijven aan
accredited, er'kend
accrue, toenemen
accumulate, (zich) ophopen
accumulator, accu(mu'lator)
accuracy, nauw'keurigheid
accurate, nauw'keurig; pre'cies
accursed, ver'vloekt
accusation, be'schuldiging
accuse, be'schuldigen
accused, ver'dachte
accustom, wennen aan
accustomed, ge'wend; ge'woon
ace, aas
acerbity, scherpheid
ache, pijn (doen); hunkeren (naar)
achieve, be'reiken
achievement, pres'tatie;
bereiken
acid, zuur
acknowledge, er'kennen;
be'antwoorden
acknowledgement, er'kenning;
be'antwoording; be'richt van
ont'vangst
acolyte, volgeling, aanhanger
acorn, eikel
acoustic, akoestiek
acquaint, in kennis stellen
acquaintance, kennis
acquainted, be'kend, op de
hoogte

acquiesce in, instemmen met; be'rusten in

acquire, ver'werven, aanschaffen

acquisition, aanwinst

acquisitive, heb'zuchtig

acquit, vrijspreken; kwijten

acquittal, vrijspraak

acre, acre, 4047 vierkante meter (m²)

acrid, scherp

acrimonious, ve'nijnig, boo'saardig

acrobat, acro'baat

across, aan (or naar) de overkant (van); (dwars) over or door

act, daad; be'drijf, nummer; handelen, werken; (to'neel)spelen

acting, waar'nemend; to'neelspel

action, handeling, werking; actie

activate, aanzetten (tot)

active, ac'tief

activity, be'drijvigheid

actor, actress ac'teur, ac'trice

actual, werkelijk

actually, eigenlijk, feitelijk

acumen, scherp'zinnigheid

acute, scherp; a'cuut

adamant, onver'murwbaar

adapt, aanpassen, be'werken

adaptability, aanpassingsvermogen

adaptable, aan te passen; plooibaar

adaptation, be'werking; aanpassing

add (to), toevoegen aan, voegen bij

– to, ver'meerderen

– up, optellen; oplopen

addict, ver'slaafde

addicted, ver'slaafd

addition, optelling; toevoeging

in –, boven'dien

additional, extra

addled, be'dorven; ver'dwaasd

address, a'dres; toespraak; adres'seren; aanspreken, toespreken

adenoids, neusamandelen

adept, be'dreven(e) (in)

adequate, vol'doende, ge'schikt

adhere, (aan)kleven; aanhangen, blijven bij

adhesion, ad'hesie

adhesive, plak-; plakmiddel

adjacent, aan'grenzend

adjective, bij'voeglijk naamwoord

adjoin, grenzen aan

adjourn, ver'dagen; (uit'een)gaan

adjudicate, uitspraak doen

adjunct, aanhangsel; be'paling

adjust, bijstellen, reguleren

adjustable, ver'stelbaar

ad lib, on'voorbereid, geïmprovi'seerd

administer, be'heren; toedienen

administration, be'heer, re'gering

administrative, administra'tief

admirable, bewonderingswaardig; voor'treffelijk

admiral, admi'raal

admiration, be'wondering

admire, be'wonderen

admissible, ver'oorloofd; aan'nemelijk

admission, toegang(sprijs), toelating; er'kenning

admit, toelaten tot, opnemen in; toegeven

admittance, toegang

admittedly, weliswaar

admonish, ver'manen

ad nauseam, tot ver'velens toe

ado, drukte

adolescence, puber'teit

adolescent, puber

adopt, aannemen

adorable, aller'liefst

adoration, aan'bidding

adore, aan'bidden; dol zijn op

adorn, (ver')sieren

adornment, ver'siering, sieraad

adrift, drijvend, los

adroit(ness), handig(heid)

adulation, ophemeling

adult, vol'wassen(e)

adultery, overspel

advance, voor'uitgang; opmars; voorschot; naar voren komen, oprukken; voorschieten

  in –, van te voren

advanced, (ver)ge'vorderd

advancement, voor'uitgang, be'vordering

advantage, voordeel

  to take advantage of, ge'bruik maken van

advantageous, gunstig

advent, (aan)komst; Ad'vent

adventure, avon'tuur, onder'neming

adventurer, avontu'rier

adventurous, avon'tuurlijk; ge'waagd

adverb, bijwoord

adversary, tegenstander

adverse, on'gunstig; na'delig

adversity, tegenspoed

advertise, adver'teren, re'clame maken (voor); be'kend maken

advertisement, adver'tentie, re'clame

advice, raad

advisable, raadzaam

advise, aanraden

advisedly, met over'leg

advisor, raadsman, consulent

advisory, raadgevend

advocate, voorspraak; voorstander; be'pleiten

aerial, an'tenne

afar, verre

affable, minzaam

affair, zaak; ver'houding

affect, (be')treffen; voorwenden

affectation, ge'maaktheid; voorwendsel

affected, ge'maakt

affection, ge'negenheid

affectionate, aan'hankelijk, hartelijk; toegenegen

affidavit, be'ëdigde ver'klaring

affiliated to, aangesloten bij

affinity, ver'wantschap

affirm, plechtig ver'klaren

affirmation, be'vestiging

affirmative, be'vestigend

afflict, kwellen, teisteren

affliction, kwelling, ramp

affluent, (schat)rijk

afford, zich ver'oorloven; ver'schaffen

affront, be'lediging

afield: far –, ver weg

afloat, drijvend

afoot, aan de gang

aforementioned, aforesaid, voor'noemd

afraid, bang

afresh, op'nieuw

after, (daar')na; na'dat

after-effect(s), nawerking

aftermath, nasleep

afternoon, (na)middag
afterthought, latere over'weging
afterwards, later, nader'hand
again, weer (eens); te'rug
  again and again, telkens weer
against, tegen
age, leeftijd, ouderdom; eeuw; ouder worden
  of –, meerder'jarig
aged, be'jaard; oud
agency, a'gentschap
agenda, a'genda
agent, tussenpersoon, a'gent
agglomeration, op'eenhoping
aggrandize, ver'heffen
aggravate, (ver')ergeren
aggravating, ver'velend; ver'zwarend
aggregate, (ge'zamenlijk) to'taal
aggression, ag'gressie
aggressive, aggres'sief
aggressor, aanvaller
aghast at, ont'zet over
agile, be'hendig
agitate, a'geren; schudden
agitation, actie; be'roering; ge'jaagdheid
aglow, gloeiend
agnostic, ag'nosticus
ago, ge'leden
agog: to be –, zitten te springen
agonizing, (vreselijk) pijnlijk
agony, vreselijke pijn
agree, het eens zijn; over'eenkomen; toestemmen
  fish doesn't – with me, ik kan niet tegen vis
agreeable, aangenaam; be'reid
agreement, over'eenkomst
agricultural, landbouw-('kundig)
agriculture, landbouw

aground, aan de grond
ahead, voor'op, voor'uit; in het voor'uitzicht
aid, hulp
ail, man'keren; sukkelen
ailment, kwaal
aim, doel(einde); mikken op; munten op; streven naar
aimless, doelloos
air, lucht; schijn; wijs; luchten
  airs (and graces), airs
aircraft, vliegtuig
aircraft carrier, vliegdekschip
airfield, vliegveld
airforce, luchtmacht
airgun, windbuks
air hostess, stewardess
airily, lucht'hartig
airlift, luchtbrug
airline, luchtvaartmaatschappij
airliner, lijnvliegtuig
airplane, vliegtuig
airport, luchthaven, vliegveld
air raid, luchtaanval
airtight, luchtdicht
airy, luchtig
aisle, zijbeuk, gangpad
ajar, op een kier
akin, ver'want
alarm, a'larm; ont'steltenis; ont'stellen
alarm clock, wekker
alarmist, alar'mist(isch)
alas, he'laas
albeit, (al)hoe'wel
alcohol, alcohol
alcoholic, alco'holisch; alcoho'list
alcove, nis; al'koof
alderman, wethouder
ale, bier
alert, waakzaam
algebra, algebra

alien, vreemd(eling), buitenlander; buitenaardswezen

alienate, ver'vreemden

alight, aan(gestoken); af(*or* uit)stappen; neerstrijken

align, op één lijn plaatsen

alike, evenzeer

  to be alike, op el'kaar lijken

alive, levend, in leven; zich be'wust van

alkali(ne), al'kali(sch)

all, al(le); alles, allen; ge'heel, alle'maal

  – **along,** steeds

  – **but,** bijna

  – **in,** alles inbegrepen

  – **right,** in orde

  – **the more,** des te meer

  after –, ten'slotte

  – **in** –, al met al

  at –, über'haupt

  not at –, hele'maal niet

  for – **that,** desondanks

  for – **I know,** voor zo'ver ik weet

allay, stillen

allegation, be'wering

allege, be'weren

alleged(ly), zoge'naamd

allegiance, trouw

allegory, allego'rie

allergic, al'lergisch

alleviate, ver'lichten

alley(way), steeg

alliance, ver'bond

allied, ver'bonden; ver'want

alliteration, allite'ratie

allocate, toewijzen

allot, toebedelen

allotment, volkstuintje

allow, toestaan; rekenen

allowance, toelage

to (make) allow(ance) for, rekening houden met

alloy, le'gering

all-round, veel'zijdig

allude to, zinspelen op

alluring, aan'lokkelijk

allusion, toespeling

ally, bondgenoot; ver'binden

almighty, al'machtig

almond, a'mandel

almost, bijna

alms, aalmoes

alone, al'leen

  let alone, laat staan

along, langs; mee; voort

  – **with,** met … mee, samen met

alongside, langs'zij

aloof, op een afstand

aloud, hardop

alphabet, alfabet

alphabetical, alfa'betisch

already, al, reeds

also, ook; boven'dien

altar, altaar

alter, ver'anderen, (zich) wijzigen

alteration, ver'andering

altercation, twistgesprek

alternate, afwisselen

  on – **days,** om de andere dag

alternately, om de beurt

alternative, alterna'tief

alternatively, aan de andere kant

although, hoe'wel

altitude, hoogte

alto, alt

altogether, hele'maal; alles bij el'kaar

altruism, altru'isme

aluminium, alu'minium

always, al'tijd

amalgamate, samensmelten

amass, op'eenhopen
amateur, ama'teur
amaze, ver'bazen
amazement, ver'bazing
ambassador, (af)gezant
ambiguity, dubbel'zinnigheid
ambiguous, dubbel'zinnig
ambition, ambi'tie; aspi'ratie,
  ide'aal
ambitious, ambi'tieus; groots
  opgezet
amble, kuieren
ambulance, ziekenauto,
  ambulance
ambush, hinderlaag
amenable, ont'vankelijk (voor)
amend, ver'beteren, wijzigen
amendment, amende'ment
amends: to make –, het weer
  goedmaken
amenity, ge'mak
amiable, be'minnelijk
amicable, vriend'schappelijk
amid(st), te midden van
amiss, ver'keerd
ammonia, ammoni'ak
ammunition, (am)mu'nitie
amnesty, amnes'tie
among(st), onder, tussen
amorous, ver'liefd; liefdes-
amount, be'drag, hoe'veelheid
  to – to, be'dragen; be'tekenen
amphibian, amfi'bie
ample, ruim (vol'doende)
amplify, aanvullen; ver'sterken
amply, ruimschoots
amputate, ampu'teren
amuse, ver'maken; pret hebben
amused: to be –, grappig vinden
amusement, ver'maak,
  tijdsverdrijf
amusing, amu'sant,
  onder'houdend

anaemia, bloedarmoede
anaesthetic, ver'dovend;
  ver'dovingsmiddel
analogous, ana'loog
analogy, analo'gie
analyse, anali'seren
analysis, ana'lyse
anarchy, anar'chie
anatomy, anato'mie
ancestor, voorvader
ancestral, voorvaderlijk
ancestry, voorgeslacht;
  afstamming
anchor, anker; (ver')ankeren
anchorage, ankergrond; steun
anchovy, an'sjovis
ancient, (zeer) oud
and, en
anecdote, anek'dote
anew, op'nieuw
angel, engel
angelic(al), engelachtig, engelen-
anger, boosheid
angle, hoek; ge'zichtspunt;
  hengelen
Anglican, angli'caan(s)
angry, boos
anguish, leed, pijn
angular, hoekig
animal, dier; dierlijk, dieren-
animate, levend; be'zielen
animated, geani'meerd, levendig
  – cartoon, tekenfilm
animation, tekenfilm,
  poppenfilm; levend(ig) maken
animosity, vij'andigheid
ankle, enkel
annals, an'nalen
annex, anne'xeren; toevoegen
annexe, uitbouw, depen'dance;
  bijlage
annihilate, ver'nietigen
anniversary, jaarfeest, ge'denkdag

announce, aankondigen
announcement, aankondiging
announcer, omroeper
annoy, ergeren
annoyance, ergenis
annoying, ver'velend
annual, jaar'lijks; éénjarige plant
annuity, jaargeld, lijfrente
annul, te'nietdoen
anoint, zalven
anomaly, afwijking
anonymous, ano'niem
another, een ander(e), nog een
answer, antwoord, oplossing;
  (be')antwoorden
answerable, aan'sprakelijk; te
  be'antwoorden
ant, mier
antagonism, vijandschap
antagonist, tegenstander
antagonize, ophitsen
antarctic, zuidpool
antecedent, voor'afgaand;
  antece'dent
anthem: national –, volkslied
anthill, mierenhoop
anthology, bloemlezing
anthracite, antra'ciet
anti-aircraft, luchtafweer-
antics, streken
anticipate, ver'wachten;
  voor'uitlopen op, vóór zijn
anticipation, ver'wachting
anticlimax, anti'climax
antidote, tegengif
antipathy, antipa'thie
antiquarian, oudheid'kundig(e),
  anti'quair
antiquated, ouder'wets
antique, an'tiek; antiqui'teit
antiquity, oudheid; ouderdom
antiseptic, anti'septisch (middel)

antithesis, tegenstelling,
  tegenge'stelde
antlers, ge'wei
anvil, aanbeeld
anxiety, be'zorgdheid
anxious, be'zorgd
  to be – to, heel graag willen
any, ieder, iemand; wat (ook),
  enig
  not –, geen; niets
anybody, anyone, iemand,
  iedereen; wie ook
anyhow, hoe dan ook; zo maar
anything, iets; alles
anyway, in ieder ge'val
anywhere, ergens; over'al
apace, vlug
apart, uit el'kaar; afgezien;
  afgezonderd
apartment, etage, flat
apathetic, a'patisch
apathy, onver'schilligheid
ape, aap; na-apen
aperture, opening
apex, top(punt)
apiece, per stuk, elk
apologetic, veront'schuldigend
apologize, zich
  veront'schuldigen
apology, veront'schuldiging
apoplectic fit, be'roerte
apostle, a'postel
apostrophe, apos'trof
appal, ont'zetten
appalling, schrik'barend
apparatus, appa'raten,
  appa'raat, toestel(len)
apparel, kle'dij
apparent, duidelijk;
  ogen'schijnlijk
apparently, blijkbaar
apparition, (geest)ver'schijning

appeal, be'roep, smeekbede; aantrekkingskracht; een be'roep doen (op), smeken; in be'roep gaan (bij); aantrekken

appear, (ver')schijnen, blijken

appearance, ver'schijning, optreden; voorkomen

appease, sussen, stillen

appeasement, ver'zoening

append, (bij)voegen

appendage, aanhangsel

appendicitis, blinde'darmontsteking

appendix, ap'pendix; aanhangsel

appertain to, be'trekking hebben op; be'horen aan

appetite, (eet)lust

appetizing, smakelijk

applaud, toejuichen, applaudis'seren

applause, ap'plaus, toejuiching(en)

apple, appel

appliance, appa'raat; toepassing

applicable, toe'passelijk

applicant, sollici'tant

application, aanbrengen; (ma'nier van) toepassing, ge'bruik; sollici'tatie; ijver

applied, toegepast

apply, aanbrengen; toepassen, van toepassing zijn; zich wenden; sollici'teren; toeleggen (op)

appoint, be'noemen, aanwijzen

appointed time, vastgesteld uur

appointment, afspraak; be'noeming, ambt

apportion, ver'delen

apposite, toe'passelijk

appraisal, schatting

appreciable, aan'merkelijk

appreciate, waar'deren, ge'voelig zijn voor; stijgen

appreciation, waar'dering, ge'voel; stijging

appreciative, dankbaar

apprehend, ge'vangen nemen; vatten; vrezen

apprehension, in'hechtenisneming; be'grip; angst

apprehensive, angstig

apprentice, leerling: in de leer doen

approach, nader'bij komen; toegang(sweg); aanpak; naderen; zich wenden tot

approachable, toe'gankelijk

approbation, goedkeuring, bijval

appropriate, ge'schikt; zich toeëigenen, be'stemmen

approval, goedkeuring, bijval

approve, goedkeuren, er'kennen

approximate, be'naderen **the (approximate) length is (approximately),** de lengte is onge'veer

approximation, schatting

apricot, abri'koos

April, a'pril

apron, schort

apt, ge'neigd; passend; vlug

aptitude, aanleg

aquarium, a'quarium

aquatic, water

aqueduct, waterleiding

aquiline, arends-

Arab, Ara'bier

Arabian, Arabic, A'rabisch

arbitrary, wille'keurig

arbitration, arbi'trage

arc, boog

arcade, gale'rij
arch, boog, ge'welf; aarts
archaeology, oudheidkunde
archaic, ver'ouderd
arched, ge'bogen
archer, boogschutter
archery, boogschieten
architect, archi'tect
architectural, bouw'kundig
architecture, bouwkunde,
  bouwstijl
archives, ar'chief,
  ar'chieven
archway, poort
arctic, noordpool
ardent, vurig
arduous, zwaar
area, oppervlak, ge'bied
arena, a'rena
argue, debat'teren;
  tegenspreken; be'togen
argument, ruzie; argument,
  rede'nering; discussie
argumentative, twistziek
arid, dor, droog
arise, ont'staan, zich voordoen;
  ver'rijzen
aristocracy, aristocra'tie
aristocrat, aristo'craat
arithmetic, rekenkunde
ark, ark
arm, arm, leuning; wapen;
  be'wapenen
  – in –, ge'armd
armament, be'wapening
armchair, leunstoel
armful, vracht
armistice, wapenstilstand
armour, harnas; wapenrusting
armoured, pantser-
armoury, wapenzaal
armpit, oksel
army, leger

aroma, a'roma
aromatic, geurig
around, rond('om); over'al; in
  de buurt (van)
arouse, opwekken; wakker
  maken
arraign, aanklagen;
  be'schuldigen
arrange, (rang)schikken;
  regelen, afspreken; arran'geren
arrangement, schikking;
  afspraak; arrange'ment
array, (slag)orde; uitstalling;
  opstellen; uitdossen
arrears, achterstand
arrest, ar'rest, arres'tatie;
  arres'teren; tegenhouden
arrival, (aan)komst;
  aangekomene
arrive, (aan)komen
arrogance, arro'gantie
arrogant, arro'gant
arrow, pijl
arsenal, arse'naal
arsenic, ar'senicum
arson, brandstichting
art, kunst
artery, (slag)ader
artful, ge'slepen
arthritis, ar'tritis, jicht
artichoke, arti'sjok
article, ar'tikel; voorwerp;
  lidwoord
  – of clothing, kledingstuk
articulate, duidelijk;
  articu'leren; koppelen
artifice, kunst(greep)
artificer, handwerksman
artificial, kunst'matig,
  ge'kunsteld, kunst-
artillery, artille'rie
artisan, vakman, ambachtsman
artist, kunstenaar, schilder

artistic, kunst'zinnig, artis'tiek
artistry, kunstenaarstalent
artless, argeloos; ruw
as, (zo)als; ter'wijl; daar
 (just) – ... (–), even ... (als)
 – to, wat betreft
asbestos, as'best
ascend, (be')stijgen
ascendancy, overwicht
Ascension, hemelvaart
ascent, stijgen, be'stijging; helling
ascertain, te weten komen
ascetic, as'ceet; as'cetisch
ascribe, toeschrijven
ash, as; es
ashamed, be'schaamd
 to be –, zich schamen
ashen, lijkbleek
ashore, aan wal, aan land
ashtray, asbak
aside, op'zij, ter'zijde
ask, vragen, **– a question,** een
 vraag stellen
askance, wan'trouwend
askew, scheef
aslant, schuin
asleep, in slaap
 to be –, slapen
asparagus, as'perge
aspect, as'pect, kant; aanblik;
 ligging
asphalt, asfalt
asphyxiate, (ver')stikken
aspirant, aspi'rant
aspiration, aspi'ratie
aspire, streven (naar)
ass, ezel
assail, be'stormen, aanvallen
assailant, aanvaller
assassin, sluipmoordenaar
assassinate, ver'moorden
assault, be'storming,
 aanval(len), be'stormen

assemble, (zich) ver'zamelen,
 mon'teren
assembly, bij'eenkomst;
 mon'tering
assent, instemming; instemmen
assert, be'weren; doen gelden,
 opkomen voor
assertion, be'wering
assess, ta'xeren; aanslaan
asset, creditpost; goed, bezit,
 kwaliteit
assiduous, naarstig
assign, toewijzen; vaststellen
assignment, opdracht
assimilate, ver'werken,
 opnemen
assimilation, assimi'latie
assist, helpen
assistance, hulp
assistant, assis'tent,
 be'diende
associate, partner; ver'want;
 ver'binden, associ'ëren,
 omgaan
association, associ'atie;
 ge'nootschap
assorted, ge'mengd
assortment, sor'tering;
 ver'zameling
assuage, stillen, lessen
assume, aannemen;
 voorwenden; op zich nemen
assumption, veronder'stelling;
 aanvaarding
assurance, ver'zekering
assure, ver'zekeren
assuredly, stellig; zelfbe'wust
astonish, ver'bazen
astonishment, ver'bazing
astound, (ten hoogste)
 ver'bazen
astray, op een dwaalspoor
astride, schrijlings (op)

astronaut, astronaut, ruimtevaarder
astronomical, astro'nomisch
astronomy, sterrenkunde
astute, slim
asunder, uit el'kaar
asylum, ge'sticht; a'siel
asymmetric(al), asym'metrisch
at, aan (position); in, op, te (place); om (time); naar (direction); voor (price)
– **(my) leisure,** op mijn ge'mak
– **that moment,** op dat ogenblik
– **the time,** toen
atheism, athe'ïsme
athlete, at'leet
athletic, at'letisch
athletics, atle'tiek
Atlantic, At'lantische Oce'aan
atlas, atlas
atmosphere, dampkring; (atmo')sfeer
atmospheric, atmos'ferisch
atom, a'toom
atomic, a'tomisch, a'toom-
atone, boeten
atonement, boete(doening), ver'zoening
atrocious, af'schuwelijk
atrocity, gruwel(daad)
attach, vastmaken, ver'binden; hechten
attachment, onderdeel, ver'binding; ge'hechtheid
attack, aanval(len)
attain, be'reiken, be'halen
attainable, be'reikbaar
attainment, be'reiken; ta'lent
attempt, poging, aanslag; trachten
attend, bijwonen; verge'zellen
  attend to, opletten; ver'zorgen

attendance, opkomst; aan'wezigheid
  in attendance, aan'wezig; in het ge'volg
attendant, be'diende; be'zoeker: bege'leidend; dienstdoend
attention, aandacht; at'tentie; houding
attentive, op'lettend; at'tent
attenuate, ver'dunnen; ver'zachten
attest, ge'tuigen van, attes'teren
attic, zolder(kamer)
attire, tooi(en)
attitude, houding
attorney, gevol'machtigde, procu'reur
attract, (aan)trekken
attraction, aantrekking(skracht)
attractive, aan'trekkelijk
attribute, eigenschap, kenmerk; attri'buut; toeschrijven
attune, (over'een)stemmen met
auburn, kas'tanjebruin
auction, veiling; veilen
auctioneer, afslager
audacious, dapper; roekeloos
audacity, dapperheid, brutali'teit
audible, hoorbaar
audience, ge'hoor, toehoorders
audit, ac'countantsverslag; verifi'ëren
audition, auditie
auditor, ac'countant; toehoorder
auditorium, zaal
augment, ver'meerderen, uitbreiden
August, au'gustus
aunt, tante
aura, aura
auspices, auspiciën
auspicious, gunstig

austere, streng, sober
austerity, ver'sobering
Austria, Oostenrijk
authentic, authen'tiek
authenticate, verifi'ëren
authenticity, echtheid
author, schrijver; schepper
authoritarian, autori'tair
  (per'soon)
authoritative, autori'tair,
  ge'zaghebbend
authority, autori'teit; bron;
  machtiging
authorize, machtigen;
  be'krachtigen
autobiography, autobiogra'fie
autocracy, onbeperkte
  heerschap'pij
autograph, handtekening
automatic, auto'matisch
autonomous, auto'noom
autopsy, lijkschouwing
autumn(al), herfst(-)
auxiliary, hulp; hulpwerkwoord
avail, baten
  of no –, vruchteloos
  to – oneself of, be'nutten
available, be'schikbaar
avalanche, la'wine
avarice, gierigheid
avaricious, gierig; be'gerig
avenge, wreken
avenue, laan; weg
average, ge'middeld (doen);
  ge'middelde
averse to, af'kerig van
aversion, afkeer, tegenzin
avert, afwenden
aviary, voli'ère
aviation, luchtvaart
avid, gretig, be'gerig
avoid, (ver')mijden
avoidance, ver'mijding

avow, be'lijden, be'kennen
avowal, be'kentenis,
  be'lijdenis
await, afwachten; wachten op
awake, wakker; zich be'wust
  (worden) van; ont'waken;
  wekken
awaken, wekken
awakening: rude –,
  ont'nuchtering
award, be'kroning, prijs;
  toekennen, toewijzen
aware, be'wust
awareness, be'sef
awash, over'spoeld
away, weg; er op los
  do – with, opruimen
awe, ont'zag
awe-inspiring, ontzag'wekkend
awful, ver'schrikkelijk, vreselijk
awfully, (heel) erg
awhile, een tijdje
awkward, on'handig; lastig
awning, dekzeil, zonnescherm
awry, scheef
axe, bijl; drastisch be'perken
axis, as(lijn); spil
azure, hemelsblauw

B

babble, babbelen, kabbelen
baboon, bavi'aan
baby, kindje, baby; jong, klein
babyish, kinderachtig
bachelor, vrijge'zel
bacillus, ba'cil
back, rug, achterkant,
  rugleuning; te'rug, achter-;
  achter'uitgaan; wedden op;
  bijvallen
  – to front, achterstevoren
  at the –, achter'aan (*or*'in)

back (*continued*)
  on the –, achter'op
  to – down, zich te'rugtrekken
  to – out, te'rugkrabbelen
  to – up, steunen
backbiting, kwaadspreke'rij
backbone, ruggegraat
backfire, te'rugslaan
background, achtergrond
backing, steun; achterkant
  (bekleding)
backstage, achter de schermen
backward(s), achter'uit, te'rug-;
  achterlijk, traag
  – and forwards, heen en weer
backwater, kreek, uithoek
bacon, spek, bacon
bacteria, bac'teriën
bad, slecht, naar; vals; be'dorven
  to go –, be'derven
  – luck, pech
badge, in'signe
badger, das; lastig vallen
badly, erg; dolgraag
bad-tempered, slecht-
  gehu'meurd
baffle, ver'bijsteren
bag, zak, tas; vangst; gappen
baggage, ba'gage
baggy, uitgezakt, hang-
bagpipe, doedelzaak
bail, borg(tocht); borgstaan;
  hozen
bailiff, rentmeester; deurwaarder
bait, lokaas; van aas voor'zien
bake, bakken
baker, bakker
bakery, bakke'rij
balaclava, bivakmuts
balance, evenwicht; saldo,
  res't(ant); weegschaal; in
  evenwicht brengen, opwegen
  tegen; sluitend maken (*or* zijn)

balanced, even'wichtig
balance sheet, ba'lans
balcony, bal'kon
bald, kaal; naakt
bale, baal; in balen ver'pakken
baleful, onheil'spellend,
  ge'pijnigd
balk, balk; ver'ijdelen,
  tegenstribbelen
ball, bal(len); bal (*dance*)
ballad, bal'lade
ballast, ballast
ball bearing, kogellager
ballet, bal'let
balloon, bal'lon; bol staan
ballot, (ge'heime) stemming; lot
balm, balsem, geur
balmy, zacht, geurig; ge'tikt
balsam, balsem
balustrade, balu'strade
bamboo, bamboe
bamboozle, bedriegen
ban, ver'bod, ban(vloek);
  ver'bieden; ver'bannen
banal, ba'naal
banana, ba'naan
band, band, rand; troep; ka'pel;
  ver'enigen
bandage, ver'band
bandit, ban'diet
bandstand, mu'ziektent
bandy-legged, met o-benen
bane, vloek
bang, klap, knal; (dicht)slaan
banish, ver'bannen
banishment, ver'banning
banisters, trapleuning
banjo, banjo
bank, oever, berm; bank;
  ophopen; depo'neren;
  overhellen; afdekken
  to – on, specu'leren op
banker, ban'kier

bank holiday, offici'ële va'kantiedag

banknote, bankbiljet

bankrupt, fai'lliet

bankruptcy, faillisse'ment

banner, ba'nier, vaandel

banquet, gastmaal

banter, gekscheren

baptism, doop

Baptist, doopsge'zinde

baptize, dopen

bar, stang, reep, staaf; barri'ère; bar; balie; maat; uitgezonderd; afsluiten, ver'sperren; uitsluiten

barbarian, bar'baar(s)

barbarity, bar'baarsheid

barbarous, bar'baars

barbed, hekelend

– wire, prikkeldraad

barber, kapper

barcode, streepjescode

bard, zanger-dichter

bare, (ont')bloot, kaal; mini'maal; ont'bloten

barefaced, onbe'schaamd

barefoot(ed), bloots'voets

bareheaded, bloots'hoofds

barely, nauwelijks

bargain, over'eenkomst; koopje; dingen

into the –, op de koop toe

to – for, rekenen op

barge, schuit, sloep; botsen, zich werken

baritone, bariton

bark, schors; ge'blaf; bark; schaven; blaffen

barley, gerst

barn, schuur

barometer, barometer

baron, ba'ron; mag'naat

baroque, ba'rok(stijl)

barracks, ka'zerne(woning)

barrel, vat, ton; loop

barren, on'vruchtbaar, dor

barricade, barri'cade; barrica'deren

barrier, barri'ère, con'trole

barrister, advo'kaat

barrow, handkar; grafheuvel

barter, ruilhandel drijven; ver'kwanselen

base, basis, voetstuk; ge'meen

baseball, honkbal

basement, kelder, souter'rain

bash, dreun; stoot; slaan

bashful, schuchter, verlegen

basic, fundamen'teel, grond-

basin, kom, bak; dok

basis, basis

bask, zich koesteren

basket, mand

basketball, basketbal

bass, bas; baars

bassoon, fa'got

bastard, bastaard; on'echt

baste, met vet over'gieten

bastion, basti'on

bat, slaghout; vleermuis; batten

off one's own –, op eigen houtje

batch, par'tij, baksel; groep

bath, bad; in bad doen (or gaan)

bathe, (zich) baden

bathed (in light), baden (in licht)

bathrobe, badjas

bathroom, badkamer

baton, stok(je)

battalion, batal'jon

batten, lat

batter, be'slag

battery, batte'rij, accu

battle, (veld)slag; strijd(en)

battleaxe, strijdbijl
battlefield, slagveld
battlement, kan'teel
battleship, slagschip
bawl, schreeuwen, brullen
bay, baai; erker, hoek; blaffen
  at bay, in het nauw
bayonet, bajo'net
bazaar, ba'zaar
be, zijn; zitten, worden
  **to – hungry, sleepy, thirsty,
  cold,** honger, slaap, dorst, het
  koud hebben
  how are you? hoe maakt
  u het?
  how is it that? hoe komt het
  dat?
beach, strand
beacon, baken
bead, kraal
beak, snavel
beaker, beker(glas)
beam, balk; stralenbundel;
  stralen (van)
bean, boon
bear, beer; (ver)'dragen; baren
  to – down, neerdrukken;
  afkomen op
  to – out, staven
  to – witness, ge'tuigen
beard, baard; trot'seren
bearer, drager, brenger; toonder
bearing, houding; be'trekking;
  richting; kogellager
beast, beest
beastly, beestachtig; akelig
beat, (maat)slag; ronde;
  (ver)'slaan, kloppen; la'veren
beating, afranseling; klappen
beautiful, mooi
beautify, ver'fraaien
beauty, schoonheid;
  prachtexemplaar

beaver, bever
because, omdat
  – of, van'wege
beckon, wenken
become, worden
  to – of, ge'beuren met
becoming, be'tamelijk, flat'teus
bed, bed
bedding, beddengoed; onderlaag
bedlam, gekkenhuis
bedraggled, nat en ver'wilderd
bedridden, bed'legerig
bedroom, slaapkamer
bedspread, sprei
bedstead, ledi'kant
bee, bij
beech, beuk
beef, rundvlees
beefsteak, runderlap
beehive, bijenkorf
beer, bier
beetle, kever
beetroot, rode biet
befall, over'komen
befit, be'tamen
befog, be'nevelen
before, voor('af, 'op *or* 'uit),
  te'voren; voordat
  – long, weldra
beforehand, voor'af, van
  te'voren
befriend, vriendschap be'wijzen
befuddle, be'nevelen
beg, bedelen; smeken,
  ver'zoeken; zo vrij zijn
beget, voortbrengen
beggar, bedelaar; stakker
begin, be'ginnen
beginning, be'gin
begrudge, mis'gunnen
beguile, be'driegen; ver'drijven
behalf: on – of, ten be'hoeve
  van, uit naam van

behave (oneself), zich (netjes)
  ge'dragen
behaviour, ge'drag
behead, ont'hoofden
behind, achter(ste)
behold, aan'schouwen
beige, beige
being, wezen
  to come into –, ont'staan
  for the time –, voor'lopig
belated, (ver')laat
belch, boeren; uitbraken
belfry, klokkentoren
Belgium, België
belie, logenstraffen
belief, ge'loof
believe, ge'loven
believer, ge'lovige; voorstander
  (van)
belittle, klei'neren
bell, bel, klok
bellicose, oorlogs'zuchtig
belligerent, strijd'lustig
bellow, ge'brul; brullen
bellows, blaasbalg
belly, buik
belong, (be')horen
  to – to, (toebe)horen aan
belongings, spullen
beloved, ge'liefd(e)
below, onder, be'neden
belt, gordel, riem; zone;
  afranselen
bemoan, be'jammeren
bench, (recht)bank
bend, bocht; (zich) buigen;
  ver'buigen
beneath, be'neden, onder
benediction, zegen
benefactor, weldoener
beneficial, heilzaam
benefit, voordeel; uitkering;
  goed doen, voordeel trekken

benevolent, wel'willend
benign, goed('aard)ig, wel'dadig
bent, ge'bogen; be'sloten, uit
  op; aanleg
benumb, ver'kleumen
bequeath, ver'maken
bequest, le'gaat
bereave, be'roven
bereaved, diep be'droefd
bereavement, zwaar ver'lies
beret, ba'ret
berry, bes
berth, ligplaats; kooi
beseech, smeken
beside, naast
  – oneself with, buiten zichzelf
  van
besides, boven'dien; be'halve
besiege, be'legeren; be'stormen
besmirch, be'vuilen; be'zoedelen
best, (het) best
  – man, getuige (at a wedding)
  – part of, bijna
  at –, in het gunstigste ge'val
  to make the – of, zich schikken
  in
bestial, beestachtig
bestow, ver'lenen, schenken
bet, wedden(schap)
betray, ver'raden
betrayal, ver'raad
better, beter; ver'beteren
  better off, er beter aan toe
  had better, moet(en) maar
between, tussen
beverage, drank
bewail, be'jammeren
beware of, oppassen voor
bewilder, ver'bijsteren
bewitch, be'heksen
beyond, voor'bij; boven;
  meer dan
  it is – me, het gaat mijn
  verstand te boven

bias, neiging; bevoor'oordelen
bib, slabbetje
Bible, bijbel
bibliography, bibliogra'fie
bicker, kibbelen
bicycle, fiets
bid, bod; beiden; ge'lasten
big, groot
bigamy, biga'mie
big-headed, verwaand
bigot(ed), kwezel(achtig)
bill, rekening; wetsontwerp;
  aanplakbiljet; snavel
billiards, bil'jart
billion, bil'joen
billow, bollen; in wolken
  opstijgen
bin, bak
bind, (in-, vast- *or* ver')binden;
  ver'plichten
binder, (boek)binder; omslag
binding, band; bindend
binoculars, verrekijker
biography, levensbeschrijving,
  biografie
biology, biolo'gie
birch, berk
bird, vogel
birth, ge'boorte
  to give – to, het leven
  schenken aan
birthday, ver'jaardag
birth rate, ge'boortecijfer
biscuit, koekje, biskwietje
bishop, bisschop
bit, beetje, stukje; bit
  wait a –, even wachten
bitch, (term of abuse) teef,
  kreng; teef (female dog)
bite, beet, hap; bijten
bitter, bitter
blab, ver'klikken
black, zwart, blauw (eye)

blackberry, braam
blackbird, merel
blackboard, schoolbord
blackmail, chan'tage; geld afpersen
blackout, ver'duistering;
  tijdelijke bewuste'loosheid
blacksmith, smid
bladder, blaas
blade, kling, lemmet, mesje;
  spriet
blame, (de) schuld (geven)
blameless, onbe'rispelijk
blanch, (ver')bleken, pellen
bland, nietszeggend; flauw
blank, blanco; wezenloos; los
  (cartridge)
  to draw a –, botvangen
blanket, deken
blare, schallen
blasphemy, godslastering
blast, rukwind, luchtdruk; laten
  springen
blast furnace, hoogoven
blatant, over'duidelijk
blaze, laaiend vuur,
  (vlammen)zee; opvlammen, in
  lichterlaaie staan
bleach, (doen ver')bleken
bleak, troosteloos
bleat, blaten
bleed, bloeden; uitzuigen
blemish, smet, ont'siering;
  be'kladden
blend, mengsel; (zich)
  ver'mengen, harmoni'ëren
bless, zegenen
blessing, zegen(ing)
blight, plantenziekte; be'derf
blind, blind; doodlopend;
  rolgordijn; foefje; ver'blinden
blindfold, ge'blinddoekt;
  blinddoeken
blindness, blindheid

blink, knipperen
bliss, geluk'zaligheid
blister, blaar
blizzard, sneeuwjacht
block, blok; (ver')stoppen
blockade, blok'kade; blok'keren
blockhead, domkop
blond(e), blon'd(ine)
blood, bloed
bloodshed, bloedvergieten
bloodshot, met bloed be'lopen
bloody, bloed(er)ig; ver'domd
bloom, bloem; waas; bloei(en)
blossom, bloesem; bloeien
blot, vlek, smet; afvloeien;
  be'kladden
  to – out, ver'nietigen
blotting paper, vloeipapier
blouse, bloes
blow, slag; waaien, blazen;
  snuiten
  to – up, opblazen; opvliegen,
  uitschelden; opsteken
blowlamp, brander
blue, blauw
blueprint, blauwdruk; plan
bluff, bluf(fen); steil(e oever)
bluish, blauwachtig
blunder, blunder; struikelen
blunt, stomp, bot (maken);
  ab'rupt
blur, ver'vagen
blurt out, er'uit flappen
blush, blos; blozen, zich
  schamen
bluster, bulderen
boar, zwijn
board, plank, bord; kost(geld);
  be'stuur
  to (go on) –, aan boord gaan
  above –, bona fide
boarding school, kostschool
boast, pochen; bogen (op)

boat, boot
bob, dobberen
bode ill (well), wat slechts
  (goeds) be'loven
bodily, li'chamelijk; in zijn
  ge'heel
body, lichaam, lijf; sub'stantie;
  carrosse'rie; groep
bodyguard, lijfwacht
bog, moe'ras
  to be bogged (down),
  vastzitten
bogey, boeman, schrikbeeld
bogus, vals
boil, kook; steenpuist; koken
  to – down, inkoken; neer
  komen (op)
boiler, ketel, boiler
boisterous, on'stuimig
bold, stout('moedig)
bolt, bout; grendel(en); ervan
  doorgaan
  bolt upright, kaarsrecht
bomb(ard), bom(bar'deren)
bombastic, bom'bastisch
bomber, bommenwerper
bomb scare, bommelding
bond, band; obli'gatie;
  entre'pot; ver'binden
bondage, slaver'nij;
  onderworpenheid; bondage
bone, been, graat
bone-dry, kurkdroog
bonfire, (vreugde)vuur
bonnet, kap
bonny, leuk, fris, knap
bonus, premie
bony, knokig, vol benen (*or*
  graten)
boob, flater, blunder; borst, (inf)
  tiet
book, boek(je); reser'veren,
  boeken

bookcase, boekenkast
bookish, leesgraag; boekachtig, stijf, saai
bookkeeping, boekhouden
bookseller, boekhandelaar
boom, ge'dreun; dreunen
boon, weldaad
boost, aanjagen, opdrijven; een zetje geven
boot, laars; bak; trappen
  to boot, op de koop toe
booth, kraam
booty, buit
booze, (sterke) drank
border, grens; rand; bloembed; om'zomen; **to – on,** grenzen aan
bore, boren; ver'velen
  to be bored, zich ver'velen
boredom, ver'veling
born, ge'boren
borough, (stads)ge'meente
borrow, lenen (van), ont'lenen (aan)
bosom, boezem; schoot
boss, baas; comman'deren
botany, plantkunde
both, beide, allebei
  – ... and, zo'wel ... als
bother, last, drukte; bah!; lastig vallen
bottle, fles; inmaken, bottelen
  to – up, opkroppen
bottom, achterste; bodem; onderste; basis
bough, (grote) tak
boulder, grote kei
bounce, stuiten; springen
bound, ver'bonden; ver'plicht; sprong; springen; be'grenzen
  to be –, moeten; op weg zijn
boundary, grens(lijn)
boundless, onbe'grensd

bountiful, vrijgevig, gul; overvloedig
bout, par'tij; peri'ode, vlaag
bow, buiging; boeg; boog; strik; strijkstok; buigen
bowels, ingewanden
bower, pri'eel
bowl, schaal, bak; bowlen
  to – over, om'vergooien; van (zijn) stuk brengen
bow-legged: he is –, hij heeft o-benen
box, doos(je), kist(je); loge; oorvijg; boksen
Boxing Day, tweede kerstdag
box office, lo'ket, kassa
boy, jongen
boycott, boycot(ten)
boyish, jongens(achtig)
bra, be'ha
brace, klamp; (zich) scherp zetten
bracelet, armband
braces, bre'tels
bracing, op'wekkend
bracket, steun; haakje
  in –s, tussen haakjes
brag, opscheppen
braggart, opschepper
braid, vlecht(en)
braille, braille
brain, hersenen
brains, hersens, ver'stand
brainwave, lumi'neus idee
brainy, knap, slim
braise, smoren
brake, rem(men)
bramble, braam(struik)
bran, zemelen
branch, tak; bijkantoor; fili'aal; afdeling; zich ver'takken
brand, merk; brandmerk(en)
brandish, (dreigend) zwaaien

brand-new, splinternieuw
brandy, co'gnac
brass, (geel)koper(en)
– **band,** fan'farekorps
brat, snotaap, rotkind
bravado, bra'voure
brave, moedig; trot'seren
bravery, moed
brawl, vechtpartij
brawn, spieren
bray, balken
brazen, bru'taal
breach, (in)breuk, schending;
bres; door'breken
bread, brood
slice of – **and butter,** boterham
breadth, breedte; ruimte
break, breuk, onder'breking,
pauze; (ver)breken
to – **down,** afbreken; weigeren;
vastlopen; over'stuur raken
to – **up,** stukbreken; zich (or
doen) ver'spreiden; eindigen
breakdown, de'fect;
mis'lukking; instorting
breakers, branding
breakfast, ont'bijt(en)
breakwater, golfbreker
breast, borst
breath, adem; zuchtje
out of –, buiten adem
breathalyser, blaaspijpje
breathe, ademen, ademhalen
breathless, ademloos, buiten
adem
breed, ras; voortbrengen,
fokken
breeding, fokken; goede
manieren
breeze, bries
breezy, winderig; vrolijk
brevity, kortheid
brew, brouwsel; brouwen; broeien

brewery, brouwe'rij
bribe, omkoopgeld; omkopen
bribery, omkope'rij
brick, baksteen, blok
to drop a –, een flater be'gaan
bricklayer, metselaar
brickwork, metselwerk
bridal, bruids-
bride(groom), bruid(egom)
bridesmaid, bruidsmeisje
bridge, brug; bridge;
over'bruggen
bridle, teugel, toom; tomen
brief, kort; instru'eren
briefcase, aktentas
brigade, bri'gade
brigand, ban'diet
bright, hel(der); pienter;
hoopvol
brighten, oplichten; opvrolijken
brilliance, schittering; geniali'teit
brilliant, schitterend; bril'jant
brim, rand
brimful, boordevol
brine, pekel; zout water
bring, (mee)brengen
to – **about,** te'weegbrengen
to – **back,** te'rugbrengen;
oproepen
to – **on,** ver'oorzaken
to – **out,** doen uitkomen
to – **round,** bijbrengen;
overhalen
to – **up,** bovenbrengen;
grootbrengen; te berde
brengen
brink, rand
brisk, kwiek
bristle, borstel(haar); gaan
over'eind staan
Britain, Groot Brit'tannië, VK,
Verenigd Koninkrijk
British, Brits

Briton, Brit(se)
brittle, broos, bros
broach, aansteken; ter sprake
brengen
broad, breed; ruim
broadcast, uitzending;
uitzenden; ver'spreiden
broaden, (zich) ver'breden;
ver'ruimen
broad-minded, ruimdenkend,
tolerant
brocade, bro'kaat
broil, roosteren
broke, blut
broken-hearted, diep
onge'lukkig
broker, makelaar
bronchitis, bron'chitis
bronze, brons; bronzen
brooch, broche
brood, kroost, gebroed; tobben,
piekeren; broeden
brook, beek
broom, bezem; brem
broth, boui'llon
brothel, bor'deel
brother, broer, broeder
brotherhood, broederschap
brother-in-law, zwager
brow, voorhoofd; rand
browbeat, intimi'deren
brown, bruin
– **paper,** pakpapier
browse, grasduinen
bruise, (blauwe) plek; kneuzen
bruiser, rouwdouwer
brunette, bru'nette
brunt, volle kracht
brush, borstel, kwast, pen'seel;
staart; (af)borstelen, (af)vegen
to – **past,** rakelings gaan langs
brush(wood), kreupelhout
brusque, bruusk

Brussels sprouts, spruitjes
brutal, beestachtig
brutality, wreedheid
brute, bruut
BSE, gekkekoeienziekte (mad
cow disease)
bubble, (lucht)bel
bucket, emmer
buckle, gesp; vastgespen;
krommen
bud, knop; uitbotten
Buddhism, boed'dhisme
budding, in de dop
budge, (zich) ver'roeren
budget, be'groting
buff, okergeel; po'lijsten
buffalo, buffel
buffet, buf'fet; stomp(en)
buffoon, pi'as
bug, beestje
bugle, si'gnaalhoorn
build, bouw(en)
to – **up,** opbouwen;
be'bouwen
builder, aannemer
building, ge'bouw
bulb, (bloem)bol; gloeilamp
bulge, uitpuiling; uitpuilen
bulk, massa; grootste deel
bulky, lijvig, groot
bull, stier; bul
bullet, kogel
bulletin, bulle'tin
bullion, (goud)staven
bullock, os
bull's eye, roos; schot in de
roos; rake opmerking
bully, beul, pestkop;
intimi'deren
bulwark, bolwerk
bumble-bee, hommel
bump, stoten, botsen (tegen),
schokken; buil, bult, hobbel;

to – into, tegen het lijf lopen
bumpy, hobbelig
bun, luxe broodje
bunch, bos(je), tros;
op'eenhopen
bundle, pak, bos; samenbinden
bungalow, bungalow
bungle, (ver')knoeien
bunk, kooi; kletspraat; er
vandoor gaan
bunkbed, stapelbed
bunting, vlaggen
buoy, boei
buoyant: to be –, drijven;
veerkracht hebben
burden, last; laden; drukken
bureau, bu'reau
burglar, inbreker
burglary, inbraak
burial, be'grafenis
burly, stoer
burn, brandwond;
(ver')branden; aanbranden
burnish, po'lijsten
burrow, hol; wroeten
burst, barst(en); vlaag; springen
bury, be'graven; ver'bergen
bus, bus
bush, struik; rimboe
business, zaak, zaken
businesslike, zakelijk
busker, straatmuzikant
bust, borstbeeld, buste
bustle, drukte; druk in de weer
zijn
busy (druk) bezig
to be –, het druk hebben
busybody, be'moeial
but, maar; be'halve
butch, (vulg) pot (lesbian);
macho, stoer
butcher, slager; beul; afslachten
butler, hoofdbediende

butt, ton; kolf; peukje;
schietbaan; stoten
butter, boter; smeren
buttercup, boterbloem
butterfly, vlinder
buttocks, billen
button, knoop; knopen
buttonhole, knoopsgat;
aanklampen
buttress, beer; steunen
buxom, mollig
buy, koop; kopen
buyer, (in)koper
buzz, ge'gons; gonzen
by, door; bij; langs; per; volgens
– train, met de trein
– night and by day, 's nachts en
over'dag
– and large, over het
alge'meen
by-election, tussentijdse
ver'kiezing
by-law, plaatselijke ver'ordening
bypass, ringweg; omloopleiding
by-product, nevenprodukt
bystander, toeschouwer

C

cab, taxi; ca'bine
cabbage, kool
cabin, hut; ca'bine
cabinet, kabi'net, kastje;
mi'nisterraad
cable, kabel; telegra'feren
caboodle, rataplan
cackle, kakelen
cacophony, tegen'strijdig
ge'schetter
cactus, cactus
cad, ploert
caddie, golfjongen
caddy, (thee)busje

cadence, ca'dans
cadet, ca'det
cadge, schooieren
café, ca'fé(-restaurant)
cage, kooi; opsluiten
cajole, aftroggelen
cake, cake, ge'bak(je); taart
koek(en)
calamity, ramp
calculate, (be')rekenen
calendar, ka'lender
calf, kalf; kuit
calibre, ka'liber
call, tele'foontje; roepen;
noemen
  to give a –, roepen
  to pay a –, een be'zoek
  afleggen
  to be called, heten
  to – off, aflasten
  to – on, be'zoeken; een be'roep
  doen op
calling, roeping
callous, onge'voelig
calm, kalm(te); be'daren
calumny, laster
camel, ka'meel
camera, fototoestel
camouflage, camou'flage;
camou'fleren
camp, kamp('eren)
campaign, veldtocht;
cam'pagne
can, kan, blik; kunnen
canal, ka'naal, gracht
canary, ka'narie
cancel, schrappen, afzeggen
cancer, kanker
candid, open('hartig)
candidate, kandi'daat
candle, kaars
candlestick, kaarsenstandaard
candour, op'rechtheid

candy, kan'dij; kon'fijten
  candied peel, su'kade
cane, rotting; riet(en);
afranselen
cannibal, kanni'baal
cannon, ka'non; ge'schut
canny, slim
canoe, kano
canoodle, knuffelen,
scharrelen
canopy, balda'kijn
cantankerous, cha'grijning
canteen, kan'tine
canter, (in) korte ga'lop
  (draven)
canvas, (zeil)doek
canvass, stemmen werven
canyon, diep ra'vijn
cap, pet; dop; over'treffen
  capped, ge'huld (in)
capable, be'kwaam, flink
  capable of, in staat tot;
  vatbaar voor
capacious, ruim
capacity, inhoud; ver'mogen;
hoe'danigheid
cape, kaap; cape
caper, capri'olen maken
capital, hoofdstad; kapi'taal;
hoofdletter; kapi'teel; prima
capitalist, kapita'list
capitulate, capitu'leren
caprice, gril
capsize, omslaan
captain, kapi'tein,
ge'zagvoerder, aanvoerder
caption, onderschrift
captivate, be'toveren
captive, ge'vangen(e)
captivity, ge'vangenschap
capture, ver'overing; ver'overen,
ge'vangennemen
car, auto

caravan, woonwagen,
kam'peerwagen; kara'vaan
carbon, koolstof;
doorslag(papier)
card, kaart(je)
cardboard, kar'ton
cardigan, vest
cardinal, kardi'naal; hoofd-
cards, kaartspel
  to play –, kaarten
care, zorg; lust hebben
  to take – of, zorgen voor;
passen op
  I don't –, het kan me niets
schelen
  to – about, geven om
  to – for, (iets) voelen voor
career, loopbaan, carri'ère
carefree, onbe'zorgd
careful, voor'zichtig; zorg'vuldig
careless, slordig
caress, liefkozing; liefkozen
caretaker, conci'ërge
cargo, lading, vracht
cargo boat, vrachtschip
caricature, karika'tuur
carillon, klokkenspel
carnage, slachting
carnal, vleselijk
carnation, anjer
carnival, carnaval
carol, (kerst)lied
carp, karper; vitten
carpenter, timmerman;
timmeren
carriage, rijtuig, wa'gon;
ver'voer; houding
carrion, kadaver
carrot, wortel
carry, dragen, houden
  to – away, meeslepen
  to – off, in de wacht slepen;
klaarspelen

  to – on, doorgaan; uitoefenen
  to – out, uitvoeren
cart, kar; ver'voeren
cartilage, kraakbeen
carton, kar'ton
cartoon, (spot)prent; tekenfilm
cartridge, pa'troon
cartwheel, karrenwiel; radslag
carve, snijden; beeldhouwen
carving, snijwerk
cascade, kleine waterval;
stortvloed; neerstorten
case, koker, koffer, kist; ge'val;
zaak
  in –, voor het ge'val dat
cash, contant geld;
(om)wisselen
cash dispenser, geldautomaat
cashier, kas'sier; cas'seren
cask, vat
cast, worp; afgietsel;
rolverdeling; werpen;
gieten
cast iron, ge'goten ijzer
castle, kas'teel
castor, rolletje
casual, noncha'lant; toe'vallig;
vluchtig
casualty, ongeval
  casualties, doden en
ge'wonden
cat, kat
catalogue, ca'talogus
catapult, katapult
cataract, waterval; staar
catastrophe, cata'strofe, ramp
catch, vangst; valstrik; haak;
(op)vangen; halen; be'trappen;
vatten; (blijven) haken; treffen
  to – on, ingang vinden
  to – up, inhalen
categorical, cate'gorisch
category, catego'rie

cater, maaltijden ver'zorgen; rekening houden (met)
caterpillar, rups
cathedral, kathe'draal
catholic, katho'liek
cattle, vee
cauliflower, bloemkool
cause, oorzaak, (be'weeg)reden; zaak; ver'oorzaken
causeway, dam
caustic, brandend; bijtend
caution, voor'zichtigheid; waarschuwen
cautious, voor'zichtig
cavalry, cavale'rie
cave(rn), grot
  to cave in, inzakken
cavity, holte
cease, ophouden (met)
ceaseless, voort'durend
cedar, ceder(hout)
cede, afstaan
ceiling, pla'fond; maximum
celebrate, vieren
celebration, viering, feest
celebrity, be'roemdheid
celery, selderij
celestial, hemels, hemel-
celibacy, celi'baat
cell, cello
cellar, kelder
cello, cel
cellophane, cello'faan
cellulose, cellu'lose
cement, ce'ment
cemetery, be'graafplaats
censor, censor; censu'reren
censure, be'risping; bekriti'seren
census, volkstelling
centenary, eeuwfeest
centigrade, Celsius
central, cen'traal, midden-, hoofd-

centralize, centrali'seren
centre, middelpunt, centrum
  in the – of, midden in
century, eeuw
cereal, graan(pro'duct)
ceremonial, ceremoni'eel
ceremony, cere'monie, formali'teit(en)
certain(ty), zeker(heid)
certificate, di'ploma, akte, at'test
certify, (plechtig) ver'klaren
chafe, schuren
chaff, kaf
chagrin, ergernis
chain, ketting; keten(en); reeks
chair, stoel
chairman(ship), voorzitter(schap)
chalice, kelk
chalk, krijt
challenge, uitdaging; uitdagen, aanroepen, be'twisten
chamber, kamer
champion, kampi'oen, voorstander; voorstaan
chance, kans; toeval; toe'vallig; wagen
chancellor, kanse'lier
chandelier, kroon(luchter)
change, ver'andering, overgang; kleingeld; ver'anderen; (ver)wisselen, ver')ruilen; (zich) ver'kleden; overstappen
  to – one's mind, zich be'denken
changeable, ver'anderlijk
channel, ka'naal; vaargeul, goot; weg
chant, (be')zingen; dreunen
chaos, chaos
chap, kerel; barsten
chapel, ka'pel

chaplain (to the forces), (leger)-
predi'kant
chapter, hoofdstuk; epi'sode
char, schroeien, ver'kolen
character, ka'rakter; type
characteristic, kenmerk(end)
(voor)
characterize, kenmerken
charcoal, houtskool
charge, aanval(len);
(be')last(en); lading;
be'schuldiging; laden;
be'schuldigen
  to be in – of, de leiding hebben
  van; be'last zijn met
  to (make a) –, rekenen
charitable, mens'lievend
charity, lief'dadigheid(s-),
naastenliefde
charm, charme; tovermiddel;
be'koren; be'toveren
charming, char'mant;
aller'aardigst
chart, kaart; grafische
voorstelling; in kaart brengen
charter, recht; handvest;
charteren, huren
chase, jacht; (na)jagen; drijven
chasm, kloof
chassis, chassis
chaste, kuis
chasten, chastize, kas'tijden
chat, babbeltje; babbelen
chatline, babbellijn
chatter, kletsen, ratelen
chatterbox, kletskous
cheap, goed'koop, waardeloos
cheat, valsspeler; be'driegen,
valsspelen
check, rem; ruit; stuiten;
contro'leren
  –(mate), schaak(mat) (zetten)
  in –, in toom

to – up, nagaan
cheek, wang; brutali'teit
cheekbone, jukbeen
cheer, juichkreet; (toe)juichen;
opmonteren
  three cheers, een hoe'raatje;
  lang leve …
cheerful, vrolijk
cheerless, troosteloos
cheese, kaas
chemical, chemisch(e stof);
schei'kundig
chemist, schei'kundige; dro'gist
chemistry, scheikunde
cheque, cheque
chequered, af'wisselend
cherish, koesteren
cherry, kers
cherub, cheru'bijn
chess: to play –, schaken
chess (set), schaakspel
chest, borst(kas); kist
chestnut, kas'tanje(boom)
chew, kauwen
chick, kuiken; meisje, grietje
chicken, kip
chicken pox, waterpokken
chicory, witlof
chide, be'rispen
chief, hoofd(-); voor'naamste
chiefly, voor'namelijk
chieftain, opperhoofd
child(ren), kind(eren)
childbirth, be'valling
childhood, kinderjaren
childish, kinderachtig, kinderlijk
childlike, kinderlijk
chill, kou; afkoelen
chill(y), kil; koel
chime, klokkenspel, klokslag;
luiden
chimney, schoorsteen
chin, kin

china, porse'lein(en)

chink, spleet; rinkelen

chip, scherf; fiche; stoten, bikken

chiropodist, pedi'cure

chirp, tjilpen

chisel, beitel(en)

chivalrous, ridderlijk

chivalry, ridderlijkheid

chlorine, chloor

chocolate, choco'la(de), choco'laatje

choice, keus; prima

choir, koor

choke, (doen) stikken, zich ver'slikken; ver'stoppen

choose, (uit)kiezen, ver'kiezen

chop, karbo'nade; (fijn)hakken

choppy, woelig

chord, ak'koord; snaar

chortle, hardop grinniken van pret

chorus, koor; re'frein

christen, dopen

christening, doop(dienst)

Christian, christelijk; christen
  Christian name, voornaam

Christianity, christendom; christelijkheid

Christmas, kerst

Christmas Day, eerste kerstdag

chromium(-plated), (ver')chroom(d)

chronic, chronisch

chronical, kro'niek; boekstaven

chronological, chrono'logisch

chubby, mollig

chuck, smijten

chuckle, ge'grinnik; grinniken (om)

chug, puffen

chum, maat

chunk, klomp, homp

church, kerk

Church of England, angli'caanse kerk

churchyard, kerkhof

churlish, lomp

churn, karn, melkbus; karnen; woelen

chute, glijbaan, glijkoker

cider, cider

cigar, si'gaar

cigarette, siga'ret

cinder, sintel

cinema, bios'coop

cinnamon, ka'neel

cipher, cijferschrift; nul

circle, cirkel(en); kring; groep; om cirkelen

circuit, kring(loop); (stroom)-baan

circuitous, om'slachtig

circular, cirkel'vormig, rond(gaand); circu'laire

circulate, (laten) circu'leren

circulation, circu'latie; bloedsomloop; oplaag

circumference, omtrek

circumscribe, om'schrijven

circumspect, om'zichtig

circumstance, om'standigheid, bij'zonderheid

circus, circus

cistern, waterreservoir

cite, ci'teren; noemen

citizen, (staats)burger

city, stad(s-)

civic, burger-, stads-

civil, burgerlijk, burger-; be'leefd

civilian, burger

civilization, be'schaving

civilize, be'schaven

civil servant, ambtenaar

clad, ge'kleed

claim, aanspraak (maken op);
  vordering; (op)eisen; be'weren
clamber, klauteren
clammy, klam
clamorous, luid('ruchtig)
clamour, ge'tier; schreeuwen
clamp, klamp(en)
clan, stam
clang, galm; kletteren
clap, slag; klap(pen (met)),
  applaudis'seren; slaan
clarify, klaren; ophelderen
clarity, duidelijkheid
clash, botsing; botsen; vloeken
clasp, gesp(en); (vast)grijpen
class, klas(se); stand; lesuur;
  plaatsen
classic, klas'siek (werk)
classical, klas'siek
classify, klassifi'ceren
classroom, klaslokaal
clatter, ge'kletter; kletteren
clause, clau'sule, bijzin
claw, klauw(en), poot
clay, klei
clean, schoon(maken),
  rein(igen); zindelijk
cleaner,
  schoonmaker/schoonmaakster,
  werkster
cleanliness, zindelijkheid
cleanse, zuiveren
clear, helder, duidelijk;
  vrij(maken); ophelderen;
  vrijspreken; ont'ruimen
  to – off, maken dat men
  wegkomt
  to – up, ver'duidelijken;
  opruimen; ophelderen
clear-cut, scherp om'lijnd
clearing, open plek
cleavage, scheiding; gleuf
  (between breasts), decolleté

cleave, kloven; kleven
cleft, kloof; ge'spleten
clemency, mildheid
clench, ballen; vastklemmen
  clenched teeth, tanden op
  el'kaar
clergy, geestelijkheid
clergyman, dominee
clerical, administra'tief;
  geestelijk
clerk, klerk, grif'fier
clever, knap
click, klik(ken)
client, klant, cliënt
cliff, klif
climate, kli'maat
climax, climax
climb, (be')klim(men)
  to climb down, afklimmen;
  inbinden
clinch, vastklinken; be'klinken,
  be'slechten
cling, zich vastklemmen,
  plakken
clinic, kli'niek
clink, klink(en)
clip, klem(metje); mep;
  klemmen; knippen
clippers, schaar, ton'deuse;
  klippers
clipping, (uit)knipsel
cloak, (dek)mantel; hullen
cloakroom, garde'robe
clock, klok
clockwise, met de klok mee
clockwork, (met) mecha'niek
clod, (aard)kluit
clog, klomp; ver'stoppen
cloister, klooster(gang)
close, dicht'bij; scherp; nauw;
  in'tiem; ingesloten ruimte;
  einde; (af)sluiten
  to – down (or up), sluiten

closed-circuit: – television, videobewaking
close-fisted, gierig
closet, kabi'net; opsluiten
clot, kluit; klonteren, stollen
cloth, stof; kleed, doek
clothe, kleden
clothes, kleren
clothesline, drooglijn
clothes-peg, knijper
clothing, kleding
cloud, wolk; ver'troebelen
  to – over, be'trekken
cloudy, be'wolkt; troebel
clout, invloed, macht; mep, klap
clove, kruidnagel
clover, klaver
clown, clown
club, knots; club, socië'tiet; klaver; knuppelen
cluck, klokken
clue, aanwijzing, sleutel
clump, groep, brok; klossen
clumsy, on'handig
cluster, tros, bos, groep; zich scharen
clutch, klauw; koppeling; (vast)pakken
clutter, warboel; volproppen
coach, koets; spoorwagon; (reis)bus; trainer, coach; trainen, coachen
coagulate, stremmen, stollen
coal, kolen(-); steenkool
coalesce, samensmelten
coalition, coa'litie
coarse, grof
coast, kust; glijden, freewheelen
coat, jas, mantel; vel; (verf)laag; bedekken
  – of arms, wapen
  – hanger, kleerhanger
co-author, medeauteur
coax, vleiend be'praten

cobble(-stone), keisteen
cobbler, schoenlapper
cobweb, spinnenweb
cock, haan; de haan spannen van; scheefhouden
cock-eyed, scheef
cockpit, cockpit
cocktail, cocktail
cocky, bru'taal
cocoa, ca'cao
coconut, kokosnoot
cod, kabel'jauw
code, code(stelsel); wet
coercion, dwang
coffee, koffie
coffin, doodkist
cog, tandrad
cogent, over'tuigend
cogitate, nadenken
coherent, samenhangend, logisch
coil, tros, spi'raal; oprollen
coin, munt(stuk); smeden
coincide, samenvallen
coincidence, samenloop van om'standigheden
coke, cokes, coke
colander, ver'giet
cold, koud; koel; ver'koudheid
  to have a –, ver'kouden zijn
collaborate, samenwerken
collapse, in'storting; in el'kaar zakken
collapsible, op'vouwbaar
collar, kraag, boord, halsband
colleague, col'lega
collect, (zich) ver'zamelen
collection, ver'zameling, col'lecte; buslichting
collector, ver'zamelaar
college, college, (hoge')school
collide, botsen
colliery, kolenmijn

collision, botsing, aanvaring
colon, dubbele punt
colonel, kolo'nel
colonial, koloni'aal
colonize, koloni'seren
colonnade, zuilengang
colony, ko'lonie
colossal, reus'achtig
colour, kleur(en), verf
colourful, kleurrijk
colt, (hengst)veulen
column, zuil; ko'lom
coma, coma
comb, kam(men); afzoeken
combat, strijd; be'strijden
combination, combi'natie
combine, syndi'caat; com'bine;
  combi'neren
combustion, ver'branding
come, komen, meegaan
  to – **about,** ge'beuren
  to – **across,** overkomen;
  tegenkomen
  to – **round,** aanlopen;
  (bij)draaien; bijkomen
  to – **in,** binnenkomen; mode
  worden
  to – **off,** afkomen; doorgaan,
  lukken
comedian, ko'miek, komedi'ant
comedy, blijspel
comely, be'vallig
comet, ko'meet
comfort, troost(en); ge'mak,
  welstand
comfortable, be'hagelijk
  to be –, ge'makkelijk zitten
  (*or* liggen)
comfortably off, in goede doen
comic, komisch;
  (kinder)krantje
coming, (op)komend; komst
comma, komma

command, be'vel(en);
  com'mando (voeren);
  be'schikking; be'schikken over;
  be'strijken
commanding officer,
  comman'dant
commandeer, (op)vorderen
commander, be'velhebber;
  kapi'tein-luitenant
commandment, ge'bod
commemorate, her'denken
commence, be'ginnen
commend, prijzen; aanbevelen
commendable, prijzens'waardig
comment, kritiek, aantekening;
  becommentariëren
commentary, commen'taar
commentator, ver'slaggever
commerce, handel(sverkeer)
commercial, commer'cieel,
  handels-
commiserate, sympathi'seren
commission, opdracht (geven);
  (offi'ciers) aanstelling;
  pro'visie; machtigen;
  aanstellen; in dienst stellen
commissioner, ge'volmachtigde,
  (hoofd)commis'saris
commit, plegen, be'gaan;
  toevertrouwen
  to – **oneself,** zich ver'binden
commitment, ver'plichting
committee, comi'té, be'stuur
  com'missie
commodious, ruim
commodity, ge'bruiksartikel
common, ge'meen('schappelijk),
  ge'woon, algemeen
  – **sense,** ge'zond ver'stand
  in –, ge'meen
commonplace, alle'daags;
  ge'meenplaats
commonwealth, gemene'best

commotion, opschudding
communal, gemeen'schappelijk
communicate, ver'binding
hebben, zich in ver'binding
stellen; mededelen
communication, mededeling;
communicatie
communicative, mede'deelzaam
communion, gemeenschap;
communie, Avondmaal
communism, commu'nisme
community, ge'meenschap;
broederschap
compact, com'pact;
over'eenkomst
companion, metgezel
companionable, ge'zellig
companionship, ge'zelschap,
vriendschap
company, gezelschap; bezoek;
onder'neming, firma,
be'drijf
comparable, te verge'lijken
comparative, be'trekkelijk,
verge'lijkend
compare, (te) verge'lijken (zijn)
comparison, verge'lijking
compartment, afdeling; cou'pé
compass, kom'pas; passer;
vatten
compassion, medelijden
compassionate, mee'warig
compatriot, landgenoot
compel, (af)dwingen
compensate for, schadeloos
stellen voor, ver'goeden;
opwegen tegen
compensation, ver'goeding,
compen'satie
compete, wedijveren,
me(d)edingen (naar)
competence, be'voegdheid,
be'kwaamheid

competent, be'kwaam,
be'voegd
competition, wedstrijd;
concur'rentie
competitive, verge'lijkend
competitor, deelnemer,
concur'rent
compile, samenstellen
complacent, gauw te'vreden
complain, klagen
complaint, (aan)klacht; kwaal
complement, aanvulling;
be'manning
complete, vol'ledig, vol'tallig,
vol'slagen; vol'tooien;
be'sluiten, aanvullen
complex, com'plex
complexion, gelaatskleur, teint
compliance, mee'gaandheid;
inwilliging
complicate, compli'ceren
complicated, inge'wikkeld
complication, compli'catie
complicity, mede'plichtigheid
compliment, compli'ment('eren)
complimentary, complimen'teus;
pre'sent-, vrij-
comply with, vol'doen aan
component, be'standdeel;
samenstellend
compose, samenstellen,
compo'neren
to be composed of, be'staan
uit
to – oneself, be'daren
composer, compo'nist
composite, samengesteld
composition, samenstelling;
compo'sitie; opstel
composure, zelfbeheersing
compound, samengesteld;
samenstelling, ver'binding; erf;
(ver')mengen

comprehend, (om')vatten
comprehension, be'grip
comprehensive, veelom'vattend
compress, kom'pres:
  samenpersen, compri'meren
comprise, be'vatten
compromise, compro'mis; tot
  een schikking komen;
  compromit'teren
compulsion, dwang
compulsory, ver'plicht
compunction, scru'pules
compute, be'rekenen
computer, com'puter
comrade, kame'raad
concave, hol
conceal, ver'bergen
concede, toegeven, toestaan
conceit, ver'waandheid;
  spits'vondigheid
conceited, ver'waand
conceivable, denkbaar
conceive, zich een voorstelling
  maken van; be'vrucht worden
concentrate, (zich)
  concen'treren
concentric, con'centrisch
concept, be'grip
conception, voorstelling,
  opvatting; be'vruchting
concern, zaak, be'lang;
  be'zorgdheid; onder'neming;
  aangaan
  to be concerned, be'lang
  hebben bij; be'trokken zijn bij;
  zich bezighouden met;
  be'zorgd zijn over
  as far as I'm concerned, wat
  mij be'treft
concerning, be'treffende
concert(o), con'cert
concerted, ge'zamenlijk
concession, con'cessie

conciliate, gunstig stemmen
concise, be'knopt
conclude, (be')sluiten; opmaken
conclusion, be'sluit, slot;
  ge'volgtrekking
conclusive, af'doend, beslissend
concoct, brouwen; ver'zinnen
concord, eendracht
concrete, be'ton(nen); con'creet
concubine, concubine
concur, het eens zijn; bijdragen
concurrence, instemming;
  samenwerking
concurrent, gelijk'tijdig
concussion, (hersen)schudding
condemn, ver'oordelen,
  afkeuren
condensation, conden'satie
condense, conden'seren;
  samenvatten
condescend, zich
  ver'waardigen
condescending, neer'buigend
condition, voorwaarde;
  con'ditie, staat, toestand
  (weather) conditions, (weers)-
  om'standigheden
condolence, deelneming
condone, ver'goelijken
conducive, be'vorderlijk
conduct, ge'drag(en);
  be'handeling; (ge')leiden;
  diri'geren
conductor, (ge')leider; diri'gent;
  conduc'teur
cone, kegel; (denne)appel
confectionery, suikergoed
confederate, mede'plichtige;
  ver'bonden
confederation, ver'bond
confer, ver'lenen (aan);
  be'raadslagen
conference, confe'rentie

confess, be'kennen; be'lijden;
biechten
confession, be'kentenis; biecht
confidant(e), ver'trouweling(e)
confide (in), in ver'trouwen
nemen
confide (to), toevertrouwen
confidence, ver'trouwen
confident, vol
('zelf)ver'trouwen; over'tuigd
confidential, ver'trouwelijk
confine, grens; be'perken
confinement, be'valling;
ge'vangenschap
confirm, be'vestigen;
be'krachtigen; vormen
confirmed, vaststaand;
chronisch, ver'stokt
confiscate, ver'beurd ver'klaren
conflagration, vlammenzee
conflict, con'flict; in strijd zijn
conflicting, (tegen')strijdig
conform, zich schikken (naar);
over'eenkomen
confound, in de war brengen;
ver'vloeken
confront, confron'teren
to be confronted by, komen te
staan tegen'over; zich
ge'plaatst zien in
confuse, ver'warren
confusion, ver'warring
confute, weer'leggen
congeal, stollen
congenial, prettig, sympa'thiek
congenital, (aan)ge'boren
congest, (zich) ophopen
conglomeration, conglome'raat
congratulate, ge'lukwensen
congratulation, ge'lukwens
congregate, (zich) ver'zamelen
congregation, ge'meente;
verzameling

congress, con'gres
conical, kegelvormig
coniferous, kegeldragend
conjecture, gissing
conjugate, ver'voegen
conjunction, voegwoord
in – with, samen met
conjure, goochelen; be'zweren
to – up, oproepen
conjurer, goochelaar
connect, (aan el'kaar)
ver'binden; in ver'band
brengen; aansluiten (op)
connection, ver'binding;
ver'band; re'latie
connive at, door de vingers zien;
– (with), in ge'heime
ver'standhouding staan (met)
connoisseur, fijnproever, kenner
connote, (tege'lijk) be'tekenen
conquer, ver'overen,
over'winnen; meester worden
conscience, ge'weten
conscientious, plichtsgetrouw
conscious, (zich) be'wust (zijn);
bij kennis
consciousness, be'wustzijn
conscript, dienst'plichtig(e);
oproepen, vorderen
conscription, con'scriptie
consecrate, (in)wijden
consecutive, op'eenvolgend,
samenhangend
consent, toestemming,
instemming; toe(*or*
in)stemmen
consequence, ge'volg
in –, dientenge'volge
of –, be'langrijk
consequent, daaruit
voortvloeiend
conservation, in'standhouding,
be'houd

conservative, conserva'tief
conservatory, serre
conserve, op peil houden;
   conser'veren
consider, over'wegen;
   beschouwen als, in
   aanmerking nemen, rekening
   houden met; menen
   all things considered, alles
   welbe'schouwd
considerable, aan'zienlijk
considerate, at'tent
consideration, over'weging;
   factor; conside'ratie;
   ver'goeding
considered, welover'wogen;
   ge'acht
considering, ge'zien; (alles)
   welbe'schouwd
consign, depo'neren;
   overleveren, toevertrouwen
consignment, zending
consist (of), be'staan (uit)
consistency, consis'tentie
consistent, conse'quent; op één
   lijn met
consolation, troost
consolidate, ver'sterken;
   consoli'deren
consonant, medeklinker
consort, metgezel, partner
   to – with, omgaan met
conspicuous, in het oog lopend;
   treffend
conspiracy, samenzwering
conspirator, samenzweerder
conspire, samenzweren
constable, po'litieagent
constancy, stand'vastigheid;
   trouw
constant, vast; voort'durend;
   trouw; con'stante
constellation, sterrenbeeld

consternation, ont'steltenis
constipation, consti'patie
constituency, kiesdistrict
constituent, be'standdeel;
   kiezer
constitute, vormen; aanstellen
constitution, ge'stel;
   samenstelling; grondwet
constitutional, aangeboren, voor
   het ge'stel; constitutio'neel
constrain, be'dwingen
constraint, (be')dwang;
   ge'dwongenheid
constrict, be'klemmen; binden;
   samentrekken
construct, (op)bouwen
construction, (aan)bouw,
   con'structie; uitleg
constructive, opbouwend
construe, ver'klaren,
   constru'eren
consul(ate), consul('aat)
consult, raadplegen
consultation, raadpleging,
   con'sult; be'raadslaging
consume, ver'bruiken,
   ver'orberen; ver'teren,
   ver'nietigen
consummate, vol'maakt: in
   ver'vulling doen gaan
consumption, ver'bruik,
   con'sumptie; (ver)tering
contact, con'tact; zich in
   ver'binding stellen met
contagious, be'smettelijk;
   aan'stekelijk
contain, be'vatten; inhouden
container, blik, doos
contaminate, veront'reinigen
contemplate, (over')peinzen;
   be'schouwen; van plan zijn
contemplation, ge'peins,
   over'weging; be'spiegeling

contemporary, van de'zelfde tijd, hedendaags; tijdgenoot
contempt, ver'achting
contemptible, ver'achtelijk
contemptuous, minachtend
contend, be'togen
  to contend with, kampen met, aankunnen
content(s), inhoud; ge'halte
content(ed), te'vreden
contention, twist; be'wering
contentment, te'vredenheid
contest, (wed)strijd; be'twisten
contestant, mededinger, deelnemer
context, ver'band
continent, vaste'land, werelddeel
continental, continen'taal
contingency, eventuali'teit
contingent, af'hankelijk, eventu'eel; contin'gent; situ'atie
continual(ly), voort'durend, her'haald(elijk)
continuance, voortzetting
continuation, voortzetting, ver'volg
continue, voortgaan (met); voortzetten
continuity, samenhang; continui'teit
continuous, on'afgebroken, door'lopend
contort, (ver')draaien
contour, con'tour
contraband, contrabande
contract, con'tract (aangaan); (zich) samentrekken; aannemen, oplopen
contraction, inkrimping, samentrekking
contractor, aannemer

contradict, tegenspreken, ont'kennen
contradiction, tegenspraak, tegen'strijdigheid
contradictory, (tegen')strijdig, weer'spannig
contraption, geval, ding, apparaat
contrary, tegengesteld(e), tegen-; ba'lorig
  – to, tegen ... in
  on the –, in'tegendeel
contrast, tegenstelling; tegenover el'kaar stellen, een con'trast vormen
contravene, in strijd zijn met
contribute, bijdragen
contribution, bijdrage
contributory, secun'dair, zij-
contrition, diep be'rouw
contrivance, apparaat; handigheid
contrive, be'ramen; ervoor zorgen
contrived, ge'maakt, gefor'ceerd
control, be'heer(sing); con'trole; stuurinrichting; in be'dwang houden, be'heersen, be'heren, regelen
controversial, controver'sieel, om'streden
controversy, ge'schil; on'enigheid
convalescence, her'stel
convene, bij'eenroepen, bij'eenkomen
convenience, ge'rief(elijkheid), ge'mak
convenient, ge'schikt, ge'riefelijk
convent, nonnenklooster; zusterschool
convention, con'ventie; samenkomst; over'eenkomst

conventional, conventio'neel
converge, conver'geren; zich
  concen'treren
conversant, ver'trouwd
conversation, ge'sprek
converse, omgekeerd(e);
  conver'seren
conversion, omzetting;
  be'kering
convert, be'keerling; omzetten,
  ver'anderen; be'keren
convex, bol
convey, ver'voeren, overdragen;
  betekenen, overbrengen
conveyance, ver'voer(middel);
  overdracht; overbrengen
convict, dwangarbeider;
  schuldig ver'klaren
conviction, over'tuiging;
  schuldigverklaring
convince, over'tuigen
convivial, feestelijk
convoy, kon'vooi
convulse, (doen) schudden;
  samentrekken; stuiptrekken
coo, kirren
cook, kok('kin); koken; knoeien
  met
cooker, for'nuis
cookery, koken; kook-
cooking, koken, keuken
cool, koel(te); kalm, bru'taal;
  ver'koelen, afkoelen
coop, hok; opsluiten
cooperate, samenwerken
cooperative, be'hulpzaam;
  coöpera'tief
coordinate, coördi'neren
cope, klaarspelen
 to – (with it), het aankunnen
copious, ruim
copper, (rood)koper(en);
  kopergeld; smeris

copse, kreupelbosje
copy, ko'pie; exem'plaar;
  namaken, nadoen
 to – out, overschrijven
copyright, auteursrecht
coquetry, kokette'rie
coral, ko'raal; ko'ralen
cord, koord
cordial, hartelijk;
  limo'nadesiroop
corduroy, ribfluweel
core, klokhuis; kern
cork, kurk(en)
corkscrew, kurkentrekker
corn, koren; likdoorn
corner, hoek; in het nauw
  drijven
cornflour, mai'zena
coronation, kroning
coroner, magi'straat bij een
  lijkschouwing
coronet, kroontje
corporal, korpo'raal; lijf-
corporate, collectief; bedrijfs-,
  ondernemings-
 – identity, bedrijfsidentiteit
corporation, corpo'ratie,
  lichaam (legal body);
  onder'neming; ge'meenteraad
corps, korps
corpse, lijk
corpulent, zwaar'lijvig
correct, juist, goed, cor'rect;
  corri'geren
correction, cor'rectie
corrective, ver'beterend;
  correc'tief
correspond, over'eenkomen;
  correspon'deren
correspondence,
  correspon'dentie;
  over'eenkomst
correspondent, correspon'dent

corresponding, overeen'komstig
corridor, gang
corroborate, be'vestigen
corrode, aantasten,
  ver'roesten
corrosion, cor'rosie, roest
corrugated, golf-
corrupt, cor'rupt, ver'dorven;
  be'derven
corruption, cor'ruptie,
  ver'derf
corset(s), kor'set
cosmetic, kos'metisch;
  schoonheidsmiddel
cosmonaut, kosmo'naut
cosmopolitan, kosmopo'litisch
cost, prijs, kosten
costly, duur, kostbaar
costume, kos'tuum,
  klederdracht
cosy, knus; muts
cot, kinderbedje
cottage, huisje
cottage cheese, hüttenkäse
cotton, ka'toen(en), garen;
  snappen
cotton wool, watten
couch, (rust)bank; stellen
cough, hoest(en)
council, raad
counsel, raad(geven),
  be'raadslaging; advo'caat
count, tel(ling); graaf;
  (mee)tellen; rekenen
  to – out, uittellen;
  uitschakelen
countenance,
  ge'laat(suitdrukking);
  sanctio'neren
counter, toonbank; balie,
  lo'ket; fiche; teller; tegen ... in;
  be'antwoorden
counter-, tegen-

counteract, neutrali'seren,
  tegenwerken
counterbalance, tegenwicht;
  opwegen tegen
counterfeit, nagemaakt;
  namaken
counterfoil, strook
counterpart, tegenhanger
countersign,
  medeondertekenen
countess, gra'vin
countless, talloos
country, (platte')land, streek;
  landelijk
  in the –, buiten
countryman, landgenoot;
  buitenman
countryside, landschap
county, graafschap
couple, paar, stel; koppelen;
  combi'neren
coupon, bon, cou'pon
courage(ous), moed(ig)
courier, koe'rier
course, (be')loop, koers,
  richting; gang; renbaan;
  cursus; ge'dragslijn
  in due –, te zijner tijd
  in the – of, in de loop van
  of –, na'tuurlijk
court, hof(houding),
  (binnen)plaats; rechtbank,
  rechtszaal; baan; het hof
  maken; zoeken
courteous, hoffelijk
courtesy, hoffelijkheid; gunst
courtier, hoveling
court martial, (voor de)
  krijgsraad (brengen)
courtyard, binnenplaats
cousin, neef, nicht
cove, inham
covenant, ver'bond; con'tract

cover, deksel; (buiten)band; dekking; (be')dekken; ver'bergen; afleggen; onder vuur hebben; ver'slaan

covert, heimelijk; schuilplaats

covet, be'geren

cow, koe; intimi'deren

coward, lafaard

cowardice, lafheid

cower, in'eenkrimpen

cowhide, rundleer

coxswain, stuurman

coy, schuchter, koket

crab, krab

crack, barst(en), kier; klap(pen); krieken; prima; kraken; tappen (jokes); overslaan
to – up, be'zwijken; ophemelen

cracker, knalbonbon, voetzoeker; cracker

crackle, knappen, kraken

cradle, wieg; bakermat

craft, ambacht, kunst'vaardigheid; sluwheid; vaartuig(en)

craftsman(ship), vakman(schap)

crafty, listig, sluw

crag, steile rots(punt)

cram, (vol)proppen, schrokken; (in)pompen

cramp, kram(p); opsluiten, be'krimpen; be'lemmeren

crane, kraan(vogel); uitrekken

crank, slinger; zonderling; aanslingeren

crash, klap, slag; botsing, neerstorting; in('een)storten, neerstorten; over de kop gaan

crass, grof

crate, krat

crater, krater

crave, hunkeren; smeken

craving, be'geerte

crawl, slakkengang; kruipen; wemelen

crayon, kleurpotlood; kleuren

craze, rage

crazy, gek; fanta'sie-

creak, kraken

cream, (slag)room, crème; puik; afromen

creamy, romig

crease, vouw(en); kreuken

create, scheppen; te'weegbrengen

creation, schepping; cre'atie

creative, scheppend

creature, schepsel

credentials, ge'loofs (or intro'ductie)brieven

credible, geloof'waardig

credit, kre'diet, te'goed, batig saldo; ge'loof, eer; credi'teren; ge'loven; toeschrijven

creditor, schuldeiser

credulous, lichtge'lovig

creed, ge'loofsbelijdenis

creek, kreek

creep, kruipen, sluipen

creeper, klimplant

cremate, cre'meren

crepe, crêpe

crescent, wassende maan; ge'bogen straat

cress, sterrekers

crest, kuif, pluim; hemelteken; top

crestfallen, ter'neergeslagen

crevice, scheur

crew, be'manning, ploeg; troep

crib, kribbe; spiekbriefje; spieken

crick, kramp

cricket, cricket; krekel

crime, misdaad, misdrijf

criminal, mis'dadig, straf-;
misdadiger
crimson, karmo'zijn(rood)
cringe, in'eenkrimpen, kruipen
crinkle, kronkel(en)
cripple, ge'brekkige;
ver'minken; ont'wrichten,
ver'lammen
crisis, crisis
crisp, bros; scherp
criss-cross, kriskras
criterion, criterium
critic, criticus, recensent
critical, kritisch; kri'tiek
criticism, kri'tiek
criticize, (be)kriti'seren
croak, ge'kwaak; kwaken,
krassen
crochet, haken
crock, aarden pot; wrak
crockery, ser'viesgoed
crocodile, kroko'dil
crocus, krokus
crony, makker, gabber
crook, staf; oplichter;
krommen
crooked, scheef, krom; vals
crop, oogst, ge'was; krop;
zweep; afvreten; kortknippen
croquet, croquet
croquette, kroket
cross, kruis(ing); dwars-; boos;
(el'kaar) kruisen; tegenwerken
to – oneself, een kruis slaan
to – out, doorhalen
to – (over), oversteken
it crossed my mind, het schoot
me door het hoofd
cross-country, dwars door het
land
cross-examination,
kruisverhoor
cross-eyed, scheel

crossing, kruispunt; overtocht;
oversteekplaats
cross purposes: at –, langs
el'kaar heen
crossroads, kruispunt;
tweesprong
cross-section, (dwars)doorsnee
crosswise, kruiselings
crotchet, kwartnoot
crouch, in el'kaar duiken
croup, kroep
crow, kraai(en)
crowbar, koevoet
crowd, menigte; (zich)
(ver')dringen
crowded, vol, druk
crown, kroon, krans; kruin, bol;
kronen (tot); be'kronen
crucial, cruciaal
crucible, smeltkroes
crucifix, kruisbeeld
crucifixion, kruisiging
crucify, kruisigen
crude, ruw; grof
cruel(ty), wreed(heid)
cruise, cruise, (zee)reis; kruisen
cruise missile, kruisraket
cruiser, kruiser
crumb, kruimel(en)
crumble, (ver')kruimelen;
afbrokkelen
crumple, ver'frommelen
crunch, (fijn)kauwen, knarsen
crusade, kruistocht; cam'pagne
crush, ge'drang; (samen)persen,
ver'brijzelen; ver'pletteren
crust, (met een) korst
(be'dekken)
crutch, kruk; kruis; vork
crux, kern
cry, kreet; leus; huilen;
schreeuwen, roepen
crying, ge'huil; schreeuwend

crypt, crypt
cryptic, ge'heim ('zinnig)
crystal, kris'tal(len)
crystallize, kristalli'seren
cub, welp, jong
cube, kubus, blokje;
   derde'macht
cubic, kubusvormig; ku'biek,
   inhouds-; derde'machts-
cuckoo, koekoek; sul
cucumber, kom'kommer
cuddle, pakkerd; knuffelen
cudgel, knuppel(en)
cue, signaal, wachtwoord; keu
cuff, man'chet; oorveeg (geven)
cufflink, man'chetknoop
culinary, keuken-, kook-
cull, plukken; uitzoeken
culminate, culmi'neren
culpable, be'rispelijk
culprit, schuldige
cult, cultus
cultivate, be(or ver)'bouwen;
   aankweken, ont'wikkelen
cultural, cultu'reel
culture, cul'tuur, be'schaving;
   aankweking; teelt
cultured, be'schaafd; ge'kweekt
cumbersome, on'handelbaar
cumulative, cumula'tief
cunning, listig(heid)
cup, kopje; kelk; hol maken
cupboard, kast
cupid, cupido(otje)
curb, be'teugelen
curdle, schiften
cure, ge'nezing, ge'neesmiddel,
   kuur; ge'nezen; zouten en
   roken
curfew, avondklok; spertijd
curio, curiosi'teit
curiosity, nieuws'gierigheid;
   curiosi'teit

curious, nieuws'gierig; vreemd,
   curi'eus
curl, krul(len)
currant, krent, bes
currency, be'taalmiddel;
   ruchtbaarheid
current, stroom; stroming;
   cou'rant, actu'eel; in omloop,
   heersend
curriculum, leerplan
curry, kerrie(schotel); met kerrie
   kruiden
curse, ver'vloeking, vloek(en),
   ver'vloeken
cursory, vluchtig
curt, bruusk, kort'af
curtail, ver'korten; be'knotten
curtain, gor'dijn, doek
curtsy, révé'rence (maken)
curve, bocht, kromming,
   ronding; (zich) buigen
cushion, kussen; bil'jartband
custard, custard, vla
custody, zorg, be'waring;
   hechtenis
custom, ge'woonte, (oud)
   ge'bruik; klan'dizie
customs, dou'ane(rechten)
customary, ge'bruikelijk
customer, klant
cut, snee, knip; ver'mindering;
   snit; (door)snijden,
   (af)knippen; slijpen; graven;
   banen; (door')klieven;
   ver'minderen; ne'geren;
   ver'zuimen; maaien
to – across, oversteken
to – down, vellen;
   ver'minderen
to – in, snijden; in de rede
vallen
to – off, afsnijden; afsluiten,
   iso'leren; ver'breken

cut (*continued*)
  to – out, (uit)knippen,
    ver'wijderen; afslaan;
    schrappen, uitscheiden met
  to – up, kleinsnijden,
    ver'snipperen; erg aangrijpen;
    opspelen
cuticle, nagelriem
cutlery, be'stek
cutting, scherp; holle weg;
  uitknipsel; stek
cycle, kringloop, cyclus; fietsen
cyclist, fietser
cyclone, cy'cloon
cygnet, jonge zwaan
cylinder, ci'linder
cymbal, cim'baal
cynic, cynicus
cynical, cynisch
cyst, cyste
Czech, Tsjech(isch)

D

dab, tik, likje; deppen,
  aantippen
dabble: to ~ in, (wat) rommelen
  in
dachshund, tekel
dad(dy), papa, vader
daffodil, (gele) nar'cis
daft, dwaas
dagger, dolk
daily, dagelijks, dag-
dainty, sierlijk, fijn, tenger;
  kies'keurig; lekker'nij
dairy, melkinrichting, melker'ij;
  melk-, zuivel-
daisy, made'liefje, mar'griet
dale, dal
dally, talmen; spelen
dam, dam; afdammen
damage, schade(n);

be'schadigen
damages, schadevergoeding
damask, da'mast(en)
dame, vrouwe
damn, donder; ver'domme!;
  (ver')doemen
damnable, ver'vloekt
damp, vochtig(heid);
  be'vochtigen; doen dempen
  be'koelen
damson, pruim
dance, dans(partij), bal; dansen
dandelion, paardenbloem
dandruff, roos
dandy, fat; reuze
danger(ous), ge'vaar(lijk)
dangle, bengelen
Danish, Deens
dank, muf en vochtig
dapper, kwiek
dappled, be'vlekt
dare, (aan)durven; tarten
daredevil, waaghals
daring, durf; ge'durfd
dark, donker; duister
darken, donker maken (*or*
  worden)
darkness, donker
darling, lieveling; liefste
darn, stop(pen); ver'dikkeme!
dart, pijl(tje); schieten
dash, streepje; scheutje, snuifje;
  run; zwier; slaan; hollen;
  ver'nietigen
dastardly, laf'hartig
data, ge'gevens
date, datum, jaartal; afspraak;
  dadel(palm); da'teren,
  ver'ouderen
  out of –, uit de tijd; ver'lopen
  to –, tot op heden
  up to –, tot dusver; op de
    hoogte; mo'dern

daub, (be')smeren; kladschilderen

daughter, dochter

daughter-in-law, schoondochter

daunt, afschrikken

dauntless, onver'vaard

dawdle, treuzelen

dawn, dageraad; aanbreken; doordringen tot

day, dag; tijd
  all –, de hele dag

daybreak, het aanbreken van de dag

daycare, dagopvang

daydream, mijmeren, dromen

daylight, daglicht

daytime: in the –, over'dag

daze, ver'bijstering; ver'doven, ver'bijsteren

dazzle, ver'blinden

dead, dood(s), levenloos, ge'voelloos, abso'luut; pal; dode(n); holst (of the night)
  – beat, doodop

deaden, dempen, ver'doven

deadlock, im'passe

deadly, dodelijk; dood(s)-, ver'schrik'elijk

deaf, doof

deafen, ver'doven

deafening, oorver'dovend

deal, trans'actie, be'handeling; handelen; geven; toebrengen
  a good (or **great deal),** nogal (or heel) veel
  to – out, uitdelen
  to – with, te doen hebben met, be'handelen, helpen; afrekenen met

dealer, handelaar; gever

dealings, zaken, omgang

dean, deken

dear, lief, dierbaar; duur; ach!

dearly, dolgraag, innig; duur

dearth, schaarste, ge'brek

death, dood; sterfgeval
  to (bleed) to –, dood(bloeden)

death duties, suc'cessierechten

debar, uitsluiten, be'letten

debase, ver'lagen; ver'nederen

debatable, be'twistbaar

debate, de'bat('teren (over)); be'twisten

debauched, liederlijk

debauchery, los'bandigheid

debility, ge'brek

debit, debet(saldo); debi'teren

debris, puin, rommel

debt(or), schuld(enaar)
  to be in –, schuld(en) hebben

début, de'buut

decade, de'cennium

decadence, deca'dentie

decamp, opbreken; zijn biezen pakken

decant, overgieten

decanter, ka'raf

decapitate, ont'hoofden

decay, ver'rotting; (in) ver'val (raken); (doen) ver'rotten

decease, over'lijden

deceased, over'leden(e)

deceit, be'drog

deceitful, vals

deceive, be'driegen

decency, fat'soen

decennial, tienjaarlijks

decent, net(jes), aardig; be'hoorlijk

deception, be'drog

deceptive, be'drieglijk

decide, (doen) be'sluiten; be'slissen

decided, be'slist; vastbesloten

deciduous tree, loofboom

decimal, decimaal

decipher, ont'cijferen
decision, be'slissing, be'sluit;
  be'slistheid
decisive, be'slissend; be'slist
deck, dek; tooien
deckchair, ligstoel
declaim, decla'meren
declaration, ver'klaring; aangifte
declare, ver'klaren,
  be'kendmaken; aangeven
decline, daling, achter'uitgang;
  be'danken (voor); afdalen,
  achter'uitgaan; ver'buigen
decompose, ont'binden
decorate, ver'sieren; schilderen
  (en be'hangen); deco'reren
decoration, ver'siering;
  deco'ratie
decorative, decora'tief
decorous, correct, fatsoenlijk
decorum, de'corum
decoy, lok(aas); in de val
  lokken
decrease, afname; ver'minderen
decree, de'creet; decre'teren
decrepit, af'tands
decry, afkeuren, in diskrediet
  brengen
dedicate, wijden; opdragen
dedication, (toe)wijding;
  opdracht
deduce, afleiden
deduct, aftrekken
deduction, aftrek, korting;
  ge'volgtrekking
deed, daad, akte
deem, achten
deep, diep
deepen, dieper worden (or
  maken)
deer, hert(en)
deface, ont'sieren
defamatory, lasterlijk

defame, be'lasteren
default, ver'zuim; in ge'breke
  blijven
defeat, nederlaag; ver'slaan;
  ver'ijdelen
defect, ge'brek
defection, af'valligheid
defective, ge'brekkig, de'fect
defence, ver'dediging
defenceless, weerloos
defend, ver'dedigen
defendant, ge'daagde
defensive, ver'dedigend
defer, uitstellen; zich
  onder'werpen aan
deference, eerbied
defiance, tarting
  in – of ..., ... ten spijt
defiant, uit'dagend
deficiency, te'kort
deficient, ontoe'reikend
deficit, te'kort
defile, bergengte; defi'leren;
  be'vuilen, be'zoedelen
define, defini'ëren
definite, be'paald, defini'tief,
  vast
definition, om'schrijving;
  scherpte
deflate, laten leeglopen; de'flatie
  tot stand brengen van
deflect, ombuigen
deform, mis'vormen
deformed, mis'maakt
defraud, bedriegen
defray, be'strijden
deft, vaardig
defunct, over'leden; ver'ouderd
defy, trot'seren
degenerate, ont'aard(en)
degradation, degra'datie
degrade, degra'deren;
  ver'nederen

degree, graad, mate, rang

dehydrate, (uit-, ver-)drogen

deify, ver'goddelijken

deign, zich ver'waardigen

deity, godheid

dejected, neer'slachtig

delay, ver'traging, uitstel(len);
ver'tragen

delectable, ge'notvol

delegate, afgevaardigde;
afvaardigen, overdragen

delegation, dele'gatie

delete, doorhalen, de'leten

deli, delica'tessenwinkel

deliberate, op'zettelijk,
weloverwogen, be'dachtzaam;
over'wegen, be'raadslagen

delicacy, fijnheid; hachelijkheid;
zwak ge'stel; delica'tesse

delicate, fijn(ge'voelig); teer

delicious, heerlijk

delight, ge'not, ver'rukking;
ver'rukken, ge'noegen
be'zorgen

delightful, ver'rukkelijk, enig

delineation, tekening, omtrek

delinquent, schuldig(e)

delirious, aan het ijlen;
waan'zinnig

deliver, be'zorgen, overleveren;
geven; ver'lossen

delivery, be'zorging,
over'handiging; voordracht;
ver'lossing

delude, mis'leiden, be'goochelen

deluge, wolkbreuk, (stort)vloed;
over'stromen, over'stelpen

delusion, be'drog, waan

de luxe, luxe

delve, delven; vorsen

demagogue, dema'goog

demand, vraag, aanspraak;
eisen, vragen

demarcation, afbakening

demeanour, optreden

demented, gek, gestoord;
dement

demigod, halfgod

demise, over'lijden; overdracht

demobilize, demobili'seren

democracy, democra'tie

democratic, demo'cratisch

demolish, afbreken

demolition, afbraak

demon, boze geest, duivel

demonic, de'monisch

demonstrate, demon'streren,
aantonen

demonstration, demon'stratie,
be'wijs, ver'toon

demonstrative, demonstra'tief;
aan'wijzend

demoralize, demorali'seren

demur, pro'test('eren)

demure, zedig; preuts

den, hol; hok

denial, ont'kenning,
ver'loochening

Denmark, Denemarken

denomination, be'naming;
ge'loofsrichting

denote, duiden op, aanduiden

denouement, ont'knoping

denounce, openlijk
ver'oordelen, aanbrengen

dense, dicht; dom

density, dichtheid; domheid

dent, (in)deuk(en)

dental, tand-

dentist, tandarts

dentures, kunstgebit

deny, ont'kennen,
ver'loochenen; ont'houden

depart, ver'trekken

departed, over'ledene

department, afdeling

departure, ver'trek; afwijking

depend (on), af'hankelijk zijn (van), ver'trouwen (op), afhangen (van)

dependable, be'trouwbaar

dependant, af'hankelijk persoon

dependent, af'hankelijk

depict, afbeelden

deplete, ver'minderen, uitputten

deplorable, betreurens'waardig

deplore, be'treuren

deploy, ont'plooien

depopulate, ont'volken

deport, depor'teren; ge'dragen

depose, afzetten

deposit, be'zinksel, laag; storting, waarborgsom; achterlaten; depo'neren

depot, de'pot

depraved, ont'aard

depravity, ver'dorvenheid

deprecate, (ernstig) afkeuren

depreciate, in waarde (doen) dalen; onder'schatten

depreciation, waardevermindering; ge'ringschatting

depress, neerdrukken; depri'meren

depression, daling, uitholling; ma'laise; neer'slachtigheid

deprive of, ont'nemen

depth, diepte, hoogte

deputation, afvaardiging

deputize, waarnemen

deputy, afgevaardigde; plaatsvervanger; plaatsvervangend

derail, (doen) ontsporen

derange, in de war brengen

derelict, ver'laten; ver'vallen

deride, honend uitlachen

derision, be'spotting

derisive, spottend

derive, afleiden; ont'lenen, ver'krijgen

derogatory, ge'ringschattend

descend, afdalen

descendant, afstammeling

descent, (af)daling; afstamming

describe, be'schrijven

description, be'schrijving, signale'ment; soort

descriptive, be'schrijvend

desecrate, ont'wijden

desert, woes'tijn; ver'diende loon; ver'laten; deser'teren

deserter, deser'teur, af'vallige

deserve, ver'dienen

deservedly, te'recht

deserving, waardevol, ver'dienstelijk

design, ont'werp(en), des'sin; oogmerk, opzet

designate, be'noemd; aanduiden; (be')noemen

designer, ont'werper

desirable, wenselijk

desire, ver'langen, be'geerte; be'geren

desist, ophouden (met)

desk, bu'reau, lessenaar; kas

desolate, ver'laten, triest; ver'woesten

desolation, woeste'nij; troosteloosheid; ver'woesting

despair, wanhoop; wanhopen

desperado, woesteling

desperate, tot het uiterste ge'dreven, wanhopig, schreeuwend

desperation, wanhoop, ver'twijfeling

despicable, ver'achtelijk

despise, ver'achten, ver'smaden

despite, on'danks
despondent, moedeloos
despot, des'poot
despotism, despo'tisme
dessert, des'sert
destination, (plaats van) be'stemming
destine, be'stemmen
he was destined for, hij was bestemd voor
destiny, (nood)lot; be'stemming
destitute, be'hoeftig, be'rooid
destroy, ver'nietigen, ver'nielen
destroyer, tor'pedojager
destruction, ver'nietiging, ver'woesting; ver'derf
destructive, ver'nielziek, schadelijk; afbrekend
detach, scheiden, losmaken; deta'cheren
detached, los(geraakt), vrijstaand; onbe'vangen
detachment, detachering; scheiding; gereser'veerdheid
detail, de'tail
detailed, uit'voerig
detain, ophouden, vasthouden
detect, be'speuren, be'trappen
detective, detec'tive, recher'cheur
detention, oponthoud; ge'vangenhouden, schoolblijven, nablijven
deter, afschrikken
detergent, wasmiddel
deteriorate, achter'uitgaan
deterioration, achter'uitgang
determination, vastbe'radenheid; vaststellen; be'slissing
determine, be'sluiten; vaststellen, be'palen

determined, vastbe'sloten, vastbe'raden
deterrent, afschrikkend (middel)
detest, ver'afschuwen
detestable, ver'foeilijk
dethrone, ont'tronen
detonate, (doen) ont'ploffen
detour, omweg
detract from, afbreuk doen aan
detriment(al), schade(lijk)
devastate, ver'woesten
develop, (zich) ont'wikkelen, uitwerken
development, ont'wikkeling
deviate, afwijken
device, toestel; list; sym'bool, de'vies
devil, duivel
devilish, duivels; ver'duiveld
devious, om'slachtig
devise, ver'zinnen
devoid of, zonder
devolve, overdragen (aan), overgaan (op)
devote, (toe)wijden
devoted, (toe)gewijd, ver'knocht
devotee, enthousi'ast
devotion, toewijding, ver'knochtheid; de'votie; ge'bed
devour, ver'slinden
devout, vroom
dew, dauw
dexterous, be'hendig
diabetes, suikerziekte
diabolic(al), duivels
diagnose, diag'nose opmaken
diagnosis, diag'nose
diagonal, diago'naal
diagram, dia'gram
dial, wijzer(plaat), schijf; facie; draaien

dialect, dia'lect
dialogue, dia'loog
diameter, middellijn
diametrically, diame'traal;
lijnrecht
diamond, dia'mant(en); ruit
(-'vormig)
diaphragm, middenrif;
dia'fragma
diarrhoea, dia'rree
diary, dagboek, a'genda
dice, dobbelstenen; dobbelen
dictate, voorschrift; stem;
dic'teren; voorschrijven
dictation, dic'teren; dic'tee;
voorschrift
dictator, dic'tator
dictatorial, dictatori'aal
dictatorship, dicta'tuur
dictionary, woordenboek
didactic, di'dactisch
die, sterven, doodgaan; snakken
naar
to – out, uitsterven
die-hard, onver'zettelijk
diesel, diesel
diet, di'eet (houden)
dietician, diëtiste
differ, ver'schillen; het niet eens
zijn
difference, ver'schil
different, ver'schillend, anders
differentiate, onder'scheiden;
onderscheid maken
difficult, moeilijk
difficulty, moeilijkheid, be'zwaar
diffident, terughoudend
diffuse, dif'fuus; (zich)
ver'spreiden
dig, por; steek; graven,
omspitten, porren
digest, ver'teren; ver'werken
digestion, (spijs)ver'tering

digit, vinger; cijfer
dignified, waardig
dignify, opluisteren
dignitary, waardigheidsbekleder
dignity, waardigheid
digress, afdwalen, uitweiden
dilapidated, bouw'vallig
dilate, (zich) uitzetten
dilemma, di'lemma
diligence, vlijt; dili'gence
diligent, vlijtig
dilute, ver'dund; ver'dunnen
dim, flauw, vaag, schemerig;
dom; dof worden,
ver'flauwen, ver'zwakken
dimension, afmeting, di'mensie
diminish, ver'minderen
diminutive, klein;
ver'kleinwoord
dimple, kuiltje
din, la'waai
dine, di'neren
diner, eter
dinghy, kleine boot; opblaasbare
boot
dingy, vuil, goor
dinner, warme maaltijd, di'ner
dip, duik(en); inzinking;
dompelen; dalen
diploma, di'ploma
diplomacy, diploma'tie
diplomat, diplo'maat
diplomatic, diploma'tiek
dire, ver'schrikkelijk
direct, rechtstreeks, di'rect;
on'middellijk; open'hartig;
leiden; ge'lasten; de weg
wijzen; richten; adres'seren
direction, richting; aanwijzing;
leiding
directly, on'middellijk; pre'cies
director, direc'teur; raadsman
directory, a'dresboek, gids

dirge, klaagzang

dirt, vuil; aarde

dirt cheap, spotgoedkoop

dirty, vuil(maken); ge'meen

disability, onvermogen

disabled, inva'lide

disablement, invalidi'teit

disadvantage, nadeel
  at a –, in een na'delige po'sitie

disadvantageous, na'delig

disagree (with), het on'eens zijn
  (met)

disagreeable, on'aangenaam

disagreement,
  (menings)verschil

disallow, niet toestaan, ongeldig
  verklaren

disappear(ance),
  ver'dwijnen

disappoint, te'leurstellen
  to be disappointing,
  tegenvallen

disappointment, te'leurstelling,
  tegenvaller

disapproval, afkeuring

disapprove, afkeuren; erop
  tegen zijn

disarm, ont'wapenen

disarmament, ont'wapening

disaster, ramp

disastrous, ramp'spoedig

disband, ont'binden

disbelief, ongeloof

disbelieve, onge'lovig zijn, in
  twijfel trekken

disc, schijf

discard, ver'werpen, afdanken;
  uittrekken; wegleggen

discern, onder'scheiden

discernible, waar'neembaar

discernment,
  onder'scheidingsvermogen,
  inzicht

discharge, ont'lading;
  ont'ploffing; ont'slag; afvoer;
  etteren; zich kwijten van;
  lossen; afschieten; ont'laden;
  ont'slaan; uitmonden; afdoen

disciple, dis'cipel

disciplinary, discipli'nair, tucht-

discipline, disci'pline;
  discipli'neren

disclaim, van de hand wijzen,
  ont'kennen

disclose, ont'hullen,
  blootleggen; loslaten

discolour, (doen) ver'kleuren

discomfort, onbe'haaglijkheid

disconcert, van de wijs brengen

disconcerting, storend

disconnect, uitschakelen,
  afkoppelen

disconnected,
  on'samenhangend

disconsolate, troosteloos

discontent(ment),
  onte'vredenheid

discontented, onte'vreden

discontinue, opheffen,
  ophouden met, staken;
  opzeggen

discord, tweedracht; disso'nant

discordance, wangeluid

discordant, dishar'monisch;
  tegen'strijdig

discotheque, discotheek

discount, korting; discon'teren;
  buiten be'schouwing laten

discourage, ont'moedigen;
  afraden; weer'houden

discouragement,
  ont'moediging; tegenwerping;
  afschrikking

discourse, ver'handeling
  (houden)

discourteous, onbeleefd

discover, ont'dekken
discovery, ont'dekking
discredit, schande; in diskrediet
  brengen; geen ge'loof hechten
  aan
discreet, dis'creet
discrepancy, onregel'matigheid,
  ver'schil
discretion, goedvinden; tact;
  onderscheid
discriminate, discrimineren;
  onderscheid maken
discrimination, discrimi'natie;
  onderscheid
discursive, discursief
discuss, be'spreken
discussion, be'spreking,
  dis'cussie
disdain, ver'achting; ver'smaden
disdainful, minachtend
disease, ziekte; kwaal
diseased, ziek, be'smet
disembark, (zich) ont'schepen
disengage, losmaken
disengaged, onbe'zet
disentangle, ont'warren
disfigure, ont'sieren,
  mis'vormen
disgorge, uitbraken; uitstorten
disgrace, schande; ongenade; te
  schande maken
disgraceful, schandelijk
disgruntled, ver'zuurd
disguise, (ver')mom(ming);
  ver'mommen, ver'bloemen
disgust, afkeer, walging; doen
  walgen
  to be disgusted at, walgen van
  to be disgusted with, meer dan
  ge'noeg hebben van
disgusting, walgelijk,
  af'schuwelijk
dish, schaal; ge'recht

to – up, opdienen, serveren
disharmony, disharmo'nie
dishcloth, vaatdoek
dishearten, ont'moedigen
dishevelled, ver'fomfaaid
dishonest(y), on'eerlijk(heid)
dishonour, oneer, schande;
  ont'eren
dishonourable, ont'erend;
  on'eervol
disillusion, ont'goochelen
disillusionment, ont'goocheling
disinclination, tegenzin
disinclined, onge'negen
disinfect, ont'smetten
disinfectant, ont'smettingsmiddel
disinherit, ont'erven
disintegrate, uitel'kaar vallen,
  (zich) ont'binden
disinterested, be'langeloos
disjointed, onsamen'hangend
dislike, afkeer; on'prettig vinden
dislocate, ont'wrichten
dislodge, losmaken, ver'drijven
disloyal(ty), ontrouw
dismal, triest
dismantle, ont'mantelen
dismay, ont'zetting; ont'stellen
dismiss, ont'slaan, wegsturen;
  afwijzen
dismissal, ont'slag
dismount, afstijgen;
  demon'teren
disobedience,
  onge'hoorzaamheid
disobedient, onge'hoorzaam
disobey, geen ge'hoor geven
  (aan), onge'hoorzaam zijn
disorder, wanorde;
  onge'regeldheid;
  onge'steldheid
disorderly, wan'orderlijk;
  op'roerig

disorganize, in de war sturen

disown, ver'loochenen

disparage, klei'neren

disparity, onge'lijkheid

dispassionate, onpar'tijdig, objec'tief

dispatch, ver'zending; (offici'eel) be'richt; spoed; ver'zenden; afmaken; ver'orberen

dispel, ver'drijven

dispensary, apo'theek

dispensation, uitdeling; dispen'satie; be'schikking

dispense, uitdelen; klaarmaken

  to dispense with, het stellen zonder

dispersal, ver'spreiding

disperse, ver'strooien

dispirit, ont'moedigen

displace, ver'plaatsen, ver'vangen

displacement, ver'plaatsing

display, ver'toon, demon'stratie; (ver')tonen, ten'toonspreiden; ont'plooien

displease, mis'hagen

displeased, ont'stemd

displeasing, on'aangenaam

displeasure, mis'noegen

disposal, opruimen; (be')-schikking

dispose, (rang)schikken; be'wegen

  to – of, van de hand doen

disposed, ge'neigd, ge'stemd

disposition, rangschikking; aard, neiging

dispossess, uit het be'zit stoten

disproportionate, oneven'redig

disprove, weer'leggen

dispute, woordentwist, dis'puut;

(be')twisten, dispu'teren; be'strijden

disqualification, diskwalifi'catie; be'lemmering

disqualify, diskwalifi'ceren; onge'schikt maken

disquiet, onrust; veront'rusten

disregard, veron'achtzaming; veron'achtzamen

disrepair, ver'val

disreputable, be'rucht; haveloos

disrespect, oneer'biedigheid

disrupt, ver'storen, ont'wrichten

dissatisfaction, onte'vredenheid

dissatisfied, onte'vreden

dissect, ont'leden

disseminate, ver'spreiden

dissent, van mening ver'schillen

dissertation, ver'handeling

dissident, dissident, andersdenkend(e)

dissimilar(ity), onge'lijk(heid)

dissipate, ver'strooien; ver'doen

dissipated, ver'lopen, los'bandig

dissociate, (af)scheiden, niet stellen achter

dissolute, liederlijk

dissolution, opheffing

dissolve, (zich) oplossen; ont'binden; wegsmelten

dissonant, wan'luidend

dissuade, afraden, afbrengen (van)

distance, afstand; verte

distant, ver; weg; koel

distaste, afkeer

distasteful, on'smakelijk

distil, distil'leren

distillery, distilleerde'rij

distinct, duidelijk; ver'schillend; be'slist

distinction, onderscheid, onder'scheiding; aanzien

distinctive, kenmerkend
distinguish, onder'scheiden, onderscheid maken
distinguished, aan'zienlijk
distort, ver'wringen; ver'draaien
distract, afleiden; krank'zinnig maken
distraction, afleiding; rade'loosheid
distraught, radeloos
distress, ellende, smart; be'droeven
distribute, uitdelen, ver'spreiden
distribution, uitreiking, ver'deling
district, streek, wijk
distrust, wantrouwen
disturb, storen; komen aan; veront'rusten
disturbance, storing; ver'warring; stoornis
disuse, onbruik
disused, oud, in onbruik ge'raakt
ditch, sloot; lozen
dive, duik(en); tent; tasten
diver, duiker; duikvogel
diverge, uit'eenlopen
divergence, ver'schil
diverse, ver'scheiden
diversion, ver'legging, wegomlegging; ont'spanning
diversity, ver'scheidenheid
divert, ver'leggen; afleiden
divest, ont'doen
divide, (zich) ver'delen; stemmen
dividend, divi'dend; deeltal
divider, (steek)passer
divine, goddelijk, gods-; aanbiddelijk; godgeleerde; peilen, gissen

divinity, god(delijk)heid; godgeleerdheid
divisible, deelbaar
division, (ver')deling, afdeling; di'visie; ver'deeldheid; stemming
divorce, (echt)scheiding; (zich laten) scheiden (van)
divulge, be'kend maken
dizzy, duizelig, duizeling'wekkend
do, doen
   to – away with, afschaffen
   to – up, vastmaken, inpakken; opknappen
   to – with, ge'bruiken; te maken met
   to do without, het stellen zonder
docile, volgzaam
dock, dok(ken); be'klaagdenbank; korten
dockyard, scheepswerf
doctor, dokter; doctor; be'handelen
doctrine, leer(stuk)
document, docu'ment('eren)
documentary, documen'tair(e film)
dodge, foefje; op'zijspringen; ont'wijken
dog, hond; (achter)volgen
dogged, hard'nekkig
dogma, dogma
dogmatic, dog'matisch
doings, ge'doe; spul(len)
dole, werk'loosheidsuitkering
   to – out, uitdelen
doleful, somber
doll, pop
dollar, dollar
dolphin, dol'fijn
domain, do'mein, landgoed; ge'bied

dome, koepel

domestic, huis('houd)elijk, huis(houd)-; binnenlands

domesticated, huiselijk; ge'temd

domicile, domi'cilie

dominant, (over')heersend; domi'nerend; domi'nant

dominate, (over')heersen, be'heersen; be'strijken

domination, over'heersing

domineer, de baas spelen over

domineering, bazig

dominion, heerschap'pij; ge'bied (met zelfbestuur)

dominoes, dominospel

don, ge'leerde; aandoen

donate, schenken

donation, do'natie

done, klaar, af; gaar

done for, er ge'weest

donkey, ezel

donor, schenker, donor

doom, noodlot, ondergang; laatste oordeel; doemen

door, deur, ingang

out of doors, buiten

doorstep, stoep

doorway, deuropening

dope, drugs; doping; sufferd (person)

dormant, slapend

dormer window, dakkapel

dormitory, slaapzaal

dose, dosis; do'seren

dot, stip(pelen), punt

dote, kinds zijn; ver'zot zijn op

dotty, niet goed snik

double, dubbel, tweepersoons-; dubbele, dubbelganger; (zich)ver'dubbelen, dubbelvouwen; zich omwenden

doubt, twijfel(en), be'twijfelen

doubtful, twijfelachtig

doubtless, onge'twijfeld

douche, douche

dough, deeg; geld

doughnut, donut

dour, stug

douse, drijfnat maken

dove, duif(je)

dovecote, duiventil

dowdy, truttig

down, naar be'neden, neder; af; down; dons

  – and out, door en door; aan lager wal

  – payment, bedrag in'eens

  – with, weg met

downcast, (ter')neergeslagen

downfall, val; zware bui

down-hearted, neer'slachtig

downhill, de heuvel af; berg'afwaarts

downpour, stortbui

downright, uitgesproken

downstairs, (naar) be'neden

downstream, stroom'afwaarts

downtrodden, plategetrapt; ver'trapt

downward(s), naar be'neden

downy, donzig

dowry, bruidschat

doze, dutje; dutten

dozen, do'zijn

drab, saai; vaal(bruin)

draft, schets, klad; inlijven, deta'cheren

draftsman, ont'werper

drag, (mee)slepen, (voort)zeulen; kruipen (time); rem; saai gedoe

  in –, als vrouw verkleed

dragon, draak

drain, afvoer(buis), ri'ool;
afvoeren, lopen; droogleggen;
ont'trekken
to be a – on, veel vergen van
drainage, afwatering; afvoer
draining board, aanrecht
drainpipe, afvoerbuis
drama, drama('tiek)
dramatic, dra'matisch
dramatics, to'neelkunst
dramatize, (zich laten)
dramati'seren
drape, drape'rie; dra'peren
drastic, drastisch
draught, tocht, trek; vangst;
diepgang; teug; trek-; ge'tapt
draughts, damspel
draughty, tochtig
draw, ge'lijkspel(en); at'tractie;
ver'loting; trekken; tekenen
to – near, naderen
to – up, stilhouden; opstellen;
bijschuiven
drawback, be'zwaar, nadeel
drawbridge, ophaalbrug
drawer, la(de); tekenaar
drawing, tekening, tekenen
drawing pin, pu'naise
drawing room, sa'lon
drawl, lijzige manier
van praten
drawn, afgetobd; onbe'slist
dread, (met) angst (en beven
tege'moetzien)
dreadful, vreselijk
dream, droom; dromen
dreamy, dromerig; vaag
dreary, somber
dredge, baggermolen;
(uit)baggeren
dregs, be'zinksel
drench, door'weken

dress, ja'pon; kleding, te'nue;
gala-; (zich) (aan)kleden;
tooien; ver'binden
to – up, (zich) opdirken
dresser, (keuken)buf'fet
dressing, verband; slasaus
dressing gown, kamerjas
dressmaker, naaister
dressmaking, naaien
dress rehearsal, gene'rale
repe'titie
dribble, druppelen, kwijlen;
dribbelen
drift, drijven; jachtsneeuw;
neiging, strekking; zich laten
meeslepen, dwalen
driftwood, drijfhout
drill, dril(boor); oefening,
exer'citie; (door')boren; drillen
drink, (iets te) drinken, borreltje
to – to, drinken op
drip, druppel(en), druipen
dripping, braadvet
drive, rit; oprijlaan; drijfkracht;
cam'pagne; slag;
(voort)drijven; rijden; slaan
to – at, doelen op
drivel, ge'wauwel; wauwelen
driver, be'stuurder
driving licence, rijbewijs
drizzle, motregen(en)
droll, grappig, zot
drone, ge'gons; gonzen, dreunen
droop, hangen; omvallen
drop, drupel; glaasje; daling;
hoogte: (laten) vallen; (laten)
dalen; weglaten; afzetten
to – in, (even) langskomen
to – off, in slaap vallen
dross, afval
drought, droogte
drown, ver'drinken;
over'stemmen

to be drowned, ver'dronken
drowse, dommelen
drowsy, slaperig; slaap'wekkend
drudge, werkezel; sloven
drudgery, ge'zwoeg
drug, be'dwelmend middel;
  be'dwelmen
drum, trom(mel), ton;
  trommelen
drunk, dronken
drunkard, dronkaard
dry, droog; (af)drogen
dry clean(ing), chemisch reinigen
dual, twee'ledig, dubbel
dub, tot ridder slaan; dubben
dubious, twijfelachtig, dubi'eus
duchess, herto'gin
duchy, hertogdom
duck, eend; duik; (onder)duiken
duct, ka'naal, buis
dud, prul; blindganger (bomb)
due, ver'schuldigd, ver'diend,
  ge'past; ver'wacht; wat
  iemand toekomt
  – to, dankzij, ten ge'volge van
duel, du'el; duel'leren
dug-out, uitgegraven
  schuilplaats
duke, hertog
dull, dof; saai; traag; somber
  afstompen
duly, dan ook; dus, naar
  be'horen
dumb, stom, sprakeloos
dumbfound, ver'stomd doen
  staan
dummy, pop; blinde; namaak-
dump, belt, stortplaats;
  opslagplaats storten,
  neerzetten
dunce, domkop
dune, duin

dung, (be')mest(en)
dungarees, over'all
dungeon, kerker
dupe, dupe; be'driegen
duplicate, dupli'caat;
  ver'dubbelen
  in –, in duplo
duplicity, dubbel'hartigheid
durable, duurzaam
duration, duur
duress, dwang
during, tijdens
dusk, schemering
dusky, donker, schemerig
dust, stof; afstoffen; be'stuiven
dustbin, vuilnisbak
dustman, vuilnisman
dustpan (and brush), (veger en)
  blik
dusty, stoffig; poeierig
Dutch, Nederlands;
  Nederlanders
dutiful, plichtsgetrouw
duty, plicht; functie; (invoer)-
  rechten
dwarf, dwerg; minia'tuur;
  over'schaduwen
dwell, wonen
  to – on, lang stilstaan bij
dweller, be'woner
dwelling, woning
dwelling place, woonplaats
dwindle (away), wegteren;
  uitsterven, ver'dwijnen
dye, verf(stof); verven, kleuren
dynamic, dy'namisch
dynamite, dyna'miet
dynamo, dy'namo
dynasty, dynas'tie
dysentery, dysente'rie

E

each, elk, ieder; per stuk
– **other,** el'kaar
eager, enthousi'ast, gretig,
ver'langend
to be –, dolgraag (zouden)
willen
eagerness, enthousi'asme,
ver'langen
eagle, arend
ear, oor; ge'hoor; aar
eardrum, trommelvlies
earl, graaf
early, (te) vroeg, vroeger,
vroeg'tijdig
earmark, be'stemmen
earn, ver'dienen; ver'werven,
be'zorgen
earnest, ernstig, vurig
in –, in (alle) ernst
earnings, verdiensten
earring, oorbel
ear-splitting, oorver'dovend
earth, aarde, grond; hol;
aardverbinding
what (*or* **how**) **on** – ... wat (*or*
hoe) in vredesnaam ...
earthenware, aardewerk
earthly, aards, stoffelijk
earthquake, aardbeving
earthworm, aardworm
earthy, grond-; laag bij de
gronds
ease, ge'mak; ver'lichten; losser
maken; voor'zichtig schuiven;
ver'minderen
easel, ezel
easily, (ge')makkelijk; verreweg
east, oosten; oost(waarts)
Easter, pasen
– **Day,** eerste paasdag
easterly, oostelijk, ooster-
eastern, oosters, oostelijk

easy, (ge')makkelijk; kalm
easy-going, gemak'zuchtig;
flegma'tiek
eat, (op)eten; vreten
eaves, overhangende dakrand
eavesdrop, afluisteren
ebb, eb(ben); ver'val; afnemen
ebony, ebbenhout(en)
eccentric, ex'centrisch;
excen'triek; zonderling
ecclesiastical, geestelijk,
kerkelijk
echo, echo; weerklank;
weer'klinken; weergeven,
her'halen
eclipse, ver'duistering;
ver'duisteren; in de schaduw
stellen
economic, eco'nomisch
economical, zuinig, voor'delig;
eco'nomisch
economics, econo'mie
economist, eco'noom
economize, be'zuinigen
economy, zuinigheid; be'heer
ecstasy, ex'tase
ecstatic, geest'driftig
eddy, draaikolk; dwarrelen
edge, rand; scherpe kant
on edge, zenuwachtig
edible, eetbaar
edict, e'dict
edifice, ge'bouw
edify, stichten
edit, uitgeven; redi'geren
edition, uitgave, e'ditie
editor, redac'teur, be'werker
editorial, hoofdartikel
editorial board (staff), re'dactie
educate, onder'wijzen,
opvoeden
education, onderwijs,
ont'wikkeling

educational, opvoedings-, onderwijs-
eel, paling
eerie, griezelig
efface, uitwissen; wegcijferen
effect, ge'volg, uitwerking, resul'taat; ef'fect; be'werkstelligen
in –, in feite; van kracht
effective, ge'slaagd, treffend; af'doend; van kracht
effeminate, ver'wijfd
effervesce, mous'seren; bruisen
efficacy, doel'treffendheid
efficiency, vaardigheid; nuttig ef'fect
effigy, beeltenis, beeldenaar
effort, krachtsinspanning, poging; pres'tatie
effrontery, brutali'teit
effusive, uit'bundig
egg, ei
to – on, aanzetten
egoist, ego'ïst
egotism, egotisme, egoïsme
eiderdown, donzen dekbed
eight(h), acht(ste)
eighteen(th), achttien(de)
eighty, tachtig
Eire, Ierland
either, één (van beide); beide; elk; ook
– ... or, of ... of
ejaculation, zaadlozing; uitroep
eject, uitwerpen, uitzetten
eke out, rekken
elaborate, inge'wikkeld, door'wrocht, uitgebreid; be'werken, bijwerken; uitweiden
elapse, ver'strijken, ver'lopen
elastic, e'lastisch; rekbaar; elas'tiek

elasticity, elastici'teit; rekbaarheid
elated, opgetogen
elbow, elleboog; door'heenwerken
– grease, zwaar werk; schoonmaakwerk
elder, ouder(e), oudst(e); ouderling
elderly, op leeftijd
elect, ge'kozen(e), uitverkoren(e); (ver')kiezen (als), uitkiezen
election, (uit)ver'kiezing
elector(ate), kiezer(s)
electric(al), e'lektrisch
electrician, elektri'cien
electricity, elektrici'teit
electrify, elektrifi'ceren; elektri'seren
elegant, ele'gant
elegy, ele'gie
element, ele'ment; be'standdeel
elemental, na'tuur-, essen'tieel
elementary, elemen'tair; een'voudig
– school, basisschool
elephant, olifant
elevate, ver'heffen
elevation, ver'hoging, hoogte; ver'heffing; opstand
eleven, elf(tal)
elf, elf, ka'bouter
elicit, ont'lokken
eligible, ver'kiesbaar; be'voegd; ge'schikt
eliminate, uitschakelen
ellipse, el'lips
elm, iep(enhout)
elongate, (zich) ver'lengen, uitrekken
elope, weglopen
eloquence, wel'sprekendheid

else, anders; verder
elsewhere, ergens anders
elucidate, toelichten
elude, ont'wijken, ont'duiken, ont'gaan
elusive, moelijk te vinden (*or* vatten)
emaciate, uitmergelen
e-mail, e-mail, email
emanate from, voortkomen uit, uitstralen van
emancipation, emanci'patie
embalm, balsemen
embankment, kade
embargo, be'slag, ver'bod, embargo
embark, (zich) inschepen
   to embark on, aanvangen
embarrass, ver'legen maken, in ver'legenheid brengen; be'moeilijken
embarrassing, pijnlijk
embarrassment, ver'legenheid
embassy, ambas'sade, ge'zantschap
embedded, ge'nesteld, vastge'raakt
embellish, ver'fraaien
ember, gloeiend kooltje (*or* stuk hout)
embezzle, ver'duisteren
embitter, ver'bitteren, ver'gallen
embody, be'lichamen; be'vatten
embossed, in re'liëf
embrace, om'helzing; (el'kaar) om'helzen; om'sluiten; zich eigen maken
embroider, bor'duren
embroidery, bor'duurwerk
embroil, ver'wikkelen
embryo, embryo
emerald, sma'ragd(en)
emerge, te voorschijn komen

emergency, nood(geval), noodtoestand
emigrant, emi'grant; emi'grerend
emigrate, emi'greren
eminence, emi'nentie, ver'maardheid
eminent, uit'zonderlijk (ver'maard)
emissary, ge'zant
emit, uitstralen, afgeven; uiten
emotion, (ge'moeds)aandoening, e'motie
emotional, emotio'neel, ge'voels-
emperor, keizer
emphasis, nadruk
emphasize, de nadruk leggen op, duidelijk doen uitkomen
emphatic, na'drukkelijk
empire, (keizer)rijk
employ, (in)dienst(hebben); ge'bruiken, bezighouden
employee, werknemer
employer, werkgever
employment, werk; ge'bruik
empower, machtigen
empty, leeg (maken *or* worden); niets'zeggend; lozen
emulate, nastreven
emulsion, e'mulsie
enable, in staat stellen
enact, tot wet ver'heffen; opvoeren
enamel, e'mail('leren), brandverf, gla'zuur; lakken
enamour, be'koren; ver'zotten
encamp, een kamp opslaan; legeren
encase, om'sluiten, opsluiten
enchant, be'toveren; ver'rukken

enchanting, sprookjesachtig, char'mant; be'toverend

encircle, om'ringen, om'singelen

enclose, insluiten

enclosure, om'sloten ruimte; bijlage

encompass, om'sluiten; be'vatten

encounter, ont'moeting; treffen; tegenkomen; onder'vinden

encourage, aanmoedigen

encouragement, aanmoediging

encroach on, doordringen tot; inbreuk maken op

encrust, be'slaan; be'zetten

encumber, be'lasten

encyclopaedia, encyclope'die

end, eind(igen); doel

  no – of, vreselijk veel

  in the –, ten'slotte

  make both ends meet, rondkomen

endanger, in ge'vaar brengen

endear, ge'liefd maken, innemen

endeavour, poging; trachten

ending, eind; uitgang

endless, eindeloos, zonder einde

endorse, endos'seren; onder'schrijven

endow, be'giftigen

endowment, gave, gift

endurance, uithoudingsvermogen; ver'dragen

endure, ver'dragen; ver'duren

enemy, vijand(elijk)

energetic, ener'giek; krachtig

energy, ener'gie

enfold, om'wikkelen; om'helzen, om'strengelen

enforce, (krachtig) uitvoeren; dwingen tot

enforcement, handhaving

enfranchise, vrijmaken; kiesrecht ver'lenen

engage, in dienst nemen; in be'slag nemen; slaags raken met; in el'kaar grijpen

engaged, ver'loofd; in ge'sprek, be'zet, bezig

  to get engaged, zich ver'loven met

engagement, afspraak; ver'loving; in'dienstneming; ge'vecht

engaging, in'nemend

engender, ver'wekken; ver'oorzaken

engine, ma'chine, motor, locomo'tief

engineer, inge'nieur, technicus, machi'nist, lid van de ge'nietroepen; klaarspelen

engineering, tech'niek

England, Engeland

English(man), Engels(man)

engraving, gra'vure, gra'veren

engross, ver'diepen; fasci'neren

engulf, ver'zwelgen

enhance, ver'hogen

enigma(tic)(al), raadsel(achtig)

enjoy, ge'nieten (van)

enjoyable, prettig

enjoyment, ple'zier, ge'nieten

enlarge, (zich) ver'groten

  to – on, uitweiden over

enlighten, opheldering geven aan; ver'lichten

enlist, (in) dienst nemen; een be'roep doen op

enliven, opvrolijken

enmity, vijandschap

enormous, e'norm

enormously, e'norm

enough, ge'noeg; heel

  kind –, zo vriendelijk

enrage, woedend maken
enrapture, in ver'voering brengen
enrich, ver'rijken
enrol, (zich laten) inschrijven; lid worden
ensue, het ge'volg zijn, volgen
ensure, veiligstellen; garanderen
entail, met zich meebrengen
entangle, vastraken; ver'strikken
enter, binnengaan, binnenkomen; gaan in; opgeven; boeken
enterprise, onder'neming(sgeest)
enterprising, onder'nemend
entertain, ver'maken, onder'houden; ont'halen, ont'vangen; over'wegen; koesteren
entertaining, amu'sant; so'ciale plichten
entertainment, amuse'ment
enthrall, boeien
enthrone, op de troon plaatsen, wijden
enthusiasm, enthousi'asme
enthusiast(ic), enthousi'ast
entice, (ver')lokken
entire, (ge')heel
entirely, helemaal
entirety, ge'heel
entitle, (be')titelen; het recht geven
entity, eenheid, entiteit, bestaan
entomb, be'graven
entrails, ingewanden
entrance, ingang; opkomen; in ver'voering brengen
entreat, smeken
entreaty, smeekbede
entrust, toevertrouwen

entry, intocht, ingang; boeking; inschrijving
enumerate, opnoemen
envelop, hullen
envelope, enve'loppe
enviable, benijdens'waardig
envious, af'gunstig
environment, om'geving
envisage, voor'zien
envoy, (af)ge'zant
envy, afgunst; be'nijden
ephemeral, kort'stondig
epic, epos, heldendaden; episch
epicure, gastro'noom
epidemic, epide'mie; rage
epilepsy, epilep'sie
epilogue, epi'loog
episode, epi'sode
epitaph, grafschrift
epoch, tijdperk
equal, ge'lijk (zijn aan); eve'naren
– to, opgewassen tegen
equality, ge'lijkheid
equalize, ge'lijk maken
equally, even('zeer)
equation, verge'lijking
equator, evenaar
equilateral, gelijk'zijdig
equilibrium, evenwicht
equip, uitrusten, toerusten
equitable, billijk
equity, billijkheid, aandelenvermogen
equivalent, equivalent
equivocal, dubbel'zinnig, twijfelachtig
era, tijdperk, jaartelling
eradicate, uitroeien
erase, schrappen; uitwissen
erect, over'eind (zetten); oprichten

erection, erectie; gebouw; het oprichten, het opbouwen
erode, uitschuren
erosion, e'rosie
erotic, e'rotisch
err, dwalen
errand, boodschap
erratic, inconse'quent, onregel'matig
erroneous, on'juist
error, fout, a'buis
erudite, ge'leerd
erupt, uitbarsten, uitspuwen
escalator, roltrap
escapade, esca'pade
escape, ont'vluchting; ont'snappen, ont'komen aan; ont'gaan
escarpment, steile wand
escort, ge'leide, es'corte; bege'leiden, escor'teren
especial, bij'zonder
especially, bijzonder, voor'al
espionage, spion'nage
essay, opstel
essence, wezen, es'sentie; es'sence
essential, essen'tieel; hoofdzaak
essentially, in wezen
establish, oprichten; (vast)stellen; vestigen; instellen
establishment, (handels)huis, instelling; oprichten; gevestigde orde
estate, landgoed, vastgoed
– agent, makelaar
esteem, achting; achten
estimable, achtens'waardig; te be'rekenen
estimate, schatting; schatten
estimation, mening; schatting, achting
estrange, ver'vreemden

estuary, ri'viermond
etc(etera), enz(ovoorts)
etch, etsen
etching, ets
eternal, eeuwig
eternity, eeuwigheid
ether, ether
ethereal, e'therisch
ethical, ethisch
ethics, ethica
euro, euro (pl: euro's)
Europe, Eu'ropa
European, Euro'pees; Europe'aan
evacuate, evacu'eren
evacuation, evacu'atie
evade, ont'wijken
evaluate, ta'xeren, schatten
evangelic(al), evan'gelisch
evangelist, evange'list
evaporate, ver'dampen; ver'dwijnen
evasion, ont'wijking, ont'duiking
evasive, ont'wijkend
eve, (voor)avond, dag voor
even, ge'lijk('matig); effen; even; quitte; gelijk'moedig; zelfs; pre'cies; nog; ge'lijkmaken
– so, maar toch
evening, avond
event, ge'beurtenis, ge'val; nummer
at all events, in ieder ge'val
eventful, veelbe'wogen
eventual, uit'eindelijk; eventu'eel
eventually, ten'slotte
ever, ooit, te allen tijde
evergreen, altijd groen(e plant)
everlasting, eeuwig('durend)
evermore, altijd

every, ieder; alle
  – other week, om de twee weken
  – now and then, af en toe
everybody, everyone, ieder'een
everyday, alle'daags, dagelijks
everything, alles
everywhere, overal (waar)
evict, uitzetten
evidence, be'wijs(materi'aal),
  ge'tuigenis; blijk
  to give –, ge'tuigenis afleggen
evident, duidelijk,
  klaar'blijkelijk
evil, kwaad; onheil, euvel
evildoer, boosdoener
evince, (aan)tonen
evoke, oproepen
evolution, evo'lutie
evolve, (zich) ont'plooien
exact, pre'cies; eisen
exacting, veel'eisend
exactitude, nauw'keurigheid
exaggerate, over'drijven
exaltation, ver'heerlijking;
  (geest)ver'voering
examination, e'xamen;
  onderzoek; ver'hoor
examine, exami'neren;
  onder'zoeken, onder'vragen;
  goed be'kijken
example, voorbeeld, mo'del
  to set an –, een voorbeeld
  geven
exasperate, ergeren, irriteren
excavate, uitgraven, opgraven
excavation, opgraving
exceed, te boven gaan,
  over'schrijden
exceedingly, bij'zonder
excel, uitmunten; over'treffen
excellence, voor'treffelijkheid
excellent, uit'stekend
except, be'halve; uitzonderen

exception, uitzondering
  to take – to, bezwaar maken
  tegen
exceptional, onge'woon,
  exceptio'neel
excerpt, (aangehaalde) passage
excess, overmaat; surplus;
  uitspatting; extra
excessive, over'dadig,
  buiten'sporig
exchange, ruil(en); beurs;
  cen'trale; (uit)wisseling;
  (in)wisselen
exchequer, schatkist
excise, ac'cijns; uitsnijden
excitable, gauw opgewonden
excite, opwinden, prikkelen;
  opwekken
excitement, opwinding
exclaim, uitroepen
exclamation, uitroep
exclude, uitsluiten, buitensluiten
exclusive, uit'sluitend; exclu'sief
excommunicate, in de ban doen
excrements, uitwerpselen
excretion, afscheiding
excruciating, folterend, pijnlijk
excursion, ex'cursie, uitstapje;
  uitweiding
excusable, be'grijpelijk
excuse, ex'cuus; excu'seren, niet
  kwalijk nemen;
  veront'schuldigen; vrijstellen
  – me, par'don; neem me niet
  kwalijk
execute, uitvoeren; ter dood
  brengen
execution, uitvoering;
  te'rechtstelling
executioner, beul
executive, uitvoerend(e macht);
  be'drijfsleider
executor, execu'teur

exemplary, voor'beeldig

exemplify, als voorbeeld dienen van, be'lichamen

exempt, vrij(gesteld); vrijstellen

exercise, oefening; (uit)oefenen; in acht nemen

exert, aanwenden, inspannen

exertion, inspanning; ge'bruik

exhale, uitademen

exhaust, uitlaat; uitputten

exhaustion, uitputting

exhibit, inzending, be'wijsstuk; ten'toonstellen; (ver')tonen

exhibition, ten'toonstelling; ver'toon, ver'toning

exhibitor, expo'sant

exhilarate, stimu'leren, opvrolijken

exhort, aansporen, ver'manen

exhume, opgraven

exile, balling(schap)

exist, be'staan

existence, be'staan

exit, uitgang; aftreden

exonerate, zuiveren

exorbitant, buiten'sporig

exorcize, be'vrijden; uitdrijven

exotic, uit'heems

expand, (doen) uitzetten, (zich) uitbreiden, (zich) uitspreiden; uitwerken

expanse, uitge'strektheid

expansion, expansie, uitbreiding

expatriate, ver'bannen

expect, ver'wachten; denken

expectant, vol verwachting

– mother, aanstaande moeder

expectation, ver'wachting

expedient, be'vorderlijk, raadzaam, redmiddel

expedite, be'spoedigen

expedition, expe'ditie

expel, uitdrijven; wegsturen

expend, uitgeven; be'steden

expenditure, uitgeven, be'steden; uitgaven

expense, (on)kosten, uitgave

expensive, duur

experience, er'varing; onder'vinden

experienced, er'varen

experiment, proef; experimen'teren

experimental, proef(onder'vindelijk)

expert, des'kundig(e); be'dreven

expiate, boeten voor

expire, aflopen; de laatste adem uitblazen; uitademen

expiry, afloop

explain, uitleggen

explanation, ver'klaring

explanatory, ver'klarend

explicit, uit'drukkelijk

explode, (doen) ont'ploffen; losbarsten; ont'zenuwen

exploit, (helden)daad; exploi'teren

exploration, onder'zoeking(stocht)

explore, ver'kennen, onder'zoeken

explorer, ont'dekkingsreiziger

explosion, ont'ploffing; uitbarsting

explosive, springstof; ont'plofbaar; op'vliegend

exponent, expo'nent

export, export(eren); uitvoer(artikel); uitvoeren

expose, blootstellen; uitstallen; ont'hullen, aan de dag brengen; be'lichten

exposed, onbe'schut

exposition, uit'eenzetting;
ten'toonstelling
exposure, ont'maskering;
blootstellen; be'lichting
expound, uit'eenzetten
express, uit'drukkelijk,
speci'aal, op'zettelijk;
ex'pres(trein); uitdrukken;
uitpersen
expression, uitdrukking
expressive, expres'sief;
veel'zeggend
expulsion, uitdrijving;
wegsturen
expunge, uitwissen
exquisite, buitengewoon fijn;
zeer ver'fijnd
extend, (zich) uitstrekken,
ver'lengen; uitbreiden;
ver'lenen
extension, bijgebouw;
ver'lenging; lijn
extensive, uitgebreid,
uitgestrekt
extent, uitge'strektheid; omvang
to what (or this) –, in hoe- (or
zo)'verre
extenuate, ver'zachten,
ver'goelijken
exterior, buiten(kant),
uit'wendig
exterminate, uitroeien
external, uit'wendig,
buiten(lands); uiterlijk(heid)
extinct, uitgestorven
extinguish, blussen, doven; een
eind maken aan
extort, afpersen
extortionate, buiten'sporig
extra, extra
extract, passage; ex'tract;
(uit)trekken, uithalen; afpersen
extraction, ex'tractie; afkomst

extraneous, vreemd, niet ter
zake dienend
extraordinary, buitenge'woon,
extra
extravagance,
buiten'sporigheid,
ver'kwisting; uitspatting
extravagant, ver'kwistend;
extravagant, over'dreven
extreme, uiterst(e)
extremely, uitermate
extremist, extre'mist(isch)
extremity, uiterste (nood),
uiteinde
extricate, loswerken, losmaken,
ont'warren
exuberant, uit'bundig
exude, afscheiden; ver'spreiden
exult, jubelen
exultant, triom'fantelijk,
opgetogen
exultation, tri'omf,
opge'togenheid
eye, oog; aankijken
to catch a person's eye,
de aandacht van iemand
trekken
to see eye to eye, het ge'heel
eens zijn
eyebrow, wenkbrauw
eyelash, wimper
eyelid, ooglid
eye-opener, open'baring
eyesight, ge'zicht (svermogen)
eyesore, gruwel (voor het oog)

F

fable, fabel
fabric, stof, weefsel; struc'tuur
fabricate, fabri'ceren; ver'zinnen
fabulous, legen'darisch;
fabelachtig

façade, gevel; voorwendsel

face, ge'zicht; wijzerplaat; oppervlakte; pres'tige; nominaal; liggen op; het ge'zicht keren naar; onder de ogen zien; be'dekken
 – to –, tegenover elkaar
 in the – of, ondanks, tegenover
 on the – of it, ogen'schijnlijk
 faced with, ge'plaatst voor (*or* in)

facecloth, washandje

facet, fa'cet

facetious, gek(scherend), schertsend

facial, ge'zichts-

facile, (licht')vaardig, opper'vlakkig

facilitate, verge'makkelijken

facility, voor'ziening, facili'teit; ta'lent

facing, tegen'over, met het ge'zicht naar (*or* op)

fact, feit
 in (point of) –, in feite, eigenlijk, zelfs, immers

faction, par'tij(strijd)

factor, factor

factory, fa'briek

factual, feitelijk

faculty, ver'mogen, aanleg; facul'teit; ver'gunning

fad, be'vlieging

fade, (doen) ver'schieten; ver'weken; wegsterven

faggot, bundel houtjes; bal gehakt; flikker (gay man)

fail, mis'lukken, (laten) zakken; nalaten; in de steek laten; opraken
 without –, zonder man'keren

failing, ge'brek; bij ge'brek aan

failure, mis'lukk(el)ing

faint, flauw(te), vaag, zwak; flauwvallen

fair, billijk, eerlijk; be'hoorlijk; blond; mooi, net; kermis, markt

fairly, tamelijk; eerlijk

fairy, fee

fairytale, sprookje

faith, ge'loof; ver'trouwen; trouw

faithful, trouw; ge'lovig(en)

faithless, onge'lovig; trouweloos

fake, be'drog; namaak; knoeien met; namaken; fin'geren

falcon, valk

fall, val(len), daling; overgave, ondergang; ver'val; be'zwijken; dalen
 to – back on, zijn toevlucht nemen tot; te'rugtrekken op
 to – out, ruzie krijgen
 to – short, te'kortschieten
 to – to, aanpakken, toetasten; dichtvallen; ten deel vallen

fallow, braak; geelbruin

false, on'juist; vals; on'trouw; scheef; loos
 – teeth, kunstgebit

falsehood, on'waarheid

falsify, ver'valsen

falter, wankelen, weifelen; stamelen

fame, roem, ver'maardheid

famed, be'roemd

familiar, be'kend, ver'trouwd; famili'aar

familiarity, familiari'teit

family, ge'zin, fa'milie; ge'slacht; kinderen

famine, hongersnood; schaarste

famish, uithongeren, ver'hongeren

famous, be'roemd; prachtig

fan, waaier, venti'lator;
enthousi'ast; waaieren;
aanwakkeren

fanatic, dweper, fana'tiek(eling)

fanaticism, fana'tisme

fanciful, fan'tastisch; grillig

fancy, ver'beelding(skracht);
be'vlieging; fanta'sie-, luxe;
zich in(or ver')beelden; een
i'dee hebben; zin hebben in

fancy dress, gecostu'meerd

fanfare, fan'fare

fantastic, fan'tastisch, grillig

fantasy, fanta'sie

far, ver; veel
 – off, ver weg
 the – side, de overkant
 as – as, voor zo'ver; tot aan
 by –, – and away, verreweg
 – and wide, heinde en ver

farce, klucht; farce,
schijnvertoning

farcical, be'spottelijk

fare, ta'rief, vracht(je);
ver'voerskosten; kost; gaan

farewell, afscheid(s-)

far-fetched, verge'zocht

farm, boerde'rij, fokke'rij,
kweke'rij; een boerde'rij
hebben (van)

farmer, boer

farmhouse, boerde'rij

farmyard, (boeren')erf

far-off, ver

far-reaching, verstrekkend

far-sighted, verziend;
voor'uitziend

farther, verder

farthest, verst

fascinate, boeien,
fasci'neren

fascination, iets boeiends,
be'koring; ge'boeide
be'langstelling

fashion, mode; ma'nier;
scheppen, vormen

fashionable, modi'eus, deftig,
(in de) mode

fast, snel, hard; vóór;
ge'raffi'neerd; vast; wasecht;
trouw; vasten
 to be – asleep; als een roos
slapen

fasten, vastmaken; gooien

fastening, sluiting, knip

fastidious, kies'keurig

fat, dik, vet

fatal, dodelijk; nood'lottig;
be'slissend

fatalist(ic), fata'list(isch)

fate, lot; dood

fateful, nood'lottig

father, vader

fathom, vadem; peilen

fathomless, peilloos

fatigue, ver'moeidheid,
ver'moeienis; afmatten

fatten, aanzetten; vetmesten

fatty, vet(tig); dikkerd

fatuous, stom, dwars

fault, fout, de'fect; schuld
 to find – with, vitten op;
aanmerkingen maken op

faultless, onbe'rispelijk, feilloos

faulty, ge'brekkig, de'fect

favour, (be')gunst(igen); ingang;
voorliefde; in'signe; de
voorkeur geven aan
 in – of, vóór; ten gunste van
 to do someone a –, iemand
een ge'noegen doen

favourable, gunstig

favourite, gunsteling, favo'riet;
lievelings-

favouritism, be'voorrechting
fax, fax; faxen
fear, angst, vrees; vrezen, bang
zijn
fearful, vreselijk
fearless, onbe'vreesd
feasible, uit'voerbaar;
aan'nemelijk
feast, feest(maal); zich
ver'gasten aan, ont'halen
feat, pres'tatie
feather, veer, pluim; veren
feature, (ge'laats)trek;
onderdeel, (op'vallende)
eigenschap; gaan over
feature film, speelfilm
February, febru'ari
fecund(ity), vruchtbaar(heid)
federal, fede'raal
federation, fede'ratie
fed up: to be –, er meer dan
genoeg van hebben
fee, hono'rarium, be'drag,
(school)geld
feeble, zwak, flauw
feed, voer(en); voeding; eten
feel, ge'voel; (zich) voelen;
(be')tasten; aanvoelen;
ge'loven; (meelij) hebben
to – like, aanvoelen als; zich
voelen (als); zin hebben in
feeling, ge'voel, voelen
feign, veinzen
felicitous, ge'lukkig
felicity, ge'luk('zaligheid)
feline, katachtig
fell, hevig; (neer)vellen
fellow, kerel; mede-
fellowship, ge'meenschap
felony, zware misdaad
felt, vilt(en)
female, vrouwelijk; vrouw
feminine, vrouwelijk

fen, moe'rasland, polder
fence, om'heining, schutting;
om'heinen; schermen
fend for oneself, voor zich'zelf
zorgen
to – off, afweren
ferment, gist(ing); be'roering;
(doen) gisten
fern, varen
ferocious, woest
ferret, fret; opsporen; snuffelen
ferry, veer(pont); overzetten
fertile, vruchtbaar; rijk
fertilize, vruchtbaar maken;
be'vruchten
fertilizer, (kunst)mest
fervent, vurig, innig
fervid, heftig
fervour, vuur
fester, zweren; woekeren
festival, feest
festive, feestelijk, feest-
festivity, festivi'teit
festoon, slinger; met slingers
tooien
fetch, (af)halen; opbrengen
fetish, fetisj
fetter, keten(en)
feud, vete
feudal, feo'daal
fever, koorts(achtige opwinding)
feverish, koorts(achtig)
few, weinig(en)
a –, een paar, enkele
fiancé(e), ver'loofde
fiasco, fi'asco
fib, leugentje; jokken
fibre, vezel; stoerheid, aard
fibreglass, glasvezel
fickle, wispel'turig
fiction, ro'mans en korte
ver'halen; fictie, ver'dichtsel
fictitious, fic'tief, gefin'geerd

fiddle, vi'ool (spelen); scharrelen
fidelity, trouw, ge'trouwheid
fidget, draaitol; wiebelen
field, veld, akker; ge'bied
fiend, duivel; mani'ak
fiendish, duivels
fierce, woest, fel
fiery, vuur(rood); vurig
fifteen(th), vijftien(de)
fifty, vijftig
fig, vijg
fight, ge'vecht, strijd; vechtlust;
    (be')vechten
figment, ver'zinsel
figurative, fi'guurlijk
figure, cijfer; prijs; ge'daante,
    fi'guur; voorkomen
    – of speech, zegswijze
    to – out, uitkienen
figurehead, boegbeeld; leider in
    naam
filament, (gloei)draad
filch, kapen
file, dos'sier, map; file; vijl(en);
    opbergen; (een voor een)
    trekken
fill, (op)vullen; stoppen
fillet, fi'let; fi'leren
filling, vulling
film, film, vlies(je), waas;
    (ver')filmen
filmy, dun, wazig
filter, filter; fil'treren; sijpelen
    – through, uitlekken
filth, vuiligheid; vuile taal
filthy, vuil, vies
fin, vin
final, laatste, eind-, slot-;
    defini'tief; eindwedstrijd
finally, ten'slotte
finance, fi'nanciën;
    finan'cieren
financial, finan'cieel

financier, finan'cier
find, vondst; (be')vinden;
    ont'dekken; merken;
    (op)zoeken
finding, be'vinding
fine, mooi; (haar)fijn; best;
    geldboete
finery, opschik
finesse, fi'nesse
finger, vinger; be'tasten
fingernail, nagel
fingerprint, vingerafdruk
finicky, kies'keurig,
    piete'peuterig
finish, eind(igen); afwerking: af
    (or op)maken; afwerken
finite, eindig
Finn(ish), Fin(s)
fiord, fjord
fir, den(nenboom)
fire, vuur, brand; haard;
    (af)vuren, (af)schieten, lossen;
    bakken; aanwakkeren; op
    straat zetten
    to catch –, vlam vatten
    on –, in brand; brandend
    (van ver'langen)
    to set – to, to set on –, in
    brand steken
firearm, vuurwapen
fire escape, brandtrap
fire extinguisher, blusapparaat
firefighter, brandweerman
fireside, (open) haard
fireworks, vuurwerk
firm, vast(be'raden), stevig,
    hecht; stand'vastig; firma
first, (voor het) eerst; ten eerste
    at –, in het be'gin
    – of all, eerst, om te be'ginnen
first aid, eerste hulp
first-rate, eersteklas, prima
fiscal, fis'caal, be'lasting-

fish, vis(sen); opdiepen
fisher(man), visser, hengelaar
fishery, visse'rij
fishing, vissen; visge'legenheid
fishing rod, hengel
fishmonger, visboer, viswinkel
fishy, visachtig, vis-; ver'dacht
fissure, kloof, spleet
fist, vuist
fit, ge'zond, fit; ge'schikt; klaar;
  aanval; bui, toeval; passen;
  kloppen met; voor'zien,
  uitrusten
  to – in, plaats (*or* tijd) vinden
  voor; zich aanpassen, passen
  bij
fitful, on'rustig, grillig
fitting, ge'past; pas; fitting
fittings, toebehoren,
  be'nodigdheden
five, vijf
fix, knel; vastmaken;
  vaststellen; vestigen;
  opknappen; fi'xeren
fixed, vast
fixture, vaste fitting; wedstrijd,
  vaste datum
fizz, sissen
fizzle, sissen, sputteren
  to – out, met een sisser aflopen
flabbergast, stomverbaasd doen
  staan
flabby, pafferig
flag, vlag; pla'vuis;
  ver'slappen
flagpole, vlaggenstok
flagrant, schandelijk
flagship, vlaggenschip
flake, volk; (af)schilferen
flamboyant, zwierig, op'zichtig
flame, vlam(men); vuurrood
  zijn
flank, flank('eren)

flannel, fla'nel(len); waslapje
flap, klep, (tafel)blad, pand;
  klapperen; (op en neer) slaan
  met
flare, opflikkering; fakkel,
  si'gnaalvlam
  to – up, opvlammen;
  opstuiven
flash, flits(en); flikkeren; schieten
flashlight, zaklantaren
flashy, op'zichtig
flask, fla'con
flat, plat, vlak; vierkant
  (refusal); standaard (rate);
  ver'schaald; mat; te laag; flat,
  é'tage
flatten, plat maken
flatter, vleien, flat'teren
flattery, vleie'rij
flatulence, opgeblazen ge'voel
flaunt, geuren met
flavour, smaak; tintje; kruiden,
  toebereiden
flavouring, a'roma
flaw, fout; leemte
flawless, gaaf; onbe'rispelijk
flax(en), vlass(ig)
flay, villen
flea, vlo
fleck, (be')spikkel(en)
flee, vluchten
fleece, vacht; villen
fleecy, wollig; schapen-
fleet, vloot; leger; snel
fleeting, bliksemsnel,
  voor'bijflitsend
Flemish, Vlaams
flesh, vlees
fleshy, vlezig
flex, snoer; buigen
flexible, buigzaam; soepel
flexitime, variabele werktijden
flick, tik(ken), knip(pen)

flicker, flikkeren

flight, vlucht; groep, zwerm; trap

flighty, wuft

flimsy, broos, fragiel

flinch, te'rugdeinzen; (in'een)krimpen

fling, korte affaire; gooien

flip, (weg)slaan

flippant, onge'past spottend

flirt, flirt(en)

flit, fladderen, dartelen

float, dobber, drijver; (laten) drijven, vlot maken

floating, vlottend

flock, kudde, schare; (samen)stromen

flog, (af)ranselen
    to – sth, iets ver'patsen/aansmeren

flood, over'stroming; (zond)vloed, zee; (doen) over'stromen; stromen

floodlight, floodlight; ver'lichten

floor, vloer, ver'dieping; over'donderen

flop, fi'asco; (in el'kaar) ploffen

floral, bloemen-

florid, bloemrijk

florist, bloe'mist

flounder, ploeteren, spartelen; worstelen

flour, bloem, meel

flourish, zwierig ge'baar, krul; ge'dijen; zwaaien; geuren met

flout, in de wind slaan

flow, stroom; vloed; stromen

flower, bloem, bloei(en)

fluctuate, schommelen, op en neer gaan

flue, rookkanaal

fluent, vloeiend

fluff, pluisjes; pluizen

fluffy, donzig

fluid, vloeibaar; on'vast; vloeistof

fluke, meevaller, mazzel, stom geluk

fluorescent, fluore'scerend

flurry, vlaag; trilling; zenuwachtig maken

flush, blos; opwelling, ge'lijk; blozen; (schoon)spoelen

fluster, ner'veus maken

flute, fluit; groef; groeven

flutter, ge'klapwiek; fladderen, klapwieken; flikkeren

flux, voort'durende ver'andering

fly, vlieg(en); gulp; vluchten (uit); oplaten; voeren

foal, veulen

foam, schuim(en)

foamy, schuimend

focus, brandpunt scherpte; scherp stellen; zich concentreren

fodder, (vee)voer

foe, vijand

fog, mist; be'nevelen

foggy, mistig; vaag

foible, zwak(ke punt)

foil, folie; verhinderen

foist off on, aansmeren

fold, vouw(en), plooi; kooi, kudde; slaan

folder, map; folder

folding, op'vouwbaar, vouw-

foliage, ge'bladerte

folio, folio

folk, mensen; volks-

follow, volgen (op), opvolgen; be'grijpen

follower, volgeling

following, aanhang

folly, dwaasheid

fond, innig
    to be – of, houden van

fondle, liefkozen

font, lettertype; doopvont

food, voedsel, eten; stof

foodstuffs, voedingsmiddelen

fool, dwaas; voor de gek houden

foolhardy, roekeloos

foolish, dwaas

foot, voet, poot; voeteneinde; voetvolk; lopen; be'talen
  on –, te voet; aan de gang
  to put one's – in it, een blunder begaan

football(er), voetbal(ler)

foothold, vaste voet

footing, houvast; (vaste) voet

footlights, voetlicht

footpath, voetpad

footprint, voetafdruk

footstep, voetstap

footwear, schoeisel

for, voor; naar; ge'durende; wegens; ondanks; want; (om)dat

foray, rooftocht; plunderen

forbear, nalaten

forbid, ver'bieden; ver'hoeden

forbidding, afschrik'wekkend

force, (strijd) kracht, ge'weld; dwingen, for'ceren
  in –, van kracht

forceful, krachtig

forceps, tang

forcible, geweld'dadig; krachtig

ford, door'waden

fore, voor('aan); voorgrond

forearm, onderarm

forebear, voorzaat

forebode, voor'spellen

foreboding, voorgevoel; voor'spelling

forecast, voor'spelling; voor'spellen

forefather, voorvader

forefinger, wijsvinger

foregoing, voor'afgaand(e)

foregone conclusion, uitgemaakte zaak

foreground, voorgrond

forehead, voorhoofd

foreign, buitenlands; vreemd

foreigner, vreemdeling, buitenlander

foreman, (ploeg)baas

foremost, voorste, eerste

foresee, voor'zien

foreshadow, de voorbode zijn van

foreshorten, ver'korten

foresight, voorzorg

forest, woud, bos

forestall, voor'komen, voorzijn

forestry, bosbouw

foretaste, voorsmaak

foretell, voor'spellen

forethought, voorzorg

forever, (voor) altijd

forfeit, boete, pand; ver'spelen

forge, smidsvuur, smidse; smeden; ver'valsen

forgery, ver'valsing

forget, ver'geten

forgetful, ver'geetachtig

forgive, ver'geven

forgiveness, ver'giffenis

forgiving, vergevensge'zind

forgo, opgeven

fork, vork; tweesprong, ver'takking; zich splitsen
  to – out, dokken

forked, ge'vorkt; zigzag

forlorn, troosteloos, zielig

form, vorm, ge'daante, lichaam; klas; bank; formu'lier; stijl; formali'teit; con'ditie; (zich) vormen, (zich) opstellen

formal, for'meel
formality, formali'teit
formation, vorming, for'matie
former, eerst(genoemd); vroeger
formidable, ge'ducht,
  ontzag'wekkend
formula, for'mule; vorm
formulate, formu'leren
fornication, ontucht
forsake, ver'laten
fort, fort
forth, voort; uit; te voorschijn
  and so –, enzovoorts
forthcoming,
  (tege'moet)komend
forthright, open'hartig
forthwith, ter'stond
fortification, ver'sterking
fortify, ver'sterken
fortitude, stand'vastigheid
fortnight, veertien dagen
fortress, vesting
fortuitous, toe'vallig
fortunate, ge'lukkig
fortune, for'tuin
  good fortune, ge'luk
forty, veertig
forward, voor'uit, voorwaarts;
  naar voren; voorst; voorlijk;
  vrij'postig; voor(speler);
  doorsturen, ver'zenden;
  voor'uithelpen
fossil, fos'siel
fossilize, ver'stenen
foster, kweken; koesteren
foster(-mother),
  pleeg(moeder)
foul, vies; laag; vals, ge'meen;
  be'vuilen; onklaar raken (*or*
  maken)
found, stichten, oprichten;
  ba'seren

foundation, funda'ment;
  oprichting; stichting;
  grond(slag)
founder, stichter, oprichter;
  grondlegger; ver'gaan;
  mis'lukken
foundling, vondeling
foundry, (me'taal)gieter'ij
fount, bron; lettertype
fountain, fon'tein; bron
fountain pen, vulpen
four, vier(tal)
  on all fours, op handen en
  voeten
fourteen(th), veertien(de)
fourth, vierde (man); kwart
fowl, ge'vogelte; hoender
fox, vos; be'driegen
foxglove, vingerhoedskruid
fraction, breuk; mi'niem
  ge'deelte, onderdeel
fractious, humeurig,
  prikkelbaar
fracture, breuk; breken
fragile, broos, breekbaar
fragment, frag'ment,
  brokstuk
fragrance, geur
fragrant, geurig
frail, teer
frailty, zwakheid
frame, lijst, mon'tuur, ko'zijn;
  lichaamsbouw; inlijsten;
  (op)stellen
  – of mind, ge'moedstoestand
framework, schema, kader;
  frame
France, Frankrijk
franchise, recht; con'cessie
frank, open'hartig
frantic, dol, razend, wild,
  radeloos

fraternal, broederlijk
fraud, be'drog, fraude; oplichter
fraudulent, fraudu'leus
fraught with, vol (van)
fray, strijd; (uit)rafelen,
    ver'slijten
freak, gril, ge'drocht
freckle(d), (vol) sproet(en)
free, vrij; gratis; los(lippig);
    open(lijk); over'vloedig;
    be'vrijden, vrijlaten
    – from (or **of),** zonder, be'vrijd
    van
    to set –, be'vrijden
freebie, weggevertje
freedom, vrijheid
freehand, met de hand
freehold, vrij (grondbezit)
freeze, (doen) (be')vriezen
freighter, vrachtboot,
    vrachtschip
French, Frans(en)
    – bean, sperzieboon
    – polish, poli'toeren
    – windows, openslaande
    deuren
Frenchman, Fransman
frenzied, razend
frenzy, razer'nij
frequency, veel-vuldigheid,
    fre'quentie
frequent, veel'voorkomend,
    ge'regeld; dikwijls be'zoeken
frequently, her'haaldelijk
fresco, fresco
fresh, vers, fris; nieuw; zoet
freshman, eerste'jaars (stu'dent)
fret, kniezen, pruilen;
    wegvreten
fretwork, uitgezaagd werk
friar, monnik
friction, wrijving
Friday, vrijdag

friend, vriend('in), kennis
    to make friends with, be'vriend
    raken met
friendly, vriend('schapp)elijk
friendship, vriendschap
frieze, rand, fries
fright, schrik
frighten, doen schrikken
frightful, ver'schrikkelijk
frigid, ijzig; kil
frill, ge'rimpelde strook;
    tierelan'tijntje
fringe, franje; pony; buitenkant;
    om'zomen; grenzen (aan)
frisky, vrolijk, speels
fritter, bei'gnet; ver'snipperen
frivolous, licht'zinnig;
    onbelangrijk
frizzle, sissen; bakken
fro: to and –, heen en weer, op
    en neer
frock, jurk(je)
frog, kikvors
frolic, pret, lol; stoeien
from, van('daan), van'af; uit;
    wegens
front, voorkant, voorste deel;
    voor-, voorste
    at the – (of), voor'aan (in)
    in – of, voor
    in the – (of), voor'in (in)
frontier, grens
frost, vorst; rijp
frostbite, be'vriezing
froth, schuim
frown, frons; het voorhoofd
    fronsen
    to – upon, niet graag zien
frugal, sober, karig
fruit, vrucht(en), fruit
fruitful, vruchtbaar
fruition, ver'vulling
fruitless, vruchteloos

frustrate, ver'ijdelen; tegenwerken

frustrated, te'leurgesteld en onbe'vredigd

frustration, frustratie

fry, bakken, braden

fuck, (vulg) neuken, naaien, wippen

fuddle, be'nevelen

fuel, brand(stof); tanken

fugitive, vluchteling: (voort')- vluchtig

fulfil, ver'vullen; waarmaken; be'antwoorden aan

full, vol('ledig)

– of, vol

in –, ten volle; vol'uit

fully, vol'komen, ten volle

fumble, tasten; frommelen

fume, damp(en); koken

fumigate, uitroken

fun, pret

for (or in) –, voor de grap

to make – of, de gek steken met

function, functie; functio'neren

functional, functio'neel; praktisch

fund, fonds; voorraad

funds, geld

fundamental, fundamen'teel grond(beginsel)

funeral, be'grafenis(-); lijk-, graf-

fungus, zwam

funky, funky, lekker, gevoelsmatig (music)

funnel, trechter; pijp

funny, grappig; raar

fur, bont; be'slag, ketelsteen

furious, woedend

furl, oprollen

furnace, (smelt)oven, kachel

furnish, meubi'leren; voor'zien van, ver'schaffen

furnishings, stof'fering (en meubi'lering)

furniture, meubelen

furrow, voor; groef

further, verder, nader; be'vorderen

furtive, steels, heimelijk

fury, woede, razer'nij

fuse, (doorgeslagen) stop; lont; samensmelten

fuselage, romp

fusion, samensmelting; fusie

fuss, drukte; zich druk maken; zenuwachtig maken

fussy, lastig; druk

fusty, muf

futile, ver'geefs, zinloos, onbe'nullig

future, toekomst; toe'komstig

in future, voortaan

G

gabble, kakelen

– away, erop los kletsen

gable, gevelspits

gadget, snufje, ge'val

gag, prop; mop; knevelen

gaiety, vrolijkheid

gain, winst; be'halen; toenemen; ver'werven; be'reiken; voorlopen

gait, gang

gala, feest; gala-

galaxy, melkweg

gale, storm

gall, gal; gruwelijk ergeren

gallantry, dapperheid; hoffelijkheid

gallery, gale'rij; mu'seum

galley, ga'lei; kom'buis

gallon, gallon, 4½ liter
gallop, ga'lop('peren)
gallows, galg
galore, in overvloed
galvanize, galvani'seren
gamble, gokje; gokken
gambler, gokker
game, spel(letje); par'tij(tje); wild; flink; be'reid; lam; gokken
gamekeeper, jachtopziener
gang, troep, bende
gangster, gangster
gangway, pad; loopplank
gap, gat, opening, hi'aat
gape, gapen
garage, ga'rage
garb, kle'dij
garbage, vuilnis
garden, tuin('ieren)
gardener, tuinman, tui'nier
gargle, gorgelen
garish, schel, op'zichtig
garlic, knoflook
garment, kledingstuk, ge'waad
garnish, gar'neren
garrison, garni'zoen; legeren
garrulous, praatziek
garter, kouseband
gas, gas; ver'gassen
gash, snee; snijden, scheuren
gasp, snak(ken)
gastric, maag-
gate, hek, poort; ingang
gatecrash, binnenvallen
gateway, poort, hek
gather, (zich) ver'zamelen; binnenhalen; krijgen (speed); samentrekken; opmaken (uit)
gathering, bij'eenkomst
gauche, links

gaudy, op'zichtig
gauge, (standard)maat; meetinstrument; meten, ijken; schatten
gaunt, (brood)mager
gauntlet, (kap)handschoen; spitsroede
gauze, gaas
gawky, slungelig
gay, homo; vrolijk
gaze, starre blik; staren
gear, ver'snelling; inrichting; tuig; instellen
  to change –, overschakelen
  out of –, uitgeschakeld; in de war
gelatine, gela'tine
gem, edelsteen; ju'weel
gender, ge'slacht
gene, gen
general, algemeen; gene'raal
  in –, over het algemeen
generalize, generali'seren
generally, ge'woonlijk; (over het) algemeen
generate, opwekken
generation, gene'ratie; opwekking
generator, gene'rator
generosity, edel'moedigheid
generous, edel'moedig; ro'yaal
genetic, ge'netisch
genial, vriendelijk; groeizaam
genitalia, geslachtsorganen
genitive, genitief
genius, ge'nie; ta'lent
gentle, licht, zacht('aardig); matig
gentleman, gentleman, heer
genuine, echt, op'recht
geographic(al), aardrijks'kundig
geography, aardrijkskunde

geology, geolo'gie
geometry, meetkunde
geranium, ge'ranium
germ, kiem, ba'cil
German, Duits(er)
  – measles, rode hond
Germany, Duitsland
gesticulate, gesticu'leren
gesture, ge'baar
get, krijgen; komen; worden
  I have got, ik heb
  I have got to, ik moet
  to – something done, iets
  (laten) doen; iets ge'daan
  krijgen
  to – about, buitenkomen,
  rondlopen
  to – along, (weg)gaan;
  opschieten; het maken
  to – around, overal komen;
  be'kend worden; om'zeilen
  to – at, be'reiken; achter
  komen; be'doelen
  to – away, wegkomen;
  ont'snappen
  to – back, te'rugkomen;
  te'rugkrijgen
  to – in, binnenkomen,
  instappen
  to – off, (er) afkomen (van),
  afstappen van; afkrijgen
  to – on, opstappen; aankrijgen;
  opschieten; het stellen; het
  maken
  to – out, (onder')uitkomen,
  uitstappen; voor de dag halen
  to – over, te boven komen
  to – through, doorkomen;
  antwoord krijgen
  to – to, komen in (*or* aan)
  to – up, opstaan; opsteken; op
  touw zetten
  geyser, geiser

ghastly, af'grijselijk, doodsbleek
ghost, spook; zweem
giant, reus('achtig)
gibber, brabbelen
gibberish, koeter'waals
giblets, inwendige organen van
  ge'vogelte
giddy, duizelig;
  duizeling'wekkend; mal
gift, ge'schenk; gave
gifted, be'gaafd
gig, optreden, concert
gigantic, gigantisch, enorm
giggle, giechelen
gild, ver'gulden
gill, kieuw
gilt, ver'guld(sel)
gin, jonge jenever
ginger, gember
gingerly, be'hoedzaam
giraffe, gi'raffe
girder, (stalen) balk
girdle, gordel
girl, meisje
girlfriend, vriendin(netje)
girlish, meisjesachtig
giro, giro(dienst), giro(cheque)
girth, omvang; buikriem
gist, kern
give, geven; doorzakken, buigen
  to – away, weggeven;
  ver'klappen
  to – in, zich ge'wonnen geven
  to – out, uitdelen;
  aankondigen; be'zwijken
  to – up, overgeven; (het)
  opgeven
given, be'paald; ge'neigd (tot)
glacier, gletsjer
glad, blij(de)
gladden, ver'blijden
glade, open plek, moerassig
  gebied

gladly, graag
glamorous, aantrekkelijk, be'toverend
glamour, be'tovering
glance, (vluchtige) blik; een blik werpen; afschampen
gland, klier
glare, ver'blindend licht; woeste blik; woest kijken
glaring, schel; vlammend; in het oog springend
glass, glas(werk); glazen
  glasses, bril
glaze, gla'zuur; van glas voor'zien; gla'zuren
gleam, schijnsel, straaltje, glans; glimmen
glean, lezen; ver'garen
glee, vreugde, leedvermaak
glen, bergdal
glib, glad, rad van tong
glide, zweven, glijden
glider, zweefvliegtuig
glimmer, flikkering; glimp; flikkeren
glimpse, glimp
glint, glinstering
glisten, glinsteren
glitter, ge'schitter; schitteren
gloat, zich ver'lustigen, leedvermaak hebben
globe, (aard)bol
gloom, duister; droef'geestigheid
gloomy, duister, somber; droef'geestig
glorify, ver'heerlijken
glorious, roemrijk; heerlijk
glory, glorie, heerlijkheid
gloss, glans
  to – over, ver'doezelen
glossy, glanzend
glove, handschoen

glow, gloed; blos; gloeien; stralen
glower, dreigend kijken
glue, (hout)lijm; lijmen
glum, mistroostig
glut, (over)ver'zadiging; over'voeren
glutton, gulzigaard
gnarled, knoestig, knokig
gnash one's teeth, knarsetanden
gnat, mug
gnaw, (af)knagen
gnome, aardmannetje
go, (weg)gaan; lopen; worden; horen
  as things –, verge'leken bij anderen
  to – by, gaan per (*or* over); voor'bijgaan; zich laten leiden door; be'kend staan onder
  to – down, afgaan; naar be'neden gaan, ondergaan, zinken, er'in gaan
  to – into, binnengaan; ingaan (op); treden in (details); zich ver'diepen in
  to – off, af (*or* weg)gaan; aflopen
  to – on, gaan op; voor'uitgaan, voortgaan
  to – up, stijgen
  to – with, meegaan met; passen bij, horen bij
  to – without, het stellen zonder
  to let –, loslaten
goad, prikkel(en); aanzetten
go-ahead, toestemming
goal, doel(punt)
goat, geit
gobble, schrokken; klokken
goblet, bo'kaal
goblin, ka'bouter
god, god

goddess, go'din
godmother, peettante
godsend, zegen
gobble, schrokken
going: to get (or **to keep) –,** aan de gang brengen, (or houden); lopen
gold, goud(en)
golden, gouden; gulden
goldfish, goudvis
golf, golf
gondola, gondel
gone, weg; op; zoek; dood
gong, gong
good, goed; zoet; bestwil
    a – deal, vrij veel
    for –, voor'goed; ten goede
goodbye, dag
goodies, iets lekkers
good-looking, knap
good-natured, ge'moedelijk, goed'aardig
goodness, goedheid; voeding
good night, welterusten
goods, goederen, spullen
goodwill, wel'willendheid; klan'dizie
goody-goody, schijnheilige
goose, gans
gooseberry, kruisbes(sen)
gore, ge'ronnen bloed; spietsen
gorge, bergengte: (zich) volstoppen
gorgeous, magni'fiek
gospel, evan'gelie
gossip, ge'roddel; roddelaar(ster); roddelen, kletsen
gothic, gotisch
govern, re'geren; leiden
government, re'gering; be'leid
governor, gouver'neur; cu'rator

gown, ja'pon; toga
grab, greep; grijpen naar
grace, gratie; ge'nade; tafelgebed; res'pijt; ver'eren
graceful, graci'eus
gracious, minzaam, hoffelijk
grade, graad, kwali'teit; sor'teren
gradient, helling(shoek)
gradual, ge'leidelijk
graft, (poli'tieke) knoeie'rij; enten, transplan'teren
grain, graan, korrel; greintje; nerf
grammar, gram'matica
grammar school, gym'nasium
granary, graanschuur
grand, groot(s), prachtig
grandchild, kleinkind
grandeur, grootsheid
grandiose, grandi'oos
grandmother, grootmoeder
granite, gra'niet(en)
grant, toelage; (toe)geven; ver'lenen; inwilligen
grape, druif
grapefruit, grapefruit
graph, gra'fiek
graphic, grafisch; aan'schouwelijk
graphite, gra'fiet
grapple, worstelen
grasp, greep; begrip; be'reik; vastpakken
grass, gras
grasshopper, sprinkhaan
grassy, gras(rijk)
grate, rooster; raspen; knarsen; tegen de borst stuiten
grateful, dankbaar
gratification, vol'doening
gratify, strelen; be'vredigen

gratifying, be'vredigend, dankbaar

grating, traliewerk; knarsen

gratitude, dankbaarheid

gratuitous, gratis; ongegrond

gratuity, fooi

grave, graf; ernstig

gravel, grint(-)

graveyard, kerkhof

gravitation, aantrekking(skracht)

gravity, zwaartekracht; ernst

  centre of –, zwaartepunt

gravy, jus

graze, schaafwond; even aanraken; schaven; grazen, weiden

grease, smeer, vet; (in)smeren, invetten

greasy, vet(tig), vuil

great, groot; voor'naamste; nobel; enthousi'aste

  a – deal (of), heel veel

great-grandchild, achterkleinkind

great-grandmother, overgrootmoeder

greatly, zeer

greed, gulzigheid, hebzucht

greedy, gulzig, hebberig

Greek, Griek(s)

green, groen; brink

greens, bladgroenten

greengrocer, groenteboer

greenhouse, broeikas

greet, (be')groeten

greeting, groet

grey, grijs (worden), grauw

greyhound, haze'wind; windhonden-

grid, (braad)rooster; hoogspanningsnet

grief, ver'driet

grievance, grief, klacht

grieve, treuren; be'droeven

grievous, erg; verschrikkelijk

grill, rooster(en)

grim, onver'biddelijk; onaan'lokkelijk; akelig

grimace, gri'mas

grime, vuil; be'vuilen

grin, grijns; grijnzen

grind, ge'zwoeg; malen; slijpen; knarsen (op)

grindstone, slijpsteen

grip, (hand)greep, vat, houvast; tas; be'grip; (vast)pakken

gristle, kraakbeen

grit, gruis; durf

grizzly, grijs(achtig)

groan, ge'kreun; kreunen

grocer, kruide'nier

groceries, levensmiddelen

groggy, suf, wankel op de benen

groin, lies

groom, ver'zorgen

groove, groef; sleur; groeven

grope, (rond)tasten

gross, bruto; grof; gros

grotesque, gro'tesk

grotto, grot

ground, grond(-); ter'rein; aan de grond lopen; grondig onder'leggen

  to cover –, ter'rein be'strijken

  to give –, wijken

  to stand one's –, standhouden; voet bij stuk houden

ground floor, be'nedenver'dieping

groundless, onge'grond

grounds, ter'rein, park; reden(en)

group, groep('eren)

grouse, korhoen(ders); kankeren
grove, bos(je)
grovel, kruipen
grow, (aan)groeien; ver'bouwen, kweken; worden
  to – up, opgroeien, ouder worden; ont'staan
growing, toenemend
growl, grom(men)
grown-up, vol'wassene
growth, groei; aanwas; gezwel
grub, larve; kost; wroeten
grudge, wrok; mis'gunnen
grudgingly, met tegenzin
gruel, gruwel
gruelling, af'mattend
gruesome, gruwelijk
gruff, bars
grumble, mopperen
grunt, ge'knor; ge'brom; knorren; brommen
guarantee, (waar)borg, ga'rantie; waarborgen, garan'deren
guard, wacht; scherm, be'scherming; hoede; conduc'teur; (be')waken; be'schermen
guarded, voor'zichtig
guardian, voogd, be'waarder; be'scherm-
guess, gis(sing); raden
guest, gast, lo'gé(e)
guidance, leiding, ad'vies
guide, gids; padvindster; leiden
guild, gilde
guilder, gulden
guile, list
guileless, argeloos
guillotine, guillo'tine
guilt, schuld
guiltless, on'schuldig

guilty, schuldig, schuldbe'wust
guitar, gi'taar
gulf, golf; kloof
gull, meeuw; beetnemen
gullet, slokdarm, keel
gullible, lichtge'lovig
gully, geul
gulp, slok, teug; opslokken; inslikken
gum, gom(men); tandvlees
gun, ka'non, ge'weer, pis'tool
gurgle, kabbelen, klokken, kirren
gush, stroom; gutsen, stromen
gushing, dwepend
gust, vlaag
gusto, animo
gusty, stormachtig
gut, darm; schoonmaken; uitbranden
gutter, goot
guttersnipe, straatkind
guy, vent, man; **–s,** jongens, mensen
guzzle, opschrokken
gymnasium, gymnas'tiekzaal
gymnastics, gymnas'tiek
gypsy, zi'geuner('in)

H

haberdashery, fourni'turen(winkel)
habit, ge'woonte; pij
habitable, be'woonbaar
habitation, woonplaats
habitual, ge'woon(lijk), ge'woonte-, regel'matig
hack, hakken
hackneyed, afgezaagd
haddock, schelvis
haemorrhage, bloeding
haggard, uitgeteerd

haggle, knibbelen

hail, hagel(en); toejuichen, (luidkeels) be'groeten; aanroepen; af'komstig zijn

hair, haar; haren
  to split hairs, muggenziften

hairdresser, kapper

hairy, harig, be'haard

half, half; (de) helft
  half past one, half twee

halfway, halver'wege

hall, hal, zaal

hallmark, keur; stempel(en)

hallow, heiligen

hallucination, halluci'natie

halo, aure'ool, halo

halt, halt (houden); stoppen, pauzeren

halter, halster

halve, hal'veren

ham, ham

hamlet, ge'hucht

hammer, hamer(en)

hammock, hangmat

hamper, mand; be'lemmeren

hand, hand; wijzer; arbeider; spel; over'handigen, aangeven
  at –, bij de hand; op handen
  in –, in be'dwang; onder handen; over
  on the other –, aan de andere kant
  to – down, overleveren
  to – in, inleveren
  to – out, uitdelen
  to – over, overdragen, over'handigen
  to – round, ronddienen, ronddelen

handbag, handtas

handcuff, handboei

handful, hand(je)vol

handicap, handicap(pen)

handicraft, handwerk, handenarbeid

handiwork, (hand)werk

handkerchief, zakdoek

handle, handvat, knop, oor; be'dienen, han'teren; aanpakken; be'handelen; handelen in

handle bars, stuur

handmade, handgemaakt

handshake, handdruk

handsome, knap; flink, ro'yaal

handwriting, (hand)schrift

handy, handig; bij de hand; van pas

hang, slag; (op)hangen; laten hangen; be'hangen
  to – about, rondlummelen
  to – on, (zich) vasthouden; wachten

hangar, han'gar

hangover, kater

haphazard, luk'raak

happen, (toe'vallig) ge'beuren
  I – to … ik … toe'vallig; ik … nu eenmaal

happenings, ge'beurtenissen

happiness, ge'luk

happy, ge'lukkig

harass, be'stoken; kwellen

harbour, haven; (ver')bergen, koesteren

hard, hard('vochtig); moeilijk; vast
  to try –, zijn best doen

harden, harder worden (*or* maken)

hard-hearted, hard'vochtig

hardly, nauwelijks; hard

hardship, ont'bering, last

hardware, ijzerwaren

hardwood, hardhout(en)

hardy, ge'hard, sterk

hare, haas
harlequin, harle'kijn
harm, schade, letsel; kwaad doen
harmful, na'delig, schadelijk
harmless, on'schadelijk; argeloos
harmonic, har'monisch
harmonica, mondharmonika
harmonious, har'monisch, harmoni'eus
harmonize, (doen) harmoni'ëren; harmoni'seren
harmony, harmo'nie
harness (paarden)tuig; ga'reel; optuigen
harp, harp; hameren
harpoon, har'poen('eren)
harpsichord, klave'cimbel
harsh, ruw, wrang; hard
harvest, oogst(tijd); oogsten
hash, mengelmoes; hasj(iesj)
haste, haast
hasten, zich haasten, ver'haasten
hasty, haastig; driftig
hat, hoed
hatch, luik; uitbroeden, uitkomen
hatchet, bijl
hate, haat; haten, een hekel hebben aan
hateful, akelig
hatred, haat
haughty, hoog'hartig
haul, vangst; slepen, halen
haunch, lende, hurk
haunt, oord, speelplaats; hol; veel'vuldig be'zoeken; achter'volgen
haunted, spook-, door geesten be'zocht

have, hebben; laten; moeten; nemen; krijgen
haven, (veilige) haven
havoc, ver'woesting
hawk, havik; venten
hawthorn, haagdoorn
hay, hooi
haystack, hooiberg
hazard, risico; wagen
hazardous, ris'kant
haze, waas, nevel
hazel, hazelaar; lichtbruin
hazy, wazig; vaag
he, hij
head, hoofd(-), kop; spits; tegen-; leiden; sturen
   to keep one's –, zijn ver'stand bij el'kaar houden
   to lose one's –, in de war raken
headache, hoofdpijn
headgear, hoofdtooi
heading, ru'briek, opschrift
headlight, koplamp
headline, kop
headlong, hals over kop
headmaster, direc'teur, (school)hoofd
headquarters, hoofdkantoor
headstrong, koppig
headway, voortgang
heal, ge'nezen
health, ge'zondheid
healthy, ge'zond
heap, hoop, massa; ophopen
hear, horen; luisteren
hearing, ge'hoor; ver'hoor
hearsay, praatjes
hearse, lijkwagen
heart, hart; moed; kern, binnenste
   by –, uit het hoofd
   to take –, moed scheppen

heart-breaking, hartver'scheurend

heartbroken, ge'broken

hearten, opbeuren

heartfelt, innig

hearth, haard

heartless, harteloos

hearty, hartelijk; ge'zond; stevig; hart'grondig

heat, hitte; vuur; loop; ver'warmen; opwinden

heater, ver'warmingsapparaat

heath, heide

heathen, heiden(s)

heather, heide

heave, hijsen, lichten; trekken; slaken; deinen

heaven, hemel

heavenly, hemels, hemel-

heavy, zwaar, klef

Hebrew, Hebreeuws; Ivriet

heckle, jouwen, scherp onder'vragen

hectic, koortsachtig

hedge, heg; om'heinen; er omheen draaien

hedgehog, egel

hedgerow, haag

heed, aandacht; letten op

heedless, achteloos

heel, hiel, hak; overhellen

hefty, stoer

height, hoogte; top(punt)

heighten, ver'hogen; ver'sterken

heinous, gruwelijk

heir, erfgenaam

heiress, erfgename

heirloom, erfstuk

helicopter, heli'kopter

hell, hel

hello, hal'lo

helm, roer

helmet, helm

help, hulp; steun, helper(s); helpen; nalaten

I can't – it, ik kan er niets aan doen

helpful, hulp'vaardig; be'vorderlijk, ge'makkelijk

helping, portie

helpless, hulpeloos

hem, zoom; zomen

hemisphere, halfrond

hemp, hennep

hen, kip

hence, van'daar (dat); hier van'daan, van nu af aan

henceforth, van nu af aan

henchman, handlanger

henpeck, op de kop zitten

her, haar

herald, her'aut, voorbode; aankondigen

heraldry, heral'diek

herb, kruid

herd, kudde; (samen-)drijven

here, hier

hereabout(s), hier in de buurt

hereafter, hier'na(maals)

hereby, hierbij, hierdoor

hereditary, erfelijk, erf-

heredity, erfelijkheid, over'erving

heretic(al), ketter(s), her'metisch

hermit, kluizenaar

hero, held

heroic, held'haftig, helden-

heroics, bombast

heroine, hel'din

heron, reiger

herring, haring

hesitant, aarzelend

hesitate, aarzelen

hesitation, aarzeling

heterogeneous, hetero'geen

heyday, bloeitijd

hiatus, hi'aat
hibernate, winterslaap doen
hiccup(s), hik(ken)
  to have –, de hik hebben
hide, huid; afrossen; (zich) ver'bergen
hide-and-seek, ver'stoppertje
hideous, af'zichtelijk, af'schuwelijk
hierarchy, hiërar'chie
high, hoog; adellijk
highland, hoogland(s)
highly, hoog-, zeer
high-pitched, hoog, schel
highway, grote weg
hike, trektocht; trekken
hilarious, uitgelaten
hill, heuvel, berg
hilly, heuvelachtig
him, hem
hind, achter(ste); hinde
hinder, (ver)hinderen
hindrance, belemmering
hinge, schar'nier; spil; draaien
hint, wenk; zweem; laten doorschemeren
  to – at, zinspelen op
hip, heup; rozebottel; hip
hippopotamus, nijlpaard
hire, huur; (ver')huren
hire purchase, huurkoop; op afbetaling kopen
his, zijn, van hem
hiss, sissen; (uit)fluiten
historian, ge'schiedschrijver
historic, his'torisch; ge'wichtig
historical, his'torisch
history, ge'schiedenis
hit, slag, treffer; suc'ces; slaan; raken, treffen
  to – upon, treffen, vinden
hitch, ruk; kink in de kabel; (op)trekken; vastmaken

hitchhike, liften
hither, hier(heen)
hitherto, tot nu toe
hive, korf
hoard, voorraad; opsparen, hamsteren
hoarding, re'clamebord
hoar frost, rijp
hoarse, hees, schor
hoax, bedrog; om de tuin leiden
hobble, strompelen
hobby, liefhebbe'rij
hockey, hockey
hog, varken; zwijn
hoist, hijstoestel; (op)hijsen
hold, houvast, vat; invloed; ruim; (vast)houden; be'vatten; (in zijn be'zit) hebben; opgaan
  to – out, geven; volhouden; in leven blijven
  to – up, ophouden; aanhouden
  to – with, goedkeuren, het eens zijn met
  to get – of, te pakken krijgen; vastpakken
hole, gat, hol
holiday, vakantie(dag); feestdag
Holland, Nederland
hollow, hol(te); leeg
  to – out, uithollen
holly, hulst
holocaust, holocaust, vernietiging
holster, holster
holy, heilig
homage, hulde(betuiging)
home, (t)huis, tehuis; binnenlands; naar huis; raak
  at –, thuis
homeland, ge'boorteland
homeless, dakloos
homely, huiselijk; ge'moedelijk
homemade, eigengemaakt

homesick: to be –, heimwee hebben
homicide, doodslag
homogeneous, homo'geen
homosexual, homoseksueel
honest(y), eerlijk(heid)
honey, honing
honeycomb, honingraat
honeymoon, huwelijksreis
honeysuckle, kamper'foelie
honk, toeteren; snateren
honorary, ere-
honour, eer(gevoel); eerbewijs; (ver')eren
honourable, eervol
hood, kap
hoodwink, zand in de ogen strooien
hoof, hoef
hook, haak; aan de haak slaan
hooligan, hooligan, van'daal, herrieschopper
hoop, hoepel
hoot, krassen; toeteren; uitjouwen
hop, sprong; hop(plant); hinken, springen
hope, hoop(volle ver'wachting); hopen
hopeful, hoopvol
hopeless, hopeloos, wan'hopig
horde, horde
horizon, horizon
horizontal, horizon'taal
horn, horen
horoscope, horos'coop
horrible, horrid, af'grijselijk, af'schuwelijk
horrify, ont'zetten
horror, afgrijzen; gruwel(daad)
horse, paard
horseback: on –, te paard
horseshoe, hoefijzer

horticulture, tuinbouw
hose, (tuin)slang
hospitable, gastvrij
hospital, ziekenhuis
hospitality, gast'vrijheid
host, gastheer/gastvrouw; massa, horde(n); optreden als gastheer/vrouw
hostage, gijzelaar
hostel, te'huis
hostess, gastvrouw
hostile, vij'andelijk, vij'andig
hostility, vij'andelijkheid, vij'andigheid
hot, heet, warm
hotel, ho'tel
hothouse, broeikas
hound, (jacht)hond
hour, uur
house, huis: huisvesten
  to keep –, de huishouding doen
household, huisgezin; huis('houd)elijk
householder, ge'zinshoofd
housekeeper, huishoudster
housekeeping, huishouden; huishoud(geld)
housewife, huisvrouw
housework, huishoudelijk werk
housing, woning-, woon-; huisvesting
hovel, krot
hover, zweven, hangen
how, hoe
however, hoe dan ook; echter
howl, huilen, janken; gillen, joelen
howler, flater; giller
hub, naaf; middelpunt
hubbub, herrie
huddle, (bij *or* in el'kaar) kruipen

hue, tint
hug, pakken; tegen zich aandrukken; koesteren
huge, reus'achtig
hulk, romp
hulking, log
hull, romp
hum, ge'gons; gonzen, snorren; neuriën
human, menselijk, mens(en-)
 – being, menselijk wezen
humane, mens'lievend
humanitarian, humani'tair
humanity, het mensdom
humanly, menselijkerwijs
humble, nederig; ver'nederen
humbug, bedrieger('ij)
humdrum, saai(e sleur)
humid(ity), vochtig(heid)
humiliate, ver'nederen
humility, nederigheid
humorist, humo'rist
humorous, grappig, humo'ristisch
humour, humor; hu'meur; luim; toegeven aan
hump, bult
hunch, samentrekken, krommen
hunchback, ge'bochelde
hundred(th), honderd(ste)
hunger, honger
hungry, hongerig
 to be –, trek (*or* honger) hebben
hunk, homp
hunt, jacht(stoet); jagen (op); (af)zoeken
 to – down, in het nauw drijven; opsporen
hunter, jager
hurdle, horde; hindernis
hurl, slingeren

hurricane, or'kaan
hurried, haastig, ge'haast
hurry, (zich) haasten
 to be in a –, haast hebben
hurt, pijn doen; deren, kwetsen
hurtle, ratelen, schieten
husband, man, echtgenoot
hush, stilte; stil!; tot zwijgen brengen
husky, schor
hustle, ge'jacht; jachten, drijven; dringen
hut, hut, ba'rak
hybrid, hy'bride; bastaard-
hydraulic, hy'draulisch
hydrogen, waterstof
hygiene, hygiëne
hygienic, hygi'ënisch
hymn, hymne
hyphen(ate), (door een) streepje (ver'binden)
hypnotize, hypnoti'seren
hypocrite, huichelaar
hypocritical, huichelachtig
hypothesis, hypo'these
hysterical, hys'terisch
hysterics, zenuwaanval

I

I, ik
ice, ijs(je); (doen) be'vriezen; gla'ceren
iceberg, ijsberg
ice cream, roomijs; ijsje
iced, ijskoud; gegla'ceerd
icicle, ijskegel
icing sugar, poedersuiker
icy, ijskoud, glad; ijs-, ijzig
idea, i'dee
ideal, ide'aal
idealism, idea'lisme

idealist(ic), idea'list(isch)
idealize, ideali'seren
identical, iden'tiek
identification identifi'catie
identify, identifi'ceren,
  vereen'zelvigen
identity, identi'teit
idiom, idi'oom
idiosyncracy, eigen'aardigheid
idiot(ic), idi'oot
idle, nietsdoend; lui; leeg; niets
  doen
  to be –, niets doen; stilliggen
idler, leegloper
idol, afgod (sbeeld)
idolize, ver'afgoden
idyll, i'dylle
if, als, in'dien, of
iffy, on'zeker, dubi'eus
ignite, in brand steken (*or*
  raken)
ignoble, laag
ignominious, smadelijk
ignorance, on'wetendheid
ignorant, on'wetend, on'kundig
ignore, ne'geren
ill, ziek; slecht, kwaad; kwalijk
  to cause – feeling, kwaad
  bloed zetten
ill-advised, onver'standig
illegal, on'wettig, onrecht'matig
illegible, on'leesbaar
illegitimate, on'wettig;
  onge'oorloofd
ill-fated, ramp'spoedig
illicit, on'wettig
illiterate, onge'letterd;
  analfa'beet
illness, ziekte
illogical, on'logisch
ill-tempered, slecht
  gehu'meurd
ill-treat, slecht be'handelen

illuminate, ver (*or* be)'lichten,
  toelichten; ver'luchten
illumination, ver'lichting;
  ver'luchting
illusion, il'lusie
illustrate, illu'streren; toelichten
illustration, ilu'stratie,
  toelichting
illustrious, gerenommeerd
image, beeld; imago, repu'tatie
imaginable, denkbaar
imaginary, denk'beeldig
imagination, ver'beelding-
  (skracht)
imaginative, vindingrijk, rijk
  aan ver'beelding; fan'tastisch
imagine, zich voorstellen
imam, imam
imbecile, imbe'ciel
imbibe, drinken; (in zich)
  opnemen
imbue, door'drenken
imitate, nabootsen
imitation, nabootsing; namaak-
immaculate, onbe'rispelijk
immaterial, on'stoffelijk;
  onver'schillig; onbe'langrijk
immature, on'rijp
immeasurable, on'meetbaar;
  niet te over'zien, on'noemelijk
immediate, on'middellijk, naast
immense, on'metelijk
immerse, onderdompelen,
  indompelen
immersed, onder'water;
  ver'diept
immigrant, immi'grant;
  immi'grerend
immigration, immi'gratie
imminent, op handen,
  dreigend
immobile, onbe'weeglijk
immoderate, on'matig

immodest, onbe'scheiden, on'zedig

immoral, immo'reel

immortal(ity), on'sterfelijk(heid)

immovable, on'beweeglijk

immune, im'muun (voor); vrijgesteld

immutable, onver'anderlijk

impact, botsing, samentreffen; ef'fect

impair, na'delig be'invloeden, schaden

impart, ver'lenen; mededelen

impartial(ity), onpar'tijdig(heid)

impassable, onbe'gaanbaar

impassioned, harts'tochtelijk

impassive, onver'stoorbaar; ge'voelloos

impatient, onge'duldig

impeach, in twijfel trekken; aanklagen

impeccable, onbe'rispelijk, feilloos

impede, be'lemmeren

impediment, be'letsel, ge'brek

impel, voortdrijven, aanzetten

impend, dreigen

impenetrable, ondoor'dringbaar

imperative, hoogstnood'zakelijk; ge'biedend

imperceptible, on'merkbaar

imperfect, imper'fect(um); afwijkend, on'gaaf

imperial, keizerlijk, keizer(s)-, rijks-

imperialism, imperia'lisme

imperious, aan'matigend

impermeable, ondoor'dringbaar

impersonal, onper'soonlijk

impersonate, voorstellen

impertinent, onbe'schaamd

imperturbable, onver'stoorbaar

impervious, ondoor'dringbaar; doof (voor)

impetuous, on'stuimig

impetus, drijfkracht; stuwkracht

impinge on, raken

implacable, onver'zoenlijk

implant, inplanten

implement, werktuig; uitvoeren

implicate, ver'wikkelen, be'trekken (bij)

implication, bijgedachte, implicatie

implicit, impli'ciet, onvoor'waardelijk

implore, (af)smeken

imply, impli'ceren, inhouden, te ver'staan geven

impolite, onbe'leefd

import, invoer(en)

importance, be'tekenis, be'lang

important, be'langrijk, gewichtig(doend)

importunity, op'dringerigheid

impose on, opleggen; misbruik maken van

imposing, indruk'wekkend

impossible, on'mogelijk

impostor, be'drieger

impotent, impo'tent, machteloos

impoverish, ver'armen, uitputten

impracticable, onuit'voerbaar

impregnable, on'neembaar; onaan'tastbaar

impregnate, impreg'neren; be'vruchten

impress, stempel(en); indruk maken op, op het hart drukken

impression, indruk, i'dee; afdruk; oplage

impressionable, ont'vankelijk

impressive, indruk'wekkend

imprint, afdruk; stempel(en); inprenten

imprison, ge'vangen zetten (*or* houden)

imprisonment, ge'vangenschap

improbable, onwaar'schijnlijk

impromptu, voor de vuist

improper, incor'rect, onfat'soenlijk

improve, ver'beteren; voor'uitgaan

improvement, ver'betering; voor'uitgang

improvise, improvi'seren

imprudent, onvoor'zichtig

impudence, brutali'teit

impudent, bru'taal

impulse, im'puls; opwelling, aandrift

impulsive, stuw-; impul'sief

impunity: with –, onge'straft

impure, on'zuiver; on'kuis

impute, toeschrijven

in, in, (naar) binnen

inability, onvermogen

inaccessible, onbe'reikbaar; onge'naakbaar

inaccurate, onnauw'keurig

inactive, nietsdoend

inactivity, nietsdoen

inadequate, ontoe'reikend

inadvertent, onop'zettelijk

inadvisable, onver'standig

inalienable, onver'vreemdbaar

inane, zinloos

inanimate, levenloos

inappropriate, onge'schikt

inarticulate, ongearticu'leerd; sprakeloos

inasmuch as, voorzo'ver; aange'zien

inattentive, onop'lettend; onat'tent

inaudible, on'hoorbaar

inaugural, inaugu'reel

inaugurate, inhuldigen; inluiden

inbreeding, inteelt

incalculable, onbe'rekenbaar

incandescent, gloei-

incantation, toverformule

incapable, onbe'kwaam; niet in staat

incapacitate, onge'schikt maken; ver'hinderen

incense, wierook; boos maken

incensed, woedend zijn

incentive, prikkel

inception, ont'staan

incessant, onop'houdelijk

incest, incest

inch, inch, duim(breed); beetje

inch forward, zich een weg banen

incident, voorval; epi'sode

incidental, toe'vallig; bij'komstig

incidentally, ter'loops, tussen twee haakjes

incision, insnijding

incite, aanzetten

inclination, buiging, helling; neiging

incline, helling; overhellen (tot)

to be inclined, ge'neigd zijn, de neiging hebben

include, be (*or* om)'vatten; meerekenen

to be included, (er'bij) inbegrepen zijn

including, met inbegrip van, waar'onder

inclusive, allesom'vattend, inclu'sief; tot en met

incoherent, onsamen'hangend

income, inkomen, inkomsten

income tax, inkomstenbelasting

incomparable, niet te
verge'lijken; weergaloos

incompatible, onver'enigbaar

incompetent, onbe'voegd;
ineffici'ënt

incomplete, onvol'ledig

incomprehensible,
onbe'grijpelijk

inconceivable, on'denkbaar

inconclusive, niet be'slissend,
niet over'tuigend

incongruous, niet passend,
onge'rijmd

inconsiderate, onat'tent

inconsistent, inconse'quent,
tegen'strijdig

inconspicuous, onop'vallend

incontestable, onbe'twistbaar

inconvenience, ongemak;
ongerief bezorgen

inconvenient, lastig, onge'legen;
onge'riefelijk

incorporate, opnemen;
ver'enigen

incorrect, on'juist

incorrigible, onver'beterlijk

increase, toename, ver'hoging;
toenemen, ver'hogen

increasingly, steeds meer

incredible, onge'lofelijk

incredulous, onge'lovig

incriminate, be'schuldigen

incubator, broedmachine

inculcate, inprenten

incur, zich op de hals halen;
oplopen

incurable, onge'neeslijk(e zieke)

indebted, schuldig, ver'plicht

indecent, on'zedelijk;
onwel'voeglijk

indecision, be'sluiteloosheid

indecisive, onbe'slist;
be'sluiteloos

indeed, inder'daad; werkelijk,
(ja) zelfs

indefatigable, onver'moeibaar,
onver'moeid

indefinite, onbe'paald

indelible, onuit'wisbaar; inkt-

indemnity, schadeloosstelling

independence,
onaf'hankelijkheid

independent, onaf'hankelijk

indescribable, onbe'schrijfelijk

index, re'gister; aanwijzing

indicate, aanwijzen; wijzen op

indication, aanwijzing

indicator, wijzer

indictment, aanklacht

indifferent, onver'schillig;
(middel')matig

indigenous, in'heems

indigestible, onver'teerbaar

indigestion, indi'gestie

indignant, veront'waardigd

indignation, veront'waardiging

indignity, smaad

indirect, indi'rect

indiscreet, indis'creet

indiscretion, indiscretie

indiscriminate, luk'raak, zonder
onderscheid; ver'ward

indispensable, on'misbaar

indisposed, onwel; onge'negen

indisputable, onbe'twistbaar

indistinct, on'duidelijk

individual, individu'eel;
indivi'du

individuality, individuali'teit

indolence, traagheid

indomitable, onover'winnelijk,
on'tembaar

indoor(s), binnen(s'huis)

induce, brengen tot;
veroorzaken, opwekken
(of birth)

inducement, stimu'lans,
  lokmiddel
induction, in'ductie; aanvoering;
  instal'latie
indulge, toegeven aan
  to – in, zich permit'teren
indulgence, toe'geeflijkheid;
  uitspatting; aflaat
industrial, industri'eel, be'drijfs
industrialist, industri'eel
industrious, vlijtig
industry, indust'rie, be'drijf-
  (sleven); vlijt
inebriated, dronken
inedible, on'eetbaar
ineffective, ineffectual,
  ondoel'treffend, vruchteloos
inefficient, ondoel'matig,
  onbe'kwaam
inept, onge'rijmd, dwaas
inequality, onge'lijkheid
inert(ia), in'ert(ie); stil(stand)
inestimable, on'schatbaar
inevitable, onver'mijdelijk
inexcusable, onver'geeflijk
inexhaustible, onuit'puttelijk
inexorable, onver'biddelijk
inexpensive, voor'delig
inexperienced, oner'varen
inexplicable, onver'klaarbaar
inexpressible, onuit'sprekelijk
infallible, on'feilbaar
infamous, schandelijk, be'rucht
infancy, kindsheid
infant, zuigeling, kind(er-)
infantry, infante'rie
infatuated, verliefd/gek (zijn) (op)
infect, be'smetten; aansteken
infection, in'fectie
infectious, be'smettelijk;
  aan'stekelijk
infer, afleiden; laten
  doorschemeren

inference, ge'volgtrekking
inferior, inferi'eur;
  onderge'schikt(e)
  to be – to, lager zijn dan;
  onderdoen voor
inferiority,
  minder'waardigheid(s-)
inferno, hel
infest, teisteren
infidel, onge'lovig(e)
infidelity, ontrouw
infinite, on'eindig (veel)
infinitesimal, on'eindig klein
infinity, on'eindigheid
infirmary, ziekenafdeling,
  ziekenhuis
infirmity, ge'brek
inflammable, ont'vlambaar
inflammation, ont'steking
inflate, opblazen, oppompen;
  opdrijven
inflation, in'flatie
inflexible, onver'zettelijk,
  rotsvast, star
inflict, toebrengen, opleggen,
  ver'oorzaken; lastig vallen met
influence, invloed; be'invloeden
influential, invloedrijk
influenza, griep
influx, toevloed, instroming
inform, informeren, be'richten;
  aanbrengen
informal, infor'meel
information, informatie,
  inlichting(en), be'richt(en)
infrequent, zeldzaam
infringe, inbreuk maken;
  over'treden
infuriate, woedend maken
infuse, laten trekken; be'zielen
ingenious, ver'nuftig
ingenuity, ver'nuft
ingenuous, onge'kunsteld

ingrained, inge'worteld

ingratiate, zich in de gunst dringen

ingratitude, on'dankbaarheid

ingredient, be'standdeel

inhabit, wonen in

inhabitant, in(*or* be')woner

inhale, inha'leren

inherent, inhe'rent

inherit, erven

inheritance, erfenis

inhibition, remming

inhospitable, ongast'vrij, onher'bergzaam

inhuman, on'menselijk

inimitable, onna'volgbaar

iniquity, onrecht'vaardigheid, ver'derf

initial, be'gin-, eerst; voorletter; para'feren

initially, in het be'gin

initiate, inwijden

initiative, initia'tief

inject, inspuiten

injudicious, onverstandig

injunction, be'vel

injure, (ver)wonden; schade doen; kwetsen

injurious, schadelijk

injury, ver'wonding; schade; be'lediging

injustice, onrecht('vaardigheid)

ink, inkt

inkling, flauw vermoeden

inlaid, ingelegd

inland, binnen(land)(s); het land in

in-laws, schoonfamilie

  father-(mother- *or* sister-) in-law, schoonvader(moeder *or* zuster)

inlet, inham, zeegat

inmate, (tijdelijk) ('mede)be'woner

inn, herberg

innate, aangeboren

inner, binnen-; innerlijk

innermost, binnenste

innkeeper, waard

innocence, onschuld

innocent, on'schuldig

innocuous, on'schadelijk

innovation, nieuwigheid

innuendo, (hatelijke) toespeling

innumerable, on'telbaar

inoculate, inenten

inoffensive, geen ergernis wekkend

inopportune, onge'legen

inordinate, buiten'sporig

inquest, ge'rechtelijk onderzoek naar de doodsoorzaak

inquire, infor'meren (naar), vragen (naar)

inquiry, vraag, poging (om inlichtingen in te winnen); onderzoek

inquisitive, nieuws'gierig

inroad, inval, ver'overing; gat

insane, krank'zinnig

insatiable, onver'zadelijk

inscribe, schrijven op, gra'veren; inschrijven

inscription, opschrift; opdracht

inscrutable, ondoor'grondelijk

insect, in'sekt

insemination, be'vruchting

  artificial –, kunst'matige insemi'natie

insensible, onge'voelig (voor); onbe'wust

inseparable, onaf'scheidelijk

insert, inlas(sen), insteken, plaatsen

inside, binnen(kant); naar binnen; in

insidious, ge'niepig

insight, inzicht
insignia, onder'scheidingstekens
insignificant, zonder be'tekenis,
  onbe'tekenend, onbe'duidend
insincere, onop'recht
insinuate, indringen; insinu'eren
insipid, flauw
insist, er op staan; (blijven)
  volhouden; (er op) aandringen
insistent, vol'hardend; dringend
insolent, onbe'schoft
insoluble, onop'losbaar
insomnia, slape'loosheid
inspect, onder'zoeken;
  inspec'teren
inspection, in'spectie; onderzoek
inspector, inspec'teur
inspiration, inspi'ratie; bezielend
  voorbeeld; ingeving
inspire, inspi'reren; inblazen;
  inboezemen
install, instal'leren
instalment, ter'mijn; ge'deelte,
  aflevering
instance, voorbeeld; ver'zoek;
  aanhalen
instant, ogenblik;
  ogen'blikkelijk
instantaneous, on'middellijk
instead of, in plaats van
instep, wreef
instigate, aanstichten
instil, bijbrengen
instinct(ive), in'stinct('ief)
institute, insti'tuut; instellen
institution, instelling; tra'ditie
instruct, onder'richten;
  ge'lasten; mededelen
instruction, onderricht;
  in'structie
instructive, leerzaam
instrument, instru'ment

instrumental, instrumen'taal;
  be'vorderlijk (voor)
insubordinate, weer'spannig
insufferable, onuit'staanbaar
insufficient, onvol'doende
insular, eiland-; geïso'leerd,
  be'krompen
insulate, iso'leren
insult, be'lediging; be'ledigen
insuperable, onover'komelijk
insurance, ver'zekering
insure, ver'zekeren
insurrection, opstand
intact, in'tact, gaaf
intake, inlaat; aanvoer
intangible, on'tastbaar
integral, inte'grerend; inte'graal
integrate, inte'greren
integrity, on'kreukbaarheid
intellect(ual), intel'lect(u'eel)
intelligence, intelli'gentie;
  inlichtingen
intelligent, intelli'gent,
  be'vattelijk
intelligible, be'grijpelijk
intemperate, on'matig
intend, van plan zijn; be'doelen
intense, in'tens
intensify, ver'hogen,
  ver'scherpen
intensity, intensi'teit
intensive, inten'sief
intent, ('in)ge'spannen;
  be'doeling
intention, be'doeling
intentional, op'zettelijk
inter, ter aarde be'stellen
interaction, wisselwerking
intercept, onder'scheppen, de
  pas afsnijden
interchange, ver'wisselen,
  afwisselen

interchangeable, ver'wisselbaar

intercom, intercom

intercourse, omgang, sociaal verkeer; ge'slachtsgemeenschap

interest, be'lang(stelling); aandeel; rente; interes'seren
to be interested in, be'lang stellen in (*or* hebben bij)

interfere, tussen'beide komen; zich mengen in

interference, be'moeienis; stoornis; storing

interim, interim; tijdelijk; tussentijd(s)

interior, inwendig, binnen(s)huis, binnenland(s)

interlock, interlock; in el'kaar grijpen

interlude, pauze, tussenperiode; tussenspel

intermediary, be'middelaar; be'middeling

intermediate, tussen-

interminable, eindeloos

intermingle, (zich) ver'mengen

intermittent, met tussenpozen

intern, in'tern; inter'neren

internal, in'wendig; binnenlands

international, internatio'naal

interplay, wisselwerking

interpose, tussenbeide komen

interpret, (ver)'tolken, uitleggen

interpreter, tolk

interrogate, onder'vragen

interrupt, onder'breken, in de rede vallen; be'lemmeren

intersect, door'snijden; el'kaar snijden

intersperse, door'spekken; ver'spreiden

interval, pause, tussentijd(*or* ruimte)

intervene, tussen'beide komen; liggen (tussen)

intervention, tussenkomst

interview, inter'view(en)

intestine, darm
intestines, ingewanden

intimate, in'tiem, ver'trouwd; laten merken

intimation, aanduiding

intimidate, intimi'deren

into, in, tot (in)

intolerable, onver'draaglijk

intolerant, onver'draagzaam

intonation, into'natie

intoxicant, be'dwelmend (middel)

intoxicate, dronken maken

intoxication, dronkenschap; roes

intractable, on'handelbaar; hard'nekkig

intrepid, onver'saagd

intricate, inge'wikkeld

intrigue, in'trige, ge'konkel; intri'geren

intrinsic, intrin'siek

introduce, introdu'ceren; brengen in; indienen

introduction, invoeren; inleiding

intrude, (zich) in(*or* op)dringen; storen

intuition, intu'ïtie; ingeving

intuitive, intuï'tief

inundate, overstelpen

invade, binnenvallen

invalid, zieke, inva'lide; on'geldig

invaluable, on'schatbaar

invariable, con'stant

invariably, zonder uitzondering

invasion, in'vasie, inval; inbreuk

invent, uitvinden, ver'zinnen

invention, uitvinding, ver'zinsel

inventive, vindingrijk

inventor, uitvinder
inventory, inven'taris
inverse, omgekeerd
invert, omkeren, omzetten
invest, be'leggen; ver'lenen
investigate, onderzoeken
investigation, onderzoek
investment, (geld)be'legging
inveterate, ver'stokt
invigorate, kracht geven
invincible, onover'winnelijk
invisible, on'zichtbaar
invitation, uitnodiging
invite, uitnodigen; vragen om
inviting, aan'lokkelijk
invoice, fac'tuur
invoke, aan(*or* op)roepen; een
    be'roep doen op
involuntary, onwille'keurig
involve, met zich meebrengen,
    be'trekken
    involved, (in)ge'wikkeld
invulnerable, on'kwetsbaar
inward, naar binnen; innerlijk
irate, woedend
Ireland, Ierland
Irish, Iers
iron, (strijk)ijzer; ijzeren; strijken
ironic(al), i'ronisch
ironmongery, ijzerwaren
irony, iro'nie
irreconcilable, onver'zoenlijk
irrefutable, onweer'legbaar
irregular, onregel'matig; tegen
    de regel
irrelevant, niet ter zake dienend
irreparable, onher'stelbaar
irrepressible, onbe'dwingbaar
irreproachable, onbe'rispelijk
irresistible, onweer'staanbaar
irresolute, be'sluiteloos
irrespective of, afgezien van,
    ongeacht

irresponsible,
    onverant'woordelijk
irretrievable, onher'stelbaar;
    reddeloos
irreverent, oneer'biedig
irrevocable, onher'roepelijk
irrigate, be'vloeien
irrigation, irri'gatie
irritable, prikkelbaar
irritate, prikkelen; irri'teren
irritation, irritatie,
    ge'prikkeldheid; branderigheid
Islam, islam
Islamic, islamitisch
island, eiland; vluchtheuvel
isle, eiland
isolate, iso'leren
issue, uitgifte, nummer;
    uitkomst; kwestie;
    ver'strekken; uitgeven;
    (voort)komen uit
it, het
Italian, Itali'aan(s)
italic, cur'sief
Italy, I'talië
itch, jeuk(en), verlangen
item, stuk, punt; be'richt
itinerant, rondtrekkend
itinerary, reisplan
its, zijn
itself, (zich')zelf
ivory, i'voor; i'voren
ivy, klimop

J

jab, steek; steken
jack, (op)krik(ken); boer
jacket, jasje; omslag
jagged, ruw, ge'tand, puntig
jam, jam; opstopping; (samen)
    duwen, klemmen; storen
January, janu'ari

Japanese, Ja'pans; Ja'panner
jar, pot; schok; krassen; een
  schok geven
jargon, jargon, vaktaal
jaundice, geelzucht
jaunt, uitstapje
jaunty, zwierig
jaw, kaak
jazz, jazz
jealous, ja'loers; angst'vallig
  be'zorgd
jeer, schimpen
jelly, ge'lei, gela'tinepudding
jellyfish, kwal
jeopardize, in ge'vaar brengen
jerk, ruk, schok; (vulg) lul, zak;
  schokken, rukken
jersey, trui(tje)
jest, scherts(en)
jettison, over'boord werpen
jetty, pier
Jew, jood
jewel, (edel)steen, ju'weel
jewellery, ju'welen
Jewish, joods
jigsaw puzzle, legpuzzel
jihad, jihad
jilt, de bons geven
jingle, (laten) rinkelen
job, kar'wei, werk(je), baan(tje)
jockey, jockey; manoeu'vreren
jocular, schertsend
jog, stoten; wippen; sukkelen;
  opfrissen
join, ver'binding, naad;
  ver'binden, ver'enigen,
  samenkomen, in elkaar slaan;
  zich voegen bij, meedoen,
  komen bij
joint, ge'wricht; ver'binding,
  naad; groot stuk vlees;
  ge'zamenlijk
joke, grap(pen maken)

joker, grappenmaker; joker
jolly, jolig; reuze
jolt, schok; hotsen
jostle, (ver')dringen
jot, jota; vlug no'teren
journal, dagboek; tijdschrift
journalism, journalis'tiek
journalist, journa'list
journey, reis (maken)
jovial, jovi'aal
joy(ful), vreugde(vol)
jubilant, jubelend, in de wolken
jubilee, jubi'leum
judge, rechter, jurylid, kenner;
  (be')oordelen
judgement, uitspraak, oordeel,
  vonnis
judicial, ge'rechtelijk
judicious, oordeel'kundig
jug, kan
juggle, goochelen
juice, sap
juicy, sappig
July, juli
jumble, warboel; door el'kaar
  gooien
jump, sprong; springen;
  opschrikken
jumper, jumper; springer
junction, knooppunt, kruispunt
June, juni
jungle, jungle, oerwoud;
  warboel
junior, junior, jonger(e)
junk, (oude) rommel
jurisdiction, juris'dictie
jury, jury
just, recht'vaardig;
  welverdiend; ge'grond;
  pre'cies; net; maar; even;
  een'voudig
justice, recht('vaardigheid),
  ge'rechtigheid; jus'titie; rechter

to do –, billijk be'handelen; eer
  aandoen, goed doen uitkomen
justifiable, gerecht'vaardigd;
  ver'dedigbaar
justification, grond,
  recht'vaardiging
justify, recht'vaardigen
jut out, uitsteken
jute, jute
juvenile, jeugd(ig), jong(eling)

K

kangaroo, kangoeroe
karaoke, kara'oke
keel, kiel
keen, scherp('zinnig);
  enthousi'ast
keep, kost; slottoren;
  (onder')houden), be'waren;
  weer'houden; (goed)blijven
  to – away, wegblijven
  to – on, blijven, door-; aan (*or*
  op)houden
  to – up, volhouden;
  onder'houden
  to – up with; bijhouden
keeper, oppasser, opzichter
keeping, hoede;
  over'eenstemming
kennel, hondenhok, kennel
kerb, stoeprand
kernel, kern
kettle, ketel
key, sleutel(-); toets; toonaard
keyboard, toetsenbord;
  toetsinstrument
keynote, grondtoon
keypad, toetsenpaneel
khaki, kaki
kick, schop(pen); te'rugstoot;
  trappen; stoten

kid, geitje; kind; voor de gek
  houden
kidnap, ont'voeren
kidney, nier
kill, doden
  to be killed, sneuvelen,
  omkomen
kiln, oven
kilt, kilt
kin, fa'milie
kind, soort; vriendelijk
kind-hearted, goed'hartig
kindle, aansteken
kindly, goed'aardig, vriendelijk
kindness, vriendelijkheid
kindred, ver'want(en)
king, koning
kingdom, koninkrijk
kink, slag, kink; kronkel
kinky, perverse; sexy,
  op'windend
kinship, ver'wantschap
kiosk, ki'osk
kiss, kus(sen)
kit, uitrusting; ba'gage;
  ge'reedschap
kitchen, keuken
kite, vlieger
kitten, katje
kiwi, kiwi(vrucht)
knack, slag, kneep
knackered, bekaf, doodop
knave, schurk; boer
knead, kneden
knee, knie
kneel, knielen, ge'knield liggen
knell, doodsklok
knickers, slipje, broekje
knickknack, snuisterij
knife, mes; door'steken
knight, (tot) ridder (slaan)
knighthood, ridderorde,
  ridderschap

knit, breien; samengroeien
knitting, breiwerk
knob, knop; knobbel
knock, slag, klop(pen), slaan
  stoten
  to – down, om'vergooien,
  aanrijden; toeslaan
  to – off, afslaan; ophouden,
  schaften
  to – out, uitkloppen;
  be'wusteloos slaan
  to – over, om'vergooien
knocker, klopper
knot, knoop; kwast; knopen
knotty, vol knopen; vol
  kwasten; lastig
know, (het) weten; (her')kennen
knowing, schrander;
  veelbe'tekenend
knowledge, (voor)kennis;
  wetenschap
knuckle, knokkel

L

label, eti'ket, label; van (een)
  eti'ket(ten) voor'zien
laboratory, labora'torium
laborious, afmattend; zwaar
labour, arbeid(en);
  werkkrachten; weeën;
  doorzagen over
labourer, arbeider
labyrinth, doolhof
lace, kant; veter; vastrijgen
lacerate, (ver')scheuren
lack, ge'brek (hebben aan)
  to be lacking, ont'breken
laconic, laco'niek
lacquer, lak(werk)
lad, knaap
ladder, ladder
laden, be'laden

ladle, scheplepel; opscheppen
lady, dame
lag, achterblijven; be'kleden
lagoon, la'gune
laid-back, ont'spannen, re'laxed
lair, hol
lake, meer
lamb, lam(svlees); lammeren
lame, kreupel; zwak
lament, weeklacht; be'treuren
lamentable, jammerlijk
lamentation, weeklacht
lamp, lamp, lan'taren
lamp post, lan'tarenpaal
lance, lans; lan'ceren
land, land(e'rij); neerkomen;
  (doen) be'landen; aan land
  zetten
landed, land-, grond-
landing, landing; overloop
  landing stage, steiger
landlady, hospita
landlord, huisbaas, landheer;
  hospes, waard
landmark, baken, be'kend punt;
  mijlpaal
land owner, grondbezitter
landscape, landschap
landslide, (aard)ver'schuiving
lane, landweg(getje); rijbaan;
  vaargeul
language, taal
languid, loom, flauw
languish, ver'slappen;
  wegkwijnen; smachten (naar)
lank, schraal; sluik
lanky, slungelachtig
lantern, lan'taren
lap, schoot; ronde; (op)leppen;
  kabbelen
lapse, foutje; periode, tijdje;
  afnemen, ver'vallen
lard, reuzel

larder, pro'visiekamer (or -kast)

large, groot

largely, grotendeels

lark, leeuwerik; pretje; lol maken

larva, larve

lash, zweepkoord; zweepslag; geselen; (doen) zwiepen; vastsjorren

lass, meisje

lassitude, matheid

last, (het) laatst; ver'leden; leest; duren, het uithouden
– **straw,** laatste druppel
at –, ten'slotte; eindelijk

lasting, blijvend; duurzaam

lastly, ten'slotte

latch, klink, slot

late, (te) laat; re'cent; wijlen, ge'wezen

lately, (in de) laatst(e tijd)

latent, la'tent

lateral, zij(delings)

lathe, draaibank

lather, schuim(en)

Latin, La'tijn(s)

latitude, breedte; speling

latter, laatst(genoemd)(e)

latterly, tegen het eind; in de laatste tijd

lattice, traliewerk

laudable, lof'waardig

laugh, lach(en)
to – **at,** lachen om; uitlachen

laughable, lach'wekkend

laughter, ge'lach

launch, (zware) sloep; te water laten; insturen; afschieten; op touw zetten, ont'ketenen

laundry, wasse'rij; was(goed)

laurel, lau'rier; lauwer-
laurels, lauweren

lava, lava

lavatory, WC, toilet

lavender, la'vendel

lavish, kwistig; over'laden

law, recht(en); wet

law-abiding, orde'lievend

law court, rechtbank

lawful, wettig, recht'matig

lawless, los'bandig

lawn, ga'zon

lawsuit, pro'ces

lawyer, advo'caat

lax(ity), laks(heid)

laxative, la'xeermiddel

lay, lied; leke(n)-; leggen; dekken
to – **down,** voorschrijven; geven; neerleggen
to – **in,** inslaan

layer, laag

layman, leek

layout, plan, aanleg

laze, luieren

lazy, lui

lead, leiding; eerste plaats, voorsprong; riem; voorbeeld; lood; leiden, ertoe brengen; voor('op)gaan; aanvoeren

leaden, loodzwaar

leader, leider; hoofdartikel

leadership, leiding; leiderschap

leading, voor'aanstaand, hoofd-

leaf, blad

leaflet, blaadje, folder

leafy, be'bladerd

league, (ver')bond

leak, lek(ken)

leakage, lek; uitlekking

lean, mager; schraal; overhellen; leunen; zetten

leaning, neiging

lean-to, afdak

leap, sprong; springen

leap year, schrikkeljaar

learn, leren; ver'nemen
learned, ge'leerd
learner, leerling
learning, ge'leerdheid, wetenschap
lease, huurcontract, pacht; huurtijd; (ver')huren
leasehold, pacht(goed)
leash, riem
least, minst
  at –, ten'minste, minstens
leather, leer; leren
leave, ver'lof; afscheid; ver'trekken (uit), weggaan; (ver')laten; achter(*or* na)laten; overlaten
  to – alone, afblijven van; met rust laten
  to – off, ophouden (met)
  to – out, weglaten; er buiten laten
lecture, lezing (houden), col'lege (geven); de les lezen
lecturer, universitair docent
ledge, richel, rand
leek, prei
leer, gluren
left, linker(hand); links(handig)
left-handed, links
leg, been, poot; (broeks)pijp; e'tappe
legacy, le'gaat; erfenis
legal, rechts'kundig, rechterlijk; wettig; wettelijk; rechts'geldig
legend, le'gende; onderschrift
legendary, legen'darisch
legible, leesbaar
legion, legi'oen; legio
legislation, wetgeving
legitimate, wettig; gerecht'vaardigd; recht'matig
leisure, vrije tijd
leisurely, be'daard

lemon(ade), ci'troen(limo'nade)
lend, (uit)lenen; ver'lenen
length, lengte, duur; eind(je)
  at length, eindelijk; uit'voerig
lengthen, ver'lengen; langer worden
lengthwise, in de lengte
lengthy, lang('durig)
lenient, cle'ment
lens, lens
lentil, linze
leopard, luipaard
leotard, tricot, balletpakje
leprosy, me'laatsheid
lesbian, lesbisch; lesbienne
less, min(der)
lessen, ver'minderen, (doen) afnemen
lesser, minder
lesson, les; schriftlezing
lest, voor het ge'val dat; opdat niet; dat
let, laten, toestaan; ver'huren
  to – down, neerlaten; uitleggen; du'peren, in de steek laten
  to – go, loslaten; laten gaan
  to – in, binnen laten
  to – off, laten gaan
lethargic, slaperig, loom
letter, brief; letter
lettuce, (krop)sla
level, vlak, ge'lijk (met); hoogte; ni'veau; ge'lijk maken
level-headed, ver'standig, nuchter
lever, hefboom
levy, heffing, lichting; heffen, werven
lewd, on'tuchtig, ob'sceen
liability, aan'sprakelijkheid, ver'antwoording; blok aan het been

liable, verplicht; vatbaar; aan'sprakelijk; de neiging hebben
– to, strafbaar, last hebben v an
liaison, ver'binding(s-); liai'son
liar, leugenaar
libel, smaadschrift; op schrift be'lasteren
liberal, roy'aal, ruim'denkend; liberaal
liberate, be'vrijden
liberty, vrijheid
librarian, bibliothe'caris
library, biblio'theek
licence, ver'gunning; vrijheid
licentious, los'bandig
lick, (af)likken
lid, deksel
lie, leugen; liegen; (gaan) liggen
to – down, gaan liggen; liggen te rusten
lieutenant, luitenant
life, leven(sbeschrijving)
lifebelt, reddingsgordel
lifeboat, reddingsboot
lifeless, levenloos
lifelike, na'tuurgetrouw
lifelong, levenslang
lifetime, leven(sduur)
lift, lift; (op)tillen; optrekken; pikken
ligament, band, pees
light, licht; vuurtje; aansteken; ver'lichten; ver'helderen
lighten, lichter worden; ophelderen; weerlichten; ver'lichten
lighter, aansteker; lichter
light-hearted, luchtig
lighthouse, vuurtoren
lighting, ver'lichting

lightly, zachtjes; licht('vaardig); luchtig
lightning, bliksem(snel)
lightweight, licht ge'wicht
like, (zo)als; houden van, aardig vinden; graag willen
it is just – him, het is echt iets voor hem; het lijkt sprekend op hem
nothing –, lang niet
something –, onge'veer, zo(iets) als
likeable, prettig
likelihood, kans
likely, waar'schijnlijk
he is – to, het is aan'nemelijk dat hij
likeness, ge'lijkenis
likewise, even'eens; insge'lijks
liking, voorliefde, zin
lilac, se'ring; lila
lily, lelie
limb, lid; tak
limbs, ledematen
lime, kalk; li'moen; linde
limelight, voorgrond
limit, grens; be'perken
limitation, be'perking; grens, te'kortkoming
limited company, naamloze vennootschap
limp, slap; mank lopen
limpid, helder
line, lijn; linie; rij; regel; spoor; lini'ëren; voeren, be'kleden
linen, linnen(goed)
linger, dralen
linguistic, taal('kundig)-
lining, voering, be'kleding
link, schakel(en); inhaken; ver'binden; met elkaar in ver'band brengen
lion(ess), leeuw('in)

lip, lip; rand
lipstick, lippenstift
liqueur, li'keur
liquid, vloeibaar; vloeistof
liquidate, liqui'deren
liquor, (sterke) drank
liquorice, drop
lisp, ge'lispel; lispelen
list, lijst; slagzij; overhellen
listen, luisteren
listless, lusteloos
literal, letterlijk
literary, lite'rair
literature, litera'tuur
lithe, soepel
litre, liter
litter, afval, rommel; nest, worp;
  (met rommel) be'zaaien
little, klein; weinig; beetje
  a little late, wat laat
liturgy, litur'gie
live, levend(ig); ge'laden, scherp;
  (blijven) leven; wonen
liveable, be'woonbaar; leefbaar
livelihood, kost, be'staan
lively, levendig, be'drijvig, druk
liver, lever
livery, li'vrei
livestock, vee
livid, razend; lijkbleek
living, levend, levens-; kost;
  leven
living room, huiskamer
lizard, hage'dis
load, vracht, lading; (in)laden,
  be'laden; over'laden
loaf, brood; lummelen
loan, lening; (uit)lenen
loath, onge'negen
loathe, walgen van
loathsome, walgelijk
lobby, hal, fo'yer
lobe, lel

lobster, kreeft
local, plaatselijk; lo'kaal
locality, om'geving
localize, lokali'seren
locate, opsporen, thuisbrengen;
  vestigen
location, ligging; plaatslokatie
lock, slot; sluis; lok; op slot
  doen (or gaan), (op)sluiten;
  vastraken
locker, kastje
locket, medail'lon
locomotive, locomo'tief;
  be'wegings-
locust, sprinkhaan
lodge, (por'tiers)woning;
  lo'geren, in de kost zijn,
  onderbrengen; blijven steken;
  indienen
lodger, kostganger
lodgings, (ge'huurde) kamers
loft, zolder; gale'rij
lofty, hoog; ver'heven
log, blok hout; log(boek); blok-;
  no'teren; afleggen
loggerheads, to be at –,
  over'hoop liggen
logic, logica
logical, logisch
loin, lende(stuk)
loiter, omhangen
loll, hangen
London, Londen(s)
lone(ly), eenzaam, ver'laten
long, lang; door; ver'langen
longing, ver'langen
longitude, lengte
long-winded, lang'dradig
look, (aan)blik; voorkomen;
  kijken; er uitzien
  to – after, zorgen voor
  to – at, be'kijken, kijken naar
  to – back, omzien; te'rugzien

to – for, zoeken (naar); ver'wachten
to – forward to, zich ver'heugen op
to – into, onder'zoeken
to – like, lijken op, er uitzien als
to – on, toekijken
to – out, uitkijken
to – up, opkijken; opzoeken; opknappen
look-alike, evenbeeld, dubbelganger
lookout, uitkijk
keep a – for, uitkijken naar
looks, uiterlijk
loom, weefgetouw; opdoemen
loony, gek, getikt; gek, dwaas (person)
loop, lus
loophole, uitvlucht
legal –s, mazen in de wet
loose, los, vrij
loosen, los(ser) maken
loot, buit; plunderen
lop, (af)snoeien
lop-sided, scheef
lord, heer, lord
lorry, vrachtauto
lose, (doen) ver'liezen, kwijtraken; missen; voor'bij laten gaan
loss, ver'lies
lost, ver'loren; ver'dwaald; ver'ongelukt
to get –, ver'dwalen
lot, lot; perceel; stel; heel wat
lotion, lotion
lottery, lote'rij
loud, luid('ruchtig)
loudspeaker, luidspreker; box
lounge, sa'lon, conver'satiezaal; leunen, liggen

louse, luis
lout, lummel, hufter
lovable, lief
love, liefde; liefje; houden van; dolgraag (willen)
(to fall) in – with, ver'liefd (worden) op
to make –, vrijen
lovely, prachtig, mooi; heerlijk
lover, minnaar
loving, aan'hankelijk; liefhebbend
low, laag; bijna op (or leeg); loeien
lower, laten zakken; strijken; dreigend kijken
lowland, laagland
lowly, nederig
loyal(ty), trouw
lubricant, smeermiddel
lubricate, smeren
lucid(ity), helder(heid)
luck, ge'luk
bad –, pech
good –, ge'luk; suc'ces!
lucky: to be –, boffen; ge'luk hebben
lucrative, winstgevend
ludicrous, be'lachelijk
lug, slepen
luggage, ba'gage
lugubrious, lu'guber
lukewarm, lauw
lull, stilte; sussen
lullaby, wiegeliedje
lumber, ge'kapt hout; rommel; dreunen
luminous, lichtgevend
lump, klomp, brok, klontje, knobbel; rond
lunacy, krank'zinnigheid
lunar, maan-
lunatic, krank'zinnig(e)

lunch, lunch(en)
lung, long
lunge, uitval (doen); dres'seren
lurch, stoot; steek; voor'uit (or op'zij)schieten, slingeren
lure, lokstem; (ver')lokken
lurid, gloeiend; gruwelijk
lurk, zich schuil houden, ver'borgen zijn, loeren
luscious, heerlijk sappig
lush, mals
lust, (wel)lust, zucht; be'geren
lustre, glans; luister
lusty, wellustig; flink
luxurious, weelderig
luxury, weelde, luxe
lying, leugenachtig
lynch, lynchen
lyric, lyrisch (ge'dicht)
lyrical, lyrisch

M

machine, ma'chine; organi'satie
machinery, machine'rieën; mecha'nisme; organi'satie(s)
mackerel, ma'kreel
mad, gek; dol
madam, me'vrouw, juf'frouw
madden, gek maken; gruwelijk ergeren
madman, gek
madness, krank'zinnig(heid); gekkigheid
madrigal, madri'gaal
magazine, tijdschrift
maggot, made
magic, toverkunst, tove'rij; tover(achtig)
magician, tovenaar
magistrate, magis'traat
magnanimous, groot'moedig
magnate, mag'naat

magnet, mag'neet
magnetic, mag'netisch
magnificence, luister, pracht
magnificent, luisterrijk, groots
magnify, ver'groten
magnitude, grootte
magpie, ekster
mahogany, ma'honie(hout)
maiden, maagd(elijk); onge'trouwd, meisjes-; eerste
mail, post
maim, ver'minken
main, hoofd-, voor'naamste
mains, hoofdleiding, net
mainland, vaste'land
mainly, hoofd'zakelijk
mainsail, grootzeil
maintain, handhaven; onder'houden; be'weren
maintenance, onderhoud
maize, maïs
majestic, majestu'eus
majesty, majesteit
major, groot(ste), hoofd-; ma'joor; majeur
majority, meerder('jarig)heid
make, merk; maken; dwingen, laten; ver'dienen; schatten, denken; halen; opmaken (a bed); zetten (tea); doen (a promise)
to – out, opstellen; be'weren; snappen; ont'cijferen; onder'scheiden urÿen
to – up, maken; ver'zinnen; ver'goeden, aanvullen; het weer goedmaken; (zich) opmaken
to – up for, goedmaken; inhalen
make-believe, een spelletje; ver'zonnen
maker, schepper, fabri'kant

makeshift, geïmprovi'seerd
    (lapmiddel)
make-up, schmink; make-up
malady, kwaal
malaria, ma'laria
male, mannelijk (per'soon *or*
    dier), mannen-
malevolent, boos'aardig
malice, boos opzet, haat
malicious, boos'aardig
malign, be'lasteren
malignant, kwaad'aardig
malleable, kneedbaar
malnutrition, onder'voeding
malt, mout(en)
mammal, zoogdier
mammoth, mammoet; reuzen-
man, man; (de) mens;
    be'mannen, be'zetten
manage, aankunnen; managen;
    leiden; klaarspelen
management, be'heer; di'rectie,
    be'stuur, management
manager, direc'teur, chef,
    manager
mandate, opdracht;
    man'daat(gebied)
mane, manen
manger, voerbak, kribbe
mangle, mangel(en);
    ver'scheuren
manhandle, ver'sjouwen,
    toetakelen
manhood, mannelijkheid,
    vol'wassenheid
mania, waanzin; manie
maniac, waan'zinnige
manicure, mani'cure
manifest, duidelijk; mani'fest;
    tonen
manifestation, uiting
manifesto, mani'fest
manifold, veel'vuldig

manipulate, manipu'leren,
    han'teren; be'werken; knoeien
    met
manipulation, han'tering;
    manipu'latie
mankind, mensdom, mensheid
manly, man'haftig, mannelijk
manner, ma'nier (van doen);
    soort
mannerism, hebbelijkheid
manoeuvre, ma'noeuvre;
    manoeu'vreren
manor, manor, groot
    (heren)huis met grondgebied
mansion, herenhuis
manslaughter, doodslag
mantelpiece, schoorsteenmantel
mantle, mantel; gloeikousje
manual, hand(en)-; manu'aal;
    handboek, handleiding
manufacture, fabri'cage,
    fabri'kaat; fabri'ceren
manure, mest; be'mesten
manuscript, handschrift;
    manuscript
many, veel; velen
    a good –, heel wat
    a great –, heel veel, heel wat
map, (land)kaart, platte'grond
maple, esdoorn
mar, ont'sieren; be'derven
maraud, plunderen
marble, marmer(en); knikker
march, mars; (doen)
    mar'cheren; oprukken
March, maart
mare, merrie
margarine, marga'rine
margin, kant(lijn); speling
marginal, kant-; onbeduidend
marijuana, marihu'ana
marigold, goudsbloem
marine, zee-, scheeps-; mari'nier

mariner, zeeman
marital, echtelijk
maritime, zee(vaart)-
mark, plek, streep, vlek, spoor;
moet, put; merk; stempel,
(ken)teken; doel; peil; een vlek
(etc) achterlaten; aanduiden;
(ken)merken; prijzen;
corri'geren; letten op
marked, duidelijk; ver'dacht
market, markt; afzetgebied; op
de markt brengen
market place, markt(plein)
marksman, scherpschutter
marmalade, marme'lade
maroon, paars'rood
to be marooned, stranden
marquis, mar'kies
marriage, huwelijk
marrow, merg; pom'poen
marry, trouwen (met);
uithuwelijken
marsh(y), moe'ras(sig)
marshal, maarschalk; ordenen;
ge'leiden
martial, krijgs('haftig)
martyr, martelaar; de
marteldood doen sterven
martyrdom, martelaarschap;
marteling
marvel, wonder; zich
ver'wonderen
marvellous, wonder'baarlijk,
fan'tastisch; heerlijk
masculine, mannelijk
mash, pap; (fijn)stampen
mask, masker(en); mas'keren
mason, steenhouwer, metselaar
masquerade, maske'rade; zich
ver'mommen
mass, massa; mis
massacre, massamoord;
slachting

massage, mas'sage; mas'seren
massive, mas'saal
mast, mast
master, (jonge) heer;
ge'zagvoerder; leraar;
meester(-); hoofd-; meester
worden
masterful, bazig
masterly, meesterlijk
masterpiece, meesterstuk
mastery, overhand;
meesterschap
masturbate, mastur'beren
mat, mat(je), kleed(je); mat, dof
match, lucifer; par'tij,
combi'natie; wedstrijd;
eve'naren; bij el'kaar passen
matchless, onverge'lijkelijk
mate, maat; levensgezel('in);
stuurman; (zich) paren
material, stof(felijk), materi'aal,
materi'eel; essenti'eel
materialist(ic), materia'list(isch)
materialize, ver'wezenlijkt
worden; ver'wezenlijken;
ver'schijnen
maternal, moederlijk, moeder-
maternity, moederschap; kraam-
mathematical, wis'kundig
mathematician, wis'kundige
mathematics, wiskunde
matrimonial, huwelijks-
matrimony, huwelijk(se staat)
matron, ma'trone; moeder;
direc'trice
matter, stof; kwestie; pus; van
be'lang zijn
as a – of fact, eigenlijk;
overigens
as a – of course, als
vanzelf'sprekend
for that –, wat dat be'treft,
trouwens

it does not –, het geeft niets, het doet er niet toe

what is the –? wat scheelt er aan?

matter-of-fact, zakelijk

mattress, ma'tras

mature, rijp(en); ver'vallen

maturity, rijpheid; ver'valtijd

maul, toetakelen

mauve, lichtpaars

maxim, stelregel

may, mogen, mis'schien kunnen

May, mei

maybe, mis'schien

mayonnaise, mayon'naise

mayor, burge'meester

maze, doolhof

me, mij, me

meadow, wei(de)

meagre, schraal

meal, maal(tijd); meel

mean, ge'meen, krenterig; ge'ring, schriel; middenweg, ge'middelde; be'doelen, menen; be'tekenen

meander, kronkelen; dolen

meaning, be'tekenis; be'doeling; veelbe'tekenend

meaningless, niets'zeggend

means, middel(en)

by all –, ge'rust

by no –, geenszins

meantime: in the –, in'tussen

meanwhile, onder'tussen

measles, mazelen

measure, maat(regel); (op)meten; zijn

measurement, maat

meat, vlees

mechanic, mecani'cien

mechanical, me'chanisch, machi'naal, werktuig'kundig; werk'tuiglijk

mechanics, werktuigkunde

mechanism, mecha'nisme, mecha'niek

mechanize, mechani'seren

medal, me'daille

meddle (with), zich be'moeien (met); komen aan

meddlesome, be'moeiziek

mediaeval, middeleeuws

mediate, als be'middelaar optreden

medical, medisch; keuring

medicinal, genees'krachtig

medicine, ge'neesmiddel; ge'neeskunde, medi'cijnen

mediocre, middel'matig

mediocrity, middel'matigheid

meditate, be'peinzen, over'peinzen

meditation, over'peinzing; medi'tatie

Mediterranean, Middellandse Zee

medium, middel('matig); medium

medley, mengelmoes; potpour'ri

meek, zacht'moedig

meet, (el'kaar) ont'moeten; (aan)treffen; samenkomen; afhalen; vol'doen aan

meeting, ver'gadering, samenkomst; ont'moeting

megaphone, mega'foon

melancholy, zwaar'moedig(heid)

mellow, zacht (en sappig); rijp

melodious, wel'luidend

melodrama, melo'drama

melody, melo'die

melon, me'loen

melt, (doen) smelten

member, lid(maat)

membership, lidmaatschap; ledental

membrane, vlies
memento, aandenken
memoirs, me'moires
memorable, gedenk'waardig
memorandum, memo'randum; nota
memorial, ge'denkteken; monument
memorize, uit het hoofd leren
memory, ge'heugen; her'innering; nagedachtenis
menace, be'dreiging; gevaar
menagerie, menage'rie
mend, repa'reren
menial, nederig, onderge'schikt
mental, geestelijk, men'taal, psychisch; met het hoofd; psychi'atrisch
– **hospital,** psychiatrische inrichting
mentality, mentali'teit
mention, (ver')melding; ver'melden
mentor, mentor
menu, me'nu
mercantile, handels-
mercenary, geld'zuchtig; huurling
merchandise, koopwaar
merchant, koopman; koopvaar'dij-
merciful, ge'nadig; ge'zegend
merciless, mee'dogenloos
mercury, kwik(zilver)
mercy, ge'nade; zegen
merely, alleen maar
merge, opgaan (in), samengaan (met), fu'seren (met); (ge'leidelijk) overgaan (in el'kaar)
merger, samensmelting; fusie
meridian, meridi'aan
meringue, schuim(gebak)

merit, ver'dienste; ver'dienen
mermaid, zeemeermin
merriment, vrolijkheid
merry, vrolijk
merry-go-round, draaimolen
mesh, maas
mess, rommel, bende; lelijke toestand; (offi'ciers)tafel; vuil maken
– **about,** prutsen, (lui) rondhangen; rotzooien met, be'lazeren
to – up, ver'knoeien
message, boodschap, be'richt
messenger, (voor)bode
Messiah, Mes'sias
messy, slordig, vuil
metal, me'taal; me'talen
metabolism, metabo'lisme, stofwisseling
metallic, me'talen, me'taalachtig
metamorphosis, ge'daanteverwisseling
metaphor, beeldspraak
metaphorical, fi'guurlijk
meteor, mete'oor
meteorological, meteoro'logisch
meter, meter
method, me'thode; sys'teem
methodical, syste'matisch
meticulous, (al te) zeer; nauwge'zet
metre, meter; metrum
metropolis, wereldstad
metropolitan, hoofd'stedelijk
mew, mi'auwen
mews, stal(woning)
microbe, mi'crobe
microphone, micro'foon
microprocessor, microprocessor
microscope, micro'scoop
microwave, magne'tron, microgolf

mid, midden
midday, twaalf uur; middag-
middle, middel(ste), midden
 – **classes,** middenstand
middle-aged, van middelbare
 leeftijd
Middle Ages, middeleeuwen
middleman, tussenpersoon
midge, mug
midget, dwerg; minia'tuur
midnight, midder'nacht(elijk)
midriff, middenrif
midst, midden
midsummer, mid'zomer
midway, halver'wege
midwife, verlos'kundige
might(y), macht(ig)
migrate, mi'greren, trekken
migration, mi'gratie, trek
mild, zacht('aardig); licht
mildew, (be')schimmel(en)
mile, mijl
mileage, afstand in mijlen
milestone, mijlpaal
militant, strijdend;
 strijd'lustig
militarism, milita'risme
military, mili'tair, krijgs-
militate, (tegen)werken
militia, mi'litie
milk, melk(en)
milkman, melkboer
Milky Way, melkweg
mill, molen; fa'briek; malen;
 kri'oelen
miller, molenaar
million, mil'joen
millionaire, miljo'nair
mime, ge'barenspel; met
 ge'baren uitbeelden
mimic, mimicus; nabootsen
mince, ge'hakt; fijnhakken

mind, geest, ver'stand,
 ge'dachte; zin; er iets op tegen
 hebben; letten op; oppassen
 to make up one's –, be'sluiten
mind-blowing, fan'tastisch,
 duizeling'wekkend
mindful, ge'dachtig (aan)
mine, van mij, het (or de) mijne;
 mijn; bron; delven
miner, mijnwerker
mineral, delfstof; mine'raal
mingle, (zich) mengen; omgaan
miniature, minia'tuur
minimize, zo klein mogelijk
 maken; ge'ringschatten
minimum, minimum
mining, mijn(bouw)
minister, predi'kant; mi'nister;
 ge'zant; ver'zorgen
ministry, mini'sterie; dienst;
 geestelijk ambt
mink, nerts
minor, klein, minder
 (be'langrijk); mineur;
 minder'jarige
minority, minder('jarig)heid
minstrel, min'streel
mint, munt(en)
minus, min; zonder
minute, mi'nuut; ogenblik;
 notule; mi'niem; minuti'eus
miracle, wonder
miraculous, wonder'baarlijk
mirage, fata mor'gana;
 zinsbegoocheling
mirror, spiegel; weer'kaatsen
mirth, vrolijkheid
misadventure, ongeluk;
 onge'lukkig voorval
misapprehension, misvatting
misbehave, zich mis'dragen
misbehaviour, wangedrag

miscalculate, zich ver'rekenen; misrekenen

miscarriage, mis'lukking; miskraam

miscarry, mis'lukken; ver'loren gaan

miscellaneous, ge'mengd; veelzijdig

miscellany, ge'mengde ver'zameling

mischief, (katte)kwaad; on'deugendheid

mischievous, on'deugend; kwaa'daardig

misconception, ve'rkeerde opvatting, mis'vatting

misconduct, wangedrag; wanbeheer; slecht be'heren

misconstrue, ver'keerd opvatten

misdeed, misdaad

misdemeanour, wangedrag

miser, vrek

miserable, diep onge'lukkig; naar'geestig; el'lendig

misery, el'lende

misfire, ketsen; overslaan

misfit: to be a –, niet passen; uit de toon vallen

misfortune, ongeluk

misgiving, bang ver'moeden

misguided, onver'standig

mishap, ongeluk(je)

misinform, ver'keerd inlichten

misinterpret, ver'keerd uitleggen

misjudge, ver'keerd (be')oordelen

mislay, kwijtraken

mislead, mis'leiden

mismanagement, wanbeheer

misnomer, ver'keerde be'naming

misplace, ver'keerd plaatsen

misplaced, mis'plaatst

misprint, drukfout; ver'keerd drukken

misrepresent, een ver'keerde voorstelling geven van

miss, juffrouw; misslaan; mislopen; missen; ver'zuimen

misshapen, mis'vormd

missile, projec'tiel

mission, missie; zending

missionary, zendeling(s-)

mist, nevel, lage wolk; waas

mistake, ver'gissing; fout; aanzien, ver'keerd be'grijpen, mis'kennen

to be mistaken, zich ver'gissen; mis'plaatst zijn

mistress, me'vrouw; juffrouw, lera'res; mai'tresse

mistrust, wantrouwen

misty, nevelachtig, wazig; be'grijpen, be'slagen

misunderstand, ver'keerd

misunderstanding, misverstand

misuse, misbruik; mis'bruiken; mis'handelen

mitigate, ver'zachten, ver'lichten

mitre, mijter; ver'stek

mitt(en), want

mix, (ver')mengen; zich laten mengen; omgaan met

to – up, ver'warren

mixture, mengsel, mengeling

moan, ge'kerm; ge'jammer; kermen, suizen; jammeren

moat, gracht

mob, (mensen)massa; ge'peupel; bende; zich ver'dringen om, als één man te lijf gaan

mobile, be'weeglijk, rondtrekkend, mo'biel; mo'bieltje, mo'biele te'léfoon mobilize, mobili'seren

mock, schijn-, kunst-; (be')spotten; be'spottelijk maken; naäpen

mockery, spot; aanfluiting

mode, mode; ma'nier

model, mo'del; model'leren, boet'seren

moderate, (ge')matig(d); matigen; be'daren

moderation, matigheid
in –, met mate

modern(ize), mo'dern(i'seren)

modest, be'scheiden; zedig

modification, wijziging

modify, wijzigen; matigen

moist(en), vochtig (maken)

moisture, vocht(igheid)

mole, mol; moedervlek

molecule, mole'cule

molest, lastig vallen

mollify, ver'tederen

moment, ogenblik; be'lang

momentarily, voor een ogenblik

momentary, kort'stondig

momentous, ge'wichtig

momentum, arbeidsvermogen van be'weging, vaart

monarch, vorst('in)

monarchy, monar'chie

monastery, klooster

Monday, maandag

monetary, munt-, geldelijk

money, geld

mongrel, bastaard(hond)

monk, monnik

monkey, aap

monocle, mo'nocle

monogram, mono'gram

monologue, al'leenspraak

monopolize, monopoli'seren

monopoly, mono'polie

monotonous, een'tonig

monotony, een'tonigheid

monsoon, moesson

monster, monster; ge'drocht

monstrosity, wanproduct

monstrous, monsterachtig

month(ly), maand(elijks)

monument, monu'ment

monumental, monumen'taal

mood, stemming, hu'meur; wijs

moody, hu'meurig; ont'stemd

moon(light), maan(licht); zwartwerken

moor, hei(de); veenmoeras; meren

moorings, meertouwen; ligplaats

moot, be'twistbaar

mop, zwabber; (afwas)kwast; dweilen, zwabberen; afgeven

mope, mokken

moral, zedelijk, zeden-, mo'reel; mo'raal
morals, zeden

morale, mo'reel

morality, zedelijke be'ginselen; zedelijkheid; morali'teit

moralize, morali'seren

morbid, ziekelijk; patho'logisch

more, meer, nog (meer)
some –, nog wat
– or less, min of meer

moreover, boven'dien

morning, morgen, ochtend
in the –, 's ochtends
tomorrow –, morgenochtend

morose, gemelijk

mortal, sterfelijk; dodelijk, doods; sterveling

mortality, sterfte(cijfer)

mortally, dodelijk

mortar, mor'tier; vijzel

mortgage, hypo'theek (nemen op)

mortify, diep ver'nederen; kas'tijden

mortuary, lijkenhuis
mosaic, moza'iek
mosque, mos'kee
mosquito, mus'kiet
moss, mos
most, meest; bij'zonder; het (or de) meeste
  at the –, op zijn hoogst (or meest)
  to make the – of, zoveel mogelijk profi'teren van
mostly, groten'deels; meestal
MOT, APK, verplichte jaarlijkse keuring
moth, nachtvlinder, mot
mother, moeder
motherly, moederlijk
mother of pearl, paarle'moer(en)
motif, mo'tief
motion, be'weging; motie; stoelgang; wenken
motionless, onbe'weeglijk
motivate, moti'veren
motive, be'weegreden
motley, bont
motor, motor; rijden
motor cycle, motorfiets
motorist, automobi'list
motto, motto
mould, vorm(en); schimmel; boet'seren
mouldy, be'schimmeld
moult, ruien
mound, wal, terp
mount, berg; rijdier; (be')stijgen
mountain(eer), berg(beklimmer)
mountainous, bergachtig
mourn, (be')treuren
mourner, rouwdrager
mournful, treurig; droevig
mourning, rouw
mouse, muis

mousetrap, muizeval
moustache, snor
mouth, mond(ing); opening
mouthful, hapje
mouthpiece, mondstuk; woordvoerder
movable, be'weegbaar; ver'anderlijk
move, zet; stap; ver'huizing; (zich) be'wegen; ver'huizen; ont'roeren
movement, be'weging
moving, roerend
mow, maaien
much, veel; zeer; vaak; vrijwel
muck, drek, vuil
mud, modder
muddle, warboel; in de war brengen, door el'kaar gooien; scharrelen
muddy, modderig
mudguard, spatbord
muff, mof; be'derven
muffle, instoppen; dempen
mug, mok, beker, kroes; sul; smoel
mulberry, moerbei
mule, muildier
multifarious, veel'soortig
multiple, veel'voudig; veelvoud
multiplex, megabioscoop
multiplication, vermenig'vuldiging
multiply, (zich) vermenig'vuldigen
multitude, menigte; groot aantal
mum: to keep –, stilzwijgen
mumble, mompelen
mummy, mummie; mammie
mumps, de bof
munch, (hoorbaar) k(n)auwen (op)
mundane, werelds

municipal, ge'meente-, stedelijk, stads-
municipality, ge'meente
munition, krijgsvoorraad
mural, muurschildering
murder, moord; ver'moorden
murderer, moordenaar
murderous, moord'dadig
murky, zwart, somber
murmur, ge'murmel; murmelen; mopperen
muscle, spier
muscular, ge'spierd; spier-
muse, muze; mijmeren
museum, mu'seum
mush, moes; ge'wauwel
mushroom, champi'gnon
music, mu'ziek
musical, muzi'kaal; mu'ziek-
musician, musicus; muzi'kant
muslin, neteldoek
mussel, mossel
must, moet(en), moest(en)
mustard, mosterd
muster, monstering; monsteren; ver'zamelen
musty, muf, schimmelig
mute, stom; dempen
mutilate, ver'minken
mutineer, muiter
mutiny, muite'rij, opstand
mutter, mompelen, prevelen
mutton, schapenvlees
mutual, onderling, weder'zijds; weder'kerig
muzzle, muil(band); mond
my, mijn
myriad, on'telbaar; tien'duizendtal
myself, me('zelf), (ik')zelf
mysterious, geheim'zinnig
mystery, ge'heim; raadsel
mystic, mysticus

mystic(al), ver'borgen; mys'tiek
mysticism, mys'tiek
mystify, ver'bijsteren
myth, mythe; ver'dichtsel
mythical, mythisch; ver'dicht
mythology, mytholo'gie

N

nag, zeuren; vitten
nail, spijker; nagel; vastspijkeren
naïve, na'ïef
naked, naakt; bloot
name, naam; (be')noemen; opnoemen; thuisbrengen
nameless, onbe'kend; ano'niem, naamloos
namely, namelijk
namesake, naamgenoot
nap, dutje; nop; dutten
nape, nek
napkin, ser'vet; luier
narcissus, nar'cis
narcotic, slaap'wekkend middel; ver'dovend
narrate, ver'halen
narrative, ver'haal; ver'halend
narrow, smal, nauw; klein
narrow-minded, klein'geestig
nasal, na'saal, neus-
nasty, akelig; smerig; naar, lelijk
nation, volk, natie
national, natio'naal; volks-, staats-
nationalist(ic), nationa'list(isch)
nationality, nationali'teit
nationalize, nationali'seren
native, autoch'toon; aangeboren; in'heems
nativity, ge'boorte (van Christus)
natural, na'tuurlijk, na'tuur-
naturalist, natura'list
naturalize, naturali'seren

naturally, na'tuurlijk; van
  na'ture
nature, na'tuur; aard
naught, nul; niets
naughty, on'deugend
nausea, misselijkheid; walging
nauseate, misselijk maken
nautical, zee(vaart'kundig)
naval, ma'rine-, zee-
navel, navel
navigable, be'vaarbaar
navigate, be'sturen
navigation, stuurmanskunst,
  navi'gatie
navigator, navi'gator
navy, ma'rine, vloot
near, dichtbij, na'bij
nearly, bijna
  not –, lang niet
neat, net(jes); handig; puur
necessarily,
  nood'zakelijk(erwijs)
necessary, nood'zakelijk;
  be'hoefte
necessitate, nood'zakelijk
  maken
necessity, nood(zaak); be'hoefte
neck, hals(stuk)
necklace, (hals)ketting,
  (hals)snoer
necktie, (strop)das
nectar, nectar
need, be'hoefte, nood(zaak);
  nodig hebben; hoeven,
  moeten
  there is no – het is niet nodig
needful, nodig
needle, naald
needless, on'nodig
needlework, naaiwerk,
  handwerk(en)
needy, be'hoeftig
negation, ont'kenning,

ver'loochening
negative, ont'kennend; negatief
neglect, ver'zuim(en),
  ver'waarlozing; ver'waarlozen
negligence, ver'waarlozing,
  on'achtzaamheid
negligent, achteloos
negligible, niet noemens'waard
negotiate, onder'handelen
negotiation, onder'handeling
neigh, hinniken
neighbour, buurman (*or*
  -vrouw); naaste
neighbourhood, buurt,
  om'geving
neighbouring, na'burig
neighbourly, vriendelijk
neither, geen van beide;
  even'min
  – ... nor, noch ... noch
nephew, neef(je)
nerve, zenuw; geestkracht;
  (bru'tale) moed; ver'mannen
nervous, zenuw(achtig); bang
nest, nest; (zich) nestelen
nestle, zich nestelen
net, net; tule, vi'trage; met een
  net vangen
nether, onder
Netherlands, Nederland(s)
netting, gaas
nettle, (brand)netel
neurotic, neu'rotisch;
  zenuwlijder, neu'root
neuter, on'zijdig
neutral, neu'traal (land)
neutralize, neutrali'seren;
  neu'traal ver'klaren
never, (nog) nooit; niet eens
nevertheless, desondanks
new, nieuw, vers
newborn, pasgeboren
newcomer, nieuweling

newly, pas, opnieuw

news, nieuws(berichten),
  be'richt; journal

newspaper, krant

New Year's Day, nieuwjaars'dag

New Year's Eve, oudejaars'avond,
  oudejaars'dag

next, volgend, aan'staande;
  daar'na
  – door, hier'naast
  – (door) to, naast

nib, pen

nibble, knabbelen

nice, aardig; lekker; net(jes);
  fijn

nicety, nauwge'zetheid; fi'nesse

niche, nis, hoekje

nickname, bijnaam

nicotine, nico'tine

niece, nicht(je)

night, nacht, avond
  at (or in the) –, 's nachts

nightdress, nachtjapon

nightfall, het vallen van
  de avond

nightingale, nachtegaal

nightmare, nachtmerrie

nimble, kwiek

nine(teen), negen(tien)

ninety, negentig

nipple, tepel

nitrogen, stikstof

nitwit, domoor

no, neen; niet, geen
  – one, niemand

nobility, adel(stand)

noble, edel(man), adelijk;
  groots; nobel

nobody, niemand; nul

nocturnal, nachtelijk, nacht-

nod, knik(ken); knikkebollen

noise, la'waai, ge'luid

noiseless, ge'ruisloos

noisy, luid'ruchtig, druk

nomad, no'made; zwerver

nominal, in naam; nomi'naal

nominate, be'noemen;
  kandi'daat stellen

nomination, be'noeming;
  kandi'daatstelling

nonchalant, onver'schillig

non-committal, (op'zettelijk)
  vaag

nondescript, onbe'paald;
  onop'vallend

none, geen (enkele), niemand,
  niets; geenszins

nonentity, nul

nonsense, onzin

nook, hoekje, plekje

noon, twaalf uur ('s middags)

noose, strop, strik

nor, noch, en … ook niet

normal, nor'maal

normally, ge'woonlijk

north, (naar het) noorden;
  noord(en)-

northerly, northern, noordelijk

Norway, Noorwegen

Norwegian, Noor(s)

nose, neus

nostril, neusgat

not, niet

notable, op'merkelijk,
  aan'zienlijk; no'tabele

notably, met name, voor'al

notch, kerf; kerven

note, aantekening, no'titie;
  briefje; nota; toon, noot;
  be'tekenis; no'teren;
  opmerken

notebook, no'titieboekje;
  notebook

noted, be'kend, be'roemd

noteworthy, opmerkens'waardig

nothing, niets

notice, aandacht; aankondiging; (op)merken
  to give –, de dienst (*or* huur) opzeggen; kennis geven
  to take – of, aandacht schenken aan
noticeable, merkbaar
notification, kennisgeving
notify, ver'wittigen; be'kend maken
notion, i'dee
notorious, be'rucht
notwithstanding, (des)ondanks
nought, niets; nul
nourish, voeden; koesteren
nourishment, voeding, voedsel
novel, ro'man; nieuw
novelist, ro'manschrijver
novelty, nieuwigheid
November, november
novice, nieuweling
now, nu
nowadays, tegen'woordig
nowhere, nergens
noxious, schadelijk
nozzle, tuit
nuclear, kern-, nucleair, atoom-
  – waste, kernafval
nucleus, kern
nude, naakt; naakstudie
nudge, duwtje; zachtjes aanstoten
nugget, (goud)klomp
nuisance: to be a –, lastig zijn
null and void, van nul en gener waarde
nullify, nietig ver'klaren; opheffen
numb, ver'kleumd, ver'doofd; ver'doven
number, ge'tal; aantal; nummer(en); tellen, rekenen
numeral, cijfer; telwoord

numerical, nume'riek
numerous, talrijk
nun, non
nuptial, huwelijks-
nurse, ver'pleegster; kindermeisje; ver'plegen; zogen; ver'zorgen; koesteren
nursery, crèche, kinder'dagverblijf; kinderkamer; kweke'rij
nurture, (op)voeden; koesteren
nut, noot; moer
nutcase, mafkees
nutmeg, nootmus'kaat
nutrition, voeding(s'leer)
nutritional, voedings
nutritive, voedzaam
nymph, nimf

O

oaf, pummel
oak, eik(enhout)(en)
oar, riem
oasis, o'ase
oath, eed; vloek
oatmeal, havermeel, havermout
oats, haver
obedience, ge'hoorzaamheid
obedient, ge'hoorzaam
obese, zwaar'lijvig
obey, ge'hoorzamen
object, voorwerp; doel; be'zwaar hebben (*or* maken) (tegen)
objection, be'zwaar, tegenwerping
objectionable, on'aangenaam, afkeurens'waardig
objective, objec'tief
obligation, ver'plichting
obligatory, ver'plicht
oblige, ver'plichten; ge'noegen

doen

obliging, voor'komend
oblique, schuin; zijdelings
obliterate, uitwissen
oblivion, ver'getelheid
oblivious, onbe'wust
oblong, lang'werpig; rechthoek
obnoxious, aan'stotelijk
oboe, hobo
obscene, on'zedelijk
obscure, ob'scuur; onbe'kend;
  ver'borgen; on'duidelijk;
  on'zichtbaar maken;
  be'lemmeren; ver'doezelen
obscurity, on'duidelijkheid;
  onbe'kendheid
observance, in'achtneming
observant, op'merkzaam
observation, waarneming,
  obser'vatie; opmerking
observatory, sterrenwacht
observe, observeren,
  (op)merken, waarnemen; in
  acht nemen
obsess, (ge'heel) ver'vullen
obsession, ob'sessie
obsolete, ver'ouderd
obstacle, hindernis; be'letsel
obstetrics, ver'loskunde
obstinate, hard'nekkig
obstruct, ver'sperren,
  be'lemmeren
obstruction, hindernis, be'letsel;
  be'lemmering
obtain, ver'krijgen, ver'werven,
  be'halen; gelden
obtainable, ver'krijgbaar;
  haalbaar
obtuse, stomp('zinnig)
obvious, overduidelijk
occasion, ge'legenheid;
  aanleiding (geven tot)
occasionally, nu en dan

occult, oc'cult
occupant, be'woner,
  inzittende
occupation, be'roep, bezigheid;
  be'zetting
occupy, be'zetten, innemen;
  be'wonen
occur, voorkomen; opkomen
  (bij)
occurrence, voorval,
  ge'beurtenis
ocean, oce'aan
o'clock, uur
octagonal, acht'hoekig
octave, oc'taaf
October, oc'tober
octopus, inktvis
odd, on'even; los; over; vreemd
  – job, kar'weitje
  – moment, ver'loren ogenblik
oddity, eigen'aardigheid,
  vreemde snuiter
oddment, res'tant
odd, oneven
odds, kans; conflict; ver'schil
odious, ver'foeilijk
odorous, kwalijk (*or*
  wel')riekend
odour, reuk; lucht(je)
of, van, uit; met; over
off, van (… af); weg; af; vrij
offal, afval
offence, over'treding; aanstoot,
  be'lediging; aanval
offend, be'ledigen, ergeren
offensive, be'ledigend;
  on'aangenaam; aanval(s-)
offer, (aan)bod; (aan)bieden;
  aanvoeren; zich voordoen
offering, gift
offhand, op het eerste ge'zicht
office, kan'toor, ambt, functie;
  zorg

officer, offi'cier; functio'naris

official, offici'eel; ambtenaar, be'ambte

officiate, dienst doen; de dienst leiden

officious, be'moeiziek

offset, (laten) opwegen tegen

offspring, kroost

often, vaak

ogle, (toe)lonken

ogre, boeman

oil, olie, pe'troleum; smeren

oil painting, schilde'rij in olieverf

oily, olieachtig

ointment, zalf

old, oud

old-fashioned, ouder'wets

olive, o'lijf(boom)

omelet, ome'let

omen, voorteken

ominous, onheil'spellend

omission, ver'zuim, weglating

omit, weglaten; nalaten

omnipotent, al'machtig

omniscient, al'wetend

on, op; aan; bij; met; over; verder; aan de gang

once, eens, één keer; eenmaal
  at –, on'middellijk
  – in a while, zo nu en dan
  – or twice, een paar keer

one, één; men

onerous, zwaar

oneself, (zich')zelf, zich

one-sided, een'zijdig

onion, ui

onlooker, toeschouwer

only, slechts, (al'leen) maar; pas, nog; enig
  – too, maar al te

onset, aanval; aanvang

onslaught, woeste aanval

onto, op

onus, last, plicht, schuld

onward(s), voorwaarts

ooze, (door)sijpelen

opal, o'paal

opaque, ondoor'schijnend

open, open('baar); open'hartig; blootgesteld; openlucht; opengaan; opendoen

opening, opening; be'gin; kans; inleidend

opera, opera

operate, ope'reren; werken; be'dienen

operation, ope'ratie; handeling

operator, telefo'nist(e); be'diener

opinion, oordeel, mening
  – poll, o'pinieonderzoek, o'piniepeiling

opinionated, koppig, eigen'wijs

opium, opium

opponent, tegenstander

opportune, gunstig

opportunist, opportu'nist

opportunity, ge'legenheid

oppose, tegenwerken; stellen tegen'over

opposite, tegen'over(gesteld)

opposition, tegenstand; oppo'sitie

oppress, (onder')drukken

oppression, onder(*or* ver')drukking

oppressive, drukkend

optic, ge'zichts-, oog-

optical, ge'zichts-

optimistic, opti'mistisch

option, keus

optional, faculta'tief

opulence, rijkdom

or, of

oracle, o'rakel

oral, mondeling; mond-

orange, sinaasappel; o'ranje

oration, rede
orator, redenaar
oratorio, ora'torium
orb, bol
orbit, baan; kring
orchard, boomgaard
orchestra(l), or'kest(-)
orchid, orchi'dee
ordain, voorschrijven; wijden
ordeal, be'proeving, proef
order, (volg)orde; stand;
  be'vel(en); be'stelling; ordenen;
  be'stellen
  in – that, op'dat
  in – to, om te
  out of –, niet op volgorde; niet
  in orde
orderly, ordelijk; ordon'nans
ordinance, ver'ordening
ordinarily, ge'woonlijk
ordinary, ge'woon
organ, orgel; or'gaan
organic, or'ganisch
organism, orga'nisme
organist, orga'nist
organization, organi'satie
organize, organi'seren
orgy, orgie, uitspatting
Orient, Oosten
oriental, oosters; oosterling
orientate, oriën'teren
orifice, opening
origin, oorsprong; afkomst
original, oor'spronkelijk;
  origi'neel
originate, ont'staan (uit);
  in het leven roepen
ornament, sieraad, ver'siersel
ornamental, sier-
ornate, sierlijk
orphan, wees(-), ouderloos
orphanage, weeshuis
orthodox, ortho'dox;
  ge'bruikelijk
ostensible, ogen'schijnlijk
ostentation, uiterlijk ver'toon
ostentatious, praalziek
ostracize, doodverklaren
ostrich, struisvogel
other, ander; nog
  the – day, onlangs
otherwise, anders
otter, otter
ought to, (eigenlijk) moeten,
  zou (eigenlijk) moeten
  you – to go home, je zou naar
  huis moeten gaan
ounce, (approx.) kwart ons
our(selves), ons(zelf)
ours, de (*or* het) onze, van ons
out, (er')uit; (naar) buiten; weg
  – and –, door en door
  – of, uit; buiten; zonder
outbreak, uitbarsting; oproer
outbuilding, bijgebouw
outburst, uitbarsting
outcast, ver'stoteling
outcome, resul'taat
outcry, luid pro'test
outdoor, openlucht-
outer, buiten-
outfit, uitrusting, uitzet
outgoing, uitgaand, aftredend;
  uitgave
outgrow, groeien uit; ont'groeien
outhouse, bijgebouw, schuurtje
outing, uitstapje
outlandish, vreemd'soortig
outlaw, banneling; vogel'vrij
  ver'klaren
outlay, uitgave(n)
outlet, uitlaat(klep),
  afvoerkanaal; vestiging,
  verkooppunt; markt,
  afzetgebied; con'tactdoos,
  stopcontact

outline, omtrek; schets(en); aftekenen
outlive, over'leven
outlook, (voor')uitzicht; opvatting
outlying, afgelegen
outnumber, (in aantal) over'treffen
out-of-date, ver'ouderd
out-of-the-way, afgelegen; buite'nissig
outpost, buiten(*or* voor)post
output, opbrengst
outrage, aanranding; schande, veront'waarding
outrageous, schan'dalig
outright, in'eens; rond'uit
outset, be'gin
outside, buiten(kant)
outsider, buitenstaander
outskirts, buitenkant
outspoken, open'hartig
outstanding, voor'treffelijk, onbe'taald, onbe'slist
outstrip, achter zich laten; over'treffen
outward, uit-, naar buiten **(to all) – appearances,** uiterlijk
outwardly, uiterlijk
outweigh, zwaarder wegen dan
oval, o'vaal
ovation, o'vatie
oven, oven
over, boven; over('heen); door; meer dan; om **– again,** nog eens
overalls, over'all
overbearing, aan'matigend
overboard, over'boord
overcast, be'trokken
overcharge, te veel vragen
overcoat, overjas
overcome, over'stelpt, be'vangen; over'winnen

overcrowded, over'vol
overdo, te veel doen; over'drijven
overdue, achter'stallig, te laat
overflow, overloop; over'stromen, overlopen
overgrown, over'woekerd
overhang, uitstekende rand; overhangen
overhaul, nakijken en repa'reren; inhalen
overhead, boven (het hoofd); boven'gronds, lucht-
overheads, algemene onkosten
overhear, horen; afluisteren
overjoyed, dolblij
overlap, ten dele be'dekken, ge'deeltelijk samenvallen
overlook, over'zien; over het hoofd zien
overnight, in één nacht; de avond te'voren
overpower, over'weldigen
overrate, over'schatten
overrule, ver'werpen
overrun, over'stromen, over'woekeren
overseas, over'zee(s)
overseer, opzichter
overshadow, over'schaduwen
oversight, ver'gissing, onop'lettendheid; super'visie
oversleep, zich ver'slapen
overstep, over'schrijden
overtake, inhalen
overthrow, ten val brengen
overtime, overwerk
overture, voorstel; ouver'ture
overturn, om'verwerpen, omslaan
overweight, te zwaar, te dik; over(ge)wicht, te zware last
overwhelm, over'stelpen

overwork, zich over'werken
overwrought, over'spannen
owe, schuldig zijn
owing to, dank zij
owl, uil
own, eigen(dom); be'zitten;
   er'kennen
owner, eigenaar
ownership, eigendom(srecht)
ox, os
oxygen, zuurstof
oyster, oester
ozone, ozone; frisse lucht

P

pace, pas, tempo; stappen
pacific, vrede'lievend
pacifist, paci'fist
pacify, tot be'daren brengen
pack, pak(ken); hoop; spel;
   ver'(or in)pakken; proppen
package, pak
packet, pakje
packing, ver'pakking
pact, ver'drag
pad, kussen(tje); blok; opvullen
paddle, pootje baden
padlock, hangslot
pagan, heiden(s)
page, bladzijde
pageant, ver'toning; optocht
pager, pieper, sema'foon
pail, emmer
pain, pijn (doen)
   to take pains moeite doen
painful, pijnlijk
painstaking, nauwge'zet
paint, verf; verven; schilderen
paintbrush, verfkwast, pen'seel
painter, schilder
painting, schilde'rij; schilderkunst
pair, paar

pal, maat
palace, pa'leis
palatable, smakelijk
palate, ge'hemelte; smaak
palatial, vorstelijk
palaver, gewauwel
pale, bleek, licht; paal;
   ver'bleken
Palestinian, Pale'stijns; Pale'stijn
palette, pa'let
paling, om'heining
pallid, bleek
pallor, bleekheid
palm, palm(tak)
   to – off on, aansmeren
palpable, voelbaar
palpitate, snel klóppen; trillen
paltry, nietig
pamper, ver'wennen
pamphlet, pam'flet
pan, pan
panacea, wondermiddel
pancake, pannenkoek
pandemonium, pande'monium
pane, ruit
panel, pa'neel, vak
pang, steek; plotseling ge'voel
panic, pa'niek; het hoofd
   ver'liezen
panic-stricken, ver'lamd van
   schrik
panorama, pano'rama
pansy, vi'ooltje
pant, hijgen; snakken (naar)
pantomime,
   sprookjesvoorstelling;
   panto'mime
pantry, pro'visiekast
pants: (pair of) –, onderbroek
papal, pauselijk
paper, pa'pier(en); krant;
   ver'handeling;
   (e'xamen)opgave; be'hangen

par, gelijkheid
  on a –, ge'lijk
parable, ge'lijkenis, pa'rabel
parachute, para'chute
parade, pa'rade; ap'pel;
  ver'toon; para'deren;
  aantreden; pronken met
paradise, para'dijs
paradox, para'dox
paraffin, pe'troleum
paragraph, a'linea
parallel, paral'lel, even'wijdig;
  eve'naren
paralyse, ver'lammen
paralysis, ver'lamming
paramount, hoogst
paranoid, parano'ïde
paraphernalia, spullen
parasite, para'siet
parasol, para'sol
parcel, pakje, pak'ket
parch, ver'dorren, uitdrogen
parchment, perka'ment
pardon, ver'giffenis; gratie
  (ver'lenen); ver'geven; par'don!
parent, ouder
parentage, afkomst
parental, ouder(lijk)
parenthood, ouderschap
parish, pa'rochie
park, park('eren)
parking fine, par'keerboete
parliament, parle'ment
parliamentary, parlemen'tair
parochial, parochi'aal;
  klein'burgerlijk
parody, pa'rodie
parole, erewoord,
  voor'waardelijke vrijlating
paroxysm, hevige aanval
parrot, pape'gaai
parry, afweren
parsley, peter'selie

parson, dominee
part, deel, ge'deelte; rol; stem;
  scheiden
partake, deel hebben aan
partial, ge'deeltelijk; par'tijdig;
  ge'steld (op)
partially, ten dele
participant, deelnemer
participate, deelnemen (aan)
particle, deeltje, par'tikel
particular, bij'zonder(heid);
  kies'keurig, pre'cies
  that – one, die ene daar; die
  be'paalde
 in particular, in het bij'zonder
particularly, (in het) bij'zonder,
  voor'al
parting, afscheid; scheiding
partisan, aanhanger; par'tijdig
partition, ver'deling;
  tussenschot; vak; ver'delen
partly, ge'deeltelijk, deels
partner, partner
partnership, ven'nootschap
partridge, pa'trijs
part-time job, deeltijdbaan,
  parttimebaan
party, ge'zelschap;
  par'tij(tje)
pass, pas; stand van zaken;
  pas'seren, voor'bijgaan;
  aangeven; slagen; vellen
  (judgement); doorbrengen;
  goedkeuren; ge'beuren; ermee
  doorkunnen
passable, redelijk; be'gaanbaar
passage, (door)gang; pas'sage;
  voor'bijgaan
passenger, passa'gier
passer-by, voor'bijganger
passing, voor'bijgaand;
  over'lijden
 in –, ter'loops

passion, hartstocht(elijke liefde); lijden(sverhaal)
passionate, harts'tochtelijk
passive, pas'sief
passport, paspoort
password, wachtwoord
past, voor'bij; ver'leden; vorig; over
pasta, pasta
paste, kleefpasta(or pap); pas'tei; plakken
pastel, pas'tel(tekening)
pastime, tijdverdrijf
pastoral, herderlijk, herders-, landelijk
pastry, korstdeeg; ge'bakje
pasture, weide; gras
pat, tikje; kluitje; zachtjes kloppen
patch, lap(je); plek(je); oplappen
patent, pa'tent; duidelijk
paternal, vader(lijk)
path, pad; baan
pathetic, aan'doenlijk; zielig
pathology, patholo'gie
pathos, pathos
pathway, pad
patience, ge'duld
patient, ge'duldig; pa'tient
patriarch, patri'arch
patriot, patri'ot
patriotic, vaderlands'lievend, patriottisch
patrol, pa'trouille; patroui'lleren
patron, vaste klant; be'schermheer(or vrouw); be'scherm-
patronize, be'schermen; uit de hoogte be'handelen; klei'neren; klant zijn van, vaak be'zoeken
patronizing, neer'buigend

patter, ge'kletter, ge'trippel; ge'babbel; kletteren, trippelen
pattern, pa'troon; voorbeeld
paunch, buik
pauper, arme
pause, rust, onder'breking; pau'seren, (even) wachten
pave, pla'veien; banen
pavement, trot'toir, rijweg (Am.)
pavilion, pavil'joen
paw, poot; krabben; aanraken
pawn, pi'on; werktuig; pand; ver'panden
pay, loon; (uit)be'talen; schenken (attention); maken (compliments); afleggen (visit); lonen
it does not –, het loont de moeite niet; het heeft geen zin
payment, be'taling; loon
pea, erwt
peace, vrede; rust
peaceable, vrede'lievend, vreedzaam
peaceful, rustig; vreedzaam
peach, perzik
peacock, pauw
peak, piek; klep; hoogtepunt
peanut (butter), pinda(kaas)
pear, peer
pearl, parel
peasant, boer
pebble, kiezelsteen
peculiar(ity), eigen'aardig(heid)
pedagogue, peda'goog
pedal, pe'daal; peddelen
pedant(ic), pe'dant
peddle, venten
pedestal, voetstuk
pedestrian, voetganger; alle'daags
pedigree, stamboom, ras-

pee, plassen, een plas(je) doen; plas, u'rine
peek, kijkje; gluren
peel, schil(len)
peep, gluren
peer, turen; gelijke
peerage, adelstand
peerless, weergaloos
peeved, gepi'keerd
peevish, chag'rijnig
peg, pen, haak, knijper, haring
to – away, ploeteren
pelican, peli'kaan
pelt, vel; be'kogelen; kletteren
pen, pen; kooi
penal, straf-, strafbaar
penalize, straffen
penalty, (geld/ge'vangenis)straf; (geld)boete; ge'volg, nadeel, schade; handicap, achterstand, strafpunt; strafschop
penance, boete(doening)
pencil, potlood
pendant, hanger; luchter
pending, hangend; in afwachting van
pendulum, slinger
penetrate, doodringen, door'boren
penetrating, scherp('zinnig)
penguin, pinguïn
peninsula, schiereiland
penis, penis
penitence, be'rouw
penitent, be'rouwvol; boeteling
penknife, zakmes
penniless, straat'arm
pension, pen'sioen, uitkering
pensioner, gepensio'neerde
pensive, peinzend; somber
penthouse, penthouse, dakappartement
pent-up, opgekropt; opgesloten

people, mensen; volk; fa'milie
pepper, peper; paprika
peppermint, peper'munt
per, per
perceive, waarnemen, be'merken
percent, pro'cent
percentage, percen'tage
perceptible, waar'neembaar, merkbaar
perception, waar'neming(svermogen)
perch, stok(je), zitplaats; baars; gaan zitten
percussion, slag(-)
perennial, overblijvend; altijd durend, eeuwig
perfect, perfect, vol'maakt, vol'slagen; perfectio'neren
perfection, vol'maaktheid, per'fectie
perfectly, vol'maakt, vol'komen
perforate, perfo'reren
perform, doen; opvoeren, ten beste geven, uitvoeren
performance, opvoering, uitvoering; optreden; pres'tatie
perfume, par'fum; geur
perfunctory, noncha'lant, vluchtig
perhaps, mis'schien
peril(ous), ge'vaar(lijk)
perimeter, omtrek; perife'rie
period, peri'ode, uur
periodical, perio'diek; tijdschrift
periodically, van tijd tot tijd
periphery, omtrek; perife'rie
periscope, peri'scoop
perish, omkomen, ver'gaan
perishable, aan be'derf onder'hevig; ver'gankelijk
perjure oneself, meineed plegen
perjury, meineed

perk up, opleven
perky, levendig, opgewekt, geest'driftig; ver'waand
permanent, vast, perma'nent
permeate, (door')dringen, (door')trekken
permissible, ge'oorloofd
permission, ver'lof
permit, ver'gunning; toestaan
perpendicular, loodrecht; loodlijn
perpetrate, be'gaan
perpetual, aan'houdend, eeuwig('durend)
perpetually, con'stant
perpetuate, ver'eeuwigen
perplex, ver'warren; compli'ceren
perplexity, ver'bijstering
persecute, ver'volgen
perseverance, vol'harding
persevere, vol'harden
Persian, Per'zisch; Pers
persist, hard'nekkig doorgaan, volhouden
persistent, hard'nekkig
person, per'soon, mens
personal, per'soonlijk
personality, per'soonlijkheid
personally, per'soonlijk; wat mij be'treft
personification, verper'soonlijking
personnel, perso'neel, staf, werknemers; perso'nele hulpmiddelen, troepen, manschappen; perso'neelsafdeling
perspective, perspec'tief
perspiration, transpi'ratie
perspire, transpi'reren
persuade, over'reden, over'tuigen

persuasion, over'reding(skracht)
persuasive, over'twigend
perturb, veront'rusten
peruse, bestu'deren; doorlezen
pervade, ver'vullen, trekken door
perverse, per'vers; dwars; eigen'zinnig
pervert, per'vers per'soon; ver'storen; ver'draaien
pessimism, pessi'misme
pessimist(ic), pessi'mist(isch)
pest, plaag
pester, plagen; lastig vallen
pet, huisdier, lieveling; lievelings-; ver'troetelen
petal, bloemblad
petite, klein en tenger
petition, ver'zoek(schrift), smeekbede
petrify, ver'lammen
petrol, ben'zine
petty, klein, nietig
petulant, kribbig
pew, kerkbank
pewter, tin(nen)
phantom, spook; schijn; fan'toom
phase, fase; stadium; schijngestalte
pheasant, fa'zant
phenomenal, fenome'naal
phenomenon, ver'schijnsel; wonder
philanthropist, filan'troop
philosopher, filo'soof
philosophic(al), filo'sofisch
philosophy, filoso'fie
phlegm, slijm
phosphorescent, fosfores'cerend
photograph, foto(gra'feren)

photographer, foto'graaf
photography, fotogra'fie
phrase, frase; uitdrukking; uitdrukken
physical, li'chamelijk, lichaams-; na'tuur('kundig)
physician, arts, dokter, inter'nist
physicist, natuur'kundige
physics, na'tuurkunde
physique, lichaamsbouw, fy'siek
pianist, pia'nist
piano, pi'ano
pick, keus; beste; hou'weel; kiezen, selec'teren; plukken; peuteren; uitzoeken
to – up, oprapen; op de kop tikken; oppikken; ophalen
pickaxe, hou'weel
pickpocket, zakkenroller
picnic, picknick(en)
pictorial, in beeld; geïllus'treerd tijdschrift
picture, afbeelding, schilderij, foto; plaatje, iets beeldschoons; toonbeeld; (speel)film; beeld; afbeelden, schilderen, be'schrijven; zich voorstellen, zich inbeelden
go to the pictures, naar de bioscoop gaan
can you – it? kun je het jezelf voorstellen?
picturesque, schilderachtig
pie, pas'tei, taart
piece, stuk(je)
pier, pier
pierce, door'boren; door'zien
piercing, door'dringend, onder'zoekend; scherp, snijdend (wind/cold), stekend (pain), snerpend (sound); piercing

piety, vroomheid
pig, varken
pigeon, duif
pigeonhole, (post)vak(je)
pig-headed, eigen'wijs
pigtail, vlecht
pike, piek; snoek
pile, stapel; hoop; aambei; nop; heipaal; (op)stapelen, ophopen
pilgrim(age), pelgrim(stocht)
pill, pil
pillage, plunderen
pillar, (steun)pi'laar, zuil
pillow, (hoofd)kussen
pillowcase, kussensloop
pilot, loods(en); pi'loot; be'sturen
pimple, puistje
pin, speld(en); pen; vastgekneld houden
pinafore, schortje
pincers, nijptang; schaar
pinch, kneep; snuifje; nood; knijpen, klemmen; gappen
pine, pijnboom; pijnhout; smachten (naar), kwijnen
pineapple, ana'nas
pink, roze; kleine anjer
pinnacle, (berg)spits, torentje; toppunt
pint, (approx) halve liter
pioneer, pio'nier(en)
pious, vroom
pip, pit
pipe, pijp, buis; fluit(en)
piper, doedelzakspeler
piquant, pi'kant
pique, pi'keren; prikkelen
pirate, zeerover(sschip), pi'raat
pistol, pis'tool
piston, zuiger
pit, kuil; mijn, groeve
pitted, vol kuiltjes; pok'dalig

pitch, pek; toonhoogte; graad; pik-; gooien; opslaan; stampen; storten

pitcher, kan

pitchfork, hooivork

piteous, beklagens'waardig

pitfall, val(strik)

pitiable, pitiful, beklagen'swaardig; jammerlijk

pitiless, mee'dogenloos

pittance, schijntje

pity, medelijden (hebben met)
  what a –, wat jammer

pivot, spil; draaien

pizza, pizza

placard, plak'kaat; re'clame maken voor, be'plakken

place, plaats(en); thuisbrengen
  to take –, plaatsvinden

placid, kalm

plague, pest; plaag; plagen; lastig vallen

plain, duidelijk; een'voudig; effen; onaan'trekkelijk; vlakte

plaintiff, aanklager

plait, vlecht(en)

plan, plan, platte'grond; ont'werpen, uitwerken, op touw zetten; van plan zijn

plane, vlak; peil; vliegtuig; schaaf; pla'taan; schaven

planet, pla'neet

plank, plank

plant, plant(en); instal'latie

plantation, plan'tage

planter, planter

plaque, (ge'denk)plaat; tandaanslag; vlek

plasma, plasma

plaster, pleister(en); be'smeren

plastic, plastic; plastisch

plate, bord; plaat; goud en zilver

plateau, pla'teau, hoogvlakte

platform, platform; per'ron (at railway station); podium; bal'kon (in bus/tram); par'tijprogramma

platinum, platina

platoon, pelo'ton

platter, schotel

plausible, geloof'waardig

play, spel(en); to'neelstuk; speling

player, (to'neel)speler

playful, speels, schertsend

playground, speelplaats

playmate, speelmakker

playpen, box

plaything, stuk speelgoed; speelbal

playwright, to'neelschrijver

plea, (dringend) ver'zoek; veront'schuldiging; pleit

plead, aanvoeren; smeken; (be')pleiten

pleasant, prettig, aardig

pleasantry, geestigheid, aardigheid

please, een ple'zier doen, be'hagen; ver'kiezen; alstublieft
  be pleased to ..., met ge'noegen ...

pleasing, aangenaam; in'nemend

pleasure, ge'noegen, ple'zier

pleat, plooi(en)

pledge, ge'lofte; be'loven, ver'binden

plentiful, overvloedig

plenty (of), ruim vol'doende, veel

pliable, pliant, buigzaam; plooibaar

pliers, buigtang

plight, toestand

plod, zwoegen

plop, plons; plonzen

plot, com'plot, in'trige; stukje grond; be'ramen, samenspannen; in kaart brengen

plough, ploeg(en)

pluck, moed; plukken; tokkelen

plucky, flink

plug, stop(contact), prop; (dicht)stoppen

plum, pruim

plumage, ge'vederte

plumb, loodrecht; pre'cies; peilen

plumber, loodgieter

plumbing, loodgieterswerk

plume, pluim

plump, mollig; (neer)ploffen

plunder, buit; plunderen

plunge, sprong; indompelen; (zich) storten

plural, meervoud

plus, plus

ply, han'teren; uitoefenen; over'laden (met); ge'regeld rijden, be'varen

pneumonia, longontsteking

poach, stropen; po'cheren

pocket, zak(-); in de zak steken; (in)slikken

pock-marked, pok'dalig

pod, peul, co'con

poem, ge'dicht

poet(ic), dichter(lijk)

poetry, poëzie, dichtwerk, ge'dichten

poignant, schrijnend; scherp; aan'grijpend

point, punt; zin; wissel; wijzen, richten

– of view, ge'zichtspunt

to – out, aanwijzen; er op wijzen

point-blank, bot'weg, van dichtbij

pointed, puntig; scherp; ad rem

pointer, wijzer; aanwijzing

pointless, zinloos

poise, houding

poised, in evenwicht

poison, ver'gift(igen)

poisonous, giftig

poke, (op)por(ren); steken; slag

poker, pook; poker

poky, benauwd, klein

polar, pool-

pole, paal, stok; pool

police, po'litie

policeman, (po'litie)a'gent

policy, be'leid; polis

polish, was, smeerpoets; glans; wrijven, poetsen; be'schaven, opknappen

Polish, Pools

polite, be'leefd

political, poli'tiek; staats-

politician, po'liticus

politics, poli'tiek, staatkunde

polka, polka

poll, stemming; opiniepeiling; aantal stemmen; stemmen (ver'krijgen)

pollen, stuifmeel

pollinate, be'stuiven

pollute, be'zoedelen, veront'reinigen

polo, polo

pompous, gewichtig; pompeus; hoog'dravend

pond, vijver

ponder, (be')peinzen

ponderous, zwaar'wichtig; zwaar op de hand

pontifical, pauselijk; pontifi'caal
pony, pony
poo (vulg), poep; poepen
poodle, poedel
pool, plas; poel; zwembad; bij el'kaar doen
poor, arm('zalig); slecht
poorly, arm('zalig); niet lekker, minnetjes
pop, knallen; wippen; puilen
pope, paus
poplar, popu'lier
poppy, klaproos
popular, popu'lair; volks-
populate, be'volken
population, be'volking
porcelain, porse'lein(en)
porch, por'tiek
pore, porie; turen
pork, varkensvlees
porn(ography), porno(gra'fie)
porous, po'reus
porridge, (havermout)pap
port, haven; bakboord; port
portable, koffer-, draagbaar
porter, kruier; por'tier
portfolio, porte'feuille, portfolio
portion, deel, portie
portrait, por'tret
portray, (af)schilderen
pose, houding; aanstelle'rij; po'seren; zich voordoen als; stellen
position, po'sitie; houding; stelling
positive, posi'tief; stellig
positively, abso'luut
possess, be'zitten
possession(s), be'zit(tingen)
possessive, hebberig; be'zittelijk
possibility, mogelijkheid
possible, mogelijk

possibly, mis'schien
post, stijl, paal; post; be'trekking; op de post doen; (over)plaatsen; aanplakken
postage, port; post-
postal, post-
postcard, briefkaart
post code, postcode
poster, poster
posterity, nageslacht
posthumous, pos'tuum
postman, postbode
post mortem, lijkschouwing
postpone, uitstellen
posture, houding
post-war, naoorlogs
pot, pot(ten); fuik; bom (duiten); inmaken
potato, aardappel
potent, krachtig
potential, potenti'eel; potenti'aal
potter, pottenbakker; aanrommelen
pottery, aardewerk; pottenbakkerij
pouch, zak, buidel
poultry, pluimvee
pounce, zich storten
pound, (approx) half kilogram, pond; beuken (op); bonzen (op); fijnstampen
pour, gieten, schenken; stromen
pout, pruilen
poverty, armoede
poverty-stricken, arm(oedig)
powder, poeier(en), (be')poeder(en); buskruit
power, macht, kracht; mogendheid
powerful, machtig, krachtig
powerless, machteloos
power station, elektrici'teitscentrale

practicable, uit'voerbaar
practical, praktisch
practically, bijna, in de praktijk
practice, oefening; prak'tijk;
  ge'woonte
practise, (be')oefenen;
  (prak'tijk) uitoefenen
prairie, prairie
praise, lof; prijzen, loven
pram, kinderwagen
prank, streek, grap
prattle, babbelen
prawn, garnaal
pray, bidden
prayer, ge'bed
preach, preken, prediken
preacher, prediker
preamble, inleiding
precarious, hachelijk
precaution,
  voorzorg(smaatregel)
precede, voor('af)gaan
precedence, voorrang,
  priori'teit, het voorgaan
precedent, prece'dent
precinct, ter'rein
precious, kostbaar, dierbaar;
  edel; ge'wild
precipice, hoge rotswand
precipitate, plotseling; overijld,
  onbe'zonnen; neerslag;
  ver'haasten
precipitous, zeer steil
precise, juist, pre'cies
precision, nauw'keurigheid,
  pre'cisie
preclude, uitsluiten
precocious, vroeg(njp)
preconceived, voor'opgezet
precursor, voorloper
predatory, roof-
predecessor, voorganger
predicament, hachelijke po'sitie

predict, voor'spellen
predominant, over'heersend,
  over'wegend
pre-eminence, superiori'teit
pre-eminent, uitblinkend
pre-eminently, bij uitstek
preen, gladstrijken, (zich)
  mooimaken
preface, voorwoord, inleiding;
  van een voorwoord voorzien,
  inleiden; leiden tot, het begin
  zijn van
prefer, de voorkeur geven aan,
  liever willen
preferable, beter (dan)
preferably, bij voorkeur
preference, voorkeur
pregnancy, zwangerschap
pregnant, zwanger; ge'laden
prehistoric, voorhis'torisch
prejudice, voor'oordeel;
  bevoor'oordelen
prejudicial, schadelijk
preliminary, voorbereidend;
  voorronde; inleidende
prelude, voorspel; pre'lude
premature, vroeg'tijdig,
  voor'barig
premeditated, voor'opgezet
premier, eerste minister,
  minister-presi'dent, pre'mier;
  eerste, voor'naamste
premise, vooronderstellling,
  pre'misse; pand, per'ceel
premium, premie
premonition, voorgevoel
preoccupation, af'wezige
  ge'dachten
preoccupy, in be'slag nemen
preparation, (voor)bereiding
preparatory, voorbereidend
prepare, (zich) voorbereiden,
  be'reiden

preposterous, ab'surd
prescribe, voorschrijven
prescription, re'cept;
  voorschrift
presence, aan'wezigheid
present, aan'wezig,
  tegen'woordig; heden;
  ca'deau; schenken;
  presen'teren; ver'tonen;
  opvoeren; voorstellen
  at –, op het ogenblik
presentable, presen'tabel
presentation, schenking;
  veerstelling; presen'tatie,
  uitreiking; opvoering
present-day, heden'daags
presently, straks
preservation, be'houd; con'ditie
preserve, wildpark; ge'bied;
  redden; be'waren,
  goedhouden, conser'veren
preserves, con'serven
preside, presi'deren, de leiding
  hebben
presidency, presi'dentschap
president, presi'dent; voorzitter
press, pers(en); drukken;
  (aan)dringen; pressen
pressure, druk(ken); drang;
  pressie
prestige, pres'tige
presumably, ver'moedelijk
presume, veronder'stellen; zo
  vrij zijn; ge'bruik maken (van)
presumption, veronder'stelling;
  aanmatiging
presumptuous, aan'matigend
pretence, voorwendsel;
  aanstelle'rij
pretend, doen alsof; aanspraak
  maken (op)
pretension, pre'tentie
pretentious, pretenti'eus

pretext, voorwendsel
pretty, lief, knap, mooi; nogal
prevail, heersen; zegevieren
  to – upon, overhalen
prevalent, heersend;
  veel'voorkomend
prevent, voor'komen,
  ver'hinderen
prevention, préventie,
  voor'komen
preventive, prevent'ief
previous, voor'afgaand, vorig
previously, vroeger; van te
  voren, al eerder
pre-war, voor'oorlogs
prey, prooi
price, prijs; prijzen
priceless, on'schatbaar;
  kostelijk
prick, prik; (inf) lul, eikel,
  schoft; prikken, steken;
  (door)steken, prikkelen
prickle, stekel(tje); prikkel
prickly, stekelig; kriebelig
pride, trots, hoogmoed
  to – oneself, prat gaan
priest, priester
prim, stijf, preuts
primarily, in de eerste plaats
primary, pri'mair
prime, eerst; bloei(tijd);
  voorbereiden
primeval, oor'spronkelijk, oer-
primitive, primi'tief
prince, prins, vorst
princely, vorstelijk
princess, prin'ses
principal, voor'naamst; hoofd(-)
principally, voor'namelijk
principle, prin'cipe
print, druk(ken); prent; afdruk;
  afdrukken; be'drukken;
  prenten

print-out, uitdraai, print-out
printer, drukker, printer
prior, voor'afgaand, eerste; prior
priority, voorrang
prism, prisma
prison, ge'vangenis
prisoner, ge'vangene
privacy, vrijheid;
  ge'heimhouding
private, vrij, pri'vé, per'soonlijk;
  particu'lier; ge'heim; sol'daat
privatize, privati'seren
privilege, voorrecht, privi'lege;
  be'voorrechten
prize, prijs; be'kroond;
  waar'deren
probability, waar'schijnlijkheid
probable, waar'schijnlijk,
  ver'moedelijk
probation, proef(tijd)
probe, peilen; doordringen
problem, pro'bleem, vraagstuk
problematic(al), proble'matisch;
  twijfelachtig
procedure, proce'dure,
  me'thode, werkwijze
proceed, doorgaan;
  voortkomen
  he proceeded to tell me, hij
  ver'telde me ver'volgens
proceedings, ge'beurtenissen;
  no'tulen
proceeds, opbrengst
process, pro'ces, procédé;
  be'handelen
procession, stoet, optocht,
  pro'cessie
proclaim, af(*or* ver')kondigen;
  uitroepen tot
procrastinate, talmen
procure, (zich) ver'(*or*
  aan)schaffen
prod, (aan)porren

prodigious, ge'weldig
prodigy, wonder
produce, pro'ducten;
  produ'ceren, opleveren,
  voortbrengen; te voorschijn
  halen; aanvoeren; opvoeren;
  ver'lengen
producer, produ'cent; regis'seur
product, pro'duct,
  voortbrengsel
production, pro'ductie
productive, produ'ctief
profane, pro'faan; ont'heiligen
profess, be'weren, be'tuigen,
  be'lijden
profession, be'roep; be'tuiging,
  be'lijdenis
professional, be'roeps(speler);
  vak'kundig; professio'neel
professor, pro'fessor
proffer, aanbieden
proficiency, be'kwaamheid
profile, pro'fiel
profit, winst; zijn voordeel doen
  (met)
profitable, winst'gevend,
  voor'delig, nuttig
profiteer, woekeraar;
  woekerwinst maken
profound, diep('zinnig *or* gaand)
profuse, over'vloedig,
  over'dadig
program,
  (com'puter)pro'gramma;
  program'meren
programme, program'ma;
  program'meren, een schema
  opstellen voor
progress, voor'uitgang,
  voortgang; loop; vorderingen;
  vorderen, voor'uitgaan,
  vorderingen maken
progressive, progres'sief (per'soon)

prohibition, ver'bod
prohibitive, schrik'wekkend
  hoog
project, plan, onderneming;
  slingeren; projec'teren;
  ont'werpen
projectile, projec'tiel
projection, uitsteeksel;
  pro'jectie
proletariat, proletari'aat
prolific, zeer vruchtbaar
prologue, pro'loog; inleiding
prolong, ver'lengen, rekken
promenade, prome'nade
prominence, be'lang;
  ver'hoging, uitsteeksel
prominent, voor'aanstaand; in
  het oog vallend; prominent
promise, be'lofte; be'loven
promising, veelbe'lovend
promote, be'vorderen
promotion, pro'motie;
  be'vordering
prompt, on'middelijk, stipt;
  nopen (tot); souf'fleren,
  voorzeggen
prone, ge'neigd; languit
  voor'over
pronoun, voornaamwoord
pronounce, uitspreken;
  uitspraak doen
pronunciation, uitspraak
proof, be'wijs; proef; be'stand
propaganda, propa'ganda
propagate, zich voortplanten;
  ver'spreiden, propa'geren
propel, voortdrijven
propeller, propeller
proper, juist; ge'past
properly, op de juiste ma'nier,
  netjes, goed; eigenlijk
property, eigendom, bezit;
  eigenschap

prophecy, voor'spelling
prophet, pro'feet
proportion, (juiste) ver'houding;
  deel; proportio'neren
  proportions, pro'porties
proportional, even'redig
proposal, voorstel; aanzoek
propose, voorstellen; zich
  voornemen; een aanzoek doen
proposition, voorstel; stelling;
  ge'val
propound, opperen
proprietary, pa'tent-, merk-,
  eigendoms-; eigenaars-
proprietor, eigenaar
propriety, goede vorm
propulsion, stuwkracht
prosaic, pro'zaïsch
pros and cons, voor en tegen
proscribe, ver'bieden;
  ver'bannen
prose, proza
prosecute, ver'volgen; uitvoeren
prosecutor, aanklager
prospect, (voor')uitzicht;
  zoeken
prospective, eventu'eel;
  aan'staande
prospector, pros'pector
prosper, ge'dijen
prosperity, voorspoed, welvaart
prosperous, voor'spoedig
prostitute, prostitu'ée
prostitution, prosti'tutie
prostrate, voor'overliggend;
  ver'slagen; neerwerpen
protect, be'schermen
protection, be'scherming
protective, be'schermend
protein, eiwit, proteïne
protest, pro'test('eren)
Protestant, protes'tant(s)
prototype, prototype

protract, ver'lengen, rekken
protracted, langge'rekt
protrude, (voor')uitsteken; zich
opdringen
proud, trots (op); groot
prove, be'wijzen; blijken
proverb, spreekwoord
proverbial, spreek'woordelijk
provide, voor'zien; zorgen
provided (that), mits
providence, (de) voor'zienigheid
province, pro'vincie; ge'bied
provincial, provinci'aal;
pro'vincie-
provision, voor'ziening;
voorwaarde; be'paling;
voorzorg(smaatregel);
voorraad
 provisions, levensmiddelen
provisional, voor'lopig
proviso, voorbehoud
provocation, aanleiding
provocative, provo'cerend
provoke, uitdagen, uitlokken;
tergen
prow, voorsteven
prowess, dapperheid;
vaardigheid
prowl, rondsluipen
proximity, na'bijheid
proxy, volmacht;
gevol'machtigde
prudence, voor'zichtigheid,
be'leid
prudent, be'dachtzaam,
ver'standig
prudish, preuts
prune, pruime'dant;
(be')snoeien
pry, snuffelen; (open)breken
psalm, psalm
pseudo(nym), pseudo('niem)
psychiatrist, psychi'ater

psychic, psychisch, geestelijk;
paranor'maal,
boven'natuurlijk;
paranor'maal be'gaafd
psychological, psycho'logisch
psychology, psycholo'gie
pub, ca'fé, bar, kroeg
puberty, puber'teit
public, open'baar, pu'bliek; volk
in –, in het open'baar
publication, publi'katie
publicity, publici'teit
publish, uitgeven; be'kend
maken
publisher, uitgever
pudding, pudding, toetje
puddle, plas
puerile, kinderachtig
puff, wolkje, stoot; soes; puffen;
opblazen
pugnacious, strijd'lustig
pull, ruk(ken); trek(ken) (aan)
to – up, uit(or op)trekken;
stilhouden
pulley, ka'trol
pullover, slipover
pulp, vruchtvlees; pap
pulpit, preekstoel
pulsate, kloppen; trillen
pulse, pols(slag)
pulverize, ver'brijzelen
pumice stone, puimsteen
pump, pomp(en); uithoren
pun, woordspeling
punch, stomp(en) drevel;
punch; knipppen
Punch and Judy, Jan Klaassen
en Ka'trijn
punctual, punctu'eel, stipt
punctuate, onder'breken
punctuation, inter'punctie
puncture, lekke band, gaatje;
(door)prikken

pungent, scherp, prikkelend
punish, straffen
punishment, straf
puny, nietig
pup, jong(e hond)
pupil, leerling; pu'pil
puppet, mario'net; speelpop
purchase, (aan)koop; houvast;
  (aan)kopen
pure, zuiver, rein; louter
purgatory, vagevuur
purify, zuiveren
purity, zuiverheid, reinheid
purple, paars, purper
purport, strekking; be'weren,
  be'doelen
purpose, doel, be'doeling
purposely, on purpose,
  op'zettelijk
purr, spinnen; snorren
purse, portemon'nee, beurs;
  samentrekken
pursue, (achter')volgen
pursuit, achter'volging; jacht;
  bezigheid
push, duw(en), zetje; dringen
puss(y), poes(je)
put, zetten, leggen; brengen;
  zeggen; doen
  to – down, neerzetten;
  onder'drukken; opschrijven;
  toeschrijven (aan)
  to – off, uitstellen; van zijn
  stuk brengen, afschrikken;
  uitdoen
  to – on, aantrekken
  to – out, uitsteken; uitdoen;
  blussen; lastig vallen
  to – up, ophangen; opsteken;
  (aan)bieden; maken; bouwen;
  ver'hogen; bergen, lo'geren;
  aanpraten
  to – up with, dulden

putty, stopverf
puzzle, (een) raadsel (zijn);
  piekeren
pyjamas, py'jama
pyramid, pira'mide

Q

quack, kwak(en);
  kwakzalver
quadrangle, binnenplein
quadruped, vier'voetig (dier)
quail, kwartel; (te'rug)
  schrikken
quaint, typisch, eigen'aardig
quake, beven
qualification, kwalifi'catie;
  re'strictie
qualified, be'voegd
qualify, ge'schikt maken; de
  be'voegdheid ver'werven;
  kwalifi'ceren
quality, kwali'teit; eigenschap
qualm, onbe'haaglijk ge'voel;
  scru'pule
quandary, lastig par'ket
quantity, (grote) hoe'veelheid;
  grootheid
quarantine, quaran'taine
quarrel, (reden tot) twist, ruzie;
  twisten
quarrelsome, twistziek
quarry, wild, prooi; slachtoffer;
  steengroeve; (uit)graven
quarter, kwart('aal); windstreek;
  wijk; ge'nade; in vieren delen;
  inkwartieren
  – of an hour, kwar'tier
quarters, kwar'tier(en); kringen
quarterly, drie'maandelijks per
  kwar'taal
quartet, kwar'tet
quartz, kwartz

quasi, quasi, zoge'naamd

quaver, trilling; achtste noot; trillen

quay, kaai, kade

queen, koning'in; (in chess) koning'in, dame; (in cards) vrouw, dame; (inf) nicht, ver'wijfde flikker

queer, vreemd, raar, zonderling; ver'dacht, onbe'trouwbaar; onwel, niet lekker; (inf) homoseksu'eel; (inf) homo, flikker

quell, onder'drukken

quench, lessen; blussen

querulous, knorrig, klagend

query, vraag(teken); twijfel; in twijfel trekken; een vraagteken zetten achter

quest: in – of, op zoek naar

question, vraag; kwestie; sprake; twijfel; onder'vragen; be'twijfelen

questionable, twijfelachtig

queue, rij; in de rij staan

quibble, spits'vondigheid; haarkloven

quick, vlug

quicken, levend worden; sneller worden

quicksand, drijfzand

quicksilver, kwik(zilver)

quick-tempered, op'vliegend

quiet, rust(ig), stil

quieten, sussen, be'daren

quilt, gewat'teerde deken; wat'teren, doorstikken

quip, geestigheid; steek

quit, ophouden, stoppen; opgeven; ophouden met, stoppen met; ver'laten, ver'trekken/heengaan van

she has – her job, zij heeft haar baan opgegeven/opgezegd

I've had enough, I –, ik heb er genoeg van, ik stop/kap ermee

to be – of, af zijn van

quite, helemaal; verreweg; vrij; juist, ja

quits, quitte

we're –, we staan quitte

quiver, peilkoker; trillen

quiz, onder'vraging, ver'hoor; test, kort examen; quiz; onder'vragen, uithoren; mondeling exami'neren

quota, quota, aandeel; (maximum) aantal

quotation, aanhaling(s-), ci'taat; no'tering

quote, ci'teren, aanhalen; opgeven (a price); ci'taat, aanhaling; no'tering (on stock exchange, etc.)

R

rabbit, ko'nijn

rabble, ge'spuis

rabid, dol

race, wedloop, wedren; ras; racen; om het hardst lopen; rennen

racecourse, renbaan

racehorse, renpaard

racetrack, renbaan, cir'cuit

racial, raci'aal, ras-, rassen- – **discrimination,** rassendiscriminatie

racing, wedrennen

racist, ra'cistisch; ra'cist

rack, rek; pijnbank; folteren; afpijnigen

racket, racket; herrie; afzette'rij

racketeer, afzetter

radiance, straling

radiant, stralend

radiate, (uit)stralen; straalsgewijs uitlopen

radiator, radi'ator

radical, radi'caal

radio, radio(-)

radioactive, radioac'tief

radish, ra'dijs

radius, straal; cirkel

raffle, ver'loting; ver'loten

raft, vlot

rafter, dakspant

rag, lapje, vod; jool; keet maken, te grazen nemen

rage, woede; rage; tieren

ragged, haveloos

raid, in(or over)val (doen)

rail, stang, spaak; rail; spoor; uitvaren (tegen)

railing(s), hek

railway, spoorweg, spoorbaan

rain, regen(en)

rainbow, regenboog

rainfall, regenval

rainy, regenachtig

raise, oplichten; ver'heffen; ver'hogen; bij'eenbrengen, opbrengen; fokken; ver'wekken; grootbrengen

raisin, ro'zijn

rake, hark(en); losbol; doorzoeken

rally, bij'eenkomst; (zich) ver'zamelen; bijkomen

ram, ram(men)

ramble, zwerftocht; zwerven; zich slingeren; bazelen, afdwalen

ramp, helling, glooiing; oprit, afrit; verkeersdrempel

rampant: to be –, woekeren; hoogtij vieren

rampart, wal; bolwerk

ramshackle, gammel

ranch, (vee)fokke'rij

rancid, ranzig

rancour, wrok

random, luk'raak

  at random, op goed ge'luk

range, ruimte, veld, kring; draagwijdte; baan; keten; for'nuis; vari'ëren; zwerven (over); (zich) opstellen

rank, rij; ge'lid; rang, stand; be'horen (tot)

rankle, iemand dwars zitten

ransack, plunderen

ransom, losgeld

rant, tekeer gaan

rap, tik(ken); duit; gooien

rape, ver'krachting; roof; ver'krachten

rapid, snel

rapids, stroomversnelling

rapt, opgetogen, ver'rukt

rapture, ver'voering

rapturous, opgetogen, ver'rukkelijk

rare, zeldzaam; niet gaar (meat)

rarely, zelden

rarity, zeldzaamheid

rascal, schelm

rash, onbe'zonnen; uitslag

rasp, rasp(en)

raspberry, fram'boos

rat, rat; onderkruiper; overlopen

rate, koers, cijfer, snelheid, prijs; klas; plaatselijke be'lasting; ge'val; schatten; be'rispen

rather, liever, eerder; nog'al; nou en of!

ratify, be'krachtigen

ratio, ver'houding
ration, rant'soen('eren)
rational, ratio'neel, redelijk
rattle, rammelaar, ratel;
ge'kletter; rammelen, ratelen;
van streek brengen
raucous, schor, rauw
ravage, ver'woesten,
ver'nietigen, teisteren;
leegplunderen, leegroven;
ver'woesting(en), ver'nietiging
rave, razen (tegen, op), ijlen,
(als een gek) te'keergaan
(tegen), lyrisch worden (over),
dwepen (met); zich gek
maken; juichende bespreking;
wild feest, dansfeest, rave
raven, raaf
ravenous, uitgehongerd
ravine, ra'vijn
ravishing, be'toverend
raw, rauw; ruw; groen; guur
– materials, grondstoffen
ray, straal; rog (fish)
razor, scheerapparaat(*or* mes)
razor-blade, scheermesje
re-, op'nieuw
reach, be'reik(en); ge'deelte;
(zich) uitstrekken; reiken; er
(bij) komen
react, rea'geren
reaction, re'actie
reactionary, reactio'nair
read, (voor)lezen; zeggen,
aanwijzen; stu'deren; opvatten
readily, ge'makkelijk; gaarne
readiness, ge'reedheid;
bereid'willigheid
reading, lezen, lezing; stand;
interpre'tatie; lec'tuur; lees-
ready, klaar; be'reid('willig);
ge'makkelijk

ready-made, con'fectie,
pasklaar, kant-en-klaar
real, werkelijk, echt
realism, rea'lisme
realist(ic), rea'list(isch)
reality, werkelijkheid
realization, be'sef;
ver'wezenlijking, reali'satie
realize, be'seffen;
ver'wezenlijken; reali'seren;
opbrengen
really, (in) werkelijk(heid)
realm, (konink)rijk
reanimation, reani'matie
reap, maaien; oogsten
reappear, op'nieuw ver'schijnen
rear, achter-; achterhoede,
achterkant
reason, rede(n); (be)rede'neren
(with)in –, redelijk(erwijs)
it stands to –, het spreekt
van'zelf
reasonable, redelijk
reasoning, rede'nering
reassurance, ver'zekering
reassure, ver'zekeren;
ge'ruststellen
rebate, korting; te'ruggave
rebel, re'bel; in opstand komen,
rebel'leren
rebellion, opstand
rebellious, op'standig
rebound, te'rugstoot;
te'rugstuiten
rebuff, koude douche; voor het
hoofd stoten
rebuke, be'risping; be'rispen
recalcitrant, weer'spannig
recant, her'roepen; er van
te'rugkomen
recapitulate, recapitu'leren
recapture, her'overen, op'nieuw
ge'vangennemen; weer oproepen

recede, te'rugwijken,
te'ruglopen
receipt, re'cu, kwi'tantie;
ont'vangst; kwi'teren
receive, ont'vangen
receiver, ont'vanger hoorn
recent, re'cent
recently, on'langs, de
laatste tijd
receptacle, (ver'gaar)bak
reception, ont'vangst; re'ceptie
receptive, ont'vankelijk (voor)
recess, re'ces; nis; schuilhoek
recipe, re'cept
recipient, ont'vanger
reciprocal, weder'kerig;
omgekeerde
reciprocate, be'antwoorden;
heen en weer gaan
recital, voordracht; opsomming;
re'cital
recite, voordragen; opsommen
reckless, roekeloos
reckon, (be')rekenen;
be'schouwen
reclaim, her'winnen,
droogleggen, redden
recline, achter'over liggen
recluse, kluizenaar
recognition, (h)er'kenning;
waar'dering
recognizable, her'kenbaar
recognize, (h)er'kennen
recoil, te'rugloop; te'rugdeinzen;
te'ruglopen
recollect, zich her'inneren
recollection, her'innering
recommend, aanbevelen;
aanraden
recommendation, aanbeveling;
ad'vies
recompense, be'loning;
be'lonen; schadeloosstellen

reconcile, ver'zoenen;
over'eenbrengen
reconciliation, ver'zoening
reconnaissance, ver'kenning(s-)
reconstruct, opbouwen,
reconstru'eren
reconstruction, weder'opbouw;
recon'structie
record, offici'ële ver'melding;
no'titie; (grammo'foon)plaat;
re'cord; repu'tatie;
ongeëve'naard; optekenen;
opnemen, te boek stellen
recount, nieuwe telling;
ver'halen
recover, te'rugkrijgen; inhalen;
her'stellen
recovery, her'stel
recreation, recre'atie,
ont'spanning, hobby
recreational, recrea'tief,
recre'atie-, ont'spannings-
recrimination,
tegenbeschuldiging
recruit, re'kruut, nieuweling;
rekru'teren
rectangle, rechthoek
rectangular, recht'hoekig
rectify, her'stellen
rector, dominee; rector
rectory, pasto'rie
recuperate, her'stellen
recur, te'rugkeren
recurrence, her'haling
recurrent, steeds te'rugkerend
red(den), rood (maken *or*
worden)
reddish, roodachtig
redeem, aflossen; ver'vullen;
ver'lossen; ver'zachten
red-handed, op heter daad
red-hot, rood'gloeiend
redouble, ver'dubbelen

redoubtable, ge'ducht
redress, ver'goeding; weer goedmaken
reduce, ver'minderen; ver'lagen
reduction, afname, ver'mindering; korting; re'ductie
redundant, over'bodig
reed, riet
reek, stinken
reel, klos(je); duizelen, wankelen
refer, ver'wijzen; zinspelen (op); be'trekking hebben (op); raadplegen
referee, scheidsrechter
reference, ver'wijzing; be'trekking; toespeling; ge'tuigschrift; hand-
refine, raffi'neren
refined, geraffi'neerd; be'schaafd
refinery, raffinade'rij
reflect, te'rugkaatsen; weer'spiegelen; weergeven; nadenken
reflection, re'flectie, weer'spiegeling, weer'kaatsing; over'denking, over'weging
  on –, bij nader inzien
reflector, re'flector
reflex, re'flex(-)
reform, ver'betering; ver'beteren; (zich) beteren
reformation, her'vorming; Refor'matie
refractory, weer'barstig
refrain, re'frein; zich ont'houden (van)
refresh, ver'kwikken; opfrissen
refreshing, ver'frissend; op'wekkend
refreshment, ver'frissing, restau'ratie; con'sumptie

refrigerator, koelkast
refuge, toevlucht(soord)
refugee, vluchteling
refund, te'rugbetaling; te'rugbetalen
refusal, weigering
refuse, vuilnis; weigeren
refute, weer'leggen
regain, her'winnen; weer be'reiken
regal, koninklijk
regard, aandacht; achting; be'schouwen; in acht nemen; be'treffen
regards, groeten
regardless of, ongeacht
regent, re'gent('es)
regime, re'gime
regiment, regi'ment
region, streek, ge'west, ge'bied
regional, ge'westelijk
register, re'gister; registeren; inschrijven; aangeven, te kennen geven; (laten) aantekenen
registration, regis'tratie
regret, spijt; be'treuren
regretfully, met spijt
regrettable, betreurens'waardig
regular, ge'regeld, regel'matig, vast; echt; be'roeps(sol'daat)
regularity, regelmaat
regulate, regelen
regulation, voorschrift, be'paling; regeling
rehabilitation, rehabili'tatie
rehearsal, repe'titie
rehearse, repe'teren, instuderen
reign, re'gering; be'wind
reimburse, ver'goeden
rein, teugel; inhouden; be'teugelen
reindeer, rendier(en)

reinforce, ver'sterken
reinforcement, ver'sterking
reinstate, her'stellen
reiterate, her'halen
reject, afgekeurd voorwerp;
  afkeuren, van de hand wijzen
rejoice, ver'heugd zijn
rejoin, zich weer voegen bij
rejoinder, re'pliek
rejuvenate, ver'jongen
relapse, instorting, te'rugval;
  weer instorten, weer ver'vallen
relate, ver'halen; in ver'band
  brengen (met)
related, ver'want
relation, be'trekking, re'latie,
  ver'houding; fa'milielid
relationship, ver'wantschap;
  ver'houding
relative, fa'milielid; relatief,
  be'trekkelijk; respec'tief
relax, (zich) ont'spannen,
  re'laxen; ver'slappen,
  ver'minderen, ont'dooien
relaxation, ont'spanning;
  ver'slapping
release, vrijlating; be'vrijding;
  vrij(*or* los)laten; bevrijden;
  vrijgeven
relegate, te'rugzetten;
  ver'bannen
relent, zich laten ver'murwen
relentless, mee'dogenloos
relevant, van toepassing (op),
  toe'passelijk
reliable, be'trouwbaar
reliance, ver'trouwen
relic, reli'kwie; overblijfsel
relief, ver'lichting; opluchting;
  hulp, aflossing(sploeg); reli'ëf;
  extra
relieve, ver'lichten; ont'lasten;
  ont'zetten; aflossen; afwisselen

religion, godsdienst, re'ligie
religious, godsdienst-,
  gods'dienstig, religi'eus;
  klooster-; plichtsgetrouw
relinquish, opgeven; afstand
  doen van
relish, smaak; pi'kante
  lekker'nij; ge;nieten van
reluctance, tegenzin
reluctant, on'willig
rely, ver'trouwen (op)
remain, (over)blijven
remains, overblijfselen
remainder, rest
remark, opmerking;
  opmerken
remarkable, merk'waardig;
  op'merkelijk
remedy, (hulp)middel;
  ver'helpen
remember, zich her'inneren;
  ont'houden, denken om; de
  groeten doen van
remembrance, nagedachtenis
remind, her'inneren (aan)
reminder, (vriendelijke)
  aanmaning
reminiscent: to be – of,
  her'inneren aan
remiss, na'latig
remit, overmaken;
  kwijtschelden
remnant, res'tant
remonstrate, protes'teren
remorse, wroeging
remorseless, onbarm'hartig
remote, afgelegen; ver; ge'ring
remotely, in de verte, enigs'zins
removal, ver'wijderen;
  ver'huizing
remove, ver'wijderen, afnemen,
  uittrekken; afzetten
remuneration, ver'goeding

remunerative, winst'gevend

Renaissance, Renais'sance

rend, (ver')scheuren

render, geven; be'tuigen; maken; ver'tolken; klaren

renegade, af'vallig(e)

renew, ver(or her)'nieuwen; ver'lengen

renounce, afstand doen van; ver'stoten

renovate, ver'nieuwen, opknappen, reno'veren

renown, ver'maardheid, roem

renowned, ver'maard

rent, huur, pacht; scheur; huren, pachten

rental, huur

renunciation, afstand doen; ver'werping, ver'loochening

reopen, her'openen; her'vatten

reorganize, reorgani'seren

repair, repar'atie; con'ditie; her'stellen

reparation, schadeloosstelling

repartee, puntigheid, ge'vatheid

repatriation, repatri'ëring

repay, te'rugbetalen

repeal, afschaffing; her'roepen, afschaffen

repeat, her'haling; her'halen; nazeggen, navertellen; opzeggen

repeated(ly), her'haald(elijk)

repel, te'rug(or af)slaan; afstoten

repellent, af'stotend

repent, be'rouw hebben

repentance, be'rouw

repentant, be'rouwvol

repercussion, re'actie, te'rugslag

repertoire, reper'toire

repetition, her'haling

replace, ver'vangen, ver'nieuwen; te'rugzetten

replacement, ver'vanging; nieuwe

replenish, aan(or bij)vullen

replica, ko'pie

reply, antwoorden

report, ver'slag (doen), rap'port, be'richt; rappor'teren; (zich) melden

reporter, ver'slaggever

repose, rust(en)

repository, opslagplaats; schatkamer

represent, voorstellen; vertegen'woordigen

representation, voorstelling; vertegen'woordiging

representative, vertegen'woordiger; representa'tief; typisch

repress, onder'drukken

reprieve, uitstel, gratie

reprimand, be'risping; be'rispen

reprint, herdruk; her'drukken

reprisal, repre'saille

reproach, ver'wijt(en); schande

reprobate, onverlaat

reproduce, weergeven; (zich) voortplanten, vermenig'vuldigen

reprove, be'rispen

reptile, rep'tiel

republic, repu'bliek

republican, republi'kein(s)

repudiate, ver'werpen; niet er'kennen; ver'stoten

repugnant, weerzin'wekkend

repulse, afslaan; afwijzen

repulsive, weerzin'wekkend

reputable, respec'tabel

reputation, repu'tatie; (goede) naam

repute, aanzien; houden voor

request, ver'zoek(en), aanvraag; vragen om

require, nodig hebben; ver'langen

requirement, be'hoefte, ver'eiste; eis

requisite, ver'eist(e); be'hoefte

requisition, vordering; vorderen

requite, ver'gelden

rescind, intrekken

rescue, redding; redden
   to come to the –, te hulp komen

research, weten'schappelijk onderzoek

resemblance, ge'lijkenis; over'eenkomst

resemble, (ge)'lijken (op)

resent, kwalijk nemen

resentful, ge'belgd, boos

resentment, wrevel

reservation, middenberm, middenstrook; reser'vaat; reser'vering, plaatsbespreking; gereser'veerde plaats; re'serve, voorbehoud, be'denking

reserve, re'serve; reser'vaat; gereser'veerdheid; be'waren, reser'veren

reserved, gereser'veerd; te'rughoudend

reservoir, reser'voir

reside, woon'achtig zijn

residence, woonplaats, woning; ver'blijf

resident, inwoner; gast; resi'dent; inwonend

residential, woon-

residue, overschot; resi'du

resign, aftreden; neerleggen
   to – oneself to, be'rusten in

resignation, ont'slag; be'rusting

resilience, veerkracht

resin, hars

resist, zich ver'zetten, weerstand bieden; zich weer'houden (van); weer'staan

resistance, ver'zet; weerstand(svermogen)

resolute, vastbe'raden

resolution, be'sluit, voornemen; voorstel; vastbe'radenheid

resolve, be'sluit(en); vastbe'radenheid; (zich) oplossen

resonance, reso'nantie

resonant, reso'nerend

resort, (va'kantie)oord; redmiddel; zijn toevlucht nemen (tot)

resound, weer'galmen; weer'kaatsen

resource, (red)middel, rijkdom, (hulp)bron

resourceful, vindingrijk

respect, eerbied, res'pect; opzicht; be'trekking; respec'teren, eer'biedigen

respectable, fat'soenlijk; respec'tabel

respectful, eer'biedig

respecting, aan'gaande

respective, respec'tief

respectively, respec'tievelijk

respiration, ademhaling

respite, ver'ademing; uitstel

resplendent, glansrijk, schitterend

respond, rea'geren (op); be'antwoorden

response, antwoord, weerklank; tegenzang

responsibility, verant'woordelijkheid

responsible 374

responsible, verant'woordelijk
responsive, ont'vankelijk (voor)
rest, rust (geven); steun; rest;
(uit)rusten, liggen; leunen
(met); be'rusten
restaurant, restau'rant
restful, rustig, kal'merend
restitution, resti'tutie,
ver'goeding
restive, on'rustig
restless, onge'durig, on'rustig,
rusteloos
restoration, restau'ratie; her'stel,
te'ruggave
restore, restau'reren; her'stellen,
te'ruggeven, terug'zetten
restrain, be'dwingen, in
be'dwang houden
restrict, be'perken
restriction, be'perking;
voorbehoud
resuscitate, reani'meren,
bijbrengen
result, resul'taat, uitslag,
ge'volg; uitkomst; uitlopen
(op); komen
resume, her'vatten
resumption, her'vatting
resurrection, opstanding
retail, klein(handel), de'tail
(handel) de'tailhandebar
retailer, detail'list, leveran'cier
retain, (vast *or* ont')houden
retaliate, re'vanche nemen
retaliation, wraak
retard, achterlijke; tegen(*or*
op)houden
reticent, terug'houdend
retina, retina
retinue, ge'volg
retire, met pen'sioen gaan,
aftreden; naar bed gaan; (zich)
te'rugtrekken

retired, gepensio'neerd;
afgelegen
retirement, ont'slag;
pensio'nering; afzondering
retiring, te'ruggetrokken
retort, vinnig (*or* ge'wiekst)
antwoord(en); re'tort
retrace, te'rugkeren op
retract, her'roepen
retreat, te'rug(*or* af)tocht; a'siel;
zich te'rugtrekken
retribution, ver'gelding
retrieve, te'rugvinden; her'stellen
retrospect: in –, achter'af
be'schouwd
return, te'rugkomst, te'rugkeer;
te'rugbrengen(*or* geven *or*
zenden); opbrengst; rap'port;
re'tour-; te'ruggaan(*or* keren
or komen)
by –, per omgaande
in –, in ruil
many happy returns, nog vele
jaren!
reunion, her'eniging; reü'nie
reunite, (zich) her'enigen
reveal, ont'hullen, open'baren;
aan het licht brengen; kenbaar
maken
revel, zich ver'lustigen;
feestvieren
revelation, open'baring
revenge, wraak(zucht)
**to revenge oneself, to be
revenged,** zich wreken (op)
revenue, (rijks)inkomsten
reverberate, weer'galmen
reverberation, nagalm
revere, (ver')eren
reverence, eerbied;
buiging
reverent, eer'biedig
reverie, mijmering

reverse, omgekeerd(e);
tegendeel; keerzijde; tegenslag,
nederlaag; omkeren;
her'roepen; achter'uitrijden
revert, weer te'rugkeren;
ver'vallen (in)
review, re'visie; te'rugblik;
re'censie; op'nieuw in
ogenschouw nemen; te'rugzien
op; her'zien; recen'seren
revile, (be')schimpen
revise, nazien; her'zien
revision, repe'teren; her'ziening
revival, opleving;
weder'opvoering
revive, (doen) her'leven,
bijkomen; op'nieuw
invoeren/ingevoerd worden
revoke, her'roepen; niet
be'kennen
revolt, opstand; in opstand
komen; doen walgen
revolting, walgelijk
revolution, revo'lutie;
omwenteling
revolutionary, revolutio'nair
revolutionize, een ommekeer
te'weegbrengen
revolve, (om)wentelen
revolver, re'volver
revulsion, ommekeer; walging
reward, be'loning; be'lonen
rhapsody, rapso'die
rhetoric, re'torica; reto'riek
rhetorical, re'torisch
rheumatic, reu'matisch
rheumatism, reuma'tiek
rhinoceros, neushoorn
rhubarb, ra'barber
rhyme, rijm(pje); rijmen
rhythm, ritme
rhythmic, ritmisch

rib, rib(stuk); ba'lein; nerf
ribbon, lint; flard
rice, rijst
rich, rijk; machtig, extra fijn;
warm
riches, rijkdom(men)
richly, rijkelijk
rickety, wankel
rid, af; afhelpen
  to get – of, kwijt raken,
ver'drijven
riddle, raadsel; grove zeef;
door'zeven
ride, rit(je), tocht(je);
(paard)rijden
rider, ruiter, be'rijder
ridge, kam; nok; rug
ridicule, spot; be'spotten
ridiculous, be'lachelijk
rife, wijdver'breid
riffraff, uitschot
rifle, ge'weer; plunderen
rift, scheur, kloof
right, juist; goed; in orde; vlak,
helemaal; pre'cies; recht;
rechterzijde; rechtzetten
  to be –, ge'lijk hebben
  on the –, rechts
  to the –, aan de rechterkant;
rechts('af)
  – away, on'middellijk
righteous, recht'schapen;
(ge)recht'vaardig(d)
rightful, recht'matig
right-hand, rechter-
rightly, te'recht; goed
rigid, vast, stijf; star
rigmarole, ge'klets
rigorous, zeer streng
rigour, strengheid
rim, rand, velg
rime, rijp
rind, korst, zwoerd, schil

ring, ring; piste; kliek;
tele'foontje; luiden; bellen;
weer'galmen
rink, baan
rinse, (om)spoelen
riot, oproer (maken)
riotous, op'roerig; los'bandig
rip, scheur(en)
ripe, rijp; be'legen
ripen, rijp worden (or maken)
ripple, golfje; lichte golfslag;
kabbelen
rise, stijgen; stijging; opkomst;
opslag; toenemen; opstaan;
opstijgen; om'hooglopen;
stijgen; opkomen
  to give – to, ver'oorzaken
risk, ge'vaar, risico; wagen,
ris'keren
risky, ris'kant
rite, rite
ritual, ritu'eel
rival, ri'vaal, mededinger;
mededingend; concur'reren
met; wedijveren met
rivalry, rivali'teit wedijver;
concur'rentie
river, ri'vier
riverside, oever
rivet, klinknagel; klinken
rivulet, beekje
road, weg, straat
roadside, (aan de) kant van de
weg, berm
roadway, rijweg
roam, dwalen
roar, ge'brul, ge'raas; brullen,
bulderen; ronken
roast, ge'braden; braden
rob, (be')roven
robber(y), rover('ij)
robe, toga, mantel
robin, roodborstje

robust, fors
rock, rots, klip; schommelen;
wiegen; schudden
rocket, ra'ket, vuurpijl
rocky, rotsachtig; wankel
rod, roe(de)
rodent, knaagdier
rogue, schelm
roguish, schalks
role, rol
roll, rol(len); roffel(en); lijst;
broodje; slingeren
roller, rol, wals; zware golf
rollerblade, skeeleren
Roman, Ro'mein(s);
rooms(katho'liek)
romance, liefdesgeschiedenis;
ro'mance; fanta'seren
romantic, roman'tisch;
ro'manticus
romp, stoeipartij; stoeien
roof, dak; ge'welf; ver'hemelte
rook, roek
room, kamer; ruimte; aanleiding
roomy, ruim
root, wortel (schieten); oorzaak;
wortelen; omwroeten
  to – up (or out), uitroeien
rooted, vastgegroeid;
ingeworteld
rope, touw, koord
rosary, rozenkrans
rose, roos
rosette, ro'zet
rosy, roze, blozend; roos'kleurig
rot, ver'rotting; be'derf; larie;
(doen) ver'rotten
rotate, ro'teren, (doen) draaien
rotation, ro'tatie,
(om)wenteling; afwisseling
  in –, om beurten
rotten, (ver')rot; be'roerd;
ge'meen

rotund, kort en dik
rouge, rouge
rough, ruw, on'effen; ruig; hard
roughly, onge'veer
round, rond('om); om(-); ronde;
reeks; omgaan
  to – off, afronden; afmaken,
vervol'maken
roundabout, ro'tonde,
ver'keersplein; draaimolen;
indi'rect, om'slachtig
rouse, wakker maken;
prikkelen
rout, wilde vlucht; op de vlucht
drijven; snuffelen; opdiepen
route, route
routine, rou'tine; ge'bruikelijk
rove, zwerven
row, rij; herrie, rel, ruzie; roeien
rowdy, la'waaierig
royal, koninklijk; vorstelijk
royalty, leden van het koninklijk
huis; iemand van koninklijken
bloede; royalty, aandeel in de
opbrengst; koningschap
rub, wrijven; schuren
  to – out, uitgummen
rubber, rubber; robber; gum
rubbish, afval, vuilnis; rommel;
klets
rubble, puin
ruby, ro'bijn(rood)
rudder, roer(blad)
ruddy, blozend
rude, onbe'leefd; grof
rudiment(ary), rudi'ment('air)
ruff, (plooi)kraag
ruffian, woesteling
ruffle, in de war brengen,
rimpelen; ver'storen
rug, ta'pijt, vloerkleed
rugged, fors en hoekig; stoer

ruin, ru'ïne; ondergang;
be'derven; ruï'neren
ruinous, ver'derfelijk; ruïneus
rule, regel; heerschap'pij;
be'slissen; be'heren, re'geren;
lini'ëren
  as a –, ge'woonlijk
ruler, heerser, re'geerder; lini'aal
ruling, be'slissing; re'gerend;
heersend
rum, rum; raar
Rumania, Roe'menië
Rumanian, Roe'meens
rumble, ge'rommel; rommelen
ruminate, her'kauwen;
be'peinzen
rummage, snuffelen
rumour, ge'rucht
rumple, kreuken
rump steak, biefstuk
run, wedloop; reis; ritje; run;
peri'ode; (hard)lopen, rennen;
kruipen; raken; doorlopen;
laten (vol)lopen; drijven
  in the long –, op de lange duur
  to – down, afnemen; opsporen;
over'rijden; uitgeput raken;
afkammen
  to – into, tegenkomen;
oprijden (*or* lopen) tegen
  to – out, aflopen; opraken
  to – out of, door … heen raken
  to – over, over'rijden;
overlopen
  to – through, door'steken;
doorlezen
runaway, op hol ge'slagen
rung, sport
runner, hardloper; bode; loper
running, door'lopend; achter
el'kaar
runway, baan; startbaan/
landingsbaan

rupture, breuk
rural, landelijk, platte'lands-
rush, drukte, haast; toeloop;
  bies; rennen, vliegen; storten;
  zich haasten
Russia, Rusland
rust, roest; (ver')roesten
rustic, boers; rus'tiek; lande'lijk
rustle, ge'ritsel; (doen) ritselen
rusty, roestig
rut, wagenspoor; sleur
ruthless, mee'dogenloos
rye, rogge

S

sabotage, sabo'tage
sabre, sabel
sack, zak; plundering; ontslaan;
  plunderen
sacrament, sacra'ment
sacred, heilig; ge'wijd
sacrifice, offer(ande),
  opoffering; (op)offeren
sacrilege, heiligschennis
sad, be'droefd; droevig
saddle, zadel(en); opschepen
sadness, be'droefdheid
safe, veilig; zeker; brandkast
safeguard, waarborg(en)
safety, veiligheid
safety belt, veiligheidsgordel,
  veiligheidsriem
safety pin, veiligheidsspeld
sag, doorbuigen; (af *or*
  door)zakken
saga, sage
sagacious, schrander
sage, wijze; salie
sail, zeil(en); ver'trekken, varen
sailor, ma'troos, zeeman
saint, heilig(e); sint

sake: for the – of; ter wille van;
  om ... te
salad, sla
salary, sa'laris
sale, (uit)verkoop, ver'koping
salesman, be'diende;
  handelsreiziger
salient, op'vallend; treffend
saliva, speeksel
sallow, ziekelijk (geel)
salmon, zalm
saloon, sa'lon; bar; zaal
salt, zout; zouten
salutary, heilzaam
salutation, groet
salute, sa'luut; salu'eren
salvage, berging; bergloon;
  afval; bergen; redden
salvation, ver'lossing; zaligheid
salve, zalf; sussen; redden
salvo, salvo
same, zelfde
  all the –, deson'danks; allemaal
  het'zelfde (*or* eender)
sample, monster; staal(tje);
  voorproefje; keuren
sanatorium, sana'torium;
  ziekenzaal
sanctimonious, schijn'heilig
sanction, sanctie; sanctio'neren
sanctity, heiligheid
sanctuary, sanctu'arium;
  reser'vaat; a'siel
sand, zand
sands, strand
sandal, san'daal
sandpaper, schuurpapier;
  schuren
sandpit, zandgroeve; zandbak
sandwich, sandwich, dubbele
  boterham; klemmen,
  vastzetten, plaatsen
sandy, zandig, zand-

sane, ge'zond van geest, ver'standig
sanguine, opgewekt; blozend
sanitary, ge'zondheids-
sanitation, sani'tair
sanity, ge'zond ver'stand
sap, sap; uitputten
sapling, jonge boom
sapphire, saf'fier(blauw)
sarcasm, sar'casme
sarcastic, sar'castisch
sardine, sar'dine
sardonic, smalend
sash, sjerp; schuifraamkozijn
satchel, schooltas
satellite, satel'liet
satiate, (over)ver'zadigen
satin, sa'tijn(en)
satire, sa'tire
satiric(al), sa'tirisch
satirize, hekelen
satisfaction, vol'doening; ge'noegdoening
satisfactorily, naar ge'noegen
satisfactory, be'vredigend
satisfy, vol'doen aan; be'vredigen, te'vreden stellen
  to be satisfied with, te'vreden zijn over (*or* met)
saturate, ver'zadigen; door'trekken; door'weken
satyr, sater
sauce, saus; brutali'teit
saucepan, (steel)pan
saucer, scholteltje
saucy, bru'taal; vlot
saunter, slenteren
sausage, worst(je)
savage, wild(e), woest
save, redden; sparen; voor'komen
savings, spaarpenningen

saviour, redder, Heiland
savour, smaak; smaken (naar); ge'nieten van
savoury, smakelijk; pi'kant
saw, zaag; zagen
sawdust, zaagsel
saxophone, saxo'foon
say, zeggenschap; (op)zeggen; luiden
  that is to –, dat wil zeggen
  it says ... er staat ...
saying, ge'zegde
scaffold, scha'vot; steiger
scaffolding, stel'lage, steiger
scald, met kokend water be'gieten, met stoom branden
scale, schub; schilfer; ketelsteen; schaal; graadverdeling; (toon)ladder; be'klimmen
scales, weegschaal
scallop, schelp; schulp
scalp, scalp('eren)
scaly, ge'schubd; schilferig
scan, afzoeken; een vluchtige blik werpen in (*or* op); scannen; (zich laten) scan'deren
scandal, schan'daal, schande; lasterpraat
scandalize, aanstoot geven
scandalous, schandelijk; lasterlijk
Scandinavian, Scandi'navisch; Scandi'naviër
scant, schraal; karig (zijn met)
scanty, spaarzaam, onvol'doende, dun
scapegoat, zondebok
scar, litteken; rotswand
scarce, schaars
scarcely, nauwelijks
scarcity, schaarste

scare, schrik('barend be'richt);
bang maken
scarecrow, vogelverschrikker
scarf, sjaal; das
scarlet, schar'laken
scathing, bijtend
scatter, (zich) ver'strooien;
uit'eendrijven
scavenger, opruimer; aasdier;
scharrelaar
scene, tafe'reel; scène
scenery, décor; landschap,
na'tuur(schoon)
scenic, na'tuur-; toneel-
scent, geur, o'deur; reuk(zin);
spoor; ruiken; snuffelen
sceptic, scepticus
sceptical, sceptisch
sceptre, scepter
schedule, ta'bel; schema
scheme, plan; schema;
intri'geren
schism, scheuring
scholar, leerling; ge'leerde
scholarly, ge'leerd,
weten'schappelijk
scholarship, (studie)beurs;
wetenschap; ge'leerdheid
school, school
schooling, schoolopleiding
schoolmaster, leraar
schoolroom, schoollokaal
schoolteacher, onder'wijzer('es)
schooner, schoener
science, (na'tuur-)wetenschap
scientific, weten'schappelijk
scientist, ge'leerde
scintillate, fonkelen
scissors, schaar
scoff at, spotten met
scold, een uitbrander geven
scoop, schoep, schep(pen);
pri'meur

scooter, autoped
scope, be'stek; vrij spel
scorch, schroeien
score, score, stand, aantal
punten; twintig(tal); partituur;
maken, be'halen; tellen;
krassen
scorn, hoon; ver'smaden, het
be'neden zich achten
scornful, minachtend
scorpion, schorpi'oen
Scot(ch), Schot(s)
scoundrel, schurk
scour, schuren; afzoeken
scourge, gesel(en); teisteren
scout, ver'kenner; padvinder;
op zoek gaan
scowl, dreigend kijken
scraggy, mager
scramble, ge'jakker; jachten;
klauteren; zich ver'dringen
scrambled egg, roerei
scrap, stukje; oud;
afdanken
scrapbook, plakboek
scrape, knel; schrappen;
schuren, krabben; schrapen
scratch, kras(sen),
schram(men); krabben
scrawl, ge'krabbel; krabbelen
scream, gil(len)
screech, ge'krijs; krijsen
screen, scherm; koorhek;
be'schermen, mas'keren
screw, schroef; schroeven
screwdriver, schroevedraaier
scribble, ge'krabbel; krabbelen
scribe, schrijver, schriftgeleerde
script, schrift; tekst
scripture, schrift
scroll, rol; krul
scrounge, (in)pikken; klaplopen
scrub, schrobben

scruple, scru'pule,
ge'wetensbezwaar
scrupulous, angst'vallig;
nauwge'zet
scrutinize, nauw'keurig
onder'zoeken
scrutiny, kritisch onderzoek
scuffle, handgemeen
scullery, bijkeuken
sculptor, beeldhouwer
sculpture, beeldhouwkunst(or
werk); beeldhouwen
scum, schuim; uitschot,
schorem, afval
scurvy, scheurbuik; ge'meen
scuttle, bak; luik(gat); snellen
scythe, zeis; maaien
sea, zee
seafaring, zeevarend
seal, zeehond; zegel(en); ver(or
be)'zegelen, sluiten
sea level, zeespiegel
sealing-wax, zegellak
seam, naad; laag
seaman, zeeman, ma'troos
sear, ver'schroeien
search, zoeken; foui'lleren
in – of, op zoek naar
searching, onder'zoekend,
diep'gaand
searchlight, zoeklicht
seashore, kust
seaside, kust
season, sei'zoen, tijd; kruiden;
drogen
seasonal, sei'zoen-
seat, (zit)plaats; bank; zetel
seaweed, zeewier
secluded, afgezonderd
seclusion, afzondering
second, tweede; se'conde;
steunen
secondary, secun'dair; middelbaar

second-hand, tweede'hands; uit
de tweede hand
secondly, ten tweede
second-rate, tweede'rangs
secrecy, ge'heimhouding
secret, ge'heim; heimelijk;
ge'sloten
secretary, secre'taris,
secreta'resse
secrete, afscheiden; ver'bergen,
ver'duisteren
secretive, ge'sloten
secretly, in het ge'heim
sect, sekte
section, (onder)deel, afdeling;
sectie; doorsnee; para'graaf;
tra'ject
sector, sector
secular, secu'lier, wereldlijk
secure, veilig; ver'zekerd; vast-
(maken); zich ver'zekeren van
security, veiligheid;
veiligheidsmaatregel(en),
veiligheidsvoorziening,
ver'zekering; be'veiliging,
(openbare) veiligheid;
obli'gatie, ef'fect, aandeel;
(waar)borg, onderpand
tight –, strenge
veiligheidsmaatregelen
– check, veiligheidscontrole
– council, Veiligheidsraad
sedate, be'zadigd, waardig
sedative, pijnstillend (or
kal'merend) (middel)
sedentary, zittend
sediment, be'zinksel
seduce, ver'leiden
see, zien, kijken (naar); zien,
begrijpen, inzien; toezien (op),
opletten, ervoor zorgen,
zorgen voor; nadenken,
be'kijken, zien; zich

see (*continued*)
voorstellen; tegenkomen,
ont'moeten; ont'vangen,
spreken; be'zoeken, opzoeken,
langs gaan bij; raadplegen;
bege'leiden, (weg)brengen
we shall –, we zien wel/wie
weet
as far as I can –, volgens mij
I am seeing Joan next week,
ik heb volgende week met
Joan afgesproken
have you seen a doctor yet?
ben je al bij een dokter
geweest?
– someone out, iemand uitlaten
seed, zaad
seeing that, aange'zien
seek, zoeken; trachten
seem, (toe)schijnen
seemingly, ogen'schijnlijk
seemly, be'tamelijk
seep, sijpelen
seesaw, wip
seethe, zieden; gisten
segment, seg'ment, partje
segregate, (zich) afzonderen
seize, pakken; nemen;
aangrijpen
seizure, nemen; be'slaglegging;
aanval
seldom, zelden
select, uitgelezen; chic; se'lect;
(uit)kiezen
selection, se'lectie; keus
self, zelf
self-assured, zelfbe'wust
self-centred, ego'centrisch
self-confidence, zelfvertrouwen
self-conscious, ver'legen
self-contained, vrij;
onafhankelijk
self-control, zelfbeheersing

self-defence, zelfverdediging
self-denial, zelfverloochening
self-evident, vanzelf'sprekend
self-government, zelfbestuur
self-interest, eigenbelang
selfish, zelf'zuchtig, ego'ïstisch
selfless, onbaat'zuchtig
self-pity, zelfbeklag
self-preservation, zelfbehoud
self-respect, zelfrespect
self-righteous, eigenge'rechtigd
self-sacrifice, zelfopoffering
selfsame: the -, pre'cies de(or
het)'zelfde
self-satisfied, zelfvol'daan
self-service, zelfbediening
self-service restaurant,
zelfbedieningsrestaurant
self-supporting: to be –, in eigen
be'hoefte kunnen voor'zien
sell, ver'kopen
semblance, schijn, voorkomen
semicircle, halve cirkel
semi-detached, twee onder één
kap
senate, se'naat
senator, se'nator
send, sturen, zenden
to – for, laten komen
senile, se'niel
senior, oudste, ouder
sensation, ge'voel,
ge'waarwording; sen'satie
sensational, opzien'barend;
sensatio'neel
sense, zin(tuig); ge'voel;
ver'stand; (aan)voelen
in a –, in zekere zin
senses, ver'stand
senseless, be'wusteloos;
on'zinnig
sensible, ver'standig, praktisch
sensitive, ge'voelig (voor)

sensual, sensuous, zin'tuiglijk;
   sensueel, zinnelijk
sentence, zin; vonnis;
   ver'oordelen
sentiment, ge'voel(en)
sentimental, sentimen'teel
sentinel, sentry, schildwacht
separate, af'zonderlijk;
   (af)scheiden
separation, scheiding
September, sep'tember
septic, septisch
sequel, ver'volg; ge'volg
sequence, op'eenvolging,
   volgorde
serenade, sere'nade (brengen)
serene, kalm, se'reen
serenity, vreedzaamheid
sergeant, ser'geant
serial killer, seriemoordenaar
series, serie, reeks,
   op'eenvolging
serious, ernstig; ge'wichtig
seriously, ernstig, in alle ernst,
   au séri'eux
sermon, preek
serpent, slang
serrated, ge'karteld
serum, serum
servant, be'diende; knecht,
   dienstmeisje; dienaar

serve, (be')dienen; opscheppen;
   ser'veren
service, dienst; strijdkracht;
   service; ser'vies
serviceable, nuttig
servile, slaafs, kruipend
servitude, slaver'nij;
   dwangarbeid
session, zitting
set¹, zetten, plaatsen, stellen,
   leggen; be'palen,

voorschrijven; ge'lijkzetten
(clock); opleggen, opdragen,
opgeven, stellen; stijf worden;
dekken (table); situ'eren;
vestigen (a record); ondergaan
(moon/sun)
set², stel, set, reeks; kring,
   groep; toestel, radio(toestel),
   tv(-toestel); ver'zameling;
   to'neelopbouw, scène, dé'cor,
   set
set³, vast, be'paald, vastgesteld;
   vastbesloten; opgelegd,
   voorgeschreven; strak, koppig,
   hard'nekkig; klaar, ge'reed
   – phrase, vaste uitdrukking
   I'm all –, ik ben er helemaal
   klaar voor
set-back, tegenslag
settee, bank
setting, zetting; (tijd en) plaats,
   om'geving
settle, regelen; zich vestigen;
   gaan zitten; ver'zakken
   to – down, tot rust komen
settlement, schikking;
   ver'effening; nederzetting
settler, kolo'nist
seven(teen)(th), zeven('tien)(de)
seventy, zeventig
sever, scheiden, ver'breken;
   doorsnijden
several, ver'scheiden;
   af'zonderlijk
severe, streng; ernstig; sober;
   hevig; zwaar
sew, naaien
sewage, afvalwater, rioolwater
sewer, ri'ool
sewing, naaien, naaiwerk
sex, ge'slacht, sekse; seks,
   ero'tiek; seksu'ele omgang,
   geslachtsgemeenschap\

sex (*continued*)
  have – with someone, met
  iemand naar bed gaan/vrijen
sexist, sek'sistisch; sek'sist
sexual, ge'slachts-, seksu'eel
sexuality, seksuali'teit
sexy, sexy, op'windend
shabby, haveloos; min
shack, keet
shackle, boei(en)
shade, schaduw; achtergrond;
  scherm, kap; tint; tikje,
  nu'ance; be'schutten,
  be'schaduwen
shadow, schaduw(en); zweem
shadowy, schaduwrijk, vaag
shady, schaduwrijk; ver'dacht
shaft, schacht; straal; pijl
shaggy, ruig
shake, schudden
shaky, on'vast, wankel
shall, zal, zullen
shallow, on'diep; opper'vlakkig
sham, namaak; schijn;
  voorwenden
shamble, schuifelen
shambles, troep, bende, zooi
shame, schaamte; schande;
  be'schaamd maken; te schande
  maken
  a –, jammer
shameful, schandelijk
shape, ge'daante; vorm(en);
  zich ont'wikkelen
shapeless, vormeloos
shapely, goed ge'vormd
share, (aan)deel; samen delen,
  ver'delen
shark, haai; oplichter
sharp, scherp; bij de'hand;
  pre'cies; kruis
sharpen, slijpen
shatter, ver'brijzelen; ver'nietigen

shave, (zich) scheren
shaving, krul; scheren
shawl, sjaal, omslagdoek
she, zij, ze
sheaf, schoof; bundel
shear, scheren
shears, schaar
sheath, schede
shed, hok, schuur(tje);
  ver'gieten, storten; afwerpen;
  ver'spreiden
sheen, glans
sheep, schaap, schapen
sheepish, schaapachtig
sheer, dun, door'schijnend;
  kinkklaar; loodrecht
sheet, laken; vel, plaat, vlak;
  schoot
shelf, plank; platte rand
shell, schaal, schelp, schil(d);
  huls; ge'raamte; doppen;
  be'schieten
shellfish, schelpdier
shelter, schutting, schuilplaats;
  be'schermen; schuilen
shelve, op de lange baan
  schuiven; op een plank zetten
shepherd, herder; ge'leiden
sheriff, sheriff
sherry, sherry
shield, schild; be'schermen
shift, ploeg, werktijd;
  ver'schuiven
shimmer, glinsteren
shin, scheen
shindy, herrie
shine, glans; (laten) schijnen;
  glimmen; uitblinken
shingle, grint
shiny, glimmend, blinkend
ship, schip; in(*or* ver')schepen
shipbuilding, scheepsbouw
shipment, ver'scheping; zending

ship owner, reder
shipping, scheepvaart, schepen
shipwreck, schipbreuk
  to be shipwrecked, schipbreuk
  lijden
shipyard, werf
shirk, zich ont'trekken aan
shirt, (over)hemd
shit, (vulg) stront, kak, poep;
  rommel, rotzooi; ge'zeik,
  onzin; hasj; schijten, poepen
shiver, rilling; rillen
shoal, on'diepte; school
shock, schok (geven); shock;
  bos (hair); aanstoot geven
shocking, aan'stotelijk;
  gruwelijk; schan'dalig
shoddy, prul-, snert-
shoe, schoen
shoot, uitloper; (dood)schieten;
  afschieten; storten
shop, winkel(en)
shopkeeper, winke'lier
shoplifter, winkeldief
shore, kust, oever; stut(ten)
short, kort; krap; bros
  to cut –, onder'breken
  in –, kort'om
  to run –, opraken
  to be – of, ge'brek hebben aan;
  te'kort komen
shortage, te'kort
short circuit, kortsluiting
  (ver'oorzaken)
shortcoming, te'kortkoming
shorten, (ver')korten
shorthand, steno(gra'fie)
short-lived, kort'stondig
shortly, (binnen)kort
shorts, korte broek
short-sighted, bij'ziend;
  kort'zichtig
short-tempered, prikkelbaar

shot, schot; schroot; poging;
  kiekje; slag
shotgun, jachtgeweer
should, zou moeten; moest(en);
  be'horen; zou(den); mocht(en)
shoulder, schouder; op zich
  nemen
shout, schreeuw(en); brullen
shove, schuiven
shovel, schop; scheppen
show, ver'toon, show, schijn;
  ten'toonstelling, amuse'ments-
  voorstelling, schouwspel, show;
  (ver')tonen; te zien zijn; laten
  zien; (be')wijzen; blijk geven van
  to – off, zich aanstellen;
  pronken met
shower, bui; douche; regen;
  over'stelpen
shrapnel, gra'naatscherven
shred, flard; schijn
shrew, feeks
shrewd, schrander
shriek, gil(len)
shrill, schel
shrimp, gar'naal
shrine, schrijn; heilige plaats
shrink, (doen) krimpen, (doen)
  afnemen; wegkruipen,
  in'eenkrimpen; zielenknijper,
  psychi'ater
shrivel, (doen) ver'schrompelen
shroud, doodskleed; sluier;
  hullen
shrub, heester
shrubbery, struikgewas
shrug, schoudersophalen
shudder, huiveren; schudden
shuffle, schuifelen; wassen
shun, schuwen
shut, dicht (doen); sluiten
  to – up, (op)sluiten; zijn mond
  houden

shutter 386

shutter, luik; sluiter
shuttle, schietspoel; pendel-
shy, ver'legen, schuw; schrikken
sick, ziek(en); misselijk; beu
　to be –, overgeven
sickening, walgelijk; ver'velend
sickle, sikkel
sickly, ziekelijk; onge'zond
sickness, ziekte; misselijkheid
side, (zij)kant; zij(de); par'tij
　(kiezen)
　– by –, naast el'kaar
sideboard, buf'fet
sidetrack, zijspoor; van zijn
　onderwerp afbrengen or
　afdwalen
sideways, zijdelings
siding, zijspoor
sidle up to, schuchter
　be'naderen
siege, be'leg
sieve, zeef; zeven
sift, zeven; ziften
sigh, zucht(en)
sight, ge'zicht;
　beziens'waardigheid; vi'zier;
　(in) zicht (krijgen)
　at first –, op het eerste ge'zicht
　to catch – of, in het oog
　krijgen
sign, (uithang)bord; wenk,
　teken; (onder')tekenen; een
　teken geven
signal, sein(en); een teken geven
signature, handtekening
signet (ring), zegel(ring)
significance, be'tekenis;
　be'lang
significant, veelbe'tekenend;
　be'langrijk
signify, be'tekenen; te kennen
　geven
signpost, wegwijzer

silence, stilte; stilwijgend; tot
　zwijgen brengen
silent, stil(zwijgend), zwijgzaam;
　stom
　to be –, zwijgen
silently, in stilte, ge'ruisloos
silhouette, silhou'et
silk, zij(de); zijden
silky, zijdeachtig
sill, vensterbank, drempel
silly, on'nozel, dwaas, flauw
silt, slib; dichtslibben
silver, zilver(werk); zilveren
similar, ge'lijk, dergelijk
similarity, over'eenkomst
simile, verge'lijking
simmer, zachtjes (laten)
　sudderen; pruttelen; gisten
simper, meesmuilen
simple, een'voudig;
　enkel'voudig; simpel;
　on'nozel
simpleton, on'nozele hals
simplicity, eenvoud
simplify, vereen'voudigen
simply, een'voudig;
　ge'woonweg, al'leen
simulate, voorwenden;
　nabootsen
simultaneous, gelijk'tijdig
sin, zonde; zondigen
since, sinds('dien), na'dien;
　van'af; daar
sincere, op'recht
sincerity, op'rechtheid
sinew, pees
sinful, zondig
sing, zingen
singe, (af)schroeien
singer, zanger('es)
single, enkel; eenpersoons-;
　onge'trouwd
　to – out, uitpikken

singly, af'zonderlijk; al'leen
singular, bij'zonder; enkelvoud
sinister, si'nister
sink, gootsteen; (ver')zinken.
  ondergaan; tot zinken brengen
sinner, zondaar
sinuous, kronkelend, lenig
sip, teugje; met teugjes drinken
sir, mijnheer; sir
  Dear Sir, Geachte Heer
sire, (voor)vader; sire
siren, si'rene
sister, zusje; zuster
sit, (gaan) zitten; zitting houden;
  po'seren
  to – down, gaan zitten
  to – up, rech'top (gaan) zitten;
  opblijven
site, bouwgrond,
  (bouw)ter'rein; ligging
sitting room, zitkamer
situated, ge'legen
situation, ligging; situ'atie;
  be'trekking
six(teen)(th), zes(tien)(de)
sixty, zestig
size, grootte, omvang; maat;
  lijmwater
sizeable, flink
sizzle, sissen
skate, schaats(enrijden); vleet
skein, streng
skeleton, ske'let; ge'raamte
sketch, schets(en)
skewer, vleespen, spies;
  door'steken
ski, ski(ën)
skid, slippen
skilful, be'kwaam, knap
skill, be'kwaamheid,
  vaardigheid
skilled, ge'schoold

skim, afscheppen, afromen;
  scheren over; doorbladeren
skimp, zuinig zijn (met)
skin, huid; vel; pels; villen
skinny, broodmager
skip, afvalcon'tainer; springen;
  overslaan
skipper, schipper
skirmish, scher'mutseling
skirt, rok; trekken (om)
skull, schedel; doodskop
sky, lucht, hemel
skyscraper, wolkenkrabber
slab, plak, plaat
slack, slap; laks; stil; gruis
slacken, ver'slappen; laten
  vieren
slam, bons; dichtslaan
slander, (be')laster(en)
slanderous, lasterlijk
slang, slang, zeer informele
  taal
slant, helling; hellen
slap, klap (geven); par'does;
  kwakken
slapdash, noncha'lant
slash, houw, jaap; (er'op los)
  maaien (or slaan); drastisch
  ver'minderen
slat, lat, reep
slate, lei(steen); leien; ervan
  langs geven
slaughter, slachting; slachten;
  afmaken
slave, slaaf; zich afbeulen
slavery, slaver'nij
slavish, slaafs
slay, doodslaan
sledge, slede; voorhamer; sleeën
sleek, glanzig, glad
sleep, slaap; slapen
sleeper, slaper; slaapwagen;
  dwarsligger

sleeping, slapen; slapend; slaap-
sleepless, slapeloos
sleepy, slaperig; doods; melig
sleet, natte sneeuw
sleeve, mouw
sleigh, arreslee
slender, slank, dun; karig, zwak, klein
slice, snee(tje); snijden
slick, vlot, glad
slide, glijbaan; glijkoker; plaatje; glijden
slight, ge'ring, licht; tenger; klei'nering; klei'neren
slightly, iets; opper'vlakkig
slim, slank
slime, slijk, slijm
slimy, slijmerig
sling, slingerverband, mi'tella; lus; slinger(en); gooien
slink, sluipen
slip, sloop; onderjurk; ver'gissing; strookje; helling; (uit)glijden; uitschieten; schuiven; laten glijden; aan(*or* uit)doen; voor'bijgaan; ont'schieten
slipper, pan'toffel
slippery, glibberig, glad
slipshod, slordig
slit, spleet, scheur(en); snijden
slobber, kwijlen
slogan, leus
sloop, sloep
slop, morsen
slope, helling; hellen, schuin lopen
sloppy, drassig; dun; slordig; zoetelijk
slot, gleuf
sloth, luiheid; luiaard
slouch, slungelen, hangen
slovenly, slonzig, slordig

slow, langzaam, traag; achter
to – down, ver'tragen, ophouden; vaart ver'minderen
slug, slak
sluggish, traag
sluice, sluis; spoelen
slum, slop, achterbuurt
slumber, sluimering; sluimeren
slump, ma'laise
slur, vlek, smet; onduidelijk spreken
slush, halfge'smolten sneeuw; bagger
slut, slet
sly, sluw
smack, klap, smak, pats; bijsmaak; zweem; een klap geven; smakken met; zwemen naar
small, klein
smallpox, pokken
smart, vinnig; flink; bijde'hand, handig; chic, keurig; zeer doen
smash, botsing; cata'strofe; ver'pletteren, stukslaan; breken; botsen (tegen)
smattering, mondjevol
smear, veeg; (be')smeren; be'smeuren
smell, reuk, lucht; ruiken (naar); rieken (naar)
smelt, smelten
smile, (glim)lach(en)
smirk, grijns (*or* grijnzen) van vol'doening
smith, smid
smithereens, gruzele'menten
smoke, rook; roken; walmen
smoky, rokerig
smooth, glad, vlak; kalm; vlot; gladstrijken
smother, smoren; stikken; be'delven; doven

smoulder, smeulen
smudge, vlek(ken)
smug, zelf'ingenomen
smuggle, smokkelen
smut, roetdeeltje;
schunnigheden
snack, hapje
snackbar, snackbar
snag, uitsteeksel; moeilijkheid
snail, (huisjes)slak
snake, slang
snap, klap, krak; drukknoop;
kiekje; knappen; happen;
snauwen; pikken
snapshot, kiekje;
momentopname
snare, (val)strik; (ver')strikken
snarl, grauw(en); snauw(en)
snatch, brokstuk; grissen
sneak, klikspaan; klikken;
sluipen; gappen
sneer, schimplach; be'schimpen;
smalen (op)
sneeze, niezen
sniff, snuiven; de neus ophalen
(voor); snuffelen; ruiken aan
snigger, grinniken
snip, snipper; knip(pen)
snipe, snip; ter'sluiks één voor
één neerschieten
sniper, sluipschutter
snob, snob
snooze, dutje; dutten
snore, snurken
snort, snuiven
snout, snuit
snow, sneeuw(en)
snowdrift, sneeuwbank
snowflake, sneeuwvlok
snowy, sneeuw-
snub, brute afwijzing; bits
afwijzen
– nose, mopneus

snuff, snuif; snuiven; snuiten
snug, knus
snuggle, (zich) nestelen
so, zo; dus; ook
or –, onge'veer
– that, zodat; opdat
soak, (door')weken; in de week
zetten (or staan); (laten)
trekken
to – up, opnemen, absor'beren
soap, zeep
soapsuds, zeepsop
soar, om'hoogvliegen; de
hoogte invliegen
sob, snik(ken)
sober, nuchter; sober;
ont'nuchteren
so-called, zoge'naamd
soccer, voetbal
sociable, soci'aal; ge'zellig
social, soci'aal
socialism, socia'lisme
society, ver'eniging;
maatschap'pij;
ge'zelschap
sock, sok
socket, gat, kas, holte
sod, zode
soda, soda
sodden, doornat
sofa, sofa
soft, zacht; week
soften, zacht maken (or
worden); ver'zachten
software, software,
(com'puter)programma(tuur)
soggy, door'weekt, drassig, klef
soil, grond, bodem; vuil maken
solace, troost
solar, zonne-, zons-
solder, sol'deersel; sol'deren
soldier, sol'daat; mili'tair
sole, enig; zool; tong (fish)

solely, al'leen
solemn, ernstig; plechtig
solemnity, plechtigheid
solicit, ver'zoeken om
solicitor, rechts'kundig advi'seur, procu'reur
solicitous, be'zorgd; ver'langend
solid, vast (lichaam); mas'sief stevig; soli'dair
solidarity, saam'horigheidsgevoel, solidari'teit
solidify, mas'sief (doen) worden
soliloquy, al'leenspraak, mono'loog
solitary, eenzaam
solitude, eenzaamheid
solo, solo
soluble, op'losbaar
solution, oplossing
solve, oplossen
solvent, sol'vent; oplossend; oplosmiddel
sombre, somber
some, sommige; enige; (er) wat (van); een (of ander); onge'veer
– **such,** een dergelijk, zo'n
– **day,** weleens
somebody, (een zeker) iemand
somehow, op de een of andere ma'nier; hoe dan ook
someone, iemand
somersault, buiteling, salto mortale
something, iets
sometime, wel eens
sometimes, soms
somewhat, enigs'zins; iets, wat
somewhere, ergens; een plaats (waar)
son, zoon

sonata, so'nate
song, lied
sonnet, son'net
sonorous, diepklinkend; weids
soon, spoedig, vroeg; lief
as – as, zo'dra
no sooner ... than, nauwelijks ... of
I would sooner, ik zou liever
soot, roet
soothe, sussen; ver'zachten
sophisticated, mon'dain
soporific, slaap'wekkend
sopping wet, drijfnat
soprano, so'praan
sorcerer, tovenaar
sorcery, tovena'rij
sordid, vuil; on'smakelijk
sore, zeer; gepi'keerd; teer; zere plek
sorrow, smart; treuren
sorrowful, droevig
sorry, treurig
I am –, het spijt me
sort, soort; sor'teren
soul, ziel; sterveling
soul-destroying, geest'dodend
sound, ge'luid, klank; zeeëngte; degelijk, gaaf, ge'zond, be'trouwbaar; flink, vast; (doen) klinken; peilen; polsen
sounding, klinkend; peiling
soup, soep
sour, zuur
source, bron
south, zuid(er), zuiden(-), naar het zuiden, ten zuiden van
southerly, zuidelijk
souvenir, souve'nir
sovereign, vorst; soeve'rein
sovereignty, soevereini'teit

sow, zeug; (be')zaaien

soy, soja

space, (tijd)ruimte; spatie; spati'ëren, ver'delen

space bar, spatiebalk

spacecraft, ruimtevaartuig

spaced out, zweverig, high, onder invloed; wereld'vreemd, excen'triek

spacious, ruim

spade, schop

span, spanwijdte; spanne

spangle, lovertje; be'zaaien

spaniel, spaniël

spank, voor zijn broek geven; patsen

spanner, moersleutel

spar, rondhout; (oefenend) boksen; redetwisten

spare, vrij; re'serve; schraal; (re'serve)onderdeel; sparen; missen; ont'zien

spark, vonk(en); greintje

sparkle, vonken schieten; fonkelen; tintelen; mous'seren

sparrow, mus

sparse, dun(ge'zaaid)

spasm, kramp('achtige be'weging); vlaag

spasmodic, kram'pachtig; bij vlagen

spate, stroom, vlaag, hoop

spatter, spatten; plassen (tegen)

speak, spreken; uitdrukken

speaker, spreker; voorzitter

spear, speer

special, bij'zonder, speci'aal

specialism, specia'lisme, speciali'satie

specialist, specia'list

specialization, speciali'satie

specialize, speciali'seren

specially, in het bij'zonder, voor'al

species, soort(en), ge'slacht(en)

specific, be'paald; uit'drukkelijk; speci'fiek

specification, specifi'catie

specify, specifi'ceren; ver'melden

specimen, proef; staaltje

speck, spikkel; vuiltje

speckle, spikkel, stippel, vlekje; be'spikkelen, stippelen

spectacle, schouwspel

spectacles, bril

spectacular, spectacu'lair, groots, grandi'oos

spectator, toeschouwer

spectre, spook; schim

spectrum, spectrum

speculate, be'spiegelingen houden; specu'leren

speculation, be'spiegeling; specu'latie

speculator, specu'lant

speech, (toe)spraak

speechless, sprakeloos

speed, vaart; snelheid; ver'snelling; snel rijden

– bump, verkeers'drempel

speed(il)y, spoedig

spell, beurt; peri'ode; be'tovering; spellen; be'tekenen

spend, uitgeven; be'steden, doorbrengen; uitputten

spew, (uit)braken

sphere, bol; hemellichaam; ge'bied, sfeer

spherical, bol'vorming

spice, spece'rij

spicy, ge'kruid; pi'kant

spider, spin

spike, (ijzeren) punt; stekel

spill, doen overlopen, laten overstromen, morsen, omgooien, ver'spillen; ver'gieten (blood); overlopen, over'stromen

spin, ritje; spinnen; draaien

spinach, spi'nazie

spinal, ruggegraats-

spindle, klos; spil

spine, ruggegraat; stekel

spinster, ongetrouwde vrouw

spiral, spi'raal(vormig)

spire, torenspits

spirit, geest; fut

  spirits, stemming; levenslust; sterke drank

spirited, vurig; geani'meerd

spiritual, geestelijk (lied)

spit, spuug; spit; landtong; spuwen; druppelen

spite, kwaa'daardigheid; ergeren

spiteful, hatelijk

splash, spat; be'spatten; plassen; uit el'kaar spatten; natmaken

spleen, milt; gal

splendid, schitterend, prachtig

splendour, pracht

splice, splitsen; lassen

splint, spalk(en)

splinter, splinter

split, spleet; scheuring; splijten; splitsen; (ver')delen

splitting, barstend

splutter, sputteren

spoil, buit; be'derven; ver'wennen

spoilsport, spelbreker

spoke, spaak; sport

spokesman, woordvoerder

sponge, spons; mos'covisch ge'bak; sponzen; klaplopen

sponsor, sponsor; peet; op touw zetten

spontaneous, spon'taan; zelf-

spool, spoel

spoon(ful), lepel

sporadic, spo'radisch

spore, spoor

sport, sport; grap; sportieve vent (or meid); spelen

sporting, sport-; spor'tief; aardig

sportsman, sportliefhebber

spot, vlek; stip(pelen); plek; scheutje; in de gaten krijgen

spotless, smetteloos; brandschoon

spotlight, zoeklicht

spouse, gade

spout, tuit; straal; spuiten

sprain, ver'stuiken

sprawl, uitgestrekt (gaan) liggen; wijd uit'eenlopen, zich wan'orderlijk ver'spreiden

spray, spuitbus; takje; (be')sproeien

spread, wijdte; ont'haal; (zich) (uit)spreiden; (zich) ver'spreiden; (be')smeren

sprig, twigje

sprightly, opgewekt

spring, veer(kracht); lente; bron; springen; ont'staan (uit); (uit de grond) schieten

sprinkle, (be')sprenkelen, strooien

sprint, sprint(en)

sprout, spruit(en)

spruce, spar(rehout); keurig; opknappen

spry, kwiek

spur, spoor; uitloper; prikkel; de sporen geven; aansporen

  on the – of the moment, in de eerste opwelling

spurious, on'echt

spurn, ver'smaden

spurt, guts; vlaag; spuiten (met);
spurten

sputter, sputteren, spatten

spy, spi'on; (be)spio'neren;
be'speuren

squabble, ge'kibbel; kibbelen

squad, (sport)ploeg

squadron, eska'dron; es'kader

squalid, vuil en ar'moedig

squall, (wind)vlaag; schreeuwen

squalor, vuile armoede

squander, ver'spillen

square, vierkant; plein;
kwa'draat; recht('hoekig);
quitte; eerlijk; in het kwa'draat
brengen; afrekenen

squash, pletten, platdrukken;
ge'plet worden; squash; siroop
ge'drang, oploop

squat, ge'drongen; neerhurken;
kraakpand; kraken

squawk, krijsen

squeak, piepen

squeal, gillen

squeamish, overdreven
ge'voelig

squeeze, ge'drang; knijpen,
uitpersen; bijstoppen; afpersen

squint, scheel kijken; gluren;
(vluchtige) blik

squirm, zich in allerlei bochten
wringen; in el'kaar kruipen

squirrel, eekhoorn

squirt, spuiten

stab, steek(wond); (door)steken

stability, stabili'teit

stabilize, stabili'seren

stable, stal(len); sta'biel, vast

stack, stapel; opstapelen

stadium, stadion

staff, staf, stok

stag, mannetjeshert

stag-night, vrijge'zellenavond

stage, e'tappe, stadium; to'neel;
tra'ject; ten to'nele brengen;
op touw zetten

stagger, (doen) wankelen;
ver'bijsteren; spreiden

stagnant, stilstaand

stagnation, stilstand; stremming

staid, be'zadigd

stain, (be')vlek(ken); smet;
beits(en); kleurstof; afgeven;
brandschilderen

stainless, smetteloos; roestvrij

stair, trede; trap-

staircase, stairs, trap

stake, paal; brandstapel;
inzet(ten); staken
  at –, op het spel

stale, oud('bakken), ver'schaald,
muf; suf

stalk, stengel, steel; stronk;
be'sluipen; achter'volgen

stall, stal(letje); (laten) afslaan

stallion, hengst

stalwart, stevig, stoer; flink;
stand'vastig, trouw

stamen, meeldraad

stamina, uithoudingsvermogen

stammer, ge'stamel; stamelen,
stotteren

stamp, (post)zegel; stempel(en);
fran'keren; stampen

stampede, pa'niek; stormloop;
stormlopen; op hol slaan

stand, standard, voet, stel;
tri'bune; plaats; (gaan *or*
blijven) staan; liggen; zetten;
ver'dragen, uitstaan; van
kracht blijven; zijn
  to – back, achter'uitgaan; (van
…) af liggen
  to – out, uitsteken; opvallen

standard, standaard; maatstaf; vaandel

standardize, standaardi'seren

stand-by, re'serve, steun

standing, aanzien; permanent; (stil)staand

standpoint, standpunt

standstill, stilstand

stanza, vers, strofe

staple, hoofd-; kram, niet(je)

stapler, nietmachine

star, ster

starboard, stuurboord

starch, zetmeel; stijfsel; stijven

stare, (aan)staren

stark, grimmig; stijf, on'buigzaam; schril; kaal
 – contrast, schril contrast

starling, spreeuw

starry, sterren-

start, be'gin(nen); start(en); schok; ver'trekken; aanzetten, aanslaan; opschrikken

startle, doen schrikken

startling, verbazing'wekkend; ont'stellend

starvation, ver'hongering

starve, (laten) ver'hongeren

state, staat, toestand; staatsie; staats-; mededelen, uit'eenzetten, consta'teren

stated, ge'noemd; vastgesteld

stately, statig

statement, ver'klaring

statesman, staatsman

statesmanship, staatkunde

static, statisch

station, sta'tion; stand(plaats); plaatsen

stationary, stilstaand; statio'nair

stationer, kan'toorboekhandel(aar)

stationery, schrijfbehoeften

statistic, sta'tistisch

statistics, statis'tiek(en)

statue, standbeeld

stature, ge'stalte; ge'halte

status, status

statute, swet, sta'tuut

staunch, trouw; stelpen

stave, duig; staaf; inslaan
 to – off, afwenden

stay, ver'blijf; stut; (ver')blijven; lo'geren

steadfast, stand'vastig

steady, stevig, vast; so'lide; stand'vastig; kalm; vasthouden

steak, runderlapje, biefstuk; moot

steal, stelen; sluipen

steam, stoom; dampen; stomen

steamer, stoomboot; stomer

steed, ros

steel, staal; stalen

steep, steil; sterk; (in)dompelen

steeple, toren(spits)

steer, sturen

steering wheel, stuur

stem, stengel, steel; (voor)steven; stuiten

stench, stank

stencil, stencil(en)

stenographer, steno'graaf

step, stap(pen); pas; trede, stoep, step-, stief-

step-, stief-

stereo, stereo

stereotype, stereo'tiep

sterile, ste'riel; on'vruchtbaar

sterilize, sterili'seren

sterling, sterling; recht'schapen

stern, achtersteven; streng

stew, stoofschotel; stoven

steward, hofmeester; official, be'diende

stick, stok; plakken; (blijven) steken; volhouden

sticky, kleverig

stiff, stijf, stroef; stevig; moeilijk

stiffen, stijver (or moeilijker) maken

stifle, (ver')stikken; onder'drukken

stigma, brandmerk, (schand)vlek, stigma

stile, overstap

still, stil(te); distil'leerketel; nog (al'tijd); toch; kal'meren

stillness, stilte

stilt, stelt

stilted, hoog'dravend; stijf

stipend, be'zoldiging

stipulate, be'dingen

stipulation, voorwaarde

stir, ophef; (be')roeren, zich ver'roeren; aanzetten

stirfry, roerbakken; roergebakken ge'recht/eten

stirring, veelbe'wogen; op'windend

stirrup, stijgbeugel

stitch, steek, hechting; stikken, hechten

stock, voorraad; ef'fecten; afkomst; bouil'lon; standaard, voor'zien (van), voorraad inslaan; in voorraad hebben

stockade, palis'sade

stockbroker, ef'fectenmakelaar

stocking, kous

stodgy, onver'teerbaar; zwaar

stoic(al), stoï'cijns

stoke, stoken

stolid, standvastig

stomach, maag; ver'dragen

stone, (edel)steen; pit; 6,35 kilo; stenen; stenigen; ont'pitten

stone-deaf, stokdoof

stony, steenachtig; steenhard; doods, koud

stool, kruk; stoelgang

stoop, ronde rug; bukken; zich ver'lagen

stop, oponthoud; halte; re'gister; (dicht)stoppen; blijven (staan); stilstaan; ophouden (met); stopzetten; stelpen

  to put a – to, een eind maken aan

stoppage, oponthoud; opstopping

stopper, stop

storage, opslaan; bergruimte; opslag-

store, warenhuis; ba'zaar; voorraad; maga'zijn; opslaan; opbergen

  to lay in a – of, inslaan

storeroom, bergruimte, pro'visiekamer

stork, ooievaar

storm, storm, (flinke) bui, onweer; razen; stuiven; be'stormen

stormy, stormachtig, onweersachtig

story, ver'haal, ge'schiedenis; ver'dieping

stout, ge'zet; stevig; flink

stove, kachel, for'nuis

stow, stouwen; opbergen

stowaway, ver'stekeling

straddle, schrijlings staan (or zitten); spreiden over

straight, recht; eerlijk; in orde; puur

  – away, di'rect

straighten, rechttrekken(or zetten); in orde brengen

straightforward, op'recht; een'voudig

strain, (in)spanning; toon; afkomst; trek; (over' *or* in)spannen; (ver')rekken; afgieten

strained, ge'dwongen, gefor'ceerd, onna'tuurlijk

strainer, ver'giet, zeefje

straits, zee'ëngte, Straat; moeilijkheden

strand, streng; stranden

to be stranded, stranden; hulpeloos staan

strange, vreemd

stranger, vreemde; onbe'kende

strangle, wurgen; onder'drukken, smoren

strap, riem, band; vastmaken (met een riem)

strapping, potig, flink

strategic, stra'tegisch

strategy, strate'gie

straw, stro(otje); rietje

strawberry, aardbei

stray, afgedwaald (dier); (af)dwalen

streak, streep; straal; strepen; streaken

stream, stroom; stromen

streamer, serpen'tine, wimpel

streamline(d), (ge')stroomlijn(d)

street, straat

strength, kracht(en); sterkte; ge'halte

strengthen, (ver')sterken

strenuous, inspannend

stress, spanning, druk, stress, be'lasting; klem(toon), nadruk, ac'cent; spanning, druk; be'nadrukken, de nadruk leggen op; be'lasten, onder druk zetten

be under –, onder druk staan

lay – on, benadrukken

stretch, uitge'strektheid; (zich) (uit)rekken; spannen; uitsteken

at a –, achter el'kaar

stretcher, bran'card

strew, strooien; be'zaaien

stricken, ge'troffen

strict, streng; pre'cies; strikt

stride, schrede; schrijden

strident, krassend

strife, twist, strijd

strike, staking; slaan; aansteken; (toe)schijnen, opkomen bij; treffen; staken; doorhalen

striking, treffend

string, touw; snoer; snaar; file; strijkinstrument; (aan'een)rijgen

stringent, streng

strip, strook; (af)stropen; (zich) uitkleden; ont'doen; afhalen

– lighting, tl-verlichting

stripe, streep; strepen

strive, streven (naar); worstelen

stroke, slag; haal; be'roerte; zet; strelen

stroll, wandeling; kuieren; trekken

strong, sterk

stronghold, bolwerk

structure, struc'tuur, (ge')bouw; samenstelling

struggle, strijd; krachtsinspanning; vechten; strompelen

strum, trommelen

strut, stijl; trots stappen

stub, stomp, stronk, peukje

stubble, stoppels

stubborn, hard'nekkig, hals'starrig

stud, (sier)spijker, sierknopje; knoop(je); (ren)stal, fokbedrijf; fokhengst, dekhengst (also

figuratively); nop
student, stu'dent(e)
studied, welover'wogen
studio, atel'ier, studio
studious, leer'gierig
study, studie; stu'deerkamer;
(be)stu'deren
stuff, materi'aal, (grond)stof;
spul; troep, rommel;
(op)vullen, volstoppen;
proppen, stoppen, steken;
opzetten
all that – can go, al die troep
kan wel weg
I'm stuffed, ik zit vol
you can – it!, je kan de pot op!
stuffy, be'nauwd
stumble, struikelen, strompelen
stump, stomp, stronk;
stommelen
stun, wezenloos slaan;
ver'bluffen
stunt, stunt; be'lemmeren
stupefy, ver'stomd doen staan
stupendous, over'weldigend,
machtig
stupid, dom, on'zinnig
stupor, ver'doving
sturdy, fors
stutter, stotteren
sty, hok; strontje
style, stijl
stylish, stijlvol; deftig
subconscious,
onderbe'wust(zijn)
subdivision, onderverdeling;
onderafdeling
subdue, onder'werpen;
onder'drukken; dempen
subject, onderwerp; vak;
onderdaan; onder'hevig (aan);
onder'werpen; blootstellen
(aan)

subjection, onder'werping;
onder'worpenheid
subjective, subjec'tief
subjugate, onder'werpen
sublime, su'bliem
submarine, onder'zeeboot
submerge, over'stromen,
ver'zwelgen
submission, onder'werping;
onder'danigheid; be'wering
submissive, onder'danig
submit, (zich) onder'werpen;
overleggen; zou(den) naar
voren willen brengen;
voorleggen
subordinate, onderge'schikt(e)
subscribe, teke̕nen voor;·
onder'schrijven; zich
abon'neren (op)
subsequent, later
subservient, onderge'schikt;
onder'danig
subside, zakken; afnemen;
zinken
subsidiary, dochter-,
bij('komstig)
subsidize, subsidiëren
subsidy, sub'sidie
subsist, be'staan; leven
subsistence, be'staan;
onderhoud
substance, stof; hoofdzaak;
wezen; sub'stantie
substantial, substan'ti'eel,
aan'zienlijk; so'lide
substantially, in wezen
substantiate, be'wijzen
substitute, plaatsver'vanger,
surro'gaat; in de plaats stellen
substitution, substi'tutie
subterfuge, uitvlucht
subterranean, onderaards
subtle, sub'tiel, fijn, spits'vondig

subtract, aftrekken
suburb, voorstad, buitenwijk
suburban, fo'renzen-, van de
   voorstad
succeed, slagen; (op)volgen
success, suc'ces
successful, suc'cesrÿk/vol,
   ge'slaagd; ge'lukkig
succession, op(een)volging;
   suc'cessie
   in –, achter el'kaar
successive, opeen'volgend
successor, opvolger
succinct, kort en bondig
succulent, sappig
succumb, be'zwijken
such, zulk; zo('n); zo'danig
   – as, zo'als; wat
suck, zuigen (op)
   to – up, vleien; opzuigen
suckle, zogen
suction, zuiging; zuig-
sudden, plotseling
sue, ge'rechtelijk ver'volgen;
   smeken
suede, suède
suffer, lijden; boeten
suffering, lijden
suffice, vol'doende zijn
sufficient, vol'doende
suffocate, (doen) stikken
suffocation, ver'stikking
suffrage, kiesrecht
sugar, suiker(en)
suggest, doen denken aan;
   voorstellen; sugge'reren
suggestion, voorstel; sug'gestie;
   spoor
suggestive, sugge'rerend;
   sugges'tief
suicide, zelfmoord
suit, pak; kleur;
   huwelijksaanzoek;

(aan)passen; ge'schikt zijn
voor; schikken; goed staan
(bij)
suitable, ge'schikt
suitcase, (hand)koffer
suite, ge'volg; ameuble'ment;
   aparte'menten
suitor, minnaar; eiser
sulk, mokken, chag'rijnig zijn;
   boze/chag'rijnige bui
sullen, stuurs; somber
sully, be'zoedelen
sulphur, zwavel
sultan, sultan
sultana, rozijn
sultry, zwoel
sum, som
   to – up, samenvatten;
   opsommen
summarize, samenvatten
summary, samenvatting;
   sum'mier
summer, zomer
   – time, zomertijd
summertime, zomerseizoen,
   zomer
summit, top(punt)
summon, ont'bieden,
   bij'eenroepen; ver'zamelen
summons, dagvaarding
sumptuous, weelderig
sun, zon(ne-)
sunbeam, zonnestraal
sunbed, zonnebank,
   zonnehemel
sunburn, zonnebrand
sunburnt, ver'brand
Sunday, zondag
sundial, zonnewijzer
sundown, zons'ondergang
sundry, di'vers(en)
sunken, blind; ingevallen
sunlight, zonlicht

sunny, zonnig
sunrise, zons'opgang
sunset, zons'ondergang
sunshine, zonneschijn
sunstroke, zonnesteek
super, machtig
superb, groots, schitterend
supercilious, hoog'hartig
superficial, opper'vlakkig
superfluous, over'tollig
superhuman, boven'menselijk
superintend, toezicht houden
   op
superintendent, inspec'teur
superior, superi'eur, hoger;
   arro'gant
superlative, van de hoogste
   graad; superlatief
supermarket, supermarkt
supernatural,
   bovenna'tuurlijk(e)
supersede, ver'vangen
supersonic, super'sonisch,
   sneller dan het geluid
superstition, bijgeloof
superstitious, bijge'lovig
supervise, toezicht hebben op;
   survei'lleren
supervision, toezicht
supper, (avond)eten,
   avondmaal, sou'per
supplant, ver'dringen
supple, soepel, buigzaam
supplement, supple'ment;
   aanvullen
supplementary, aanvullend
supply, voorraad; voor'ziening;
   ver'schaffen; vol'doen (aan)
support, steun;
   (onder')steunen;
   onder'houden; staven
supporter, aanhanger,
   sup'porter

suppose, (ver)onder'stellen,
   aannemen
   I – so, ik neem aan van wel
   – he isn't there? stel dat hij er
   niet is?
supposed, ver'meend;
   aangenomen
supposing (that), stel dat
supposition, veronder'stelling
suppress, onder'drukken;
   ver'bieden
supremacy, oppermacht
supreme, opper-, uiterste
surcharge, toeslag
sure, zeker
   to make –, contro'leren
surely, (toch) zeker
surety, borg
surf, branding; surfen
   – the net, internetten/op het
   net surfen
surface, oppervlak(te), vlak
surfboard, surfplank
surfeit, overdaad
surge, opwelling; golven,
   storten; stuwen; zwellen
surgeon, chi'rurg
surgery, chirur'gie; spreekkamer
surly, nors
surmise, ver'moeden
surmount, be'kronen;
   over'winnen
surname, achternaam
surpass, over'treffen
surplus, overschot;
   over('tollig)
surprise, ver'rassing, ver'bazing;
   ver'rassen; ver'wonderen,
   ver'bazen
surprising, ver'wonderlijk,
   ver'bazend
surrender, overgave; (zich)
   overgeven

surround 400

surround, om'ringen, om'singelen
surroundings, om'geving
surveillance, toezicht
survey, in'spectie; overzicht;
opmeting; inspec'teren;
over'zien; opmeten
surveyor, ex'pert; opzichter;
landmeter
survival, leven, voortbestaan;
overblijfsel
survive, over'leven; blijven
be'staan
survivor, over'levende
susceptible, vatbaar, ge'voelig
(voor)
suspect, ver'dacht(e);
ver'moeden; ver'denken
suspend, staken; schorsen;
opschorten
to be suspended, hangen
suspenders, jarre'telles
suspense, spanning
suspicion, ver'moeden;
achterdocht; ver'denking;
schijnte
suspicious, ver'dacht;
achter'dochtig
sustain, staande houden;
voeden; doorstaan; lijden
sustenance, voedsel;
onderhoud
swagger, zeilen; opscheppen
swallow, zwaluw; (door or
in)slikken, ver'zwelgen
swamp, moe'ras; over'spoelen;
over'stelpen
swampy, moe'rassig
swan, zwaan
swap, rail; (ver')ruilen
swarm, zwerm(en); wemelen
swarthy, donker
sway, invloed; schommelen,
ervan afbrengen

swear, zweren; vloeken
sweat, zweet; zweten
sweater, trui
Swedish, Zweeds
sweep, zwaai;
schoorsteenveger; (op)vegen;
voeren; schrijden
sweeping, wijds; ver'strekkend
sweet, zoet; lief; fris; snoepje
sweeten, suiker doen in
sweetheart, liefje, schat
swell, deining; (aan or
op)zwellen; toenemen
swelling, zwelling, ver'dikking
swerve, zwenken
swift, snel; gierzwaluw
swill, afval; (uit)spoelen
swim, zwemmen; duizelen
swindle, oplichte'rij; oplichten
swine, zwijn(en)
swing, zwaai(en); schommel;
animo; swing; slingeren
swirl, (doen) warrelen
swish, zoevend geluid, ge'ruis;
chic, modi'eus; zoeven, suizen,
ruizen
Swiss, Zwitser(s)
switch, schakelaar; wissel;
ommezwaai, ver'andering;
(om)schakelen, ver'anderen
(van), overgaan (op)
– off, uitschakelen, uitdoen
swoon, flauwte; be'zwijmen
swoop, zich storten
sword, zwaard
syllable, lettergreep
symbol, sym'bool
symbolic(al), sym'bolisch
symbolize, symboli'seren
symmetrical, sym'metrisch
symmetry, symme'trie
sympathetic, vol medeleven;
wel'willend

sympathize, meevoelen
sympathy, sympa'thie
symphony, symfo'nie
symptom, symp'toom
synagogue, syna'goge
synchronize, (doen) samenvallen; ge'lijkzetten
syndicate, syndi'caat
synod, sy'node
synonym(ous), syno'niem
synopsis, sy'nopsis
syntax, syn'taxis
synthesis, syn'these
synthetic, syn'thetisch
syringe, spuit(je); uitspuiten
syrup, stroop, si'roop
system, sys'teem; stelsel; net; lichaam
systematic, syste'matisch

T

tab, label; lus; rekening
table, tafel; ta'bel
tablespoon, eetlepel
table tennis, tafeltennis
tablet, ta'blet(je); ge'denkplaat
taboo, ta'boe (ver'klaren)
tacit, stil'zwijgend
taciturn, zwijgzaam
tack, kopspijker; spoor; koers; rijgen; toevoegen; van koers veranderen
tackle, tuig; takel; aanpakken; tekkelen
tact(ful), tact(vol)
tactical, tac'tisch
tactics, tac'tiek
tactless, tactloos
taffeta, tafzij
tag, eti'ketje; eindje, bandje
  to – on to, zich aansluiten bij
tail, staart; pand; achter-

tailor, kleermaker
taint, smet; be'derven
take, (aan, in, mee *or* op)nemen; brengen; kosten (time)
  to – down, opschrijven
  to – for, houden voor
  to – in, herbergen; innemen; in zich opnemen; beetnemen
  to – off, uittrekken; opstijgen
  to – on, aannemen; op zich nemen
  taken aback, van zijn stuk ge'bracht
takings, ont'vangsten
talc(um), talk
tale, ver'haal; praatje
talent(ed), ta'lent(vol)
talk, ge'sprek; sprake; be'spreking; praten, spreken
  to – over, be'spreken, be'praten
talkative, praatziek
tall, lang, hoog
tally, eti'ket; kloppen
talon, klauw
tame, tam; temmen
tamper with, knoeien met
tampon, tampon
tan, (geel)bruin; tanen; bruinen; jongebruind
tandem, tandem
  in –, achter elkaar
tang, scherpe smaak
tangerine, manda'rijn
tangible, tastbaar
tangle, knoop, war; in de war raken (*or* maken)
tank, tank, bak
tannin, looizuur
tantalize, tantali'seren
tantamount: to be – to, neerkomen op
tantrum, driftbui

tap, kraan; tik(ken), kloppen; (af)tappen

tape, band

taper, waspit; taps toelopen

tapestry, tapisse'rie; wandtapijt

tar, teer; teren

tardy, traag

target, schietschijf; mikpunt, doel

tariff, ta'rief

tarnish, be'slaan, aantasten; be'zoedelen

tarpaulin, zeil(doek)

tarry, (ver')toeven

tart, taart; slet; wrang

tartar, tandsteen; driftkop; Ta'taar

task, taak

tassel, kwast(je)

taste, smaak(je), proefje; proeven, smaken (naar)

tasteful, smaakvol

tasteless, smaakeloos

tasty, smakelijk

tattoo, tatoe'age; taptoe; tatoe'ëren

tattered, haveloos

tatters, flarden

taunt, schimpscheut; schimpen op

taut, strak

tavern, herberg

tawdry, op'zichtig, prullig

tawny, vaalgeel

tax, be'lasting; veel vergen van; be'schuldigen

  – cut, be'lastingverlaging

  – evasion, be'lastingontduiking

  to be taxed, be'lasting be'talen, onder'hevig zijn aan be'lasting

taxation, be'lasting

taxi, taxi(ën)

tax-free, belasting'vrij

taxpayer, be'lastingbetaler

tea, thee

  – towel, theedoek

teach, onder'wijzen, les geven, leren

teacher, onder'wijzer('es), leraar, lera'res

team, elftal; ploeg; span

teamwork, teamwork, samenwerking, samenspel

teapot, theepot

tear, traan; scheur(en); vliegen

tease, plagen

teaspoon, theelepeltje

teat, tepel; speen

technical, technisch, ambachts-

technicalities, tech'niek; formali'teiten

technically, technisch; strikt ge'nomen

technician, technicus

technique, tech'niek

tedious, ver'velend

teem, wemelen (van)

teetotaller, ge'heelonthouder

telecommunications, telecommunicatie; telecommuni'catietechniek

telegram, tele'gram

telegraph, tele'graaf; telegra'feren

telephone, tele'foon; telefo'neren

telephone box, tele'fooncel

telephone call, tele'foongesprek

telephone directory, tele'foongids, tele'foonboek

teleshopping, (het) telewinkelen, (het) teleshoppen

telescope, tele'scoop; in el'kaar schuiven

television, tele'visie

television commercial,
re'clamespot(je)
tell, (het) ver'tellen, (het) zeggen;
onder'scheiden
telling, raak; veel'zeggend
temper, aard, hu'meur;
drift(bui); hardheid;
ver'zachten; harden
temperament, aard;
tempera'ment
temperamental,
tempera'mentvol, vol kuren
temperance, matigheid;
ont'houding
temperate, ge'matigd, matig
temperature, tempera'tuur;
ver'hoging
tempest, hevige storm
tempestuous, stormachtig,
on'stuimig
temple, tempel; slaap
temporal, tijdelijk; wereldlijk
temporary, tijdelijk, voor'lopig
tempt, ver'leiden; lokken
temptation, ver'leiding;
aanvechting
tempting, ver'leidelijk
tenth, tiende
tenable, ver'dedigbaar
tenacious, vast'houdend;
hard'nekkig
tenant, huurder, pachter
tend, ge'neigd zijn; lopen;
overhellen; (licht) kunnen;
passen op
tendency, neiging
tender, mals; te(d)er; ge'voelig;
of'ferte; be'taalmiddel; tender;
aanbieden
tendon, pees
tendril, rank
tenement, pachtgoed;
(huur)kamer, apparte'ment

tennis (court), tennis(baan)
tenor, te'nor; loop; strekking
tense, strak; ge'spannen,
spannend; tijd
tension, spanning
tent, tent
tentacle, voelhoorn; vangarm
tentative, voorlopig; aarzelend
tenterhooks: on –, op hete kolen
(zitten)
tenuous, ijl, schraal
tenure, be'zit; tijd
tepid, lauw
term, tri'mester, se'mester,
onderwijsperiode; ter'mijn,
peri'ode; (vak)term, woord
terminal, eind('station);
terminal; terminaal
terminate, (be')ëindigen,
aflopen; opzeggen
terminology, terminolo'gie
terminus, eindstation (*or* punt)
terms, voorwaarden, con'dities,
be'palingen
  come to – with, zich verzoenen
  met, zich neerleggen bij
terrace, ter'ras; huizenrij
terrestrial, aard-; land-
terrible, vreselijk,
ver'schrikkelijk
terrier, terriër
terrific, ge'weldig
terrify, schrik aanjagen
  to be terrified, in doodsangst
  ver'keren, zich doodschrikken
territorial, territori'aal
territory, (grond)gebied
terror, schrik, angst
terrorism, terro'risme
terrorist, terro'ristisch, ter'reur;
terro'rist
terrorize, terrori'seren, schrik
aanjagen

terse, kort en bondig

test, proef(werk), e'xamen; be'proeving; testen, exami'neren; op de proef stellen

– tube, rea'geerbuis

testament, testa'ment

testify, ge'tuigen (van); onder ede ver'klaren

testimonial, ge'tuigschrift, ver'klaring

testimony, ge'tuigenis

text, tekst

textbook, leerboek, studieboek, schoolboek

textile, tex'tiel

texture, weefsel; samenstel, bouw

than, dan

thank, (be')danken

  thanks, be'dankt; dank

thankful, dankbaar

thankless, on'dankbaar

thanksgiving, dankbétuiging; Thanksgiving

that, dat; die; wat; daar-

thatch(ed roof), riet(en dak)

thaw, dooi(en); (doen) ont'dooien

the, de, het

theatre, the'ater, schouwburg; to'neel; zaal

theatrical, to'neel-; thea'traal

thee, U

theft, diefstal

their, hun

theirs, (die *or* dat) van hun

them, hen, ze

theme, onderwerp; thema

themselves, zich(zelf), zelf

then, toen('malig); dan; boven'dien

  by –, tegen die tijd

but –, maar … (dan ook)

– and there, on'middellijk

thence, van'daar; daaruit

theologian, theo'loog

theological, theo'logisch

theology, godge'leerdheid

theoretical, theo'retisch

theory, theo'rie

there, daar('heen); er

thereabouts, daar in de buurt; daarom'trent

therefore, daarom

thermometer, thermometer

these, deze; hier-

thesis, stelling; disser'tatie

they, zij

thick, dik; dicht

thicken, dikker worden; binden

thicket, struikgewas

thickness, dikte; laag

thick-skinned, dik'huidig

thief, dief

thieve, stelen

thigh, dij

thimble, vingerhoed

thin, dun; mager; ijl; ver'dunnen

thing, ding

  a –, iets

  the – that, wat

  things, spullen; (de) dingen

think, denken (aan *or* over); nadenken; ge'loven; een i'dee hebben; vinden

thinnish, vrij dun

third, derde; terts

thirdly, ten derde

thirst, dorst(en); zucht (naar)

thirsty: to be –, dorst hebben; dorstig zijn

thirteen(th), dertien(de)

thirty, dertig

this, deze, dit; hier-

thistle, distel

thorn, doorn

thorny, doornig; netelig

thorough, grondig; echt

those, die; de'genen; er; daar-

though, hoe'wel; al (… ook);
  (ja) maar, (en) toch
  as –, als'of

thought, i'dee, ge'dachte;
  (na)denken; at'tentie

thoughtful, in ge'dachten
  ver'zonken; at'tent

thoughtless, onbe'zonnen;
  onat'tent

thousand, duizend

thrash, geselen, aframmelen;
  ver'slaan, niets heel laten van

thread, garen; draad; de draad
  steken door; zich (een weg)
  banen

threadbare, kaal; afgezaagd

threat, be'dreiging

threaten, dreigen met;
  be'dreigen

three, drie

thresh, dorsen

threshold, drempel

thrice, driemaal

thrift, zuinigheid

thrifty, spaarzaam

thrill, sen'satie; aangrijpen;
  ver'rukken

thrilling, aan'grijpend; (erg)
  op'windend

thrive, ge'dijen; bloeien

throat, keel

throb, bonzen, kloppen

throne, troon

throng, ge'drang; (zich
  ver')dringen (op)

throttle, smoorklep; smoren

through, door('heen);
  doorgaand

throughout, door heel

– the day, de hele dag door

throw, worp; werpen; (toe *or*
  af)gooien; gooien met

thrust, stoot, steek; stoten,
  steken; werpen

thud, plof

thug, misdadiger, moordenaar

thumb, duim; be'duimelen

thump, bons; stomp(en);
  bonken (op), bonzen (op)

thunder, donder(en), onweer
  – storm, onweer(sbui)

thunderbolt, bliksemflits;
  donderslag

thundercloud, onweerswolk

thunderous, daverend

Thursday, donderdag

thus, (al')dus; zo

thwart, dwarsbomen, ver'ijdelen

tick, tik(ken); streepje;
  ogenblikje; teek; tijk;
  aftekenen

ticket, kaartje, ticket

tickle, kietelen; jeuken;
  amu'seren

ticklish, kietelig; netelig

tidal, ge'tij-, vloed-

tide, ge'tij, stroom; helpen

tidings, nieuws

tidy, net(jes); flink; opruimen

tie, (strop)das; band; onbesliste
  wedstrijd; (vast)binden;
  strikken, knopen; ge'lijkstaan,
  ge'lijk aankomen

tier, rang, ver'dieping

tiger, tijger

tight, vast; dicht op el'kaar;
  strak; kachel

tighten, strakker aanhalen;
  ver'scherpen

tile, tegel; dakpan; be'tegelen

till, tot(dat); geldlade;
  be'ploegen

till (*continued*)
  up –, tot (aan)
  not ... –, pas
tilt, overhellen; kantelen; schuinhouden (*or* zetten)
  full –, met volle vaart
timber, timmerhout; balk
time, (de) tijd; keer; ge'legenheid; maat, tempo; de tijd opnemen van; uitrekenen
  at the same –, tege'lijkertijd; desondanks
  for the – being, voor'lopig
  in –, op tijd; op den duur; in de maat
timely, tijdig
timid, timorous, schuchter
tin, tin; blik(ken); bus, trommel
tinge, tint(en); tikje
tingle, tintelen
tinker, ketellapper; prutsen
tinkle, tingelen
tinned, in blik
tinsel, klatergoud
tint, tint(en)
tiny, heel klein
tip, punt, top; (een) fooi (geven); wenk, optillen, kantelen; storten
tipsy, aangeschoten
tiptoe: on –, op de tenen; in spanning
tire, band; ver'moeien; moe (*or* beu) worden
tired, moe; beu
tireless, onvermoeid
tiresome, ver'velend
tissue, weefsel; vloei-
tit, mees; (inf) tiet; tepel; sukkel, klier
titbit, lekker hapje
title, titel; aanspraak (op); be'titelen

titled, adellijk
titter, giechelen
to, naar; tot (aan); (om) te; in; aan; dicht
  – and fro, heen en weer
toad, pad
toadstool, paddestoel
toast, ge'roosterd brood; toost; roosteren; drinken op
tobacco, ta'bak
tobacconist, si'garenhandelaar
today, van'daag; tegen'woordig
toddle, dribbelen
toe, teen
toffee, toffee
together, samen; tege'lijk
toil, arbeid; zwoegen; zich slepen
toilet, toi'let
  – bag, toi'lettas
token, teken, blijk, bewijs; bon, ca'deaubon; munt, fiche, penning; aandenken
tolerable, draaglijk; redelijk
tolerance, ver'draagzaamheid
tolerant, ver'draagzaam
tolerate, dulden
toll, tol; luiden
tomato, to'maat
  – juice, to'matensap
  – ketchup, (to'maten)ketchup
tomb, graftombe
tombstone, grafsteen
tomorrow, morgen
tom-tom, tam-tam
ton, ton
tone, toon, klank; tint; harmoni'ëren
tongs, tang
tongue, tong; taal; klepel
tonic, ver'sterkend middel
tonight, van'avond, van'nacht
tonsil, a'mandel

too, ook (nog); (al) te
tool, ge'reedschap, werktuig
tooth, tand, kies
toothache, kiespijn
toothbrush, tandenborstel
toothpaste, tandpasta
toothpick, tandenstoker
top, top; tol; bovenste,
   bovenaan
topic, onderwerp
topical, actu'eel
topography, topogra'fie
topple, (bijna)
   omvallen/kantelen; (bijna)
   doen omvallen/kantelen
topsy-turvy, op zijn kop
torch, zaklantaren; fakkel
torment, foltering; kwellen
tornado, tor'nado, wervelstorm
torpedo, tor'pedo; torpe'deren
torrent, (berg)stroom; stortvloed
torrential, stort-
torrid, heet
torso, torso, romp
tortoise, schildpad
tortuous, kronkelend; draaiend
torture, foltering; kwelling;
   folteren; kwellen
toss, toss; opgooien; slingeren;
   de lucht in gooien
tot, peuter
 – up, optellen
total, to'taal; be'dragen
totally, vol'komen
totter, wankelen
touch, aanraking; con'tact; tikje;
   trekje; aanslag; (aan)raken;
   el'kaar raken; (aan)roeren
touching, roerend
tough, taai; zuur; hard;
   moeilijk; ruwe klant
tour, (rond)reis; rondtoer; (op)
   tour'nee (zijn); (af)reizen

tourist, toe'rist
tournament, toer'nooi
tousle, ver'fomfaaien
tow, sleeptouw; slepen
toward(s), naar ... toe, in de
   richting van; jegens; tegen
towel, handdoek
tower, toren; zich torenhoog
   ver'heffen
town, stad
townhall, stad'huis
toxic, ver'giftig
toy, (stuk) speelgoed; speelbal;
   spelen
trace, spoor; tikje; opsporen,
   vinden; overtrekken, schetsen
track, spoor; pad; baan;
   opsporen
tracksuit, trainingspak
tractor, tractor
trade, handel(en); vak; zaken;
   handeldrijven
trademark, handelsmerk
trader, handelaar;
   handelsvaartuig
tradesman, leveran'cier
trades union, (vak)bond,
   vakvereniging
tradition, tra'ditie
traditional, traditio'neel
traffic, ver'keer; handel(en)
 – jam, (ver'keers)opstopping,
   file
 – lane, rijstrook
 – sign, ver'keersteken,
   ver'keersbord
tragedy, treurspel; trage'die
tragic, treurspel; trage'die
trail, spoor; nasleep; pad; (laten)
   slepen; kruipen; opsporen
 to – off (*or* **away),** wegsterven
trailer, kruipplant;
   aanhangwagen

train, trein; sleep; ge'volg; reeks;
opleiden; trainen; (af)richten
trainee, stagi'air(e)
trainer, trainer
training, opleiding; training
trait, trek
traitor(ous), ver'rader(lijk)
tram, tram
tramp, landloper; wandeling;
sjouwen; lopen; trappen
trample, trappen
trance, trance; geestvervoering
tranquil, rustig
tranquillity, rust
transact, doen, sluiten
transaction, trans'actie;
ver'richten
transcend, te boven gaan
transfer, overplaatsing;
overdruk; overdragen,
overbrengen, over(*or*
ver')plaatsen; transfer (sport)
transfigure, een andere
ge'daante geven
transfix, door'steken; aan de
grond nagelen
transform, (ge'heel) ver'anderen;
transfor'meren
transgress, over'treden; te
buiten gaan
transient, kort'stondig
transit: in –, onder'weg
transition(al), overgang(s-)
transitory, ver'gankelijk
translate, ver'talen; omzetten
translation, ver'taling
translucent, door'schijnend
transmission, trans'missie;
overbrengen; gangwissel
transmit, overbrengen;
uitzenden
transparent, door'zichtig,
transpa'rant

transpire, blijken; zich
voordoen
transplant, ver'planten,
overplanten; transplan'teren;
getransplan'teerd orgaan,
transplan'taat; transplan'tatie
transport, ver'voer, trans'port;
ver'voeren
transport café, wegrestaurant
transpose, ver'wisselen;
transpo'neren
transsexual, transseksu'eel
transverse, dwars
transvestite, traves'tiet
trap, val(strik), hinderlaag; sjees;
in de val laten lopen; opsluiten
trapdoor, valluik
trash, prullen, prul'laria; afval;
rotzooi
travel, reizen; zich voortplanten
– agency, reisbureau
traveller, reiziger
– cheque, reischeque
traverse, dwars; doortrekken
travesty, tra'vestie; aanfluiting
trawler, treiler
tray, blad; bak
treacherous, ver'raderlijk; vals
treachery, ver'raad
tread, tred(en); loopvlak;
be'treden; trappen
treason, (land)verraad
treasure, schat(ten); ju'weel;
hoogschatten; angst'vallig
be'waren
treasurer, penningmeester
treasury, schatkist; minis'terie
van fi'nanciën
treat, trak'tatie; feestje;
be'handelen; trak'teren
treatise, ver'handeling
treatment, be'handeling
treaty, ver'drag

treble, drie'voudig; so'praan; verdrie'voudigen
tree, boom; leest
trek, trek(ken)
trellis, latwerk
tremble, beven
tremendous, e'norm
tremor, trilling
trench, loopgraaf; voor
trenchant, snijdend; krachtig
trend, neiging; loop, richting
trepidation, schroom, beven
trespass, op ver'boden ter'rein zijn (*or* komen); be'slag leggen
tress, lok
trestle, schraag
trial, ver'hoor; proef(neming); be'proeving; lastpost
triangle, driehoek; tri'angel
triangular, drie'hoekig
triathlon, triatlon
tribe, stam
tribulation, be'proeving
tribunal, rechtbank; tribu'naal
tributary, zijrivier; bij-
tribute, hulde(blijk); schatting
trick, truc; kunstje; streek; slag; be'driegen
trickle, straaltje; sijpelen, biggelen; druppelen
tricky, lastig, netelig
tricycle, driewieler
trifle, kleinigheid; klein beetje; fruit en cake met custard en room; spotten
trifling, onbe'duidend
trigger, trekker
trim, net(jes); con'ditie; bijwerken, bijknippen; gar'neren
trimming, gar'nering, versiering
Trinity, drie'ëenheid
trinket, kleinood

trip, tocht(je); (doen) struikelen; trippelen
   to – up, struikelen; zich in de vingers snijden
triple, drie'delig; drie'dubbel
tripod, drievoet
trite, afgezaagd
triumph, tri'omf; zegevieren
triumphal, tri'omf-
triumphant, zegevierend, triom'fantelijk
trivial, onbe'duidend
trolley, trolley; rolwagen(tje), theewagen
troop, troep; pelo'ton; zich scharen; allen (tege'lijk) gaan
trophy, prijs, tro'fee; zegeteken
tropics, tropen
tropical, tropisch
trot, draf; draven
trouble, zorg; moeite (nemen); hinderen; lastig vallen
troublesome, lastig
trough, trog; dal
trousers, broek
trout, fo'rel(len)
trowel, troffel; schopje
truant: to play –, spijbelen
truce, wapenstilstand
truck, vrachtauto; (goederen)wagen
trudge, sjokken
true, waar; echt; (ge')trouw; zuiver
truism, afgezaagde waarheid
truly, heus
trump, troef; troeven
   to – up, ver'zinnen
trumpet, trom'pet(ten)
truncheon, stok
trundle, rollen
trunk, stam, romp; hutkoffer; slurf; interlo'kaal

truss, bundel, spant;
   (vast)binden
trust, ver'trouwen (op);
   be'waring; trust; hopen
trustee, execu'teur;
   gevol'machtigde
trustful, goed van ver'trouwen
trustworthy, be'trouwbaar
trusty, trouw
truth, waarheid
truthful, eerlijk
try, poging; pro'beren;
   be'proeven; op de proef
   stellen; ver'horen
trying, moeilijk
T-shirt, t-shirt
tub, kuip, ton
tube, buis, slang; (binnen)band;
   tube; onder'grondse
tuberculosis, tubercu'lose
tuck, plooi; stoppen
Tuesday, dinsdag
tuft, bosje
tug, ruk(ken); sleepboot;
   trekken
tuition, onderwijs
tulip, tulp
tumble, tuimelen
tumbledown, bouw'vallig
tumble dryer, droogtrommel
tumbler, (limo'nade)glas
tumour, tumor
tumult, tumult
tumultuous, tumultu'eus,
   ru'moerig
tune, wijsje, melo'die; stemmen
tuneful, wel'luidend
tunic, overgooier; tu'niek
tunnel, tunnel (maken)
turban, tulband
turbine, tur'bine
turbulent, woelig, wild,
   turbu'lent

turf, zode(n), gras; renbaan
turkey, kal'koen; Tur'kije
turmoil, be'roering
turn, draai; bocht; ommekeer;
   beurt; dienst; kunstje;
   (om)draaien; omslaan;
   omkeren; worden;
   ver'anderen; omzetten;
   wenden
to – down, om'vouwen;
   afwijzen
to – out, uitdraaien; aantreden,
   opstaan; (er) uitzetten;
   produ'ceren; aflopen; blijken
to – over, omslaan; (zich)
   omkeren; overdragen;
   over'denken
to – to, overgaan op; zich
   wenden tot; aanpakken
to – up, omslaan, optrekken;
   opdraaien; ver'schijnen
turnip, knol, raap
turnover, omzet
turnpike, tolhek
turpentine, terpen'tijn
turquoise, tur'koois
turret, torentje; ge'schuttoren
turtle, zeeschildpad
tusk, slagtand
tussle, worsteling; worstelen
tutor, pri'véleraar
tut tut, nou nou
twaddle, ge'wauwel; wauwelen
twang, ping; neusgeluid; tingelen
tweed, tweed
tweezers, pin'cet
twelve, twaalf
twenty, twintig
twice, tweemaal
twiddle, draaien
twig, twijgje
twilight, schemering
twin, tweeling

twinge, steek
twinkle, fonkelen
twirl, (rond)draaien
twist, kromming; (ver')draaien;
  zich slingeren; ver'trekken
twitch, zenuwtrekking; trekken
twitter, tjilpen
two, twee
twofold, twee'voudig
type, type; letter(type); tikken
typewriter, schrijfmachine,
  typemachine
typhoid, tyfus
typhoon, ty'foon
typical, typisch
typify, ty'peren
tyrannical, tiran'niek
tyranny, tiran'nie
tyrant, ti'ran

U

ubiquitous, alomheersend
udder, uier
UFO, ufo, vliegende schotel
ugly, lelijk
ulcer, zweer
ulterior, heimelijk, bij-
ultimate, laatste; uit'eindelijk;
  essen'tieel, grond-; ul'tiem
ultimatum, ulti'matum
ultra-violet, ultravio'let
umbrella, para'plu; tuinparasol
umpire, scheidsrechter
UN, VN (Verenigde Naties)
un-, on-
unable, niet in staat
unaccompanied, zonder
  bege'leiding; a-ca'pella
unaccountable, onver'klaarbaar
unaccustomed, niet ge'wend
unanimous, een'stemmig,
  eensge'zind

unassuming, be'scheiden
unattended, onbe'heerd
unauthorized, onbe'voegd
unavailing, ver'geefs
unavoidable, onver'mijdelijk
unaware, niet be'wust
unawares, onbe'wust;
  onver'hoeds
unbearable, on'draaglijk
unbelievable, onge'looflijk
unbound, niet ge'bonden
unbroken, onver'broken;
  on'afgebroken
unbutton, losknopen
uncalled-for, onge'vraagd;
  mis'plaatst
uncanny, griezelig, onge'looflijk,
  geheim'zinnig
uncertain, on'zeker
unchecked, onbe'lemmerd
uncle, oom
uncommon, onge'woon
uncompromising, on'buigzaam,
  rotsvast
unconcerned, onver'schillig;
  onbe'kommerd
unconditional,
  onvoor'waardelijk
unconquerable,
  onover'winnelijk
unconscious, be'wusteloos;
  onbe'wust
uncontrollable, onbe'dwingbaar,
  onbe'daarlijk
uncork, ont'kurken
uncouth, lomp
uncover, ont'bloten; aan het
  licht brengen
undaunted, onver'saagd
undecided, onbe'slist; in dubio
undeniable, ontegen'zeggelijk,
  onbe'twistbaar
under, onder(-)

undercurrent, onderstroom;
ver'borgen stroming
underdone, on'gaar
undergraduate, stu'dent
underground, onder de grond;
onder'gronds(e)
undergrowth, kreupelhout
underhand, onder'hands
underlying, grond-,
undermine, onder'mijnen
underneath, onder, be'neden;
onderkant
understand, be'grijpen; horen;
aannemen
understanding, be'grip;
ver'standhouding; sympa'thiek
undertake, onder'nemen; op
zich nemen
undertaker,
be'grafenisondernemer
undertaking, onder'neming;
be'lofte
undertone, ge'dempte stem;
grondkleur; ondergrond
underwear, ondergoed
undesirable, onge'wenst
undo, los(or open)maken;
onge'daan maken
undoing, ondergang
undoubtedly, onge'twijfeld
undress, (zich) uitkleden
undue, over'matig
undulate, golven
unearth, opgraven; aan het licht
brengen
unearthly, boven'aards;
on'mogelijk
uneasy, onge'rust, on'rustig
uneducated, onge'schoold
unemployed, werkloos
unemployment, werk'loosheid
unemployment benefit,
werk'loosheidsuitkering

unending, eindeloos
unequal, onge'lijk; niet
opgewassen (tegen)
unerring, on'feilbaar
uneven, on'effen; onge'lijk;
on'even
uneventful, onbe'wogen, saai
unexpected(ly), onver'wacht(s),
onvoor'zien
unfailing, on'feilbaar;
onuit'puttelijk; zeker
unfamiliar, onbe'kend; niet op
de hoogte
unfasten, los(or open)maken
unfathomable,
ondoor'grondelijk
unfeeling, onge'voelig
unfetter, ont'ketenen
unfinished, onvol'tooid
unfit, onge'schikt
unfold, ont'vouwen, (zich)
ont'plooien
unforgettable, onver'getelijk
unforgivable, onver'geeflijk
unfortunately, jammer ge'noeg,
he'laas
unfounded, onge'grond
unfurl, (zich) ont'plooien
ungainly, lomp
ungodly, goddeloos
ungovernable, on'tembaar
ungracious, on'hoffelijk
unhappiness, ver'driet
unharmed, onge'deerd,
onbe'schadigd
unheard-of, onge'kend;
onge'hoord
unheeded, on'opgemerkt;
onge'merkt, ver'waarloosd
unholy, goddeloos; heidens
unicorn, eenhoorn
uniform, ge'lijk('matig);
uni'form

unify, ver'enigen

unimaginative, zonder fanta'sie; fanta'sieloos

unimpaired, on'aangetast

uninformed, niet op de hoogte, on'wetend

uninhabitable, onbe'woonbaar

unintelligent, dom

unintelligible, onver'staanbaar, onbe'grijpelijk

uninvited, onge'nood

union, ver'bond, unie; (vak)bond; stu'dentenvereniging

unique, u'niek

unison: in –, een'stemmig; tege'lijk

unit, eenheid; afdeling

unite, (zich) ver'enigen

united, ver'enigd; saam'horig; ge'zamenlijk

United Kingdom, Ver'enigd Koninkrijk

United States of America, Ver'enigde Staten van A'merika

unity, eenheid; eensge'zindheid

universal, univer'seel; alge'meen

universe, heel'al

university, universi'teit

unkempt, onver'zorgd

unkind, on'aardig

unknown, onbe'kend(e)

unless, ten'zij

unlike, ver'schillend, anders dan

   it is – him to forget, het is niets voor hem het te ver'geten

unload, ont'laden, lossen

unlock, ont'sluiten

unmanageable, on'handelbaar

unmask, ont'maskeren, onthullen

unmistakable, onmis'kenbaar

unmitigated, onver'minderd; onver'valst

unnerve, ont'zenuwen

unobtrusive, be'scheiden

unoccupied, onbe'zet; onbe'woond; niet bezig

unofficial, niet offi'cieel

unpack, uitpakken

unpalatable, on'smakelijk; on'aangenaam

unparalleled, weergaloos, ongeëve'naard

unpardonable, onver'geeflijk

unpleasant, on'aangenaam

unprecedented, onge'hoord

unpredictable, onbe'rekenbaar

unprincipled, ge'wetenloos

unprofitable, on'vruchtbaar

unquestionable, onbe'twistbaar

unquestionably, onge'twijfeld

unravel, ont'warren

unreasoned, onberede'neerd

unreservedly, zonder voorbehoud

unrestrained, onbe'teugeld; onge'dwongen

unrivalled, ongeëve'naard

unruly, on'ordelijk, on'handelbaar

unsavoury, smakeloos; on'smakelijk; onver'kwikkelijk

unscathed, onge'deerd

unscrew, losschroeven

unscrupulous, ge'wetenloos

unselfish, onbaat'zuchtig

unsettled, on'zeker

unsightly, on'ooglijk

unsparing, kwistig, mild; mee'dogenloos

unspeakable, onbe'schrijf(e)lijk

unsuccessful, ver'geefs

   to be –, geen suc'ces hebben

unsuspicious, argeloos

untangle, ont'warren

untenable, on'houdbaar

unthinkable, on'denkbaar

untidy, slordig, wan'ordelijk

untie, losmaken

until, tot(dat)

untimely, on'tijdig; onge'legen

untiring, onver'moeid

unto, tot (aan)

untold, onver'teld; on'telbaar

untoward, on'gunstig

unused, onge'bruikt; niet
ge'wend (aan)

unusual, onge'woon,
onge'bruikelijk

unutterable, onuit'sprekelijk

unvaried, unvarying,
onver'anderlijk

unveil, ont'hullen; ont'sluieren

unwarranted,
ongerecht'vaardigd

unwavering, stand'vastig

unwieldy, log

unwind, afwinden; (zich)
ont'rollen

unwittingly, onop'zettelijk,
onbe'wust

unwonted, onge'woon

unwrap, uitpakken

unyielding, onver'zettelijk

up, (verder) op; (naar) boven;
om'hoog; over'eind;
ver'streken
  to be – to, in staat zijn; in de
zin hebben, uitvoeren; zijn aan

upbringing, opvoeding

upheaval, opschudding

uphill, de heuvel op, opwaarts;
zwaar

uphold, hooghouden; steunen

upholstery, be'kleding

upkeep, onderhoud

uplift, ver'heffen

upon, op

upper, boven(ste); superieur

uppermost, hoogst; bovenst; op
de voorgrond

upright, recht'op; op'recht

uprising, opstand

uproar, tu'mult

uproarious, ru'moerig;
stormachtig

uproot, ont'wortelen; uitroeien

upset, om'verwerpen; in de war
sturen; van streek maken

upshot, resul'taat

upside down, onderste'boven

upstairs, (naar) boven

upstart, parve'nu(achtig);
poen(ig)

upstream, stroom'opwaarts

up-to-date, bijgewerkt, op de
hoogte; mo'dern, heden'daags

upturn, verbetering, ommekeer

upward(s), opwaarts, naar
boven; (en) hoger, (en) ouder

uranium, u'ranium

urban, stedelijk, stads-, steeds

urchin, kwa'jongen

urge, (aan)drang; aanzetten;
aandringen (op)

urgent, dringend

urn, urn

us, ons

usable, bruikbaar

usage, ge'bruik; be'handeling

use, ge'bruik(en); toepassing;
nut; ver'bruiken
  to be used to, ge'wend zijn
(aan)
  it used to be, het was
vroeger

useful, nuttig, handig

useless, nutteloos

usher, plaatsaanwijzer; leiden

usual, ge'bruikelijk, ge'woon
  as −, zoals ge'woonlijk
usually, ge'woonlijk
usurp, usur'peren
utensils, ge'rei; werktuigen,
  ge'reedschap
utility, (openbare) voorziening,
  nut(tigheids-)
utilize, be'nutten
utmost, uiterste, hoogste
utter, vol'slagen; uiten
utterance, uiting; uitspraak
uttermost, uiterst

V

vacancy, vaca'ture, leemte
vacant, va'cant; onbe'woond;
  wezenloos
vacate, ont'ruimen
vacation, va'kantie
vaccinate, inenten
vacuum, vacuüm, leegte;
  stofzuigen
vacuum cleaner, stofzuiger
vagabond, vagebond
vagrant, ronddolend
vague, vaag
vain, ijdel; ver'geefs
  in −, tever'geefs
vale, dal
valet, be'diende
valid, (rechts')geldig
validity, (rechts)geldigheid
valley, dal
valour, moed
valuable, waardevol;
  kostbaar(heid)
valuation, ta'xatie
value, waarde; ta'xeren; op prijs
  stellen
valve, klep, ven'tiel

van, (be'stel)wagen; voorhoede
vandalism, vanda'lisme
vane, vaantje; wiek, schoep
vanguard, voorhoede
vanilla, va'nille
vanish, (spoorloos) ver'dwijnen;
  uitsterven
vanity, ijdelheid
vanquish, over'winnen
vantage, voorsprong; gunstig
vapour, damp
variable, ver'anderlijk;
  ver'stelbaar
variation, afwisseling;
  ver'andering; vari'atie
variety, ver'scheidenheid
  afwisseling; soort; varié'té
various, ver'scheiden
varnish, ver'nis(sen)
vary, vari'ëren
vase, vaas
vast, on'metelijk, kolos'saal
vastly, e'norm
VAT, btw (be'lasting op de
  toegevoegde waarde)
vat, vat
Vatican, Vati'caan
vault, ge'welf, kluis; sprong;
  springen
veal, kalfsvlees
veer, draaien; vieren; van
  richting ver'anderen
vegetable, groente(-);
  plant'aardig
vegetarian, vegetariër;
  vege'tarisch
vegetation, vege'tatie,
  plantengroei
vehement, hevig
vehicle, voertuig; drager
veil, sluier(en)
vein, ader; neiging, trek;
  stemming

velocity, snelheid
velvet, flu'weel; flu'welen
vendor, ver'koper
veneer, fi'neer(hout); ver'nisje;
 fi'neren
venerable, eerbied'waardig;
 eer'waard
venerate, diep ver'eren
venereal, ge'slachts-
Venetian, Vene'tiaans
venetian blind, jaloe'zie
vengeance, wraak
vengeful, wraak'gierig
Venice, Venetië
venom(ous), ve'nijn(ig)
vent, opening, luchtgaatje;
 uitweg; luchten
ventilate, venti'leren
ventilation, venti'latie
ventriloquist, buikspreker
venture, onder'heming;
 waagstuk; (het) wagen
venturesome, venturous,
 stout'moedig
verb, werkwoord
verbal, in woorden; mondeling;
 werk'woordelijk
verbatim, woordelijk
verdict, uitspraak; oordeel,
 vonnis; be'slissing
verge, rand; grenzen (aan)
verify, verifi'ëren
veritable, waar
vermilion, vermil'joen
vermin, ongedierte
vernacular, moedertaal
versatile, veel'zijdig
verse, poëzie; cou'plet
versed, be'dreven
version, ver'taling, versie, lezing,
 be'werking
vertebrate, ge'werveeld (dier)
vertical, verti'caal; loodlijn

very, zeer, erg; pre'cies; al'leen al
vessel, vaartuig; vat
vest, hemd; vest; (be')kleden
vestry, sacris'tie
veteran, vete'raan; er'varen
vet(erinary), veearts(e'nij)
veto, veto; ver'werpen
vex, ergeren
vexation, ergernis
viaduct, via'duct
vial, flesje
vibrate, vi'breren
vibration, trilling
vicar, dominee, pas'toor
vice, ondeugd; bankschroef;
 vice-
vice versa, vice versa,
 omgekeerd
vicinity, na'bijheid, buurt
vicious, boos'aardig; vici'eus
victim, slachtoffer
victor, over'winnaar
victorious, zegevierend
victory, over'winning
video, video; videorecorder; op
 (de) video opnemen
video recorder, videorecorder
videotape, videoband
vie, wedijveren
Vienna, Wenen
Viennese, Weens
view, uitzicht, ge'zicht; mening;
 be'schouwen
 in –, in het ge'zicht; voor ogen
 in – of, ge'zien
viewpoint, uitzichtpunt;
 ge'zichtspunt
vigil, wacht, waken, wake
vigilance, waakzaamheid
vigorous, krachtig, ener'giek
vigour, kracht, ener'gie
vile, af'schuwelijk
villa, villa

village, dorp
villain, schurk
villainous, schurkachtig, heel
  slecht, ge'meen
vindicate, wrekend, handhaven,
  recht'-vaardigen, zuiveren (van
  blaam)
vindictive, wraak'gierig
vine, wijnstok; wingerd
vinegar, a'zijn
vineyard, wijngaard
vintage, jaar; wijnoogst
viola, altviool; vi'ooltje
violate, schenden
violation, schennis
violence, ge'weld
violent, hevig, heftig,
  geweld'dadig
violet, vi'ooltje; vio'let
violin, vi'ool
violinist, vio'list
viper, adder
virgin, maagd(elijk); onge'rept
virile, man'moedig, krachtig
virtual, eigenlijk
virtually, praktisch
virtue, deugd; ver'dienste
virtuous, deugdzaam
virulent, kwad'aardig; ve'nijnig
visa, visum
visibility, zicht
visible, zichtbaar
visibly, zienderogen
vision, ge'zicht; vérziende blik;
  visi'oen
visit, be'zoek(en)
visitor, be'zoeker, gast
visual, ge'zichts-
vital, essen'tieel; vi'taal; levens-
vitality, vitali'teit
vitamin, vita'mine
vivacious, levendig
vivid, helder; levendig

vocabulary, woordenlijst;
  woordenschat, vocabu'laire
vocal, stem-, zang-
vocation, roeping; be'roep
vogue, zwang; populari'teit
voice, stem; uiten
void, on'geldig; ont'bloot; leegte
volatile, vluchtig; wispel'turig
volcano, vul'kaan
volley, regen, stroom; volley
volt(age), volt('age)
volume, (boek)deel; vo'lume,
  omvang; massa
voluminous, volumi'neus
voluntary, vrij'willig;
  wille'keurig; lief'dadigheids-
volunteer, vrij'williger; vrij'willig
  in dienst treden; aanbieden
voluptuous, wel'lustig;
  weelderig
vomit, overgeven, (uit)braken;
  braaksel, overgeefsel
vote, stem(recht); motie;
  stemmen; toestaan
voter, kiezer
vouch, instaan
vow, ge'lofte; plechtig be'loven
vowel, klinker
voyage, reis
vulgar, vul'gair, plat
vulgarity, vulgari'teit, platheid
vulnerable, kwetsbaar
vulture, gier

W

wad, prop; pakje
waddle, waggelen
wade, waden
wafer, wafel; hostie
waft, drijven, zweven
wag, kwispelen (tail)
wage, loon; voeren

wager, weddenschap; wedden om

wagon, wagen, wa'gon

wail, weeklagen; loeien

waist, taille

waistcoat, vest

wait, wachten; dienen

waiter, kelner

waiting room, wachtkamer

waitress, ser'verster

waive, afstand doen van, afzien van

wake, kielzog; spoor
 to – up, wakker worden (*or* maken)

walk, wandeling, eind lopen; loop; laan; sfeer; lopen, wandelen
 to go for a –, gaan wandelen

wall, muur, wand, wal

wallet, porte'feuille, portemon'nee

wallpaper, be'hang

walnut, walnoot; notenhout(en)

waltz, wals(en)

wan, bleek; flets

wand, toverstaf

wander, zwerven; dwalen

wane, afnemen

wangle, klaarspelen; knoeien met

want, be'hoefte; ge'brek, nood; willen (hebben); nodig hebben, moeten worden

wanton, bal'dadig; wild

war, oorlog; strijden

ward, pu'pil; zaal; stadswijk
 to – off, afweren

warden, direc'teur

warder, ci'pier

wardrobe, klerenkast; garde'robe

ware, waar, goed

warehouse, pakhuis

warlike, oorlogs'zuchtig

warm, warm; (ver')warmen

warmth, warmte

warn, waarschuwen

warning, waarschuwing

warp, kromtrekken; ver'draaien

warrant, be'vel; waarborgen

warrior, krijgsman

wart, wrat

wartime, oorlogs(tijd)

wary, voor'zichtig

wash, was; golfslag; (zich) wassen; spoelen
 to – up, afwassen

washable, wasbaar

wash basin, wastafel

washer, wasser; sluitring, leertje

washing, was(goed); was-

washing machine, wasautomaat, wasmachine

washing up, afwas, vaat

wasp, wesp

wastage, ver'spilling

waste, ver'spilling; afval(-); woeste'nij; ver'spillen; (weg)kwijnen
 to lay –, ver'woesten

wasteful, ver'kwistend

wastepaper basket, prullenmand

watch, wacht; hor'loge; uitkijken; gadeslaan; opletten

watchful, waakzaam

watchman, waker

water, water (geven); wateren

watercolour, waterverf; aqua'rel

waterfall, waterval

watertight, waterproof, waterdicht

watery, water(acht)ig; regen-

wave, golf; wuiven (met); watergolven, perma'nenten

waver, flikkeren; weifelen; beven
wavy, golvend
wax, was(sen); wassen; worden
way, ma'nier, wijze; opzicht;
   kant, weg, eind; zin; vaart
   by the –, tussen haakjes
   to give –, toegeven; wegzakken
   in a –, in zekere zin
   to make one's own –, zijn weg
   vinden; voor'uitkomen
wayfarer, reiziger, zwerver
waylay, aanranden; aanklampen
wayside, (aan de) kant van de
   weg
wayward, eigen'zinnig
we, wij, we
weak, zwak; slap
weaken, ver'zwakken;
   ver'slappen
weakling, zwakkeling
weakness, zwakte; zwak (punt)
wealth, rijkdom; schat
wealthy, rijk
weapon, wapen
wear, dracht, kleding; slij'tage;
   dragen; slijten; zich houden
   to – out, (ver')slijten, afdragen;
   afmatten
weariness, ver'moeidheid
weary, moe
weather, weer; ver'weren;
   door'staan
weather-beaten, door storm
   ge'teisterd; ver'weerd
weathercock, weerhaant
weave, weven;
   (samen)vlechten; zich
   slingerend banen
web, web; weefsel
website, website
wedding,
   huwelijk(splechtigheid), bruiloft
wedge, wig; vastzetten

wee, heel klein
weed, onkruid; ta'bak,
   marihu'ana, hasj; lange
   slapjanus; wieden,
   ver'wijderen, schoffelen;
   zuiveren
weedy, vol onkruid; spichtig
week, week
weekend, weekend, weekeinde
weekly, wekelijks, week-
weep, wenen, huilen; huilbui
weigh, (af)wegen; drukken;
   lichten
weight, ge'wicht
weighty, zwaar; ge'wichtig
weird, raar, gek, vreemd, eng
welcome, welkom,
   ver'welkoming; ver'welkomen
weld, las(sen)
welfare, welzijn; soci'aal,
   weten'schappelijk
well, goed; ver; wel; put, bron;
   wellen
   as –, ook; even'goed; zo'wel
well-bred, wel'opgevoed
well-known, be'kend
well-nigh, nage'noeg
well-off, welge'steld; goed'af
well-read, be'lezen
west, west(en), west(waards)
   – of, ten westen van
westerly, westelijk, wester-
western, westers, westelijk
wet, nat (maken)
whack, mep; slaan
whale, walvis
wharf, kade, aanlegsteiger
what, wat (voor (een)), welk;
   waar-
   – is the time? hoe laat is het?
   – is it called? hoe heet het?
whatever, wat (*or* welk) dan
   ook; wat … toch

wheat, tarwe
wheel, wiel, rad; zwenken; duwen
wheelbarrow, kruiwagen
wheel clamp, wielklem
wheeze, piepen, hijgen
whelp, welp; kwa'jongen
when, wan'neer; (en) toen
whence, van'waar
whenever, wan'neer ook; telkens wan'neer
where, waar (naar toe)
whereabouts, waar onge'veer; ver'blijfplaats, ligging
whereas, ter'wijl
wherever, waar (... ook *or* toch); overal waar
whether, of
whew! oef!
which, welk, wat; die, dat; wie
whiff, vleugje, wolkje
while, tijd; ter'wijl; hoe'wel
  to – away, ver'slijten
whilst, ter'wijl; alhoe'wel
whim(sical), gril(lig)
whimper, grienen, janken
whine, jengelen, janken
whinny, hinniken
whip, zweep; (met de zweep) slaan; wippen, schieten; kloppen
whir, ge'snor; snorren
whirl, roes; dwarrelen; tollen, slingeren, stormen
whirlpool, draaikolk
whirlwind, wervelwind
whisk, klopper; (weg)wippen
whiskers, bakkebaarden; snor
whisky, whisky
whisper, ge'fluister; fluisteren
whistle, fluit(je); fluiten
white, wit; blank
whitewash, witkalk; witten

Whitsun, Pinksteren
whittle down, ge'leidelijk ver'minderen
whiz, suizen, zoeven
who, wie; die
whoever, wie ... ook; al wie
whole, (ge')heel; vol'ledig
  on the –, over het ge'heel ge'nomen, in het algemeen
wholesale, groothandel; inkoops-; op grote schaal
wholesome, ge'zond
wholly, to'taal
whoop, kreet; schreeuwen
whooping cough, kinkhoest
whore, hoer
whose, wiens, wier; van wie
why, waarom; wel
wick, pit, ka'toentje
wicked, slecht; on'deugend; schan'dalig; cool
wicker, rieten
wide, breed, wijd
  wide-awake, klaar wakker
widely, wijd en zijd; zeer
widen, (zich) ver'wijden
widespread, uitgestrekt; wijd ver'spreid
widow, weduwe
widower, weduwnaar
width, breedte, wijdte
wield, zwaaien; uitoefenen
wife, vrouw
wig, pruik
wiggle, wiebelen met
wild, wild; woest
wilderness, wildernis
wilful, eigen'zinnig; moed'willig
will, wil(len); testa'ment; zal, zult, zullen; kunnen
willing, be'reid('willig), ge'willig
willow, wilg

wilt, ver'leppen
wily, slim, sluw
wimp, doetje, lulletje
win, winnen, be'halen
wince, in'eenkrimpen, zijn ge'zicht ver'trekken
wind, wind; blaas-; kronkelen; winden
windfall, afgewaaide vrucht; buitenkansje
window, raam
window pane, ruit
windowsill, vensterbank
windscreen, voorruit
windshield, voorruit
windshield wiper, ruitenwisser
windsurfing, windsurfen
windy, winderig
wine, wijn
wing, vleugel; cou'lisse; flank
wink, knipoogje; knipogen
winner, winnaar
winning, winnend; in'nemend
winter, winter(-)
wintry, winters
wipe, (af)vegen
wire, (ijzer)draad; tele'gram
wireless, radio; draadloos
wisdom, wijsheid
wise, wijs, ver'standig; wijze
wish, ver'langen; wens(en);
   I – that you were here, ik wou dat je hier was
   I – to speak to him, ik zou hem willen spreken
wistful, ver'langend, wee'moedig
wit, ver'nuft, ver'stand; geest(igheid)
   at one's wits' end, ten einde raad
witch, heks
witchcraft, tovena'rij

with, met, bij; van
withdraw, (zich) te'rugtrekken
wither, ver'welken; ver'nietigen
withhold, ont'houden
within, binnen(in)
without, zonder; buiten
withstand, weer'staan
witness, ge'tuige(nis); ge'tuige zijn van; ge'tuigen (van)
witticism, geestigheid
witty, geestig
wizard, tovenaar
wobble, wiebelen
woeful, ramp'zalig
wolf, wolf; opschrokken
woman, vrouw; mens
womb, baarmoeder; schoot
wonder, wonder; ver'wondering; (zich) ver'wonderen; zich afvragen
wonderful, wonder'baarlijk; prachtig
woo, het hof maken
wood, hout; bos
wooded, be'bost
wooden, houten; houterig
woodland, bosland; bos-
woodwork, houtwerk; houtbe'werking
woody, bosrijk
wool(len), wol(len)
woolly, wollig
word, woord; be'richt
   – processor, tekstverwerker
wording, re'dactie, woordkeus
work, werk(en); han'teren
   – experience, werkervaring
worker, arbeider, werker
working, werking
workmanship, vakmanschap
workout, training
workshop, werkplaats

world(ly), wereld(s)
world record, wereldrecord
world war, wereldoorlog
worldwide, wereldwijd, over de
hele wereld
worm, wurm(en); kruipen;
indringen
worn-out, ver'sleten; uitgeput
worry, zorg; (zich) be'zorgd
maken; lastig vallen
worse, erger, slechter
worship, aan'bidding;
godsdienst(oefening);
aan'bidden; ver'eren
worst, ergst, slechtst
worth, waard(e)
  – while, – doing (seeing etc.),
de moeite waard
worthless, waardeloos;
ver'achtelijk
worthy, (achtens')waardig,
waard
would, zou(den) (willen);
wilde(n); wou
would-be, zoge'naamd;
toe'komstig, poten'tieel,
mogelijk
  a – buyer, een mogelijke koper
wound, wond(en)
wrangle, ruzie (maken)
wrap, sjaal, cape; wikkelen,
inpakken; hullen, ver'zinken
  to – around, omslaan
wrapping, ver'pakking
wrath(ful), toorn(ig)
wreak, uit'storten; ver'oorzaken,
aanrichten
wreath, krans
wreck, wrak; ver'nielen
wrench, ruk(ken); schroefsleutel
wrest, ont'wringen, afpersen
wrestle, worstelen
wretch, stakker

wretched, el'lendig; be'roerd
wriggle, draaien, wriemelen;
zich wringen
wring, (uit)wringen; afdwingen;
omdraaien
wrinkle, rimpel(en)
wrist, pols
writ, (be'vel)schrift, dagvaarding
write, schrijven
writer, schrijver
writhe, (zich ver')wringen
writing, (ge')schrift, schrijven;
schrijf-
wrong, ver'keerd; on'juist; niet
in orde; kwaad, onrecht
(aandoen)
  what is –? wat man'keert
eraan? wat is er?
  to go –, misgaan; ver'keerd
gaan; de'fect raken; de
ver'keerde weg opgaan
wrought iron, smeedijzer
wry, zuur

X

X-ray, röntgenfoto, doorlichten
xenophobia, vreemdelingen-
haat

Y

yacht, jacht; zeilen
yap, keffen; snauwen
yard, plaats(je), erf; kleine meter
(91,44 cm)
yarn, garen; ver'haal
yawn, geeuw(en); gapen
year, jaar
yearly, jaarlijks
yearn, vurig ver'langen (naar)
yeast, gist
yell, gil(len)

yellow, geel
yelp, janken
yes, ja
yesterday, gisteren

yet, nog; al; toch
  as –, tot nu toe
yield, opbrengst; (zich)
  overgeven; (be'z)wijken (voor);
  opleveren
yogurt, yoghurt
yoke, juk; schouder(*or*
  heup)stuk
yolk, dooier
you, u; jij, je, jou; jullie
young, jong(en); jeugd
youngster, jong'mens,
  jonge'man; jochie
your, uw; je, jouw; jullie
yours, (die *or* dat) van u, (die *or*
  dat) van jou, (die *or* dat) van
  jullie
yourself, (u')zelf, zich; je('zelf)
youth, jeugd; tiener
youthful, jeugdig

Z

zeal, vuur; lijver
zealot, dweper
zealous, ijverig; vurig
zenith, zenit; toppunt
zero, nul(punt)
zest, animo
zigzag, zigzag
zinc, zink
zip, rits(sluiting); ritsen; zoeven,
  scheuren; snel gaan
ZIP code, postcode
zipper, rits(sluiting)
zodiac, dierenriem
zone, zone
zoo, dierentuin
zoological, zoö'logisch

teach
yourself

beginner's dutch
gerdi quist & dennis strik

- Are you new to language learning?
- Do you want lots of practice and examples?
- Do you want to improve your confidence to speak?

Beginner's Dutch is written for the complete beginner who
wants to move at a steady pace and have lots of opportunity to
practise. The grammar is explained clearly and does not assume
that you have studied a language before. You will learn
everything you need to get the most out of a holiday or to go on
to further study.

teach
yourself

dutch
gerdi quist & dennis strik

- Do you want to cover the basics then progress fast?
- Do you want to communicate in a range of situations?
- Do you need to reach a high standard?

Dutch starts with the basics but moves at a lively pace to give you a good level of understanding, speaking and writing. You will have lots of opportunity to practise the kind of language you will need to be able to communicate with confidence and understand Dutch culture.

dutch grammar
gerdi quist & dennis strik

- Are you looking for an accessible guide to Dutch grammar?
- Do you want a book you can use either as a reference or as a course?
- Would you like exercises to reinforce your learning?

Dutch Grammar explains the most important structures in a clear and jargon-free way, with plenty of examples to show how they work in context. Use the book as a comprehensive reference to dip in and out of or work through it to build your knowledge.

teach
yourself

dutch conversation
marleen owen

- Do you want to talk with confidence?
- Are you looking for basic conversation skills?
- Do you want to understand what people say to you?

Dutch Conversation is a three-hour, all-audio course which
you can use at any time, whether you want a quick refresher
before a trip or whether you are a complete beginner. The 20
dialogues on CDs 1 and 2 will teach you the Dutch you will
need to speak and understand, without getting bogged down
with grammar. CD 3, uniquely, teaches skills for listening and
understanding. This is the perfect accompaniment to
Beginner's Dutch and **Dutch** in the **teach yourself** range.